S0-AJK-588

Mushrooms Demystified

David Arora

Mushrooms Demystified

A Comprehensive Guide to the Fleshy Fungi of the Central California Coast

Ten Speed Press

Berkeley

Cover Design by Brenton Beck,
Fifth Street Design Associates.
Illustrations by Michael Cabaniss.
All photographs by the author
unless otherwise indicated.
Front cover photograph of
Agaricus augustus (The Prince), page 295,
by Bill Donaldson

Grateful acknowledgement is made to the *Peoples Press,*
in whose pages some of the introductory material
originally appeared.

Printed in the United States of America.
Library of Congress Catalog Number 79-8513
ISBN: 0-89815-009-4 (paper), 0-89815-010-8 (cloth)

The information in this book is accurate to the best of the author's knowledge. However, neither the author nor the publisher can accept responsibility for mistakes in identification or idiosyncratic reactions to mushrooms. It is certainly not necessary to eat mushrooms in order to enjoy them. People who choose to eat mushrooms do so at their own risk.

PREFACE

FOR the last eight years people taking my courses on wild mushroom identification have expressed the wish for a comprehensive popular field guide to the mushrooms of California. *Mushrooms Demystified* is designed to satisfy that need. The subtitle specifies the "Central California Coast" because my studies have been centered in the coastal area from Marin County south to San Luis Obispo County and east to the Central Valley. However, since nearly all of the mushrooms described in this book have a wider distribution, mushroom hunters will find *Mushrooms Demystified* useful in the Sierra Nevada (hereafter referred to colloquially as "the Sierras"), as well as in the rest of California, Oregon, and even Washington. In fact, *Mushrooms Demystified* can serve almost anywhere as a general introduction to wild mushrooms, especially when used in conjunction with other regional guides. However, the farther you stray from the central California coast ("our area"), the more likely you are to encounter species that are *not* included in this book, and the greater the likelihood that the seasonal occurence and habitats of the included species will vary due to differences in climate, vegetation, and altitude.

Many general mushroom field guides have been published in recent years. Some are excellent, but they share one serious limitation—in striving to cover a large geographical area they have sacrificed comprehensiveness. As a result, the user becomes discouraged because only a fraction of the mushrooms he or she finds can be identified with any one book. Precisely because this book is a *regional* field guide, it includes many species *not* described in the general field guides, while excluding species depicted in those same field guides but not found in our area. In addition, special regional information is provided on the habitat and seasonal occurence of each mushroom, which is not possible in a book dealing with the entire country.

In using this book it is important to realize that the identification of mushrooms differs in several key respects from the identification of, say, birds or wildflowers. There is no book that "has them all." More than 700 species are described or mentioned here, including practically all of the common species that can be identified without a microscope. However, it will be many years before we have a definitive inventory of California mushrooms.

More than anything this is a tribute to the elusive and ephemeral nature of mushrooms. They are difficult to study because they're so unpredictable, and so much depends upon being in the right place at the right time.

It is also a comment on the fact that relatively few people study mushrooms seriously. In other words, the documented distribution of the lesser-known mushrooms corresponds to the undocumented distribution of the better-known mycologists. Furthermore, many kinds of mushrooms haven't been formally classified. While this makes identification more difficult, it also adds an element of mystery to the hunt. One is always encountering species that are new to science, or new to California, or new to the area, or at least new to oneself.

Another important point to realize is that many mushrooms can't be positively identified unless you have access to a microscope and know how to use one. Microscopic characteristics are not stressed in this book, which means that a substantial percentage of the species described are actually species "complexes"—that is, groups of closely related species whose exact identities are a matter for the specialist. Many amateurs, however, would like to apply names to these species complexes even if they are unequipped to make the subtler distinctions between species within a complex.

Therefore, I have chosen to sacrifice a certain degree of scientific accuracy by interpreting many species broadly. For example, the description of *Amanita strobiliformis* embraces a confusing group of white Amanitas with prominent warts on the cap. It may be that the "true" *A. strobiliformis* does not occur in California, but I see no harm in applying the name to the complex, *providing readers are made aware of the situation and are not misled.* Those who wish to pursue the matter further can then make use of the existing technical literature.

In view of the rapidly increasing popularity of mushroom hunting, I believe that a field guide ought to be as accessible as it is comprehensive. Thus I have made a special effort to keep the terminology simple and the language entertaining. For the uninitiated, special chapters have been provided on mushroom terminology and classification, when and where to find mushrooms, how to collect and identify mushrooms, and how to use the keys (which are the backbone of this book). For those who wish to learn a few safe edible types without wrestling with the rest, a chart of fifty distinctive mushrooms has been included on pages 36-41. In addition to being a field guide, *Mushrooms Demystified* is also a vehicle for expressing my love for mushrooms, for people who love mushrooms, my respect for life, and for people who respect life. Much of the pleasure in getting to know wild mushrooms is directly attributable to the companionship of fellow fungophiles, and I have paid tribute to these folks wherever possible.

Many people have helped make this book a reality. First and foremost, I'd like to express my gratitude to the many professional mycologists whose monographs and papers form the factual foundation of this book. If at times I seem irreverent in my discussions of taxonomy and taxonomists, it is only because I am so by nature. I fully realize that without their dedicated efforts, this venture would not have been possible. Specifically, I'd like to extend special thanks to Ralph and Mildred Buchsbaum, whose initial interest in the project made it possible; to Michael Cabaniss for his fine artwork; to Herb Saylor for his photographs and critical suggestions on the Clavariaceae; to the staff of the Santa Cruz City Museum for their continued support and loan of facilities; to Joel Leivick, Bill Everson, Nancy Burnett, Ray Gipson, Rick Kerrigan, Bob Tally, and Betty Barnhart, for their photographs; to Stanley Dudek and Hugo Sloane for their editorial suggestions; to Nancy MacGlashan and Rosalie Hunt for their help in typing and editing the manuscript; to Tinker, for her companionship; to my mother and father, for their timely support; to Mark Hildebrand, Pavel Machotka, Joe Czarnecki, John Cage, Luen, Reggie, Willie, Duke, Honus, Hank, and the countless other friends and colleagues who have brought me rare and interesting fungi; and finally, to the Milazzos, for everything else.

David Arora

Santa Cruz
1979

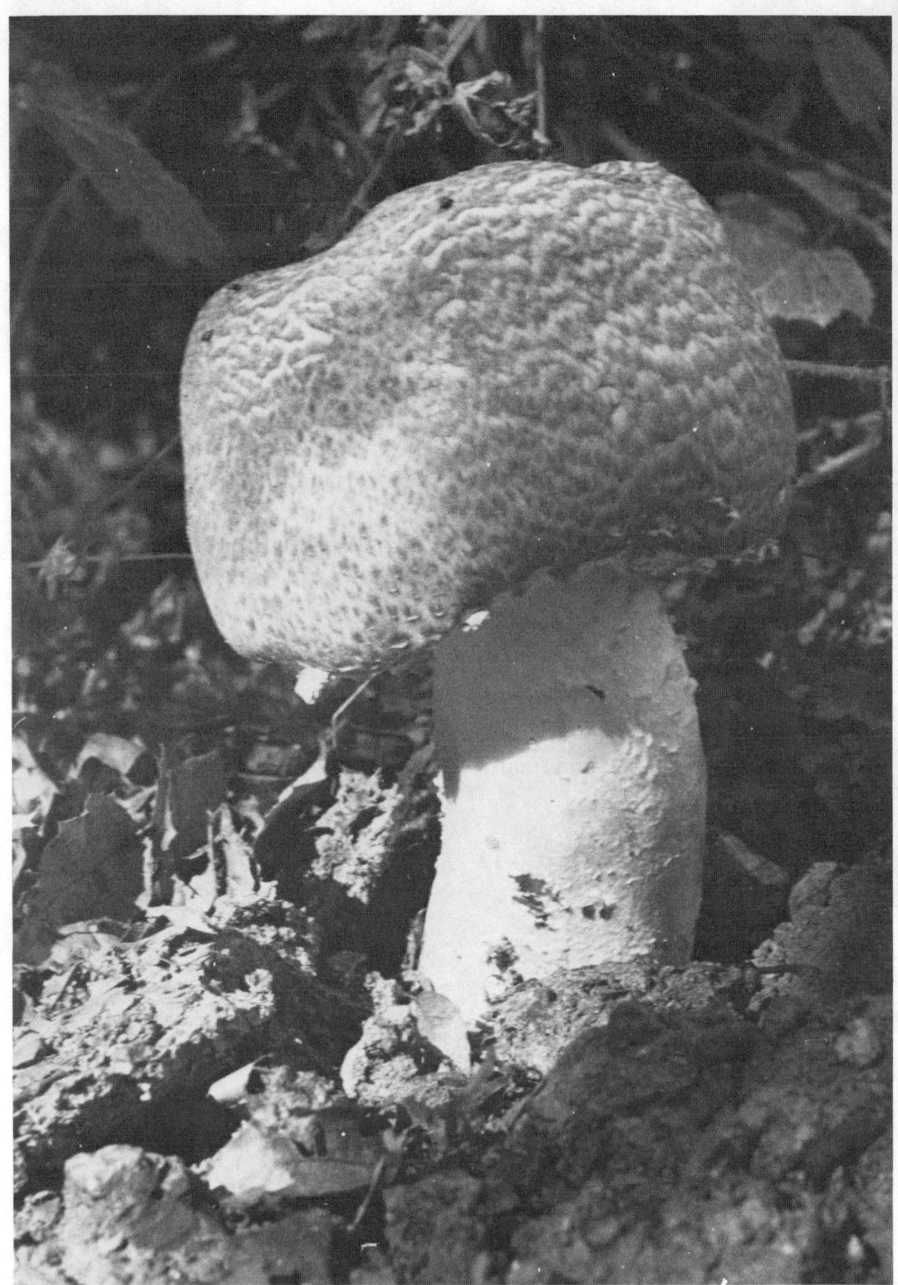

Agaricus augustus, The Prince, is one of our most delicious fleshy fungi.

CONTENTS

FUNGOPHOBIA

BRING HOME what looks like a wild onion for dinner, and no one gives it a second thought—despite the fact it might be a death camas you have, especially if you didn't bother to smell it. But bring home a wild mushroom for dinner, and watch the faces of your friends crawl with various combinations of fear, anxiety, loathing, and distrust. Appetites are suddenly and mysteriously misplaced, vague announcements are hurriedly mumbled as to dinner engagements elsewhere, until you're finally left alone to "enjoy" your meal in total silence.

For there are few things that strike as much fear in your average American as the mere mention of wild mushrooms or "toadstools." Like snakes, slugs, worms, and spiders, they're regarded as unearthly and unworthy, despicable and inexplicable—the vermin of the vegetable world. And yet, consider this: out of several thousand different kinds of wild mushrooms in North America, only five or six are deadly poisonous! And once you know what to look for, it's about as difficult to tell a deadly *Amanita* from a savory chanterelle as it is a lima bean from an artichoke.

This irrational fear of fungi is certainly *not* a universal trait. The media and medical profession have in some cases helped to perpetuate it, but they are certainly not responsible for its origin. To a large extent, we inherited our fungophobia from the British. William Delisle Hays, an astute Englishman writing in the 1800s, expressed it this way:

> (All mushrooms) . . . are lumped together in one sweeping condemnation. They are looked upon as vegetable vermin only made to be destroyed. No English eye can see their beauties, their office is unknown, their varieties not regarded. They are hardly allowed a place among nature's lawful children, but are considered something abnormal, worthless, and inexplicable. By precept and example children are taught from earliest infancy to despise, loathe, and avoid all kinds of "toadstools." The individual who desires to engage in the study of them must boldly face a good deal of scorn. He is laughed at for his strange taste among the better classes, and is actually regarded as a sort of idiot among the lower orders. No fad or hobby is esteemed so contemptible as that of "fungus-hunter," or "toadstool-eater."
>
> This popular sentiment, which we may coin the word "fungophobia" to express, is very curious. If it were human—that is, universal—one would be inclined to set it down as an instinct, and to revere it accordingly. But it is not human—it is merely British. It is so

> deep and intense a prejudice that it amounts to a national superstition . . .
>
> It is a striking instance of the confused popular notions of fungi in England that hardly any species have or ever had colloquial English names. They are all "toadstools," and therefore are thought unworthy of baptism. Can anything more fully demonstrate the existence of that deep-rooted prejudice called here "fungophobia"? . . .

Mushrooms can be every bit as beautiful as birds, butterflies, shells, and flowers, yet we never think to describe them in such flattering terms. When novelists or poets want to conjure up an emotion of fear, loathing, total revulsion, and imminent decay, they inevitably drag in the mushrooms and toadstools—malignant instruments of death and disease that appear only in the dankest and most abominable of situations. Witness Shelley:

> And agarics and fungi, with mildew and mould
> Started like mist from the wet ground cold
> Pale, fleshy, as if the decaying dead
> With a spirit of growth had been animated . . .

Or Sir Arthur Conan Doyle, bygone creator of Sherlock Holmes:

> . . . A sickly autumn shone upon the land. Wet and rotten leaves reeked and festered under the foul haze. The fields were spotted with monstrous fungi of a size and colour never matched before—scarlet and mauve and liver and black—it was as though the sick earth had burst into foul pustules. Mildew and lichen mottled the walls and with that filthy crop, death sprang also from the watersoaked earth.

Or that prim American poet Emily Dickinson:

> Had nature any outcast face
> Could she a son condemn
> Had nature an Iscariot
> That mushroom—it is him.

Has any group of organisms been so unjustly maligned? Actually, Dickinson's effort should come as no surprise, since she was a virtual recluse. Prejudice, among other things, is a measure of ignorance!

And yet, if you go to the continent, you'll find that fungophobia is the exception and not the rule. Most Europeans, especially those who live close to the woods, know which mushrooms to pick and how to cook them. They bestow upon each species an individual name and sell them at the markets. Many Americans, on the other hand, are completely oblivious to the fact that there is more than one fungus among us—those of recent European ancestry being notable exceptions.

The farther east you go in Europe, the more passionate the love for mushrooms. Which brings us to Russia. The Russians go absolutely bananas over fungus. Mushrooming is a commonplace tradition there, not the hallowed turf of the academic or connoisseur. Instead of talking about the weather, strangers talk about how the mushroom season is progressing. And Russian children are raised on mushrooms from earliest infancy. Many family names are derived from fungi: Bribov, Borovikov, Gruzdjov, Ryshikov, Opjonkin. Another one is Griboyedev, or "Mr. Mushroom-eater." The poet Majokovsky was a mushroom addict. (Poetry, like mushrooms, is a great tradition there. A Russian poet draws 5,000 to a poetry reading—here you're lucky to draw fifty.) Even Lenin is said to have been possessed by a *razh* or "mushroom passion."

In this country, it is only with the renewal of interest in natural foods and the desire to return to the earth (and what's good for you) that mushrooms are being noticed again. Mycological societies are sprouting up in the major cities. And of course, business is capitalizing on the trend. Polka-dotted mushrooms have appeared in startling profusion on curtains and calendars, pottery and stationery, potholders and incense holders, bumper stickers and birthday cakes.

And yet, when it comes down to actually eating wild mushrooms, most Americans are still afraid. Instead they opt for something more familiar and not half as good, such as Grape Nuts or Malt Balls. Yet it stands to reason that if mushroom-eating were an inherently dangerous activity, it could not exist to the extent it does in Europe. And the mycological societies would be in dire need of new members, their ranks depleted annually by the "Mushroom Menace." Like driving, swimming, walking, or breathing, mushroom-eating *is only made dangerous by those who approach it frivolously.*

If you treat mushrooms with discrimination and respect, you can learn to pick your own edible wild mushrooms without fear of confusing them with poisonous types—mushrooms which are nutritious, far more flavorful than the mass-produced commercial variety, and best of all, free! It does, however, require time and effort—a willingness to plunge into the woods, to uncover their secrets, to learn their characteristics, to penetrate their haunts. That's what this book is about.

WHAT IS A MUSHROOM?

FUNGI ARE neither plants nor animals. They don't contain chlorophyll like green plants, and as a result cannot manufacture their own food. In this respect they resemble animals, because they feed themselves by digesting other organic matter. However, they lack the nervous system, specialized organs, and mobility characteristic of most animals. Furthermore, fungi reproduce by means of microscopic reproductive units called **spores.** These usually consist of a single cell, and are far simpler in structure than seeds or eggs.

The term **mushroom** is usually used to describe the reproductive structure **(fruiting body)** of a fungus. In this sense a mushroom, like a potato or persimmon, is *not* an organism, but a *part* of an organism. However, the term "mushroom" can also mean any fungus which produces a fleshy fruiting body (that is, one that has substance). By this definition, not all fungi qualify as mushrooms. Athlete's foot fungus, bread molds, water molds, yeasts, mildews, and slime molds are examples of fungi which do *not* form fleshy fruiting bodies. The term "mushroom" can also be applied in a more restricted sense to those fungi (like the commercial mushroom) whose fruiting bodies are furnished with radiating blades or **gills.**

Many fungi are exquisitely constructed, and their life cycles are among the most complex to be found. It is not the purpose of this book to explore their biology, but it *is* necessary to consider briefly how mushrooms grow and reproduce. The mushrooms described in this book belong to two classes of fungi. The vast majority produce their spores on the *exterior* of microscopic club-shaped cells called **basidia** (singular: **basidium**), hence they are called **Basidiomycetes.** The remainder produce their spores *inside* microscopic saclike mother cells called **asci** (singular: **ascus**), hence they are called **Ascomycetes.**

basidium

ascus

Spore formation. At left is a typical club-shaped basidium, with four small stalks (sterigmata) on which the spores form. At right is an ascus, inside of which spores (usually 8) form.

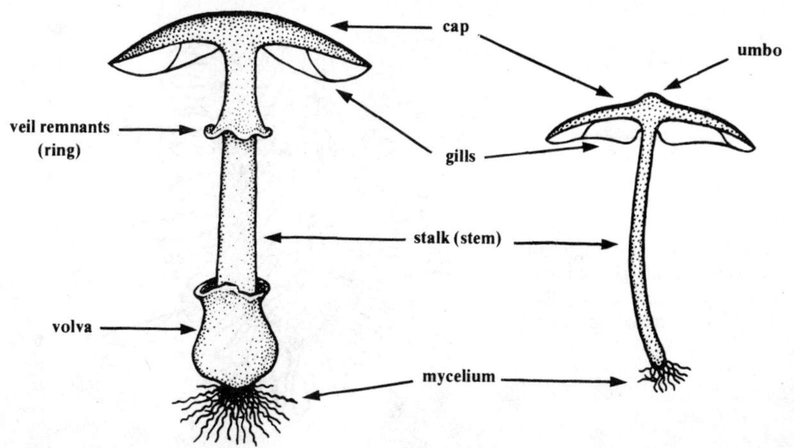

Parts of a gilled mushroom. Mature *Amanita* at left has cap, stalk, gills, ring, and volva. The veil covers the gills when young and breaks to form a ring on the stalk, while the volva envelops entire fruiting body and breaks to form a sack, collar, or series of concentric rings at base of stalk. Development of fruiting body is shown on pp. 232-233. At right is a mature *Marasmius*, which lacks both veil and volva, but has an umbo (knob) on cap.

The fruiting bodies of Basidiomycetes and Ascomycetes vary greatly in detail and design, but their function is always the same—to perpetuate their species by disseminating spores. A typical gilled mushroom (the most common type of fruiting body) is a rather simple structure consisting of a **cap, gills,** and (usually) a **stalk.** A **ring** or **volva** (or both) may also be present. The parts of a gilled mushroom are discussed in more detail on pp. 16-22. Fruiting bodies of a radically different structure, such as puffballs, are illustrated and discussed in their respective chapters.

In a gilled mushroom, millions of spores are produced on basidia which line the gills. These spores are subsequently discharged and carried by air currents to new localities. Each is theoretically capable of germination, but only a small percentage land in a favorable environment. Spores germinate by sending out a **germ tube** which branches to form many threadlike cells **(hyphae)**. When two spores of opposite strains (or "sexes") germinate in close proximity to each other, their hyphae merge to form hyphae with two nuclei (one from each parent). These hyphae grow rapidly, forming an intricate network of filaments called the **mycelium** (or **spawn**). The mycelium is the *vegetative portion of the fungus.* The tips of the mycelial hyphae liberate enzymes which digest food to support growth.

After the mycelium has established itself and built up an adequate food reserve, it is capable of producing mushrooms. Periodically, when conditions are favorable (damp but not soggy, cool but not cold), hyphae bundle together to form knots which gradually develop into fruiting bodies. When these fruiting bodies are differentiated but not

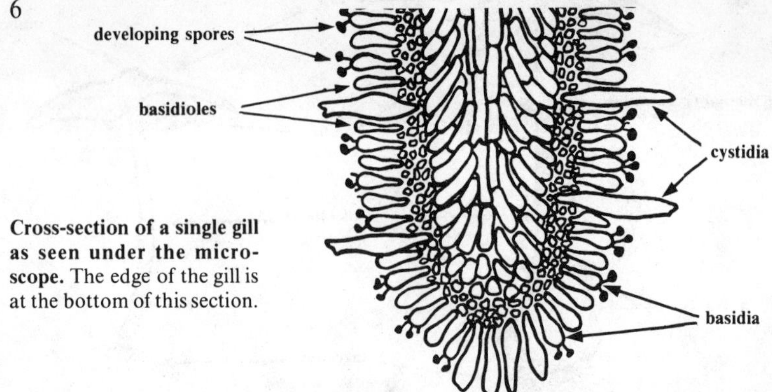

Cross-section of a single gill as seen under the microscope. The edge of the gill is at the bottom of this section.

fully developed (that is, before the mushroom expands), they are called **buttons.** The stalk then elongates, pushing the cap above the surface of the ground. Then the cap opens and the veil (if present) breaks, exposing the gills. The mature fruiting body is essentially a bundle of filamentous hyphae (each with two nuclei), but the filaments in the bundle terminate in either special spore-producing cells (**basidia**), specialized sterile cells (**cystidia**), or unspecialized sterile cells (**paraphyses,** or in the case of gilled mushrooms, **basidioles**).

Though they lack the sexual organs of plants and animals, mushrooms reproduce sexually. That is, genes are recombined so that *offspring are not genetically identical with parents.* In mushrooms the sexual act takes place in the basidium (or ascus) where the two nuclei fuse, doubling the chromosome number, and then divide twice—reducing the chromosome number to half that before fusion. The four resulting nuclei migrate to the tip of the basidium. Walls form behind them to produce four spores—two of each strain ("sex"), each with one nucleus. With their subsequent discharge the cycle is completed.

This life cycle holds for most mushrooms, except that it is often complicated by the presence of more than two strains (just as our life cycle would be unimaginably complicated by the existence of more than two sexes). Also, some mushrooms are capable of forming spores asexually.

MUSHROOMS AND THE ENVIRONMENT

IT IS the "role" of fungi to break things down, to give things back. One of the more obvious laws of nature is that existing life must die if new life is to flourish. Stale air must go out the window if fresh air is to come in. If there were no vehicle for the disposal of dead matter, there would soon be no need for one—we would all be buried under a blanket of dead, inert matter. Fungi (along with bacteria) are that vehicle. They are nature's recyclers, the soil's replenishers. Plants deplete the soil by extracting minerals to manufacture their food. Animals in turn devour plants. In feeding on dead (or occasionally living) matter, fungi and bacteria reduce complex organic compounds to raw materials, thereby enabling plants to re-use them. Thus, in a very profound sense, fungi are life-givers as well as destroyers. To associate them only with death and decay is to do them (as well as your own ability to perceive) an injustice.

Fungi can be divided into three categories based on their relationship to their immediate environment **(substrate). Parasitic** fungi feed on living organisms. Most serious fungus pests (such as wheat rust) fall in this category, but relatively few mushrooms are parasitic. Their ranks include *Cordyceps* species (on insects, insect pupae, and larvae); *Asterophora, Hypomyces,* and *Sepedonium* (on other mushrooms); several polypores (on trees); and *Sparassis radicata* on tree roots. Some, like the common honey mushroom, *Armillariella mellea,* are parasitic under certain conditions and saprophytic (see below) under others.

Saprophytic fungi subsist on dead or decaying matter (wood, humus, soil, debris, and dung). When there is an even distribution of nutrients in the environment, the mycelium of a terrestrial fungus may grow outward at the same rate in all directions, periodically producing circles of mushrooms on its outer fringes. These circles or arcs are called **fairy rings,** presumably because people once thought fairies danced in them. Many mushrooms are capable of forming fairy rings, including the aptly named fairy ring mushroom, *Marasmius oreades,* which grows on

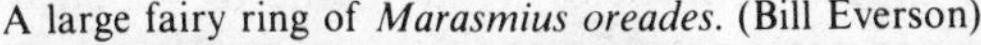
A large fairy ring of *Marasmius oreades.* (Bill Everson)

lawns. Each year the fairy ring gets larger as the mycelium grows outward, until something finally impedes its progress (usually a lack of food), and the mycelium dies. By measuring the annual rate of growth, it has been estimated that some fairy rings in the Midwest prairies are four hundred years old!

Mycorrhizal fungi comprise the third category. They form a symbiotic (mutually beneficial) relationship with the rootlets of plants (mostly trees) called **mycorrhiza** (*myco,* fungus and *rhiza,* root). The mycelium forms a sheath of hyphae around the rootlets of the host and an exchange of nutrients takes place. The rootlets provide the fungus with moisture and organic compounds (such as carbohydrates), while the fungus aids the roots in the absorption of phosphorus, inorganic nitrogen, and other minerals. As a rule the fungus cannot grow without the trees, and studies have shown that trees deprived of their mycorrhizal partners cannot compete successfully with those that have their normal complement. In poor soil trees are especially dependent on mycorrhiza, and mycorrhizal fungi have proved invaluable in reforestation projects.

Many mycorrhiza-formers are very specific in their habitat requirements. They often grow only with one kind of tree. For instance, *Suillus pungens* grows only with Monterey and knobcone (rarely ponderosa) pine, while *Amanita rubescens* is monogamous (in our area) with oak. A tree, however, may have several mycorrhizal associates, whose relationships with the tree are qualitatively different. In other words, each type of mushroom occupies a different **ecological niche.** Many factors are encompassed by the concept of niche, some of which we don't understand. A niche is not so much an organism's habitat as its "profession"—the "role" it plays in its biological community. Each kind of mushroom reproduces and germinates successfully within a certain humidity and temperature spectrum. Each extracts particular nutrients from its environment. Thus two species may occur in the same habitat, but occupy different niches. One may be digesting the lignin from a log, another the cellulose. Or one may be feeding on the heartwood, another on the sapwood. Or returning to the mycorrhizal fungi, one may be supplying phosphorus to a tree, and another, inorganic nitrogen.

Succession also occurs—as one type of mushroom exhausts its nutrient supply, another takes its place. A living tree may harbor certain types of fungal growth. As soon as it falls, new species will appear. Eventually the wood is reduced to fragments or powder, at which point still other mushrooms take over, with growth habits suited to the changed conditions.

NAMES AND CLASSIFICATION

NAMES, like automobiles, are largely vehicles of convenience. You can't claim to have a profound knowledge of human beings without knowing at least *some* of them on an individual basis. Recognition is a prerequisite to getting to know someone, and a name is helpful in associating that person with a unique set of identifying characteristics, whether it be his big nose and hairy face, or her long legs and swift smile. Rather than saying "the 6 ft. 7 in. acrobatic forward of the Philadelphia 76ers," we say "Julius Erving" or "Doctor J." Instead of "the bright red mushroom with the white spots that grows under pine," we say *Amanita muscaria,* or "fly agaric."

Names can also be descriptive. For instance, the red-headed woodpecker has a red head and pecks wood. What's more, names can reflect common bonds. Your last name identifies you as a member of a group with similar genes, and provides a clue to your origins. Your first name defines you as an individual entity within that group.

Unfortunately, relatively few mushrooms have colloquial English names. As pointed out previously, this can be attributed to our fungophobic past. In some cases I have capriciously coined common names, but to do so in every case would only create confusion, as there is no assurance they would be accepted. Therefore, it is necessary to learn the scientific names of mushrooms. People usually groan when they hear this, and to be sure, the long Latin names are intimidating at first. But so is a can opener—it's just a question of familiarity. In fact, most people have mastered a great number of Latin (scientific) names without realizing it—e.g., *Eucalyptus, Rhododendron, Hippopotamus.* Memorization is made easier by learning the meanings of the names—*lac* means "milk" and *sanguis* means "blood," and sure enough, *Lactarius sanguifluus* exudes a bloody "milk" when cut. Don't get bogged down in pronunciation. Accent marks are included in the index for selected names, but it doesn't really matter *how* you say something, so long as you *communicate* it. Even scientists don't agree on the "correct" pronunciation of many names!

As you begin to use scientific nomenclature, you'll discover its many advantages. Common names do *not* necessarily reflect natural affinities. Hedge nettle is not a nettle, and poison oak is by no means an oak. Likewise, the names meadow mushroom, honey mushroom, matsutake, and horse mushroom provide no clues as to which, if any, have common bonds or similar characteristics. Also, common names are *not* universal. For instance, *Boletus edulis* has dozens of regional names. Memorizing all of them would be almost as difficult as getting people to agree on one of them!

In contrast, scientific nomenclature transcends cultural and regional barriers. It is used by naturalists and biologists throughout the world, and it is designed to reflect natural relationships. It employs a **binomial system** in which each kind of organism has two names. The second name, the **species,** is the *kind* of organism; the first name, the **genus** (plural: **genera**) is a collection of species with very similar traits. The species epithet is meaningless without the genus name (or its abbreviation) attached (we never sign a check with only our first name!). The names are in Latin because that language was universally fashionable in learned circles when the binomial system was devised. The beauty of the binomial system is that it indicates commonality while simultaneously expressing singularity.* *Amanita calyptroderma* (the coccora) and *Amanita phalloides* (the death cap) are different mushrooms belonging to the same genus, just as *Canis lupis* (wolf), *Canis latrans* (coyote), and *Canis familiaris* (dog) belong to the same genus. Yet their common names don't reflect this!

Some kinds of similarities are clearly more fundamental than others. Therefore, it was deemed necessary to erect a hierarchy of classification to indicate the *degree of commonality.* Genus and species are only two levels in that hierarchy. Just as species with common characteristics are grouped in a genus, several genera with common characteristics are grouped in a **family** (e.g., the red fox, *Vulpes fulva,* belongs to the same family as the dog, but *not* the same genus). Families are in turn grouped in an **order,** orders in a **class,** classes in a **division** (or phylum), and **divisions** in a kingdom. At the other end of the scale, slightly different populations of a single species are designated as **subspecies, varieties,** or **forms.**** Here is the complete classification scheme for three mushrooms—the blewitt, shaggy mane, and inky cap.

Category	Blewitt	Shaggy mane	Inky cap
Kingdom	Fungi	Fungi	Fungi
Division	Eumycota	Eumycota	Eumycota
Class	Basidiomycetes	Basidiomycetes	Basidiomycetes
Order	Agaricales	Agaricales	Agaricales
Family	Tricholomataceae	Coprinaceae	Coprinaceae
Genus	*Lepista*	*Coprinus*	*Coprinus*
Species	*nuda*	*comatus*	*atramentarius*

* the singularity of a *population* of organisms; our personal names, on the other hand, indicate the singularity of *individual* organisms

** In this book the term "variety" is used in its ordinary English sense to mean a "type" of organism. Only when *one* species is being discussed and "variety" is abbreviated (var.) is it applied in its scientific sense. The same goes for "form."

All three are fungi—they possess neither photosynthetic compounds nor seeds, and their vegetative phase is comprised of filamentous cells (hyphae). Since none are amoeba-like, they belong to the division Eumycota. All three produce their spores on microscopic cells called basidia, hence they belong to the class Basidiomycetes. All form their basidia on radiating bladelike gills, therefore they belong to the order Agaricales. However, the blewitt has pinkish spores while the shaggy mane and inky cap have black spores—which is one reason they are placed in different families. Not only do the shaggy mane and inky cap belong to the same family (Coprinaceae), but to the same *(Coprinus)*, because both have gills that liquefy at maturity. However, the shaggy mane has a tall, shaggy, cylindrical cap while the inky cap has a smooth, broad, oval cap; consequently they are recognized as distinct species.

Note the suffixes at the levels above genus: *—ceae* denotes a family; *—ales* denotes an order; and *—cetes* denotes anything above an order and below a division (all three of the above belong to the "sub-class" Homobasidiomy*cetes* and the "super-order" Hymenomy*cetes*).

It must be remembered, however, that this elaborate classification scheme is contrived. *It is our attempt at imposing order on nature.* There are common gene pools and definite evolutionary trends, but no such clearcut categories exist. Thus, the definition and interpretation of species, genera, families, etc., *is largely a matter of opinion.* Disputes invariably arise, many of which have not been resolved. For instance, at the genus level and above, there is the problem of deciding which similarities among fungi are fundamental (indicators of common origin), and which are coincidental or superficial, or the result of convergent evolution.* The advent of the microscope has exacerbated the confusion by introducing a vast new set of criteria on which to pass judgment. The result is a nomenclatural nightmare, from the upper echelons of the hierarchy right on down to the species level.

Mycological literature is as riddled with contradictions as a *Suillus pungens* is with maggots. Anyone who has used more than one mushroom book can testify to the frustration at finding different names applied to the same fungus (synonyms), or one name applied to several different fungi (homonyms). For instance, *Lepista nuda* (the blewitt) was formerly known as *Tricholoma nudum,* is known in Europe as *Rhodopaxillus nudus,* has recently been rechristened *Clitocybe nuda,* and has been incorrectly called *Tricholoma personatum*!

* The fins and torpedo-shaped bodies of sharks and killer whales are independent adaptations to a similar environment, *not* indicators of common origin. This phenomenon is called convergent evolution.

This confusion is largely the result of disagreement as to what exactly constitutes a "genus" or "species"—a difference in philosophy that is known in taxonomic circles as the battle between the "lumpers" and "splitters." The "lumpers" are conservative in their approach. They interpret genera and species broadly, allowing for a good deal of variation—in other words, they tend to stress similarities between mushrooms rather than differences. "Splitters," on the other hand, are forever describing new genera and species based on the most minute (but not necessarily insignificant) differences. Both approaches have their advantages and disadvantages, and carried to an extreme both are self-defeating.

The important thing to realize is that the system of classification used in this book is *by no means definitive*. It represents an amalgamation of various investigators' views of the fleshy fungi. Some names will undoubtedly be invalidated in the near future. Others have been used tentatively (placed in quotations). Synonyms have been provided and homonyms elucidated. But the inherent advantages of the binomial system of nomenclature will not be fully realized until stabilization is achieved and one name is agreed upon for each kind of mushroom. In exceptional cases like that of the blewitt, it is perhaps easiest in the meantime to use the common English name (if there is one).

COLLECTING MUSHROOMS

MUSHROOM HUNTING is not simply a matter of traipsing through the woods in winter. It is an art, a skill, a meditation, and a process. If you proceed at a careful, deliberate rate, you'll enjoy much more success than if you rush around blindly picking whatever mushrooms you see, then stuff them in your basket, bring the whole mess home and dump it on your table. Mushrooms collected in this manner are likely to wind up in the garbage, unidentified and unappreciated.

Don't just collect, but *observe*—the mushrooms and their surroundings. In the process you'll discover many other clandestine wonders you were previously unaware of. *Be selective*—pick only distinctive species in good condition. You enhance your chances of correct identification immeasurably by collecting *several specimens of each kind of mushroom*. This is absolutely essential, because you have no other means of assessing variation within a given species. Since identification is a time-consuming process and mushrooms decay rapidly, don't pick every kind you see. It's far better to fill your basket with many specimens of a few species (in which case your chances of identification are good), than with one or two specimens of many species (in which case your chances of identification are almost nil).

Don't assume, however, that two mushrooms are the same species simply because they grow together. Judge each on its own merits. If you're uncertain, *assume for safety's sake* that they're different, and treat them as such. As you become more adept at observation, your ability to identify fleshy fungi will "mushroom"—but only after a solid foundation ("mycelium") is laid.

It is far better to learn a few species well than a large number superficially. The novelty of the Easter egg approach wears off quickly as its futility becomes apparent. If possible, choose a specific quarry for the hunt. Suppose it's January and you're going for a walk in a live oak woodland. By consulting the chart on pp. 36-41, you find that the blewitt *(Lepista nuda)* is *usually* abundant under oak in January. The next step is to familiarize yourself with the blewitt's identifying characteristics: bluish-purple color, stocky stature, absence of a veil, citrus odor, etc. Your mushroom hunt is thus transformed into a *blewitt* hunt. Of course, nothing stops you from gathering other interesting fungi you encounter, but focusing your attention on the blewitt insures that you'll learn something about blewitts *even if you don't find any* (namely, that the locality or weather conditions were not conducive to its fruiting).

The desirability of this approach is underscored by the excitement it lends to the hunt. It is much more gratifying to find something you are specifically looking for. And you'll be more likely to remember what it looks like and where it grows, so you can return to harvest more. By focusing on several species as the season unfolds, you will develop a quicker and keener appreciation of what grows where and what weather factors they respond to. Many of the more distinctive species occur throughout the world, so the knowledge is useful practically everywhere.

EQUIPMENT

Foraging for fungi requires little in the way of sophisticated paraphernalia. The bare necessities are:

A rigid container for carrying the mushrooms. There's no point in picking mushrooms unless you transport them home in decent condition. A broad, shallow basket is best, but a cardboard box or bucket will do unless it's raining. Paper bags sag and the mushrooms get crushed. NEVER USE PLASTIC BAGS! Mushrooms, like people, have to "breathe." Plastic bags trap moisture, making the mushrooms "sweat" and rot rapidly.

Waxed paper is necessary when collecting mushrooms for identification. It provides support for mushrooms within the basket and also keeps them separated. *Never mix unknown species together.* Wrap each type separately and arrange them carefully in the basket with the heavier ones on the bottom. Tall specimens like *Agaricus* and *Amanita* will bend unless placed upright

Always dig up unknown mushrooms so as not to miss the volva, if present. There's no room for carelessness, as evidenced here: *Agaricus arvensis* at left lacks a volva and is edible; *Amanita ocreata* at right is furnished with a volva and is deadly poisonous!

(mushrooms exhibit negative geotropism: their caps will turn away from gravity so as to orient the gills properly). Small paper bags are useful when harvesting familiar edible species.

A **knife** is necessary for digging up mushrooms or detaching them from trees. It's also handy for cleaning edible species you are already familiar with, but *always* dig up unknown mushrooms so as not to leave behind the volva or "tap root," if present. (The telltale volva of a deadly *Amanita* is usually buried in the ground!)

A pencil and small notebook (or index cards) are useful for taking field notes and spore prints.

Bread, cheese, and fruit are essential if you're always hungry like I am. I make a practice of stocking my basket generously—then each time I put a mushroom in my basket, I'm compelled to put something from the basket in my mouth. If you find some *Agaricus* buttons, put them in a sandwich! Not known for wasting opportunities, the French carry this tradition one step further—they bring wine, wine glasses, and a table cloth, and pause for a picnic every half hour. The advantage of this strategy is obvious—you needn't find any mushrooms to have a good time!

Binoculars are handy in open country (e.g., pastures). They enable you to distinguish at a distance giant puffballs (*Calvatia* species) and horse mushrooms *(Agaricus arvensis)* from rocks and other assorted "pseudocarps." And of course, they allow you to watch birds and mammals as well.

Other optional equipment includes: a hand lens, compass, stick (for probing brambles and "mushrumps"), field guide (for leisurely use on a sunny day), small jars or vials (for delicate specimens such as Mycenas), rainboots and other rain gear, gloves for frigid winter mornings, and camera equipment (usually too cumbersome except for special picture-taking expeditions).

FIELD NOTES

Is it growing on the ground or on a log? Is it near a tree? What kind(s)? Are familiar types of mushrooms growing nearby? Which ones? If it's growing on wood, is the wood coniferous or hardwood? Recently felled or in an advanced stage of decay? If on the ground, is the humus layer deep? Is the ground disturbed? Is there a road, trail, or parking lot nearby?

You should automatically ask yourself these questions every time you find a mushroom. *Observation begins in the field.* After all, in picking a mushroom you are leaving the vegetative portion of the fungus behind. It is folly to depart without some idea of the niche that fungus occupies in the larger scheme of things. Field (or mental) notes should include:

> **Date, weather conditions, abundance** (how many times you observed a particular species), **growth habit** (solitary, scattered, gregarious, clustered, in fairy rings, etc.), **substrate** (humus, soil, grass, moss, dung, wood, etc.), **vegetation** (trees and shrubs within 50 feet).
>
> If growing on wood: **stage of decomposition, type of wood** (hardwood or conifer), **type of tree** (if discernible), **effects on the wood** (see chapter on polypores, p. 437).
>
> If growing on dung: **type of dung, stage of decomposition**
>
> If growing on ground: **type of ground** (disturbed, cultivated, sandy, charred, etc.)

Don't restrict your observations to specimens that you collect. After you have a representative sampling of a particular species, continue to note its habitat each time you encounter it.

With terrestrial fungi, it is important to note all types of trees within 50 feet because mycorrhizal species grow in association with rootlets that may be quite a distance from the trunk of the host. Usually there are several kinds of trees in the vicinity, and you have no way of knowing which (if any) is the mycorrhizal associate. However, through repeated observation many possibilities can be eliminated. For instance, if you find *Suillus pungens* growing under a pine, you *cannot* conclude that there is a relationship between the two. But if you find that *Suillus pungens* always grows with pine *and nowhere else,* then an intimate relationship of some kind can be inferred.

IDENTIFICATION AND TERMINOLOGY

IF YOU take the time to seek mushrooms out, it only makes sense to exercise the extra care and trouble necessary to get them home in beautiful condition. Handle them gingerly, don't store them in stuffy places (like cars), and don't shift them unnecessarily from place to place. *Always* conduct your studies on fresh material, preferably the day you pick them. *Coprinus* species digest themselves in a few hours, and many types are devoured overnight by maggots. If you're pressed for time, at least sort them out, and separate worm-riddled specimens. Then refrigerate the ones you wish to save or spread them out in a cool, dry place where they can "breathe."

Now let's assume you've taken field notes, brought several species home, and are ready to study them. For the diligent and disciplined taxonomist, a detailed written description of each species is a definitive must. For most people, compiling a written description is a tedious affair which tends to detract from the enjoyment and spontaneity of the hunt. However, it is an ideal tool for learning *how* to look at mushrooms critically, so try it a few times.

The basic terminology for identifying and describing gilled mushrooms is outlined here. (Fruiting bodies with a radically different structure, such as puffballs, are illustrated and discussed in their respective chapters.) Unfamiliar terms are illustrated or defined in the glossary. Remember to base your observations on *as many specimens of each species* as possible. The value of written descriptions is enhanced when accompanied by sketches, photographs, and spore prints of fresh material.

MACROSCOPIC CHARACTERISTICS

SIZE

Size is important for purposes of comparison. The terms **large, medium, small,** and **minute** cannot be given absolute measurements, but they communicate a characteristic *size range* that you will quickly learn to appreciate. The size of a fruiting body is dependent on three major factors: age, amount of moisture available, and genes. Since mushrooms grow very quickly, those that fruit during a period of prolonged rainfall are apt to be larger than those that fruit during a dry spell—subject, of course, to genetic constraints.

Measurements given in descriptions and keys do *not* take into account extremes due to extraordinary conditions. For the sake of uniformity, the metric system is used. It is not familiar to everyone, but a conversion rule is provided on the inside back cover of this book. It's also easy to remember that 1 inch equals approximately 2½ centimeters, or 2 inches equal 5 centimeters.

COLOR

Color is one of the most noticeable features of any fungus, but is also one of the most deceptive and variable. Unfortunately, beginners tend to attach undue importance to color at the expense of more critical characteristics. This inevitably leads to misidentification because many mushroom pigments are highly sensitive to environmental influence. Direct sunlight or prolonged rain can bleach a mushroom drastically, and I will never forget my experience following a prolonged rainy spell in which practically every mushroom growing under redwood had a reddish cap! Apparently the redwood pigments had dissolved in the drip-off and been absorbed by the mushrooms. None of these mushrooms would have keyed out properly unless this phenomenon were taken into account! Color may also depend on age. An immature sea gull is brown, while an adult is black and white. Likewise, an immature *Hygrophorus conicus* is red or yellow, but blackens as it ages.

Therefore, color should always be used *in conjunction with other characteristics.* The most striking feature of *Amanita muscaria* is its bright red cap, but a slew of other mushrooms are also bright red. Furthermore, its cap may fade to orange or even whitish. It is the red cap *combined with the presence of warts and a volva* that render *A. muscaria* distinct.

The stalk color is not as variable because it is sheltered by the cap, but the gill color often changes as the spores mature. In fact, the disparity in gill color may be so great that young and old specimens can be mistaken for different species unless intervening stages are found.

Describing color is another problem. Even color pictures can't show the degree of variation within a given species. Standardized color charts are available, but they represent an extra expense. In this book, colors are described using familiar terms where possible, plus a few specific ones (e.g., vinaceous) defined in the glossary.

COLOR CHANGES

The tissue of many mushrooms oxidizes when exposed to the air—that is, it undergoes a color change when bruised. This may occur instantaneously (like the blueing of the tubes in many boletes), or slowly, like the reddening ("blushing") of the flesh in *Amanita rubescens.* Bruising reactions should be looked for on the surface of the cap and stalk, and on the flesh.

TEXTURE

The texture of the fruiting body is often significant—i.e., soft, watery, spongy, brittle, tough, leathery, corky, woody, etc. The dried fruiting bodies of some types (notably *Marasmius*) revive completely when moistened.

ODOR AND TASTE

It comes as a pleasant surprise to many people that mushrooms have distinctive tastes and odors. For instance, *Lactarius insulsus* is excruciatingly acrid (peppery), while *Agaricus augustus* is sweet. *Marasmius scorodonius* reeks of garlic (and is usually smelled before it is seen!); *Clitocybe suaveolens* smells like anise, and *Russula fragrantissima* like maraschino cherries, while *Armillaria ponderosa* is spicy—a provocative compromise between red hots and dirty socks.

The problem with odor and taste is terminology. They are essentially chemical tests, but each person's "laboratory" is different. What smells like sauerkraut to one person smells like sewer gas to the next. Moreover, mushrooms with a "mild" odor may be very pungent when crushed, or may only develop an odor at maturity. For this reason, odor and taste are not noted in this book except where crucial to identification.

Incidentally, any mushroom can be safely tasted by chewing on a small piece of the cap *and then spitting it out.* However, it is *not* a good policy to sample unknown mushrooms, particularly Amanitas. Do so only when it is called for in keys or descriptions.

CAP

The **cap** (or **pileus**) is the structure that supports the spore-producing surface (gills, pores, etc.). The skin of the cap is called the **cuticle** (or **pellicle** if it peels easily). A **viscid** cap is sticky when moist, often **slimy** (glutinous) when wet, and sometimes assumes a glossy appearance as it dries. Debris stuck to the cap surface is a telltale sign that it was viscid when moist. Also, if you moisten your finger and press it against the surface, it will feel sticky. A **hygrophanous** cap appears watery (or even translucent) when moist and opaque when dry, and fades dramatically in the process of drying *(Psathyrella candolleana,* a common lawn lover, is a good example.). A **dry** cap is neither viscid nor hygrophanous. It often has a dull, unpolished appearance, but will naturally be moist or soggy in wet weather.

Other features to note are: **size; shape** (p. 19); **color and color changes; surface characteristics** (smooth, scaly, granulose, fibrillose, warty, etc.); and **margin** (inrolled, incurved, straight, or uplifted; striate, translucent-striate, or not striate).

FLESH

Note **color, color changes, texture, thickness, odor when crushed,** and **taste** (if called for).

GILLS

Gills (or **lamellae**) are the thin, radiating blades found on the underside of most mushrooms, including the commercial variety. Shorter gills (**lamellulae**) are often interspersed with longer ones, but they usually don't have taxonomic significance. Features to note include: **mode of attachment to the stalk** (p. 19), **spacing, thickness, depth, forking pattern** (if any), and **color** (in both mature and immature specimens).

STALK

The **stalk** is the stemlike structure on which the cap is mounted. Its function is to thrust the cap above the ground so spores can be released into the air. Many wood-inhabiting forms lack a stalk because the wood serves the same purpose. The technical term for stalk is **stipe,** but I see no reason to clutter our vocabulary with yet another monosyllable starting with *st-*. Hereafter, the terms **stalk** and **stem** are used interchangeably.

SHAPE OF THE CAP

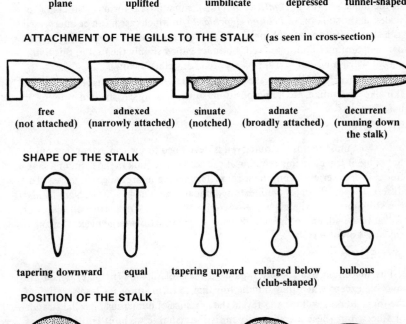

cylindrical conical bell-shaped umbonate convex

plane uplifted umbilicate depressed funnel-shaped

ATTACHMENT OF THE GILLS TO THE STALK (as seen in cross-section)

free (not attached) adnexed (narrowly attached) sinuate (notched) adnate (broadly attached) decurrent (running down the stalk)

SHAPE OF THE STALK

tapering downward equal tapering upward enlarged below (club-shaped) bulbous

POSITION OF THE STALK

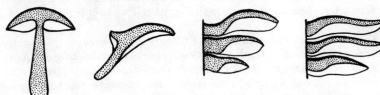

central off-center (eccentric) lateral absent (sessile)

Features to note include: **size, color and color changes, shape** (p. 19), **position** (p. 19), **texture** (fleshy or cartilaginous), **surface characteristics** (fibrillose, scaly, etc.), **viscidity**, and **presence or absence of a ring and volva** (see below).

VEIL

An **inner** (or **partial**) **veil** is a protective covering extending from the *margin* of the cap to the stalk. It hides the gills (or pores) when young, and breaks up or collapses as the cap spreads out. A **persistent** veil leaves visible remnants upon breaking. An **evanescent** veil disappears; consequently it can be detected only in the button stage. Many mushrooms lack a veil altogether. A **membranous** veil usually forms a **ring** (or **annulus**) on the stalk. A **fibrillose** veil is hairy and either disappears or forms a belt of collapsed hairs on the stalk. A **cortina** is a cobwebby fibrillose veil. A **slimy (glutinous)** veil either disappears or deposits a layer of slime on the stalk.

An **outer** (or **universal**) **veil** resembles an inner veil, but surrounds the entire mushroom in the button stage. Sometimes it adheres to the underside of the inner veil (as in *Agaricus arvensis*); sometimes it forms a "stocking" of scales on the stalk (as in *Lepiota clypeolaria*), in which case it can be interpreted as a sheathlike (**peronate**) inner veil. Since it is not always easy to distinguish between an inner and outer veil, both are called simply the **veil** in this book, except when an outer veil forms a **volva** (described below).

If a ring is formed, note the **color, texture** (see above), **shape** (collarlike, skirtlike, sheathlike, etc.), and **position** (superior or apical, median, inferior or basal).

VOLVA

In some mushrooms the outer veil is developed to such an extent that, upon breaking, it leaves visible remains at the base of the stalk in the form of a sack, free collar, or series of concentric rings. These remains are called the **volva.** The different types of volvas are illustrated under *Amanita,* p. 226. *Volvariella* and the stinkhorns (Phallales) are also equipped with a volva. If small pieces of volval tissue adhere to the cap, they are called **warts;** a large piece of tissue is called a **volval patch.**

MYCELIUM

The mycelium is a loosely organized mass of threads (hyphae) which are invisible except when they bundle together to form strands. Close scrutiny of the forest humus will usually reveal the presence of numerous mycelial strands or fibers, but these are virtually indistinguishable without fruiting bodies present.

There are a few exceptions, like *Chlorosplenium aeruginascens,* an Ascomycete which stains its substrate (a log or piece of wood) bluish-green. As a rule, however, it is the fruiting body alone that provides clues to the identity of a fungus. This is one reason why the classification of mushrooms has lagged behind that of other organisms—we're handicapped at the outset because our studies are restricted to only one aspect of the organism.

SPORE COLOR AND SPORE PRINTS

Unlike the color of the fruiting body, the spore color is constant for each species. Though individual spores cannot be seen with the naked eye, their color in mass can be ascertained by taking a **spore print**. Just cut off the cap of any mature mushroom and lay it gills down on a piece of *white* paper (covering it with a glass or bowl helps protect it from air currents). In 2-6 hours you'll *usually* have a spore print. Spore prints can also be obtained from boletes, teeth fungi, chanterelles, corals, and sometimes polypores. Fruiting bodies which are too young or too old will not give spore prints, and sterile specimens are sometimes encountered.

Always take a spore print to determine the spore color of an unknown mushroom, especially if you want to eat it. The color of the mature gills often corresponds to the spore color, but not often enough to be a reliable indicator. If you are frustrated by the two-hour delay, carry white index cards with you when you forage. Each time you collect several individuals of the same species, decapitate one, place it on a card, wrap it in waxed paper, and place it gills down in the basket in such a way that it won't be crushed. By the time you get home you'll have a spore print!

There are several shortcuts for determining spore color, but I recommend them only for experienced collectors because these methods are not completely reliable. If mushrooms are growing in a cluster, the lowermost caps will often be covered with spore dust from the upper ones. Spores borne aloft by air currents will often coat the cap of any mushroom, and falling spores are often trapped by the veil (if present) or the stalk, if it is sticky.

Deciding into which color category your spore print falls can be tricky. For instance, don't expect "pinkish" spores to be bright pink or "purple-brown"

Black spore prints of *Panaeolus campanulatus*.

spores to be purple. “Pinkish” spores are really closer to flesh color while “purple-brown” describes spores which could just as well be called “oil-slick aubergine” (deep brown in mass and dark reddish-brown under the microscope). Only through practice and comparison will you learn to assess the spore color correctly. The thickness of the spore print also affects the color, i.e., the heavier the deposit, the darker it will be.

Always take a spore print on white paper. A colored background distorts color perception. White spores will show up on white paper when viewed at an angle. Or you may wish to position the cap so that half of it is on white paper and half on black. Special cards can be designed for this purpose.

MICROSCOPIC CHARACTERISTICS

The microscope has had a great impact on the taxonomy of fungi, especially in the last fifty years. But since the vast majority of people do not have access to a microscope, microscopic features are not stressed in this book. For those who do have a microscope, spore characteristics (shape, size, and ornamentation) have been listed for each species. Spore size is measured in **microns** (= **micrometers:** μm). A micron is one thousandth of a millimeter. For each family or order of mushrooms, some typical spores have been illustrated—not for the purpose of identification so much as to give those without a microscope an idea of what they look like.

Other microscopic criteria used in the taxonomy of gilled mushrooms include: **orientation of the hyphae in the gill tissue, structure of the cap cuticle,** and **shape and size of cystidia** (specialized sterile cells) on the gills, stalk, and cap.

ARRANGEMENT OF THE GILL HYPHAE (as seen in cross-section)

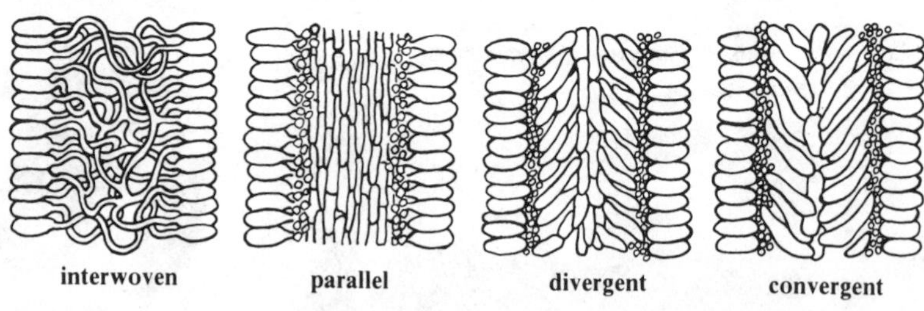

interwoven — parallel — divergent — convergent

STRUCTURE OF THE CAP CUTICLE

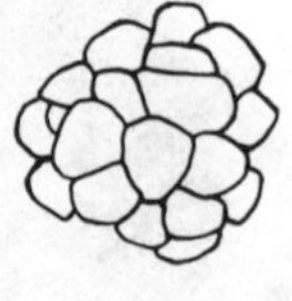

cellular

filamentous

CYSTIDIA

lance-shaped

flask-shaped

horned

harpoon-like

Spores can be examined by taking spore dust from a spore print and mounting it on a slide with a drop of water and a cover slip. Cystidia, basidia, and gill hyphae are best observed by making a thin cross-section of a gill with a razor blade and mounting it in a similar manner. The cap cuticle and tissue are also best seen in cross-section.

CHEMICAL CHARACTERISTICS

The ways in which mushrooms react to different chemicals have also assumed great importance in their classification. For instance, the genus *Lyophyllum* was erected to encompass those white-spored gilled mushrooms whose basidia contain granules that darken when treated with heated acetocarmine. Since most people are not equipped to conduct tests of this sort, they are not stressed. But there are two particularly useful chemicals: a 5-10% solution of potassium hydroxide (KOH), and an iodine solution called Melzer's reagent (see glossary for formula). Spores which stain bluish-gray to bluish-black in Melzer's are said to be **amyloid.** Spores which turn brown or reddish-brown are **dextrinoid.** Many spores are neither amyloid nor dextrinoid. The test is only useful on spores that are not deeply colored to begin with. It is easily observed under the microscope, but can also be assessed by placing spore dust on a glass slide, treating it with Melzer's, then holding the slide over a piece of white paper. The reaction (if any) will take place within a few minutes.

PRESERVING MUSHROOMS FOR FUTURE STUDY

Part of mushrooms' mystique is their ephemerality—they're literally here today and gone tomorrow, and there is no adequate means of preserving their beauty. For scientific purposes, drying is the best way to preserve them—they shrink and fade, but their microscopic features remain intact. Of course, for dried material to have value it must be accompanied by a spore print and precise description of the fresh fruiting bodies. Drying is best accomplished on a rack or screen, using a light bulb or hot plate as a heat source. It is more important for the air to circulate freely (carrying off the moisture), than for the temperature to be extremely hot. For this reason ovens are not suitable.

For ornamental purposes mushrooms can be freeze-dried or encased in cubes of plastic resin. Or they can be sectioned and pressed in a book, like these *Chroogomphus*. Preserving mushrooms for consumption is discussed in chapter on mushroom cookery.

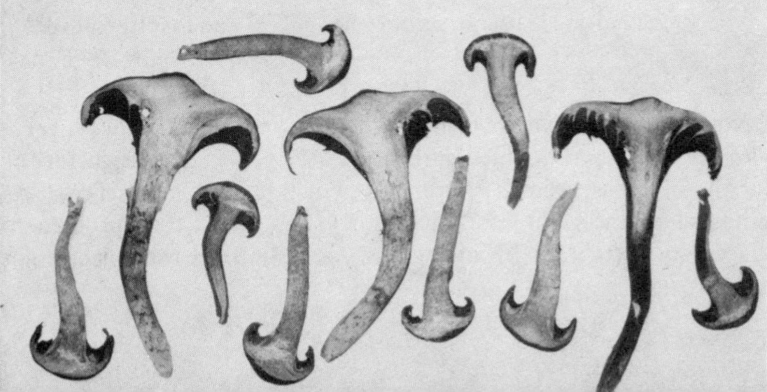

HOW TO USE THE KEYS

IF DESCRIPTIONS and illustrations are the meat of this book, then **keys** are its skeletal structure. Keys are tools designed to aid in the identification process. With the exception of the two pictorial keys, all the keys in this book are **dichotomous.** That is, they consist of a series of *contrasting paired statements* **(couplets).** You are asked to decide which statement in a given couplet is applicable to the mushroom in question. Having made your choice, you are then referred to the number of another couplet, where you again make a choice. This process is repeated until you are given the name of a mushroom (or group of mushrooms) and its appropriate page number.

The dichotomous keys in this book begin at the bottom of p. 55 with "Key to the Classes of Fleshy Fungi." Under each major group of fungi you'll find a key to families; under each family a key to genera; under each genus, a key to species. Keying will be a laborious process at first. However, as you gain experience, you can take shortcuts. For instance, if you already know that your mushroom is an *Agaricus,* you needn't consult the keys to families and genera of gilled mushrooms. You can proceed directly to the *Agaricus* key in order to determine the species.

The *key* to the proper use of a dichotomous key is an understanding of its limitations. The following key to a banana, banana slug, hat, rabbit, and sea urchin will admirably illustrate the assets and pitfalls of the dichotomous key. It is designed for the express use of creatures from the planet Fazoog, but I'm sure they won't mind if we use it here.

1. Object yellow 2
1. Object not yellow 4

2. Object more or less cylindrical 3
2. Object not cylindrical .... **hat**

3. Object peeling easily .... **banana**
3. Object not peeling easily .... **banana slug**

4. Object purple and spiny .... **sea urchin**
4. Not as above 5

5. Object moving of its own accord when poked; with four stumplike projections on underside .... **rabbit**
5. Not as above .... **hat**

Now let's pretend you're trying to identify a rabbit. You *always begin with the first couplet,* which in this case asks you to decide whether or not the object is yellow. Presumably, you'll choose "not yellow." As indicated to the right of "object not yellow," you then proceed to couplet no. 4 (thereby bypassing nos. 2 and 3). Since the object is not purple *and* spiny, you move on to number 5. At this juncture you are confronted with a more difficult decision. Does the object move of its own accord when poked, *and* have four "stumps" (legs)? If so, it is a rabbit, at least according to the key.

But *keys alone are worthless unless accompanied by detailed descriptions.* For instance, if you tried to identify a tiger using this key, you would arrive at "rabbit." Unless a definitive description of a rabbit is provided, you have no way of knowing whether it is indeed a rabbit you have, or an object *not included in the key.* Furthermore, if the word "edible" appeared next to "rabbit," you would find yourself in serious trouble. Imagine the consequences of attempting to eat a tiger under the mistaken impression that it is a rabbit (more likely the tiger would eat you!). Similarly, a good key to mushrooms does *not* contain information on their edibility. Instead, it refers you to a detailed description of the mushroom. *Always* compare the mushroom you are trying to identify with the appropriate description as indicated by the key. Resist the urge to "fit" the mushroom to the description or vice-versa. A major discrepancy between your mushroom and the description has *three possible explanations:*

(1) **IT IS THE MUSHROOM'S "FAULT."** Mushrooms have not seen pictures or descriptions of themselves, and do not know what they are "supposed" to look like. We can only summarize what a given species *usually* looks like. A good key will allow for a certain degree of variation. For instance, you will notice in the sample key that "hat" appears twice, because some hats are yellow and some are not. The key does *not* account for other possibilities, however. Suppose you have a *dead rabbit.* Since it does not move of its own accord when poked, it would be a *hat* according to the key. Or supposing you find a *peeled banana,* or a *blackened banana* (the kind my father likes to eat). It will not be yellow, and consequently will not key out properly. A better key would account for these possibilities, but *a key cannot account for all possible variations without becoming hopelessly unwieldy.* At first you'll have difficulty assessing what is typical and what is not. The only solution to this problem is to use *several specimens of each type of mushroom*—at different stages of development if possible. You are then in a better position to decide what is typical and what is not (i.e., if you have ten rabbits and one of them is dead, you can conclude that something is "wrong" with the dead one, and still use the key correctly).

(2) **IT IS YOUR FAULT.** People often go astray because they misread a couplet or inadvertently go to the wrong number, or exercise poor judgment. There are several ways to minimize these mistakes. First

and foremost, *always read both statements in a couplet* before deciding which one is true. Second, if you are unsure of a choice, make a notation and choose the one that seems most likely. If it later proves to be wrong, you can go back and try the other choice. Remember, the purpose of a key is not to identify, but to eliminate. There are more than 1000 possibilities as to what any unknown mushroom can be. If the keys eliminate 996 of these possibilities, they have done their job. It is then up to you to carefully compare the descriptions of the remaining three or four species, and decide which (if any) is the correct one. In this respect, keys are like mazes—if you arrive at a dead end, you can always turn around and go back!

Another possible pitfall to be aware of is language. Be wary of qualifiers such as *and, if, usually, sometimes, generally, typically, when young,* and *at maturity;* i.e., "often" does *not* mean "always," and "typically" means "most often." Also watch out for the statement "not as above," as in the following excerpt from a dichotomous key to the poems of an obscure but brilliant Santa Cruz poet.

1. Poem with a pointed social comment 2
1. Not as above 77

"Not as above" in this case means "social comment absent, *or if present, then not pointed."* However, if the first statement said "social comment present, often pointed," then "not as above" would translate as "social comment absent."

(3) **IT IS THE KEY'S FAULT.** As already pointed out, our inventory of California mushrooms is still in the preliminary stages. No mushroom book (or key) is complete, and none should pretend to be. If you have followed the key correctly, and are certain your mushroom(s) is not an aberration, then a discrepancy between the mushroom and the description means that it's probably a species not included in this book. You may then either consult another book in hopes of finding it, discard it altogether, or give it an informal name of your own.

In addition to aiding in identification, keys can be effective teaching devices. In keying out a mushroom (instead of being told what it is or leafing through a bunch of pictures), you are forced to judge critically and develop an eye for detail. By the time you have keyed out a mushroom, you will have accumulated a considerable amount of information on what it is, *as well as what it is not.* And you learn things about it you might not otherwise have noticed. For instance, in keying out a banana slug using the sample key, *you must try to peel it*—something you ordinarily would *not* do. You will then learn that a banana slug does *not* peel easily. A challenging way to familiarize yourself with keys is to devise one yourself—to household objects or common mushrooms. You'll discover it's not as easy as it looks.

QUESTIONS ABOUT MUSHROOMS

WHICH MUSHROOMS ARE GOOD TO EAT?

Fortunately, there is no easy answer to this question. If there were, everybody would pick mushrooms and there wouldn't be enough to go around. *The only way to determine the edibility of a mushroom is to eat it.* O.K. But who wants to risk their life for the sake of one lousy (or marvelous) meal? Well, through just such a trial-and-error process we humans have painstakingly accumulated a reliable body of information on the edibility of certain mushrooms. *By systematically learning the identifying characteristics of these mushrooms,* you can take advantage of other people's experiences (many of them unfortunate) and seek out the most savory types while avoiding the poisonous ones.

If possible, seek out the help of an experienced mushroom hunter. There's a subtle gap between the mushroom in the book and the mushroom in the bush, and he or she can help you bridge that gap. If you don't have a mushroom mentor, proceed with caution. If you identify a mushroom as an edible species, it's best to collect it several times before eating it. When you misidentify a bird or lizard, it doesn't really matter, because you're not (hopefully) going to eat the thing. With mushrooms, it's different. The cardinal rule is: DON'T EAT ANY MUSHROOM UNLESS YOU ARE ABSOLUTELY SURE OF ITS IDENTITY! Or—WHEN IN DOUBT, THROW IT OUT! In other words, you're better off not eating an edible mushroom than eating a poisonous one, and you're better off not eating a poisonous mushroom than eating an edible one.

Empirical approaches such as the "silver coin" test are *without exception* pure poppycock. The lethal Amanitas do *not* blacken silver (fortunately, silver coins are a rarity nowadays, so this fallacious test is more difficult to carry out). Mushrooms partially eaten by animals or insects are *not* necessarily fit for human consumption (one animal's meat is another's poison). Mushrooms that smell and taste good are *not* necessarily edible (again, the deadly Amanitas are said to be delicious). Most insidious of all is the "intuitive" approach now in vogue. Intuition can play an important part in finding mushrooms, but *not* in determining their edibility. It is a sad comment on our times that

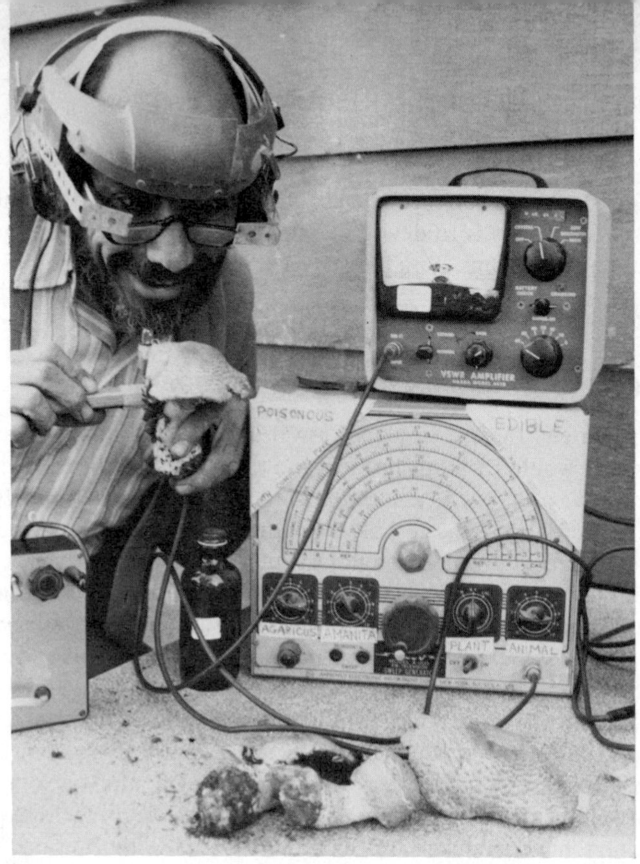

Even relatively sophisticated devices such as this "Toadstool Tester" are unreliable. There is no substitute for caution, experience, and a fundamental familiarity with the fleshy fungi.

intuition is so often peddled as a *substitute* for critical observation. If our intuitions were infallible insofar as mushrooms are concerned, there would be no need for books on the subject. It takes time and conscious effort to identify mushrooms. The "intuitive" approach is appealing, I suspect, precisely because it promises a maximum amount of satisfaction for a minimum amount of effort.

WHAT'S THE DIFFERENCE BETWEEN A MUSHROOM AND A TOADSTOOL?

"Toadstool" usually carries the connotation of being poisonous, but since many people think that *all* wild mushrooms are poisonous, the two terms in popular usage are virtually interchangeable. The word "toadstool" is perhaps a testament to the old folk belief that toads gave warts to people who handled them, and made mushrooms poisonous by sitting on them.

WHEN AND WHERE DO MUSHROOMS GROW?

Learning to recognize a mushroom should not be an end in itself, but a means of getting to know the *fungus.* A field guide can teach you the physical features of the fruiting body (the *mushroom*), but you must discover for yourself the traits of the *fungus*—its fruiting behavior and ecological idiosyncrasies. This can only be appreciated by spending a good deal of time in the woods and fields, and yet it is this aspect of fungi that is ultimately the most rewarding—getting to know organisms you can't see on an intimate basis.

Fungally speaking, we are smiled upon most favorably. Our mild climate allows for a long mushroom season (late October through March) compared to most regions. And at least a few species can be found every month of the year. *Agaricus augustus,* for instance, fruits prolifically in the dry summer months, but the peak months for most mushrooms are the wettest ones—November through February. As you move north along the coast, the season is progressively earlier (September through December) and more compressed; as you move south it is correspondingly later and more erratic.

Just as some wildflowers bloom in March and others in June, so each kind of mushroom has its own biological clock. The sulfur shelf *(Laetiporus sulphureus)* fruits in September and October on eucalyptus stumps *before* the fall rains arrive, while the horn of plenty *(Craterellus cornucopioides)* seldom shows up before January, morels (*Morchella* species) appear in the spring, and the blewitt *(Lepista nuda)* fruits continuously throughout the mushroom season.

Since rainfall and temperature are major determining factors, no two mushroom seasons are alike. There are good mushroom years and bad mushroom years, but most typical is a year which favors the fruiting of some types at the expense of others. For instance, the warm winter rains of 1977-78 produced a bumper crop of *Agaricus*, whereas *Chroogomphus* was practically absent. The previous year there was a preponderance of *Chroogomphus* and only a smattering of *Agaricus.* Thus, the terms "common" and "rare" are misleading. "Rare" actually means "rarely common" because some species may be absent for many years and then, at the beckoning of some obscure signal, fruit suddenly in unprecedented quantity. You can search the same locality for years and still find new species!

To the beginner practically every mushroom is "rare." Experienced hunters always find more mushrooms because they know exactly where to go. They stake out secret patches which they visit regularly and guard

Poison oak is the bane of many a would-be mushroom hunter. The leaves always grow in threes, but during the winter it loses its leaves! If you're allergic to it, shower thoroughly after every mushroom hunt and don't wear the same clothes the next day. Ticks and boletivores (p. 434) may also cause problems.

zealously. So unless it's the peak of the season, you're likely to find little in the way of choice edibles unless you know exactly what you are looking for and where it is likely to grow. For instance, you don't go looking for manzanita boletes *(Leccinum manzanitae)* under pine. If you do, you'll come home emptyhanded, although without realizing it you may pass up some delicious hedgehog mushrooms *(Dentinum repandum),* especially if the area you searched was overgrown with brambles and poison oak. The more you hunt, the more patches you accumulate and the more you develop an intuitive feel for when and where mushrooms grow. You learn to hunt as much with your nose and fingers and belly as with your eyes. Eventually you can walk through the woods in the summer, when there are no mushrooms about, and successfully predict which ones will come up in the fall and where.

And yet, a large part of mushroom hunting is timing, and a large part of timing is luck. So much depends on where you happen to be at what time. If you're one day too early, the mushrooms will be invisible, still under the mulch. If you're one day too late, they'll be riddled with maggots or too old to eat. Make as many generalizations or specifications as you like, and mushrooms will still defy them.

This principle of uncertainty, though at times the cause of considerable frustration, is also the reason for much of the excitement. No matter how experienced you are, you can never really be sure of what you'll find—you can only increase to some degree your chances of success. There is the acute despair of not finding what you hoped for, the frenzied delight and disbelief at finding more than you dreamed possible, the sure and comfortable satisfaction of finding exactly what you "knew" would be there.

CAN PEOPLE HARM MUSHROOMS BY PICKING THEM?

Mushrooms are a renewable resource. Since the mushroom is only the "fruit" of the fungus, picking mushrooms is like picking apples or blackberries or figs—no harm is done providing you pick them carefully and do not unduly disturb the environment. Nor does selective picking interfere seriously with their ability to reproduce. Most mushrooms you find have already begun to shed their spores (unlike flowers, which have yet to form seeds), and will continue to shed spores after they're picked. The mycelium lives from year to year and produces new mushrooms periodically. In Europe, species such as *Boletus edulis* that have been harvested for centuries continue to fruit year after year in the same localities. The only sure way to eradicate a species is to eliminate its habitat, which, unfortunately, is becoming a common practice as wild areas succumb to development.

So don't feel guilty about picking mushrooms. But don't, on the other hand, pick more than you can use. Respect the environment and be considerate of those who follow in your footsteps. You may be one of them!

CAN PEOPLE HARM THEMSELVES BY PICKING MUSHROOMS?

No. Handling wild mushrooms is not dangerous. You may want to wash your hands after prolonged contact with deadly Amanitas, but poisonous mushrooms can cause harm *only* if ingested.

DO OTHER ANIMALS EAT MUSHROOMS?

Yes. Many a marvellous meaty mushroom has been reduced in a matter of hours to a writhing mass of beatific maggots. These wiggly white "worms" with the black heads are the larvae of fungus gnats (Mycetophiladae). Eggs are usually laid at the base of the stalk, and the newly hatched maggots work their way up to the cap, gorging themselves along the way. Many other insects feed on fungi, including certain ants which cultivate and harvest the mycelia.

Sowbugs are fond of *Agaricus augustus*. Slugs gormandize mushrooms whenever possible, and have special "fungus-detectors" for this purpose. Tortoises have been known to interrupt their imperturbable peregrinations to munch on a mushroom or two. Rodents (particularly squirrels and chipmunks) are confirmed fungophiles. They're fanatically fond of boletes and the odoriferous underground fungi called truffles and false truffles. Pigs have a passion for true truffles. In fact, they are used in Europe to hunt them down, but are muzzled so they don't devour them! Even the ruminants—cattle, deer, etc.—occasionally indulge. Siberian reindeer are addicted to *Amanita muscaria* (like humans, they experience profound mental disturbances after eating it). They are also extremely fond of human urine. (Is it a coincidence that Siberians who ate *A. muscaria* also made a practice of drinking their own urine to recycle the intoxicants?) R. Gordon

Wasson, in *SOMA: The Divine Mushroom of Immortality,* quotes Vladimir Jochelson, a Russian anthropologist:

> The reindeer have a keen sense of hearing and smell, but their sight is rather poor. A man stopping to urinate in the open attracts reindeer from afar, which, following the sense of smell, will run to the urine, hardly discerning the man, and paying no attention to him. The position of a man standing up in the open while urinating is rather critical when he becomes the object of attention from reindeer coming down on him from all sides at full speed.

WHAT IS THE NUTRITIONAL VALUE OF MUSHROOMS?

Mushrooms are esteemed primarily for their flavor, but they can also be a healthy supplement to your diet. Each type, of course, has a different chemical composition. In general their nutritive value compares favorably with that of most vegetables. They are rich in the B vitamins (including choline, which acts as a protective agent for your liver in case of mushroom poisoning), vitamin D, and vitamin K. Some are also high in vitamin A (e.g., the chanterelle, *Cantharellus cibarius*), and a few (like the beefsteak fungus, *Fistulina hepatica*) contain vitamin C. They are also rich in minerals such as iron and copper, and even contain some trace elements.

Like fruits and vegetables, mushrooms are mostly water (85-95%). They have a low fat and carbohydrate content and as a result, almost no calories (unless, of course, they are cooked in oil or butter). Some types are high in protein (especially *Agaricus, Lepiota,* and *Calvatia*), and on a dry weight basis *Boletus edulis* contains more protein than any common vegetable except soybeans. However, not all of this protein is digestible, so mushrooms are *not* a viable substitute for meat, eggs, and other high-protein foods.

Mushrooms may pose digestive problems, especially for those who don't eat them regularly. As with most foods, proper cooking increases their digestibility, but overcooking removes some of the vitamins and flavor.

WHAT IS THE MEDICINAL VALUE OF MUSHROOMS?

Very little investigation has been conducted in this area. Fungi contain many unique substances—for instance, the antibiotic penicillin, which was accidentally discovered in the bread mold *Penicillium.* Several mushrooms also contain antibiotics. One of our most common woodland species, *Leucopaxillus albissimus,* is remarkably resistant to decay—a property which has been attributed to the presence of antibiotics that inhibit bacterial growth.

CAN YOU GROW WILD MUSHROOMS?

This complex subject is beyond the scope of this book. Certain wild mushrooms have been successfully cultivated, e.g., *Pleurotus ostreatus, Lepista nuda, Lentinus edodes, Psilocybe cubensis,* and *Agaricus* species. Others have stubbornly resisted attempts to raise them, e.g., *Boletus edulis, Cantharellus cibarius,* and *Morchella* species. As a rule the mycorrhizal types don't lend themselves readily to cultivation because it is difficult to duplicate their natural environment (tree rootlets). For more information, see Suggested Readings.

HEY, MAAAAAAN, DO ANY PSILOCYBIN MUSHROOMS GROW AROUND HERE?

I am asked this question more often than any other, and it irritates me—not because I object to the use of hallucinogenic drugs per se—but because of the attitude that usually (but not necessarily) accompanies it. Most of the people who ask this question would rather change their way of looking at reality than face the difficult and discouraging task of transforming reality itself. Hence they see mushrooms as a means to their own ends. They go out to the pastures and stuff their plastic bags with all the little brown mushrooms they can find, bring them home, then either pop the whole rotten mess into their mouth (a dangerous practice!), or expect someone like me to sort them out. While clinging to the moronic belief that they constitute a "counterculture," they share our society's urge for expediency. They make no attempt to learn about the organisms they are eating, and it is indeed ironic that people with such a low level of consciousness should be seeking "higher consciousness."

Excerpts from *Good Times* (January 1971) epitomize their line of thinking: "Amanita Reality"; "us genetic revolutionaries the longhairs"; "circumcision of the second charka"; "magic mushroom generation"; ". . . I could relate the black hole notion to the notion of total pollution in that either experience would seem kind of freaky"; and "*Amanita muscaria* is total revolt, and the revolution is just about won." From these statements it is clear why Marge Piercy laments:

> We grew up in Disneyland with ads for friends
> and believed we could be made new by taking a pill.
> We wanted instant revolution, where all we had to add
> was a little smoke
> But there is no tribe who dance and then sit down
> and wait for the crops to harvest themselves
> and supper to roll over before the pot . . .

To answer the original question—yes, there are hallucinogenic mushrooms in California, most of which contain psilocybin and psilocin. But if you're just looking for a new high, you really ought to take up hang-gliding or bottle-throttling, or take your chances with what you get on the street. If, on the other hand, you have a genuine interest in our co-inhabitants on this planet, and you wish to explore altered states of consciousness, then the safest approach is to buy a *responsible* field guide to hallucinogenic mushrooms and use it in conjunction with this book. Possession of psilocybin and psilocin, incidentally, is prohibited by federal law (the Comprehensive Drug Abuse and Control Act).

LBM'S: LITTLE BROWN MUSHROOMS

THE CAP is brown, the stem a shade browner, the gills browner still. This can be said of roughly one half of all the mushrooms you find. On even the most casual jaunt through the woods, you will find dozens and dozens of Little Brown Mushrooms sprouting at your feet, and very likely under them as well. The fact is, Little Brown Mushrooms are so overwhelmingly abundant and uncompromisingly undistinguished that it is more than just futile for the beginner to attempt to identify them—it is downright foolish.

After spending a good 25% of my waking existence being downright foolish, I have come to the painful but inescapable conclusion that the only possible reason for there being more than one kind of Little Brown Mushroom is that their "creator" has an inexplicable fondness for prospective professionals in search of a profession, i.e., Little Brown Mushrooms provide an ever-expanding plethora of pleasant possibilities for lengthy treatises with intriguing and titillating titles such as "A Preliminary Contribution toward a Partial Monograph of the Section Ignobiles of Subgenus Obfustucantes, Genus Immobilaria as It Occurs in Outer New Brunswick."

I wouldn't begrudge this in the least were it not for the fact that this same "creator" is unequivocally cruel when it comes to rank amateurs such as you and I, who are not paid to peer down the narrow barrel of a microscope until we are bug-eyed or get scholar's thumb from flipping through all those worn-out stacks of abstruse Ph.D. theses—and whose curiosity must consequently be swallowed rather than satiated as we slam our big red mushroom book against the wall and decapitate that unpretentious little brown thing that didn't ask to be picked and demystified in the first place, but which we went ahead and picked anyway, and have ever since been attempting in vain to identify.

An LBM (Little Brown Mushroom).

Though each new Little Brown Mushroom you find will bear a striking resemblance to the last Little Brown Mushroom you threw away, don't let this deceive you into assuming they are identical. Far from it! Somehow, each one finds a new and more minute way to be different, whether it be that the incrustation of the pileal epidermis is cheeriose rather than pretzeloid, or that the hymenial pleurocystidia contain mysterious particles with a high refractive content when mounted in Pepto-Bismol. It is almost as if they were deliberately challenging the taxonomist, who must tax his or her creative powers to their utmost in order to uncover the differences.

Actually, thanks to the diligence and expertise of the professionals, we are slowly accumulating a large mass of knowledge on the Little Brown Mushrooms. Not a completely coherent mass, mind you (in some ways it still resembles a mess more than a mass), but six hours' painstaking perusal of the current literature will produce the name of at least one out of 50 of the featureless fellows instead of one out of 51, as it used to be. Part of the problem, I suspect, is that new species are being designed and disseminated at approximately the same rate that old ones are being defined and differentiated, so that we will never attain the level of taxonomic command that we have of, say, the Little Brown Limpets or the Big Brown Toads.

Incidentally, to qualify as a bonafide Little Brown Mushroom, you ought to be little, and you most definitely have to be a mushroom, but you *don't* necessarily have to be brown, though it certainly simplifies things for you (by making it more difficult for us) if you are. That is to say, there are any number of dingy buff Little Brown Mushrooms, wishy-washy white Little Brown Mushrooms, and dismal gray Little Brown Mushrooms (to say nothing of those whose color is so neutral as to defy description), but there are no breathtakingly blue Little Brown Mushrooms, and by and large Little Brown Mushrooms are simply and unequivocally *brown.*

The point of all this is that it's sheer folly to embark upon the purchase of a field guide with the expectation of identifying each and every fleshy fungal fructification you find. Please, for your sake, don't expect the "pegs" to fit neatly into the "holes." *The "holes" are made by human beings and the "pegs" are not!* Some "pegs" will fit a number of holes, some won't fit anywhere and must wait for a hole to be gouged out. A few will fit snugly into one hole and one hole only, and these are the ones you should get to know. By concentrating on these larger and more distinctive types (see chart below), and proceeding at a deliberate pace, you will experience a mounting satisfaction at your ability to demystify, identify, appreciate (and hopefully eat) some of the mushrooms you gather. Remember, what we know of mushrooms (or anything, for that matter) is substantially more than what we knew fifty years ago, but is still precious little compared to what we don't know.

The bulk of this book deals with the larger, more easily recognizable fleshy fungi. However, in the interests of providing a broad overview, some of the more noteworthy (or rather, less unnoteworthy) Little Brown Mushrooms have been included. Almost every genus boasts a few, but the majority belong to *Inocybe, Galerina, Psathyrella, Collybia, Mycena,* and *Cortinarius.*

FIFTY DISTINCTIVE EDIBLE

COMMON NAME	LATIN NAME	EDIBILITY
Delicious Milk Cap	*Lactarius deliciosus* *p. 65*	edible
Bleeding Milk Cap	*Lactarius sanguifluus* *p. 66*	edible
Candy Cap	*Lactarius camphoratus* *p. 73*	edible
Short-Stemmed Russula	*Russula brevipes* *p. 78*	edible
Emetic Russula	*Russula emetica* *p. 88*	poisonous
Rosy Russula	*Russula rosacea* *p. 89*	poisonous
Witch's Hat	*Hygrophorus conicus* *p. 104*	questionable
Ivory Waxy Cap	*Hygrophorus eburneus* *p. 107*	edible
Oyster Mushroom	*Pleurotus ostreatus* *p. 120*	edible
Jack-O-Lantern Mushroom	*Omphalotus olivascens* *p. 130*	poisonous

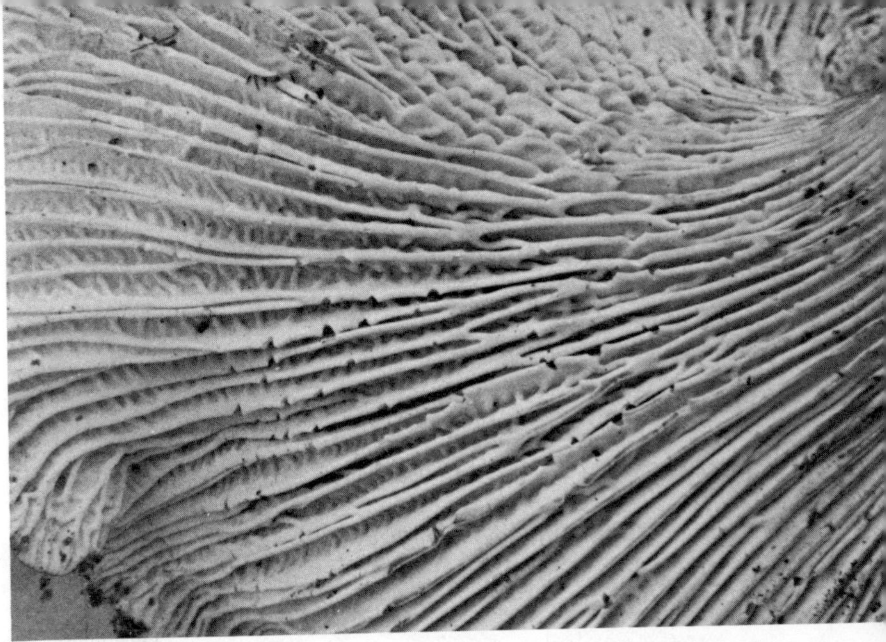

Cantharellus cibarius, gill detail. One of our most popular edible wild mushrooms, the chanterelle can be recognized by its orange color and shallow, blunt, veined, foldlike gills.

AND POISONOUS MUSHROOMS

PRINCIPAL HABITAT	PRINCIPAL SEASON
mostly pine	late fall and winter
Douglas-fir	late fall and winter
mostly hardwoods	winter and spring
woods	fall and winter
woods (mostly madrone-manzanita)	late fall and winter
pine	late fall and winter
woods (mostly redwood)	fall and winter
woods (mostly hardwoods)	fall and winter
hardwood logs, stumps	mostly in fall
hardwoods (esp. madrone)	fall and winter

COMMON NAME	LATIN NAME	EDIBILITY
Blewitt	*Lepista nuda* *p. 133*	edible
Clustered Lyophyllum	*Lyophyllum decastes* *p. 154*	edible with caution
Man On Horseback	*Tricholoma flavovirens* *p. 158*	edible
Matsutake	*Armillaria ponderosa* *p. 169*	edible
Honey Mushroom	*Armillariella mellea* *p. 171*	edible
Fairy Ring Mushroom	*Marasmius oreades* *p. 185*	edible
Death Cap	*Amanita phalloides* *p. 231*	deadly poisonous
Destroying Angel	*Amanita ocreata* *p. 232*	deadly poisonous
Fly Agaric	*Amanita muscaria* *p. 242*	poisonous/ hallucinogenic
Coccora	*Amanita calyptroderma* *p. 246*	edible
Shaggy Parasol	*Lepiota rachodes* *p. 259*	edible
Smooth Lepiota	*Lepiota naucina* *p. 261*	edible with caution
Meadow Mushroom	*Agaricus campestris* *p. 278*	edible
California Agaricus	*Agaricus "californicus"* *p. 287*	mildly poisonous
Horse Mushroom	*Agaricus arvensis* *p. 292*	edible
The Prince	*Agaricus augustus* *p. 295*	edible
Clustered Woodlover	*Naematoloma fasciculare* *p. 305*	poisonous
Shaggy Mane	*Coprinus comatus* *p. 316*	edible
Pine Mushroom	*Chroogomphus* species *p. 397*	edible
Pungent Slippery Jack	*Suillus pungens* *p. 408*	edible

PRINCIPAL HABITAT	PRINCIPAL SEASON
woods (mostly oak, cypress, pine)	fall, winter, spring
disturbed ground (near roads, paths)	fall, winter
pine, occasionally madrone	late fall, winter
manzanita, tanoak-madrone, conifers	late fall, early winter
cosmopolitan (stumps, logs, roots, buried wood)	fall, winter, early spring
lawns	fall, spring, summer (winter if warm)
oak	fall, early winter
oak, possibly madrone	winter, spring
pine, occasionally oak or madrone	late fall, winter
mostly hardwoods, esp. madrone	fall, winter
disturbed ground, usually under conifers such as cypress	year-round
lawns, pastures, disturbed ground	mostly in fall
lawns, pastures	fall, early winter
cosmopolitan (lawns, gardens, etc.)	year-round
lawns, pastures	fall, spring (winter if it's warm)
disturbed ground under trees (along roads, paths, etc.)	fall, spring, summer (winter if warm)
on stumps, logs, buried wood	fall, winter
disturbed ground (along roads, paths, parking lots, etc.)	fall, winter
pine	fall, winter, spring
pine	fall, winter, early spring

COMMON NAME	LATIN NAME	EDIBILITY
Butter Boletus	*Boletus appendiculatus* *p. 420*	edible
Satan's Boletus	*Boletus satanas* *p. 422*	poisonous
King Boletus	*Boletus edulis* *p. 424*	edible
Manzanita Bolete	*Leccinum manzanitae* *p. 429*	edible
Sulfur Shelf	*Laetiporus sulphureus* *p. 446*	edible
Many-Colored Polypore	*Coriolus versicolor* *p. 451*	inedible
Artist's Fungus	*Ganoderma applanatum* *p. 456*	inedible
Hericium	*Hericium* species *p. 481*	edible
Hedgehog Mushroom	*Dentinum repandum* *p. 485*	edible
Pink-Tipped Coral	*Ramaria botrytis* *p. 513*	edible
Cauliflower Mushroom	*Sparassis radicata* *p. 515*	edible
Chanterelle	*Cantharellus cibarius* *p. 520*	edible
Horn of Plenty	*Craterellus cornucopioides* *p. 523*	edible
Giant Puffball	*Calvatia gigantea* *p. 530*	edible
Common Puffball	*Lycoperdon perlatum* *p. 540*	edible
Stinkhorn	*Phallus impudicus* *p. 563*	inedible
Witch's Butter	*Tremella mesenterica* *p. 580*	inedible
Orange Peel Fungus	*Aleuria aurantia* *p. 591*	edible
Black Elfin Saddle	*Helvella lacunosa* *p. 601*	edible when cooked
Morel	*Morchella* species *p. 608*	edible

PRINCIPAL HABITAT	PRINCIPAL SEASON
hardwoods	fall
oak	fall
pine, sometimes oak	fall, early winter, occasionally spring
manzanita, madrone	fall, winter
stumps, logs, trees, esp. eucalyptus	late summer, fall
hardwood stumps, logs, branches	fall, winter, spring, summer
hardwood trees, esp. bay laurel	fall, winter, spring, summer
stumps, logs, trees, branches	fall, winter
mostly pine	winter, spring
woods, especially tanoak	late fall, winter
at base of conifers, esp. pine	late fall, winter
woods, especially oak, also conifers	fall, winter, spring
hardwoods, esp. oak	winter
pastures, open ground	fall, spring
woods	fall, winter, spring
lawns, gardens, disturbed ground	fall, winter, spring, summer
hardwood logs, branches, stumps	fall, winter, spring
disturbed ground, woods	late fall, winter, spring
pine and oak	late fall, winter, early spring
gardens, sandy soil, streamsides, burned ground, orchards, etc.	mostly spring

An oak woodland, with cluster of honey mushrooms, *Armillariella mellea*, in foreground.

HABITATS

DEVELOPING AN AWARENESS of biological communities is essential to any nature study. In this chapter, the more common or distinctive mushrooms have been grouped according to habitat—the type of place where they're most likely to be found, or the type of tree with which they commonly grow. This aspect of collecting is frequently neglected by mushroom hunters, who eagerly remove mushrooms from their place of growth without taking note of their surroundings. In many instances the place of growth will provide clues to the identity of the mushroom—and you'll soon discover that certain mushrooms always seem to grow together; that is, they are indicators of a certain habitat or biological community.

Most of the habitats are listed here on the basis of the dominant vegetation (redwood, oak, grass, etc.). Since only a few of our trees are significant in mushroom identification, it is better to learn those trees *before* you learn the mushrooms, rather than trying to differentiate between several hundred kinds of mushrooms before learning the basic trees.

Always bear in mind that the different habitats discussed here overlap. In a given area there are usually several habitats present. For instance, a lawn with a Monterey pine will feature lawn-inhabiting fungi as well as species mycorrhizal with pine. And a road through the woods will offer several types of trees plus disturbed ground (the roadside). Be sure to check the list of cosmopolitan mushrooms ("Anywhere and Everywhere"), for these will turn up in almost any habitat. Also remember that mycorrhizal fungi do not necessarily grow *under* their host—they are associated with the tree's rootlets, which may be quite a distance away from the trunk.

PINE (*Pinus* species)

Pine forests are favored by a melange of mycorrhizal mushrooms, plus multitudes of minute, saprophytic Mycenas. When the needle carpet is dry ("potato chip conditions"), the larger mushrooms often hide underneath, manifesting themselves as low mounds or "mushrumps." Prized edible species include *Boletus edulis, Dentinum repandum, Lepista nuda, Sparassis radicata,* and *Tricholoma flavovirens. Suillus* and *Chroogomphus* species often fruit together in enormous quantities, along with the green and orange *Lactarius deliciosus* and the bright red *Russula rosacea.* But the most spectacular fungal feature of our pine forests is unquestionably *Amanita muscaria,* with its fiery red cap and white "stars."

The different pines exhibit some differences in mycorrhizal partners. For instance, *Suillus pseudobrevipes* and *Chroogomphus pseudovinicolor* grow with ponderosa pine, *Suillus pungens* with Monterey and knobcone pine, and *Suillus fuscotomentosus* with knobcone and ponderosa pine. *Hygrophorus gliocyclus* is abundant inland under digger pine but is also common under Monterey pine along the coast.

Agaricus subrutilescens
Amanita aspera
Amanita muscaria
Amanita pantherina
Amanita strobiliformis
Boletus edulis
Chroogomphus species
Clitocybe sclerotoidea
Clitocybe suaveolens
Collybia butyracea
Collybia dryophila
Cortinarius cinnamomeus
Cortinarius croceofolius
Cryptoporus volvatus
Dentinum repandum
Gymnopilus spectabilis
Hebeloma crustuliniforme
Hebeloma sinapizans
Helvella lacunosa
Hirschioporus abietinus
Hydnellum species
Hygrophoropsis aurantiacus
Hygrophorus gliocyclus
Hygrophorus hypothejus
Inocybe geophylla var. *lilacina*
Inocybe pudica
Laccaria amethystina
Laccaria laccata
Lactarius camphoratus
Lactarius chrysorheus
Lactarius deliciosus
Lepista nuda
Mycena species
Naematoloma fasciculare
Phaeolus schweinitzii
Phellinus pini
Pholiota velaglutinosa
Ramariopsis kunzei
Rhizopogon species
Russula alutacea
Russula pectinatoides
Russula rosacea
Sparassis radicata
Suillus brevipes
Suillus fuscotomentosus
Suillus pseudobrevipes
Suillus pungens
Tricholoma flavovirens
Tricholoma imbricatum
Tricholoma terreum
Tricholomopsis rutilans

DOUGLAS-FIR (*Pseudotsuga menziesii*)

The great Douglas-fir forests of the Pacific Northwest are among the best fungal foraging grounds in the world. In our region, however, the Douglas-fir habitat is no better than average. There are a number of mycorrhizal associates, the most prominent of which are *Suillus* and *Gomphidius* species. *Russula xerampelina* is the only choice edible species that grows exclusively with Douglas-fir. *Lateiporus sulphureus* is occasionally found on logs and stumps;

Cantharellus cibarius and *Cantharellus subalbidus* are abundant under Douglas-fir farther north.

Douglas-fir is hyphenated in this book because it is not a true fir. It is easily told from redwood (with which it often grows) by its browner bark, spurred cones, and habit of dropping needles *without* the twigs intact (redwood drops twigs with the reddish needles intact).

Agaricus hondensis
Amanita pantherina
Fomes pinicola
Fomes subroseus
Gomphidius species
Hirschioporus abietinus
Hygrophorus agathosmus
Inocybe species
Lactarius chrysorheus
Lactarius sanguifluus
Laetiporus sulphureus
Lepiota clypeolaria
Mycena species
Phaeolus schweinitzii
Phellinus pini
Rhizopogon species
Russula placita
Russula xerampelina
Suillus caerulescens
Suillus lakei
Suillus ponderosus
Tricholoma terreum

REDWOOD (*Sequoia sempervirens*)

Ironically, our largest tree supports a fungal phantasmagoria of dainty, fragile fungi, but only a scattering of large, fleshy types. Relatively few are wood-rotters, and even fewer (if any) are mycorrhizal—a tribute to the redwood's unique position among the conifers.

Collybia umbonata, with its conical cap and long "tap root," is perhaps the most distinctive redwood lover. Colorful waxy caps (*Hygrophorus* species) abound, but pickings for the table are meager, at least south of San Francisco—*Agaricus augustus* (but always near roads or trails), *Agaricus subrutilescens,* occasionally *Cantharellus cibarius,* and *Clitocybe suaveolens.* The largest inhabitant of our redwood forests is *Leucopaxillus albissimus,* which often forms gigantic fairy rings.

Agaricus augustus
Agaricus hondensis
Agaricus meleagris
Agaricus subrutilescens
Boletus zelleri
Cantharellus cibarius
Clitocybe nebularis
Clitocybe suaveolens
Collybia umbonata
Entoloma madidum
Entoloma nitidum
Hygrophoropsis aurantiacus
Hygrophorus acutoconicus
Hygrophorus borealis
Hygrophorus calyptraeformis
Hygrophorus coccineus
Hygrophorus conicus
Hygrophorus flavescens
Hygrophorus pratensis
Hygrophorus psittacinus
Hygrophorus puniceus
Lepiota species
Leptonia parva
Leucopaxillus albissimus
Mycena species
Tricholomopsis rutilans
Xeromphalina cauticinalis

CYPRESS (*Cupressus* species)

Our cypress groves do not qualify as "woods" because all but two (at Point Lobos and Cypress Point) were planted. However, they do have characteristic fungal associates, though few (if any) are mycorrhizal. The harsh winds and salt spray to which cypresses are subjected make for unpredictable hunting, but under favorable conditions there is a large burst of *Agaricus* and *Lepiota* species, many of them unclassified and/or endemic to California. From a gastronomic standpoint the best cypress lovers are *Agaricus bisporus, Agaricus rodmani, Lepiota rachodes,* and *Lepista nuda.*

Agaricus "annae"
Agaricus bisporus
Agaricus "californicus"
Agaricus haemorrhoidarius
Agaricus rodmani
Agaricus xanthodermus
Battaraea phalloides
Geastrum species
Lepiota rachodes
Lepiota species
Lepista nuda

OAK (*Quercus* species)

Oaks are endowed with a rich array of fleshy fungi that differ drastically from the conifer-lovers typical of northern California and the Pacific Northwest. In fact, oaks appear to have more mycorrhizal associates than any other hardwoods. And since live oaks are the dominant forest trees of the Central California Coast, mushroom lovers are indeed fortunate. To inveterate fungus fans, oak woodlands are synonymous with chanterelles and blewitts *(Cantharellus cibarius* and *Lepista nuda)*—the two not only grow together, they go together. Other choice edibles include *Boletus appendiculatus, Craterellus cornucopioides, Lactarius camphoratus, Pleurotus ostreatus, Tricholoma portentosum,* and an occasional *Boletus edulis.* But beginners beware—our most dangerous mushrooms, *Amanita phalloides* and *Amanita ocreata,* are also associated with live oak! Other kinds of oaks found inland offer a comparable but more modest selection of fleshy fungi—perhaps because they receive less rain.

Oaks also boast the longest mushroom season of any forest type. The major fruiting, naturally, is in the fall and early winter, but there is a characteristic spring crop highlighted by *Lactarius camphoratus* and a trio of Amanitas—*Amanita ocreata, A. rubescens,* and *A. velosa.* Wood-inhabiting bracket fungi are also prominent—*Coriolus versicolor, Lenzites betulina, Stereum hirsutum,* etc.

Agaricus albolutescens
Agaricus hondensis
Amanita baccata
Amanita ocreata
Amanita phalloides
Amanita rubescens
Amanita strobiliformis
Amanita velosa
Boletus appendiculatus
Boletus dryophilus
Boletus edulis
Boletus erythropus
Boletus "marshii"
Boletus satanas
Cantharellus cibarius
Clavariadelphus pistillaris
Collybia dryophila
Coriolus versicolor
Cortinarius fulmineus
Cortinarius glaucopus
Craterellus cinereus
Craterellus cornucopioides
Crepidotus mollis
Daldinia grandis
Entoloma rhodopolium
Ganoderma applanatum
Hebeloma crustuliniforme
Helvella lacunosa
Hygrophorus eburneus
Hygrophorus roseibrunneus
Hygrophorus sordidus
Lactarius camphoratus
Lactarius insulsus
Lenzites betulina
Lepista nuda
Naematoloma fasciculare
Phellinus gilvus
Pleurotus ostreatus
Russula "adusta"
Russula brevipes
Russula fragrantissima
Russula pectinatoides
Stereum species
Tremella foliacea
Tremella mesenterica
Tricholoma pessundatum
Tricholoma portentosum
Tricholoma saponaceum
Tuber species

TANOAK (*Lithocarpus densiflorus*)

This relative of the oaks forms dense stands at higher elevations in the coastal mountains (where it often mingles with madrone), and also in sheltered basins where it grows with redwood. Among the prominent fungi of our tanoak woods are the lovely coral mushrooms (*Ramaria* species) and the minute garlic mushroom *(Marasmius scorodonius),* which is often smelled before it is seen. The best edibles are *Agaricus silvicola, Armillaria ponderosa, Pleurotus ostreatus* (on decaying logs), and *Russula cyanoxantha.*

Agaricus hondensis
Agaricus silvicola
Armillaria ponderosa
Armillaria zelleri
Cortinarius collinitus
Cortinarius infractus
Entoloma madidum
Entoloma rhodopolium
Limacella glischra
Marasmius scorodonius
Phaeobulgaria inquinans
Phellinus gilvus
Pleurotus ostreatus
Ramaria species
Russula cyanoxantha

MADRONE and MANZANITA (*Arbutus menziesii* and *Arctostaphylos* species)

Madrone woods are my favorite foraging grounds. They boast their share of gastronomic delights *(Amanita calyptroderma, Craterellus cornucopioides, Leccinum manzanitae),* but their chief attraction is their beauty. They don't blot out the sun like redwoods, and they're more colorful (though not quite as venerable) as oaks. Every year madrones shed their reddish barks in sheets, revealing smooth, yellow, musclebound limbs beneath. In the summer the rags of stripped bark sizzle audibly in the sunlight as they curl up like pencil shavings. In the fall, the bark combines with the large scarlet leaves and clusters of bittersweet orange-red berries to form a deep, incomparably rich, reddish-black humus. In such splendid company, it's hard to keep your mind on mushrooms!

Manzanitas are essentially miniature madrones. The most that can be said for fungus-foraging in manzanita thickets is that it's different—you spend most of the time on your hands and knees wishing you'd taken up stamp collecting or basket weaving or stayed home and watched the ball game.

It is interesting to note that a number of mushrooms normally associated with conifers cross over to madrone (they just can't resist!) These include *Amanita aspera, Amanita muscaria, Armillaria ponderosa, Hygrophorus chrysodon, Hygrophorus eburneus, Tricholoma aurantium,* and *Tricholoma flavovirens.*

Amanita aspera
Amanita calyptroderma
Armillaria ponderosa
Craterellus cornucopioides
Entoloma rhodopolium
Hygrophorus chrysodon
Hygrophorus eburneus
Lactarius chrysorheus
Leccinum manzanitae
Lepiota atrodisca
Omphalotus olivascens
Russula emetica
Russula raoultii
Tricholoma aurantium
Tricholoma flavovirens
Tricholoma saponaceum

EUCALYPTUS (*Eucalyptus* species)

This messy, aggressive intruder was originally brought to this country in the hope that its noxious fumes would combat malaria. It grows quickly, and its greedy, shallow roots inhibit the growth of many native plants and mushrooms. However, dried eucalyptus makes fairly good firewood, and if you chop them down, you're liable to get succulent sulfur shelves *(Laetiporus sulphureus)* sprouting from the stumps.

RIPARIAN WOODLAND

Streams and rivers being indisputably damp, many people assume they constitute an ideal setting for mushrooms. The mixed hardwoods (alder, cottonwood, willow, maple, etc.) of our stream valleys do indeed support a characteristic fungus flora, but it is a very modest one that does not yield the bountiful harvests of our oak and pine forests. Log-rotters abound (*Pholiota, Psathyrella, Naematoloma, Pleurotus, Armillariella,* etc.), while the best edibles are *Armillariella mellea* and *Pleurotus ostreatus* in the fall, *Verpa* and *Morchella* species in the spring.

Armillariella mellea
Flammulina velutipes
Hebeloma mesophaeum
Marasmius candidus
Morchella species
Mycena species
Naematoloma species
Pholiota species
Pleurotus ostreatus
Pluteus cervinus
Psathyrella species
Sarcoscypha coccinea
Stropharia ambigua
Verpa species

OTHER TREES

Only a fraction of our native trees have been discussed so far, but the remaining trees are not particularly significant from a mushroom identification standpoint. The few mushrooms they harbor (either beneath them or on them) are likely to be cosmopolitan. There are several exceptions, however, including: *Fistulina hepatica,* on chinquapin stumps and trunks; *Ganoderma applanatum,* on bay laurel, as well as many other hardwoods; *Flammulina velutipes,* on bush lupine; *Laccaria laccata,* in droves under acacia; and *Lactarius torminosus,* in yards and parks where birch has been planted.

In northern California and the Sierras, the presence of true firs *(Abies),* spruce *(Picea),* and hemlock *(Tsuga)* makes for large numbers of mushrooms not treated in this book. *Abies,* however, is represented in central California by the remarkable Santa Lucia fir *(Abies bracteata),* in the canyons and rugged peaks behind Big Sur. This remote area, which also harbors sugar pine and Coulter pine, undoubtedly has many unique fungi, but has not been intensively studied to my knowledge.

DUNG and MANURE

Cow pies (or any kind of dung) are miniature mushroom gardens. If kept in a humid environment, they will yield a fascinating succession of dainty fungi, none large enough to eat. The mycelium of a dung-inhabiting fungus has a shorter life span than that of other fungi due to the transient nature of the substrate. The spores are presumably ingested by cows (or other animals). They pass through the digestive tract unscathed, and into the dung, where they germinate. In addition to the common dung addicts listed below, you'll find a multitude of minute Ascomycetes not treated in this book. Some of these are extremely specialized, living only on lizard dung, frog feces, opposum excrement, etc.

Bolbitius vitellinus
Coprinus species
Cyathus stercoreus
Lepista tarda
Panaeolus species
Peziza fimeti
Peziza vesiculosa
Psilocybe coprophila
Stropharia semiglobata

PASTURES

Pastures offer a wide selection of easily identified edible mushrooms, notably *Agaricus campestris, Agaricus arvensis, Agaricus crocodilinus, Lepiota naucina,* and *Calvatia gigantea.* Every fall there is a period of about one month when our cow pastures are literally chock-full of mushrooms, and there is generally another, smaller crop in the spring. The following list excludes mushrooms associated with trees (such as *Amanita velosa*), which frequently fruit at the edges of pastures, as well as those that grow on dung. It's interesting to note that several species which appear in pastures do *not* grow on lawns (and vice versa).

Agaricus arvensis
Agaricus campestris
Agaricus crocodilinus
Agaricus micromegathus
Agaricus xanthodermus
Agrocybe pediades
Amanita sp. (unidentified)
Bovista plumbea
Calvatia bovista
Calvatia cyathiformis
Calvatia gigantea
Clitocybe dealbata
Lepiota naucina
Lepista subconnexa
Lepista tarda
Lepista sp. (unidentified)
Melanoleuca melaleuca
Nolanea sericea
Panaeolus campanulatus
Stropharia coronilla
Vascellum depressum

LAWNS and GARDENS

To many people mushroom-hunting is synonymous with a day in the woods—plunging into the dripping depths of a forest, lunging through manzanita thickets, or meandering through ravines and puffball-pocked pastures. However, a mushroom hunt can (and should) begin in the mundane confines of your own yard (assuming you have one), and radiate outward gradually, like the mycelium of a fairy ring. After all, some of the most delicious *(Marasmius oreades, Agaricus campestris)* and bizarre *(Phallus impudicus)* mushrooms might be growing right outside your door!

Agaricus is the most prominent group of mushrooms in lawns and gardens, and more than one species of *Agaricus* often grow together. *Agaricus campestris, A. bisporus,* and *A. rodmani* are delicious, but care must be taken not to confuse them with *A. californicus* and *A. xanthodermus,* which are poisonous to some people. Other choice morsels include *Lepiota rachodes, L. barssii, L. naucina,* the omnipresent *Marasmius oreades,* and an occasional morel *(Morchella).*

Lawns and gardens are actually two different habitats. *Volvariella speciosa* and *Agaricus bisporus,* for instance, grow in gardens but not on lawns, whereas *Agaricus campestris* and *Marasmius oreades* grow on lawns but not in gardens. But since many yards incorporate elements of both, they are listed together here. Also, mushrooms associated with trees are excluded from this list though they often appear in people's yards. Most yards also qualify as "disturbed ground."

Agaricus arvensis
Agaricus bisporus
Agaricus "californicus"
Agaricus campestris
Agaricus micromegathus
Agaricus rodmani
Agaricus xanthodermus
Agrocybe pediades
Agrocybe praecox
Bovista plumbea
Chlorophyllum molybdites
Conocybe lactea
Coprinus species
Lepiota barssii
Lepiota naucina
Lepiota rachodes
Lepista sp. (unidentified)
Marasmius oreades
Melanoleuca melaleuca
Morchella species
Panaeolus foenisecii
Panaeolus papilionaceus
Phallus impudicus
Scleroderma species
Stropharia coronilla
Vascellum depressum
Volvariella speciosa

INDOORS

In some cases a mushroom hunt can begin inside your house. The brown cup fungus, *Peziza domiciliana,* is commonly found indoors, growing out of walls, floors, tile, and plaster. *Lepiota lutea* consistently pops up in flower pots, though it sometimes finds its way outdoors. A mysterious *Coprinus* invaded the floor of my '67 Chevy Nova, but the majority of fungi found indoors occur outside as well.

Coprinus micaceus
Gymnopilus species
Lepiota lutea
Lepiota rachodes
Morchella species
Mycena species
Peziza domiciliana
Poria species
Serpula lacrymans
Sphaerobolus stellatus
Volvariella species

DISTURBED GROUND

"Disturbed" ground means roadsides, pathsides, gardens, vacant lots, building sites, and the perimeters of parking lots. Of course, it overlaps with lawns and gardens ("cultivated ground"), but we do have a very distinct roadside fungus flora exemplified by the shaggy mane, *Coprinus comatus.*

Just what makes certain mushrooms prefer (or even require) disturbed ground is a mystery. Obviously, the process of disrupting, overturning, or paving the soil must release certain otherwise inaccessible nutrients. An unsurpassed edible mushroom like *Agaricus augustus* could be raised commercially if this puzzle is solved. Some mushrooms, such as *Lyophyllum decastes,* seem to *require* disturbed ground whereas others merely *prefer* it. Some show a liking for asphalt and will even poke up through it—notably *Coprinus comatus, Lyophyllum decastes, Pisolithus tinctorius,* and *Scleroderma geaster.* Shaggy manes have even ruined tennis courts!

Two assets of these fungi are that they're easily spotted from the road (or trail) and are consequently tailormade for people who have an extreme allergy to poison oak. And many are worth stopping for!—*Agaricus augustus, Agaricus rodmani, Coprinus comatus, Lepiota naucina, Lepiota rachodes,* and *Lyophyllum decastes.*

Agaricus augustus
Agaricus "californicus"
Agaricus meleagris
Agaricus rodmani
Agaricus xanthodermus
Aleuria aurantia
Astreus pteridis
Coprinus atramentarius
Coprinus comatus
Lepiota naucina
Lepiota rachodes
Lyophyllum decastes
Pholiota terrestris
Pisolithus tinctorius
Scleroderma bovista
Scleroderma cepa
Scleroderma geaster

SAND

Odd as it may seem, a number of mushrooms grow in sand or sandy soil, including the delicious *Morchella conica,* and *Lepiota rachodes,* which I have found on Año Nuevo Island. The deserts of California support a fascinating but exasperatingly elusive fungus flora in which Gasteromycetes figure prominently. Desert fungi are not dealt with in this book, but the sand lovers marked with an asterisk are common in the desert.

Amanita baccata
Astreus species*
*Battaraea phalloides**
Calvatia species*
Coprinus species
Geastrum species*
Laccaria species
Lepiota rachodes
Pisolithus tinctorius
*Podaxis pistillaris**
Sarcosphaera eximia
Sarcosphaera ammophila
Scleroderma species
Sepultaria arenicola
Tulostoma species*

CHARRED GROUND

Many plants are specially adapted to growing in burned-over areas. The cones of the knobcone pine, for instance, release their seeds only when subjected to extreme heat. Likewise, certain mushrooms fruit only in burnt ground. The most reliable way to cultivate the fabulous morel is to set fire to some woods and return the following spring! (This practice had to be outlawed in Europe.)

Coltrichia perennis
Morchella angusticeps
Morchella conica
Morchella esculenta
Omphalina maura
Peziza proteana
Peziza pustulata
Peziza violacea
Pholiota highlandensis
Psathyrella carbonicola
Rhizina undulata

SPECIALIZED HABITATS

Specialization is an integral part of the process of evolution—without it there would be far less diversity. All fungi are specialized, but in some cases the specialization is more bizarre or extreme—or at least more apparent to us. For instance, it is said that certain poorly known Laboulbeniomycetes grow only on the left anterior appendage (left front foot) of their insect host!

Among the fleshy fungi, *Asterophora, Collybia tuberosa,* and *Hypomyces* grow only on other mushrooms; *Cordyceps* species parasitize certain insects and underground truffle-like Ascomycetes; and several *Omphalina* species are associated with algae. Many wood-inhabiting mushrooms can grow on cones, but *Auriscalpium vulgare* (as well as several *Strobilurus* species) are *restricted* to cones. The extremely specialized niche has enabled *Auriscalpium* to survive, but if and when conifers disappear from the earth (as they are slowly doing), *Auriscalpium* will be doomed.

ANYWHERE and EVERYWHERE

No habitat list is complete without mention of some of our cosmopolitan fungi or "mushroom weeds." Most are restricted to wooded areas, but those which are likely to pop up anywhere are marked with an asterisk. The best of the lot from an edibility standpoint are *Armillariella mellea* and *Lepista nuda.*

*Agaricus "californicus"**
Agaricus hondensis
*Agaricus meleagris**
*Agaricus xanthodermus**
*Aleuria aurantia**
Amanita "constricta"
Amanita "pachycolea"
Amanita pantherina
Amanita vaginata
*Armillariella mellea**
Boletus chrysenteron
Boletus subtomentosus
Clavaria vermicularis
Clitocybe nebularis
Galerina species*
*Ganoderma applanatum**
Inocybe geophylla
Laccaria amethystina
Laccaria laccata
*Lepista nuda**
*Lepista subconnexa**
Leucopaxillus albissimus
Leucopaxillus amarus
Lycoperdon perlatum
Mycena species*
Naematoloma fasciculare
*Pholiota terrestris**
*Pluteus cervinus**
Russula albidula
Russula brevipes
*Tubaria furfuracea**

Top: An abnormality, in which one *Russula raoultii* has formed on the cap of another. Abnormalities are the result of environmental conditions or improper development, and are *not* inherited or passed on. One widespread abnormality is the development of a small rosette of gills ("rose gill") on the cap surface. Other abnormalities include aborted fruiting bodies, sterile gills, and failure of the cap or gills to form. **Bottom Left and Right:** *Amanita vaginata* emerging from its volva. (Herb Saylor)

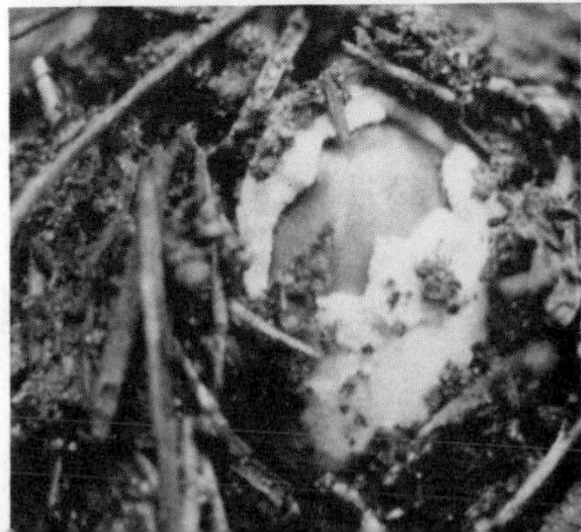

PICTORIAL KEY TO THE MAJOR GROUPS OF FLESHY FUNGI

BASIDIOMYCETES

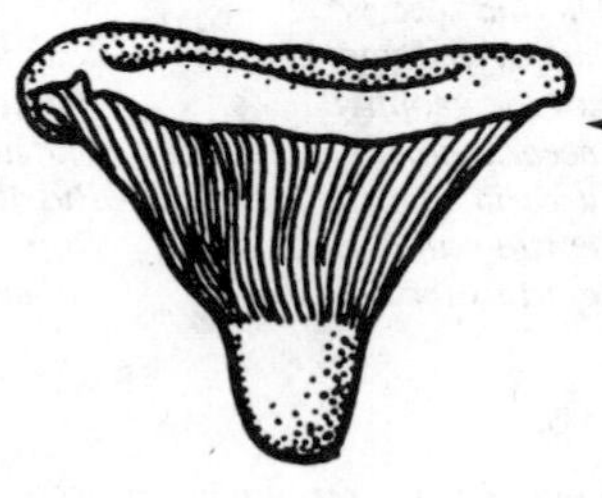

Fruiting body with a cap and stalk, or just a cap; cap with gills (radiating blades) on underside .... **AGARICS** (GILLED MUSHROOMS), p. 58

close-up of the veined underside of a chanterelle

Fruiting body with a cap and stalk, usually vase-shaped or trumpetlike at maturity; underside of cap smooth, wrinkled, veined, or with ridges .... **CHANTERELLES,** p. 516

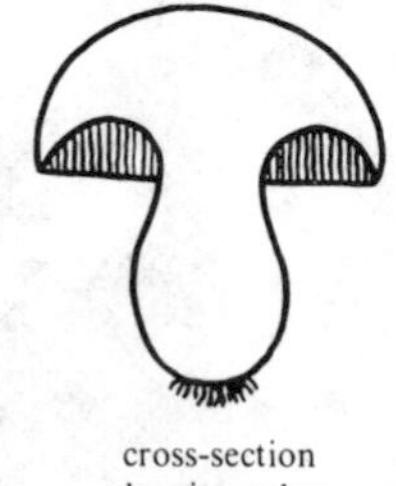
cross-section showing tubes

Fruiting body with a cap and stalk; underside of cap with a spongy layer of tubes or pores; stalk more or less central, flesh usually soft; almost always growing on ground **BOLETES,** p. 401

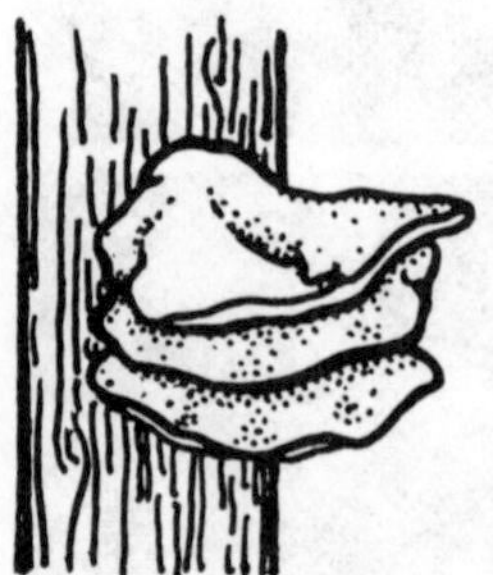
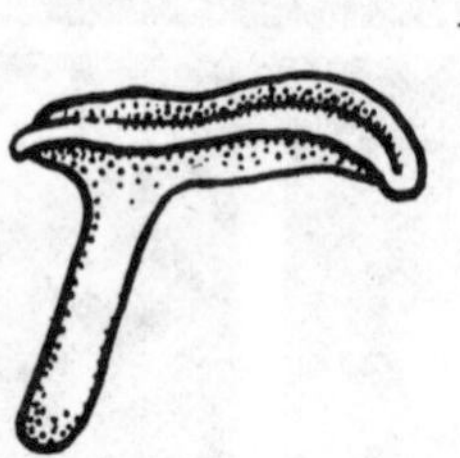

Fruiting body with a cap and stalk, or just a cap; usually bracketlike or shelf-like on wood (but *not* black and charcoal-like); if on ground, then *not* fleshy with a central stalk; underside of cap smooth, warty, or with pores .. **POLYPORES and BRACKET FUNGI,** p. 437

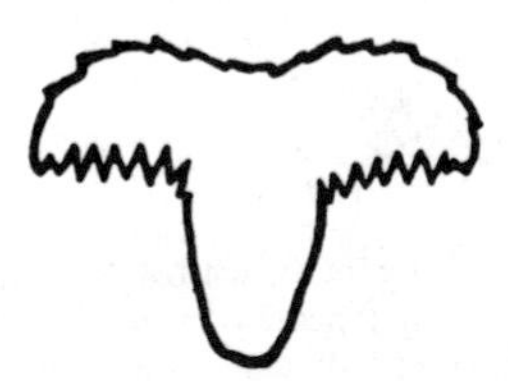

spines on underside of cap are exaggerated in this cross-section

Fruiting body with a cap and stalk and layer of spines underneath the cap, *or* with spines suspended from a fleshy base .... **TEETH FUNGI,** p. 480

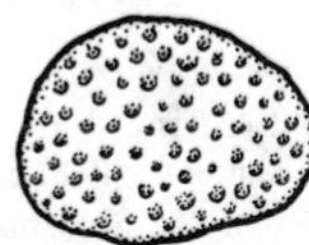

cross-section

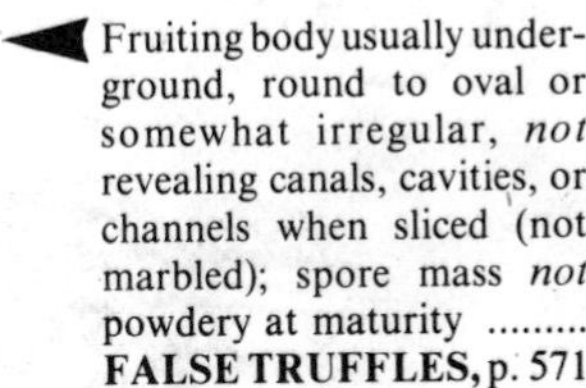

Fruiting body usually underground, round to oval or somewhat irregular, *not* revealing canals, cavities, or channels when sliced (not marbled); spore mass *not* powdery at maturity .... **FALSE TRUFFLES,** p. 571

Fruiting body minute (10 mm broad or less), shaped like miniature bird's nest, with one or more small "eggs" inside ...... **BIRD'S NEST FUNGI,** p. 567

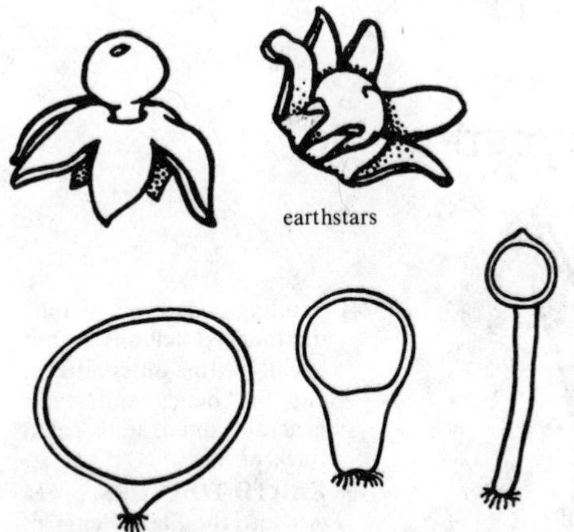

three immature puffballs in cross-section; eventually they rupture to release spores

Fruiting body usually above the ground at maturity, round to oval or pear-shaped, sometimes with a stalk or rays; spore mass powdery at maturity, held within a sac or numerous lentil-like bodies .... **PUFFBALLS and EARTHSTARS,** p. 526

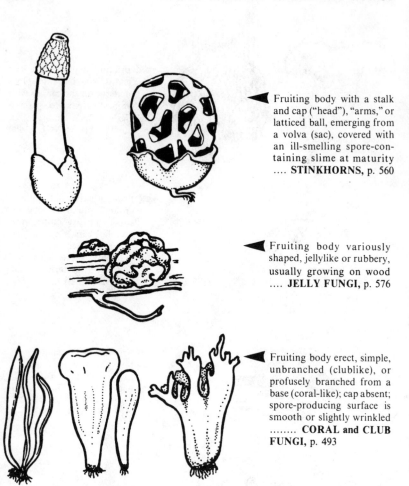

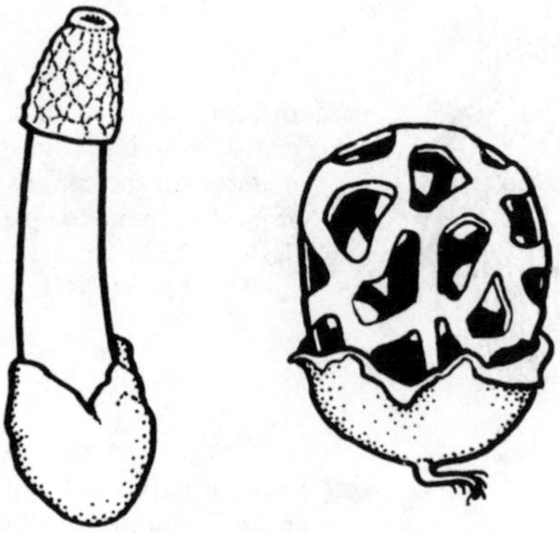

Fruiting body with a stalk and cap ("head"), "arms," or latticed ball, emerging from a volva (sac), covered with an ill-smelling spore-containing slime at maturity .... **STINKHORNS,** p. 560

Fruiting body variously shaped, jellylike or rubbery, usually growing on wood .... **JELLY FUNGI,** p. 576

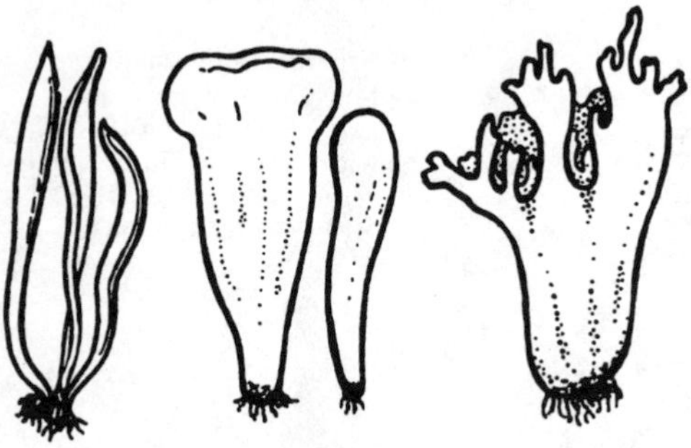

Fruiting body erect, simple, unbranched (clublike), or profusely branched from a base (coral-like); cap absent; spore-producing surface is smooth or slightly wrinkled .... **CORAL and CLUB FUNGI,** p. 493

ASCOMYCETES

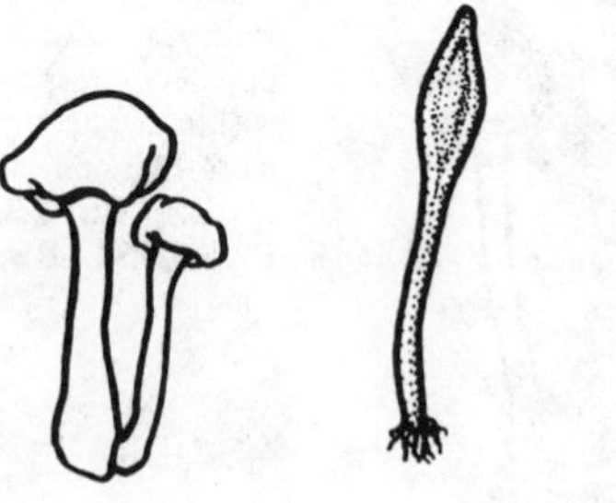

Fruiting body erect, simple, unbranched (clublike), but usually with a differentiated cap or "head" and stalk; generally small, stalk 7 mm thick or less ....
EARTH TONGUES, p. 614 (see also the **Flask Fungi,** p. 622)

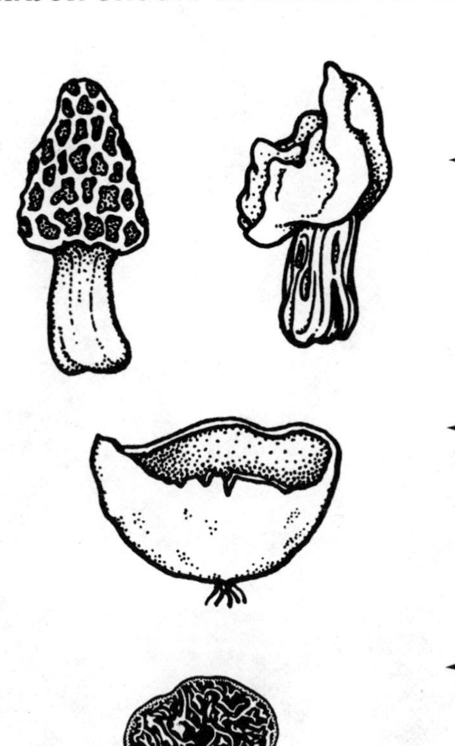

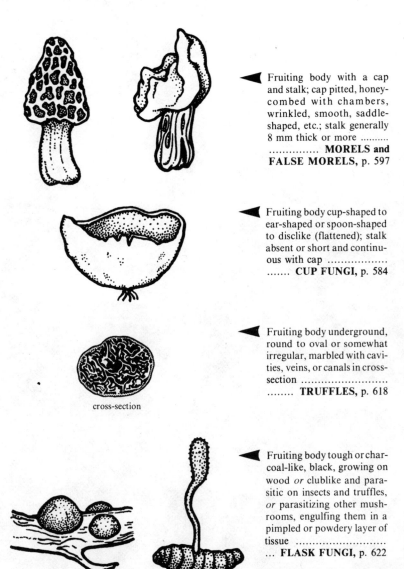

Fruiting body with a cap and stalk; cap pitted, honeycombed with chambers, wrinkled, smooth, saddle-shaped, etc.; stalk generally 8 mm thick or more .... **MORELS and FALSE MORELS,** p. 597

Fruiting body cup-shaped to ear-shaped or spoon-shaped to disclike (flattened); stalk absent or short and continuous with cap .... **CUP FUNGI,** p. 584

Fruiting body underground, round to oval or somewhat irregular, marbled with cavities, veins, or canals in cross-section .... **TRUFFLES,** p. 618

cross-section

Fruiting body tough or charcoal-like, black, growing on wood *or* clublike and parasitic on insects and truffles, *or* parasitizing other mushrooms, engulfing them in a pimpled or powdery layer of tissue .... **FLASK FUNGI,** p. 622

Key to the Classes of Fleshy Fungi

1. Spores produced on mother cells (basidia); fruiting body variously shaped (see pp. 52-54) .... **Basidiomycetes**, p. 57
1. Spores produced inside mother cells (asci); fruiting body variously shaped (see pp. 54-55) .... **Ascomycetes**, p. 583

The shaggy mane, *Coprinus comatus*, is a familiar sight along roads in the fall and winter. It is one of many Basidiomycetes.

BASIDIOMYCETES

THE Basidiomycetes are a large class of fungi that bear spores on specialized mother cells called **basidia.** Three major groups of Basidiomycetes are treated here: the Heterobasidiomycetes (jelly fungi) have partitioned or forked basidia and a gelatinous fruiting body; the Homobasidiomycetes have simple, club-shaped basidia, and are divided into the Gasteromycetes, which bear their spores internally, and the Hymenomycetes, which have an exposed spore-producing surface.

Key to the Basidiomycetes

1. Fruiting body gelatinous (jellylike) or rubbery, often translucent; gills or tubes absent; usually growing on wood; basidia partitioned or forked .... **Heterobasidiomycetes,** p. 576
1. Fruiting body not as above; basidia simple (neither partitioned nor forked) 2

2. Spores borne externally (on gills, tubes, spines, etc.), forcibly discharged at maturity (spore print usually but not always obtainable); fruiting body with a cap and stalk, or clublike, or coral-like, or bracketlike (without a stalk) on wood .... **Hymenomycetes,** below
2. Spores produced inside a spore sac, or in small pill-shaped bodies, or in a slime which covers the fruiting body at maturity; spores not forcibly discharged, thus spore print unobtainable ..... **Gasteromycetes,** p. 525

HYMENOMYCETES

IN this large division of the Homobasidiomycetes the spores are produced on an exposed surface or surfaces (the **hymenium**) and are forcibly discharged at maturity. Terrestrial forms are usually furnished with a cap and stalk, but many of the wood-inhabiting types are bracketlike. In the more primitive forms the hymenium is smooth or slightly wrinkled, while in the more advanced types it takes the form of gills, tubes, spines, or elaborate branches.

The Hymenomycetes are traditionally divided into two orders: the Agaricales include the gilled mushrooms (agarics) and fleshy tube fungi (boletes), while the Aphyllophorales are an artificial group embracing the bracket fungi, coral fungi, chanterelles, and teeth fungi.

There has been a great deal of speculation as to whether Hymenomycetes evolved from Gasteromycetes or vice-versa. The current consensus seems to be that evolution has flowed both ways. Many Hymenomycetes have adapted to harsh environments by fruiting underground—in the process losing their ability to discharge spores and becoming "gastroid." On the other hand, there seem to be clear lines of evolution leading from primitive Gasteromycetes to certain Hymenomycetes, through gradual development of a hymenium, stalk, and cap.

Key to the Hymenomycetes

1. Fruiting body with gills .... **Agaricales,** below
1. Fruiting body without gills 2

2. Fruiting body with spines or teeth .... **Hydnaceae,** p. 480
2. Not as above 3

3. Fruiting body with a layer of tubes or pores 4
3. Not as above 5

4. Fruiting body fleshy, rapidly decaying, almost always terrestrial; stalk typically central .... **Boletaceae,** p. 401
4. Fruiting body usually tough, usually growing on wood, or if fleshy *and* terrestrial, then stalk off-center and pores usually decurrent .... **Polyporaceae and relatives,** p. 437

5. Fruiting body upright: simple and clublike, or branched and coral-like, or trumpet-shaped 6
5. Fruiting body bracketlike or crustlike, usually growing on wood .... **Polyporaceae and relatives,** p. 437

6. Fruiting body with a cap and stalk, usually trumpet-shaped or vaselike at maturity .... **Cantharellaceae,** p. 516
6. Fruiting body clublike or coral-like, without a well-defined cap............. .... **Clavariaceae,** p. 493

Agarics

AGARICALES

THE agarics, or gilled mushrooms, bear their spores on radiating blades or plates called **gills.** They are by far the most numerous and complex group of fleshy fungi, and are thought to have arisen from several different sources. They were originally placed in a single massive genus, *Agaricus.* In the 19th century, however, Elias Fries (the "father" of mushroom taxonomy) divided them into several dozen genera based on macroscopic features such as attachment of the gills, texture of the stalk, presence or absence of a veil, and spore color. The "Friesian" system suits the amateur because of its simplicity, but does not necessarily express natural relationships. In recent years, microscopic and chemical characteristics have assumed a great deal of importance in the taxonomy of agarics, and more than 100 genera are now recognized.

Since their disposition is still in a state of flux, a semi-Friesian classification scheme is employed here.

The agarics have been grouped into 14 families, which are keyed below. It is necessary to know the spore color (pp. 21-22) in order to use this key. A pictorial key to gilled mushrooms has also been provided, illustrating the common genera (thereby circumventing the family category). It is by no means infallible, but neither, for that matter, is the dichotomous key. The term "agaric," incidentally, is not to be confused with *Agaricus,* the genus to which the cultivated mushroom belongs.

Key to the Agaricales

1. Spore print white to buff, yellow, yellow-orange, or lilac-tinted 2
1. Spore print some other color (pinkish, yellow-brown, brown, rusty-orange, chocolate, black, greenish, etc.) 10

2. Volva present at base of stalk *and/or* warts on cap .... **Amanitaceae,** p. 224
2. Neither volva nor warts present (cap may be scaly, however) 3

3. Gills free *and* veil present; veil usually forming a ring, if not then stalk scaly or slimy below veil 4
3. Veil absent, or if present then gills attached 5

4. Cap slimy or viscid .... **Amanitaceae,** p. 224
4. Cap dry (or slightly viscid when wet) .... **Lepiotaceae,** p. 255

5. Gills foldlike: thick, shallow, blunt, decurrent, usually veined .... (see **Cantharellaceae,** p. 516)
5. Gills platelike or bladelike, not as above 6

6. Gills and flesh exuding a latex (milk or juice) when broken; stalk stout .... **Russulaceae,** p. 63
6. Not as above 7

7. Fruiting body rigid, stout, brittle, often (but not always) squat; flesh dry; stalk fleshy; cap plane to depressed at maturity; usually terrestrial .. 8
7. Not as above 9

8. Stalk breaking like chalk, without white mycelial mat at base .... **Russulaceae,** p. 63
8. Stalk tough, fibrous, often with white mycelial mat at base .... **Tricholomataceae,** p. 116

9. Gills soft, with a waxy appearance or texture; cap brightly colored or if not, then gills usually adnate to decurrent; almost always terrestrial .... **Hygrophoraceae,** p. 94
9. Gills not waxy; color and gill attachment variable; on ground or wood .... **Tricholomataceae,** p. 116

10. Spore print pinkish to deep flesh color or sordid reddish 11
10. Spore print some shade of orange, brown, black, or green 14

11. Volva present at base of stalk .... **Volvariaceae,** p. 217
11. Volva absent 12

12. Gills purple or purple-tinted when fresh .... **Tricholomataceae,** p. 116
12. Gills not purple 13

13. Gills typically free at maturity; growing on wood (sometimes buried!), wood chips, etc; spores smooth .... **Volvariaceae,** p. 217
13. Gills typically attached; usually (but not always) on ground; spores angular or longitudinally ridged .... **Rhodophyllaceae,** p. 206

14. Spore print greenish 15
14. Spore print some shade of brown or black 16

15. Gills blood-red to dark brown .... **Agaricaceae,** p. 273
15. Gills white to dull greenish .... **Lepiotaceae,** p. 255

16. Spore print deep brown, chocolate-brown, purple-brown, purple-gray, smoky-black, smoky-olive, or black 17
16. Spore print rusty-orange, rusty-brown, yellow-brown, cinnamon-brown, dull brown, bright brown, or cigar-brown 22

17. Gills usually decurrent; spore print smoky-olive to smoky-black; associated with conifers .... **Gomphidiaceae,** p. 394
17. Not as above; gills rarely decurrent 18

18. Gills turning into an inky black mass at maturity **Coprinaceae,** p. 313
18. Gills not liquefying 19

19. Veil present, usually forming a ring; gills free or nearly free, pallid to pinkish when young, chocolate-brown at maturity .... **Agaricaceae,** p. 273
19. Not as above 20

20. Cap brightly colored (yellow, green, orange, etc.) .... **Strophariaceae,** p. 299
20. Cap dull, some shade of brown, buff, gray, or white 21

21. Cap viscid when moist .... **Strophariaceae,** p. 299
21. Cap generally not viscid; fruiting body fragile ...... **Coprinaceae,** p. 313

22. Parasitic on other mushrooms .... **Tricholomataceae,** p. 116
22. Not as above 23

23. Gills decurrent, yellowish to orange or if not, then staining brown when bruised 24
23. Not as above 25

24. Spore print rusty-orange; veil often present ...... **Cortinariaceae,** p. 345
24. Spore print not rusty-orange; veil absent .... **Paxillaceae,** p. 389

25. Fruiting body small, fragile, withering quickly, or gills liquefying somewhat in wet weather; cap egg-shaped, conical, or bell-shaped; usually growing in grass or dung .... **Bolbitiaceae,** p. 336
25. Not as above .... **Cortinariaceae,** p. 345

Principal Characteristics	Spore print white to buff, yellow, yellow-orange, greenish, or lilac-tinted	Spore print pinkish to reddish or flesh color	Spore print brown to rusty-brown, yellow-brown, or rusty-orange	Spore print purple-gray to deep brown, purple-brown, or black
1. **Volva present** **Veil (ring) present or absent** **Gills free or slightly attached**	*Amanita*	*Volvariella*		*Agaricus* *Coprinus*
2. **Volva absent** **Veil present** **Gills free at maturity**	*Amanita* *Chlorophyllum* *Lepiota* *Limacella* *Melanophyllum*			*Agaricus* *Coprinus*
3. **Volva absent** **Veil absent** **Gills free at maturity, close**	*Collybia* *Hygrophorus* *Lepiota* *Limacella* *Marasmius* *Mycena* *Russula* *Tricholoma*	*Pluteus*	*Bolbitius* *Galerina* *Inocybe*	*Agaricus* *Coprinus*
4. **Volva absent** **Veil present, persistent** **Gills attached** **Stalk fleshy**	*Amanita* *Armillaria* *Armillariella* *Cystoderma* *Hygrophorus* *Lentinus*		*Agrocybe* *Cortinarius* *Gymnopilus* *Hebeloma* *Inocybe* *Pholiota* *Rozites*	*Chroogomphus* *Gomphidius* *Naematoloma* *Psilocybe* *Stropharia*
5. **Volva absent** **Veil absent or evanescent** **Gills typically adnate to decurrent** **Stalk fleshy**	*Cantharellus* *Clitocybe* *Craterellus* *Gomphus* *Hygrophoropsis* *Hygrophorus* *Laccaria* *Lactarius* *Lentinus* *Leucopaxillus* *Lyophyllum* *Omphalotus* *Panus* *Russula* *Tricholomopsis*	*Clitopilus* *Lepista*	*Agrocybe* *Cortinarius* *Gymnopilus* *Paxillus* *Pholiota* *Phylloporus*	*Chroogomphus* *Gomphidius*

Principal Characteristics	Spore print white to buff, yellow, yellow-orange, greenish, or lilac-tinted	Spore print pinkish to reddish or flesh color	Spore print brown to rusty-brown, yellow-brown, or rusty-orange	Spore print purple-gray to deep brown, purple-brown, or black
6. Volva absent Veil absent or evanescent Gills typically notched Stalk fleshy	*Hygrophorus* *Laccaria* *Lactarius* *Leucopaxillus* *Lyophyllum* *Melanoleuca* *Russula* *Tricholoma* *Tricholomopsis*	*Entoloma* *Lepista*	*Agrocybe* *Cortinarius* *Gymnopilus* *Hebeloma* *Inocybe* *Phaeocollybia* *Pholiota*	*Naematoloma*
7. Volva absent Veil present, persistent Gills attached Stalk thin, cartilaginous	*Cystoderma* *Hygrophorus*		*Conocybe* *Galerina* *Pholiota*	*Coprinus* *Panaeolus* *Psathyrella* *Psilocybe* *Stropharia*
8. Veil and volva absent Stalk thin, cartilaginous Cap conical to bell-shaped, at least when young	*Hygrophorus* *Marasmius* *Mycena*	*Entoloma* *Nolanea*	*Bolbitius* *Conocybe* *Galerina* *Inocybe*	*Coprinus* *Panaeolus* *Psathyrella* *Psilocybe*
9. Veil and volva absent Stalk thin, cartilaginous Cap convex to plane or umbilicate	*Clitocybe* *Collybia* *Flammulina* *Hygrophorus* *Laccaria* *Marasmius* *Melanoleuca* *Omphalina* *Xeromphalina*	*Entoloma* *Leptonia* *Nolanea*	*Agrocybe* *Galerina* *Inocybe* *Naucoria* *Pholiota* *Tubaria*	*Coprinus* *Naematoloma* *Panaeolus* *Psathyrella* *Psilocybe*
10. Volva absent Veil present or absent Stalk consistently off-center, lateral, or absent Growing shelflike on wood	*Lentinellus* *Lentinus* *Lenzites* *Panellus* *Panus* *Pleurotus* *Schizophyllum*	*Claudopus* *Phyllotopsis*	*Crepidotus* *Paxillus*	

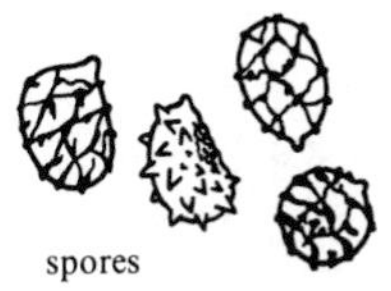

RUSSULACEAE

THE Russulaceae differ from all other gilled mushrooms in the microscopic structure of the cap tissue: nests of large, round cells called **sphaerocysts** are interspersed with the usual filamentous hyphae, giving the fruiting body a characteristic dry, brittle, rigid texture. There are two genera: *Lactarius*, which exudes a milk or juice (**latex**) when broken, and *Russula*, which does not. Though often characterized as a white-spored family, the spore color ranges from white to yellowish, buff, or ochraceous. The spores are always ornamented with strongly amyloid warts, spines, or ridges.

Lactarius and *Russula* are thought to have evolved independently of other agarics, probably from underground ancestors (see Hymenogastrales, p. 571). For this reason they are placed by some mycologists in a separate order, Russulales, rather than Agaricales.

Lactarius and *Russula* are mycorrhizal and often grow together, fruiting in spectacular abundance once or twice a year. From an edibility standpoint they are good for beginners because none of the mild forms are dangerous. But the acrid (peppery) types are best avoided since many are poisonous, at least raw. To determine whether a species is **acrid**, chew on a *small* piece of the cap for a minute or two, then spit it out. If it is acrid, you'll experience a burning sensation on your tongue—in fact, you may have to wash out your mouth to get rid of the taste! If you're not sure whether it's acrid, then it's undoubtedly "mild." Be careful—some species really pack a wallop!

Key to the Russulaceae

1. Fresh fruiting body exuding a latex (milk or juice) when broken (best seen by cutting gills near the stalk)* .... *Lactarius*, p. 64
1. Latex absent .... *Russula*, p. 74

* In dry weather, species with a scanty latex may have none at all. However, their gills are usually colored, whereas in *Russula* the gills are white to yellow (sometimes discoloring or aging reddish, brown, or black). The Lactarii that most often lack a latex are *L. sanguifluus* and *L. deliciosus*, which usually have greenish stains on the cap and gills; and *L. camphoratus*, small, with a red-brown to cinnamon cap and fragrant odor.

LACTARIUS (MILK CAPS)

Terrestrial, often squat, mostly medium-sized woodland mushrooms. CAP *usually depressed at maturity*, often with an inrolled margin when young, sometimes concentrically zoned. *Flesh rigid, brittle, usually exuding a milk or juice (latex) when broken;* taste mild or acrid. GILLS attached (usually adnate to decurrent), variously colored. STALK *stout, rigid, brittle*, often hollow, central. VEIL and VOLVA *absent*. SPORE PRINT *white to buff or yellowish*. Spores with amyloid warts or ridges. Cap tissue with nests of sphaerocysts.

LACTARIUS is readily recognized by its brittle flesh and rigid fruiting body which exudes a milky or juicy **latex** when broken. The latex is best seen by cutting the gills near the stalk. Old, dry fruiting bodies often lack a latex, leading to confusion with *Russula*. In *Russula*, however, the gills are usually white to yellow and the margin of the cap is often striate, while in *Lactarius* the gills are colored differently (at least in those species with a scanty latex), the cap is rarely striate, and the stem is often short. Some Mycenas possess a latex, but they strike a radically different pose: a conical to bell-shaped cap mounted on a long, thin, fragile stalk.

The most important feature to note on any *Lactarius* is the color of the latex and the color changes it undergoes (or produces on surrounding tissue) when exposed to the air. This should *always* be noted on fresh material. The latex may react with the air rapidly (within one minute) as in *L. chrysorheus*, or slowly (within 30 minutes) as in *L. trivialis* or *L. sanguifluus*, or not at all, as in *L. camphoratus*. The structure of the cap cuticle and pattern of ornamentation on the spores are important microscopic characters, but are not stressed here.

Lactarius contains several edible species. The candy cap, *L. camphoratus*, is the tastiest of the local varieties besides being one of the most abundant. *L. deliciosus* and *L. sanguifluus* are widely collected but require special treatment. All acrid Lactarii should be avoided—especially those with yellow- or purple-staining milk. Some acrid species can be rendered edible by pickling or parboiling, but it hardly seems worth the effort (or risk) to do so.

Lactarius is a large and complex genus. In general the species are easier to identify than their ubiquitous brethren, the Russulas, but are not as colorful. Like the Russulas, they are mycorrhizal, terrestrial woodland fungi, but often appear at the edges of pastures or on lawns where there are trees. Many are specific to certain hosts—e.g., *L. insulsus* associates only with live oak, *L. torminosus* with birch, *L. deliciosus* with pine, and *L. sanguifluus* with Douglas-fir.

They fruit in the fall and winter and sometimes rival the Russulas in abundance. However, there are far fewer species in our area. About 50 kinds are known from California, but most of these occur in the northern half of the state. Only nine are depicted here.

Key to Lactarius

1. Latex dark red to orange, scanty, slowly staining wounded areas greenish 2
1. Latex clear or white, at least *before* exposure to air 3

2. Latex dark red; associated mostly with Douglas-fir *L. sanguifluus*, p. 66
2. Latex carrot-orange; associated mostly with pine .. *L. deliciosus*, below

3. Latex changing to yellow upon exposure to air (within one minute) .... *L. chrysorheus*, p. 68
3. Not as above 4

4. Taste distinctly to excruciatingly acrid 5
4. Taste mild or slightly bitter 9

5. Margin of cap with a woolly matting of hairs when young; associated with birch (in lawns, gardens, etc.) .... *L. torminosus*, p. 70
5. Not as above 6

6. Latex slowly staining gills lilac to dull purple .... *L. uvidus*, p. 72
6. Not as above 7

7. Latex slowly staining gills greenish-gray to brownish; cap dull grayish-brown to gray or violet-gray 8
7. Not as above; cap pallid to yellowish to orange or reddish-orange, often zoned .... *L. insulsus*, p. 69

8. Spore print white; cap 5 cm broad or less, slimy when moist .... *L. mucidus*, p. 71
8. Spore print yellowish; cap 5 cm broad or more, viscid when moist, or sometimes slimy .... *L. trivialis*, p. 71

9. Odor noticeably aromatic, especially when dried *L. camphoratus*, p. 73
9. Odor mild; not common .... *L. subdulcis* (see *L. camphoratus*, p. 73)

Lactarius deliciosus (Delicious Milk Cap)

CAP 5-18 cm broad, convex becoming plane or depressed, surface viscid when moist; smooth, dull orange to carrot-orange or dark orange, sometimes blotched with green, fading in age or dry weather to dull greenish-gray or even yellowish; often zoned, margin inrolled when young. Flesh thick, brittle, light orange to greenish-gray, taste slightly bitter. **LATEX** scanty, bright carrot-orange, slowly staining wounded areas greenish. **GILLS** bright orange to dull yellowish or orange-buff,

Lactarius deliciosus, mature specimens. The scanty orange latex stains wounded tissue greenish. Note pine needles at left—it is usually associated with pine.

close, adnate to decurrent, brittle, greenish where wounded. **STALK** to 7.5 cm long but usually shorter, equal or narrowed at base, dry, smooth, stuffed then hollow, colored like cap or paler. **SPORE PRINT** tinged yellowish-buff; spores 8-11 × 7-9 μm, nearly round with amyloid ridges.

HABITAT: Scattered to gregarious under pine, fall and winter, common. A prominent fungal feature of our coastal Monterey pine forests, its occurrence is often linked with *Russula rosacea.*

EDIBILITY: Edible but not necessarily delicious. Prized in Europe, but special treatment is required to get rid of the granular texture and latent bitterness. Some ecological variants are better than others. Its abundance and distinctiveness make experimentation worthwhile. Some sources recommend slow cooking (e.g., baked in a casserole); others insist it should be cooked rapidly in a frying pan with *very* little butter. The Russians are fanatically fond of it.

COMMENTS: This vexingly variable fungus strikes a discordant note with its unlikely color combination of green and orange. The carrot-colored latex separates it from its close relative, *L. sanguifluus.* The latex is scanty and in dry weather often absent; however, the rigid, brittle flesh and greenish stains on the cap and/or gills identify it. The fruiting bodies persist for a long time and are often hollowed out by maggots. The Greeks were familiar with this fungus—it is depicted on a fresco from Herculaneum (buried in 79 A.D.).

Lactarius sanguifluus (Bleeding Milk Cap)

CAP 3-13 cm broad, convex becoming plane or depressed; surface slightly viscid when moist, smooth, reddish-brown to orange, orange-brown, or tan, dull greenish in old age, often zoned. Flesh thick, brittle, granular, brownish to buff, taste mild or slightly acrid. **LATEX**

Lactarius sanguifluus, gill detail. Note zoned cap margin. Scanty dark red latex stains wounded tissue greenish; it is usually associated with Douglas-fir. (Joel Leivick)

dark red, scanty, slowly staining wounded areas greenish. **GILLS** adnate to decurrent, reddish or dull purplish-red to tan with a dark reddish sheen, greenish where wounded or in old age, close. **STALK** to 6 cm long, equal or with narrowed base, dry, smooth, rigid, hollow, colored like cap or paler. **SPORE PRINT** pale yellowish; spores 7.5-10 × 6.5-8 µm, elliptical with amyloid ridges.

HABITAT: Scattered to gregarious in woods, associated in our area with Douglas-fir. Common in the fall, occasional in winter. Abundant at times in the Santa Cruz Mountains, but largely supplanted on the Monterey Peninsula (where pine predominates) by *L. deliciosus.* In the Pacific Northwest the mycorrhizal hosts are sometimes reversed!

EDIBILITY: Edible. As good or better than *L. deliciosus.* See comments on the edibility of that species.

COMMENTS: The telltale feature of this fetching fungus is the dark red latex which stains wounded tissue greenish. In dry weather the latex may be absent, but the greenish stains are characteristic. Mature specimens often have tiny, aborted green buttons at their base. Be sure not to confuse this species with *L. chrysorheus*, which has a white latex that turns yellow—the two often grow together.

Lactarius chrysorheus, mature specimens. The copious white latex quickly turns yellow when exposed to the air. It is rather unusual for it to grow in clusters.

Lactarius chrysorheus (Yellow-Staining Milk Cap)

CAP 2.5-10 cm broad, convex becoming plane or depressed; surface smooth, slightly viscid when moist; pinkish-buff to reddish-cinnamon or cinnamon-buff, often with watery spots or darker and lighter zones. Flesh firm, white, becoming yellow when exposed to air, odor mild, taste bitter or tardily acrid. **LATEX** white, changing quickly (within 30 seconds) to sulfur-yellow when exposed; staining wounded tissue yellowish. **GILLS** white to pinkish-cinnamon, sometimes stained reddish-brown in age, close, adnate to decurrent. **STALK** to 7 cm long, equal, dry, smooth, white to pinkish-buff, sometimes with darker spots. **SPORE PRINT** pale yellow or buff; spores 6-9 × 5-7 μm, elliptical to nearly round with amyloid ridges.

HABITAT: In groups or troops under both hardwoods and conifers. Common throughout rainy season, but especially in winter. It is abundant under pine, live oak, and manzanita, where it often mingles with *Russula emetica* and *R. raoultii*.

EDIBILITY: All yellow-staining milk caps should be strictly avoided.

COMMENTS: This ubiquitous *Lactarius* is easily identified by the prompt yellowing of the latex when exposed to the air. It superficially resembles *L. sanguifluus* and *L. camphoratus*, but is unique in this respect. We also have a confusing complex of oak-loving forms with a golden, more or less zoned cap and latex which yellows *slowly*. These resemble *L. insulsus* and may even prove to be aberrant forms of that species. They also resemble *L. alnicola*, a species with nearly white spores. Other milk caps with yellowing latex include: *L. vinaceo-rufescens*, cap vinaceous-rufous, taste only slightly bitter or acrid, spore print white, and gills reddish-stained in age; and *L. scrobiculatus*, cap golden-yellow with a woolly margin (like *L. torminosus*).

Lactarius insulsus, mature specimens. The golden zoned cap and peppery white latex typify a confusing complex of species. In our area they usually occur with oak. (Bill Everson)

Lactarius insulsus (Golden Milk Cap)

CAP 4-15 cm broad, convex with an inrolled margin becoming plane and then depressed; surface smooth, viscid when moist, distinctly zoned with alternating bands of buff, yellow-orange, pale yellow, orange-buff, and copper. Flesh thick, brittle, white to buff, taste extremely acrid. **LATEX** white, unchanging when exposed to air (but sometimes drying sordid yellowish on gills). **GILLS** adnate to decurrent, close, white or tinged cap color, darkening slightly in age, wounded areas sometimes yellowish or even brownish. **STALK** to 6.5 cm long, equal or with narrowed base, smooth, hollow or stuffed, dry, rigid, colored like cap or paler, sometimes with brighter (yellow to orange) spots. **SPORE PRINT** pale yellowish; spores 6-9 × 5-6.5 μm, broadly ellipsoid with amyloid warts and ridges (reticulate).

HABITAT: Scattered or in groups in woods or brush, monogamous with live oak. Abundant at times, fall and winter. It is the dominant *Lactarius* of live oak woods, especially around the edges of pastures.

EDIBILITY: Unknown. The acrid taste is a strong deterrent.

COMMENTS: The white unchanging latex, acrid taste, and yellowish-buff to dull orange, more or less zoned cap are the fallible fieldmarks of this prolific *Lactarius*. The above description actually encompasses a number of closely related forms, and whether ours is the "true" *L. insulsus* of Europe is for licensed lactariologists to decide. The group is easy to recognize, for the cap margin is not woolly as in *L. torminosus*, and the milk does not normally turn yellow as in the *L. chrysorheus* group. In one variety, however, the latex does eventually stain wounded tissue yellowish. In another variety the stalk is pitted or spotted. *L. zonarius* is a related species with reddish-orange bands on the cap and larger spores (9-11 μm long). *L. involutus* has a paler cap and white spores. *L. aurantiacus* has a smooth, viscid, bright orange unzoned cap, slightly acrid taste, and rather long, slender stalk. It is common farther north under conifers. Other acrid species with a white, unchanging latex include: *L. piperatus*, with a dry white cap; *L. necator* (or *L. turpis*), with an olive-brown to greenish cap; *L. rufus*, with a dark reddish cap; and *L. cinereus*, with a thin gray cap.

Lactarius torminosus (Woolly Milk Cap)

CAP 4-13 cm broad, convex with an inrolled margin, becoming plane or depressed; surface viscid when moist, yellowish-buff to pinkish-buff to whitish, the center usually tinged pale pinkish-orange; sometimes zoned; margin covered with a dense white matting of soft, woolly hairs when inrolled; hairs becoming sparse in age. Flesh thick, white or pale pinkish, crisp, odor mild, taste very acrid. **LATEX** white, unchanging. **GILLS** adnate to decurrent, close, white to yellowish or with a strong pinkish tint. **STALK** to 7 cm long but usually much shorter, equal or with narrowed base, smooth, rigid, dry, more or less cap color, sometimes with yellow spots. **SPORE PRINT** white; spores 7-10 × 5-8 μm, elliptical with amyloid warts and ridges.

HABITAT: Scattered or in groups in lawns and gardens where birch trees have been planted. Fairly common, usually fruiting after the first

Lactarius torminosus. Note the inrolled woolly-cottony margin when young; it is commonly found with birch.

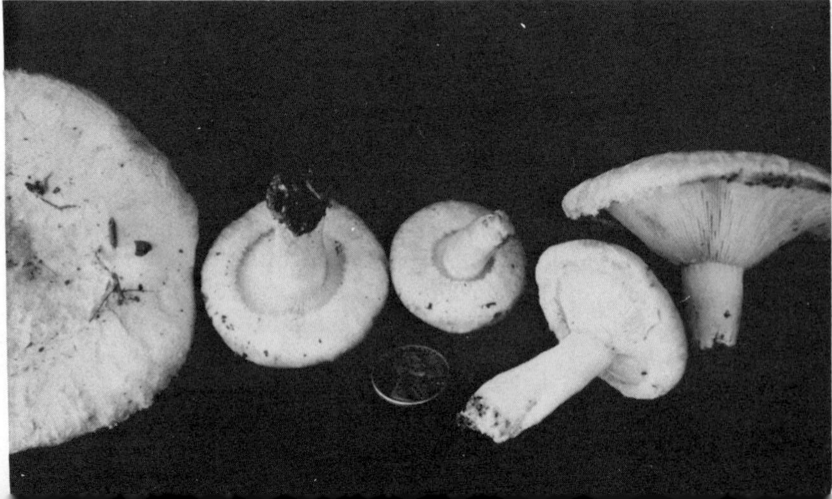

fall rains. Since it is mycorrhizal with birch, it seems likely that the mycelium is introduced on the roots of the saplings.

EDIBILITY: Not recommended. It is indigestible or poisonous unless thoroughly cooked. In Russia and Scandinavia it is pickled; in Norway it is roasted and added to coffee.

COMMENTS: The woolly cap margin and association with birch are the trademarks of this attractive *Lactarius.* Buttons with an inrolled margin are reminiscent of *Paxillus involutus*, but the presence of a latex distinguishes them. In one collection I made there was a greenish band on the gills and stalk apex, just as in *Russula brevipes.*

Lactarius trivialis (Vulgar Milk Cap)

CAP 5-20 cm broad, convex becoming plane and then depressed; surface smooth, viscid or slimy, smoky-gray or brownish-gray to violet-gray, but fading in age, sometimes obscurely zoned. Flesh thick, pallid, taste acrid. **LATEX** white, slowly staining wounded areas sordid grayish-green to brownish. **GILLS** adnate to decurrent, close, creamy-yellowish to pallid grayish-white, wounded areas greenish-gray to sordid brownish. **STALK** to 10 cm long, stout, rigid, smooth, equal, same color as cap or paler. **SPORE PRINT** yellowish; spores 9-12 × 810 μm, ellipsoid with amyloid warts and ridges.

HABITAT: Solitary or scattered in humus, usually in mixed woods, sometimes growing with *L. uvidus.* Common, late fall and winter.

EDIBILITY: Indigestible, perhaps poisonous.

COMMENTS: This is our largest and least attractive *Lactarius.* The grayish to violet-gray cap, white latex, acrid taste, and yellowish spore print are distinctive. Wounded areas stain brownish to greenish-gray as in *L. mucidus*, but the cap is larger, paler, and not as slimy.

Lactarius mucidus (Slimy Milk Cap)

CAP to 5 cm broad, convex to plane or slightly depressed; surface slimy when wet, viscid otherwise, smooth, uniformly gray-brown to slate-gray. Flesh thin, white or grayish, taste acrid. **LATEX** white, slowly staining adjacent areas dingy greenish-gray, bluish-gray, or brownish-gray. **GILLS** close, adnate or slightly decurrent, white, more or less greenish-gray where wounded. **STALK** to 7 cm long, equal, slimy or viscid when moist, colored like cap, smooth, rigid. **SPORE PRINT** white; spores 7.5-10 × 6-8 μm, nearly round with amyloid ridges.

HABITAT: Scattered in mixed woods and under conifers, especially Douglas-fir; fall and early winter, rather rare.

EDIBILITY: Inedible due to the acrid taste.

COMMENTS: The slimy-viscid grayish cap and stem, white spores, acrid taste, and white latex staining wounded areas greenish-gray to brownish-gray are the principal features of this lackluster *Lactarius*. In wet weather the layer of slime on the cap is so thick it looks like a *Hygrophorus*. The presence of a latex, however, distinguishes it. *L. trivialis* is similar, but larger, not as slimy, and has yellowish spores.

Lactarius uvidus (Purple-Staining Milk Cap)

CAP up to 10 cm broad, convex becoming plane or depressed; surface smooth, slimy or viscid, gray to brownish-gray or lilac-gray, sometimes obscurely zoned. Flesh thick, white, staining lilac, taste acrid. **LATEX** white, *slowly* staining wounded areas lilac. **GILLS** adnate to decurrent, close, white or yellowish, wounded areas lilac to lilac-brown. **STALK** to 7.5 cm long, but usually shorter, equal or slightly enlarged below, white or colored like cap, smooth, viscid when moist, rigid. **SPORE PRINT** white; spores 7-12 × 6-8 μm, elliptical with amyloid warts and ridges.

HABITAT: Solitary or scattered in woods, late fall and winter. Common, but seldom abundant. I find it most often in mixed woods of oak, tanoak, and madrone.

EDIBILITY: All lilac-staining milk caps should be avoided.

COMMENTS: The lilac-staining gills set this species apart. In other respects it resembles *L. trivialis*. Another lilac-staining species, *L. aspideus*, has a smooth yellow cap. *L. lignyotus* is a small mushroom with a velvety brownish-black cap and pinkish-staining latex.

Lactarius uvidus, mature specimens. Distinctive characters are the smooth viscid cap and white latex that stains wounded areas purplish. *L. trivialis* (not illustrated) looks similar but is larger and doesn't stain purplish.

Lactarius camphoratus (Candy Cap)

CAP 2-5 cm broad, convex to plane or slightly depressed, sometimes with a small umbo; surface smooth, dry, burnt orange to cinnamon-brown to brownish-red, not zoned. Flesh same color as cap or paler, rather thin, odor fragrant, especially when dry, taste mild. **LATEX** white or watery-white, unchanging, scanty or absent in dry weather. **GILLS** adnate to decurrent, close, brittle, colored like cap or paler. **STALK** to 7 cm long, slender, rigid, usually hollow, more or less equal, smooth, dry, same color as cap or paler. **SPORE PRINT** white; spores 6-8.5 × 6-7.5 μm, nearly round with large amyloid warts.

HABITAT: Scattered to gregarious or in small clumps in woods, especially along paths, drainage ditches, and other damp places. Very common, late fall through spring. Generally the last *Lactarius* to arrive on the scene, and one of the last mushrooms to exit. It is partial to oak but not restricted to that habitat.

EDIBILITY: Edible and excellent when its unique flavor and aroma are highlighted. Try it in pancake batter or as a stuffing for chicken, or sauteed with cinnamon, sesame seeds, and molasses (or honey) on toast. I know one person who is allergic to it, so try it cautiously the first time.

Lactarius camphoratus is our best tasting milky cap. The burnt orange to cinnamon cap, modest size, fragrant odor, and mild whitish latex set it apart.

COMMENTS: For many years the name *L. camphoratus* has been applied to a knotty group of closely related milky caps with a cinnamon cap, watery-white latex, rigid hollow stem, mild taste, and sweet odor. Whether or not ours is the "true" *L. camphoratus* of Europe is for the experts to decide. Whatever its name, it is a delicious edible that should be on the list of every fungus forager. The maple syrup odor becomes very pronounced as it cooks or dries—one mushroom can smell up a whole house. In addition to our typical form with a burnt orange to cinnamon cap and white spores, we have a beautiful brownish-red form with yellowish spores. It is also edible. *L. subdulcis* is an edible species that closely resembles *L. camphoratus* but has a mild odor. *L. acquifluus* (also called *L. helvus*) is a fragrant species with a clear latex. Its edibility has not been ascertained. I have yet to find it in our area. All of these resemble *L. chrysorheus* (a common species with yellowing latex), and *L. rufus* (a poisonous species with an excruciatingly acrid taste that is common farther north.

RUSSULA

Medium to large terrestrial woodland mushrooms. CAP plane or depressed at maturity, viscid or dry, skin often peeling easily, margin often striate. *Flesh dry, rigid, brittle*; taste mild or acrid, latex absent. GILLS attached or free, brittle, white to yellow when young (sometimes discoloring brown, reddish, gray, or black in age). STALK *stout, rigid, brittle,* central, *breaking like soft chalk.* VEIL and VOLVA *absent.* SPORE PRINT *white to yellow or ochraceous.* Spores with amyloid warts or ridges. Cap tissue (and usually gill tissue) containing nests of sphaerocysts.

RUSSULA is distinct by virtue of its dry brittle flesh, stout rigid fruiting body, white to yellow spore print, and warty amyloid spores. The stem is relatively thick and breaks like soft chalk (it snaps audibly)—in other words, it lacks the fibrous quality of most mushrooms. *Lactarius* is similar but exudes a latex when broken (at least when fresh). *Leucopaxillus* is somewhat brittle but has a tough fibrous stem that does *not* break like chalk, and often has white mycelium at the base (a feature not found in *Russula*).

Russulas also have a characteristic appearance that, though difficult to describe, makes them one of the easiest groups to recognize. The cap is plane to depressed at maturity and usually broader than the length of the stem (there are exceptions, of course).

As such *Russula* is a very clearcut group, yet mastering the vast catalog of species is an ambitious undertaking. Russulas come in a brilliant array of colors (reds, purples, pinks, yellows, and greens predominate), that is at once their most attractive and deceptive feature. The pigments are unusually sensitive to environmental and genetic caprice. As a result no two look quite alike. Identification is made more difficult by the fact that many species produce only one or two fruiting bodies per mycelium—making it hard to gauge accurately the degree of color variation. The result, of course, is that many species are still unclassified, while synonyms and homonyms abound. *Russula* researchers have resorted to measuring the spore ornamentation and pattern (a relatively constant feature) in an effort to dispel some of the confusion.

The task of getting to know the Russulas is made easier by arranging them in groups. For instance, the Compactae are comprised of large, coarse, hard-stemmed species with gills alternating long and short (*R. albonigra* and *R. brevipes* are good examples). Another group, centered around *R. fragrantissima* and *R. pectinatoides,* has a yellow-brown to brown conspicuously striate cap and a fragrant to unpleasant odor. A third section, poorly represented here, has flesh which turns grayish when exposed. The remaining Russulas can be divided into four large groups based on spore color (white or yellow) and taste (mild or acrid).

Russulas form mycorrhiza with a broad range of hardwood and conifer hosts, and are almost always terrestrial. They grow not only in the woods, but at the edges of pastures, in brushy areas, and on lawns where trees have been planted. They are the most omnipresent mushrooms of temperate forests, but are often concealed by leaves and needles and evident only as low mounds ("mushrumps") in the humus.

Russulas run rampant throughout the mushroom season, subject, of course, to the whim of the weather. A bewildering melange of species (*R. albonigra, R. xerampelina*, etc.) usually appears after the first fall rains, followed by another burst (spearheaded by *R. emetica* and *R. raoultii*) in mid-winter.

All mild-tasting Russulas are said to be edible, but this should not be taken as a signal to sample them indiscriminately. Always identify what you intend to eat. Acrid types (such as *R. emetica*) should be avoided—at least some cause vomiting and diarrhea. Though cooking may render them edible, it hardly seems worth the effort or risk. In this country Russulas are not often sought as esculents, and it is true that their dry, granular flesh does not blend well with many dishes. However, *R. xerampelina* and *R. cyanoxantha* (to name just two) are delicious delicacies in their own right.

Russulas are among the most maligned of all mushrooms. Even veteran mushroom hunters treat them mercilessly—throwing them over their shoulder or crushing them underfoot with disparaging remarks like "Oh, it's just another *Russula.*" Their omnipresence and poor culinary reputation are partly responsible, I am sure. Also, their brittle flesh is irresistible to those who like to smash things. Furthermore, they have a habit of forming "mushrumps" in the humus which resemble those made by *Boletus edulis.* Frustrated boletivores can be uncompromisingly brutal (see p. 434), and their habitual hunting grounds are inevitably strewn with the broken bodies of Russulas. However, mushrooms were not created for the exclusive enjoyment of *Homo sapiens*, and it is wrong to judge them accordingly. Try to resist the sharp temptation to mash, maim, and mutilate them. Those who follow in your footsteps will appreciate your sensitivity and self-restraint. A substantial number of Russulas are described here, but you will doubtlessly encounter many more—some of them unclassified.

Key to Russula

1. Gills alternating long and short; stalk hard; cap white, brown, gray, or black, often large 2
1. Not as above 5

2. Gills *or* stalk (or both) staining reddish in age or when bruised 3
2. Not as above 4

3. Fruiting body (especially stalk) staining reddish and then dark gray to black when bruised .... *R. densifolia,* p. 80
3. Gills slowly staining reddish; stalk staining reddish but never black .... *R. "adusta,"* p. 81

4. Fruiting body (especially stalk) staining dark gray to black in age or when bruised .... *R. albonigra,* p. 79
4. Not as above .... *R. brevipes,* p. 78

5. Cap 5-20 cm broad, yellow-brown to yellow-orange or orange-brown; odor sweet (like maraschino cherries) when young, fetid in age .... *R. fragrantissima*, p. 82
5. Not as above 6

6. Cap yellow-brown to brown or grayish-brown, margin striate with small bumps; odor usually spermatic or unpleasant, sometimes mild; taste of gills usually acrid .... *R. pectinatoides* p. 83
6. Not as above 7

7. Spore print white to creamy-white 8
7. Spore print pale yellow to yellow-orange or ochraceous (gills usually yellowish at maturity) 15

8. Cap white to yellowish-white 9
8. Cap not white 10

9. Cap margin striate; cap pale yellowish-white; usually occurring in groups or troops .... *R. raoultii*, p. 87
9. Cap margin not striate or only obscurely so; cap dull white (often buff at the center); occurring solitary or in small groups ... *R. albidula*, p. 86

10. Taste very acrid 11
10. Taste more or less mild 12

11. Cap red, fading in age .... *R. emetica*, p. 88
11. Cap purple-gray to yellow-pink or olive *R. fragilis* (see *R. emetica*, p. 88

12. Cap minutely powdery or velvety, dry, 2-7.5 cm broad, purple to purple-red .... *R. mariae*, p. 86
12. Not as above 13

13. Cap red, fading to orange .... *R. lepida* (see *R. emetica*, p. 88)
13. Cap never red 14

14. Cap predominately greenish (often with a brownish center), 3-8 cm broad .... *R. aeruginea*, p. 85
14. Cap variously tinted with lilac, pink, green, blue, yellow, etc., 6-18 cm broad .... *R. cyanoxantha*, p. 84

15. Flesh and stalk bruising grayish *R. decolorans* (see *R. alutacea*, p. 92)
15. Not as above 16

16. Taste acrid 17
16. Taste more or less mild 20

17. Cap rosy-pink to purple-pink, often tinted olive or brownish; stalk usually pinkish-tinted; associated with Douglas-fir *R. "palustris,"* p. 90
17. Not as above 18

18. Cap red; stalk rosy-red; associated with pine .... *R. rosacea*, p. 89
18. Not as above; stalk usually white or pallid 19

19. Cap more or less red .... *R. veternosa* (see *R. alutacea*, p. 92)
19. Cap brownish-lilac to brownish-red *Russula* sp. (see *R. integra*, p. 92)

20. Stalk bruising yellowish and then brownish; odor becoming fishy in age or when dried .... *R. xerampelina*, p. 93
20. Not as above 21

21. Cap predominately greenish or olive 22
21. Not as above (cap may have slight greenish tints) 23

22. Medium-sized, cap 3-8 cm broad .... *R. aeruginea*, p. 85
22. Medium to very large, cap 7-30 cm *R. olivacea* (see *R. aeruginea*, p. 85)

23. Cap whitish, tinged yellow-gray or grayish-green .... *Russula* sp. (see *R. albidula*, p. 86)
23. Not as above 24

24. Cap reddish-buff to brownish-red .... *R. integra*, p. 92
24. Cap some other color (including purple or red) 25

25. Cap minutely powdery or velvety, dry, 2-7.5 cm broad, purple to purple-red .... *R. mariae*, p. 86
25. Not as above; cap neither powdery nor velvety 26

26. Cap red to purplish-red, fading in age, 5-16 cm broad *R. alutacea*, p. 92
26. Cap dark purple to reddish-violet or purple-pink, sometimes with brown or yellowish tints, 2-7 cm broad, fragile .... *R. placita*, p. 91

Russula brevipes (Short-Stemmed Russula)

CAP 5-25 cm broad, convex becoming depressed; surface dry, minutely woolly or felty, white or whitish, often stained yellow-brown or brown and covered with dirt; margin at first inrolled. Flesh thick, crisp, dry, brittle, white, not bruising, taste mild or slightly acrid. **GILLS** thin, close, white or creamy, sometimes with a blue-green cast, adnate to decurrent, alternating long and short, sometimes brownish-stained in age. **STALK** 2-7 cm long, usually quite short and stout, equal or tapering downward, dry, smooth, dull white or brownish-stained, sometimes with a blue-green band at apex, hard and rigid. **SPORE PRINT** white or creamy-white; spores 8-11 × 6.5-8.5 μm, elliptical with amyloid warts and ridges.

Russula brevipes. Mature specimens at right have been turned upside down. Note how the specimen on the left (which has not been touched) barely pokes up above the humus—a feature typical of many Russulas. (Rick Kerrigan)

HABITAT: Solitary, more often in groups or troops on ground in woods, fall and winter, abundant. It hugs the ground closely and is often visible only as a low mound or "mushrump" in the humus. The main fruiting is typically in November or December.

EDIBILITY: Edible when cooked, but mediocre. One authority recommends stewing it slowly in soups.

COMMENTS: The most common of our large Russulas, this species is easily recognized by its white color, depressed cap with inrolled margin when young, close gills, short hard stem, and crisp dry flesh which does not redden or blacken when exposed. It has the aspect of a *Lactarius* but lacks a latex. It is larger and coarser than *R. albidula*, and has gills alternating long and short. *R. brevipes* var. *acrior* is the form with blue-green tints in the gills and stalk apex. In older books *R. brevipes* is misnamed *R. delica,* a European species with thick, well-spaced gills. A *Russula* meeting these specifications occurs in our area, but is rare.

Russula albonigra (Blackening Russula)

CAP 7-30 cm broad, convex becoming depressed; surface dry or slightly viscid when moist, sometimes polished; smooth, at first white, soon becoming gray and finally black; margin not striate. Flesh thick, dry, crisp, firm, white bruising gray to black; taste mild or slightly acrid. **GILLS** adnate to slightly decurrent, rather well-spaced, thick, brittle, alternating long and short, white staining gray or black, entirely black in old age. **STALK** up to 13 cm long and up to 5 cm thick; hard, stout, rigid, solid, smooth, equal or tapering downward, white becoming grayish or brownish-gray when wounded or in age, then black. **SPORE PRINT** white; spores 7-10 × 5.5-7.5 μm, broadly elliptical to nearly round with low amyloid warts.

HABITAT: Scattered or in troops in mixed woods (live oak, tanoak, madrone), fall and early winter. Sporadically common, at times appearing abundant because the fruiting bodies do not decay readily.

EDIBILITY: Edible when cooked—but hardly appealing.

COMMENTS: This massive *Russula* is easily identified by its large size, hard stem, and blackening of all parts in age or when handled. Young specimens are creamy-white (and reminiscent of *R. brevipes*) while elderly individuals are completely black—hence the species epithet *albonigra*, meaning "white-black." Allied species stain reddish and then black (see *R. densifolia*). *R. sordida* is a passe pseudonym.

Russula densifolia, mature specimens. Note the stains on the stalk—it turns reddish when scratched, then gray or black. *R. albonigra* (not illustrated) looks very similar but stains directly to black.

Russula densifolia (Rigid Russula)

CAP 6-24 cm broad, convex becoming depressed; surface viscid when moist, often polished when dry, smooth, dingy white becoming grayish or smoky-brown. Flesh thick, dry, crisp, white bruising reddish and then black; odor unpleasant in age, taste usually acrid. **GILLS** adnate to slightly decurrent, close, brittle, whitish, stained sordid reddish and then dark smoky-gray, alternating long and short. **STALK** to 10 cm long, thick, stout, hard, rigid, smooth, equal, whitish or stained brown, reddish-brown, or smoky; turning reddish when cut, then slowly black. **SPORE PRINT** white; spores 7-10 × 6-8 μm, nearly round with amyloid ridges,

HABITAT: Solitary, scattered, or in groups in woods, fall and winter. Fairly common, but not as abundant as *R. albonigra* or *R. "adusta."*

EDIBILITY: The sharp taste is said to disappear in the cooking process, but the end product is insipid and mediocre at best.

COMMENTS: The staining of wounded areas to reddish and then black (or sooty-gray) is the calling card of this rank *Russula*. In this sense it is a tactful compromise between *R. albonigra,* which blackens directly, and *R. "adusta"* which stains reddish but not black. The full sequence takes twenty minutes and is best seen by scratching the stalk. Two very similar species which redden before blackening are *R. nigricans*, with thick, well-spaced gills and spores 6-8 μm long, and *R. dissimulans*, with slighty closer gills and spores 7.5-11 μm long.

Russula "adusta." This large, rank *Russula* develops reddish stains on the gills, but never blackens. It always grows with oak and appears to be unclassified.

Russula "adusta" (Reddening Russula)

CAP 7-30 cm broad, convex becoming depressed; surface viscid when moist, smooth, whitish soon becoming rusty-ochraceous, sordid reddish-brown, or most often smoky-brown; margin at first inrolled. Flesh thick, crisp, dry, white bruising *slowly* reddish and then smoky-brown *or* directly to smoky-brown *or* not changing color at all; odor strong and unpleasant in age or upon drying, taste mild or slightly bitter. **GILLS** pallid soon stained sordid reddish, thick, brittle, adnate to slightly decurrent, usually alternating long and short. **STALK** up to 13 cm long and up to 5 cm thick, very hard, rigid, solid, equal or with a tapered base, smooth, white staining sordid reddish and then smoky-brown *or* directly to smoky-brownish in age or when handled. **SPORE PRINT** white; spores 6-10 μm, round or nearly round, with amyloid ridges.

HABITAT: Solitary or in small groups under live oak. Common, late summer through early winter. Chanterelles are often found in close proximity.

EDIBILITY: Unknown. The unappealing odor is a definite deterrent.

COMMENTS: This vulgar giant of the genus is easily identified by its hard stem, large size, and reddening of the gills in age or when wounded. The bruising reactions of the flesh and stalk are quite variable, however: reddish or smoky-brownish stains frequently develop but at no point does any part of the fruiting body blacken as in *R. densifolia.* The cap is usually stained with an unbecoming blend of murky gray, smoky-brown, and sordid reddish. In one collection the cap and stem were tinged bluish-green as in *R. brevipes.* Accounts of *R. adusta* are at odds with each other, and there are several discrepancies between our variety and the most definitive description. I reluctantly call our species *R. "adusta,"* but only as a matter of convenience (it could just as incorrectly be called *R. "compacta"*). Until it is critically evaluated by an expert, there seems little harm in doing so. *R. polyphylla* is a large species with a somewhat scaly cap in age and crowded buff to pinkish gills which bruise reddish-brown.

Russula fragrantissima (Fragrant Russula)

CAP 5-20 cm broad, convex becoming plane or somewhat depressed; surface viscid or slimy when moist, smooth, yellow-brown to ochraceous or orange-brown, usually darker (or reddish-spotted) at the center; margin radially grooved (conspicuously striate). Flesh white becoming pale yellowish-brown, thick, brittle, odor heavy and penetrating, at first sweet (like maraschino cherries or benzaldehyde), at length nauseating (fetid); taste mild or nauseating, taste of gills acrid. **GILLS** whitish becoming slightly yellowish or brownish-spotted in old age, often beaded with water droplets when fresh, adnexed to adnate or even free, close. **STALK** 4-10 cm long and up to 4 cm thick, stout, hard becoming spongy, equal, smooth, dry, dull white becoming yellowish or brownish-stained in age, especially near base. **SPORE PRINT** white to creamy-white; spores 6-9 $\times$ 6-8 μm, broadly ovate to nearly round, with amyloid warts, at least partially reticulate.

HABITAT: Solitary or scattered in mixed woods and under oak. Sporadically common, especially in the fall.

EDIBILITY: Unequivocally inedible, possibly poisonous. The nauseating taste and strong odor are enough to discourage most.

COMMENTS: Anyone under the mistaken impression that all mushrooms smell alike should get a whiff of this robust, odoriferous *Russula.* The penetrating odor is reminiscent of maraschino cherries,

Russula fragrantissima, young and mature individuals. Unfortunately, the overpowering maraschino cherry odor that distinguishes this hefty *Russula* cannot be communicated by a photograph. The orange-brown to yellow-brown cap is distinctly striate.

but alas, becomes putrid at maturity. The yellow-brown to yellow-orange furrowed cap, large size, and water droplets on the gills (when moist) are also distinctive. *R. foetens* is a similar European species with a nauseating odor even in youth, a hollow stem, and spores with isolated warts; *R. laurocerasi* is a yellower, slightly slimmer version whose odor is strongly fragrant through maturity (albeit sometimes with a subtle fetid component). It occurs in California also. All three of these have passed under the all-encompassing epithet *R. foetens*.

Russula pectinatoides (Comb Russula)

CAP 3-10 cm broad, convex becoming plane or somewhat depressed; surface viscid when moist, smooth, dark brown to gray-brown at the center, straw color to yellow-brown, light brown, ochraceous, or even reddish-brown toward the margin, which is radially furrowed and bumpy (tuberculate-striate). Flesh white, brittle, odor somewhat unpleasant or spermatic, taste mild or slightly acrid, taste of gills acrid. **GILLS** white or creamy, developing brownish stains, adnexed to slightly decurrent, close. **STALK** to 7.5 cm long, stout, equal or tapering downward, white or grayish, sometimes with brownish stains, the base sometimes rusty-spotted; smooth. **SPORE PRINT** creamy to pale yellow; spores 5.5-8.5 × 4.5-7 μm, elliptical with amyloid warts.

HABITAT: Scattered to densely gregarious in woods of all kinds and under trees on lawns, fall and winter, very common. The principal associates are live oak, pine, and Douglas-fir.

EDIBILITY: To be avoided. Several species in this group have not been tested. Besides, the odor and taste are unappealing.

Russula pectinatoides, mature specimens. The yellow-brown to grayish-brown cap has a striate margin which is not evident in this picture.

COMMENTS: The yellow-brown to grayish-brown cap with tuberculate-striate margin, creamy gills, unpleasant odor, and modest size are characteristic. The above description actually embraces a number of species which can only be separated with a microscope. They have long passed under the name *R. pectinata.* Among them are: *R. pectinata*, with a strong acrid taste and nauseating odor; *R. sororia*, with a grayish to olive-brown or grayish-brown cap and acrid taste; *R. foetentula*, with a pale yellow spore print and reddish stains at the stalk base; *R. amoenelens* and *R. cerolens*, with a grayer cap and strongly spermatic odor (the latter with partially reticulate spores); and *R. granulata*, with a scurfy-granulose cap. All have the general aspect of *R. fragrantissima* but are smaller, slimmer, and lack the fragrant odor.

Russula cyanoxantha (Variegated Russula)

CAP 6-18 cm broad, broadly convex becoming plane or depressed; surface viscid when moist, smooth, color variable: a mixture of rose-pink, lilac-purple, green, blue-green, and white, sometimes also yellow and brown; typically pallid to rose-pink or lilac when young (or under leaves), developing greenish tones in age or in sunlight; margin sometimes obscurely striate. Flesh firm, white, thick, dry, crisp, odor mild or pleasant, taste mild. **GILLS** attached, close, white or with a few brownish stains, lardy or slightly greasy to the touch; often forked. **STALK** 5-13 cm long and 2-5 cm thick, rather hard, stout, solid or stuffed, more or less equal, smooth, white. **SPORE PRINT** white; spores 7.5-10 $\times$ 6-8 μm, broadly elliptical to nearly round, with isolated amyloid warts.

HABITAT: Solitary or in groups or troops in mixed woods and under hardwoods, especially tanoak. Common in the fall, occasional in

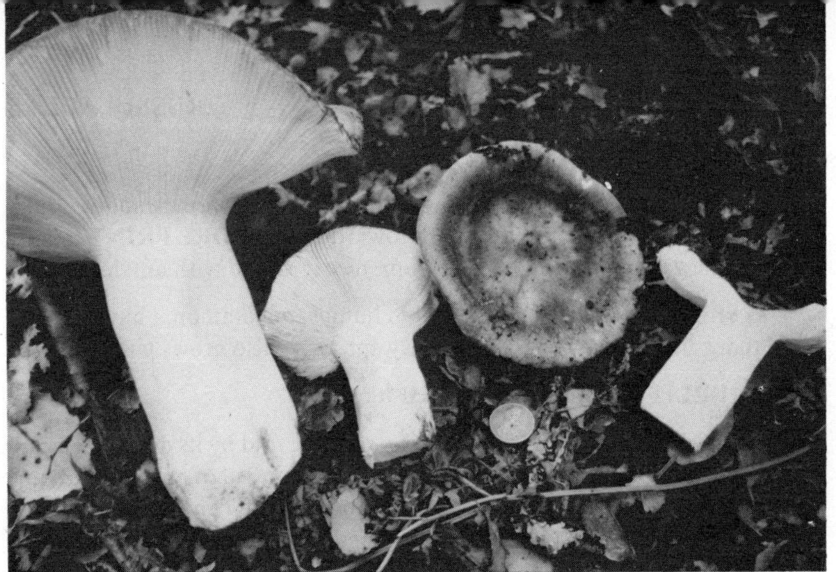

Russula cyanoxantha. Note the mottled or zoned cap, white stalk, white gills, and large size. Worm-free specimens such as the one on the right are a rarity.

winter. Often concealed by fallen leaves.

EDIBILITY: Edible. In Europe it is rated highly, but our version is invariably riddled with maggots. Hard, crisp, uninfested buttons are an excellent choice for omelets.

COMMENTS: The telltale signs of this beautiful, robust *Russula* are the large size, white spores, stout white stem, mild taste, and variegated cap—typically a mixture of pink, lilac, green, or even blue. It is one of the most conspicuous Russulas of our mixed hardwood forests, but is more finicky in its fruiting requirements than, say, *R. emetica* or *R. brevipes*. It was practically absent in the fall of 1976, then overwhelmingly abundant the following year. *R. variata (=R. cyanoxantha* var. *variata)* is identical but has an acrid taste. *R. brunneola* is a slightly smaller species without lardy gills. It, too, has forked gills, a mild taste, and white spores, and is deceptively variable in color: the cap is grayish to brownish to yellowish, olive, or grayish-red, with a striate margin.

Russula aeruginea (Green Russula)

CAP 3-8 cm broad, convex then plane or slightly depressed; surface viscid when moist, smooth, dull green, dark green, or smoky-green, darker (often brownish) at the center; margin often striate. Flesh white or greenish, dry, rather fragile, taste mild. **GILLS** adnate to free, close, brittle, white to creamy or spotted brownish. **STALK** to 7 cm long, but usually shorter, stout, equal or tapering downward, smooth, rigid, white, often discolored brownish toward base. **SPORE PRINT** creamy to pale yellow; spores 6-9 × 5-7 μm, nearly round with amyloid warts.

HABITAT: Solitary or scattered in humus, uncommon. I have found it under live oak in the fall and early spring; it also grows with conifers.

EDIBILITY: Edible. I have tried it.

COMMENTS: This modest *Russula* can be told by its deep green cap, pallid gills, and creamy spore print. There is no red or purple as in some of the larger Russulas which show green on the cap. *R. crustosa* is a similar species with a crusty-scaly cap and white spores; *R. olivascens* has a greenish cap and yellower spores; *R. olivacea* is a massive species (cap 7-30 cm broad) with a more or less dry, non-striate, olive cap, often shaded with purple or dark red. It has yellowish gills, yellow spores, a mild odor and mild taste. The stalk does not bruise yellowish or brownish like *R. xerampelina*, but stains purple-red in phenol.

Russula mariae

CAP 2-7.5 cm broad, convex becoming plane or slightly depressed; surface dry, finely powdered or velvety, purple to amethyst, reddish-purple, or maroon, sometimes overlaid with gray or olive; margin sometimes striate when old. Flesh thin, brittle, white, taste mild or very slightly acrid. **GILLS** close, white becoming creamy or pale yellowish, usually attached. **STALK** up to 7.5 cm long, equal or tapering downward, firm, rigid, spongy-stuffed, white, sometimes tinged red or purplish-red. **SPORE PRINT** creamy or faintly yellow; spores 7-10 × 6-8 μm, broadly elliptical to nearly round, with amyloid ridges, reticulate.

HABITAT: Solitary or in small groups in mixed woods, fall and early winter, not common. I have found it only once, in November.

EDIBILITY: Edible, but hardly incredible.

COMMENTS: This exquisite *Russula* is easily identified by its dry, velvety or finely powdered purplish cap, mild taste, and creamy spores. No other species really approaches it.

Russula albidula (White Russula)

CAP 3-8 cm broad, convex becoming plane or shallowly depressed; surface smooth, slightly viscid when moist, then dry, white or tinged buff at center; margin not striate or very obscurely so. Flesh fragile, dry,

Russula albidula. A dingy (and often dirty) whitish species of moderate size. *R. raoultii* (illustrated on p. 51) is usually cleaner.

white, taste acrid. **GILLS** attached, brittle, close, white or creamy. **STALK** up to 7 cm long, equal, dry, smooth, rigid, white, spongy-hollow in age. **SPORE PRINT** white or creamy-white; spores 7-10 μm, nearly round with amyloid ridges.

HABITAT: Solitary or in small groups in woods, especially oak, late summer through early spring. Common, but never in large numbers (like lips, it tends to occur in pairs). It is partial to poor or sandy soil along trails or roadcuts.

EDIBILITY: Utterly inedible due to the acrid taste.

COMMENTS: This plain, profoundly forgettable *Russula* can be recognized by its white cap and gills, modest size, and acrid taste. It is smaller and more fragile than *R. brevipes* and the stem is proportionately longer. The cap is dull white rather than yellowish-white as in *R. raoultii*, and the margin is scarcely striate. There are several similar wishy-washy Russulas, including: *R. albella*, with dry white cap (sometimes tinged pinkish) and mild taste; *R. albida*, with viscid white cap and mild taste; and *R. anomala*, with dry white (or yellowish) cap and acrid taste. An unidentified species with a whitish cap tinged grayish-green to yellow-gray, mild taste, and yellow spores also occurs. I have found it in mixed woods of tanoak and Douglas-fir, in November.

Russula raoultii

CAP 3-10 cm broad, convex becoming plane or shallowly depressed; surface viscid when moist, smooth, yellowish-white, the center often slightly darker; margin striate, sometimes obscurely so. Flesh dry, white, brittle, taste very acrid. **GILLS** brittle, close, white or creamy-white, adnate or notched, rarely free. **STALK** to 7 cm long, equal, dry, smooth, spongy-stuffed becoming hollow, with longitudinal lines, dull white. **SPORE PRINT** white; spores 6-9 × 5.5-7 μm, broadly elliptical to nearly round, with amyloid warts, more or less reticulate.

HABITAT: Scattered or gregarious (sometimes in troops), very common in chaparral hardwoods (oak, madrone, manzanita). Fruiting in late fall and winter, often mixing company with *R. emetica.*

EDIBILITY: Unknown. Presumably poisonous like *R. emetica.*

COMMENTS: This species is an exact replica of *R. emetica*, but with a pale yellowish-white rather than red cap. It is distinguished with some difficulty from *R. albidula*, but is slightly yellower, has a striate cap margin, and tends to fruit in larger numbers.

Russula emetica (Emetic Russula)

CAP 3-10 cm broad, convex becoming plane or shallowly depressed; surface viscid when moist, smooth, dark red to bright red when young, the center usually darker, fading to pinkish-red or blotched with pink and white; margin striate, sometimes obscurely so. Flesh brittle, dry, white, taste extremely acrid. **GILLS** white or creamy-white, brittle, thin, close, attached or sometimes free. **STALK** to 10 cm long, equal, hollow in age, smooth, dry, with longitudinal lines, dull white. **SPORE PRINT** white; spores 7-10 × 6.5-8 μm, broadly elliptical with amyloid warts, more or less reticulate.

HABITAT: Solitary, in groups or troops in woods, fall and winter, common. It fruits in great abundance every winter in chaparral and mixed hardwood forests (oak, madrone, manzanita, and pine), often intermingled with *R. raoultii* and *Lactarius chrysorheus.* It sometimes grows on very rotten wood—unorthodox behavior for a *Russula.*

EDIBILITY: Poisonous, at least when raw. As its name implies, it can be used to induce vomiting. Parboiling may destroy the toxins, but it hardly seems worth the trouble. It is eaten by Himalayan villagers, presumably as a spice.

COMMENTS: This attractive mushroom is easily recognized by its red cap, white stem, white gills, and brittle peppery flesh. It is pleasing to the eyes of all, to the tongues of some, but to the stomachs of none. As in many Russulas, the skin peels rather easily from the cap. For years the

Russula emetica, mature specimens. The bright red cap, white gills, white stem, and peppery taste make this species a cinch to identify.

name *R. emetica* has been indiscriminately (but quite understandably) applied to a confusing group of Russulas with the above features. The present consensus seems to be that the "real" *R. emetica* is almost exclusively restricted to boggy areas. *R. silvicola* may be a better name for our fungus, or it may be a new species altogether. Since it isn't edible, such exacting distinctions needn't concern you—at least they don't concern me. *R. fragilis* is a small fragile cousin with a purplish-gray to yellowish-pink or olive-tinted cap, white spores, white stem, and acrid taste. *R. lepida* has a red cap fading to orange or yellowish, creamy-white spores, and a mild or slightly bitter taste.

Russula rosacea (Rosy Russula)

CAP 3-10 cm broad, convex to plane or slightly depressed; surface viscid when moist, smooth, dark red to bright red, fading in old age to pink or blotched with white. Flesh white, firm, dry, brittle, taste very acrid. **GILLS** creamy-white becoming pale yellow, adnate to decurrent, close. **STALK** to 10 cm long, equal or with a narrowed base, smooth, dry, hollow in age, flushed pink or red. **SPORE PRINT** pale yellow; spores 7-9 $\times$ 6-8 μm, nearly round with amyloid warts.

HABITAT: Scattered to densely gregarious under pine. Abundant, fall through early spring; frequently found with *Lactarius deliciosus*.

EDIBILITY: To be avoided because of the acrid taste.

COMMENTS: This common, conspicuous, and colorful inhabitant of our coastal pine forests is readily recognized by its red cap, rosy stem,

Russula rosacea has a red cap and peppery taste like *R. emetica*, but the stalk is flushed pink or red. It usually grows with pine.

creamy gills, acrid taste, and dry brittle flesh. It is one of our prettiest mushrooms—the clean, creamy gills contrasting nicely with the red cap and stem. At a distance it is sometimes mistaken for *Amanita muscaria*, which has a white stem with a ring and volva. The pale yellow spores and rosy stem distinguish it from *R. emetica*, while the acrid taste separates it from *R. alutacea*. *R. sanguinea* is very similar if not the same.

Russula "palustris"

CAP 3-10 cm broad, convex becoming plane or slightly depressed; surface smooth, viscid when moist, rosy-pink to purple-pink or zoned brownish to purple-brown at the center, olivaceous in the middle, and pinkish toward the margin, which is usually striate. Flesh white, fragile, taste tardily acrid. **GILLS** creamy-white becoming creamy-yellow or dingy yellow, close, attached but not decurrent, brittle. **STALK** 5-10 cm long, equal, smooth, hollow or stuffed; pallid or tinted pink to purple, or sometimes pale greenish-gray with pinkish tints in old age. **SPORE PRINT** pale yellow; spores 7-9 $\times$ 5.5-6.5 μm, broadly elliptical to nearly round, with amyloid warts, more or less reticulate.

HABITAT: Scattered to gregarious in mixed woods and under conifers, fall and early winter, common. Douglas-fir and pine appear to be its mycorrhizal mates.

EDIBILITY: To be avoided because of the acrid taste.

COMMENTS: The yellow spores, fragile flesh, pinkish-tinted stalk, acrid taste, and peculiarly colored cap set this attractive species apart. It is probably not the genuine *R. palustris*, but that is for the *Russula* researchers to decide. It superficially resembles *R. placita*, but differs in its acrid taste. *R. fallax* has a similarly colored cap, acrid taste, and white spores.

Russula placita is one of several small fragile Russulas with purplish cap and yellow gills. It usually grows with conifers, especially Douglas-fir.

Russula placita (Pleasing Russula)

CAP 2-7 cm broad, plane or slightly depressed; surface viscid when moist, smooth, dark purple to reddish-violet or purple-pink, often paler at the margin, sometimes dark brown or yellowish at the center; margin striate, sometimes obscurely so. Flesh thin, fragile, dry, white, taste mild. **GILLS** close, at first creamy-white, soon yellow, becoming dingy yellowish-ochre in old age, adnexed to adnate. **STALK** to 7 cm long, equal or tapering downward, whitish, dry, smooth, soft and spongy inside. **SPORE PRINT** yellow; spores 7-10 $\times$ 6-9 μm, broadly elliptical to nearly round, with large amyloid warts.

HABITAT: Scattered to gregarious on ground in woods, affiliated primarily with Douglas-fir, also pine. Common in the fall, occasional in winter; often found with *R. xerampelina* and *Lactarius sanguifluus*.

EDIBILITY: Edible but forgettable. It is pleasing to the eye but not to the palate, being bland bordering on tasteless.

COMMENTS: This common species is distinguished by its purple cap, yellow gills, mild taste, and marked fragility. It is frequently wormy and it's difficult to transport a group home without crushing them. It lacks the shrimpy odor of *R. xerampelina* and doesn't stain brown on the stem. There is a slew of other small fragile Russulas with a mild taste and yellow spores. Sorting them out is best left to specialists. Their ranks include: *R. abietina*, with a purplish to greenish-purple or brownish cap and ochraceous spores, associated mainly with true firs; *R. puellaris*, with a purple to livid brown cap, pale yellow spores, and stem becoming yellowish in age; and *R. chamaeleontina*, with a small, thin, fragile, purplish to lilac or reddish cap fading to yellow or orange. The latter has proved invaluable to compulsive categorizers exasperated by the endless nuances of color in *Russula.* Any aberrant forms with yellow spores and a mild taste can be referred to *R. chamaeleontina* and conveniently forgotten about. *R. fragilis* has served the same purpose in the white-spored, acrid group.

Russula integra

CAP 5-12 cm broad, convex becoming plane or slightly depressed; surface viscid when wet, smooth, dull red to reddish-brown or reddish-buff, often mixed with yellowish-buff, olive, salmon, etc., margin striate at maturity. Flesh white, fragile, taste mild. **GILLS** close, adnate to free, creamy becoming yellowish. **STALK** up to 6.5 cm long, stout, equal, smooth, dry, white, spongy-stuffed. **SPORE PRINT** yellow; spores 7-9 × 5.5-7 μm, broadly elliptical to nearly round with amyloid warts.

HABITAT: Scattered or in small groups in mixed woods and under oak. Fairly common in the fall, less so in winter.

EDIBILITY: Edible. All the specimens I've found were wormy.

COMMENTS: The dull red to reddish-buff cap, white stem, mild taste, and yellowish spores render this rotund *Russula* distinct. It lacks the purple color of *R. placita* and is slightly larger. As usual, there are several closely related varieties which need to be critically evaluated. One has a brownish-lilac to brownish-red cap, yellow spores, and an acrid taste.

Russula alutacea

CAP 5-18 cm broad, convex becoming depressed; surface viscid when moist, smooth, red to purplish-red, fading in age (sometimes with olive or yellowish spots); margin striate at maturity. Flesh crisp, dry, white, thick, odor and taste mild. **GILLS** adnate to free, pallid becoming yellow to ochraceous-yellow, brittle, close. **STALK** 3-10 cm long, stout, more or less equal, smooth, dry, white or tinged cap color. **SPORE PRINT** dark yellow or ochraceous; spores 8-10 × 7-9 μm, nearly round with prominent, isolated amyloid warts.

HABITAT: Solitary or scattered in mixed woods and under conifers, particularly pine. Fairly common, fall and winter. I find it regularly at Point Lobos.

EDIBILITY: Edible, but not choice.

COMMENTS: This arresting reddish *Russula* belongs to a complex group of medium to large Russulas with reddish cap, mild taste, and yellow to ochraceous spores. Distinguishing between them is a job for rabid *Russula* buffs. A slightly smaller species with a red cap that fades in blotches to pink or yellow is common under hardwoods, usually alone or in twos and threes. *R. borealis* has a blood-red cap that scarcely fades; *R. amygdaloides* has a peach-colored to pinkish-yellow cap and yellow spores. For some of the small fragile Russulas with a mild taste and yellow spores, see *R. placita*. Similar to *R. alutacea* but with an acrid taste are *R. tenuiceps*, with ochraceous-yellow spores and pink stem, and *R. veternosa*, with pale yellow spores and white stem. There is also a group of yellow-spored Russulas whose stem and flesh bruise grayish. They are a characteristic component of northern coniferous forests, but poorly represented in our area. Members of the club include *R. decolorans*, with orange-red cap, and *R. ochroleuca*, with yellow cap.

Russula xerampelina (Shrimp Russula)

CAP 5-20 cm broad, convex becoming plane and finally depressed; surface viscid when moist, smooth, red to dark red to purple, often laced with olive, brown, yellow-brown, or purple-brown; margin striate (sometimes obscurely so). Flesh thick, creamy, bruising yellowish and then brown; odor mild becoming shrimpy or fishy in age, taste mild. **GILLS** close, adnate to adnexed, creamy-white or slightly yellowish, staining yellowish and then brown, becoming grayish-brown or grayish when dried. **STALK** to 13 cm long, rather stout, equal or with slightly enlarged base, often finely grooved or longitudinally wrinkled; dry, white usually flushed with pink or purple, staining yellowish where bruised and then brown; interior spongy and often discolored. **SPORE PRINT** yellowish; spores 8-11 × 6-8.5μm, ellipsoid to nearly round, with isolated amyloid warts. Flesh turning deep green in ferrous sulfate.

HABITAT: Solitary, scattered, or gregarious under conifers. Common in the fall following heavy rain, occasional otherwise. In our area it is associated principally with Douglas-fir, and occasionally with pine.

EDIBILITY: Edible and unforgettable—one of the least appreciated of our edible fungi, undoubtedly due to the mediocrity of its brethren. In contrast to *R. cyanoxantha*, it is rarely eaten by maggots. Young caps

Russula xerampelina, mature specimens. This delicious *Russula* is round and symmetrical when young and develops a shrimpy odor in age. Note Douglas-fir needles stuck to the cap (indicating it was viscid), and the brownish stains on the stalk and gills.

are superb stuffed with cheese, chives, and parsley and then broiled.

COMMENTS: This extremely variable species can be recognized by the following combination of characteristics: (1) cap viscid when wet, usually with adhering debris when dry (2) stem usually tinted pinkish and always staining yellow, then slowly brown when bruised (3) yellow spore print (4) mild taste (5) fishy odor *at maturity*, which is accentuated by cooking or drying (6) tendency of the gills to age or dry brownish to grayish. In addition, the young buttons are remarkably rotund and symmetrical—but this character can be appreciated only with experience. Given the extreme variation in color and stature, *R. xerampelina* may be a composite species. One very distinct variety with a pale greenish-yellow to yellow-buff cap is fairly common in mixed chaparral-hardwoods. Like "typical" *R. xerampelina* it has yellow spores and develops brownish stains and a shrimpy odor as it ripens.

HYGROPHORACEAE (WAXY CAPS)

Mostly small to medium-sized *terrestrial* mushrooms. CAP typically smooth, often viscid and brightly colored. Flesh soft. GILLS *soft, waxy*, usually thick and well spaced, usually attached. STALK central; fleshy or cartilaginous. VEIL absent or evanescent. VOLVA absent. SPORE PRINT *white*. Spores round to elliptical, often shaped like corn kernels when immature, smooth, rarely amyloid. Basidia long and narrow. Gill hyphae interwoven, parallel, or divergent.

THIS is an attractive and very colorful group with white spores and waxy gills. There is a single genus, *Hygrophorus*. The "waxiness" of the gills is admittedly a subjective character, but with a little experience is readily apparent. The gills are soft, clean, fleshy, and . . . they look and feel *waxy*. The cap may also have a waxy appearance, hence the name "waxy caps."

There is little else to separate them from the white-spored Tricholomataceae. The flesh is not dry and brittle as in *Russula*. The gills are not blunt as in *Cantharellus*. Laccarias may have slightly waxy gills, but they have tough, fibrous stems and spiny spores. The Gomphidiaceae also have waxy gills, but their spores are smoky-black.

The long narrow, protruding basidia (which are responsible for the "waxiness" of the gills) have led some investigators to suggest that *Hygrophorus* evolved from *Cantharellus*-like ancestors. *H. pratensis*, in fact, bears an uncanny resemblance to the chanterelle *(Cantharellus cibarius)*. A relationship to *Omphalina* is also possible.

Hygrophorus is divided into three major groups based on the microscopic arrangement of the gill hyphae. These are raised to generic rank by some mycologists *(Hygrocybe, Camarophyllus, Limacium, etc.)*. In the most primitive group (interwoven hyphae), the cap is usually dry, the gills thick, well-spaced, and decurrent. Those with parallel hyphae are the waxiest and most brilliantly colored: the cap is usually viscid and the gills rarely decurrent. The least waxy and most advanced group has divergent hyphae. The cap and stem are often slimy, the gills typically white and decurrent. An evanescent veil may be present and the stalk apex is frequently **punctate** (adorned with pointlike scales or granules). These are the ones most often mistaken for other white-spored genera. In contrast to the first two groups, which are saprophytic, many of the latter appear to be mycorrhizal.

None of the waxy caps are dangerously poisonous, but they have little to offer the mushroom-eater. Most are bland and watery (see *H. sordidus*), and a few (such as *H. conicus* and *H. puniceus*) may cause illness. However, they are notable for their beauty, if nothing else. Virtually every color of the rainbow is represented: blue or green in *H. psittacinus*, pink in *H. calyptraeformis*, yellow, orange, red and white in a great many species, black in *H. conicus*.

The waxy caps fruit throughout the mushroom season, but normally peak (in both diversity and numbers) in the cold winter months. They are primarily woodland fungi. Mycorrhizal species are common under oak, madrone, pine, and Douglas-fir, while redwoods are rich in the saprophytic types. It is interesting to note, however, that in other regions waxy caps frequent bogs and pastures. Though many species are common, only the mycorrhizal types fruit in appreciable quantity, and then only sporadically.

Hygrophorus is a large genus. More than 200 species are known from North America. About half of these occur in California. Since they always attract attention and are relatively easy to distinguish, a fairly large selection is offered here.

Key to the Hygrophoraceae (Hygrophorus)

1. Cap *and/or* top of stalk with golden-yellow to orange powder or granules; cap white .... *H. chrysodon*, p. 107
1. Not as above 2

2. Cap white or tinged yellowish when fresh, sometimes discolored in age 3
2. Cap distinctly colored, at least at center 8

3. *Both* cap *and* stalk slimy or viscid when moist; slimy veil present when young 4
3. Stalk dry; cap dry or viscid; veil absent 5

4. Stocky; cap creamy-yellowish; associated with pine *H. gliocyclus*, p. 108
4. Stalk rather slender; cap white; found only occasionally with pine .... *H. eburneus*, p. 107

5. Robust; cap large, 5-20 cm broad; stalk at least 1.5 cm thick .... *H. sordidus*, p. 109
5. Smaller; not as above 6

6. Odor aromatic .... *H. russocoriaceus* (see *H. borealis*, p. 99)
6. Odor mild 7

7. Cap distinctly viscid when moist, drying reddish-brown, 2.5-7 cm broad .... *H. albicastaneus* (see *H. eburneus*, p. 107)
7. Cap not viscid, or if viscid, then about 2 cm broad and very thin-fleshed, not drying reddish-brown .... *H. borealis*, p. 99

8. Fruiting body staining gray or black when handled or in age .... *H. conicus*, p. 104
8. Not blackening when handled 9

9. Cap bright red, yellow, or orange 10
9. Cap some other color (including pink and reddish-purple) 16

10. Both cap and stalk viscid; gills decurrent; cap convex to plane, usually olive-brown at center, at least when young; associated with pine .... *H. hypothejus*, p. 110
10. Not as above 11

11. Cap bright red when fresh, may fade in age 12
11. Cap yellow to orange, never red 15

12. Cap sharply conical, at least when young .... *H. cuspidatus* (see *H. acutoconicus*, p. 103)
12. Cap not sharply conical 13

13. Cap distinctly viscid .... *H. puniceus*, p. 101
13. Cap not distinctly viscid 14

14. Cap fading drastically to orange or yellow as it dries, less than 2.5 cm broad .... *H. miniatus*, p. 100
14. Cap fading only slightly, 2 cm broad or more .... *H. coccineus*, p. 100

15. Cap conical, at least when young .... *H. acutoconicus*, p. 103
15. Cap convex to plane, not conical .... *H. flavescens*, p. 102

16. Gills white, soon spotted or stained pinkish-red to purple-red; cap streaked with similar colors, *not* conical 17
16. Not as above 18

17. Robust; gills close or crowded; with hardwoods .... *H. russula*, p. 111
17. Not as above .... *H. erubescens*, p. 112

18. Cap and gills pink; cap sharply conical, at least when young; stalk long and slender .... *H. calyptraeformis*, p. 105
18. Not as above 19

19. Cap green (rarely blue) when young, soon fading to salmon, pink, reddish or even yellowish, but usually retaining traces of olive somewhere on fruiting body; cap small, both cap and stalk viscid or slimy when moist .... *H. psittacinus*, p. 106
19. Not as above 20

20. Gills purple to sordid pinkish-flesh color; stalk tough and fibrous; cap convex to plane, not viscid .... (see *Laccaria*, p. 151)
20. Not as above 21

21. Cap dry, dull orange to orange-buff or rufous; gills decurrent, widely spaced, same color as cap (not white) .... *H. pratensis*, p. 98
21. Not as above 22

22. Odor aromatic, sweet 23
22. Odor mild 24

23. Cap grayish-olive to grayish-brown or gray .... *H. agathosmus*, p. 114
23. Cap tawny to reddish-brown .... *H. bakerensis*, p. 114

24. Cap tawny-brown to rosy-brown to cinnamon, at least at center .... *H. roseibrunneus*, p. 113
24. Cap olive-brown to grayish-brown to dark brown, etc 25

25. Stalk dry, not viscid .... *H. calophyllus*, p. 115
25. Stalk viscid or slimy when moist 26

26. Gills decurrent, at first creamy but soon pale yellow to orange; associated with pine .... *H. hypothejus*, p. 110
26. Gills typically not decurrent, white to grayish .... *H. unguinosus* (see *H. psittacinus*, p. 106)

Hygrophorus pratensis. The entire fruiting body is dull orange to rufous-buff. The cap is *not* viscid; the gills are well-spaced and slightly waxy.

Hygrophorus pratensis (Meadow Waxy Cap)

CAP to 9 cm broad, obtuse to convex, then umbonate, turbinate, or plane; surface smooth, dry, rufous to dull cinnamon-orange to pale orange-buff or salmon-buff. Flesh thick, white or tinted cap color, odor mild. **GILLS** decurrent, same color as cap or slightly paler, well-spaced, broad, thick, waxy. **STALK** to 10 cm long, white or tinged cap color, dry, equal or tapering downward, smooth. **VEIL** absent. **SPORE PRINT** white; spores 5.5-8 $\times$ 3.5-5 μm, ellipsoid, smooth. Gill hyphae interwoven.

HABITAT: Solitary to gregarious in damp places, mostly in woods, fall through early spring. Particularly common in winter under redwood, but I have also found it in October, growing with chanterelles under oak. It has a wide distribution and is a grassland species in some regions.

EDIBILITY: Edible. Rated highly by Europeans—one author even puts it on a par with morels! My own experience with it gives me no great cause for enthusiasm, but it is rather fleshy for a *Hygrophorus*, so try it! Unlike the chanterelle, it is readily attacked by maggots.

COMMENTS: The dull orange-buff to rufous color of the cap and gills is the outstanding attribute of this clean, attractive waxy cap. The cap and stem are not viscid but the gills are thick and waxy. One variant I encountered had the unmistakable odor of Clorox bleach, but was in all other respects identical. Large, robust individuals are reminiscent of chanterelles *(Cantharellus cibarius),* but differ in their duller color and broad, well-developed gills with acute edges.

Hygrophorus borealis. A little white mushroom with a slender stem, dry cap, and adnate to decurrent gills.

Hygrophorus borealis (Snowy Waxy Cap)

CAP to 4 cm broad, convex to obtusely umbonate, expanding slightly in age; surface smooth; moist, dry, or lubricous but not viscid; watery white to dull white. Flesh thin, soft, white, odor mild. **GILLS** decurrent, white, well-spaced, soft, waxy. **STALK** to 12 cm long, slender, white, equal or tapering downward, usually long in proportion to cap, smooth, dry. **VEIL** absent. **SPORE PRINT** white; spores 7-9 × 4.5-6.5 μm, ellipsoid, smooth. Gill hyphae interwoven.

HABITAT: Scattered in damp places in woods. This species and its relatives (see below) are common throughout the mushroom season but seldom occur in the large numbers typical of, say, *H. eburneus.* The largest fruiting is usually in the winter, often in relatively dry weather.

EDIBILITY: Edible but thin-fleshed and flavorless.

COMMENTS: This is one of several slender white waxy caps with a dry to slightly viscid (never slimy) cap, long dry stalk, and interwoven gill hyphae. Others include: *H. russocoriaceus,* very common, with a piquant cedarlike odor; *H. pusillus,* with viscid cap, aromatic odor, and divergent gill hyphae; *H. niveus,* with a very thin, slightly viscid cap; *H. virgineus,* usually tinged yellow in age or upon drying and with spores 8-10 μm long; and *H. angustifolius,* dull white with small spores 5-8 μm long. These are easily confused with each other, but no harm can result. None have the slimy cap and stem of *H. eburneus. Leptonia sericella* is similar but has pinkish spores and pink gills at maturity.

Hygrophorus miniatus (Miniature Waxy Cap)

CAP 2.5 cm broad or less, convex to plane or slightly depressed; surface smooth or minutely scaly, not viscid, hygrophanous: bright red when moist, quickly fading to orange and finally pale yellow as it dries. Flesh very thin, waxy, colored like cap. **GILLS** adnexed, adnate or slightly decurrent, soft, thick, waxy, somewhat paler than cap. **STALK** to 7 cm long, slender, equal, colored like cap but fading more slowly, smooth, not viscid. **VEIL** absent. **SPORE PRINT** white; spores 6-8 × 4-5 μm, ellipsoid, smooth. Gill hyphae parallel.

HABITAT: Solitary or in groups, occasionally tufted, in moist places where there is a substantial accumulation of humus; at times on moss or rotting logs. Fairly common, late fall and winter. The one luxuriant fruiting I've seen was in a dense stand of pole-size redwood saplings.

EDIBILITY: Edible but negligible. McIlvaine says: "The gunner for partridges will not shoot rabbits; the knowing toadstool-seeker will pass all others where *H. miniatus* abounds." However, I've never found it in sufficient quantity to use it in a dish.

COMMENTS: The small size, waxy gills, and cap fading markedly from red to yellow are the far-from-infallible fieldmarks of this dainty fungus. The cap is neither viscid nor conical, and its growth (at times) on rotting logs is highly unorthodox for a *Hygrophorus*. *H. cantharellus* is a similar species with deeply decurrent gills and a long, slender stalk.

Hygrophorus coccineus (Righteous Red Waxy Cap)

CAP 2-5 cm broad, obtusely conic becoming convex or plane; surface smooth, moist or slightly tacky, deep red to bright red when fresh, fading somewhat in age. Flesh thin, reddish to orange, waxy. **GILLS** adnate to adnexed, reddish-orange to yellowish-orange, thick, soft, waxy. **STALK** to 7 cm long, slender, colored like cap or paler below, base usually yellow; smooth, equal, not viscid. **VEIL** absent. **SPORE PRINT** white; spores 7-10 × 4-5 μm, ellipsoid, smooth. Gill hyphae parallel.

HABITAT: Solitary or in small groups in woods, late fall and winter; occasional. Like *H. puniceus*, it prefers redwood, but is not as common.

EDIBILITY: Supposedly edible. I haven't tried it.

COMMENTS: This exquisite bright red mushroom is definitely worth

Hygrophorus coccineus. **Left:** Young specimens with a conical to convex cap. **Right:** Mature individuals with cap fully expanded. Cap is brilliant red when fresh.

seeking out. It is larger than *H. miniatus* but smaller and more slender than *H. puniceus.* It differs from *H. puniceus* in its moist (not distinctly viscid) cap. It does not fade dramatically to yellow like *H. miniatus.*

Hygrophorus puniceus (Scarlet Waxy Cap)

CAP 2.5-13 cm broad, obtusely conic to convex when young, then umbonate, plane, or with uplifted margin; surface smooth, distinctly viscid, deep red slowly fading to reddish-orange and finally orange, sometimes in streaky fashion. Flesh thin, waxy, watery reddish-orange to yellow-orange. **GILLS** adnate to slightly decurrent, seceding with

Hygrophorus puniceus. Large, robust individuals like those on the left are common, but smaller specimens are certainly not a rarity. Cap is bright red and distinctly viscid when moist.

age; reddish-orange to yellow, well-spaced, soft, thick, waxy. **STALK** to 7.5 cm long, often rather thick (up to 2 cm), equal or narrowed at base, reddish soon fading to orange or yellow, fibrillose-striate, base usually white. **VEIL** absent. **SPORE PRINT** white; spores 8-11 × 4-6 μm, ellipsoid to oblong, smooth. Gill hyphae parallel.

HABITAT: Scattered to gregarious in cool, damp places—mostly under redwood. Common, winter and early spring. Generally the last *Hygrophorus* to appear (mid-January or later).

EDIBILITY: Listed as edible in most books, but poisonous at least to some. I know two people who had very unpleasant experiences with it. It is an efficient concentrator of the malleable metallic element cadmium, which is decidedly deleterious when consumed regularly.

COMMENTS: The bright red sticky cap and indisputably waxy gills make this mushroom as easy to recognize as it is difficult to overlook. It stands out vividly in the dim, damp milieu where it thrives. It is larger than *H. coccineus* and the cap is equipped with a thick, viscid pellicle. A similar species known only from northern California, *H. laetissimus*, has a brilliant red viscid cap and white stalk.

Hygrophorus flavescens (Golden Waxy Cap)

CAP 2.5-5 cm broad, convex becoming plane; surface smooth, slightly viscid when moist, yellow to golden-yellow, often orange toward the center. Flesh thin, yellow, waxy. **GILLS** more or less narrowly attached, soft, thick, waxy, yellow. **STALK** to 7 cm long, slender, equal, fragile, smooth, not viscid, yellow with a whitish base. **VEIL** absent. **SPORE PRINT** white; spores 7-8 × 4-5 μm, ellipsoid, smooth. Gill hyphae parallel.

HABITAT: Solitary or scattered in woods, mostly under redwood. Common in winter, usually fruiting in the wake of *H. acutoconicus*.

EDIBILITY: Edible, but with little substance or taste.

COMMENTS: The golden-yellow color, convex to plane cap, and waxy yellow gills identify this modest mushroom. The cap is not conical as in *H. acutoconicus*, nor red as in *H. miniatus*. *H. flavifolius* is a small, yellow-orange species with a slimy-viscid cap *and* stem. I have found it under redwood at Nisene Marks. It is more closely related to *H. psittacinus* than to *H. flavescens*.

Hygrophorus acutoconicus. This common yellow to orange waxy cap does *not* blacken when handled. Cap is sharply conical when young, but eventually expands as shown at the left. *H. flavescens* (not illustrated) is similar but has a convex to plane cap.

Hygrophorus acutoconicus (Acutely Conic Waxy Cap)

CAP to 7 cm broad but usually smaller, bluntly or acutely conic when young, then more or less expanded with a pointed umbo; surface smooth, viscid, bright yellow to orange, the orange usually toward the center. Flesh soft, thin, yellow, waxy. **GILLS** free or narrowly attached, thick, soft, waxy, yellow, never blackening. **STALK** to 12 cm long, slender, colored about like cap, not blackening but occasionally grayish at very base; equal, striate, sometimes twisted. **VEIL** absent. **SPORE PRINT** white; spores 9-15 × 5-9 μm, ellipsoid, smooth. Gill hyphae parallel.

HABITAT: Scattered to gregarious in shady situations, mostly under redwood and oak; fall and early winter. It is as common as its blackening counterpart *H. conicus*, but has a shorter season.

EDIBILITY: Harmless, fleshless, flavorless—but makes a colorful (if glutinous) addition to a salad.

COMMENTS: A cute, conic *Hygrophorus*, differing from *H. conicus* in its "failure" to blacken when handled. Scientists may scoff at our tendency to anthropomorphize (attribute human qualities to inhuman beings or inanimate objects), yet our language leaves us little choice. For instance, the word "failure" (with its attendant implications of inadequacy, its connotation of "attempting to, but not succeeding") is often utilized by taxonomists to denote "absence." Before I'm accused of lending credence to this trend, let me earnestly put this question to you philosophical few among the myopic many (or you fungophilic few among the mycophobic many): Is the "failure" in this case an innate inability to succeed? An admirable example of genetic restraint? A coincidental and pointless byproduct of circumstance? Or none of the above? . . . Also found in California is *H. cuspidatus*, with a conical red cap fading to orange.

Hygrophorus conicus (Witch's Hat; Conic Waxy Cap)

CAP 1-6.5 cm broad, sharply conic to broadly conic, expanding somewhat to convex or plane with a pointed umbo, margin sometimes uplifted in old age; surface smooth, dry, moist or slighty viscid, bright red to orange, yellow, or greenish-yellow, blackening in age. Flesh thin, colored like cap, blackening. **GILLS** almost free, thick, waxy, at first whitish, soon grayish or black, sometimes tinged yellow, fairly close. **STALK** to 15 cm long, typically long and slender, equal, not viscid, longitudinally striate, often twisted, hollow, pallid to more or less cap color, whitish at base, blackening in age or upon handling. **VEIL** absent. **SPORE PRINT** white; spores 9-12 × 5.5-6.5 µm, ellipsoid, smooth. Gill hyphae parallel.

Hygrophorus conicus. **Left:** Young, sharply conical specimens. Note black stains on stem. **Right:** A mature specimen which is partially expanded. The cap margin may eventually curl up, but the center remains pointed.

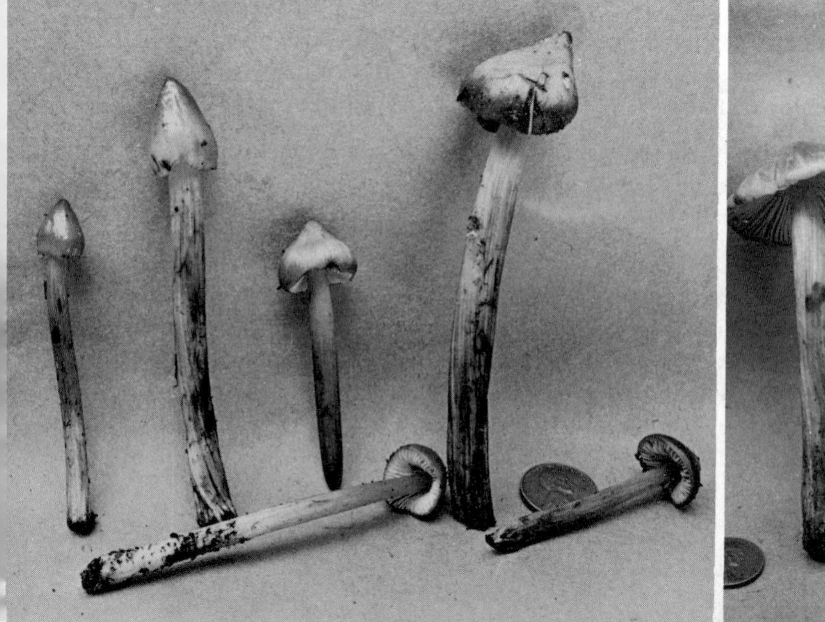

HABITAT: Solitary, scattered, or in groups in damp places, usually in woods. Common, fall through early spring. Known from a wide variety of habitats in North America, but in our area showing a definite preference for redwood.

EDIBILITY: Once considered poisonous, perhaps because of its blackening qualities; now regarded as harmless. Four deaths in China were apparently misattributed to it, and Larry Stickney of San Francisco says it "elicited an odd sensation of lightheadedness and numbness." At any rate, it hardly seems worth experimenting with such a thin-fleshed, watery, tasteless morsel.

COMMENTS: The conical cap and tendency of all parts to blacken when handled immediately identify this species. It is our most common brightly colored *Hygrophorus*, one of the first woodland mushrooms you'll encounter. Fresh specimens are quite attractive when growing in the woods, but are barely recognizable by time you get them home. Old, dried-up, completely blackened individuals are sometimes found.

Hygrophorus calyptraeformis (Shell Pink Waxy Cap)

CAP 2.5-7 cm broad; sharply conic at first, then more or less expanded with a pointed umbo; surface slightly viscid when moist, smooth, pinkish-red becoming a delicate shell-pink or salmon-pink. Flesh thin, watery pinkish. **GILLS** adnate to adnexed, pink, soft, waxy. **STALK** to 16 cm long, slender, whitish tinged cap color; equal, smooth, not truly viscid, usually longitudinally striate and sometimes twisted, often buried in humus. **VEIL** absent. **SPORE PRINT** white; spores 6.5-8 × 4.5-5 μm, ellipsoid, smooth. Gill hyphae parallel.

HABITAT: Scattered under redwoods and in mixed woods, rare. I have found it only twice, in winter.

EDIBILITY: Unknown.

COMMENTS: It is indeed a pleasure to find this striking species. In my fickle fungal opinion, it is the most elegant of all the waxy caps. Its rarity only accentuates its beauty. The pointed pink cap, waxy pink gills, and long slender stalk render it distinct. *H. psittacinus* may be pinkish but is smaller, has a slimy-viscid stem, and is never sharply conical.

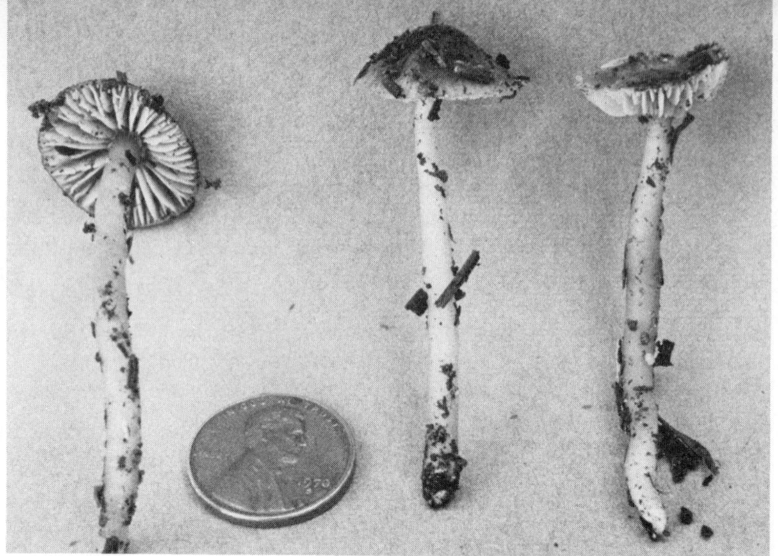

Hygrophorus psittacinus, mature specimens. Note small size, slimy cap and stem with adhering debris. Green cap fades drastically to pinkish, reddish, or even yellow.

Hygrophorus psittacinus (Parrot Green Waxy Cap)

CAP about 2 cm broad, convex or bell-shaped becoming plane in age; surface smooth, slimy or viscid when moist, hygrophanous, at first dark parrot-green, then olive-green, soon fading to rufous, pinkish-flesh, ochraceous-orange, vinaceous, or even yellowish. Flesh thin, colored like cap, waxy. **GILLS** typically adnate, well spaced, soft, thick, waxy, at first greenish, then fading like cap (or more reddish), sometimes retaining green tints. **STALK** to 10 cm long, slender, equal, smooth, slimy or viscid, greenish when young, fading to pinkish, orange, yellow, etc. **VEIL** absent. **SPORE PRINT** white; spores 6.5-8 $\times$ 4-5 μm, ellipsoid, smooth. Gill hyphae parallel.

HABITAT: Solitary or in small groups in damp places. Fairly common, late fall and winter. Its favorite abodes are on mossy banks along roadcuts, and under redwood.

EDIBILITY: Edible, but slimy and insubstantial. Raw specimens make a colorful and provocative addition to salads, but slide down your throat before you can taste them.

COMMENTS: The slimy green cap when young sets this species apart. The drastic color change is befuddling, but faint traces of olive can usually be found somewhere on the fruiting body. The slimy-viscid stem and small size are good secondary fieldmarks. Related species with a slimy-viscid cap and stem include: *H. psittacinus* var. *californicus*, rare, with a blue rather than green cap when young; *H. laetus*, with violet-gray to pinkish-orange (never green) cap and frequent skunklike odor; and *H. unguinosus*, with dark grayish-brown to nearly black cap, found under conifers.

Hygrophorus chrysodon (Golden-Flaked Waxy Cap)

CAP 2.5-10 cm broad, convex to plane; surface smooth, slimy or viscid when moist, white with golden-yellow to orange granules on the margin, or in rainy weather tinted yellow throughout. Flesh soft, white. **GILLS** decurrent, soft, white, waxy, well spaced. **STALK** to 7.5 cm long, equal, smooth, viscid, white with ring of golden-yellow granules at apex (or occasionally throughout). **VEIL** slimy, evanescent. **SPORE PRINT** white; spores 7-9 × 3.5-4.5 µm, ellipsoid, smooth. Gill hyphae divergent.

HABITAT: Solitary or in groups in oak-madrone woods, late fall and winter. Widely distributed but uncommon here. Yet another example of a mushroom normally associated with conifers that crosses over to madrone.

EDIBILITY: Edible, but slimy and bland (see *H. sordidus*).

COMMENTS: The exquisite flakes of gold on the cap margin and/or stem apex afford a good means of recognizing this species. These are most evident in young specimens. They are sometimes distributed throughout the cap or washed off by rain. In other respects it resembles *H. eburneus*, but is slightly larger and thicker.

Hygrophorus eburneus (Ivory Waxy Cap)

CAP 2-7.5 cm broad, obtuse to convex becoming plane or with uplifted margin; surface smooth, extremely slimy when wet, otherwise viscid; pure white, sometimes yellowish in old age or very rarely pinkish. Flesh soft, white, thin. **GILLS** adnate to decurrent, well-spaced, soft, waxy, pure white to very slightly yellowish in old age. **STALK** to 15 cm long, equal or tapering downward, usually slender, smooth or apex punctate, viscid or slimy, pure white, sometimes discoloring in age. **VEIL** slimy, evanescent, depositing slime on cap and stem. **SPORE PRINT** white; spores 6-8 × 3.5-5 µm, ellipsoid, smooth. Gill hyphae divergent.

HABITAT: Scattered to gregarious in woods, mostly oak-madrone-manzanita. Common, at times abundant, fall through early spring. Elsewhere, like *H. chrysodon*, it grows mainly with conifers.

Hygrophorus eburneus. A pure white waxy cap, exceedingly common under oak and madrone. Note the thick layer of slime coating the cap and stem. *H. gliocyclus* (not illustrated) is stockier and tinged creamy-yellowish.

EDIBILITY: Edible but slimy (see edibility of *H. sordidus*).

COMMENTS: The pure white slimy cap *and* slimy stem plus the soft, waxy white gills typify this cosmopolitan *Hygrophorus.* It is whiter and slimmer than *H. gliocyclus*, and does not commonly grow with pine (at least in our area). Sometimes the layer of slime is so thick that it's difficult to pick the mushroom up. At other times the slime dries out, in which case there's usually debris glued irrevocably to the cap, indicating, without a doubt, that *H. eburneus* deserves to be ranked with *Suillus pungens* (among others) as the "slipperiest and slimiest fungus amongus." *Limacella illinita* is also slimy and white, but has free gills. *H. albicastaneus* is a similar species with a dry or slightly tacky stem and viscid white cap that dries reddish-brown.

Hygrophorus gliocyclus (Slimy Waxy Cap)

CAP to 10 cm broad, convex or obtuse to plane or shallowly depressed; surface smooth, slimy or viscid, white to pale cream, the center usually more yellowish or tinged buff. Flesh white, thick at center, fairly firm. **GILLS** adnate to decurrent, fairly well spaced, soft, waxy, white becoming dingy yellowish in age. **STALK** to 6 cm long, typically short and thick, equal above, tapered at base, dingy white to creamy, solid, smooth, slimy below veil. **VEIL** slimy, evanescent or forming an obscure ring. **SPORE PRINT** white; spores 8-11 $\times$ 4.5-6 μm, ellipsoid, smooth. Gill hyphae divergent.

HABITAT: Scattered to gregarious among needles under pine. Fairly common, fall and winter, sometimes intermingled with *H. hypothejus*. I have found it along the coast with Monterey pine and in great numbers inland with digger pine.

EDIBILITY: Edible. Like *H. eburneus*, slimy and disagreeable to collect, but apparently relished by some. One book describes how to remove the slime from the *mushrooms* before cooking, but says nothing about removing the slime from your *hands*.

COMMENTS: The creamy-yellowish cap, stocky stature, thick layer of slime on the cap and stem, waxy gills, and association with pine are characteristic of this humdrum *Hygrophorus*. It is thicker and squatter than *H. eburneus* and the stem is indisputably viscid, in contrast to *H. sordidus*. A related species, *H. ponderatus*, also has a slimy cap and stem, but is larger, pure white, and has smaller spores. It is recorded from California but I haven't seen it.

Hygrophorus sordidus (Sordid Waxy Cap)

CAP 5-20 cm broad, convex then plane or with margin uplifted; surface smooth, viscid when moist, white, sometimes tinged yellowish-buff at center. Flesh thick, firm, white. **GILLS** adnate to decurrent, soft, waxy, white, sometimes dingy yellowish in old age. **STALK** to 10 cm long, and up to 2.5 cm thick, smooth, white, dry, equal or slightly pinched at base, solid. **VEIL** absent. **SPORE PRINT** white; spores 6-8 $\times$ 4-5.5 μm, elliptical, smooth. Gill hyphae divergent.

Hygrophorus sordidus. Our largest waxy cap, entirely white with a viscid cap and dry stem. Gills are slightly waxy.

HABITAT: Scattered to gregarious in mixed woods and under oak, fall and winter. Fairly abundant at Henry Cowell Redwoods State Park, occasional elsewhere in the Santa Cruz Mountains. Previously reported only from eastern North America.

EDIBILITY: Edible but undesirable—sluggish and insipid. I ruined an otherwise superb curry in my sole attempt to make it palatable. The sliced caps neither absorbed the surrounding spices nor contributed any special flavor of their own. The turmeric did turn them yellow, however, making them look for all the world like undercooked and overfed banana slugs—gummy, amorphous masses of slime that coagulated around or completely engulfed the peas and savory chunks of potato, rendering the entire dish inedible (though unforgettable). Since its attractive appearance belies its sluggish qualities, I can only conclude that the scientific soul who named it had a similar and equally sordid experience with it.

COMMENTS: Our largest *Hygrophorus*—its bulkiness alone distinguishes it from other white members of the genus. It is more likely to be mistaken for a *Clitocybe (C. robusta)* or *Russula (R. brevipes)*, but the gills are soft, fleshy, and, at least to the experienced *Hygrophorus*-hound, waxy. *H. subalpinus* is similar but grows near melting snow and has a short, bulbous stem with a flaring ring.

Hygrophorus hypothejus (Olive-Yellow Waxy Cap)

CAP to 7.5 cm broad, convex to plane or sometimes depressed; surface smooth, slimy or viscid when wet, color variable but typically olive-brown at the center, greenish-yellow to reddish-orange near the margin, brighter (redder) overall in age. Flesh thin, yellowish to whitish. **GILLS** decurrent, well spaced, soft, waxy, at first pallid but soon yellow, finally orange to reddish-orange or colored like cap margin. **STALK** to 15 cm long, equal or tapering downward, rather slender, viscid or slimy, colored more or less like cap below, paler above, smooth. **VEIL** slimy, evanescent. **SPORE PRINT** white; spores 7-9 $\times$ 4-5 μm, ellipsoid, smooth. Gill hyphae divergent.

HABITAT: Scattered to gregarious in coastal pine forests, often intermingled with *H. gliocyclus*. Fairly common, fall and winter. The largest fruiting I've seen was at New Brighton Beach State Park.

EDIBILITY: Edible, but not choice.

COMMENTS: This cheerful, attractive *Hygrophorus* is told by its viscid, convex to depressed cap, decurrent yellow to reddish-orange gills, and monogamous relationship with pine. The colors are extremely variable, and young specimens bear little resemblance to old ones until you find stages in between. Both slim and relatively robust forms can be found. *H. olivaceoalbus* is a striking species of northern coniferous forests with a slimy, smoky-brown to blackish cap, white gills, and a fibrillose stocking on the stem coated with slime.

Hygrophorus russula (Russulaceous Waxy Cap)

CAP 5-13 cm broad, convex to plane or with uplifted margin; surface viscid when wet but soon dry, coral-pink to reddish, usually streaked with purple-red fibrils, smooth or minutely scaly, occasionally staining yellowish when rubbed. Flesh thick, white or tinged pinkish, odor mild. **GILLS** adnate to decurrent, close to crowded (120-150 reach stalk); narrow, white soon flushed pink, then spotted or stained purple-red; soft, waxy. **STALK** to 7.5 cm long, thick, stout, solid, dry, smooth, equal or tapered slightly toward base, white stained or streaked pinkish, or becoming cap color. **VEIL** absent. **SPORE PRINT** white; spores 6-8 $\times$ 3-5 μm, ellipsoid, smooth. Gill hyphae divergent.

HABITAT: Gregarious in mixed hardwoods (tanoak-live oak-madrone) near Bonny Doon; fall and winter, uncommon.

EDIBILITY: Edible and highly rated by several authorities. However,

Hygrophorus russula. Entire fruiting body is stained dark reddish in age. Gills are very close together, only slightly waxy.

my lingering distaste for fleshy waxy caps (see comments on edibility of *H. sordidus*) has discouraged me from sampling it.

COMMENTS: A beautiful, robust *Hygrophorus* well worth finding. The shrimp- to coral-pink to dark reddish cap, close reddish-spotted gills, absence of a veil, and habitat under hardwoods distinguish it. As the name implies, it has the stature of a *Russula* (and was originally placed in *Tricholoma*), but the gills are soft and waxy. *H. erubescens* and relatives are similar but smaller, with well-spaced gills. *H. purpurascens*, a version with a fibrillose veil, is common under conifers in the Sierras.

Hygrophorus erubescens (Reddening Waxy Cap)

CAP 2.5-7.5 cm broad, convex becoming plane or slightly umbonate; surface smooth, viscid when wet, dark reddish at the center, paler pink toward the margin, with a somewhat streaked or fibrillose appearance, usually staining yellow, especially on the margin. Flesh white, soft, often bruising yellowish. **GILLS** adnate to decurrent, white then spotted pinkish-red, soft, waxy, fairly well-spaced. **STALK** to 10 cm long, slender or stout, equal or with tapered base, white with pinkish-red fibrils, darker in age, dry. **VEIL** absent. **SPORE PRINT** white; spores 7-11 × 5-6 μm, ellipsoid, smooth. Gill hyphae divergent.

HABITAT: Scattered to gregarious in mixed woods and under conifers; uncommon, late fall and winter. It has been found near Boulder Creek in chaparral with knobcone pine, madrone, and manzanita present.

EDIBILITY: Edible. I haven't tried it.

COMMENTS: Like *H. russula*, this species becomes reddish-spotted in age. However, it is smaller, the gills are more widely spaced, it has a more pronounced disposition to stain yellow on the cap, and it is typically found with conifers. The collection from Boulder Creek appears to fit *H. erubescens* var. *gracilis* more than the typical variety, which is stouter. However, the margin of the cap turned yellow when left in the refrigerator overnight, which is more characteristic of the typical variety. *H. capreolarius* is a similar species found in conifer forests farther north. It has well-spaced gills and is entirely purple-red at maturity.

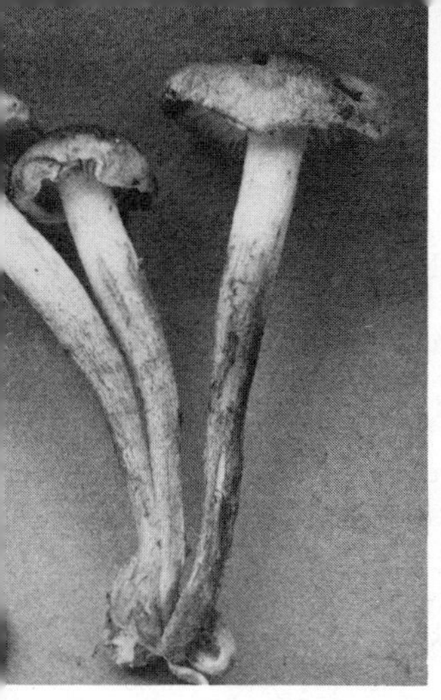
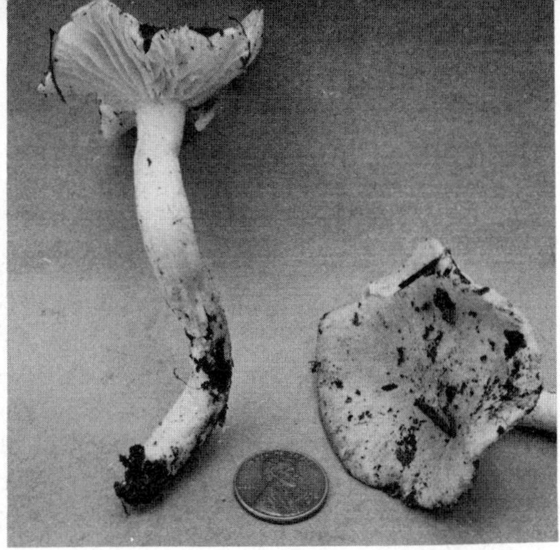

Left: *Hygrophorus erubescens.* A very slender form that develops dark reddish stains in age and turns yellow when handled or refrigerated. **Right:** *Hygrophorus roseibrunneus,* mature specimens. A common oak lover with a viscid brown to pinkish-brown cap, waxy white gills, and dry white stem.

Hygrophorus roseibrunneus (Rosy-Brown Waxy Cap)

CAP 2-10 cm broad, convex to plane or with uplifted margin in age; surface viscid when wet, tawny-brown to pinkish-cinnamon to rosy-brown (at least at center), margin usually pallid and slightly cottony when young. Flesh white, soft, odor mild. **GILLS** attached, close, white, soft, waxy. **STALK** to 12 cm long, equal or tapering downward, often curved, dry, white, prominently punctate at apex. **VEIL** absent. **SPORE PRINT** white; spores 7-8 $\times$ 3.5-5 μm, ellipsoid, smooth. Gill hyphae divergent.

HABITAT: Scattered to gregarious in leaf litter under oak. Common, fall and winter.

EDIBILITY: Edible. I have tried it.

COMMENTS: The rosy-brown to tawny cap, dry stalk, waxy white gills, and mild odor are the main features of this variable *Hygrophorus.* The punctate stem is characteristic of many waxy caps but in this species it is especially attractive. *H. laurae* is similar but has a viscid stem. *H. marianae* has a streaked pinkish-red to purple cap, well-spaced white gills and a dry, rooting stalk. It was originally decribed from Santa Barbara, under oak. *H. pudorinus* is a large, handsome species with a pinkish-salmon cap, pallid to pinkish-buff gills, and a thick punctate stalk often staining yellow. It is fairly common in the coniferous forests of northern California. *Leucopaxillus amarus* resembles these species somewhat, but has a dry cap, nonwaxy gills, and bitter taste.

Hygrophorus bakerensis (Mt. Baker Waxy Cap)

CAP 4-12 cm broad, convex to plane; surface smooth, slimy or viscid when wet, reddish-brown to cinnamon to yellow-brown, margin paler. Flesh thick, white, odor strongly aromatic and penetrating, like almond extract, maraschino cherries, or crushed peach pits. **GILLS** white to pale cream, attached, soft, thin, fairly close. **STALK** 5-18 cm long, rather thick, equal or tapering downward, dry, smooth, solid, firm, white to pale pinkish-buff, apex punctate. **VEIL** absent. **SPORE PRINT** white; spores 7-10 $\times$ 4.5-6 μm, ellipsoid, smooth. Gill hyphae divergent.

HABITAT: Solitary or in groups in mixed woods, late fall and winter. Common in the Pacific Northwest under conifers, but rare here. I have found it only once, near Bonny Doon.

EDIBILITY: Edible and according to one source, good. Unfortunately, it doesn't taste like it smells.

COMMENTS: The heavy. sweet, penetrating odor is the most remarkable aspect of this handsome *Hygrophorus.* The stalk may be very long and seated deeply in the humus. The gills and stalk are often beaded with water droplets in moist weather. It is frequently misidentified as a *Clitocybe* or *Tricholoma* because the gills are thin and not very waxy. The specimens from Bonny Doon were darker and more reddish than typical *H. bakerensis. H. agathosmus* has a sweet odor but the cap is grayish. Other fragrant waxy caps with brown caps are: *H. pacificus*, very fragrant with dry stalk and russet to tawny cap with wavy, crisped, or notched margin, yellow-buff gills, and spores 10-14 μm long; and *H. variicolor*, faintly fragrant with viscid-slimy cap and stem.

Hygrophorus agathosmus (Almond Waxy Cap)

CAP to 7.5 cm broad, convex to plane; surface smooth, slimy or viscid when wet, dull ashy-gray to grayish-olive or brownish-gray. Flesh soft, whitish, odor fragrant, like almonds. **GILLS** adnate to slightly decurrent, white to pale grayish, soft, waxy. **STALK** to 7 cm long, at first white, then grayish, smooth, dry, equal. **VEIL** absent. **SPORE PRINT** white; spores 8-10.5 $\times$ 4.5-5.5 μm, smooth, elliptical. Gill hyphae divergent.

HABITAT: In small groups in mixed woods and under conifers. Apparently restricted to Douglas-fir in the Santa Cruz Mountains. Infrequent, fall and winter.

Hygrophorus agathosmus, mature specimens. Note the Douglas-fir needles stuck to cap (indicating it was viscid). Cap is grayish, gills white and waxy, odor almondy.

EDIBILITY: Edible, but its flavor doesn't live up to its smell.

COMMENTS: The viscid grayish cap, waxy white gills, and almond odor are the telltale traits of this fine fungus. The odor is sometimes faint but if several are placed together in a closed container it usually becomes evident. Other fragrant waxy caps do not have grayish caps. *H. calophyllus* is somewhat similar but has a darker cap and lacks the odor.

Hygrophorus calophyllus

CAP 4-10 cm broad, convex to plane; surface slimy or viscid when moist, smooth, evenly colored deep olive-brown to umber. Flesh soft, white, thick, odor mild or faintly fragrant. **GILLS** white or flushed a delicate pink, well spaced, thick, soft, waxy, decurrent. **STALK** to 10 cm long, equal, smooth, dry, unpolished, colored like cap but paler, white at apex. **VEIL** absent. **SPORE PRINT** white; spores 5.5-8 $\times$ 4-5 μm, ellipsoid, smooth. Gill hyphae divergent.

HABITAT: Solitary or in small groups in woods, fall and winter, rather rare. Associated with Douglas-fir, at least in our area.

EDIBILITY: Edible. I haven't tried it.

COMMENTS: A clean, attractive species—the dark brown cap is set off sharply by the white to pale pink gills. It might be mistaken for a

Clitocybe or *Lyophyllum*, but the gills have that incomparable waxy quality peculiar to *Hygrophorus*. I have seen specimens with chanterellesque gills, their development apparently thwarted by dry weather. Of a more dingy appearance is *H. camarophyllus*, with a fuscous to grayish, practically dry, streaked cap and white to pale grayish gills. I've found it in the Santa Cruz Mountains, in mixed woods. Both *H. calophyllus* and *H. camarophyllus* are darker than *H. agathosmus* and lack the almond fragrance.

A common species in pastures and coniferous woods of northern California is *H. recurvatus*. Its cap is dry to slightly viscid, pale to dark olive-brown, sometimes with a small pointed "pimple" at the center; the gills are grayish-white, well-spaced, and decurrent, and the gill hyphae are interwoven—a character which places it close to *H. pratensis*. To the north *H. olivaceoalbus* also occurs (see *H. hypothejus* for details).

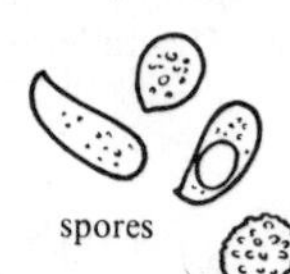

TRICHOLOMATACEAE

THIS is the largest and most complex family of gilled fungi. The spore print is usually white, but ranges to buff, yellowish, pale lilac, or pinkish. A stem is normally present but in several of the wood-inhabiting species it is lateral or even absent. The gills are typically attached to the stem, but in some of the smaller forms they are free.

The best way to recognize the family is to eliminate the other white-spored families. The gills are neither soft and waxy as in the Hygrophoraceae, nor shallow, blunt, and foldlike as in the Cantharellaceae. The fleshy forms (with the exception of *Leucopaxillus*) do not have noticeably dry, brittle flesh as in the Russulaceae. There is no volva as in the Amanitaceae, and the few species with a veil do not have free gills as in the Lepiotaceae.

The size and complexity of the Tricholomataceae is such that no generalizations can be made regarding edibility. Some (mostly Clitocybes and Tricholomas) are poisonous while many others have not been tested or are too small to be of value. The only safe approach is to learn the individual characteristics of each edible species—and there *are* some delectably delicious fungi that are well worth getting to know. The most prominent are: the oyster mushroom *(Pleurotus ostreatus)*, the man on horseback *(Tricholoma flavovirens)*, the honey mushroom *(Armillariella mellea)*, the matsutake *(Armillaria ponderosa)*, the fairy ring mushroom *(Marasmius oreades)*, and the blewitt *(Lepista nuda)*.

The Tricholomataceae comprise a significant segment of our woodland fungi. Many species grow on wood whereas the other white-spored families are almost exclusively terrestrial. A few, such as *Marasmius oreades*, grow in grass. For simplicity's sake only the major genera are keyed below. Minor genera are then keyed out under the major ones.

Key to the Tricholomataceae

1. Stalk (if present) fleshy, typically 5 mm thick or more 2
1. Stalk thin, cartilaginous (fragile or tough and usually hollow); typically *less* than 6 mm thick 16

2. Gill edges serrate or toothed; growing on wood .... *Lentinus* and *Lentinellus*, p. 126
2. Not as above; if growing on wood then gills not serrate 3

3. Gills decurrent, yellow to yellow-olive to bright orange (occasionally entirely olive); stalk present 4
3. Not as above (if stalk present and gills decurrent, then gills not colored as above) 6

4. Gills repeatedly forked or veined, deep orange to pale orange or yellowish, but not olive .... (see **Paxillaceae**, p. 389)
4. Not as above 5

5. Cap *and/or* stalk with scales of a contrasting color; gills never olive-tinted .... *Tricholomopsis*, p. 128
5. Cap and stalk smooth, without scales; gills often olive-tinted .... *Omphalotus*, p. 129

6. Stalk consistently off-center to lateral or absent; usually growing on wood .... *Pleurotus*, *Panus*, and *Panellus*, p. 119
6. Stalk more or less central; usually (but not always) on ground 7

7. Gills (or entire fruiting body) purple to bluish-purple 8
7. Gills some other color 9

8. Stalk tough and fibrous, relatively slender and usually longer than width of cap; spore print white or lilac-tinted .... *Laccaria*, p. 151
8. Stalk fleshy, rather stout; spore print dull pinkish ...... *Lepista*, p. 131

9. Veil present, usually forming a ring on stalk 10
9. Veil absent or rudimentary 11

10. Stalk (and usually the cap) covered with mealy granules below the veil; small to medium-sized .... *Cystoderma*, p. 173
10. Not as above; medium-sized to very large .... *Armillaria* and *Armillariella*, p. 167

11. Spore print pinkish to pinkish-buff .... *Lepista*, p. 131
11. Spore print white to yellowish or buff 12

12. Typically growing in dense clusters in disturbed soil (along roads, paths, etc.); cap dark brown to grayish-brown, pale brown or tan; gills and stalk white or pallid; mature caps at least 3 cm broad *Lyophyllum*, p. 154
12. Not as above 13

13. Gills more or less flesh color to pinkish, well spaced; stalk tough, fibrous, usually slender, cap typically less than 5 cm broad .. *Laccaria*, p. 151
13. Not as above 14

14. Gills and flesh yellow; cap and/or stalk usually with red, purple-red, or grayish-black scales; growing on or near conifer wood .... *Tricholomopsis*, p. 128
14. Not as above; if gills yellow then flesh white and cap smooth, without scales 15

15. Gills typically notched or narrowly attached, occasionally adnate or free .... *Tricholoma*, p. 155
15. Gills typically adnate to decurrent .... *Clitocybe*, p. 139

16. Gills purple to pinkish-flesh color; stalk tough, fibrous; cap convex to plane, never conical or bell-shaped; growing on ground *Laccaria*, p. 151
16. Not as above 17

17. Growing on decaying mushrooms .... *Collybia* and relatives, p. 176
17. Not as above 18

18. Tough; shrivelled specimens reviving completely when moistened; stalk tough or wiry or polished 19
18. Fleshy or fragile; not reviving when moistened; stalk fragile or tough, but not wiry or polished 20

19. Gills adnate to decurrent, yellow to orange .... *Omphalina* and *Xeromphalina*, p. 190
19. Gills not as above .... *Marasmius*, p. 183

20. Cap typically bell-shaped or conical when young (may expand in age); margin of cap usually straight, rarely incurved .... *Mycena*, p. 193
20. Cap typically convex to plane, depressed, or umbilicate; if conical when young then margin at first incurved 21

21. Gills narrowly attached, notched, or free; or if gills adnate, then stalk of a different texture than cap .... *Collybia* and relatives, p. 176
21. Gills typically adnate to decurrent (if adnate, then stalk more or less same texture as cap) 22

22. Gills pale yellow to orange or pink; cap usually less than 20 mm broad ....*Omphalina* and *Xeromphalina*, p. 190
22. Gills white to buff, grayish, or bluish-green; cap 12 mm broad or more .... *Clitocybe*, p. 139

PLEUROTUS, PANUS, and PANELLUS

Small to large *wood-inhabiting fungi usually growing shelflike.* CAP smooth or hairy, dry or viscid. Flesh soft *(Pleurotus)*, more or less tough *(Panus* and *Panellus).* GILLS adnate to decurrent (if stalk is present), *edges entire.* STALK *absent, lateral or off-center*, occasionally central. VEIL usually absent. VOLVA absent. SPORE PRINT *white to buff or pale lilac;* spores smooth, amyloid *(Panellus),* not amyloid *(Pleurotus* and *Panus).*

THIS group includes pale-spored wood-inhabiting agarics with entire gills and a consistently off-center to lateral stem. There are three genera: *Pleurotus* is an artificial grouping of species with a soft, fleshy fruiting body. *Panus* and *Panellus* incorporate those forms with a tough fruiting body. The latter has amyloid spores. *Lentinus* and *Lentinellus* are similar but have serrated gills. *Omphalotus* has a central to off-center stem and a bright golden-orange to yellow-olive fruiting body. *Phyllotopsis, Claudopus,* and *Crepidotus* are shelflike, but have pink to brown spores.

The oyster mushroom, *Pleurotus ostreatus*, is delicious, but most members of this group are too tough or rare to be of value. *Pleurotus* is represented in California by about ten species, while *Panus* and *Panellus* have three each. Four are described here.

Key to Pleurotus, Panus, and Panellus

1. Cap smooth or minutely hairy 2
1. Cap conspicuously hairy, woolly, or velvety 5

2. Cap viscid, green to yellow-green .... *Panellus serotinus* (see *Panus torulosus*, p. 124)
2. Not as above 3

3. Tough; stalk well developed; gills tan to buff or violet-tinted; cap tan or tinted violet, reddish-brown, or pinkish; rare .... *Panus torulosus*, p. 124
3. Soft, fleshy, not as above 4

4. Gills broad (deep); cap white to gray or brown; stalk (if present) short; common on hardwoods .... *Pleurotus ostreatus*, p. 120
4. Not as above; gills narrow, crowded ...... *Pleurotus petaloides*, p. 122

5. Cap very tough, concentrically zoned, stalk absent; gills thick, well spaced .... (see *Lenzites betulina*, p. 454)
5. Not as above; cap not concentrically zoned 6

6. Gills pale orange to orange-buff to yellowish-tan 7
6. Gills white to grayish 8

7. Stalk absent or rudimentary; odor disagreeable .... (see *Phyllotopsis nidulans*, p. 125)
7. Stalk present; taste very bitter *Panellus stypticus* (see *Panus rudis*, p. 123)
8. Cap small, white to gray; gills appearing longitudinally split or grooved, rolling back in dry weather .... (see *Schizophyllum commune*, p. 455)
8. Cap violet to reddish-brown or tan; gills not longitudinally split .... *Panus rudis*, p. 123

Pleurotus ostreatus (Oyster Mushroom)

CAP 2.5-20 cm broad; fan-shaped, shell-shaped, elongated or circular in outline, convex becoming plane or occasionally funnel-shaped; surface smooth, moist but not viscid, white to pale gray, grayish-brown, tan, bluish-gray or even dark brown; margin inrolled when young, sometimes lobed or wavy. Flesh thick, white, soft, tougher near the stalk. **GILLS** close or fairly well spaced, broad, white or pale grayish-white, sometimes discolored yellowish in old age, decurrent (if a stalk is present). **STALK** if present off-center to lateral, occasionally central; solid, firm, thick, usually hairy or downy at base, same color as cap or paler. **SPORE PRINT** white to pale lilac; spores 7-10 × 3-4 μm, oblong, smooth, not amyloid.

HABITAT: In shelving groups, columns, or rows on hardwood logs and stumps, sometimes on standing trees, rarely on conifers. Very common after the first fall rains, occasional otherwise. I have seen enormous fruitings on tanoak and live oak, but its hosts include cottonwood, alder, and sycamore. It has been raised on an astonishing variety of substrates (including shredded Time magazines), and oyster mushroom cultivation kits are now being marketed.

EDIBILITY: A universal favorite—absolutely delicious rolled in bread crumbs and egg batter and fried, with a superb fishy texture and taste. Be sure to check for small beetles between the gills (these can be removed by washing them quickly), and of course, for maggots. The tough stem or basal plug of tissue should be removed.

COMMENTS: Pure, pale, and graceful, the oyster mushroom is easily distinguished by its white gills, soft flesh, smooth cap and shelflike growth habit on wood. The cap color and position of the stem depend on the location of the fruiting body. When growing out of the side of a log, the stem is lateral or absent, since there is no need to elevate the cap. When growing on top of a log, however, the stem can be central, leading to confusion with *Clitocybe*. The cap is generally darker in sunlight and

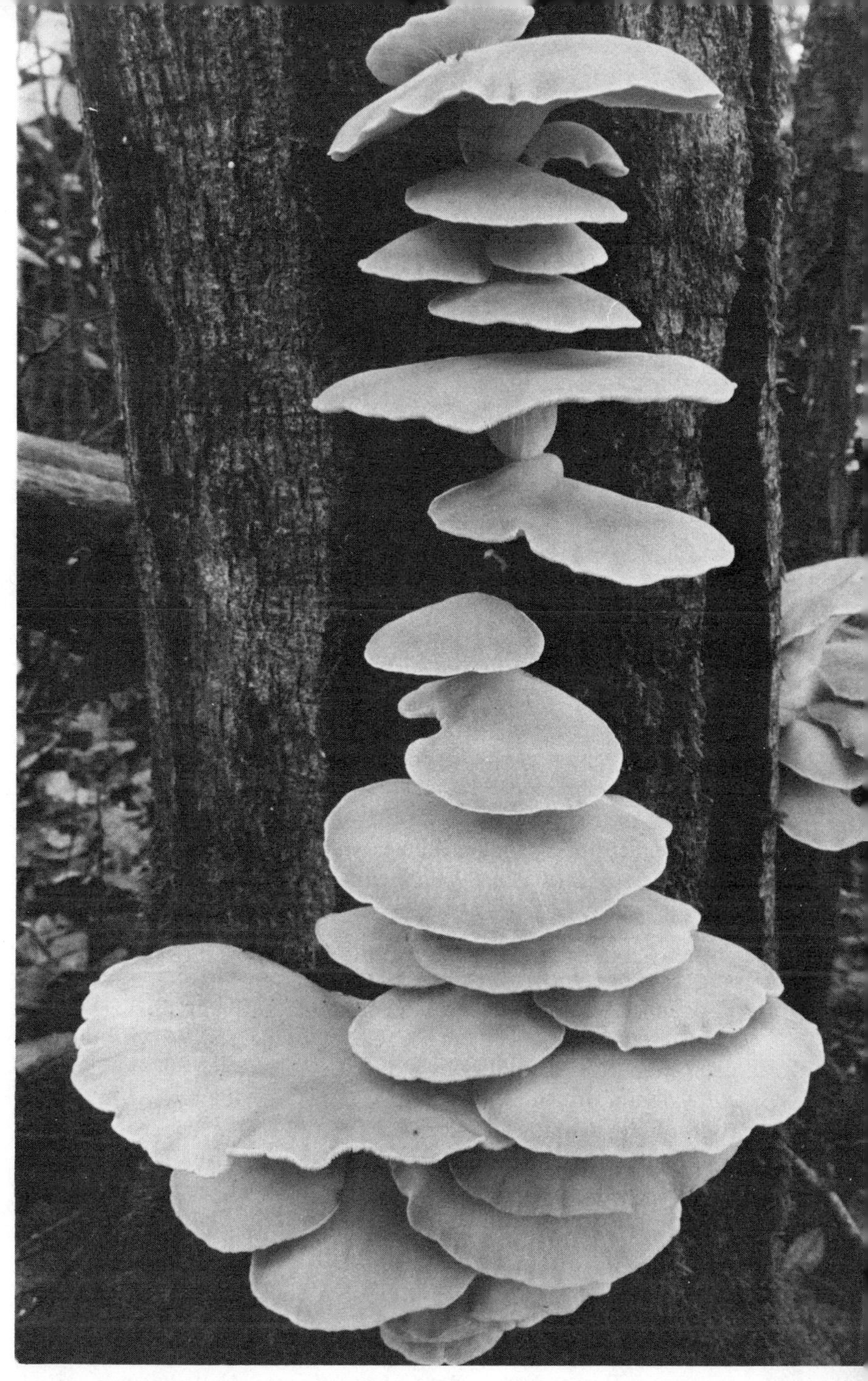

Pleurotus ostreatus growing on a dead oak. When growing on fallen logs, it's more likely to appear in rows rather than columns.

Pleurotus ostreatus, gill detail. The white gills, white or lilac-tinted spores, and soft flesh typify *Pleurotus*.

correspondingly paler in dim surroundings. The name *P. sapidus* has been given to the lilac-spored form. However, there is doubt as to whether a white-spored form actually exists, because the color of the spore print varies according to the thickness of the deposit and the amount of moisture present. If they are indeed the same, *P. ostreatus* would be the correct name. Both are equally delicious, so the distinction is academic. For a smaller, thinner white species growing on conifers, see *P. porrigens* (under *P. petaloides*).

Pleurotus petaloides (Petal-Shaped Pleurotus)

CAP up to 5 cm broad and 7.5 cm long but usually smaller; wedge-shaped, spatula-shaped, fan-shaped, or funnel-shaped with one side open, tapering to a stemlike base; surface moist or gelatinous but not viscid, smooth, brown to grayish-brown; margin often wavy, at first inrolled. Flesh pliant, white or watery tan. **GILLS** narrow, crowded, thin, decurrent, white to yellowish becoming pale grayish-buff. **STALK** lateral or off-center, continuous with cap but narrowed, tapering downward, white or grayish, short, minutely hairy. **SPORE PRINT** white; spores 7-9 × 4.5-5 μm, ellipsoid, smooth, not amyloid. Conspicuous cystidia on gills.

HABITAT: Gregarious or in small clusters on rotting or buried wood, often appearing terrestrial. Frequently in cultivated places—lawns, nurseries, flower beds, edges of woods, etc. Fall through spring, occasional.

EDIBILITY: Edible but too small and infrequent to be of value.

COMMENTS: The elongated brown cap, white spores, narrow crowded gills and lateral stemlike base distingush this species. It is apt to be looked for in *Clitocybe* since it usually appears terrestrial. The stalk is never central, however. *Pleurotus spathulatus* is a synonym. *P. angustatus* is similar but has round spores 3-4 μm in diameter. Both have been removed to a separate genus, *Acanthocystis* (or *Hohenbuehelia*). Other species include *P. lignatilis*, with a whitish cap, mealy odor, and thin crowded gills, growing gregariously on logs; *P. elongatipes*, large and white, with a very long, curved off-center stem, growing singly or clustered on decaying hardwoods; *P. mastrucatus*, with a minutely scaly, gelatinous grayish cap and no stem; and *P. porrigens* ("Angel Wings"), with a pure white cap and gills, thin flesh, narrow crowded gills, and little or no stem. The latter is common in northern California on rotting conifers, and is also known as *Pleurocybella porrigens*.

Panus rudis (Hairy Panus)

CAP 2.5-10 cm broad; fan-shaped or wedge-shaped to somewhat irregular in outline, convex becoming plane or depressed; surface dry, covered with dense, coarse, stiff, velvety hairs, violet when wet, fading to reddish-brown or tan; margin incurved, often lobed. Flesh tough, thin, white, taste slightly bitter. **GILLS** decurrent, close, narrow, edges entire; white to cream color, sometimes tinted cap color. **STALK** a short, stout plug of tissue, off-center to lateral, occasionally central; tough,

Panus rudis grows on hardwood stumps and logs. The cap is hairy, the stalk off-center to lateral. Young specimen at left has a violet cap; mature individual at right is tan.

solid, hairy like cap and about same color. **SPORE PRINT** white; spores 4.5-7 × 2-3 μm, elliptical, smooth, not amyloid.

HABITAT: Gregarious on rotting hardwood stumps and logs; fruiting in the fall, uncommon. I have seen it several times on tanoak in the Santa Cruz Mountains.

EDIBILITY: Edible but very hairy. You'd do better to brush your teeth with it than eat it.

COMMENTS: The hairy cap, tough texture, white spores, and lateral stem set this singular fungus apart. Fresh caps are a gorgeous deep violet. *P. strigosus* is a very large species with a creamy white to yellowish hairy cap. It grows from wounds on living hardwoods and is rare. *Panellus stypticus* is a widely distributed luminescent species with a small orange-buff to brown woolly or scurfy cap (up to 2.5 cm broad). It has a very unpleasant, astringent taste and is not edible.

Panus torulosus

CAP up to 10 cm broad, occasionally larger; broadly convex to plane or depressed; surface smooth, dry, minutely downy at first, pale tan to brownish or reddish-brown, often tinged violet when moist; margin at first inrolled. Flesh tough, firm, white. **GILLS** decurrent, fairly close, narrow, edges entire, tan to buff, often tinged violet when moist. **STALK** up to 5 cm long, fairly thick, solid, tough, off-center or lateral, sometimes central; covered with fine violet or grayish hairs. **SPORE PRINT** white; spores 5.5-7 × 2.5-3.5 μm, elliptical, smooth, not amyloid.

HABITAT: Solitary or in small clusters on hardwood stumps and trees. Rare. I have found it once at the base of a live oak in December.

EDIBILITY: Harmless but tough.

COMMENTS: This is a large *Panus* with a well-developed stem that is sometimes central. The mixture of tan, reddish-tan, and violet plus the growth on wood, decurrent gills, and smooth cap are good fieldmarks. The gill edges are not serrate as in *Lentinus* and there is no veil. *Panus conchatus* is a synonym. *Panellus serotinus* has a smooth, viscid olive-green to yellow-green cap and pale orange to yellowish gills. It is edible, but not choice.

PHYLLOTOPSIS

THIS genus includes one widespread species, described below. The shelflike fruiting body, pinkish sausage-shaped spores, and habitat on wood are the principal fieldmarks.

Phyllotopsis nidulans

CAP 2.5-7.5 cm, broadly convex to plane, more or less shell-shaped in outline; surface dry, densely hairy or velvety, light orange to orange-buff or yellowish, fading to buff; margin at first inrolled. Flesh duplex, orange-buff or paler; odor strong and disagreeable, like sewer gas. **GILLS** close, narrow, adnate (if stalk is present), orange-buff to orange or ochraceous. **STALK** absent or present as a narrowed, stemlike base on side of cap. **VEIL** absent. **SPORE PRINT** pale pinkish or pinkish-brown; spores 5-7 × 2-3 μm, sausage-shaped to elliptical, smooth.

HABITAT: In groups on rotting logs and stumps, fairly common but never abundant, fall and winter.

EDIBILITY: Inedible. The disgusting odor is a definite deterrent.

COMMENTS: This is a rather attractive shelving species with a pale orange hairy cap and gills. The obnoxious odor is sometimes absent. *Paxillus panuoides* is somewhat similar but has yellowish-buff spores and veined or forking gills. *Crepidotus* has brown spores and *Panellus* has white spores, while *Claudopus* species do not have orange gills. *Claudopus nidulans* and *Panellus nidulans* are synonyms.

Phyllotopsis nidulans. A common wood-inhabiter, easily recognized by its hairy cap, orange-buff to yellowish gills, and obnoxious odor. Note the absence of a stalk.

LENTINUS and LENTINELLUS

Medium-sized to large fungi *growing on wood.* CAP usually hairy or scaly. Flesh tough or fleshy-tough. GILLS attached, *edges toothed, serrate, or ragged.* STALK absent, lateral, off-center or central. VEIL absent *(Lentinellus)*; often present *(Lentinus).* VOLVA absent. SPORE PRINT *white.* Spores smooth or rough, amyloid *(Lentinellus),* not amyloid *(Lentinus).*

THESE are white-spored wood-inhabiting agarics with ragged or serrated gill edges. *Pleurotus, Panus,* and *Panellus* are similar but do not have serrated gills. In *Lentinus* the stalk is sometimes central, leading to confusion with *Tricholomopsis* and other wood-inhabiting agarics with white spores. In fact, the shiitake *(Lentinus edodes)* has been placed in *Tricholomopsis* by some mycologists. It is a highly prized delicacy but the other members of this group are not. Both *Lentinus* and *Lentinellus* are small and relatively rare. Two representatives are described here.

Key to Lentinus and Lentinellus

1. Stalk present, central to off-center .... *Lentinus lepideus*, p. 127
1. Stalk absent or rudimentary 2
2. Cap concentrically zoned, velvety or hairy, very tough; gills well spaced .... (see *Lenzites betulina*, p. 454)
2. Cap not concentrically zoned; gills close .... *Lentinellus ursinus,* below

Lentinellus ursinus

CAP up to 8 cm long and 5 cm wide, fan-shaped or elongated in outline, convex becoming plane; surface dry, with sparse to dense hairs over the center, brown to pale reddish-brown, margin at first incurved. Flesh thin, firm or rather tough, white to pinkish-buff, taste bitter. **GILLS** close, dingy white to pinkish-buff with ragged or coarsely toothed edges. **STALK** absent or rudimentary. **SPORE PRINT** white; spores 3-5 × 2-3.5 μm, nearly round, with minute amyloid spines.

HABITAT: Gregarious on rotting hardwoods and conifers, fall and winter, uncommon.

EDIBILITY: Inedible due to the bitter taste.

COMMENTS: This flaccid, fleshless, featureless fungus could be carelessly mistaken for an oyster mushroom *(Pleurotus)* were it not for the ragged gills. *Lentinellus vulpinus* is a larger species with a coarsely hairy cap and a hankering for hardwoods.

Lentinellus ursinus. Note the ragged or serrate gills. The stalk is lateral or completely absent.

Lentinus lepideus (Scaly Lentinus)

CAP 5-35 cm broad (occasionally larger), irregularly convex to plane; surface viscid when young but soon dry, whitish to buff or pale yellowish with brown scales. Flesh tough, white, not decaying readily, odor fragrant. **GILLS** whitish to buff, wounded areas rusty-brown; attached; edges serrate. **STALK** to 10 cm long, central or off-center, thick, stout, more or less equal, solid with a hard base, white above the ring, with small brownish scales below, often reddish-brown in age. **VEIL** membranous, buff, forming a superior ring which often disappears. **SPORE PRINT** white; spores 7-15 $\times$ 3.5-6.5 μm, long-elliptical, smooth, not amyloid.

HABITAT: Solitary or in small groups on conifer stumps and logs (occasionally on oak), also on fence posts and structural timber; fall and winter, infrequent. It used to be common on railroad ties and is still common in the Sierras.

EDIBILITY: Edible when young, but tough. Long cooking is required.

COMMENTS: The scaly cap, serrated gills, membranous veil, white spores, and habitat on wood set this species apart. The renowned shiitake *(Lentinus edodes)* is familiar to many people as the "Black Mushroom" of Oriental restaurants. It has long been cultivated on oak log "teepees" in Japan. Now that shiitake cultivation kits are available and it is being raised commercially in California, it might conceivably escape and establish itself on our native oaks. It has a dry, brown to ochraceous brown (or violet-tinted) cracked or scaly cap, whitish gills, a more or less central stem, and a fibrillose, evanescent veil.

TRICHOLOMOPSIS

Medium-sized fungi *found on or near wood.* CAP not viscid. GILLS *attached, usually yellow.* STALK central, *fleshy.* VEIL absent or evanescent. VOLVA absent. SPORE PRINT *white.* Spores smooth, not amyloid. Cystidia abundant on gill edges.

THIS is a small genus of wood-inhabiting agarics formerly distributed among *Tricholoma, Clitocybe,* and *Collybia.* In most species the gills are yellow, but in *Tricholomopsis platyphylla* they are white or grayish. *Tricholomopsis* may occasionally appear terrestrial, but the yellow gills and yellow flesh, absence of a veil, and central fleshy stalk are distinctive. None of its members are particularly good eating. Of the three species keyed below, only *T. rutilans* is common.

Key to Tricholomopsis

1. Gills white to gray .... *T. platyphylla* (see *T. rutilans*, below)
1. Gills yellow 2

2. Cap scales red to purple-red .... *T. rutilans*, below
2. Cap scales gray to black .... *T. decora* (see *T. rutilans*, below)

Tricholomopsis rutilans

CAP 5-13 cm broad, convex becoming plane; surface dry, yellow, covered with dark red to purple-red scales or fibrils which become sparser in age. Flesh thick, firm, pale yellow, odor mild. **GILLS** adnate or

Tricholomopsis rutilans. Dark red scales on cap and stem, yellow gills, yellow flesh are distinctive. It commonly grows on or near rotting conifers.

notched, close, yellow. **STALK** to 18 cm long, equal or enlarged slightly below, dry, yellow with reddish scales (like cap), sometimes entirely yellow in old age. **VEIL** absent. **SPORE PRINT** white; spores 5-6 × 3.5-4.5 μm, elliptical, smooth. Cystidia on gill edges numerous, club-shaped. **HABITAT:** Solitary or in small groups on or near rotting conifer wood: on logs, stumps, in wood chips and humus rich in lignin. Fairly common, late fall and winter. I find it most often with pine and redwood.

EDIBILITY: Edible. According to *Chroogomphus*-king Ciro Milazzo (who was born and raised in Brooklyn), it tastes like rotten wood. I've never tasted rotten wood, so I have no means of verifying this statement. But I wasn't born and raised in Brooklyn either.

COMMENTS: A very attractive mushroom when fresh, easily recognized by the dark red scales on a yellow background. This color combination is not found in any other white-spored agaric with a fleshy stem. Similar, but with grayish-black scales is *T. decora.* I have found it on rotting redwood, but it is rare. Of a totally different appearance is *T. platyphylla*, with a dry to moist (but not viscid) gray to blackish-brown cap and notched, well-spaced, very broad, white to grayish gills. The stalk is long and pallid, and it grows on or near rotting hardwoods and conifers. It looks somewhat like *Tricholoma portentosum* but has a dry cap. *Tricholomopsis platyphylla* was formerly placed in *Collybia, T. decora* in *Clitocybe*, and *T. rutilans* in *Tricholoma.*

OMPHALOTUS

Golden-yellow to olive-yellow to bright orange fungi. CAP smooth. GILLS *decurrent, luminescent when fresh.* STALK *central or off-center*, fleshy. VEIL and VOLVA absent. SPORE PRINT *white.* Spores smooth, not amyloid.

THESE are brightly colored agarics with decurrent gills that glow in the dark, and a fleshy stem. The luminescence is best seen by sitting with the mushroom in the dark for several minutes to allow your eyes to adjust to the low level of luminosity. If the fruiting bodies are young and fresh, an eerie silvery glow will develop, growing gradually brighter until each gill is clearly outlined.

Members of this group are wood-inhabiting but often appear terrestrial. They are poisonous, muscarine being one of the known toxins. One common species is described here.

Omphalotus olivascens often grows in clusters. Gills are decurrent and glow in the dark *when fresh.* Entire fruiting body is golden-yellow to olive-yellow or olive-orange.

Omphalotus olivascens (Jack-O-Lantern Mushroom)

CAP 5-25 cm broad, broadly convex becoming plane and then depressed; surface smooth, not viscid, dull reddish-orange to bright golden-orange with olive tones developing, sometimes entirely olive in old age. Flesh thin, pliant, colored like cap, odor mild. **GILLS** bright yellow-orange becoming olive tinted, decurrent, close, luminescent when fresh. **STALK** to 15 cm long, often off-center, stout, solid, equal or with a narrowed base, dry, more or less cap color, dingy olivaceous in age. **SPORE PRINT** creamy-white; spores 5-6.5 × 4-5.5 μm, ellipsoid to nearly round, smooth.

HABITAT: In clusters or occasionally solitary, on or around hardwood stumps and buried wood, especially oak, madrone, and manzanita. Common, fall and winter. Known only from California and Oregon.

EDIBILITY: Poisonous; profuse sweating and gastrointestinal distress are the usual symptoms.

COMMENTS: The bright golden-olive color, decurrent gills, white spores, and tendency to grow in clusters distinguish this handsome species. The chanterelle *(Cantharellus cibarius)* is vaguely similar but has thick, shallow, blunt, foldlike gills; the false chanterelle *(Hygrophoropsis aurantiacus)* has deeper orange, repeatedly forked gills, while

Gymnopilus species have rusty-orange spores. All lack the olive tones characteristic of mature *Omphalotus olivascens.*

The jack-o-lantern mushroom pictured in most books, *O. olearius (=Clitocybe illudens),* also lacks the olive tones. According to one dubious report, its luminescence is bright enough to read a newspaper by. And then there's the tale about a shipwrecked sailor on an uninhabited island, who wrote a last message by the light of a jack-o-lantern mushroom, using the ink from a shaggy mane, with the stalk of an *Agaricus* for a pen. Unfortunately, he starved to death because he was afraid to eat any of the mushrooms he found!

LEPISTA

Medium-sized terrestrial fungi. CAP convex to plane or depressed, not viscid. GILLS *attached,* often purple or bluish-purple, often dusted pinkish-buff in age. STALK *central, fleshy.* VEIL and VOLVA absent. SPORE PRINT *dull pinkish to pinkish-buff.* Spores rough but neither angular nor longitudinally ridged; not amyloid.

LEPISTA embraces a modest group of pinkish-spored mushrooms whose taxonomic history is a sterling example of human beings' unlimited capacity for quibbling (or likewise, their innate inability to agree). Most Lepistas (such as the blewitt, *L. nuda*) have more or less notched gills and were originally placed in *Tricholoma,* a white-spored genus. On the basis of their pinkish spores they were then removed to either *Lepista* or *Rhodopaxillus.* The concept of the group was broadened to include some white-spored Clitocybes with minutely prickly spores, which subsequently led to the proposal that *Lepista* be incorporated into *Clitocybe.* Until this suggestion meets with universal acceptance it seems best to retain the name *Lepista.*

The gills are attached to the stem but vary from notched (as in *Tricholoma*) to decurrent (as in *Clitocybe*). The most common species (*L. nuda*) is best recognized by its purple to bluish-purple gills. Lepistas differ from other members of the Tricholomataceae by having pinkish spores but are easily confused with pink-spored members of the Rhodophyllaceae (particularly *Entoloma*). The latter, however, has a deeper pink spore print and angular to longitudinally ridged spores. Since only a select few have access to a microscope, the four Lepistas described here are also keyed out in the Rhodophyllaceae.

Lepistas are saprophytic on dung, humus, and organic debris. So far as is known none are poisonous and the blewitt, *L. nuda,* is a popular favorite. Other species should be tested cautiously, if at all, since confusion with members of the Rhodophyllaceae is possible. Four species are described here, including one that does not have a name. If your "Lepista" has a distinct anise odor and buff spores tinted faintly pinkish, check *Clitocybe.*

Key to Lepista

1. Gills purple to bluish-purple when fresh, dull pinkish in age; cap and stalk also purple, but fading .... *L. nuda*, p. 133
1. Gills not purple 2

2. Stalk purple; robust .... *L. saeva* (see *L. nuda*, p. 133)
2. Stalk not purple 3

3. Stalk slender; gills usually tinted faintly violet; growing in or near dung, rich soil .... *L. tarda*, below
3. Not as above; fairly robust; gills never tinted violet 4

4. Usually growing in clusters; cap grayish to buff; gills adnate to decurrent .... *L. subconnexa*, p. 135
4. Not clustered (but often in groups); gills notched or adnate, occasionally decurrent 5

5. Cap white to buff; in woods .... *L. irina* (see *Lepista* sp., p. 135)
5. Cap brown to watery tan; in grass .... *Lepista* sp. (unidentified), p. 135

Lepista tarda

CAP 2.5-7 cm broad, convex with an incurved margin, becoming plane or depressed with an uplifted margin; sometimes broadly umbonate; surface smooth, moist, flesh color to tan or dull brownish, fading as it dries. Flesh thin, same color as cap or paler. **GILLS** adnate to slightly decurrent, occasionally notched, close, thin, more or less cap color but often with a slight lilac tint. **STALK** 2-8 cm long, usually rather short and slender, equal, fibrillose, same color as cap or paler. **SPORE PRINT** pale pinkish; spores 6-7.5 × 3-4.5 μm, ellipsoid, roughened.

HABITAT: Gregarious in small clusters or rings in grass, dung, manure, straw heaps, compost piles, etc. Fairly common after heavy rains, late fall and winter.

EDIBILITY: Edible but thin-fleshed. I haven't tried it.

COMMENTS: This is a smaller, slimmer version of the blewitt. It isn't purple, but the gills often have a faint lilac or vinaceous tint. It can easily be mistaken for a *Clitocybe* or *Melanoleuca*, but the spore print is pale pinkish. The cap color is difficult to characterize but is a rather sordid tan or pale grayish-brown. It used to called *Tricholoma sordidum.*

Lepista nuda. Young specimens at left are purple throughout. In age the cap expands as shown at right, and the color fades gradually to watery-brown, tan, or pinkish-tan.

Lepista nuda (Blewitt)

CAP up to 15 cm broad but usually 5-8 cm; convex with an inrolled margin when young, becoming broadly umbonate to plane or depressed with an uplifted margin in age; surface smooth, lubricous when moist but not viscid, somewhat polished when dry; deep violet when fresh soon fading to lilac gray or lilac brown, brownish or pinkish-tan in old age; margin often wavy. Flesh thick, soft, purple to lilac-buff. Odor faintly fragrant, like frozen orange juice; taste pleasant. **GILLS** attached, notched or adnate, sometimes slightly decurrent, close, purple to bluish-purple when young, fading to lilac-buff or pinkish-buff as the spores mature. **STALK** relatively stout, 2.5-9 cm long, 1-2 cm thick, usually enlarged at the base, dry, fibrillose, purple to pale lilac, fading in

Lepista nuda. The pale purple monstrosity at left is a stem which kept on growing after the cap was cut off. Large, mature individuals at right have pale purple stems and pinkish-lilac gills.

age, with copious pale purplish mycelium at base. **SPORE PRINT** dull pinkish; spores 5.5-8 × 3.5-5 μm, ellipsoid, minutely roughened.

HABITAT: Generally gregarious, often in rings or arcs—in woods, brush, gardens, practically anywhere where there is organic debris. Abundant, fall through spring. Its favorite abode is in brambles under live oak, where it is often found with chanterelles. It is also common under pine and cypress, and it grows on Año Nuevo Island in beach grass and elephant seal dung. One fairy ring near Felton is sixty feet in diameter and produces about 200 blewitts each time it fruits. Known as a "trash inhabiter" because of its fondness for virtually any type of decomposing organic matter, it has been raised on a wide range of substrates, including shredded newspaper and compost.

EDIBILITY: Edible and very popular. The most readily available of edible wild mushrooms, it is a favorite with beginners and gourmets alike. A single mycelium will produce up to a dozen crops a year, so check your patches regularly. It has the dubious distinction of being one of the few purple foods that actually tastes good. It is popular in England, where it is gathered and sold in markets.

COMMENTS: The ubiquitous blewitt is the quintessential embodiment of spunk and persistence—cut one down and two will grow back! Decapitated stems will often continue to grow as if nothing had happened. A new cap will not form, but a grotesque (and edible) cancerous looking pale purple growth will take its place. The blewitt's trademarks are its purple color, stout stature, absence of a veil, faint fruity fragrance, and dull pinkish spores. The cap has a characteristic lubricous feel when moist, but may look quite different—polished and silvery-violet—when dry. Old faded blewitts are barely recognizable but in that condition are not worth eating anyway.

Other purple mushrooms include: *Inocybe geophylla* var.*lilacina,* with brown gills, brown spores, and a small umbonate cap; many *Cortinarius* species, with a cobwebby veil and rusty-brown spores; *Mycena pura,* small and slender with white spores; and *Laccaria amethystina,* with purple gills, white to lilac-tinted spores, and a long tough fibrous stalk. Of these, only the *Inocybe* is poisonous. There are also two bluish Entolomas which may be poisonous. They are never purple, however.

Synonyms for the blewitt are almost as numerous as the blewitt itself. They include: *Tricholoma personatum, T. nudum, Rhodopaxillus nuda,* and *Clitocybe nuda.* The colloquial name "blewitt" is a contraction of "blue hat." *Lepista saeva (=Tricholoma personatum)* is an edible species very similar to the blewitt but with purple present on the stem only. It grows in grassy places, and has been found in California.

Lepista sp. (unidentified)

CAP 4-13 cm broad, convex with an inrolled margin becoming plane or slightly depressed with an uplifted margin; sometimes broadly umbonate; surface moist or lubricous but not viscid, smooth, watery brown to tan, hazel, or buff, usually darker when young. Flesh thick, pallid, odor mild or pleasant. **GILLS** attached, most often notched but often adnate or slightly decurrent; very close, dark buff to grayish-buff or pale brown, becoming dusted pinkish with spores. **STALK** up to 10 cm long, stout, relatively short and thick, fleshy, solid, dry, smooth, equal or enlarged below, pale buff to cap color (but paler). **SPORE PRINT** rosy-buff; spores 5-8 × 3-4 μm, ellipsoid, minutely roughened.

HABITAT: Gregarious in lawns and pastures, usually in rings. It was abundant around Santa Cruz in the wet winter of 1977-78, but is otherwise infrequent. I have found it in late fall, winter, and spring.

EDIBILITY: Edible and quite good. I have tried it. Be sure not to confuse it with poisonous Entolomas, however!

COMMENTS: This interesting species is apparently unnamed. The shape, stature, and characteristically lubricous feel of the cap when moist point to a close relationship to the blewitt. However, there are no purple shades anywhere on the fruiting body. It is not an aberrant form, as I have observed it many times. The gills are typically notched, but as in all Lepistas, their attachment varies considerably. I have always found it growing in grass. It is larger than *L. tarda* and not nearly as slender. It never grows in clusters like *L. subconnexa*. It can be separated from most Entolomas by its habitat. Somewhat similar, but with a white to dingy buff cap and fragrant blewitt-like odor is *L. irina*, an edible species that grows in the woods. It is widely distributed, but I have yet to find it in our area.

Lepista subconnexa (Clustered Lepista)

CAP 4-10 cm broad, convex with an incurved margin becoming plane or with margin uplifted; surface smooth, dry, opaque, grayish-white to gray to dingy buff or brownish-buff, often with a satiny luster or watery spots. Flesh thick, white or pallid, rather brittle, odor mild or mealy. **GILLS** adnate to decurrent, very close, narrow, pale buff to pale pinkish-buff to dull pinkish. **STALK** to 10 cm long, equal or with base enlarged somewhat, smooth, dry, same color as cap or paler, with whitish silky-fibrillose coating. **SPORE PRINT** pinkish-buff to flesh color; spores 4.5-6 × 3-3.5 μm, ellipsoid, rough.

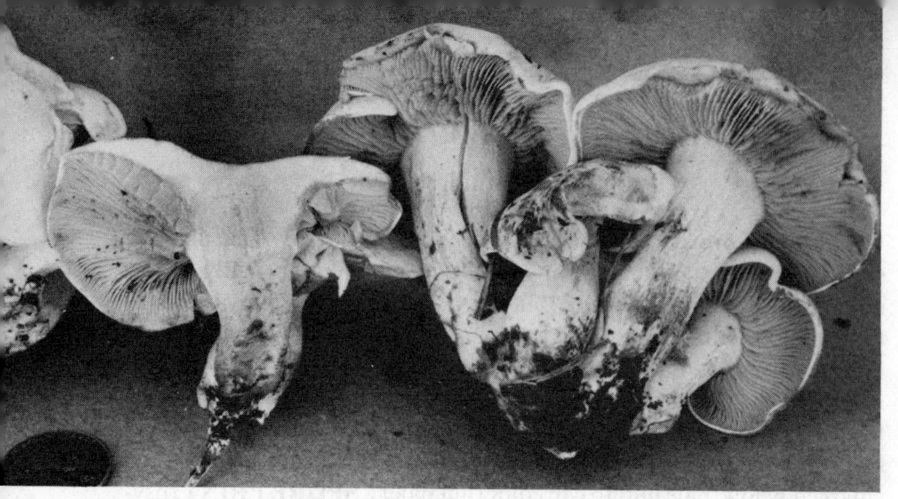

Lepista subconnexa. Clustered growth habit is an important feature of this species. Cap is gray to watery-buff, gills are decurrent, spores are pinkish.

HABITAT: In groups on ground, usually clustered—in woods, brush, pastures, and open places. Common, fall through spring.

EDIBILITY: Edible according to European sources, and good. However, I can find no information on American material, and there is the possibility of confusing it with poisonus Entolomas.

COMMENTS: This common species can be identified by its grayish-buff color, adnate to decurrent gills, and dull pinkish spores. It usually grows in clusters, but solitary fruiting bodies are sometimes found. It is larger and fleshier than *Clitopilus prunulus* and does not have longitudinally ridged spores. At times it is very abundant and, like the blewitt, seems to grow anywhere. It differs from *Lepista* sp. (unidentifed) in its more typically decurrent gills and tendency to grow in clusters. *Tricholoma panaeolum* var. *caespitosus* is one of several synonyms.

LEUCOPAXILLUS

Medium to large fleshy terrestrial fungi. CAP convex to depressed, margin usually inrolled when young; *surface dry, unpolished. Flesh dry, tough.*GILLS attached, close, *more or less white, at least when fresh.* STALK central, *fleshy, tough, often attached to conspicuous white mycelium.* VEIL and VOLVA absent.SPORE PRINT *white;* spores rough or smooth, amyloid.

THIS is a small but very conspicuous group of robust mushrooms with a dry unpolished cap, tough fleshy stem, white gills, and white amyloid spores. It is an easy genus to recognize but a difficult one to define. The flesh is rather dry and brittle, leading to confusion with *Russula*, but the stem does not break like soft chalk, there is often white mycelium at the base, and the stature is completely different.

Confusion with *Clitocybe* and *Tricholoma* (to which *Leucopaxillus* species originally belonged) is also likely. *Clitocybe* and *Tricholoma*, however, do not have amyloid spores, are soft and fleshy, and rot readily. In contrast, *Leucopaxillus* is very tough and remarkably resistant to decay (in part due to the presence of antibiotics). Like *Laccaria*, the fruiting bodies persist for weeks, thus appearing more common than they actually are.

There are only two common species in our area but both fruit prolifically and are likely to be among the first agarics you encounter. They are strictly woodland fungi, probably mycorrhizal. The white mycelium is usually visible as a moldy-looking mat that permeates the immediate vicinity.

Though large and firm, they are tough and / or bitter. None are known to be poisonous, so intrepid mushroom addicts may opt to experiment with the mild-tasting forms. It is certainly easy enough to fill your basket with them.

Key to Leucopaxillus

1. Cap brown to red-brown; taste bitter; medium-sized *L. amarus*, p. 138
1. Cap white to yellowish or tan; taste mild or bitter; medium to large .... *L. albissimus*, below

Leucopaxillus albissimus (Large White Leucopaxillus)

CAP 5-30 cm broad or larger; convex then plane; surface smooth, dry, unpolished, white to yellowish-buff or yellowish-tan, especially toward the center, usually cracking or splitting in age; margin at first inrolled. Flesh thick, dry, white, rather tough; odor aromatic to unpleasant, taste mild or bitter. **GILLS** white to slightly yellowish in old age, typically adnate to decurrent but sometimes notched, very close, rather brittle. **STALK** to 20 cm long and up to 2.5 cm thick; stout, tough, solid, equal or enlrged below, chalky white discoloring slightly in old age, smooth, dry, often with white mycelium at base. **SPORE PRINT** white; spores 5.5-8.5 $\times$ 4.5-5.5 μm, elliptical, warty, amyloid.

HABITAT: Scattered to gregarious (occasionally solitary) in woods, often forming large fairy rings, fall through early spring, very common. It favors conifers (especially redwood) and is abundant in the cold winter months.

Leucopaxillus albissimus. **Left:** Fresh white specimens. (Ralph Buchsbaum). **Right:** Old, weathered specimens which refuse to decay. The large one is nearly a foot across. Color varies from whitish to yellowish or even tan.

EDIBILITY: A tempting specimen, but I don't recommend it. Mild-tasting forms are edible but rather coarse and difficult to digest.

COMMENTS: One of our largest and most memorable mushrooms—its outstanding attribute is its resolute resistance to decay. It is white when young, but one frequently finds old, weathered yellowish specimens which persist for weeks, long after their fleshier cousins have rotted away. It is most likely to be confused with *Clitocybe*, but the dry unpolished cap, tough stem, and resistance to decay distingush it. Many varieties and forms have been described, based on taste and cap color. The common variety in our area is not bitter, but does have a distinctive odor. *L. laterarius* is a similar species with a very bitter taste, cap tinted pinkish-buff, and round spores. It is said to occur under hardwoods.

Leucopaxillus amarus (Bitter Brown Leucopaxillus)

CAP 5-15 cm broad, broadly convex to plane; surface dry, unpolished, smooth, uniformly reddish-brown to cinnamon-brown or brown, often cracked in age; margin at first inrolled. Flesh thick, firm, white, odor usually unpleasant, taste very bitter. **GILLS** typically adnate but varying from notched to slightly decurrent, close, white, rather brittle. **STALK** to 7.5 cm long, stout, equal or enlarged below, smooth, dry, white, sometimes discolored below; copious white mycelium usually present at base. **SPORE PRINT** white; spores 4-6 × 3.5-5 μm, nearly round, warted, amyloid. Cystidia numerous on gill edges.

Leucopaxillus amarus. At right is a typical, fresh, mature individual. The others are weathered and dried up, but refuse to decay. Note the white mycelium at base of specimen on left. When young the cap is convex with an inrolled margin.

HABITAT: Solitary, scattered, or gregarious (often in troops), under both hardwoods and conifers. Common, fall and winter.

EDIBILITY: Unequivocally inedible. It smells like creepy crawlers and tastes like a mildewed army tent. If you're lost in the woods and have nothing to eat, you'd do better to follow the example of Charlie Chaplin and stew your boots before venturing to make a meal of this mushroom.

COMMENTS: This ubiquitous fungus is recognized by its dry, unpolished, evenly colored brown cap, white gills, bitter taste, absence of a veil, and moldy-looking white mycelium that usually permeates the surrounding humus and frequently adheres to the base of the stalk. The cap color is similar to *Hygrophorus roseibrunneus* but the gills are not soft and waxy. The gills may discolor slightly in age but they never become reddish-spotted as in the brown-capped Tricholomas, and the cap is not depressed as in *Russula* or *Clitocybe.*

CLITOCYBE

Small to large fleshy fungi found on ground or rotten wood. CAP convex to plane or depressed, rarely viscid. GILLS *adnate to decurrent, usually white to buff or grayish.* STALK central, *usually fleshy,* but often slender. VEIL and VOLVA *absent.* SPORE PRINT *white to buff or yellowish*; spores typically smooth, not amyloid.

THIS is a large and complex group of soft, fleshy, "white"-spored mushrooms with adnate to decurrent gills, no veil, and a central, usually fleshy stem. The gill attachment (admittedly a somewhat arbitrary character since it depends to some extent on the age and shape of the cap) separates *Clitocybe* from *Tricholoma.* The spores are not pinkish as in *Lepista* or *Clitopilus*, but they may be faintly pinkish-buff. There is no veil as in *Armillaria*, the gills are not soft and waxy as in *Hygrophorus*, nor are they purple or pinkish as in *Laccaria*, nor foldlike, shallow, and blunt as in *Cantharellus.* The flesh is not dry and brittle as in *Russula.* Several other genera (such as *Leucopaxillus*) are structurally similar and are keyed out here. The smaller Clitocybes with slender stems are apt to be mistaken for *Omphalina* or *Collybia,* which have a cartilaginous stem of a different texture than the cap. In *Collybia* the gills are sometimes adnate, but not decurrent.

Clitocybes are most prevalent in coniferous woods but also occur under hardwoods and in grass. Like Tricholomas, they are cold-weather fungi, most abundant from December through February.

Clitocybe is a large but lackluster group whose aesthetic and gustatory value is pratically nil. Confirmed *Clitocybe* experts will be the first to admit that the anonymous throngs of white to grayish species which litter our wintertime woods are exceedingly difficult to identify. Several are undoubtedly poisonous, as are the small grass-inhabiting species, *C. rivulosa* and *C. dealbata.* The larger forms are slightly easier to identify but just as difficult to digest. Several have a disagreeable odor, notably *C. nebularis* and *C. robusta.* The anise-scented varieties, on the other hand, are edible and quite good.

About forty species are reported from California and many more undoubtedly exist. The larger species are described here, plus a handful of the smaller ones.

Key to Clitocybe

1. Growing in lawns, pastures, and other grassy places 2
1. Growing in woods or under trees 4

2. Cap pinkish-tan .... *C. rivulosa* (see *C. dealbata*, p. 144)
2. Cap dull white to gray or brown 3

3. Cap hygrophanous, brown fading to grayish-white, sometimes umbonate; stalk stiff; spores amyloid .... (see *Melanoleuca*, p. 175)
3. Cap neither umbonate nor hygrophanous; dull white to dingy gray; spores not amyloid .... *C. dealbata*, p. 144

4. Odor fragrant, like anise or licorice 5
4. Odor not aniselike 7

5. Fruiting body tinted blue-green .... *C. odora*, p. 142
5. Fruiting body not as above 6

6. Spore print buff to pinkish-buff .... *C. suaveolens*, p. 142
6. Spore print white .... *C. fragrans* (see *C. suaveolens*, p. 142)

7. Cap small (4 cm broad or less); growing in small, compact clumps arising from a fleshy mass of tissue; usually under pine *C. sclerotoidea*, p. 145
7. Not as above 8

8. Growing on rotting wood or stumps 9
8. Growing on ground 11

9. Some part of fruiting body tinted reddish or violet; tough .... (see *Panus torulosus*, p. 124)
9. Not as above 10

10. Stalk white, short; gills white; cap smooth, usually pale; spore print usually lilac-tinted .... (see *Pleurotus ostreatus*, p. 120)
10. Not as above 11

11. Cap orange-brown to red-brown or cinnamon 12
11. Cap some other color 14

12. Gills white; stalk often with white mycelium at base .... (see *Leucopaxillus*, p. 136)
12. Gills not white 13
13. Flesh dry, brittle; stalk rigid, hollow; odor sweet .... (see *Lactarius camphoratus*, p. 73)
13. Not as above (odor may be pepperlike) .... *C. inversa*, p. 150

14. Cap small (5 cm broad or less), white or whitish .. *C. variabilis*, p. 143
14. Larger or differently colored 15

15. Spore print yellowish to yellowish-buff; odor rancid or unpleasant; fruiting body robust 16
15. Spore print white; odor may be distinctive but not as above 17

16. Cap white, often with a satiny luster .... *C. robusta*, p. 148
16. Cap more or less grayish to watery buff .... *C. nebularis*, p. 147

17. Medium-sized to very large; cap dry, unpolished, white to yellowish, tan, or brown (never grayish); stalk tough; gills and stalk white or whitish; fruiting body not decaying readily; spores amyloid; common .... (see *Leucopaxillus*, p. 136)
17. Not as above 18

18. Cap dark brown to pale tan; stalk white, stout, fleshy; found in disturbed soil, usually near roads .... (see *Lyophyllum*, p. 154)
18. Not as above 19

19. Cap pale tan to pinkish-tan or flesh color, convex with a depressed center when young, funnel-shaped at maturity 20
19. Not as above 21

20. Stalk white or whitish .... *C. gibba*, p. 149
20. Stalk colored like cap or darker . *C. squamulosa* (see *C. gibba*, p. 149)

21. Cap small, less than 2.5 cm broad, dark brown to grayish .... *C. epichysium* (see *C. cyathiformis*, p. 146)
21. Not as above; larger 22

22. Cap often umbonate, *not* markedly depressed; stalk stiff; spores amyloid .... (see *Melanoleuca*, p. 175)
22. Not as above 23

23. Stalk slender, rather long; cap 6 cm broad or less *C. cyathiformis*, p. 146
23. Stalk stout; cap 3-20 cm broad or even larger 24

24. Growing on or near rotting wood *C. avellaneialba* (see *C. clavipes*, p. 147)
24. Growing on ground 25

25. Medium-sized to large; gills grayish; odor more or less mild .... *C. harperi* (see *C. nebularis*, p. 147)
25. Medium-sized; gills white to yellowish-buff; odor sometimes fragrant .. .. *C. clavipes*, p. 147

Clitocybe odora (Fragrant Clitocybe)

CAP 2.5-7.5 cm broad, convex then plane or with margin uplifted; surface smooth, moist but not viscid, bluish-green or gray with a blue-green tint. Flesh thin, whitish or tinted blue-green, odor fragrant, anise-like. **GILLS** adnate to decurrent, blue-green to greenish, fairly close. **STALK** to 5 cm long, rather slender, smooth, equal or slightly enlarged at base, same color as cap or paler. **SPORE PRINT** buff or pale pinkish-buff; spores 6.5-8 $\times$ 4-5 μm, elliptical, smooth.

HABITAT: Scattered to gregarious in woods, fall and early winter, rare. I have found it twice under live oak.

EDIBILITY: Edible but thin-fleshed; excellent as a flavoring agent.

COMMENTS: The blue-green color and distinct anise (or licorice) odor identify this species. The coastal variety described above has been designated *C. odora* var. *pacifica. C. odora* var. *odora* is more robust, with a bluish-green tinted cap and pallid to pinkish-buff gills. It is a prominent feature of the Rocky Mountain fungus flora, but I have not seen it here. The other anise-scented Clitocybes in our area (*C. fragrans* and *C. suaveolens*) are never bluish-green.

Clitocybe suaveolens (Anise Clitocybe)

CAP up to 6 cm broad but usually about 2.5 cm; convex becoming plane or depressed; surface smooth, not viscid, color variable: pale brown to buff or watery whitish, sometimes with a darker marginal band. Flesh thin, same color as cap, odor fragrant, aniselike. **GILLS**

Clitocybe suaveolens is distinguished from many similar species by its anise odor. *C. odora* (not illustrated) is bluish-green and somewhat larger.

adnate to slightly decurrent, same color as cap or paler, close. **STALK** to 7.5 cm long, slender, equal or with an enlarged base, smooth, more or less cap color. **SPORE PRINT** pale pinkish-buff; spores 6.5-8 × 4-4.5 μm, elliptical, smooth.

HABITAT: Scattered to gregarious in damp places under conifers, especially redwood and pine. Common to abundant, fall and winter.

EDIBILITY: Edible. Sometimes tasteless, but at least some forms have a pleasant anise flavor when sauteed. Because of its small size it is best used as a flavoring agent in cakes, breads, and cookies. Be *sure* each specimen smells like anise—similar species with a mild odor may be poisonous!

COMMENTS: The distinct anise odor separates this species from the dozens of other small, anonymous white to grayish Clitocybes. *C. fragrans* is a very similar anise-scented species with a white spore print and white to pale grayish-buff cap. It is also edible, and occurs under hardwoods as well as with conifers.

Clitocybe variabilis

CAP up to 6.5 cm broad but usually smaller; convex becoming plane or broadly umbonate; surface dry, smooth, pure white when fresh, dingier in age. Flesh thin, white, odor mild or faintly fragrant. **GILLS** more or less decurrent, white tinged buff in old age, fairly close. **STALK** to 7.5 cm long, slender, equal or enlarged below, smooth, dull white discoloring brownish-buff in age. **SPORE PRINT** white; spores 5.5-8 × 3-5 μm, ovate to elliptical, smooth.

HABITAT: Scattered to gregarious in mixed woods and under conifers, late fall and winter. Uncommon, but similar species are sometimes abundant (see below).

EDIBILITY: Unknown, to be avoided; related species are poisonous.

COMMENTS: This species along with *C. cyathiformis* is representative of a metagrobolizing myriad of small white to grayish Clitocybes that are exceedingly difficult to distinguish. *C. cerussata* is similar but has smaller spores and a dingier cap. A small (cap less than 2.5 cm broad), fragile, thin-fleshed, pure white species occurs in dense carpets under pine.

Clitocybe dealbata (Sweat-Producing Clitocybe)

CAP up to 5 cm broad, convex becoming plane or depressed; surface smooth, dingy white to grayish to buffy-white, sometimes with watery spots. Flesh thin, grayish-white, odor mild or faintly farinaceous. **GILLS** grayish-white to buff or pinkish-buff, close, adnate to decurrent. **STALK** to 5 cm long, rather short, slender, tough, colored like cap, equal or tapering downward, smooth. **SPORE PRINT** white; spores 4-5 $\times$ 2.5-3 μm, elliptical, smooth.

HABITAT: Scattered to gregarious (usually in fairy rings) in pastures and other grassy places. Common, fall and winter, often found with the meadow mushroom, *Agaricus campestris.*

EDIBILITY: Poisonous; causes profuse sweating, salivation, and diarrhea; potentially fatal to small children. Muscarine is the main toxin.

Clitocybe dealbata, gill detail at left, young specimen at right. This poisonous grayish grass lover likes to grow in circles like the edible fairy ring mushroom, *Marasmius oreades.*

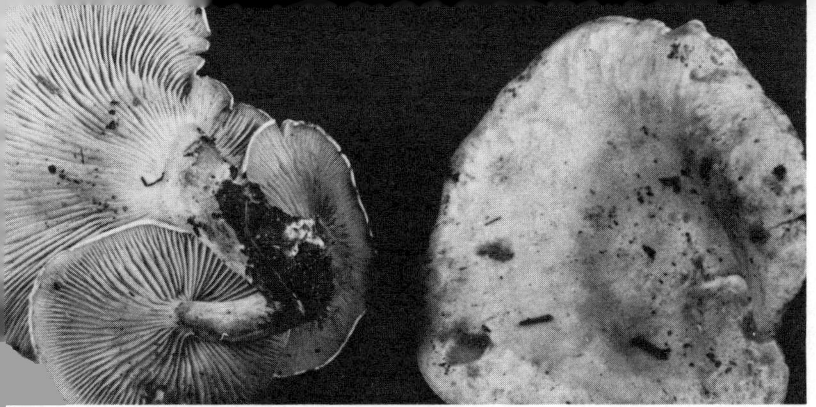

Clitocybe dealbata, gill detail at left, depressed cap of a mature specimen at right. The gills are close together and decurrent, the spores are white.

COMMENTS: The dingy grayish-white color, close decurrent gills, white spore print, small size, and habitat in grass are the distinguishing features of this drab *Clitocybe*. It is sometimes confused with the edible fairy ring mushroom *(Marasmius oreades)*, which has a somewhat umbonate cap and well-spaced gills that are never decurrent. It also resembles *Clitopilus prunulus*, but has white spores. I have found a small, fragile *Clitocybe* with a smooth, pinkish-tan cap and close, white, adnate gills growing on lawns with *Marasmius oreades*. It is very close to *Clitocybe rivulosa*, another poisonous species. Synonyms for *C. dealbata* include *C. morbifera* and *C. sudorifica*.

Clitocybe sclerotoidea

CAP up to 5 cm broad but usually smaller, convex to plane; surface dry, unpolished, with a fine whitish fibrillose coating which rubs off; pallid to sordid buff to pinkish-buff or grayish, sometimes with darker watery spots. Flesh whitish, odor mild. **GILLS** adnate or slightly notched, becoming decurrent, fairly well-spaced, more or less cap color to gray or dingy pinkish-buff. **STALK** to 5 cm long, more or less equal, solid, colored like cap or paler; with soft, matted downy hairs; arising from an underground mass of tissue ("sclerotium"). **SPORE PRINT** white; spores 8-11 $\times$ 3-4 μm, subfusiform (elongated), smooth.

HABITAT: In small, tight clumps on ground under pine, late fall until early spring (seldom appearing before January); common. The black elfin saddle *(Helvella lacunosa)* is often found nearby.

EDIBILITY: Unknown, and like myself, likely to remain so.

COMMENTS: I can find hidden virtues in almost any fungus, but this drab, undistinguished *Clitocybe* defies me—its mediocrity is downright stupefying. It serves as a compelling reminder that organisms do not

Clitocybe sclerotoidea. Note the growth habit in small, tight clumps. The mass of tissue from which the mushrooms arise is thought to be aborted *Helvella lacunosa.*

exist for our enjoyment alone, and should not be judged accordingly. It can be recognized by its small size, dingy color (or lack of it), and habit of growing in compact clumps from an underground mass of tissue. Small, aborted individuals are usually present in each clump. The gills may have a slight pinkish cast but the spores are white. The "sclerotium" is actually composed of hyphae from both *C. sclerotoidea* and *Helvella lacunosa*—suggesting that the *Clitocybe* is parasitic on the *Helvella.* It is interesting to note, however, that the *Helvella* occurs with both hardwoods and conifers, while *Clitocybe sclerotoidea* is apparently confined to pine.

Clitocybe cyathiformis

CAP up to 7 cm broad but usually 2.5-5 cm; at first plane with a depressed center and incurved margin, becoming depressed or funnel-shaped; surface smooth, not viscid, dark gray-brown to sooty-brown, fading in age to grayish. Flesh thin, soft, odor mild. **GILLS** at first adnate but soon decurrent, pallid to grayish, close. **STALK** to 10 cm long, slender, equal or tapering upward, colored like cap or paler, smooth, fibrillose, base with white down. **SPORE PRINT** white; spores 7-10.5 × 5-6 μm, elliptical, smooth.

HABITAT: Solitary or in small groups in humus, along paths, at the edges of woods, on rotting wood, etc. Frequent, fall and winter.

EDIBILITY: Unknown. Do not experiment.

COMMENTS: The above description will suffice for a number of anonymous slender-stemmed grayish Clitocybes with concave to funnel-shaped caps. *C. metachroa* is smaller with spores 4.5-5.5 μm long. *C. (Omphalina) epichysium* is a small attractive species with a dry cap about 2 cm broad, dark sooty-brown to olive-brown or ashy, and minutely scurfy-scaly at the center. It is fairly common in our area, in mixed woods and under conifers.

Clitocybe clavipes (Club-Footed Clitocybe)

CAP 2.5-10 cm broad, convex becoming plane or depressed; surface more or less smooth, not viscid, drab grayish-brown to dark gray-brown or olive-brown, often paler toward the margin. Flesh thick, pallid, odor mild or somewhat fruity. **GILLS** decurrent, fairly close, at first white, then yellowish-buff. **STALK** to 7.5 cm long, stout, usually club-shaped (enlarged below), pallid with grayish or sordid olive-buff fibrils, with white down at base. **SPORE PRINT** white; spores 6-8.5 × 3.5-5 μm, ellipsoid, smooth.

HABITAT: Solitary, scattered, or gregarious under conifers and in mixed woods, late fall and winter. It is common and widely distributed, but infrequently encountered in our area.

EDIBILITY: Edible, but not choice. Similar species haven't been tested.

COMMENTS: The drab grayish-brown cap, decurrent white gills, white spores, and club-shaped stem are characteristic. The more common *C. nebularis* is larger, paler, has an unpleasant odor and yellowish-buff spores. *C. avellaneialba* is similar but has larger, elongated spores (8-10 μm long), a darker cap, and grows on or near decayed logs (conifers and alder). *C. atrialba* (now placed in *Clitocybula*) also grows on logs, but has a blackish-brown cap, scurfy stem, and amyloid spores.

Clitocybe nebularis (Cloudy Clitocybe)

CAP 7-30 cm broad, convex to plane becoming depressed with an uplifted margin; surface dry, finely fibrillose or covered with a hoary bloom, grayish to pale grayish-brown or buff, sometimes with watery spots. Flesh thick, white, odor rancid, disagreeable. **GILLS** adnate to decurrent, close, whitish to pale buff. **STALK** to 13 cm long, thick, stout, tough, usually enlarged below; whitish with dingy brownish fibrils, the base covered with white down. **SPORE PRINT** pale buff to yellowish; spores 5.5-8 × 3.5-4.5 μm, elliptical, smooth.

HABITAT: Scattered to gregarious (often in fairy rings) in mixed woods and under conifers. Common, late fall and winter, seldom appearing before December.

EDIBILITY: Eaten in Europe, but its odor is a deterrent. Moreover, it is indigestible unless thoroughly parboiled.

Clitocybe nebularis is a large buff to grayish species with decurrent gills and a rancid odor. Cap is convex when young, depressed in age. (Nancy Burnett)

COMMENTS: The outstanding feature of this large, drab, cold-weather *Clitocybe* is the disagreeable odor, which has been variously compared to rancid flour, skunk cabbage, beer barf, mice feces, and rotten cucumbers. It decays much more rapidly than *Leucopaxillus albissimus*, is grayer, and has pale yellowish spores. Another large, undistinguished grayish species, *Clitocybe harperi*, is slightly less common. It has darker gray gills, white spores, and a mild odor. Like *C. nebularis,* it grows in the woods, usually with conifers. Its edibility is unknown.

Clitocybe robusta (Robust Clitocybe)

CAP 5-20 cm broad, convex becoming plane or shallowly depressed; surface dry, smooth, pure white with a satiny luster, duller in age. Flesh thick, white, odor rancid, disagreeable. **GILLS** adnate to decurrent, white to pale buff, close. **STALK** to 10 cm long, thick, stout, equal or enlarged below, white, dry. **SPORE PRINT** pale yellowish-buff; spores 6-7.5 × 3-4 μm, elliptical, smooth.

HABITAT: Scattered to gregarious, often in small clumps, under conifers or in mixed woods, late fall and winter, sometimes common. I have found it under pine and in mixed woods of pine, live oak, and madrone.

EDIBILITY: Edible, but should be cooked well.

COMMENTS: Also known as *C. alba*, this is essentially a pure white version of *C. nebularis*. It is one of our most attractive Clitocybes—robust, clean, and compact. I have found it growing with *Hygrophorus sordidus*, a large white mushroom with waxy gills. *Leucopaxillus albissimus* is also similar but has white amyloid spores and is much tougher.

Clitocybe gibba (Funnel-Shaped Clitocybe)

CAP to 7.5 cm broad, at first convex or plane with a slightly depressed center and inrolled margin, becoming deeply depressed or funnel-shaped in age; surface smooth, not viscid, tan to pinkish-tan or flesh color, fading in age or after heavy rain; margin often wavy. Flesh thin, whitish, odor mild. **GILLS** deeply decurrent, very close, white to pale buff or pinkish-buff. **STALK** to 7.5 cm long, slender, equal or enlarged below, smooth or finely fibrillose, white or yellowish, base with white down. **SPORE PRINT** white; spores 5-8 $\times$ 3.5-5 μm, elliptical, smooth.

HABITAT: Solitary or in small groups in woods (mostly oak), winter, infrequent.

EDIBILITY: Edible, but not a good mushroom for beginners—too many species of unknown edibility resemble it. Mushroom books generally rate it as mediocre, but it's probably a case of each author taking another's word for it. Breaded and fried it tastes like the oyster mushroom, *Pleurotus ostreatus*.

COMMENTS: The pale pinkish-tan cap which is funnel-shaped at maturity combined with the pallid, decurrent gills and whitish stem render this species distinct. It is paler than *C. inversa* and not as common. *C. infundibuliformis* is a lengthy synonym. *C. squamulosa* is a very similar species in which the stalk is the same color as the cap or darker. It is

Clitocybe gibba. The decurrent gills and pinkish-tan cap color are distinctive. Note how the cap becomes deeply depressed or funnel-shaped in old age (specimen at left).

also edible. *C. sinopica* has a red-brown cap and stem and farinaceous odor. Several unidentified species occur as well. It is interesting to note that *C. gibba* releases HCN (cyanide gas) into the atmosphere. So does the common fairy ring mushroom, *Marasmius oreades*, as well as many other mushrooms and plants (notably lupine and almond). It is not produced in sufficient quantity to harm humans, however.

Clitocybe inversa

CAP 2.5-10 cm broad, convex or plane with an inrolled margin, becoming depressed in the center, then funnel-shaped; surface dry, smooth or minutely scaly, pale orange-brown to orange-tan, reddish-tan, cinnamon-orange, or salmon-buff. Flesh paler than cap, thin, odor sharp, somewhat like pepper. **GILLS** decurrent, close, buff to more or less cap color (but paler). **STALK** to 12 cm long, rather slender, equal or slightly enlarged below, often curved, colored like cap or slightly paler, smooth. **SPORE PRINT** whitish; spores 4.5-5 × 3.5-4 μm, nearly round, minutely prickly.

Clitocybe inversa. Decurrent gills and orange-brown color typify this common wintertime woodland species. It sometimes grows in small tufts, more often in rings.

HABITAT: Scattered to gregarious in woods, sometimes in small clusters, more often in rings or arcs. Very common, late fall and winter. I have seen very large fruitings under live oak.

EDIBILITY: Edible. I haven't tried it.

COMMENTS: This common *Clitocybe*, also called *C. flaccida* and *Lepista inversa*, is easily recognized by its cheerful orange-brown color, depressed cap, decurrent gills, and white spores. A variety with slightly colored spores also occurs. *C. gibba* has a similar stature but is differently colored. *Lactarius camphoratus* is also similar (especially when its latex has dried up) but has a sweetish odor and hollow, rigid stem.

LACCARIA

Small to medium-sized terrestrial fungi. CAP not viscid, convex to plane. GILLS attached, *rather thick, slightly waxy, pinkish-flesh to purple.*STALK *tough and fibrous* usually slender, more or less central. VEIL and VOLVA absent. SPORE PRINT *white to pale lilac.* Spores usually spiny, not amyloid.

A SMALL but common genus, originally placed in *Clitocybe*, but clearly different. The pinkish-flesh to purple gills and tough, fibrous stem are good field characters. The stalk may appear cartilaginous in small individuals but is never fragile. The fruiting bodies persist for weeks without decaying. As a result they appear more common than they actually are.

Laccarias are found in a variety of woodland habitats, but are particularly fond of sandy situations under pine. Some actually grow in sand dunes. They are edible, and better than most authorities suggest. Two cosmopolitan species are keyed below.

Key to Laccaria

1. Gills deep purple when young, fading slowly in age *L. amethystina,* below
1. Gills pinkish to more or less flesh color .... *L. laccata,* p. 152

Laccaria amethystina (Amethyst Laccaria)

CAP up to 6.5 cm broad but generally smaller, convex becoming plane, the margin sometimes uplifted or wavy; surface smooth or minutely scaly, not viscid; deep violet when young, soon fading as it dries to brownish-violet, flesh color or paler. Flesh thin, lavender, odor mild. **GILLS** attached, fairly well spaced, thick, somewhat waxy, deep amethyst-purple when young, fading slowly to dull purple, then dusted

Laccaria amethystina, mature specimens. The one at the right has deep purple gills; the other two have begun to fade. Note the tough, hairy, fibrous stalk.

white with spores. **STALK** up to 13 cm long, usually slender and longer than width of cap, more or less equal, sometimes curved; tough, fibrous, more or less cap color but fading, fibrillose-striate, the fibrils whitish. **SPORE PRINT** white to pale lilac; spores 8-11 μm, round or nearly round, spiny.

HABITAT: In or near woods, mostly in poor soil under conifers, also with oak. Scattered to gregarious, fall through early spring. Common, especially in cold, dry weather when other fungi are scarce.

EDIBILITY: Edible but supposedly mediocre. The tough stems should be discarded.

COMMENTS: The deep amethyst-purple gills (when young) combined with the long, tough, fibrous stem set this beautiful species apart. The color fades in age but the gills retain their purple well into maturity. It was formerly known as *L. laccata* var. *amethystina. L. ochropurpurea* is a large (cap 4-12 cm broad) fleshy edible species with purple gills and a dull whitish to grayish cap. It grows under hardwoods but is not common. The blewitt *(Lepista nuda)* is also purple but squatter, has pinkish spores, closer gills, and a softer, fleshier stem.

Laccaria laccata (Lackadaisical Laccaria)

CAP up to 6 cm broad but usually about 3 cm; convex becoming plane or with uplifted margin; surface not viscid, smooth or minutely scaly, color variable: flesh color to orange-cinnamon to brownish-cinnamon

Laccaria laccata. Ten photographs can't show the range of variation in this species. These are rather short specimens with a cinnamon-colored stem and pinkish-flesh cap and gills.

to reddish-tan, much paler when dry; margin sometimes wavy. Flesh thin, same color as cap or paler, odor mild. **GILLS** attached, thick, well spaced, somewhat waxy, pale flesh color to pinkish or reddish-tan, then dusted white wth spores. **STALK** up to 12 cm long, slender, equal, tough, fibrous, fibrillose-striate or scurfy, same color as cap or darker (deep reddish-brown). **SPORE PRINT** white; spores 7.5-10 × 7-8.5 μm, round to broadly ellipsoid, spiny.

HABITAT: Scattered to densely gregarious in or near woods or trees; partial to poor or sandy soil. Common to abundant, especially in cold, dry weather, fall through spring, often intermixed with *L. amethystina.* I have seen luxuriant fruitings under pine and acacia.

EDIBILITY: Edible and quite good, especially when seasoned. The tough stems should be discarded.

COMMENTS: This cosmopolitan mushroom inevitably turns up when one is seeking more exotic species. In other words, it is a mushroom "weed", undistinguished and unassuming, without the brilliant color of its cousin, *L. amethystina.* It is an extremely variable fungus, but the telltale traits are: the overall color (pinkish-flesh to orange-cinnamon); thick, well-spaced gills; white spores; and tough stem. It is easily confused with a host of other brownish mushrooms, especially *Lactarius camphoratus*, which has a latex and sweet odor. Other pinkish-flesh Laccarias include: *L. striatula,* with a translucent-striate cap when fresh; and *L. tortilis*, a small moss-loving species with round, spiny spores 12-14 μm in diameter.

LYOPHYLLUM

Small to medium-sized mushrooms *often growing in dense clusters.* CAP *white to gray or brown,* convex to plane, *not viscid.* GILLS attached, usually white or grayish. STALK fleshy or cartilaginous, central. VEIL and VOLVA absent. SPORE PRINT *white.* Spores usually smooth, not amyloid. Cystidia on gills absent or inconspicuous. Basidia with carminophilous granules.

THIS is a nondescript amalgamation of white-spored mushrooms formerly dispersed among *Tricholoma, Collybia,* and *Clitocybe.* It is puzzling to the amateur because the various species appear to have little in common. Most are slender and *Collybia*-like, but others are robust and *Tricholoma*-like. The unifying characteristic is rather esoteric: the basidia contain particles which darken when heated in acetocarmine. Our one common species is best recognized by its densely clustered growth habit.

Lyophyllum decastes (Clustered Lyophyllum)

CAP 2.5-15 cm broad, convex to plane or with margin slightly uplifted; surface moist but not viscid, smooth, at first dark grayish-brown (often with a metallic luster), then fading to pale brown or watery tan; margin sometimes lobed. Flesh thick, firm, white, odor mild. **GILLS** close, attached (often notched), white or pallid, sometimes discoloring in age.

Lyophyllum decastes is abundant along roads and paths, and almost always grows in dense clumps like this one. These mature specimens have a tan cap. However, the cap is deep brown when young. Gills, stalk, and flesh are white.

STALK to 10 cm long and 2.5 cm thick; stout, equal or tapering downward, smooth, dry, white or discolored in age. **SPORE PRINT** white; spores 5-7 × 5-6 μm, round to elliptical, smooth.

HABITAT: Gregarious on ground, usually in large compact clumps along roads, paths, and other disturbed places; sometimes forcing its way up through asphalt. Common, at times abundant, from early fall through spring. It was the single most abundant mushroom on the UC Santa Cruz campus (a very disturbed place) during the dry 1976-77 season. A couple hundred pounds could have been harvested.

EDIBILITY: Edible, and according to many sources, good. It certainly fruits in enough quantity to make experimentation worthwhile. Be cautious, however—allergic reactions are reported for some variants.

COMMENTS: This exceedingly common species (or complex of species) is best recognized by its growth habit in dense clusters which may weigh up to fifteen pounds each. Solitary individuals are sometimes found, however, and these consistently confound the beginner. Since size, cap color, and gill attachment are so variable, it is best to eat only those growing in large clumps. Examine the lower caps in each cluster to make sure the spores are white. Poisonous *Entoloma* species (see *Entoloma rhodopolium*) sometimes grow in clusters, but have deep pinkish spores. *Lepista subconnexa* is another cespitose (clustered) mushroom with pinkish spores. The fondness of *Lyophyllum decastes* for disturbed soil is another telltale trait. Entolomas prefer deep woods.

TRICHOLOMA

Medium-sized to large *terrestrial* fungi. CAP viscid or dry, smooth or scaly. GILLS *notched or narrowly attached,* occasionally adnate. STALK central, *fleshy*. VEIL *absent or rudimentary*. VOLVA absent. SPORE PRINT *white*. Spores smooth, not amyloid. Cystidia on gills rare.

TRICHOLOMA is a large and prominent group of terrestrial white-spored mushrooms with notched gills and a central, fleshy stem. It corresponds anatomically to *Entoloma* (deep pinkish spores) and *Hebeloma* (brown spores), but has little else in common with those fungi. Among the white-spored genera, *Collybia* differs in its cartilaginous stalk, *Tricholomopsis* grows on or near wood, *Hygrophorus* has soft, waxy gills, *Russula* has dry, brittle flesh, and *Clitocybe* has adnate to decurrent gills. *Melanoleuca, Leucopaxillus,* and *Lyophyllum* differ microscopically, and are keyed out in *Tricholoma. Lepista* may have notched gills, but its spores are pinkish-buff.

Tricholoma contains several excellent edible species as well as some very poisonous ones. The man on horseback, *T. flavovirens*, is the only species I consider safe for beginners. The brown-capped and gray-capped species should be strictly avoided until you are intimately familiar with each and every one of them. Then, and only then, should species like *T. portentosum* and *T. terreum* become a part of your culinary repertoire. Tricholomas, incidentally, form the bulk of wild mushrooms served by Joe and Wanda Czarnecki at their fabulous wild mushroom restaurant in Reading, Pennsylvania.

Tricholomas are almost exclusively woodland fungi. Many are undoubtedly mycorrhizal—especially with pine. They fruit in cold weather, normally appearing in late November and reaching their peak in December or January. In some regions they continue to fruit after there is snow on the ground!

Though *Tricholoma* is an easy genus to recognize, its species are perplexing even to the professional. Many kinds are known only from a single locality and microscopic characteristics are not as helpful as in, say, *Mycena.* I have found more than twenty kinds in our area, half of which are described here.

Key to Tricholoma

1. Gills yellow; cap yellow to yellow-brown or brown 2
1. Not as above 3

2. Stalk sheathed with cottony scales (see *Armillaria albolanaripes*, p. 170)
2. Stalk smooth, without scales .... *T. flavovirens*, p. 158

3. Cap conical when young, umbonate in age; stalk with a narrow "tap root" extending deep into humus .... (see *Collybia umbonata*, p. 181)
3. Not as above 4

4. Stalk belted with delicate rusty-orange scales; cap viscid, orange to rusty-brown (dark green in one form); odor unpleasant or farinaceous .... *T. aurantium,* p. 166
4. Not as above 5

5. Cap olive-gray to greenish (but brown or olive-brown tones may also be present); flesh in extreme base of stalk often pinkish-orange; cap not viscid .... *T. saponaceum*, p. 162
5. Not as above 6

6. Cap smooth, not viscid, less than 7 cm broad, dark brown to grayish-brown, gray, or whitish; stalk slender, stiff; gills white to buff, crowded; common in grassy places, sometimes in woods; spores amyloid .... (see *Melanoleuca*, p. 175)
6. Not as above 7

7. Cap orange-brown to reddish, red-brown, or cinnamon-brown, *or* gills reddish-spotted *or* both 8
7. Cap some other color; gills never reddish-spotted 13

8. Fibrillose veil present, leaving a slight ring on stalk or remnants on cap margin; stalk fragile .... *T. focale,* p. 165
8. Not as above; stalk not markedly fragile 9

9. Cap viscid when moist 10
9. Cap dry 11

10. Odor farinaceous or unpleasant .... *T. pessundatum*, p. 163
10. Odor mild .... *T. ustale* (see *T. pessundatum*, p. 163)

11. Cap margin woolly or cottony .... *T. vaccinum* (see *T. focale*, p. 165)
11. Cap margin not woolly or cottony 11

12. Cap dry, unpolished; gills white, *not* reddish-spotted; taste very bitter . ... (see *Leucopaxillus*, p. 136)
12. Gills white becoming spotted or stained sordid reddish; taste not noticeably bitter .... *T. imbricatum*, p. 164

13. Medium-sized to very large, not decaying readily; cap dry, unpolished, white to yellowish-tan; gills and stalk white or whitish; stalk very tough, often with white mycelium at base; spores amyloid; common .... (see *Leucopaxillus*, p. 136)
13. Not as above 14

14. Cap white (may discolor slightly in age) .... *T. resplendens*, p. 161
14. Cap colored, or at least with colored scales 15

15. Cap viscid when moist; gray to purple-gray, usually with a streaked appearance .... *T. portentosum*, p. 159
15. Cap not viscid 16

16. Cap small, fragile, less than 5 cm broad, covered with dark gray to black hairy or scurfy scales .... *T. terreum*, p. 159
16. Not as above 17

17. Cap smooth, without scales, dark gray-brown to tan; growing in disturbed soil, usually on or near roads and paths .... (see *Lyophyllum*, p. 154)
17. Not as above 18

18. Cap convex to plane, not scaly; gills very broad (deep); growing on or near wood .... (see *Tricholomopsis*, p. 128)
18. Not as above; growing on ground 19

19. Gills whitish, at least when young 20
19. Gills grayish .... *Tricholoma* sp. (unidentified) (see *T. virgatum*, p. 160)

20. Cap conical to broadly conical when young, fibrillose *T. virgatum*, p. 160
20. Cap convex to plane, white with grayish scales, center often darker .... *T. pardinum* (see *T. virgatum*, p. 160)

Tricholoma flavovirens, mature specimens. Stalk and gills are yellow; cap is yellow to brown and viscid. Note how the gills are notched at the stem. This species is often hidden by pine needles.

Tricholoma flavovirens (Man On Horseback)

CAP 5-15 cm broad, convex to plane or with margin uplifted; surface viscid when moist, smooth, yellow to greenish-yellow or brownish-yellow, sometimes reddish-brown at the center and yellow toward the margin. Flesh thick, firm, white; odor and taste farinaceous. **GILLS** yellow, close, notched. **STALK** up to 10 cm long and to 2.5 cm thick; more or less equal, white, buff, or tinged yellow, dry, smooth, spongy when infested with maggots. **VEIL** absent. **SPORE PRINT** white; spores 6-7 $\times$ 4-5 μm, elliptical, smooth.

HABITAT: Scattered to densely gregarious in grassy or shrubby areas under pine, usually buried in the duff. Common, late fall and winter. It is also found occasionally in oak-madrone woods—still another example of a mushroom normally associated with pine crossing over to madrone.

EDIBILITY: Edible and excellent; one of the least appreciated and finest of edible fungi. The viscid cap should be cleaned in the field or the skin peeled off.

COMMENTS: Formerly known as *T. equestre*, this mushroom is as dependably yellow as the blewitt is purple. Its color, plus the sticky cap, white spores, absence of a veil, and association with pine combine to make it one of the safest (as well as tastiest) mushrooms. None of which explains the misnomer "Man on Horseback"—it doesn't look anything like a horse, and most of the horseback riders I see are women . . .

Armillaria albolanaripes is also yellow but has a veil and scaly stem. There are several yellow *Cortinarius* species, but they have a cobwebby veil and rusty spores. *Hygrophorus hypothejus* grows with pine but has waxy decurrent gills. *Tricholoma sejunctum* is a somewhat similar species with white gills. It is said to be edible, but not choice. *T. sulphureum* is a foul-smelling (like gas tar) poisonous yellow species with a dry cap.

Tricholoma portentosum, young specimen at center, mature individuals at left and right. Cap is viscid, streaked, deep grayish. Stalk is white, gills are notched.

Tricholoma portentosum (Streaked Tricholoma)

CAP 5-10 cm broad, convex to plane or with margin uplifted; surface smooth, viscid when moist, streaked with a mixture of gray, brownish-gray, and livid (purplish-gray) fibrils, center sometimes nearly black and margin often paler. Flesh white or tinged gray, odor and taste mild. **GILLS** adnexed or notched, at first white, becoming grayish or sometimes pale yellow. **STALK** to 10 cm long, stout, smooth, dry, more or less equal, white. **VEIL** absent. **SPORE PRINT** white; spores 6-7 $\times$ 3-4 μm, elliptical, smooth.

HABITAT: Scattered to gregarious under oak and in mixed woods. Fairly common, late fall and winter. January is usually the best month.

EDIBILITY: Edible and excellent, with a strong hearty flavor. The Czarnecki's serve it in their wild mushroom restaurant, along with *T. flavovirens* and *T. terreum*. However, be sure of your identification before eating it!

COMMENTS: The viscid cap separates this species from the multitude of other gray-capped Tricholomas, many of which are poisonous. The notched gills, fleshy stalk, white spores, and absence of a veil identify it as a *Tricholoma*. *Entoloma madidum* is similar but has pinkish spores (and pinkish gills in old age) and a bluish-gray stalk.

Tricholoma terreum (Mousy Tricholoma)

CAP up to 5 cm broad but usually about 3 cm, conical or bell-shaped becoming plane; surface dry, mouse-colored (gray to grayish-black), covered with small dark gray to black scales with a mealy or hairy-scaly

Tricholoma terreum. This small species with the hairy-scaly grayish to grayish-black cap is sometimes abundant under conifers. The gills are often grayer than those illustrated.

consistency. Flesh thin, fragile, white or grayish, odor and taste mild. **GILLS** adnexed or notched, close, white becoming grayish. **STALK** short (less than 5 cm), rather slender, equal, white or grayish, smooth, dry. **VEIL** absent. **SPORE PRINT** white; spores 6-7.5 × 3.5-5.5 μm, ovoid, smooth.

HABITAT: Scattered to gregarious under conifers, especially Douglas-fir and pine. Common, fall and winter. I have seen enormous fruitings under a pine on a lawn in Santa Cruz.

EDIBILITY: Edible with caution. The flavor is good but extreme care must be taken not to confuse it with *T. pardinum* and other poisonous gray Tricholomas.

COMMENTS: The small size, fragile flesh, and dry scaly mouse-colored cap are characteristic of a complex of closely related species. Since they have probably all been mistaken for *T. terreum*, it's unlikely that any are poisonous. *T. myomyces* is very similar but has a farinaceous odor and taste and smaller spores. It is also common in our area. *T. acre* is slightly larger with an acrid taste; *T. squarrulosum* has larger spores, 7-9 μm long. All of these are smaller, scalier, and more fragile than *T. pardinum* and *T. virgatum.*

Tricholoma virgatum

CAP to 7.5 cm broad, at first conical, then convex or umbonate; surface dry, grayish, gray-brown, or purplish-gray, sometimes nearly black at the center, with dark radiating fibrils. Flesh thin, whitish, odor mild, taste slightly acrid. **GILLS** adnexed or notched, white, close. **STALK** to

10 cm long, more or less equal, solid, white, smooth. **VEIL** absent. **SPORE PRINT** white; spores 6-7.5 × 4.5-5 μm, ovoid, smooth.

HABITAT: Solitary or scattered in woods, especially under conifers. Occasional, fall and winter.

EDIBILITY: There are conflicting opinions on its edibility, but its resemblance to the poisonous *T. pardinum* (see below) precludes me from recommending it.

COMMENTS: The dry fibrillose-streaked grayish cap which is conical when young affords a good means of recognizing this species. It is also known as *T. subacutum.* The cap is never viscid as in *T. portentosum. T. pardinum* is a robust species with scattered gray scales on the dry cap. I have found it several times in mixed woods. It causes severe poisoning of the gastrointestinal tract, and the adage is often heard: "Avoid all gray Tricholomas!" An unidentified species with a dry, grayish-olive fibrillose cap is common under hardwoods in the winter. It is fairly robust and has grayish gills and a mild taste.

Tricholoma resplendens (Resplendent Tricholoma)

CAP 4-8 cm broad, convex to plane; surface viscid when moist, smooth, white or whitish, discoloring slightly brownish in age, especially toward center. Flesh firm, white, odor mild. **GILLS** notched, white, fairly close. **STALK** to 7.5 cm long, equal or narrowed at base, white, smooth, dry. **VEIL** absent. **SPORE PRINT** white; spores 5-7.5 × 3.5-4.5 μm, elliptical, smooth.

HABITAT: Solitary or in small groups in mixed woods and under oak. Occasional, late fall and winter.

EDIBILITY: Edible, but not recommended. Similar species haven't been tested.

COMMENTS: The above description will suffice for several white Tricholomas whose identities are not firmly established. In *T. resplendens* the cap is slightly viscid. Species with a dry cap include: *T. album*, with a bitter taste; *T. olesonii*, robust, pure white, under oak; *T. columbetta*, a European species of questionable occurence here; and *T. venenata*, a poisonous species which discolors brownish in age. Any of these can be mistaken for *Hygrophorus* or *Russula*, but the gills are not waxy and the flesh is not dry or brittle.

Tricholoma saponaceum, mature specimens. The stalk is often stained pinkish-orange at base, a feature not evident in this photograph. The cap on the left is a lovely greenish-gray, but the color varies to brown.

Tricholoma saponaceum (Soapy Tricholoma)

CAP 5-18 cm broad, convex to plane or with uplifted margin; surface smooth, dry or slightly viscid when moist, color variable: olive-gray to greenish, sometimes with olive-brown or reddish-brown shades, sometimes cracking in age; margin often wavy. Flesh thick, white, odor somewhat soapy. **GILLS** adnate becoming notched, white or tinged slightly greenish, sometimes stained reddish, fairly well-spaced. **STALK** to 20 cm long, thick, equal or enlarged below or sometimes tapered, dry, smooth or with small scales; white, brownish-stained in age, flesh at base usually pinkish-orange. **VEIL** absent. **SPORE PRINT** white; spores 5.5-7 × 3.5-5 μm, elliptical, smooth.

HABITAT: Solitary or scattered in woods of all kinds, but particularly in tanoak-live oak-madrone. Common, late fall and winter.

EDIBILITY: Inedible; it has an insipid or soapy taste and may actually be mildly poisonous.

COMMENTS: The greenish-gray to brownish-olive cap, white gills, and pinkish-orange flesh in the base of the stalk are the fallible fieldmarks of this vexingly variable *Tricholoma*. The gills are rather soft, leading to possible confusion with *Hygrophorus*. The cap color is extremely variable but is most often grayish-green. In the Pacific Northwest and Rocky Mountains it is at times overwhelmingly abundant and as a result has been called a "mushroom weed." Here it is not as prevalent and its beauty is more readily appreciated. One especially attractive form has a bluish-green cap.

Tricholoma pessundatum

CAP 5-18 cm broad, convex to plane or with margin slightly uplifted; surface viscid when moist, reddish-brown to reddish-tan, often darker toward the center; sometimes finely scaly in age; margin often lobed, at first inrolled. Flesh thick, white, odor and taste strongly farinaceous or like linseed soil. **GILLS** white becoming reddish-spotted; typically notched or adnexed, sometimes nearly free in age, close. **STALK** to 10 cm long, stout, thick, smooth, solid; pallid above, reddish-brown below, equal or tapered at base. **VEIL** absent. **SPORE PRINT** white; spores 4-6 $\times$ 2.5-4 μm, ellipsoid, smooth.

HABITAT: Scattered to gregarious in live oak woods, late fall and winter. Sporadically common. I have seen large fruitings in December and January.

EDIBILITY: This common, viscid, red-brown *Tricholoma* is delicious stewed slowly with zucchini and served steaming hot on rice with chicken chow mein and white wine. Suffering from an acute attack of overconfidence, M. Henis and C. Cole tried it in this manner one winter evening in order to determine its edibility. They subsequently staggered through an all-night ordeal of nausea, vomiting, and diarrhea, in which

Tricholoma ustale (see *T. pessundatum*), mature specimens. Note the viscid brown cap, fleshy stem, and notched white gills.

not only the mushroom, but everything else was expelled.

It is probable, then, that this common, viscid, red-brown *Tricholoma* is poisonous, although a violent allergic reaction on the part of M. Henis and C. Cole cannot be ruled out entirely. It is suggested that those foolish enough to try it (or any other mushroom of unknown edibility) should do so in extremely small amounts—*without* the rice, chicken chow mein, and white wine, and by all means, regardless of one's nutritional needs, culinary quirks, or dietary deficiencies, *without* the zucchini.

COMMENTS: There are many Tricholomas with a viscid reddish-brown cap and notched, reddish-spotted gills. Whether ours is the true *T. pessundatum* or a very similar species is a problem best left to licensed tricholomatologists. *T. transmutans* is said to differ in its bitter-tasting cap cuticle; *T. ustale* is also similar but has a mild odor. I have found it several times in mixed woods. *T. albobrunneum* has a faintly farinaceous odor, cap minutely streaked with darker lines, and stem with small scales above. *T. populinum* grows in dense groups in sandy soil under poplar or cottonwood. None of these have the scaly stem or rudimentary veil characteristic of *T. aurantium* and *T. focale*. Until better known they are best avoided.

Tricholoma imbricatum

CAP 5-15 cm broad, convex to plane; surface dry, reddish-brown to cinnamon-brown or brown, with flattened fibrils becoming scaly toward the margin in age. Flesh thick, firm, white, odor and taste mild or faintly farinaceous. **GILLS** adnexed or notched, close, white becoming reddish-spotted. **STALK** up to 12 cm long, thick, solid, firm, dry, more or less equal, white, reddish-brown toward base, fibrillose. **VEIL** absent. **SPORE PRINT** white; spores 5-6.5 $\times$ 3.5-4 μm, elliptical, smooth.

HABITAT: Scattered to densely gregarious under pine, late fall through early spring, common.

EDIBILITY: Reportedly edible, but not recommended. As a rule brown-capped Tricholomas should be avoided (see comments on edibility of *T. pessundatum*!).

COMMENTS: This coarse, robust fungus is a prominent fungal feature of our pine forests. It differs from other red-brown Tricholomas in its

Tricholoma imbricatum. This hefty *Tricholoma* is common under pine. The notched white gills are sometimes reddish-stained in age. The dry cinnamon-brown cap becomes scalier as it ages. *T. "pessundatum"* (not illustrated) looks similar but has a viscid cap.

dry rather than viscid cap. There is no rudimentary veil as in *T. aurantium* and *T. focale.* The cap is not as scaly as in *T. vaccinum*, nor is the margin woolly. It might be mistaken for a *Russula*, but the gills are deeply notched, the stalk is rather tough and not noticeably brittle, and the spores are not amyloid. *Leucopaxillus amarus* also has a brown cap, but is very bitter and has amyloid spores.

Tricholoma focale

CAP 2.5-7.5 cm broad, bell-shaped becoming convex to nearly plane; surface smooth, slightly viscid when moist, soon dry, bright brick-red to cinnamon, somewhat scaly or torn up in age, margin often hung with veil remnants. Flesh thin, pinkish, odor pleasantly farinaceous (a cross between Pond's cold cream and raw peanuts). **GILLS** notched, close, pallid, soon tinged cap color. **STALK** to 15 cm long, rather slender, equal or with narrowed base, very fragile and soft, pallid above the veil, scaly-fibrillose below and colored like cap or paler. **VEIL** fibrillose, evanescent, forming an obscure zone on stalk or disappearing entirely. **SPORE PRINT** white; spores 3-4.5 μm, more or less round, smooth.

HABITAT: Solitary or scattered in mixed woods, fall and winter, not uncommon. I find it regularly under live oak and tanoak.

EDIBILITY: Unknown, and like myself, likely to remain so.

COMMENTS: The brick-red cap, evanescent veil, and fragile stem are the fieldmarks of this species. The stem will break at the slightest provocation and it's quite an accomplishment to transport it home in one piece. It is not nearly as robust or coarse as *T. aurantium* and does

Tricholoma focale. This poorly known species has an evanescent veil. The veil, upon breaking, leaves hairs on the stalk which are barely visible in this picture.

not have the unpleasant odor of that species. A similar species, *T. vaccinum*, has a dry, felty-scaly, reddish-brown cap with a woolly margin. It is associated primarily with conifers and is fairly common in northern California. Because of the veil *T. focale* was originally placed in *Armillaria.*

Tricholoma aurantium

CAP up to 10 cm broad; convex with an inrolled margin to nearly plane or slightly umbonate; surface viscid, smooth or with flattened fibrils or mealy scales (especially at the center); bright rusty-orange to orange-red or orange-brown (in one form deep green when young). Flesh white, thick, odor farinaceous or cucumberlike, disagreeable in age. **GILLS** adnate to adnexed or notched, occasionally almost free, close, white becoming spotted rusty-brown. **STALK** to 10 cm long, stout, thick, equal or enlarged or narrowed at base; white or pale yellow above the ring, belted with delicate rusty scales below. **VEIL** fibrillose, thin, soon disappearing or leaving an obscure hairy ring at stalk apex. **SPORE PRINT** white; spores 4-6 $\times$ 3-4 μm, broadly ellipsoid to nearly round, smooth.

HABITAT: Solitary or in groups in woods, late fall and winter, uncommon. A widely distributed species normally associated with conifers, but in our area more frequent with tanoak-madrone (just like *Armillaria zelleri* and *A. ponderosa*).

EDIBILITY: Inedible; perhaps poisonous.

COMMENTS: The belts of delicate scales on the stalk plus the viscid cap, rusty-spotted gills, and strong odor distingish this species. The cap color is more or less rusty-orange at maturity, but in the tanoak-madrone variety it is a striking deep green color when young. In this respect it resembles *Armillaria zelleri*, which has a persistent, membranous veil.

ARMILLARIA and ARMILLARIELLA

Medium-sized to large, fleshy fungi. CAP convex to plane. GILLS *attached*, edges typically entire. STALK central, *fleshy*. VEIL *present, persistent, usually forming a ring on stalk*. VOLVA *absent*. SPORE PRINT *white;* spores smooth, typically not amyloid.

ARMILLARIAS are robust, fleshy, terrestrial mushrooms with white spores and a more or less membranous veil that usually forms a distinct ring on the stem. There is no volva or warts on the cap as in *Amanita*; the gills are never free as in *Lepiota* and *Limacella*, nor are they serrated as in *Lentinus*, nor soft and waxy as in *Hygrophorus;* and the cap and stem are not covered with mealy granules as in *Cystoderma*. *Tricholoma* closely approaches *Armillaria* but as defined here does not include any species with a persistent veil.

The honey mushroom, *Armillariella mellea*, is superficially similar to *Armillaria*, but has a tough fibrous stalk and grows on wood, often in large clusters. It is listed under *Armillaria* in most books. A third genus, *Catathelasma*, is terrestrial like *Armillaria* but has a double veil, decurrent gills, and amyloid spores. Two large species are known from California but do not seem to occur in our area

Both *Armillaria* and *Armillariella* are safe to eat. The matsutake, *Armillaria ponderosa*, is a magnificent mushroom esteemed by the Japanese, while the honey mushroom, *Armillariella mellea*, is a popular and well-known favorite. Armillarias are strictly woodland fungi and are not particularly common, in contrast to *Armillariella*, which is cosmopolitan. It grows wherever there are trees and is almost as common in towns as in the woods. Neither genus is large. Four species are described here.

Key to Armillaria and Armillariella

1. Cap yellow to yellow-brown; stalk sheathed with cottony scales .... *Armillaria albolanaripes*, p. 170
1. Not as above 2

2. Growing on wood, usually in clusters .... *Armillariella mellea*, p. 171
2. Growing on ground 3

3. Cap brick red to cinnamon; veil fibrillose, usually evanescent; stalk fragile .... (see *Tricholoma focale*, p. 165)
3. Not as above; veil membranous, stalk not markedly fragile 4
4. Cap viscid, smooth, bright yellow-orange to rusty-orange to cinnamon or sometimes greenish .... *Armillaria zelleri*, below
4. Not as above 5
5. Taste bitter (sometimes latently); stalk tough, fibrous, typically longer than width of cap; cap usually with small hairs toward the center .... *Armillariella mellea*, p. 171
5. Not as above 6
6. Cap and/or stalk flushed reddish; flesh bruising reddish slowly (especially around worm holes); growing with oak (see *Amanita rubescens*, p. 239)
6. Not as above 7
7. Stalk tough, continuous with cap; odor mild or spicy-aromatic; medium-sized to very large 8
7. Stalk cleanly separable from cap, often rooting in ground; odor mild or chlorine-like; cap white to grayish .... (see *Amanita*, p. 225)
8. Odor spicy, aromatic; cap white or with brown to pinkish-brown fibrils .... *Armillaria ponderosa*, p. 169
8. Odor mild; cap smooth or cracked, cinnamon-buff to yellow-brown; tough .... *Catathelasma imperialis* (see *Armillaria ponderosa*, p. 169)

Armillaria zelleri (Zeller's Armillaria)

CAP 5-15 cm broad, convex then plane; surface viscid, bright orange, yellow-orange, or orange-brown, sometimes mottled with olive; margin at first hung with veil remnants. Flesh thick, white, bruising orange-brown, odor and taste farinaceous. **GILLS** at first white, soon spotted rusty orange-brown, close, adnate or notched. **STALK** to 12 cm long, tapering downward, dry, pallid with downy hairs above the ring, somewhat scaly with orange-brown stains below. **VEIL** white, membranous, forming a persistent, superior ring which usually collapses on the stalk. **SPORE PRINT** white; spores 4-5.5 × 3-4 μm, elliptical, smooth, not amyloid.

HABITAT: Scattered in humus in tanoak-madrone woods near Boulder Creek. Uncommon, fruiting in late fall and early winter. Elsewhere, like *A. ponderosa*, it is associated with conifers.

EDIBILITY: Edible according to some sources. I haven't tried it.

COMMENTS: The sticky bright orange to greenish-orange cap, attached gills, membranous veil, and white spores are diagnostic. It grows in the same habitats as *A. ponderosa* but is even less common. It

Armillaria zelleri, mature specimens. Note the prominent ring, attached gills, and *Tricholoma*-like stature. The viscid cap is convex when young and ranges in color from yellow-orange to orange or greenish-orange.

calls to mind *Tricholoma aurantium*, but that species has an evanescent veil. It can also be confused with *T. focale*, which has a redder cap, fibrillose veil, and fragile stem.

Armillaria ponderosa (American Matsutake)

CAP 7-40 cm broad or even larger, convex to plane; surface dry or slightly viscid, white, with flattened brown or pinkish-brown fibrils in age; margin at first inrolled, cottony from the veil. Flesh thick, tough, white, odor distinctly spicy-aromatic. **GILLS** white or creamy, spotted brownish in age, close, more or less notched. **STALK** to 24 cm long, 2-4 cm thick, solid, tough, equal or with a tapered base, smooth and white above the ring, usually scaly below with brownish stains. **VEIL** white, membranous, forming a prominent flaring or skirtlike ring. **SPORE PRINT** white; spores 5.5-7 × 4.5-5.5 μm, elliptical, smooth, not amyloid.

HABITAT: Solitary, scattered, or gregarious in mixed woods, Santa Cruz Mountains, late fall and winter, not common. I have seen three large fruitings—two in tanoak-madrone woods and one in a dense thicket of manzanita and stunted knobcone pine. It is interesting to note that both *A. ponderosa* and *A. zelleri* associate mostly with conifers to the north, but in our area cross over to tanoak, madrone, and manzanita.

Armillaria ponderosa, fairly young individuals. In age the ring in this delectable species is less prominent and the cap much broader. Its aromatic-spicy odor is very distinctive.

EDIBILITY: Edible and highly prized by the Japanese. In the Puget Sound area it is harvested commercially, going for as much as $20 a pound. It is tough, however, and does not appeal to everyone. Long, slow cooking is required. Large, *thin* slices cooked in a clear soup or broth assume a marvelous noodlelike quality.

COMMENTS: The unique spicy odor (a provocative compromise between red hots and dirty socks) is the hallmark of this magnificent mushroom. Its robust stature, white color, and prominent veil are also distinctive. From the top it looks like "just another *Russula*" (especially *R. brevipes*), but Russulas do not have a veil. Old specimens discolor brownish and look coarse and unappealing, but the young, white, cottony buttons are gorgeous. The matsutake of Japan, *A. (Tricholoma) matsutake (=A. caligata?)* has the same spicy odor and a darker cap. *A. (=Catathelasma) subcaligata*, with pinkish-brown fibrils and no odor, has been found in Santa Barbara. *Catathelasma imperialis* is a massive, hard-fleshed species with a smooth or cracked cinnamon-buff to dull yellow-brown cap, decurrent gills, and amyloid spores. I have seen it in New Mexico, Idaho, and northern California, but not here.

Armillaria albolanaripes (Sheathed Armillaria)

CAP 5-10 cm broad, convex to plane; surface moist or slightly viscid, bright yellow to golden-yellow with innate flattened cinnamon-brown scales or fibrils which darken in age. Flesh white or tinged yellowish, odor mild. **GILLS** usually notched, pallid when young but soon yellow.

Armillaria albolanaripes, mature specimens. The sheath of cottony scales on the stem and overall yellow color are characteristic.

STALK to 10 cm long, more or less equal, dry, white above the ring, sheathed with concentric zones of soft cottony scales below, the scales white at first, then yellow or yellow-brown. **VEIL** white, cottony, fragile, leaving a ragged superior ring and often remnants on the cap margin. **SPORE PRINT** white; spores 5-7 × 3-4.5 μm, elliptical, smooth, not amyloid.

HABITAT: Solitary or in small groups in woods and along paths. Occasional, fall and early winter. I find it once or twice every year. It was abundant at Yosemite in the spring of 1978.

EDIBILITY: Edible, but definitely not choice. I have tried it.

COMMENTS: This handsome mushroom is easily identified by its yellow-brown cap, creamy to yellow gills, and soft cottony scales on the stem. The veil is also a critical feature but does not always form a distinct ring. The scaly stem might be mistaken for a volva *(Amanita)*, but the gills are attached and there are no warts on the cap. *Amanita aspera* is similarly colored but has white gills.

Armillariella mellea (Honey Mushroom)

CAP to 15 cm broad (occasionally larger); convex or with a broad umbo, expanding slightly in age; surface viscid when moist, with scattered scales or erect hairs, especially toward center; color variable: yellow-brown, pinkish-brown, sometimes dark brown, honey-colored,

Armillariella mellea. This cluster of unexpanded specimens is growing on a stump. It fruits on practically any kind of tree and is regarded as a pest by many gardeners and landscapers. Note the tiny hairs on the cap. Another cluster is shown on p. 42.

etc. Flesh thick, white, brownish in old age, odor mild, taste acidic or latently bitter. **GILLS** adnate to slightly decurrent, sometimes notched; white to creamy or flesh color, often brownish-stained in old age. **STALK** to 20 cm long, very tough and fibrous, equal above, tapered below or with an enlarged base, dry, pallid above the ring, darker or yellowish below. **VEIL** membranous, white to yellowish-buff, forming a persistent superior ring, occasionally disappearing. **SPORE PRINT** white; spores 6-9.5 × 5-6 μm, elliptical, smooth, not amyloid.

HABITAT: In large clusters on stumps, logs, and living trees, or in groups (occasionally solitary) on ground, growing from roots or buried wood. Common, at times abundant, mostly in fall and winter. On both hardwoods and conifers. It is a serious parasite of timber and fruit trees but is more often saprophytic on dead wood. It is also called "shoe string root rot" because of the thick, black mycelial strands (rhizomorphs) that penetrate the roots (and/or heartwood) of the host, reducing them to a white, spongy pulp. When actively growing, these strands luminesce at night, giving the wood an eerie aura called "foxfire." Inhabitants of subarctic regions sometimes mark their trails with bits of glowing wood infected by this fungus.

EDIBILITY: Eminently edible. Use firm caps and discard the tough stalks. It is an abundant food source and an excellent substitute for the shiitake, *Lentinus edodes.* The bitter taste cooks out, but some forms are better than others. I happen to prefer the yellow-capped variety (see below); at least it's more attractive.

Armillariella mellea. Note the whitish gills attached to the stalk, presence of a ring, and hairs on the cap. Wavy gills are the result of environmental conditions. These specimens were found on the ground, presumably growing from buried wood. (Ralph Buchsbaum)

COMMENTS: There is very little that can or cannot be said about the honey mushroom. It is among the most variable and cosmopolitan of the fleshy fungi, and its innumerable guises will confound you time and time again. Especially variable are its color, shape, and manner of growth (one study recognized 14 different "species" in the *A. mellea* complex). There are several key, more or less constant features, however: the presence of a veil, the tough fibrous stalk, the scattered hairs on the cap, the bitter taste (when raw), the white spores (in any mature cluster the lower caps will be dusted white), and the habitat (often) on wood. There are at least two widespread variants: one has a yellow-brown or honey-colored cap and usually grows in clusters on hardwoods. The other, usually found with conifers, is pinkish-brown to sordid flesh color and grows either in clusters or scattered on the ground. Intermediate forms occur, however.

In view of its extreme variability, beginners should eat *only those growing in clusters on wood.* The poisonous *Galerina autumnalis* grows on wood and has a ring but is smaller, with a smooth cap, fragile stem, and brown spores. The name "Honey Mushroom" is a reference to its cap color, not its taste. *Armillaria mellea* is an older name for it.

CYSTODERMA

Small to medium-sized mostly terrestrial fungi. CAP dry, *with a coating of mealy granules.* GILLS pallid, *attached.* STALK central, not cleanly separable from cap; *lower portion sheathed with mealy granules or scales.* VEIL *present,* often forming a ring. VOLVA absent. SPORE PRINT white; spores smooth, sometimes amyloid.

THE principal feature of this genus is the layer of mealy or powdery granules that coats the cap and lower stem. A veil is always present and in several species forms a prominent ring. The Armillarias have a veil and attached gills but are larger and lack the granulose coating. *Cystoderma* closely mimics *Lepiota* but in the latter the gills are free and the stem cleanly separable from the cap. *Cystoderma* used to belong to *Lepiota* and is retained in the Lepiotaceae by some mycologists.

Cystoderma is a common fungal feature of coniferous forests in the Pacific Northwest, but is infrequently encountered here. Several species are very attractive but their edibility is unknown. Four are recorded from California. One is described here.

Cystoderma fallax

CAP 2.5-5 cm broad, convex to plane, usually with a conspicuous umbo; surface dry, granulose, cinnamon-brown to rusty orange-brown; margin at first hung with veil fragments. Flesh whitish or tinged cap color. **GILLS** adnexed to adnate, close, white to pale pinkish-buff. **STALK** to 7.5 cm long, slender, equal or enlarged below, smooth and pallid above the ring, sheathed with cinnamon-brown granules below. **VEIL** membranous, forming a large, delicate, persistent flaring ring. **SPORE PRINT** white; spores 3.5-4.5 × 3-3.5 μm, broadly ellipsoid, smooth, amyloid.

Cystoderma fallax. Note the umbonate cap, prominent ring, and dense coating of granules on the stalk and cap. It does not always grow in clusters like these.

HABITAT: Scattered to gregarious in mixed woods of oak and pine, and under conifers. Fall and winter, not common.

EDIBILITY: Unknown.

COMMENTS: One of the most attractive and delicately adorned of our woodland fungi, this *Cystoderma* is identified by its cinnamon cap, prominent ring, whitish gills attached to the stem, and granulose scales on the cap and stem. The illustration does not do it justice. Rain may wash the granules off the cap, but not the stem. Other Cystodermas reported from California include: *C. amianthinum*, with a yellowish-brown cap and stem, and *C. cinnabarinum*, with a striking cinnabar-red to reddish-orange cap and stem. Neither has the persistent, flaring ring characteristic of *C. fallax*.

MELANOLEUCA

Small to medium-sized *terrestrial* fungi. CAP *smooth, often umbonate and hygrophanous.* GILLS close, attached (usually notched), *usually white.* STALK *semi-cartilaginous,* rather slender, *stiff or rigid.* VEIL and VOLVA *absent.* SPORE PRINT *white.* Spores rough, amyloid; harpoon-shaped cystidia often present on gill edges.

THIS is a rather small group of unimposing white to gray or brown mushrooms with a stature intermediate between *Tricholoma* and *Collybia.* The stiff, semi-cartilaginous stem, frequently hygrophanous, broadly umbonate cap, amyloid spores, and preference for grass or open ground are the principal fieldmarks.

Melanoleucas grow almost anywhere, but are most often found on lawns or shaded areas in pastures. There are no reports of poisoning from this genus, but the North American species are not well known. One widespread species is depicted here.

Melanoleuca melaleuca

CAP up to 7 cm broad, convex to plane, often with a broad umbo; surface smooth, moist but not viscid, dark brown to smoky-brown, fading to pale gray in sunlight (or as it dries). Flesh thin, whitish, odor mild. **GILLS** attached (usually notched), white, close. **STALK** to 10 cm long, equal or with a slightly swollen base, rather slender, stiff, smooth, whitish with darker fibrils. **SPORE PRINT** white; spores 6-8 $\times$ 4-5 μm, ellipsoid, rough, amyloid. Harpoonlike cystidia abundant on gill edges.

Melanoleuca melaleuca, mature specimens. This variable species changes color markedly as it dries. Dark brown cap at right is fresh and moist, the one at left has begun to fade. Note how close together the gills are. It usually, but not always, grows in grass.

HABITAT: Scattered to gregarious in open places (lawns, pastures, roadsides), along trails, and in the woods. Common, fall through spring.

EDIBILITY: Edible. The caps are delicious fried in butter, but since it is not an easy mushroom to recognize, I hesitate to recommend it. Related species have not been tested.

COMMENTS: The above description has been broadened to include a number of confusing, closely related forms. All are characterized by their grayish-brown to pale gray cap, close white gills, rigid fibrillose stalk, and strongly amyloid warty spores. One large woodland variety has a dark brown cap that does not fade appreciably. Another, common in the winter and spring in grassy places, is smaller, frequently riddled with maggots, and fades drastically in color from dark grayish-brown to nearly white. Still another has larger spores (9-10 × 6 μm), adnate to slightly decurrent gills, and a grayish-white cap. *M. alboflavida* has a pale yellow-brown to buff or whitish cap and spores 7-10 μm long. *M. graminicola* is a brown-capped species common under conifers near melting snow. All of these are likely to be mistaken for a *Collybia* or small *Tricholoma*. *M. melaleuca* is also called *M. vulgaris*.

COLLYBIA and Relatives

Minute to medium-sized woodland fungi *that don't revive when moistened.* CAP *typically convex to plane at maturity; margin incurved when young.* GILLS *usually white or whitish, typically notched or narrowly attached,* occasionally free or adnate. STALK central, *cartilaginous* or fibrous, *usually slender.* VEIL and VOLVA absent. SPORE PRINT *white to pale buff.* Spores smooth, typically not amyloid.

THIS is a faceless and featureless group of white-spored little brown mushrooms with a cartilaginous stem and convex (occasionally conical) to plane cap. The margin of the cap is incurved when young, not straight as in *Mycena*. The gills are usually adnexed but in some cases are broadly attached, leading to confusion with *Clitocybe*. By definition dried specimens do not revive when moistened, but this distinction is not always clearcut. Some species, in fact, have been shuttled back and forth between *Marasmius* and *Collybia* because they revive *somewhat* when moistened. The stalk is usually thin and brittle; if thick it has a cartilaginous outer rind. In some species, such as *C. umbonata*, it roots deeply in the humus.

Collybias are among our most common woodland fungi. They are saprophytic on humus, wood, conifer cones, and decaying mushrooms. A few may be mycorrhizal. It is a difficult group from a taxonomic standpoint and has little to offer the mushroom-eater. Unless you are familiar with each species, the entire lot is best avoided. Five species are described here, including *Flammulina velutipes*, a mushroom formerly placed in *Collybia*. If your "Collybia" does not key out satisfactorily, check *Marasmius* and *Mycena*.

Key to Collybia and Relatives

1. Growing on other mushrooms (or blackened remains of mushrooms) .. .. *C. tuberosa*, p. 179
1. Not as above 2

2. Cap minute (generally 12 mm broad or less); growing on decaying cones or humus 3
2. Cap larger (generally 20 mm broad or more); on ground or wood 4

3. Gills free; veil present (but evanescent); growing in humus .... (see *Lepiota seminuda*, p. 267)
3. Gills usually attached; veil absent; usually on decaying cones .... *C. conigena* (see *C. tuberosa*, p. 179)

4. Stalk rooting deeply 5
4. Stalk not rooting deeply 6

5. Growing on ground, usually under redwood; cap yellow-brown to orange-brown to red-brown or tan, usually with a conic umbo .... *C. umbonata*, p. 181
5. Growing on or near wood; often clustered; cap buffy-brown to grayish, without a conic umbo .... (see *Mycena galericulata*, p. 199)

6. Cap pale gray to dark grayish-brown to grayish-black 7
6. Cap tan to yellow-brown, red-brown, brown, flesh color, white, etc. 11

7. Cap scaly or hairy-scaly, mouse-colored, fragile .... (see *Tricholoma terreum*, p. 159)
7. Not as above; cap more or less smooth 8

8. Growing on wood, usually clustered *C. familia* (see *C. dryophila*, p. 180)
8. Growing on ground 9

9. Cap often umbonate; stalk stiff; usually growing in grass but sometimes in woods; spores amyloid .... (see *Melanoleuca*, p. 175)
9. Not as above; in woods 10

10. Stalk smooth .... *C. asema* (see *C. dryophila*, p. 180)
10. Stalk covered with minute downy hairs .... *C. confluens*, p. 179

11. Growing in grass 12
11. Growing in woods or under trees 13

12. Gills well spaced; stalk thin and tough; cap often somewhat bell-shaped when young; spores not amyloid ..... (see *Marasmius oreades*, p. 185)
12. Gills very close; stalk stiff but not tough; cap never bell-shaped; spores amyloid .... (see *Melanoleuca*, p. 175)

13. Cap viscid; stalk velvety, brown .... *Flammulina velutipes*, p. 182
13. Cap not viscid; stalk not velvety 14

14. Cap brown to purple-brown or chocolate; gills soon tinted cap color .. .. (see *Marasmius fuscopurpureus*, p. 184)
14. Not as above; gills more or less white 15

15. Growing on or near wood in dense clusters .... *C. acervata* (see *C. dryophila*, p. 180)
15. Growing on ground 16

16. Stalk covered with minute downy hairs .... *C. confluens*, p. 179
16. Stalk smooth 17

17. Gill edges often eroded or toothed; cap usually conical when young .... *C. butyracea* (see *C. dryophila*, p. 180)
17. Gill edges entire; cap convex to plane .... *C. dryophila*, p. 180

Collybia tuberosa grows in small colonies on the blackened remains of old mushrooms. The black "stump" at the left is the stalk of the host.

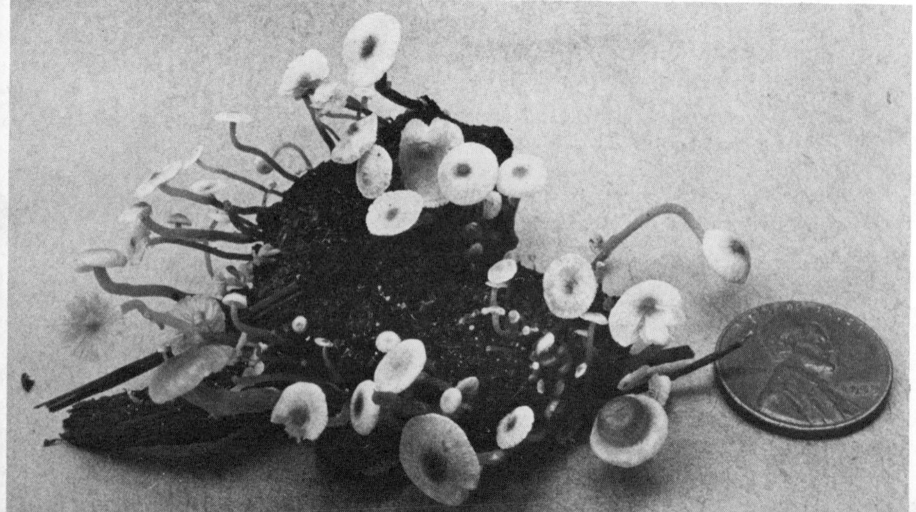

Collybia tuberosa

CAP minute, up to 1 cm broad, convex becoming plane; surface smooth, dry, whitish with a darker (yellowish or brownish) center. Flesh very thin, white. **GILLS** attached, close, white. **STALK** up to 2.5 cm long, very thin, equal, dry, minutely downy, white or tinted cap color, arising from a small reddish-brown to blackish "tuber" (sclerotium). **SPORE PRINT** white; spores 3-5.5 × 2-3 μm, elliptical, smooth.

HABITAT: In colonies on the blackened remains of old mushrooms, fall and winter, sometimes common.

EDIBILITY: Much too small to be of value.

COMMENTS: This dainty little *Collybia* is one of several species that colonize decayed mushrooms. The host mushrom may be so deteriorated, however, that it is unrecognizable. The sclerotia from which the fruiting bodies arise are small and difficult to locate. Also found on decayed mushrooms are *C. cirrhata (=C. cookei)*, with a yellow sclerotium (if present), and *C. racemosa*, an odd species with a grayish cap, black sclerotium, and small stubby branches diverging from the stem. Several minute species resembling *C. tuberosa* grow only on buried cones, including: *C. conigena (=Baeospora myosura)*, with a pinkish-cinnamon cap and amyloid spores; and *C. conigenoides (=Strobilurus kemptonae)*, with a tan to tawny cap and non-amyloid spores.

Finally, there is *Asterophora (=Nyctalis)*, an outlandish oddball that produces thick-walled brownish asexual spores that develop on hyphae instead of basidia. It is parasitic on other mushrooms, particularly *Lactarius* and *Russula*. There are two species, both rare: *A. parasitica*, with a grayish cap and adnate gills; and *A. lycoperdoides*, with gills absent or poorly formed and a round cap powdered by spores.

Collybia confluens

CAP 2-5 cm broad, convex to plane or slightly umbonate, the margin sometimes wavy or uplifted; surface smooth, hygrophanous, reddish-brown when moist, becoming watery tan to grayish-flesh color or even whitish as it dries. Flesh thin, rather tough, white. **GILLS** close, whitish, narrow, free or narrowly attached. **STALK** 5-10 cm long, slender, equal, hollow, tough, sometimes flattened or grooved, usually darker than cap (pinkish to reddish-brown under a coating of minute downy white hairs); white mycelium often at base and permeating surroundings. **SPORE PRINT** white; spores 4-7 × 3-4 μm, elliptical, smooth.

HABITAT: In groups or tufts on ground among fallen leaves or needles, fall and winter. Uncommon, but see comments below.

EDIBILITY: Edible, but similar species have not been tested.

COMMENTS: The white pubescence on the stalk separates this species from *C. dryophila.* It shrivels up in dry weather and revives somewhat when moistened, leading some mycologists to place it in *Marasmius.* A similar, unidentified species with attached gills is very common in the redwood-tanoak-madrone forests of the Santa Cruz Mountains. It sometimes rivals *C. dryophila* for abundance, but appears later in the season. Like *C. confluens,* it has minute hairs on the stem. A third pubescent species, *C. hariolorum,* has a sharp unpleasant odor when crushed.

Collybia dryophila (Oak-Loving Collybia)

CAP 2-5 cm broad, broadly convex with an incurved margin, becoming plane or with uplifted margin, sometimes slightly umbonate; surface smooth, hygrophanous, reddish-brown when young and moist, fading to tan or yellow-brown as it dries; margin often wavy. Flesh thin, white, odor pleasant. **GILLS** close, usually notched or adnexed, white, edges entire. **STALK** to 7.5 cm long, slender, equal or with a swollen base; smooth, hollow, rather tough, pale cream to cap color, white mycelium often visible in surrounding humus. **SPORE PRINT** white; spores 5-7 × 3-3.5 μm, ellipsoid, smooth.

HABITAT: Gregarious in woods, usually in arcs or rings. Abundant after the first fall rains, occasional in winter, spring, and even summer. As its name implies (*dryophila* means "oak-loving"), it prefers oak, but is also abundant under pine.

EDIBILITY: Edible, but some people are apparently sensitive to it. Only the caps are tender enough to be used. It is a proficient concentrator of mercury. Mercury is a cumulative poison, however, so occasional consumption of *C. dryophila* does not pose a threat.

COMMENTS: The appearance of *C. dryophila* in large fairy rings under oaks is a sure sign that the fall mushroom season is under way. The white gills separate it from *Laccaria laccata.* Since it likes to grow in

Collybia dryophila. This abundant little brown mushroom has a convex to depressed cap, whitish gills and spores, and usually grows in circles, groups, or small clusters.

rings, it is sometimes mistaken for the fairy ring mushroom, *Marasmius oreades.* The gills are crowded, however, the habitat is quite different, and shrivelled individuals do not revive when moistened.

The buttery collybia, *C. butyracea,* is a closely related edible species found mostly with conifers. The cap is dark reddish-brown when moist, fading to dingy pinkish-buff, and often has a pronounced umbo. The surface of the cap has a buttery feel, the gills have eroded edges and the spore print is pale buff. I have seen it in profusion under pine in late winter but its occurrence is unpredictable. *C. asema* has a similar stature but is grayish, as are several *Lyophyllum* species. Common farther north are two species which grow in large, tight clusters or fused bundles on or near rotting conifers: *C. acervata,* with a dark reddish-brown to flesh colored cap and stem; and *C. familia* (now placed in *Clitocybula*), with a gray to blackish cap and amyloid spores.

Collybia umbonata (Rooting Collybia)

CAP 2.5-15 cm broad, at first conical or bell-shaped with a pronounced umbo, expanding in age but usually retaining the umbo; surface smooth, dry, chestnut-brown to warm orange-brown, tan, or yellow-brown; margin at first incurved. Flesh thin, whitish or tinged cap color. **GILLS** typically notched, close, white to yellowish or tinged cap color. **STALK** 10-50 cm long or longer, most of it underground in the form of a long, tapered "tap root"; equal above the ground, smooth, twisted-striate, usually paler than cap (or yellowish-brown), rather tough and fibrous. **SPORE PRINT** white; spores 6-8 × 4-5 μm, ellipsoid, smooth.

HABITAT: Solitary or in groups near or under redwood; restricted to coastal California, fall and winter, very common.

EDIBILITY: Not firmly established. However, if it were poisonous we would probably know by now. I've sampled it without ill effects.

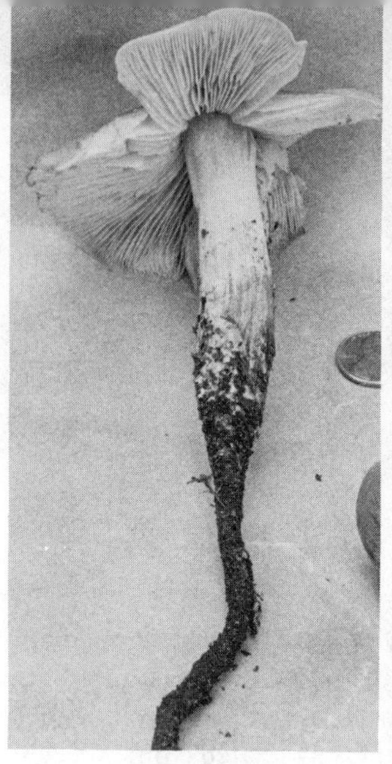

Collybia umbonata. **Left:** The long "tap root" is the outstanding feature of this redwood lover. **Right:** The cap is usually conical when young, umbonate in age.

COMMENTS: Anchored by its long "tap root", this distinctive species, like a dandelion, resists being uprooted. The rooting stem, pallid gills, and umbonate cap set it apart. The "tap root" is brittle, however, and will break off unless dug up carefully. The spores are amyloid according to Smith, an unusual feature for a *Collybia.* There are several other rooting species, including *C. hygrophoroides*, with a dry rufous to dull tan cap, occurring under hardwoods, and *C. radicata*, with a viscid grayish-brown cap. All of these are separated from the genus *Phaeocollybia* (which also has a "tap root") by their white spores.

Flammulina velutipes (Velvet Foot)

CAP 2-7 cm broad, convex becoming plane; surface smooth, slimy or viscid when moist, orange to reddish-brown to yellow-brown at the center, yellower toward the margin, fading in dry weather. Flesh thin, white to yellowish. **GILLS** cream color to pale yellow, attached. **STALK** to 7.5 cm long, slender, tough, often curved, sometimes slightly off-center; yellowish above, rich dark brown below and velvety from a coating of tiny hairs. **SPORE PRINT** white; spores 6.5-10 × 3-4 μm, elliptical, smooth, not amyloid. Cystidia present on gills.

HABITAT: In clusters on hardwood stumps and buried wood, fall through spring, fruiting mostly in cold weather; occasional. Its favorite hosts are bush lupine (along the coast), willow, and poplar.

EDIBILITY: Edible. The slimy skin should be removed. An exotic form called the snow puff mushroom ("Enoki-dake") is cultivated on a commercial basis. It looks something like a bean sprout—small and white with a long, smooth (not velvety!) stem and negligible cap.

COMMENTS: The smooth sticky yellow-brown cap, dark brown velvety stem, white spores, absence of a veil, and clustered growth habit typify this species. It originally belonged to *Collybia* but was divorced from that genus due to the viscid cap and prominent cystidia. In regions where it snows it is an important edible species because it fruits in very cold weather when other fungi are scarce—even in the middle of winter! In our balmy climate its season coincides with that of other mushrooms, so it is not as often collected.

MARASMIUS

Small to minute fungi that *shrivel up in dry weather and revive when moistened,* continuing to shed spores. CAP usually convex to plane, sometimes bell-shaped; not viscid. GILLS free or attached but rarely decurrent, usually pallid and well spaced. STALK *thin, tough, cartilaginous or wiry,* usually central. VEIL and VOLVA absent. SPORE PRINT *white.* Spores smooth, not amyloid.

THE trademark of *Marasmius* is its astonishing ability to revive when moistened. If dried-up specimens are placed in a bowl of water, they will quickly swell up, magically reassuming their original shape and dimensions. Though this characteristic is not always clearcut, it forms the basis for separating *Marasmius* from *Collybia, Mycena,* and all the other white-spored mushrooms with cartilaginous stems.

Marasmius can usually be told in the field by its tough or membranous texture and wiry, tubular, or polished stem. *Xeromphalina* is similar but has decurrent yellow-orange gills and amyloid spores.

Marasmius is a very large and complex genus centered in the tropics. Nevertheless, there are many temperate species and California is blessed with a significant number of them. They are saprophytic on sticks, leaves, grass, and other organic matter, are common but inconspicuous.

Most are too tiny to eat. Two exceptional exceptions are the fabulous fairy ring mushroom, *M. oreades* (forgive my excessive use of superlatives, but it is one of the very best of all mushrooms!), and the garlic mushroom, *M. scorodonius.* Though not as colorful as *Mycena* or *Hygrophorus,* many species are exquisitely built, particularly *M. plicatulus, M. candidus,* and *M. oreades.* Six common species are described here. If your "Marasmius" does not key out convincingly, check *Collybia.*

Key to Marasmius

1. Odor distinctly garliclike or onionlike .... *M. scorodonius*, p. 186
1. Not as above 2
2. Growing in grass (often in circles or arcs); common *M. oreades*, p. 185
2. Growing in woods or under trees 3
3. Small, white (reddish-stained in old age), gills few and far between; growing on wood, sticks .... *M. candidus*, p. 188
3. Not as above 4
4. Stalk hairlike, black, less than 1 mm thick; cap less than 14 mm broad . ... *M. androsaceus*, p. 188
4. Not as above; stalk not hairlike 5
5. Cap bell-shaped to conical, expanding somewhat, wine-red to bay-brown; stalk rigid, polished, brittle, tubular, reddish to black .... *M. plicatulus*, p. 189
5. Not as above; cap convex to plane 6
6. Cap brown to purplish-chocolate; gills soon tinted cap color .... *M. fuscopurpureus*, below
6. Cap brown or paler; gills white or whitish .... (see *Collybia*, p. 176)

Marasmius fuscopurpureus (Chocolate Marasmius)

CAP to 4 cm broad or slightly larger; convex becoming plane or slightly depressed in the center; surface dark reddish-brown, purple-brown, or chocolate when fresh, fading to tan when dry, usually radially wrinkled or finely striate. Flesh whitish or cap color, thin, reviving somewhat, odor mild. **GILLS** attached (usually notched), pallid or pale pinkish-tan becoming more or less cap color, then dusted with spores. **STALK** up to 7 cm long, thin, tough, equal, dry, same color as cap or darker, often curved at the litter-binding base; smooth or finely pubescent above, covered with minute grayish hairs below. **SPORE PRINT** white; spores 6-8 × 3-4 μm, narrowly ovoid, smooth.

HABITAT: Densely gregarious or clustered on ground in woods, under trees, along paths and roads. Common to abundant, early fall through spring.

EDIBILITY: Unknown.

COMMENTS: This exceedingly common *Marasmius* forms thick carpets of tiny parasols in leaf litter and debris, especially where the ground has been disturbed. Like most little brown mushrooms, it blends into its surroundings. The reddish-brown to chocolate colored convex to plane cap, white spores, and tendency to grow in dense

Marasmius fuscopurpureus. This ubiquitous little brown mushroom does not always grow in clusters like these, but it almost always occurs in large numbers.

groups are the principal fieldmarks. The cap is never bell-shaped as in *Mycena.* It does not revive as readily as other *Marasmius* species, causing some mycologists to place it in *Collybia.* Other species with a finely hairy or velvety stem include: *M. varicosus*, with dark rusty-brown hairs on the stem, and *M. peronatus*, slightly larger and paler, with an acrid or peppery taste.

Marasmius oreades (Fairy Ring Mushroom)

CAP up to 5 cm broad (usually 2-3 cm); at first bell-shaped or umbonate with a slightly incurved margin, becoming convex or plane but often retaining an obtuse umbo, the margin sometimes uplifted in age; surface smooth, dry, color variable: reddish-tan to light brown, tan, buff, or even white; margin faintly striate when moist. Flesh tough, pliant, pallid, reviving when moistened, odor agreeable. **GILLS** adnate to free, fairly well-spaced, broad, white to pale tan, sometimes discoloring brownish in old age. **STALK** 2.5-7.5 cm long, thin, equal or tapering downward, tough, hollow or stuffed with a pith, smooth, same color as cap or paler (whitish). **SPORE PRINT** white; spores 7-9 × 4-5.5 μm, ovate to somewhat irregular, smooth, apiculate.

HABITAT: Gregarious in grass, usually in arcs or rings. Very common in lawns, parks, baseball fields, etc., rarely in pastures. Found year-round, but most abundant in the summer (on watered lawns) and fall. Several crops are produced each year, but its presence can be detected even when it isn't fruiting: just look for "fairy rings" (patches of brown grass rimmed by a zone of lush, deeper green grass). The living mycelium on the periphery of the ring stimulates the grass to grow, while the dried-up mycelial matter within the circle inhibits growth.

Marasmius oreades. The umbonate cap at maturity and well-spaced whitish gills mark this delicious lawn "pest." The specimens in front are immature. When stored in a closed container this species develops a cyanide odor. A large fairy ring is shown on p. 7.

EDIBILITY: Delectably delicious—one of the few little brown mushrooms worth learning. What it lacks in substance it more than makes up for in abundance. Discard the tough stems and use the caps whole. It is exceptionally versatile, superb in just about anything—omelets, soups, sauces, even cookies; or simply saute in butter and serve on toast. What's more, it dries easily, doesn't decay readily, and is rarely infested by maggots. Don't pass up shrivelled, sun-dried specimens—they are easily resurrected or can be stored in an airtight jar for later use.

COMMENTS: At first glance this seems like yet another undistinguished, nondescript little brown mushroom. However, a closer look reveals that it is really quite attractive, with a lean, clean subtle symmetry all its own. Many little brown mushrooms grow on lawns, but the fairy ring mushroom can be distinguished by the following features: (1) cap obtusely umbonate in many specimens (2) white spores (the grass beneath mature caps is often dusted with white spore powder) (3) broad (deep) white to buff gills which are fairly well spaced and *never* decurrent (4) thin, *tough* stem (5) habitat in grass (6) the ability to revive dramatically when moistened. Be especially careful not to confuse it with the poisonous *Clitocybe dealbata* and *C. rivulosa*, which are white-spored and grow in grass, but have thin, crowded, adnate to decurrent gills and a convex to plane (*not* umbonate) cap.

Marasmius scorodonius (Garlic Mushroom)

CAP up to 1 cm broad, convex then plane; surface smooth or wrinkled in age, dry, reddish-tan to brown, fading as it dries to pale buff. Flesh thin, with a strong garlic odor and taste, reviving when moistened.

Marasmius scorodonius. The garlic odor and taste separate this species from the dozens of other little brown mushrooms. The cap is convex to plane, never conical as in *Mycena.* Notice its growth on old tanoak leaves.

GILLS white to creamy-buff, narrow, attached. **STALK** up to 4 cm long, very thin, equal or tapering downward, tubular, tough, smooth, brown to dark reddish-brown, the apex paler and the base blackish. **SPORE PRINT** white; spores 6-9 × 3-4.5 μm, ellipsoid, apiculate, smooth.

HABITAT: Gregarious or scattered on leaves, twigs, stems, and debris, mostly on tanoak leaves. Common, fall and early winter.

EDIBILITY: Edible. It makes up for its small size by fruiting in large numbers, and can be used as a substitute for garlic.

COMMENTS: True to its name, the garlic mushroom smells and tastes like garlic. In fact, it is often smelled before it is seen. Aside from the odor, there is little to separate it from other little brown mushrooms. The above description will actually suffice for a complex of closely related species with a garlic odor. The preference of our variety for tanoak leaves suggests it is not bonafide *M. scorodonius*, but something very similar. However, I gladly leave such exacting distinctions to future generations of meticulous marasmiologists. *M. prasiosmus* is a slightly larger species with a garlic odor and stem clothed with fine white hairs. *M. alliaceus* has a long black stem and garlic odor. Both grow on dead leaves. *M. foetidus* is a small brownish wood-inhabiting species with a strong, unpleasant odor.

Marasmius androsaceus (Horsehair Fungus)

CAP minute, less than 14 mm broad; convex soon expanding to plane with a depressed center; surface dry, radially wrinkled or striate, reddish-brown, fading in age. Flesh very thin, pliant, reviving when moistened; odor mild. **GILLS** well-spaced, flesh color or cap color, typically adnate. **STALK** up to 7 cm long, very thin (less than 1 mm), wiry or hairlike, tough, smooth, shining black, equal. **SPORE PRINT** white; spores 6-9 × 2.5-4 μm, pip-shaped, smooth.

HABITAT: Scattered on fallen needles, twigs, leaves, etc., in woods. Common but easily overlooked, fall through early spring.

EDIBILITY: Unknown. Hardly worth the trouble to find out.

COMMENTS: There are several minute *Marasmius* species with a dark hairlike stem. They are barely visible when shrivelled up, but rain revives them. *M. androsaceus* is distinguished by its thin, tough black stem and reddish-brown to flesh colored cap. The mycelium sometimes produces stems on which caps never form! *M. perforans* is similar but has a velvety stem and unpleasant odor when crushed. *Crinipellis piceae* is a minute species with dextrinoid hairs on the cap. It grows on rotting conifer logs and needles. There are also several minute Collybias that do not revive when moistened. All of these differ from *Mycena* by their convex to plane or umbilicate (never bell-shaped or conical) cap.

Marasmius candidus (Candid Marasmius)

CAP up to 2.5 cm broad, convex to broadly convex or even plane; surface dry, shining white or translucent white, deep pinkish- or reddish-stained in old age; striate or grooved at maturity. Flesh very thin, pliant, soft, reviving when moistened, odor mild. **GILLS** few and far between, usually interspersed with smaller gills or veins; adnate to slightly decurrent, white like the cap becoming reddish-stained in old age. **STALK** less than 2.5 cm long, rather short, thin, central or off-center (but not lateral), tough, smooth, often curved, equal or tapering downward, white, darkening gradually to brownish-black from the base upward. **SPORE PRINT** white; spores 10-13 × 5-6 μm, tear-shaped, smooth.

HABITAT: In groups or rows on dead sticks, branches, and berry canes. Common to abundant in fall and early winter, especially along creeks overgrown with brambles.

Marasmius candidus has widely separated gills and grows on sticks and berry canes. These specimens are white but will develop reddish stains in age.

EDIBILITY: Utterly inconsequential.

COMMENTS: This dainty mushroom is not easy to overlook—the shining white cap stands out brilliantly in the forest gloom. The exceedingly distant gills are the outstanding feature. The stem, which may be off-center, is tough and darkens at maturity. The entire fruiting body develops sordid pinkish or vinaceous tones as it ages, leading one to falsely (but reasonably) assume that the spores are pink. It has recently been given another name, *M. magnisporus.*

Marasmius plicatulus (Frosted Marasmius)

CAP to 4 cm broad, obtusely conical to bell-shaped, expanding somewhat in age; surface dry, with a velvety or frosted appearance, furrowed or wrinkled in age or upon drying: bay-brown to dark wine-red or maroon, often with a hoary sheen. Flesh thin, tough, pliant, pallid. **GILLS** attached to nearly free, widely-spaced, white to pinkish or tinted cap color, broad. **STALK** up to 13 cm long, very thin and tough, rigid, very brittle, wiry or tubular, smooth, polished or shiny, equal, pallid to pinkish above, reddish-black to deep chestnut below; white mycelium at base. **SPORE PRINT** white; spores 11-15 × 5-6.5 μm, ovoid to inequilateral, smooth.

HABITAT: Scattered to gregarious among leaves, needles, and debris in woods and brush. Common, late fall and winter. It was abundant in the winter of 1977-78 in brambles under oak and pine. Endemic to the west coast.

EDIBILITY: Like myself, too tough and thin to be edible.

COMMENTS: One of the most exquisite of all mushrooms. The frosted wine-red to bay-brown cap, widely-spaced pallid gills, and long shining reddish-black stalk are distinctive. The stalk is so brittle that the

Marasmius plicatulus is one of our most beautiful mushrooms. Note the well-spaced gills and long, slender, shiny stem. The cap is bay-brown to dark red, the stalk reddish-black.

entire mushroom must be dug up to keep it intact. The bell-shaped cap may lead to confusion with *Mycena*, but the tough, polished stem is characteristic of *Marasmius*. I have seen specimens preserved nicely in cubes of plastic resin. A related and equally exquisite species, *M. siccus*, is pictured in many mushroom books.

OMPHALINA and XEROMPHALINA

Small to minute, mostly brightly colored fungi. CAP *at maturity usually plane or depressed,* never conical; margin at first incurved. GILLS *usually yellow or orange, typically decurrent.* STALK central, *thin, cartilaginous,* tough (*Xeromphalina*). VEIL and VOLVA absent. SPORE PRINT *white to pale yellow.* Spores smooth, amyloid *(Xeromphalina),* not amyloid *(Omphalina).*

THESE are dainty, brightly colored mushrooms with decurrent gills and a cartilaginous stem. They were originally grouped together in the obsolete genus *Omphalia*, but *Xeromphalina* was created for the species with a tougher texture, ability to revive somewhat when moistened, and amyloid spores.

Omphalina is interesting from a botanical standpoint because several species grow only with lichens. It is now thought that the mushrooms are the fruiting bodies of the fungal component of the lichen (a lichen is a symbiotic relationship between an alga and a fungus). Other Omphalinas are usually found in moss, grass, or on soggy logs or charred ground. They are easily confused with Mycenas (which usually have a conical or bell-shaped cap), while even experts cannot agree on the distinctions between *Omphalina* and the small, slender Clitocybes.

Xeromphalina is found on logs and in humus. The tough stem and ability to revive are reminiscent of *Marasmius*, but the decurrent yellow-orange gills and amyloid spores are distinct.

None of the mushrooms in this group are large enough to eat. One member of each genus is depicted here. If your mushroom does not key out convincingly, check *Mycena.*

Key to Omphalina and Xeromphalina

1. Stalk tough, lower portion dark brown to reddish-brown 2
1. Stalk fragile, not as above .... *Omphalina ericetorum*, p. 192

2. Growing on wood .... *Xeromphalina campanella*, below
2. Growing on ground .... *X. cauticinalis* (see *X. campanella*, below)

Xeromphalina campanella

CAP less than 2.5 cm broad, bell-shaped or convex becoming broadly convex with a depressed center; surface smooth, not viscid, yellow-brown to orange-brown or rusty; margin striate when moist. Flesh thin, pliant, yellowish, reviving when moistened. **GILLS** yellowish to dull orange, fairly well spaced, decurrent with veins between. **STALK** up to 5 cm long, very thin, equal, pliant, tough, smooth, polished, yellowish above, brown to reddish-brown below; usually curved, base with tawny hairs. **SPORE PRINT** white to pale buff; spores 5-9 × 3-4 μm, elliptical, smooth, amyloid.

Xeromphalina campanella. A common yellow-orange inhabitant of decaying conifer wood. Note the decurrent gills, small size, and dark stalk.

HABITAT: In groups or dense clusters on rotting conifer logs and stumps. Common, fall and winter.

EDIBILITY: A miniscule morsel, much too small to be of value.

COMMENTS: The yellow-orange decurrent gills, thin polished stem, small size, and growth on conifer logs typify this dainty mushroom. It can serve as an indicator of coniferous wood. It might be mistaken for a *Mycena*, but the shape of the mature cap is quite different. It also resembles *Galerina autumnalis* but lacks a veil and has whitish spores. A related species, *X. cauticinalis*, is very common on conifer needles and twigs, especially redwood. It has a convex to plane yellowish cap, pale yellow gills, and a thin tough straight stem which is tawny above and dark brown below. It fruits in late fall and winter, often in great numbers, but never on stumps or logs. *X. fulvipes* is larger, with a tough, dry stem covered with velvety brown hairs. It occurs on wood and needles of conifers but is not common.

Omphalina ericetorum

CAP up to 2.5 cm broad, occasionally larger; at first plane with an incurved margin, becoming deeply depressed or funnel-shaped; surface smooth, not viscid, dull cinnamon to light brown to yellowish or straw color, fading in age; margin striate, often wavy. Flesh very thin, pliant, same color as cap. **GILLS** decurrent, well spaced, sometimes veined, pale yellowish. **STALK** to 4 cm long, very thin, equal, often curved, smooth, pale reddish-brown above, yellow-brown to light brown below, pale yellowish in old age. **SPORE PRINT** white or yellowish; spores 7-9 × 4-6 μm, elliptical, smooth, not amyloid.

HABITAT: In groups on old mossy or lichen-covered conifer logs, associated with the lichen *Botrydina vulgaris*. Widely distributed in temperate regions, but rare in our area.

EDIBILITY: Much too small to be of value.

COMMENTS: The small size, depressed cap, thin cartilaginous stem, decurrent gills, and habitat are distinctive. The gills may appear somewhat waxy (as in *Hygrophorus*), but the latter doesn't grow on wood. *O. umbellifera* is a synonym. There are several similar species, including an unidentified creamy to pinkish variety that is common in our area in grassy places, and *O. maura*, grayish-brown, found on burnt ground.

MYCENA

Small to minute saprophytic fungi that *do not revive when moistened.* CAP often translucent, *typically conical to bell-shaped when young*, often expanding in age; *margin usually straight*, rarely incurved. GILLS usually attached. STALK central, *thin, fragile or cartilaginous*, hollow. VEIL and VOLVA absent. SPORE PRINT *white*. Spores smooth, amyloid or not amyloid. Cystidia usually present on gills.

THIS is a very large group of very small mushrooms with a cartilaginous stem and bell-shaped to conical cap when young. The gills are not waxy as in *Hygrophorus*. The fruiting body does not revive when moistened as in *Marasmius*, and is not particularly tough. *Collybia* and *Omphalina* are similar but usually have a convex to plane or umbilicate cap. Other small mushrooms with conical to bell-shaped caps (*Coprinus, Galerina, Nolanea*, etc.) do not have white spores.

In sheer numbers Mycenas are more abundant than any other mushrooms. Yet because of their diminutive dimensions, most people are oblivious to their presence. In the wake of heavy rains they fruit in untold quantity in the woods, especially on needle beds under conifers, where they form thick carpets of delicate domes. They are strictly saprophytic—on logs, stumps, sticks, leaves, soil, and humus. They turn up occasionally in lawns, gardens, and flower pots, but do *not* grow in dung like *Coprinus* and *Bolbitius*.

The most common forms are gray or brown, but a few (such as *M. acicula*) are brightly colored. A 1947 monograph lists 218 North American species, but dozens more have been discovered since. The overwhelming majority cannot be differentiated without a microscope (some Mycenas are so small they can barely be seen with the naked eye!). The size and shape of sterile cells (cystidia) on the gills plays a crucial role in identification. However, *Mycena* can be divided into manageable groups based on gross features such as size, color, odor, habitat, and viscidity. In addition, some species exude a latex (juice) when the base of the stem is broken and squeezed. *Lactarius* species also possess a latex but are much larger and fleshier, with thicker stems.

In every mixed bag of individuals I take mushroom hunting, there's always one or two with a keen eye for detail. In the normal course of events, I begin with a brief spiel about the marvels of the mushroom world, before dispatching the group to rush about madly in search of the elusive 25-lb. *Boletus edulis* (trampling myriad Mycenas with every step), while I make a sly beeline for my secret *Boletus* patch. These one or two keen-eyed individuals, however, are content to remain where they are, meticulously examining every leaf, twig, and cone, and uncovering in the process not only a multitude of marvelously minute Mycenas, but an astonishing assortment of other clandestine creations—centipedes, spiders, snakes, slugs, salamanders, etc.

As I am rather small myself, I harbor a profound respect for these exceptional individuals. In a society where people are taught from birth to think big, it is encouraging to find some who are still able to make the distinction between quality and quantity, who appreciate the fact that size alone is not a measure of intrinsic worth.

My lust satiated and my basket laden with *Boletus*, I return later to find these patient and perceptive souls sprawled out on their bellies in the same spot where I left them—for they consider the day well spent if they discover fifty Mycenas whose composite mass is no bigger than their thumb! Finding myself in good company, I bring out the cheese and (if I'm lucky) they bring out the wine, and we proceed to have an impromptu picnic, sharing our discoveries, then savoring the silence around us while awaiting the riotous return of the rest of the group.

For the benefit of these people I have included 14 Mycenas here, though they constitute only a small fraction of what can be found. They are much too small to eat, and some may actually be poisonous. However, they deserve to be better known. They are exquisite in their daintiness and are among the most attractive of fleshy (fleshless?) fungi. If your "Mycena" does not key out convincingly, check *Marasmius* and *Collybia.*

Key to Mycena

1. Stalk and flesh "bleeding" (exuding a dark red juice when broken or squeezed) 2
1. Not as above 3

2. Usually growing on ground .... *M. sanguinolenta*, p. 203
2. Usually growing on wood *M. haematopus* (see *M. sanguinolenta*, p. 203)

3. Stalk viscid or slimy when fresh 4
3. Stalk not viscid or slimy 6

4. Stalk yellow to greenish-gray .... *M. epipterygia*, p. 205
4. Stalk not colored as above 5

5. Cap dry .... *M. rorida*, p. 206
5. Cap viscid .... *M. vulgaris* (see *M. rorida*, p. 206)

6. Cap bright yellow to coral red .... *M. acicula*, p. 196
6. Not as above 7

7. Cap minute (up to 10 mm broad but usually much less); white to gray .... *M. capillaris*, p. 196
7. Larger; cap rarely white 8

8. Gills marginate (gill edges darker and differently colored than faces) 9
8. Gills not marginate 10

9. Growing on wood or cones .... *M. purpureofusca*, p. 202
9. Growing on ground .... *M. capillaripes*, p. 202

10. Growing on ground or in humus 11
10. Growing on wood 19

11. Some part of fruiting body (especially stalk) usually lilac-tinted; cap lilac to bluish-gray to nearly white; odor radishlike .... *M. pura*, p. 197
11. Not as above 12

12. Stalk rooting deeply in humus 13
12. Stalk not rooting deeply 14

13. Cap yellow-brown to orange-brown, reddish-brown, or tan, usually with a conic umbo .... (see *Collybia umbonata,* p. 181)
13. Cap buffy-brown to grayish, without conic umbo *M. galericulata*, p. 199

14. Cap white to tan to reddish-brown; stalk rather tough 15
14. Cap dark brown to grayish-brown or gray; stalk fragile 16

15. Growing in grass .... (see *Marasmius oreades*, p. 185)
15. Growing in woods .... (see *Collybia*, p. 176)

16. Odor alkaline .... *M. leptocephala* (see *M. alcalina*, p. 198)
16. Odor not alkaline 17

17. Base of stalk exuding a droplet of juice (usually milky) when squeezed (in fresh specimens only) .... *M. galopus*, p. 204
17. Not as above 18

18. Stalk with whitish fibrils or particles .... *M. scabripes*, p. 198
18. Stalk more or less smooth .... *M. stannea* (see *M. alcalina*, p. 198)

19. Odor alkaline .... *M. alcalina*, p. 198
19. Odor usually mild, not alkaline 20

20. Gills (and sometimes cap) soon spotted sordid pinkish to reddish .... *M. maculata*, p. 200
20. Not as above (but gills may be flushed evenly pinkish in age) 21

21. Stalk usually rooting; growing on hardwoods .. *M. galericulata*, p. 199
21. Stalk not rooting; on hardwoods or conifers 22

22. Usually growing in clusters 23
22. Usually solitary or scattered, not clustered .... *M. subcana*, p. 201

23. Cap brown to grayish .... *M. occidentalis* (see *M. subcana*, p. 201)
23. Cap reddish-brown fading to flesh color .... (see *Collybia acervata*, under *C. dryophila,* p. 180)

Mycena capillaris

CAP minute, 2-8 mm broad, bluntly conic or bell-shaped to convex, sometimes plane in age; surface smooth, gray soon fading to white, translucent-striate when moist. Flesh very thin, odor mild. **GILLS** adnate to nearly free, well-spaced, grayish then white. **STALK** to 6.5 cm long, very thin, equal, very fragile, smooth, pale gray to white. **SPORE PRINT** white; spores 8-10 × 4-5 μm, ellipsoid, smooth, not amyloid.

HABITAT: Solitary to gregarious on fallen leaves, especially oak and tanoak. Common in wet weather, often growing with *M. acicula.*

EDIBILITY: Unequivocally inconsequential.

COMMENTS: This miniscule *Mycena* is recognized by its whitish color and habit of growing on leaves—the mycelium does not normally penetrate the humus below. You can pick up a leaf and carry it home, mushroom and mycelium intact. There are dozens of other minute white Mycenas, including: *M. tenerrima*, even smaller and with a shorter stem, on bark, twigs, and woody debris; *M. delicatella*, cap 3-10 mm broad, gills close, gregarious on needles and twigs under conifers; *M. albidula*, with well-spaced decurrent gills, on leaves and bark of hardwoods; and *M. ignobilis*, growing in mud.

Mycena acicula

CAP minute, up to 10 mm broad, convex or bell-shaped; surface not viscid; coral-red when young, soon fading to bright orange-yellow or yellow. Flesh thin, yellow, odor mild. **GILLS** attached, yellowish-orange to whitish. **STALK** to 7 cm long, very thin (less than 1 mm), equal, brittle, orange-yellow to yellow. **SPORE PRINT** white; spores 9-11 × 3.5-4.5 μm, elongated-elliptical, smooth, not amyloid.

HABITAT: Scattered to gregarious on leaves and debris in woods, especially along streams. Common throughout the mushroom season. I have seen it in large numbers in streamside oak and blackberry thickets.

EDIBILITY: Unknown. A great many would be needed for a mouthful.

COMMENTS: This minute *Mycena* is a delight to behold. The deep pinkish-red to yellow cap is a startling contrast to the dim backdrop of decaying leaves and humus. Similar species include: *M. oregonensis*, with cap yellow from infancy; *M. strobilinoides*, cap larger (1-2 cm), red fading to yellow; and *M. adonis*, cap red fading to yellow, and stalk 1-2 mm thick. All three occur primarily in needle beds under conifers.

Mycena pura. These specimens are young and rather small. The cap is usually broader.

Mycena pura (Pure Mycena)

CAP 2-6.5 cm broad, obtusely umbonate or convex becoming broadly convex or plane, sometimes with uplifted margin; surface smooth, hygrophanous, translucent-striate when moist, color variable: blue-gray, blue-green with a yellowish center, pinkish, lavender, purplish- or lilac-gray, sometimes even whitish tinged purple or blue at the center. Flesh pallid, soft, odor radishlike. **GILLS** adnate or adnexed, usually tinged lilac or bluish, sometimes grayish, sometimes white, edges whitish. **STALK** to 10 cm long, slender, equal or enlarged somewhat below, hollow, smooth, colored more or less like cap or paler, sometimes whitish. **SPORE PRINT** white; spores 6-9 $\times$ 3-3.5 μm, ellipsoid, smooth, amyloid.

HABITAT: Solitary or scattered in humus; common, fall through early spring. I find it most often under Douglas-fir and oak.

EDIBILITY: Ostensibly edible. I haven't tried it.

COMMENTS: This is one of the largest Mycenas as well as one of the most beautiful. The color is exceedingly variable, but there is usually a trace of lilac somewhere on the fruiting body, especially the stem. The radishlike odor is another important fieldmark. The gill edges are not purple as in *M. purpureofusca*, and it is strictly terrestrial. It never grows in clusters and does not normally fruit in dense carpets either. I have seen fairly robust specimens which resembled the blewitt *(Lepista nuda). Inocybe geophylla* var. *lilacina* is similar but has brown spores.

Mycena scabripes. Note the whitish fibrils and particles on the stalk.

Mycena scabripes (Rough-Stemmed Mycena)

CAP up to 2.5 cm broad, obtusely conic becoming convex and then plane, usually with an umbo; surface moist but not viscid, blackish-brown at the center, olive-brown toward the margin, fading somewhat in age to olive-gray; not distinctly striate. Flesh brownish-gray, thin, odor mild. **GILLS** adnate to adnexed, free in age, pallid or tinged cap color, sometimes spotted reddish-brown in age. **STALK** to 7 cm long, slender, equal, hollow, same color as cap or paler, with a distinct coating of silky white to grayish fibrils and particles. **SPORE PRINT** white; spores 7-9 × 4-5 μm, ellipsoid, smooth, not amyloid.

HABITAT: Scattered to gregarious, sometimes in small clusters, in humus and debris, fall and winter, occasional. I have found it under redwood and oak.

EDIBILITY: Unknown.

COMMENTS: The distinguishing feature of this undistinguished *Mycena* is the presence of silky white fibrils and particles on the stem. The olive-brown, more or less umbonate cap is also distinctive.

Mycena alcalina (Alkaline Mycena)

CAP up to 4 cm broad, obtusely conical to convex with an obtuse umbo; surface smooth, dark brownish-black when young, gray to grayish-brown in age, striate. Flesh thin, fragile, pallid, odor faintly to strongly alkaline. **GILLS** rather close, adnate to slightly decurrent, whitish to gray, sometimes stained reddish-brown in age. **STALK** to 10 cm long, thin, same color as cap or paler, fragile, hollow, equal. **SPORE PRINT** white; spores 8-10 × 4.5-6 μm, ellipsoid, smooth, amyloid.

HABITAT: In groups or clusters on decaying conifer logs, sometimes in humus. Common and widespread, fall and winter.

EDIBILITY: Unknown.

COMMENTS: This species differs from the throngs of other grayish Mycenas in its alkaline odor. This is best detected by crushing the cap. It is rather large for a *Mycena*, and the cap is usually umbonate. Another common species with an alkaline odor, *M. leptocephala*, is found on leaves, needles, or even grass. It is rarely umbonate. Similar terrestrial Mycenas without the alkaline odor abound. Some fruit in dense troops under conifers, others may appear in lawns, gardens, or flower pots (perhaps growing from buried bits of wood). Among these are *M. stannea*, with a blackish cap fading to gray and spores 8-11 μm long; *M. abramsii*, with a dark gray to pale gray cap and spores 11-13 μm long; *M. pseudotenax*, with a slippery cap when young; *M. metata*, with a brown to vinaceous-brown cap and sharp (but not alkaline) odor; and *M. iodiolens*, with a strong antiseptic odor, on sticks and debris.

Mycena galericulata

CAP up to 4 cm broad (rarely larger); conical when young, broadly bell-shaped to umbonate to plane or with uplifted margin in age; surface moist but not viscid, striate or radially wrinkled nearly to center; buffy-brown to watery gray or pale grayish-brown. Flesh watery gray, odor somewhat farinaceous. **GILLS** adnate to adnexed, white or grayish, with veins between, often flushed pale pinkish in age. **STALK** to 18 cm long, thin, equal, cartilaginous, hollow, smooth, usually rooting; grayish-white, darker below. **SPORE PRINT** white; spores 8-10 × 5.5-7 μm, ellipsoid, smooth, amyloid.

HABITAT: Scattered, gregarious, or in small clusters on decaying hardwood stumps, logs, and debris, fall and winter. One form is common on manzanita burls.

EDIBILITY: Edible but not recommended. It is one of the few Mycenas large enough to eat, but many of its relatives have not been tested.

COMMENTS: This widespread species can be mistaken for *Collybia* because the cap is convex to plane in age. The telltale traits are its pale

Mycena galericulata, mature specimens. Note the long, rooting stem and growth in clusters. The cap is broadly conical when young, but soon expands as shown here.

color, long rooting stem, and penchant for growing in small, loose clusters. The gills are often pinkish in age but do not become reddish-spotted as in *M. maculata.* A related species, *M. rugulosiceps*, has a mild odor and little or no "root". *M. vitilis* has a "root" covered with white hairs, and grows in humus under hardwoods.

Mycena maculata (Reddish-Spotted Mycena)

CAP 2-4 cm broad (rarely larger); obtusely conic or bell-shaped expanding to broadly convex or plane with a broad umbo; the margin sometimes uplifted; surface smooth, dark brown soon fading to brown or brownish-gray, usually spotted with sordid reddish-brown, sometimes entirely pale gray; striate. Flesh thin, firm, grayish slowly bruising reddish-brown, odor mild. **GILLS** adnate to adnexed, whitish to pale gray, soon stained with reddish spots, sometimes entirely sordid reddish in old age. **STALK** to 10 cm long or more, slender, cartilaginous, hollow, nearly equal, smooth, pallid above, cap color or paler below, the base soon stained reddish-brown, with white hairs. **SPORE PRINT** white; spores 7-10 × 4-6 μm, ellipsoid, smooth, amyloid.

HABITAT: On logs and stumps, usually in clusters, common in cool weather. I have found it on redwood and Douglas-fir.

EDIBILITY: Unknown.

COMMENTS: The reddish-spotted gills and habitat on wood distinguish this rather unattractive species. The stalk sometimes has a "tap root" like *M. galericulata.* It doesn't "bleed" like *M. haematopus* and *M. sanguinolenta*, and the gill edges aren't purple as in *M. purpureofusca.*

Left: *Mycena subcana.* A nondescript grayish *Mycena* found in small groups on rotting wood. Similar species occur in clusters. **Right:** *Mycena elegantula* (see *M. purpureofusca*) is one of several Mycenas with pinkish to reddish gill edges. (Ray Gipson)

Mycena subcana (Neutral Gray Mycena)

CAP up to 2.5 cm broad, obtusely conical to bell-shaped, convex in age; surface smooth or with a hoary sheen, grayish to pale gray, usually darker at the center; translucent-striate nearly to center. Flesh thin, grayish, odor mild. **GILLS** attached, well-spaced, whitish to pale gray. **STALK** to 4 cm long, slender, equal or slightly enlarged at base, smooth, same color as cap or paler, with downy white hairs at base. **SPORE PRINT** white; spores 8-10 $\times$ 5-6 μm, ellipsoid, smooth, amyloid.

HABITAT: Solitary or in small groups on dead sticks and branches, sometimes on living trees, fall and winter, occasional. It is said to prefer conifers, but the specimen photographed was found on tanoak.

EDIBILITY: Unknown.

COMMENTS: This indifferent species is representative of a multitude of neutral grayish wood-inhabiting Mycenas. It is futile trying to separate them without a microscope. The salient macroscopic features of *M. subcana* are the short stem, translucent-striate cap, and habitat on dead sticks. Unlike most of its kin, it shuns company, preferring to fruit alone. *M. occidentalis* is a grayish species commonly found in clusters on conifer logs and debris. *M. parabolica* has a sooty black cap fading to gray. It grows in groups or small clusters on rotting wood.

Mycena purpureofusca (Purple-Gray Mycena)

CAP up to 2.5 cm broad or occasionally larger; obtusely conical with a slightly incurved margin, becoming broadly conic to bell-shaped, sometimes expanding to nearly plane in old age; surface not viscid, dark purplish fading to purplish-gray, the margin usually paler (lilac); translucent-striate at maturity, opaque when young. Flesh thin, pliant, odor mild. **GILLS** attached, fairly close, pallid to grayish, the edges dark grayish-purple. **STALK** to 10 cm long, thin, equal, tubular, cartilaginous and rather tough, more or less cap color, the base with white hairs and sometimes rooting. **SPORE PRINT** white; spores 8-14 × 6-8.5 μm, broadly ellipsoid, smooth, amyloid.

HABITAT: Solitary or tufted on conifer wood and debris. Fairly common, fall and winter. I find it often on decaying pine cones.

EDIBILITY: Unknown, and like myself, likely to remain so.

COMMENTS: The purplish conical cap, dark purple-gray gill edges, and habitat on wood or cones typify this species. The stalk does not exude a red latex like *M. haematopus*. The color and stature are reminiscent of *Marasmius plicatulus*, which has a very tough, brittle stalk, pallid gill edges, and grows on the ground. *Marasmius fuscopurpureus* is sometimes purplish, but has a convex to plane cap and is also terrestrial. *Mycena elegantula* (illustrated on p. 201) is a similar species with dark reddish-brown to pinkish cap and pale pink gill edges. It also grows on coniferous wood and debris, including cones.

Mycena capillaripes

CAP up to 2.5 cm broad, bell-shaped or conical, often with an obtuse umbo, sometimes nearly plane in age; surface smooth, dry, usually some shade of vinaceous-gray or reddish-brown; striate or furrowed, sometimes wrinkled. Flesh thin, tinged cap color, odor nitrous, especially when crushed. **GILLS** usually adnate, well-spaced, typically vinaceous-gray with pale pink edges. **STALK** to 7 cm long, slender, equal, hollow, smooth, more or less cap color, paler at apex. **SPORE PRINT** white; spores 7-9 × 4-5 μm, ellipsoid, smooth, amyloid.

HABITAT: Densely gregarious under conifers, fall and winter, common. I have seen luxuriant fruitings under Monterey pine.

EDIBILITY: Inconsequential.

COMMENTS: This is one of several Mycenas that carpet our pine forests with a miniature "fungal jungle" of petite parasols. The reddish or vinaceous tints on the cap and stem and the pink-margined gills are distinctive. *M. rosella* has a pale rose or grayish-rose stem, pinkish cap, and pale to bright rose gills with sordid reddish edges. It also fruits in troops under conifers. Other terrestrial species with colored gill margins include: *M. aurantiomarginata,* with bright orange gill edges and yellow-orange hairs at stalk base; *M. citrinomarginata,* with pale yellow to yellow-brown gill edges and spores 8-11 μm long; and *M. olivaceo-brunnea,* smaller, with yellowish gill edges and spores 6-8 μm long.

Mycena sanguinolenta (Bleeding Mycena)

CAP up to 2.5 cm broad, conical to bell-shaped or convex; surface smooth, not viscid, color variable: light reddish-brown to bright red-brown or dull reddish-brown, furrowed at maturity. Flesh thin, reddish, exuding a dark red juice when cut, odor mild. **GILLS** typically adnate, well-spaced, pallid or tinged reddish, edges dark red-brown. **STALK** to 7.5 cm long, 1-2 mm thick, equal, hollow, fragile, colored like cap, base exuding a dark red juice when broken and squeezed. **SPORE PRINT** white; spores 8-10 × 4-5 μm, ellipsoid, smooth, weakly amyloid. Cystidia present on gill faces and edges.

HABITAT: Scattered to gregarious in leaf mold or needles. Common, fall and winter.

EDIBILITY: Unknown.

COMMENTS: True to its name, this species and its close cousin *M. haematopus* "bleed" when broken. As such they are the easiest Mycenas to recognize. The reddish-brown furrowed cap is reminiscent of *Marasmius plicatulus*, but the latter has a tough, polished stem and no

Mycena sanguinolenta. This diminutive terrestrial *Mycena* "bleeds" when broken. *M. haematopus* (not illustrated) is slightly larger and grows on wood.

latex. *Mycena haematopus* is also common here. It is larger, usually has pallid gill edges, and grows on wood. I have encountered an odd form of *M. haematopus* growing on oak in which the young caps had sterile, incurved, veil-like margins. A third species, *M. subsanguinolenta* differs microscopically from *M. sanguinolenta* in lacking cystidia on the gill faces. It is partial to needle beds under conifers.

Mycena galopus (Milky Mycena)

CAP up to 2.5 cm broad but usually smaller; conical to bell-shaped, the margin sometimes curving back in age; surface smooth, not viscid, at first grayish-black (at least at center), soon fading to dark gray, then pale gray, the margin whitish; translucent-striate when moist. Flesh thin, soft, odor mild. **GILLS** well-spaced, attached, whitish to grayish. **STALK** to 12 cm long, thin, equal, fragile, smooth, dark grayish-brown below, paler above; the hairy base exuding a milky juice when squeezed. **SPORE PRINT** white; spores 9-13 $\times$ 5-6.5 μm, ellipsoid, smooth, sometimes weakly amyloid.

HABITAT: Scattered to gregarious in humus in woods, fall through spring. Abundant at times, especially under redwood and tanoak.

EDIBILITY: Unknown; hardly worth the effort to find out.

Mycena galopus is one of innumerable grayish Mycenas. Cap is deep grayish-brown when young, pale gray in age. Base of stalk exudes a milky droplet when cut and squeezed.

COMMENTS: This ubiquitous *Mycena* will be encountered by anyone who takes his or her little brown (or gray) mushrooms seriously. At first glance there is little to distinguish it from the myriads of other anonymous grayish Mycenas. However, if you break the very base of the stalk and squeeze gently, a drop of milky fluid will emerge. This is best observed in the field, while the fruiting body is still fresh. The stem of *M. atroalboides* also exudes a liquid, but it is clear, not milky. It is not as common as *M. galopus*, and its gills are spotted reddish in old age.

Mycena epipterygia (Yellow-Stemmed Mycena)

CAP to 2.5 cm broad or slightly larger; egg-shaped to bell-shaped, convex, or umbonate; surface smooth, slimy or viscid when moist, color variable: mostly yellow with olive or grayish tones, fading in age to grayish or whitish. Flesh thin, yellowish, odor mild or faintly fragrant. **GILLS** attached, whitish or tinged yellow, fairly well-spaced. **STALK** to 7.5 cm long, equal, fragile, hollow, thin, slimy or viscid, yellow, fading to whitish in old age. **SPORE PRINT** white; spores 8-10 × 5-6 µm, ovoid, smooth, amyloid.

HABITAT: Scattered to gregarious on needles under conifers. Fairly common, fall and winter, especially in coastal pine forests. One variety occurs on decaying conifers.

EDIBILITY: Unknown,

COMMENTS: This is one of several attractive Mycenas with a viscid cap and yellow to greenish-gray viscid stem. Others include: *M. viscosa*, with a strong rancid odor and taste; *M. epipterygioides,* with a dark olive-gray cap that does not fade to white; *M. lilacifolia,* with pale lilac gills at first, found on decaying conifers; and *M. griseoviridis*, with a deep olive to olive-brown cap which blackens in age, and thorny cystidia on the gill edges. Any of these can be mistaken for a *Hygrophorus* (especially *H. psittacinus*), but the gills are not waxy.

Mycena rorida (Slippery Mycena)

CAP up to 10 mm broad, at first round or bell-shaped, then expanding to nearly plane; surface dry, pale brown or brownish-gray fading to white. Flesh thin, odor mild. **GILLS** adnate to decurrent, well-spaced, white. **STALK** to 5 cm long, thin, equal, fragile, whitish, covered with a sheath of slime when fresh. **SPORE PRINT** white; spores 8-10 × 4-5 μm, ellipsoid, smooth, amyloid.

HABITAT: Solitary or scattered on debris under conifers and in mixed woods; not common. I have found it under redwood in November.

EDIBILITY: Unknown. Too small and slippery to be of value.

COMMENTS: This species is easily identified by its pale color, dry cap, and slimy stem. Plucking it from the ground is a difficult proposition if you try to grasp it by the stem. Other Mycenas with a pallid to grayish viscid stem include: *M. tenax*, with a gray-brown to pale gray cap and strong disagreeable odor; *M. vulgaris*, similar but with an extremely viscid cap and slight odor; and *M. clavicularis*, with a dry grayish cap and mild odor. All occur in groups under conifers.

spores

RHODOPHYLLACEAE

Small to fairly large *mostly terrestrial* fungi. CAP dry or slightly viscid. GILLS *attached* (but sometimes seceding). STALK usually central (except in *Claudopus*), thick or thin, fleshy or cartilaginous, not cleanly separable from cap. VEIL and VOLVA *absent*. SPORE PRINT *pinkish* (rosy to deep flesh color or cinnamon-flesh). Spores typically angular (longitudinally ridged in *Clitopilus*), not amyloid.

THIS is the largest family of pinkish-spored mushrooms. The gills are not free as in the Volvariaceae and the stalk is not cleanly separable from the cap. The angular (many-sided) or longitudinally ridged spores serve as the main criterion for separating the Rhodophyllaceae from the pinkish-spored members of the Tricholomataceae *(Lepista).* Since this feature is microscopic, several Lepistas are keyed out here.

The family is traditionally divided into five genera: *Claudopus* is wood-inhabiting with little or no stem; *Clitopilus* (which corresponds structurally to the white-spored genus *Clitocybe*) has decurrent gills and a fleshy stem. *Entoloma* (which corresponds to *Tricholoma*) has a fleshy or semi-cartilaginous stem and non-decurrent gills. *Nolanea* and *Leptonia* (which correspond to *Mycena* and *Colybia* respectively) have a thin cartilaginous stem. In *Nolanea* the cap is usually bell-shaped or conical whereas in *Leptonia* it is convex to depressed or umbilicate.

A nebulous series of intermediate forms has led the "lumpers" to consolidate all but *Clitopilus* in a single giant genus, *Rhodophyllus*, but recent studies have revealed a chemical basis for maintaining generic distinctions along more or less conventional lines. To muddle matters more, some lumpers use *Entoloma* instead of *Rhodophyllus*. The result is that each species has an endless series of synonyms. For instance, *Leptonia sericella, Alboleptonia sericella, Entoloma sericellum,* and *Rhodophyllus sericellus* are all names for the same fungus! Human beings are certainly a confusing (or confused) lot!

The mushrooms themselves do little to ameliorate matters. They are notoriously difficult to identify, even with a microscope. One rhodophyllologist goes so far as to base generic and species concepts on whether or not the spores are symmetrical! Particularly perplexing is an interminable series of brown to grayish forms evenly divided among *Entoloma, Nolanea,* and *Leptonia.*

Not only are the Rhodophyllaceae exasperatingly difficult to identify, but many are poisonous—particularly the large, handsome, fleshy Entolomas. This clearly invalidates the old adage that "any mushroom with pink gills is edible" (a reference to *Agaricus*). Several species are strikingly beautiful, however, notably *Entoloma nitidum.*

The Rhodophyllaceae fruit throughout the mushroom season and are often in evidence when other fungi are scarce. Most are confined to the woods but some (such as *Nolanea sericea*) frequent pastures and open hillsides. The vast majority are terrestrial (unlike the pinkish-spored genus *Pluteus*), but a few grow on sticks or rotting wood. The family is treated as one entity here. Of the dozens of species known from California, a few of the common species "complexes" are described here.

Key to the Rhodophyllaceae

1. Shelflike; stalk absent or rudimentary; usually on wood 2
1. Not as above; stalk well developed, central to off-center 3

2. Gills pallid to pinkish .... *Claudopus depluens*, p. 209
2. Gills yellow-orange to orange-buff .... (see *Phyllotopsis*, p. 125)

3. Gills decurrent, stalk fleshy (though sometimes slender) 4
3. Gills not decurrent, or if decurrent then stalk thin, fragile, hollow ... 5

4. Cap dull white to gray, *not* growing in clusters; stalk slender, often off-center; odor pleasant .... *Clitopilus prunulus*, p. 209
4. Not as above .... (see *Lepista*, p. 131)

5. Cap white or whitish 6
5. Cap not white 8

6. Small and fragile; stalk thin (1-3 mm) .... *Leptonia sericella*, p. 217
6. Medium-sized; stalk thicker 7

7. Cap chalk-white, gills deep flesh color at maturity; spores *not* angular; rare .... (see *Hebeloma*, p. 352)
7. Not as above; spores angular; common *Entoloma rhodopolium*, p. 210

8. Stalk or cap (or both) blue, blue-gray, or black 9
8. Not as above; cap and stalk white, pallid, brown, etc. 13

9. Stalk thin (3 mm or less), cartilaginous, fragile 10
9. Stalk fleshy (though sometimes slender) 12

10. Cap brown to grayish-brown *Leptonia "asprella"* (see *L. parva*, p. 215)
10. Cap black to blue-black, at least when fresh (may fade to gray) 11

11. Gill edges blue-black .... *Leptonia serrulata* (see *L. parva*, p. 215)
11. Gill edges not blue-black .... *Leptonia parva*, p. 215

12. Cap indigo-blue, dry; stalk rather slender ... *Entoloma nitidum*, p. 212
12. Cap black to bluish-gray or steel-gray, viscid when moist; stalk thick, stout .... *Entoloma madidum*, p. 211

13. Stalk fleshy, usually thick and stout, white or pallid 14
13. Stalk slender (6 mm thick or less) 17

14. Cap grayish-brown streaked with darker fibrils .... *Entoloma clypeatum* (see *E. rhodopolium*, p. 210)
14. Not as above 15

15. Odor nitrous (like bleach) .... *Entoloma nidorosum* (see *E. rhodopolium*, p. 210)
15. Not as above 16

16. Usually growing in woods; stalk whitish *Entoloma rhodopolium*, p. 210
16. Growing in grass; stalk not white .... (see *Lepista*, p. 131)

17. Growing in grass (especially pastures) or manured ground 18
17. Usually growing in woods or under trees 20

18. Cap convex or umbonate to plane; gills usually lilac or vinaceous-tinted; growing in dung or grass .... (see *Lepista*, p. 131)
18. Not as above 19

19. Cap convex or umbonate to plane .... *Nolanea sericea*, p. 214
19. Cap broadly conical to bell-shaped .... *Nolanea staurospora*, p. 215

20. Cap convex becoming depressed or umbilicate; gills decurrent .... *Nolanea californica* (see *N. staurospora*, p. 215)
20. Not as above; gills not decurrent 21

21. Growing on wood .... (see *Pluteus*, p. 218)
21. Growing on ground 22

22. Cap with a prominent umbo; stalk long, thin .... *Nolanea mammosa* (see *N. staurospora*, p. 215)
22. Not as above 23

23. Stalk 2 mm thick or more .... *Entoloma peckianum*, p. 213
23. Stalk 1-2 (rarely 3) mm thick, fragile ...... *Nolanea staurospora*, p. 215

Claudopus depluens

CAP minute, up to 10 mm broad, round or shell-shaped in outline; convex to plane; surface white or grayish, dry, minutely cottony or hairy. Flesh very thin, whitish, odor mild. **GILLS** radiating from the stalk, well-spaced, pallid becoming pinkish at maturity. **STALK** absent or lateral, not well-formed. **SPORE PRINT** flesh color; spores 7-10 × 6-7.5 μm, ovoid-angular.

HABITAT: Scattered or in groups on rotting wood, rarely on soil. Fall and winter, not common.

EDIBILITY: Unknown.

COMMENTS: This fleshless, flavorless, featureless little fungus is distinguished (if one can call it that) by its white to grayish cap, pinkish spores, and rudimentary or absent stem. *C. byssisedus* is an equally forgettable fungus with a grayish cap and longer spores. *Crepidotus* species are similar but have brown spores. *Phyllotopsis nidulans* has pinkish spores but is larger and has dull orange gills.

Clitopilus prunulus (Sweetbread Mushroom)

CAP 4-10 cm broad, convex becoming plane or depressed; surface dry, unpolished, smooth, dull white to ashy-gray; margin often wavy. Flesh white, rather thin, odor pleasantly farinaceous. **GILLS** decurrent, close, narrow, whitish to gray, then dusted pinkish with spores. **STALK** to 7 cm long but usually much shorter, central or off-center, rather slender, equal or tapering downward, colored like cap. **SPORE PRINT** reddish-flesh color; spores 10-12 × 5-7 µm, elliptical, longitudinally ridged.

HABITAT: Solitary or in small groups in pastures and at their edges, occasionally in woods. Fairly common after the first fall rains.

EDIBILITY: Edible and choice, but not recommended. It is easily confused with poisonous species and is seldom abundant besides.

COMMENTS: The pinkish spores, decurrent gills, grayish cap, and odor of meal are the principal fieldmarks of this drab fungus. The poisonous *Clitocybe dealbata* closely mimics it but is smaller and has white spores. *Lepista subconnexa* has pinkish spores but grows in clusters and is thicker and more robust. *Clitopilus orcellus* is a very similar species with a viscid white to yellowish-white cap.

Entoloma rhodopolium (Poisonous Entoloma)

CAP 5-15 cm broad, broadly bell-shaped or convex becoming plane or broadly umbonate; surface smooth, dry or slightly tacky when moist, pale dingy tan to yellowish-gray to dull grayish-ochre; margin often

Entoloma rhodopolium, mature specimens. A common poisonous woodland mushroom with pinkish spores and a gray to yellow-gray or buffy-tan cap. It sometimes grows in clusters, as shown at left. Specimen at right is very old, as evidenced by depressed cap.

splitting in age. Flesh thick, firm, white, odor mild or slightly farinaceous. **GILLS** notched, fairly well separated, pallid or yellowish-gray becoming pinkish in age. **STALK** to 13 cm long, stout, fleshy, thick, equal or tapered below, smooth, dry, white. **SPORE PRINT** deep rosy-flesh color; spores 8.5-11 × 7-9 μm, nearly round, angular.

HABITAT: Scattered, gregarious, or clustered on ground in woods, mid-fall through winter. Abundant at times, especially under hardwoods.

EDIBILITY: Poisonous. Causes severe vomiting, diarrhea, and abdominal cramps that may require hospitalization. All members of this group should be strictly avoided although some are said to be edible.

COMMENTS: The above description encompasses a group of large, showy woodland Entolomas with a smooth, grayish to yellowish-tan cap, white fleshy stem, notched gills, and pinkish spores. They are the most common and conspicuous of our Entolomas as well as the most dangerous. They have the stature of a *Tricholoma* and are never as slender as *E. peckianum* or the grayish-brown Nolaneas. Distinguishing between the various species is a matter for the specialist. *E. lividum (=E. sinuatum),* the species most often pictured in mushroom books, has a farinaceous odor and tan to livid-tan cap that is *viscid* when moist. Its occurrence in California is moot. *E. grayanum* is a very common species with a farinaceous odor and whitish to watery yellow or grayish-brown non-viscid cap. *E. clypeatum* has a farinaceous odor and gray-brown cap streaked with darker fibrils. It is encountered occasionally in mixed woods and under oak, in small groups or clusters. *E. nidorosum* is distinct by virtue of its strong, unpleasant nitrous (bleachlike) odor. It is also common. Related species with white or whitish caps include: *E. prunuloides*, large, fleshy, with a viscid cap, and *E. speculum*, slender, with a dry, umbonate cap.

Entoloma madidum

CAP 5-13 cm broad, obtusely conic or convex, expanding to plane or remaining obtusely umbonate; surface viscid when moist, smooth with a fibrillose or streaked appearance; blue-gray to violet-gray to nearly black, fading in age to fuscous. Flesh thick, firm, white, odor farinaceous. **GILLS** notched, close, white or tinged cap color, becoming pinkish in age as the spores ripen. **STALK** to 13 cm long and up to 2 cm thick, stout, hard, solid, fleshy, fibrillose, blue-gray or

Entoloma madidum, mature specimens. Note the steel-gray to bluish-black cap and stalk, notched gills, and hard fleshy stem.

colored like cap or paler, occasionally whitish; more or less equal with a tapered base. **SPORE PRINT** cinnamon-flesh color; spores 7-9 × 6-7.5 μm, ovoid-angular to nearly round-angular.

HABITAT: Scattered to gregarious in woods, fall and winter. Common, especially under redwood, madrone, and tanoak. I have seen enormous fruitings at Big Basin State Park in December.

EDIBILITY: Unknown. All large Entolomas should be avoided.

COMMENTS: The bluish-gray to black cap, pinkish spores, notched gills, and hard fleshy stem set this striking species apart. It has the aspect of a *Russula*, but is not as brittle and has pinkish spores. It is much larger and fleshier than the small bluish-black Leptonias. It is never deep blue like *E. nitidum*, nor purple like the blewitt, *Lepista nuda*. *Tricholoma portentosum* is very similar but has white spores and a white stem.

Entoloma nitidum (Indigo Entoloma)

CAP 2.5-6.5 cm broad, at first conical or bell-shaped, expanding somewhat to convex or umbonate; surface dry, fibrillose or minutely scaly, deep indigo-blue. Flesh violet under cuticle, paler otherwise, odor mild. **GILLS** typically notched, at first pallid, becoming pinkish (rosy-gray to grayish-purple) as spores mature. **STALK** to 10 cm long, rather slender but fleshy, equal, minutely scaly-scurfy, dry, indigo-blue with a pallid base, sometimes violet-tinted at apex. **SPORE PRINT** pinkish; spores 7-9 × 6.5-7.5 μm, nearly round, angular.

Entoloma nitidum. The cap and stalk of this uncommon species are a striking deep indigo-blue. Gills are paler. (Joel Leivick)

HABITAT: Solitary or in small groups in woods, uncommon. I have found it several times near or under redwood in late fall and winter during an otherwise dry and uneventful season. Its deep color camouflages it well.

EDIBILITY: Undetermined.

COMMENTS: The stunning indigo-blue cap and stem render this breathtakingly beautiful mushroom distinct. Its rarity makes it all the more pleasurable to find. Its only rival for intensity of color is *Cortinarius violaceus*, which has rusty-brown spores. The stem is not as thick as in most Entolomas, but is fleshy nevertheless. The black and bluish-gray tones characteristic of *E. madidum* and *Leptonia parva* are absent, and the cap is not viscid. The blewitt *(Lepista nuda)* differs by its purple to bluish-purple gills.

Entoloma peckianum

CAP up to 5 cm broad, broadly conical to convex or umbonate, sometimes nearly plane in age; surface not viscid, appearing radially streaked when dry, hygrophanous, dark brown to grayish-brown, paler as it dries. Flesh thin, dingy brownish or pallid, odor more or less mild. **GILLS** adnexed or notched, sometimes even free, pallid becoming flesh color, fairly close. **STALK** to 13 cm long, slender, smooth or with silky longitudinal fibrils, often twisted, equal, pallid to brownish-gray, hollow, dry, splitting lengthwise easily. **SPORE PRINT** flesh color; spores 9-14 × 7.5-9 μm, elliptical-angular.

HABITAT: Solitary or in scattered groups in woods, fall through spring. Common but not numerous, usually under hardwoods.

EDIBILITY: Unknown.

COMMENTS: The above description fits any number of slender-stemmed Entolomas with dark brown to olive-brown or grayish-brown cap. They can be differentiated only with a microscope, and even then it's not easy. Similarly colored Nolaneas tend to be smaller with even thinner stems and more conical caps. Superficially, however, *Entoloma* and *Nolanea* intergrade. *E. griseum* is similar to *E. peckianum* but has smaller spores, 7-9 μm long. *E. longistriata* has a striate cap.

Nolanea sericea

CAP up to 6.5 cm broad but usually smaller, convex or convex-umbonate; surface smooth, not viscid, dark olive-brown to gray-brown when moist, paler with a silky or streaked appearance when dry; center sometimes very dark, margin sometimes wavy. Flesh thin, watery, brownish, odor faintly farinaceous. **GILLS** typically notched, pallid grayish or tinged cap color becoming pinkish as spores ripen. **STALK** to 10 cm long, slender, equal or with enlarged base, dry, longitudinally fibrillose-striate, often twisted, grayish-brown. **SPORE PRINT** deep salmon-pinkish; spores 8-10 × 6-8 μm, ovoid-angular, warted.

Nolanea sericea, rather large specimens. This common inhabitant of pastures is recognized by its pinkish spores and olive-brown to grayish-brown cap. It occasionally grows in the woods as well.

HABITAT: Scattered to gregarious in grassy places, on hillsides, sometimes in the woods. Common, fall through early spring. Contrary to most fungi, it tends to fruit during rain rather than following it.

EDIBILITY: Unknown.

COMMENTS: Only when this species is found in grassy places can it be distinguished with any certainty from the anonymous hordes of olive-brown to grayish-brown Nolaneas and Entolomas. The pinkish spores and gray-brown to olive-brown cap separate it from other grass-inhabiting mushrooms. It is a common fungal feature of our pastures but is often overlooked because it hides in the grass. *Entoloma griseum* is a similar but slightly stouter woodland species.

Nolanea staurospora

CAP up to 4 cm broad, broadly conical to bell-shaped; surface smooth, umber to date-brown when moist, fading to yellow-brown when dry; margin striate when moist. Flesh very thin, odor mild. **GILLS** at first pallid, becoming pinkish in age, close, adnate or notched. **STALK** to 10 cm long, thin, longitudinally striate, fragile, often twisted, splitting longitudinally, same color as cap but paler. **SPORE PRINT** deep flesh color; spores 9-11 × 7-9 μm, cruciate-nodulose (shaped like jacks).

HABITAT: Scattered in woods, along trails, in damp soil or occasionally in grass. Fall and winter, infrequent.

EDIBILITY: Unknown.

COMMENTS: The outstanding attribute of this little fungus is its spores, which look like jacks. It is impossible to appreciate the relief they provide unless you've spent many long, tedious hours scrutinizing the round to elliptical spores sported by the overhwelming majority of mushrooms. The thin, cartilaginous stem and conical to bell-shaped cap is reminiscent of *Mycena*, but the pinkish spores indicate *Nolanea.* There are several similar woodland Nolaneas without cruciate spores, including: *N. hirtipes*, with a grayish-brown to olive-brown cap; *N. mammosa*, with a long slender stem and convex to conical cap with a pointed umbo; and *N. californica*, a small dingy brown species with a plane to umbilicate cap and decurrent gills.

Leptonia parva (Blue-Black Leptonia)

CAP typically 2-3 cm broad, convex becoming plane or with a depressed center; surface dry, minutely scaly or fibrillose (especially at

Leptonia parva, or a very similar species. The cap and stalk are bluish-black, the gills are white becoming pinkish. Cap at left is the most typical—broadly convex with a depressed center. Later it may become depressed (second from left) and quite scaly.

center), blue-black to black, fading to bluish-gray or smoky. Flesh thin, pallid or tinted cap color, odor mild. **GILLS** adnate to adnexed or occasionally seceding to free, fairly well-spaced, white or pallid becoming pinkish in old age. **STALK** to 7.5 cm long, thin (2-3 mm), equal, smooth, blackish-blue to bluish-gray, paler gray in age. **SPORE PRINT** rosy-pinkish; spores 8-12 $\times$ 5.5-9 μm, elliptical-angular, warty.

HABITAT: Scattered or in small groups in or near woods—on humus, debris, decaying wood, etc. Very common but easily overlooked, fall through early spring. It is partial to redwood.

EDIBILITY: Unknown. Too small to be of value.

COMMENTS: The above description embraces a large group of delicate blue-black Leptonias. Identifying them is a job for rabid rhodophyllologists, but you needn't know their exact identities to appreciate their beauty. No other mushrooms have a bluish-black to black cap, thin bluish-gray to gray stem, and pinkish spores. Similarly colored Entolomas are much larger and fleshier. Other members of the club include: *L. aethiops*, with a blackish to smoky-gray (never bluish) stalk; *L. corvina*, with a pale bluish stalk fading to whitish and bluish-black cap fading to grayish-brown; *L. nigra*, a beautiful endemic version with a bluish-black convex to plane (not umbilicate) cap and bluish to bluish-gray gills; *L. serrulata*, stalk smoky-grayish and gills whitish with finely serrate, blue-black edges; *L. euchroa*, with entire blue-black gill edges, growing on wood; and *L. "asprella"*, with a gray to bluish-gray stalk and umber to gray-brown (never blue or black) cap.

Leptonia sericella (Little White Leptonia)

CAP up to 5 cm broad, convex becoming plane or depressed; surface smooth, dry, often silky, pure white or translucent-white, tinged yellow in age or sometimes pinkish. Flesh very thin, whitish, odor mild. **GILLS** attached, well-spaced, white becoming rosy-pinkish. **STALK** to 5 cm long, thin, fragile, equal, smooth, white. **SPORE PRINT** bright flesh color; spores 9-13 × 6-8 μm, ellipsoid-angular (nodulose).

HABITAT: Scattered to gregarious in damp soil in woods, thickets, along trails, etc. Common, fall and winter.

EDIBILITY: Unknown.

COMMENTS: This is the only small white mushroom with pinkish spores, thin stem, and attached gills. It has recently been given a more impressive name, *Alboleptonia sericella.* It resembles *Hygrophorus borealis* and *Inocybe geophylla*, but the spore color distinguishes it. Its fragility makes it difficult to transport without crushing. *L. (Alboleptonia) adnatifolia* is a pure white species with spores 8.5-10 μm long. *L. (Alboleptonia) ochracea* ages or bruises ochraceous.

spores

VOLVARIACEAE

THESE are small to medium-sized mushrooms with pinkish spores, a central stem, and free gills at maturity. In the other major pink-spored family (the Rhodophyllaceae) the gills are usually attached.

There are three genera: *Volvariella* has a volva but no ring; *Chameota* (extremely rare and not treated here) has a ring but no volva; *Pluteus* has neither ring nor volva.

Because of the free gills and volva (in *Volvariella*), the Volvariaceae are placed close to the Amanitaceae. Besides the disparity in spore color, however, there is a fundamental microscopic difference: the gill hyphae are convergent in the Volvariaceae, divergent in the Amanitas.

Key to the Volvariaceae

1. Volva present as a sack at base of stalk .... *Volvariella*, p. 222
1. Volva absent 2

2. Veil present, usually forming a ring .... (see *Lepiota naucina*, p. 261)
2. Veil absent .... *Pluteus*, p. 218

PLUTEUS

Small to medium-sized *wood-inhabiting* fungi. CAP convex to plane. Flesh soft, decaying rapidly. GILLS usually *close, typically free at maturity*, usually pinkish in old age. STALK central, fleshy or cartilaginous, cleanly separable from cap. VEIL and VOLVA *absent*. SPORE PRINT *flesh color to deep pinkish*. Spores smooth, mostly ellipsoid. Gill hyphae convergent.

THESE pinkish-spored mushrooms have a central stalk and free gills and grow almost exclusively on wood. The wood, however, may be buried or decomposed, making them appear terrestrial. They are most often confused with the angular-spored Rhodophyllaceae, which are typically terrestrial with gills attached to the stem.

Pluteus is sporadically common but never abundant. Most of the species have watery flesh and decay rapidly. However, the larger types such as *P. magnus* and *P. cervinus* are edible and of topnotch quality when fresh and firm. None are known to be poisonous.

It is a fair-sized genus with about twenty different kinds recorded from California. These are segregated primarily on microscopic features, such as the structure of the cap cuticle and the shape of sterile cells (cystidia) on the gills. Four species are described here.

Key to Pluteus

1. Cap entirely white .... *P. pellitus*, p. 220
1. Cap colored 2

2. Stalk yellow .... *P. lutescens*, p. 221
2. Stalk not yellow 3

3. Medium-sized (cap 4-15 cm broad); cap smooth or fibrillose; odor often radishlike .... *P. cervinus*, below
3. Small (cap 2-5 cm broad); cap granulose, wrinkled, or striate; odor not radishlike 4

4. Cap granulose, yellow at least at margin .... *P. flavofuligineus* (see *P. lutescens*, p. 221)
4. Not as above; cap never yellow .... *P. longistriatus*, p. 220

Pluteus cervinus (Deer Mushroom)

CAP 4-15 cm broad, convex becoming broadly convex or nearly plane; surface smooth or streaked with fibrils, moist but not viscid, blackish-brown to brown, gray-brown, dingy fawn, sometimes pallid except at center. Flesh watery, soft, white, odor often radishlike. **GILLS** close or crowded, soft, white becoming pink or flesh color, free at maturity.

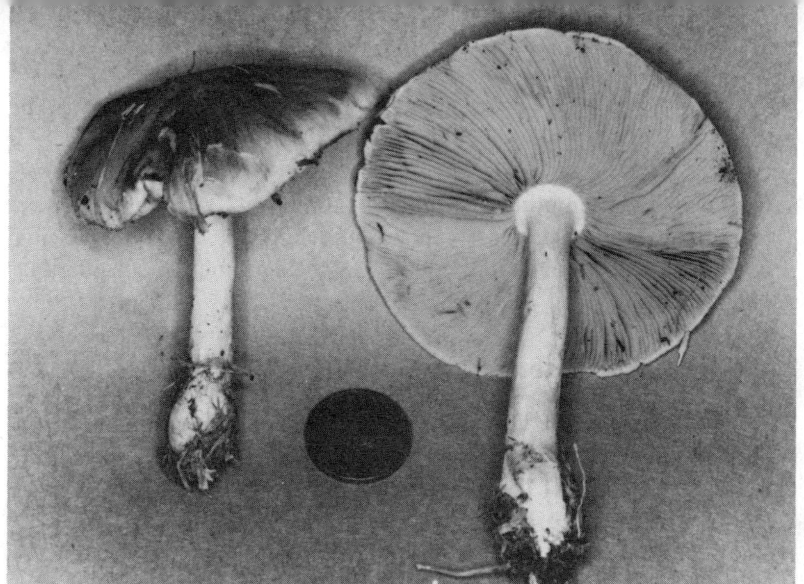

Pluteus cervinus, mature specimens. Note the free crowded gills which are deep pinkish at maturity. These rather small individuals were growing on a log, but they sometimes grow from buried wood, thus appearing terrestrial.

STALK to 13 cm long, up to 1.5 cm thick, equal or tapering upward, dry, white or with brownish fibrils, smooth. **SPORE PRINT** flesh color; spores 5-8 × 4-6 μm, ellipsoid, smooth. Cystidia on gills with long necks and 2-4 "horns."

HABITAT: Solitary or in groups on decaying wood, sawdust piles, wood chips, buried wood; fall through winter or even spring, common but never abundant. It seems to prefer hardwoods but also grows on conifers.

EDIBILITY: Edible and excellent when fresh and firm. The flaccid, waterlogged specimens one usually finds are apt to be insipid. *P. magnus* (see below) is equally good, if not better.

COMMENTS: The deer mushroom is our most common and conspicuous *Pluteus.* It is rather nondescript, but can be safely identified by its pink spores, free gills, no veil, and habitat on wood. The cap color is extremely variable but is typically some shade of brown. Special care should be taken not to confuse it with the poisonous *Entoloma rhodopolium* and relatives, which have attached (usually notched) gills and grow on the ground (*Pluteus* may have gills slightly attached when young). Until you are intimately familiar with it, eat only those clearly growing on wood.

P. magnus is a similar species whose cystidia are not horned. It tends to be larger and more robust than *P. cervinus.* I find it frequently along roads or paths, presumably growing from buried stumps. *P. magnus*, incidentally, is an excellent conductor of electricity. I discovered this the hard way, by attempting to remove a clump from under an electrified fence. Only the uppermost cap was touching the wire, but when I uprooted the lowermost individual, I received a shock of considerable magnitude.

Pluteus pellitus (White Pluteus)

CAP to 7.5 cm broad, convex to nearly plane; surface smooth, moist but not viscid, pure white when fresh, watery white in age. Flesh soft, white, odor mild. **GILLS** at first white, then flesh-colored, close, free at maturity. **STALK** to 10 cm long, equal, white, hollow, rather slender, smooth or somewhat scurfy at apex. **SPORE PRINT** flesh color; spores 6-8 × 4-6 μm, ellipsoid to nearly round, smooth.

HABITAT: Solitary or in small groups on rotting stumps and logs, rare. I have found it only once, in mixed woods near Boulder Creek.

EDIBILITY: Unknown.

COMMENTS: The pristine white cap and shining white stem combine with the free pink gills to set this showy species apart. It is similar in stature to *P. cervinus.* From a distance it looks like the deadly *Amanita ocreata,* but there is no volva and the spore print is pinkish.

Pluteus longistriatus (Striate Pluteus)

CAP up to 5 cm broad, convex becoming plane; surface minutely scaly or granulose (at least at center), not viscid, ashy-brown to brownish-gray or grayish-olive; conspicuously striate in age. Flesh thin, watery, pallid, odor mild. **GILLS** free or slightly attached, close, rather broad, pallid becoming flesh color. **STALK** to 6.5 cm long, slender, finely fibrillose-striate, pallid or tinged cap color, equal or with enlarged base, straight or curved. **SPORE PRINT** flesh color; spores 5-7 × 4-6 μm, nearly round, smooth. Cystidia on gills club-shaped or flasklike.

HABITAT: Solitary or scattered on decaying sticks and branches, late fall through early winter, sporadically common.

EDIBILITY: Unknown.

COMMENTS: The brownish-gray striate cap at maturity, small size, pinkish spores, and close, free gills are diagnostic. Actually, the gills may be slightly attached, leading to confusion with the Rhodophyllaceae, but the spores are smooth and all material I have seen was

Left: *Pluteus longistriatus*, recognized by its pinkish spores, small size, finely striate cap at maturity, and growth on decaying wood. **Right:** *Pluteus lutescens*, mature specimen. Has yellow stem, free gills, grows on rotting hardwoods.

clearly growing on wood. The above description will suffice for a number of small, undistinguished *Pluteus* species, including: *P. seticeps*, with a reddish-brown cap; *P. cyanopus*, rare, with a blue-gray to greenish-gray stem; and *P. salicinus*, tinted blue or green only at the stem base. *P. californicus* should also be mentioned.

Pluteus lutescens (Yellow-Stemmed Pluteus)

CAP less than 5 cm broad, convex becoming broadly umbonate or plane; surface finely granulose or wrinkled, sometimes nearly smooth in age, not viscid, dark olive-brown to yellowish-olive. Flesh thin, white to pale yellow, odor mild. **GILLS** free, close, white or pale yellow, becoming pinkish from maturing spores. **STALK** to 5 cm long, thin, equal, straight or curved, smooth, hollow, yellow. **SPORE PRINT** flesh color; spores 6-7 × 5-6 μm, nearly round, smooth. Cystidia on gills club-shaped to flask-shaped.

HABITAT: Solitary or scattered on rotting hardwood logs, sticks, and debris. Fairly common, late fall and winter, especially on oak.

EDIBILITY: Undetermined. Too small to be significant.

COMMENTS: This colorful, delicate *Pluteus* is easily identified by its clear yellow stem, olive-brown cap, close free gills, and pinkish spores. *P. nanus* var. *lutescens* is a synonym. I have also found a rare species, *P. flavofuligineus*, in our area. It has a more granulose cap showing yellow at least at the margin, and a whitish stem becoming pinkish (or occasionally yellowish) in age. But the critical difference is microscopic—the cap cuticle is filamentous rather than cellular as in *P. lutescens.*

VOLVARIELLA

Medium-sized fungi found on wood or rich soil. CAP smooth, convex to plane. GILLS *free at maturity*, close, *pinkish to deep flesh color in age.* STALK central, usually hollow, cleanly separable from cap. VEIL (inner) *absent.* VOLVA *present, membranous, saclike.* SPORE PRINT *pinkish to deep flesh color.* Spores smooth, elliptical. Gill hyphae convergent.

VOLVARIELLA (formerly *Volvaria*) resembles *Amanita* but has pinkish to reddish-salmon spores. The volva is always saclike and there is no ring (inner veil).

Several Volvariellas are edible. In fact, *Volvariella* is to the tropics what *Agaricus* is to temperate regions—the principal mushroom of commerce. The paddy straw mushroom, *V. volvacea*, is cultivated widely in Southeast Asia, usually on straw in rice paddies. It is shipped abroad and can be purchased at exotic food stores. I was presented with a can of it six years ago, on some unforgettable occasion I can no longer remember. I am sorry to say it has languished in the back of the cupboard ever since—there are always so many fresh mushrooms in my refrigerator!

The handful of temperate Volvariellas frequent cultivated fields, gardens, straw heaps, and greenhouses. A few grow on wood and one is parasitic on other mushrooms. Only one species is common in California. A key hardly seems necessary.

Volvariella speciosa (Common Volvariella)

CAP 5-15 cm broad, at first egg-shaped, then convex, finally plane; surface smooth, viscid when moist, dull white to pearl-gray, grayish-brown, or even fulvous, paler toward the margin; with a metallic or silky luster when dry. Flesh soft, white. **GILLS** free, white becoming pink or flesh color, finally sordid reddish. **STALK** to 20 cm long, equal or enlarged below, smooth, dry, whitish. **VEIL** (inner) absent. **VOLVA** membranous, white, forming a sack at the base of the stalk, usually buried in soil. **SPORE PRINT** deep flesh color; spores 13.5-16.5 × 7.5-9 µm, ovoid, smooth.

HABITAT: Solitary or scattered in cultivated soil—gardens, vacant lots, roadsides, occasionally at edges of woods. Common, fall through

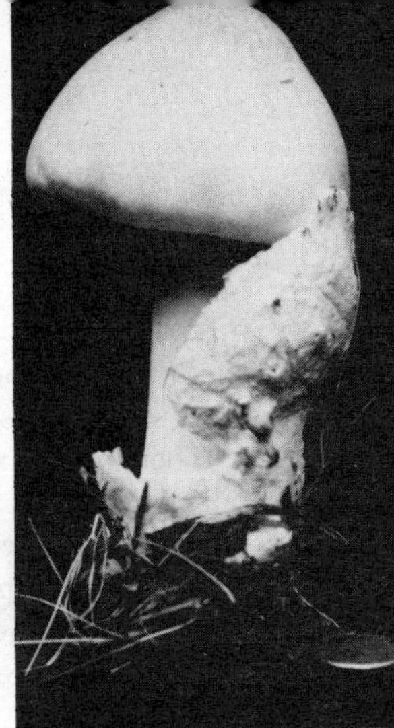

Volvariella speciosa. **Left:** Note the reddish gills on mature individual and pallid gills of younger specimen. (Nancy Burnett) **Right:** A majestic specimen emerging from its volva. Later it will become flaccid like old specimen in lefthand picture.

spring, even in summer. Especially fond of brussels sprouts fields.

EDIBILITY: Edible but mediocre (once thought to be poisonous perhaps due to its resemblance to *Amanita*). Should you try it, be sure of your identification—Amanitas can have pinkish gills in old age!

COMMENTS: This mushroom can cause quite a stir when it appears, bold and unannounced, in the middle of your cabbage bed. It is our only common *Volvariella* and is recognized as such by its saclike volva and deep pinkish spores. Though quite attractive when it first emerges, it quickly becomes flaccid and waterlogged. *V. speciosa* var. *gloicephala* is said to differ from the typical variety in its darker (pearl-gray to fulvous) pileus (cap) with a striate margin and smaller spores. One dismal day of illegal trespassing in a smelly old brussels sprouts field yielded the following: twenty soggy specimens with pale pileus and non-striate margin, six soggy specimens with dark pileus and striate margin, five soggy specimens with dark pileus and non-striate margin, and eleven soggy specimens with pale pileus and striate margin. If you can detect a meaningful mycelial thread running through all of this, then you are a better mycologist than I. (Just be thankful, as I am, that I didn't measure the spores!) . . .

The following species may occur rarely in California: in woods and gardens, *V. hypopithys*, cap small and white, and *V. taylori*, cap small, gray to grayish-tan, both with spores less than 10 µm long; in cellars, straw heaps, hothouses, compost piles, *V. volvacea*, cap large, dark gray-brown, odor aromatic, volva brown; last and least, *V. surrecta*, a small whitish species parasitic on other agarics (particularly *Clitocybe nebularis*).

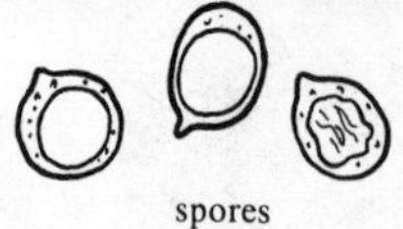

AMANITACEAE

MEMBERS of this family have white spores, white to yellow gills, and an outer veil. The majority are also furnished with an inner veil and the stalk is cleanly separable from the cap.

There are two genera: in *Amanita* the outer veil takes the form of a membranous or powdery volva which envelops the young mushroom; in *Limacella* the outer veil is glutinous, manifesting itself as a layer of slime on the cap and often the stalk.

The Amanitaceae are most likely to be confused with the white-spored Lepiotaceae, which have neither volva nor viscid cap. Microscopically the two families are distinct by virtue of the amyloid or non-amyloid spores and divergent gill hyphae of the Amanitaceae, as opposed to the typically dextrinoid spores and parallel to interwoven gill hyphae of the Lepiotaceae.

Amanita is of paramount importance to toadstool-testers because it contains the deadliest of all mushrooms, as well as some of the most delicious. *Limacella* is too rare to be of culinary value.

Key to the Amanitaceae

1. Volva present at base of stalk as a sack, free collar, or series of concentric rings .... *Amanita,* p. 225
1. Volva absent or indistinct 2

2. Cap viscid or slimy, smooth; stalk often slimy .... *Limacella,* p. 253
2. Cap usually warty or dry and cottony; occasionally viscid but not slimy; stalk never slimy .... *Amanita*, p. 225

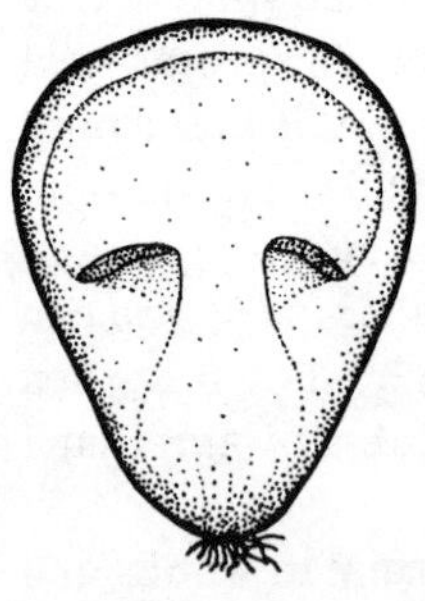
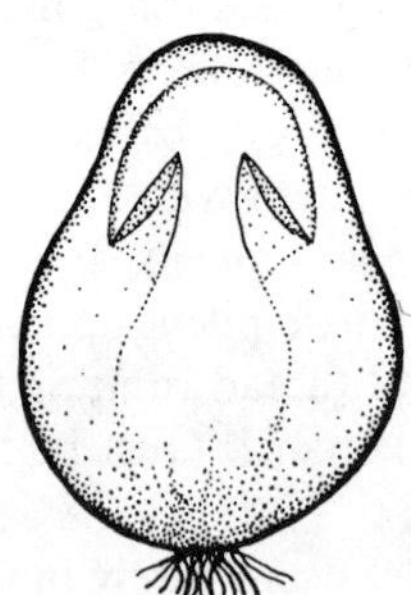
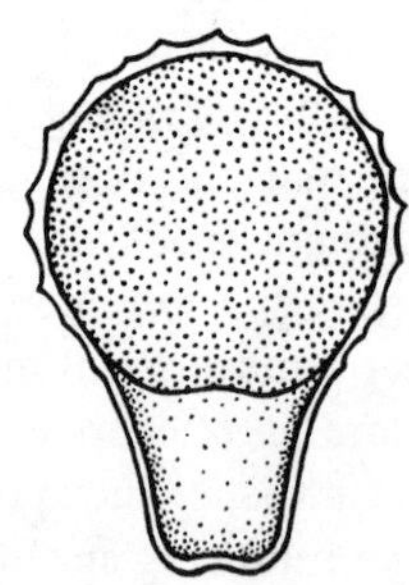

Amanita "eggs" still enveloped by the outer veil (volva) resemble puffballs. However, a longitudinal cross-section reveals the outline of cap, gills, and stalk (left and center), while a puffball (right) is solid within. Note difference in shape between the deadly *A. phalloides* "egg" (center) and the *A. calyptroderma* "egg" (left).

AMANITA (THE AMANITAS)

Medium to large terrestrial fungi found mostly in woods. CAP *smooth or with warts or a cottony patch or other remains of the volva.* GILLS *typically white, creamy, or yellow; close,* attached or free. STALK central, usually hollow or stuffed, cleanly separable from cap. VEIL (inner) *usually present,* forming a membranous ring on stalk. VOLVA *usually present as a sack, rim, collar, or series of concentric rings at base of stalk.* SPORE PRINT *white.* Spores smooth, amyloid or not amyloid. Gill hyphae divergent (at least when young).

LEARNING to recognize this genus should be an overriding priority for all mushroom hunters, since Amanitas are responsible for 90% of mushroom-induced fatalities. The outstanding attributes of any *Amanita*—what makes even a rotten *Amanita* not just another rotten mushroom, but a rotten *Amanita* (and therefore worthy of your attention and respect)—are the white spores, white to yellow gills, and presence of a **volva.** The volva (outer veil) completely envelops the young mushroom, but breaks as the stalk elongates, usually forming a sack or collar at the base of the stalk and often depositing remnants on the cap in the form of a single large piece of tissue (**volval patch**) or many smaller pieces (**warts**). Obviously, it is important to carefully dig up any unfamiliar mushroom so as not to miss the volva (if present). It is also a good idea to examine the surrounding soil to be doubly sure pieces of the volva aren't left behind.

Most Amanitas (including the deadly ones) are also furnished with an inner veil which, upon breaking, forms a skirtlike ring near the top of the stalk. Until recently those species without a ring were placed in a separate genus, *Amanitopsis.* A feature emphasized by many mushroom books is that the gills in *Amanita* are free. This is *not* always the case, however, and this feature is not stressed here.

The only other agarics consistently equipped with a volva are the pinkish-spored Volvariellas. *Agaricus* occasionally forms a volva but has chocolate spores. *Lepiota* superficially resembles *Amanita* but lacks a volva and always has free gills.

Amanita is divided into two groups (subgenera) based on whether or not the spores are amyloid. Half of the species described here (including the deadly ones!) have amyloid spores. These groups are in turn subdivided according to the type of volva (see p. 226). If the volva is **membranous** (skinlike), a loose sack or cup is formed at the base of the stalk and the cap is either bald or adorned with a volval patch. If the volva is **friable** (easily crumbling) it manifests itself as a series of concentric scales or rings around the base of the stem. If the volva is semi-friable and interwoven with the base of the stalk, it will form a

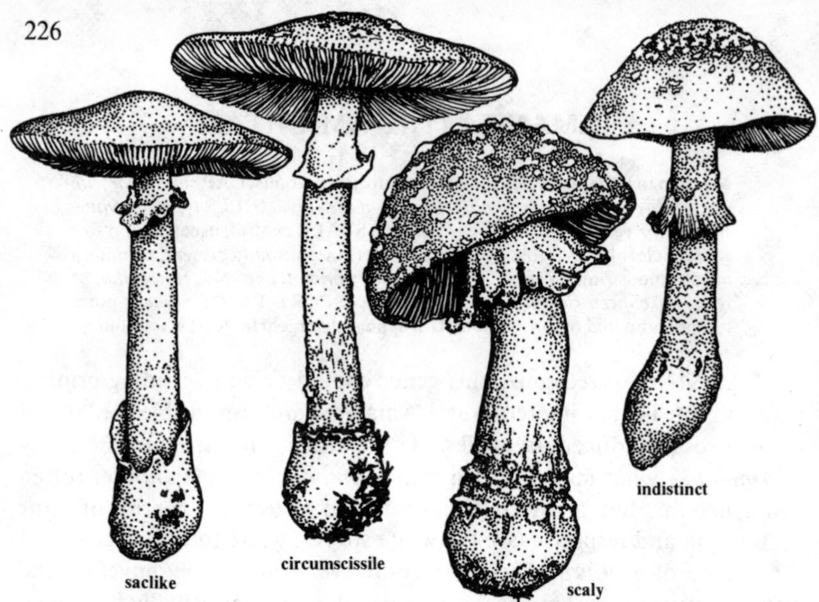

Different types of volvas in *Amanita.* Left to right: *A. phalloides, A. pantherina, A. muscaria, A. rubescens.*

collar or free rim (as in *A. pantherina*), but not a true sack. Unless the volva is membranous, numerous warts are usually deposited on the cap. These warts are typically white, gray, or yellow and, with the exception of *A. strobiliformis*, are readily removable (unlike the colored scales of an *Agaricus* or *Lepiota*). In fact, they are sometimes washed off by rain.

In some Amanitas (such as *A. rubescens* and *A. silvicola*) a distinct volva is not formed. However, vestiges of the outer veil on the cap (in the form of warts or cottony material) signify *Amanita*. In the rare instances in which neither volva nor volval remnants are visible, Amanitas can still be recognized by their uncanny "*Amanita* aura." They are so unequivocally elegant and graceful that you quickly learn to tell an *Amanita* without having to dig it up!

Amanita is a study in antithesis. At one extreme are the most poisonous of all mushrooms—the death cap and destroying angels (*A. phalloides, A. ocreata,* et al). Every fungophile should learn the telltale signs of these deadly fungi (for symptoms and treatment see p. 631). At the other end of the spectrum are two of the most exquisitely flavored of fleshy fungi—*A. caesaria* and *A. calyptroderma.* The rest of the Amanitas fall somewhere in between: several are hallucinogenic and poisonous (*A. muscaria* and *A. pantherina*); others are edible but scarcely incredible (*A. velosa* and *A. vaginata*); still others have not been tested (*A. aspera, A. silvicola,* etc.).

I for one do *not* subscribe to the wholesale philosophy (as expounded by many mushroom mentors) that Amanitas should not be eaten under any circumstances. In my humble fungal opinion, it is just as easy to carelessly overlook the volva and mistake a deadly *Amanita* for an edible mushroom of another genus as to mistake a deadly *Amanita* for the coccora *(A. calyptroderma)* or grisette *(A. vaginata)*. True, *it is sheer stupidity to risk your life for the sake of a single meal,* however delectable it may be. But the key word here is "risk"—in the case of *A. calyptroderma* and *A. vaginata*, I don't consider it a risk for *discriminating* amateurs to eat them provided they become intimately familiar with their characteristics and those of their lethal counterparts. Simplistic slogans or catchwords such as "Do not eat-a the *Amanita*" often accomplish the precise opposite of what they intend. Rather than encouraging people to use their eyes and nose and the gray mass between their ears, to approach each and every mushroom with discrimination, intelligence, and respect, such adages reinforce people's desire for expediency by fostering an unhealthy, mindless reliance on shortcuts and glib generalizations. Such rules can even be misconstrued to read "if a mushroom isn't an *Amanita* it won't kill you"—a dangerous assumption!

Too many people eat and enjoy the edible Amanitas (especially the coccora) for me not to recommend them. But at the risk of being redundant, let me reiterate some rules of the trade. Unless you are *absolutely, indisputably, and irrefutably* sure of your Amanita's identity, don't eat it! (The one adage with which I wholeheartedly concur is: "When in doubt, throw it out!"). If possible, have an experienced collector verify your identification, and collect the species several times before venturing to eat it. Above all, *don't rely on a single characteristic* (such as striate vs. non-striate margin) to distinguish between edible and deadly poisonous species. Each individual mushroom is subject to a different set of environmental and genetic factors—therefore each will be slightly different. Only by using a *combination* of critical characteristics can you rest assured that you have a savory coccora or grisette instead of a death cap or destroying angel. Finally, *don't* assume that two or more Amanitas growing together are the same species. Judge each and every mushroom on its own merits. Also remember that there is always the possibility of encountering species not included in this book.

My reason for delving into the Amanitas in such depth is that they never fail to attract attention and admiration. You certainly needn't eat them to enjoy them, for they are among the most beautiful and graceful of all fungi, the epitome of impeccability and elegance.

The fly agaric *(A. muscaria)*, with its fiery red cap and white "stars" is the most spectacular example, of course. Down through the ages it has been compared to bull testicles and male genitalia and worshipped (more for its appearance, I suspect, than for its properties) as the earthly incarnation of infinity, divinity, and virility. It is one of the commonest mushrooms of our pine forests, yet one never tires of finding it. The variation in color, size, shape, and "constellations" is such that each presents a new and deliciously different feast for the eye. It's hard to resist taking one or two home to show off to impressionable neighbors or friends, but never is the ephemerality of life so emphatically underscored as when they come the next day to pay their respects, only to find a writhing mass of beatific maggots where your blazing incarnation of the cosmos had been.

In contrast to the flamboyant splendor of the fly agaric is the subdued and radiant warmth of the coccora *(A. calyptroderma)*. I say "warmth" because in the egg stage it is so huge and soft that it looks positively warm inside. Finding a family of them in rich red madrone humus is like stumbling on the nest of a rare and secretive woodland bird. And watching a coccora "hatch"—the round, orange head emerging from its cottony cocoon—is like watching the sun rise from a blanket of clouds—a quietly inspiring reaffirmation of life best experienced alone.

Most Amanitas are mycorrhizal. Consequently they are found in the woods or near trees.A few, however, grow in pastures or open ground. *Amanita* attains its greatest diversity in warm, temperate regions such as southeastern North America. Several species are endemic to the west coast and in our region two distinct *Amanita* floras can be recognized. The first, comprised of northern species, occurs primarily with conifers in the late fall and winter. *A. muscaria, A. pantherina,* and *A. silvicola* are prominent examples. The second group has a more southerly distribution and is associated with live oak and madrone. Some members of this group fruit in the fall (*A. phalloides* and *A. calyptroderma*), others in the late winter and spring (*A. velosa, A. rubescens,* and *A. ocreata*).

Despite the large number of studies conducted on *Amanita*, no all-encompassing monograph has been published, perhaps because it is a far more complex genus than originally thought. Particularly perplexing are the Amanitas with amyloid spores and friable volvas (the "Lepidellas") and the *A. vaginata*-complex. I have found more than 20 species in our area, several of them unidentified. Sixteen are described here. Their elegance and individuality of expression make them a fascinating and rewarding group to study, even for those not armed with a microscope.

Key to Amanita

1. Volva saclike, membranous; cap smooth or with a volval patch, rarely with warts 2
1. Volva not saclike; cap usually decorated with warts or cottony volval remnants (which may be washed off or obliterated) 11

2. Cap white (may discolor pinkish, brownish, or buff in age) 3
2. Cap not white 4

3. Ring absent; cap margin markedly striate *A. alba* (see *A. vaginata*, p. 251)
3. Ring present but sometimes disappearing; cap margin not striate .... *A. ocreata*, p. 232

4. Ring present (check more than one specimen if possible); cap margin may or may not be striate 5
4. Ring absent; cap margin striate 7

5. Cap margin *not* striate; cap smooth or occasionally with a thin, silky volval patch; cap usually greenish, yellowish-green, or brownish-green, often with a metallic luster; odor unpleasant in old age .... *A. phalloides*, p. 231
5. Cap margin striate; cap usually with a thick volval patch 6

6. Cap some shade of orange, brown, or yellow *A. calyptroderma*, p. 246
6. Cap greenish; rare .... *A. calyptrata* (see *A. calyptroderma*, p. 246)

7. Cap gray, grayish-brown, or dark brown 8
7. Cap some other color 10

8. Volva forming a loose sack, attached to stalk only at very base 9
8. Not as above .... *A. inaurata*, p. 253

9. Cap usually dark brown (but fading); stalk typically tall (12-30 cm); volva large and often rusty-stained .... *A. "pachycolea,"* p. 250
9. Not as above; cap generally some shade of gray .... *A. vaginata*, p. 251

10. Cap salmon-buff to pale orange, fading in age; usually decorated with a volval patch or warts; typically found in open, but associated with oak (in our area); very common in winter and spring .... *A. velosa* , p. 248
10. Cap reddish-tan to orange-brown or tawny; rarely with a patch; found in woods; rare .... *A. fulva* (see *A. vaginata*, p. 251)

11. Cap bright red, fading in age to orange, yellow-orange, or paler; volva present as a series of concentric rings at base of stalk *A. muscaria*, p. 242
11. Not as above 12

12. Cap with large brown scales; flesh in stalk staining orange and then reddish when cut .... (see *Lepiota rachodes*, p. 259)
12. Not as above 13

13. Cap, stalk, or flesh with pink to reddish stains, or bruising reddish slowly after prolonged handling; maggot tunnels in flesh also reddish; associated with oak .... *A. rubescens*, p. 239
13. Not as above 14

14. Cap small (7 cm broad or less), grayish-white to gray or grayish-brown, with mealy or powdery warts; ring and volva fragile; growing in pastures and open ground .... *Amanita* sp. (unidentified), p. 238
14. Not as above; generally growing in or near woods 15

15. Cap more or less white; sometimes stained buff to yellowish in age 16
15. Cap not white 19

16. Volva present as a free collar at base of stalk ....
.... *A. cothurnata* (see *A. gemmata*, p. 245)
16. Volva indistinct or present as concentric warts or scales 17

17. Cap with prominent warts .... *A. strobiliformis*, p. 236
17. Warts absent or obscure, poorly developed, sparse 18

18. Stalk with a tapered, rooting base; usually growing in sandy soil ....
.... *A. baccata*, p. 235
18. Not as above; cap usually cotttony .... *A. silvicola*, p. 235

19. Cap *and* stalk with pyramidal brownish warty scales; veil *not* forming a ring .... (see *Lepiota hispida*, p. 270)
19. Not as above 20

20. Ring absent; cap gray to dark grayish-brown, margin conspicuously striate
.... *A. inaurata*, p. 253
20. Not as above 21

21. Cap smooth, yellow-brown; stalk with cottony scales below veil; gills attached, soon yellow .... (see *Armillaria albolanaripes*, p. 170)
21. Not as above 22

22. Volva and warts (when young) yellow; ring also yellow (at least partially); volva consisting of concentric rings of powdery scales *A. aspera*, p. 241
22. Not as above; warts white or pallid; volva consisting of a free rim or collar above which there may or may not be concentric rings 23

23. Stalk with grayish patches; cap often with a subtle purplish cast ....
.... *A. porphyria* (see *A. pantherina*, p. 244)
23. Stalk without grayish patches 24

24. Ring absent .... *A. exannulata* (see *A. gemmata*, p. 245)
24. Ring present 25

25. Cap yellow to creamy .... *A. gemmata*, p. 245
25. Cap dull yellowish to yellow-brown, tan, or brown *A. pantherina*, p. 244

Amanita phalloides (Death Cap)

CAP 4-16 cm broad, at first nearly egg-shaped, soon convex, finally plane; surface smooth, viscid when moist, green or yellow-green (sometimes nearly white) when fresh, fading to grayish-green, brassy olive, light brown, tan, or silvery-white in age; shiny when dry, often with a metallic luster; sometimes with a very thin silky white volval patch; margin not striate. Flesh white, odor at first mild but soon pungent (like raw potatoes or chlorine). **GILLS** free or slightly attached, close, white or tinted faintly greenish. **STALK** to 18 cm long, tapering upward with an enlarged base, stuffed or hollow, smooth, white or tinted cap color. **VEIL** membranous, white, forming a persistent but fragile superior skirtlike ring. **VOLVA** membranous, saclike, sheathing the base of the stalk; white, loose or appressed, thin and rather fragile, usually buried in ground. **SPORE PRINT** white; spores 7-12 $\times$ 6-9 μm, round or nearly round, smooth, amyloid.

HABITAT: Solitary, scattered, or in troops in leaf litter near or under live oak (sometimes on lawns if oak is nearby). Common, at times abundant, fall through early winter, occasional in summer, largely supplanted in the spring by *A. ocreata.* It used to be rare but is now the most abundant *Amanita* of our coastal live oak woodlands. Perhaps an adventitious introduction from Europe on the roots of trees, it has taken a fancy to our native live oaks and spread like the plague. I've never found it growing without live oak in the vicinity, but it has recently turned up in New Jersey and Pennsylvania under conifers (reports in older books of *A. phalloides* in eastern North America may actually refer to another species, *A. brunnescens*). Apparently *A. phalloides* can form mycorrhiza with a wide range of hosts.

EDIBILITY: DEADLY POISONOUS! Learn to recognize this species before eating any mushroom with white gills! It is particularly dangerous because the symptoms are delayed, not appearing for from six to 24 hours after ingestion, by which time there is relatively little modern medicine can do. In the last decade there have been several unfortunate deaths in California caused by this mushroom. However, none of the victims were even aware that they were picking Amanitas! For an account of symptoms and treatment, see p. 631.

COMMENTS: There is no rational reason why anyone should mistake the death cap for an edible mushroom. The telltale signs are: (1) white gills (2) white spores (3) veil forming a skirtlike ring near the top of the stalk (4) membranous white sack at the base of the stalk. The ring is

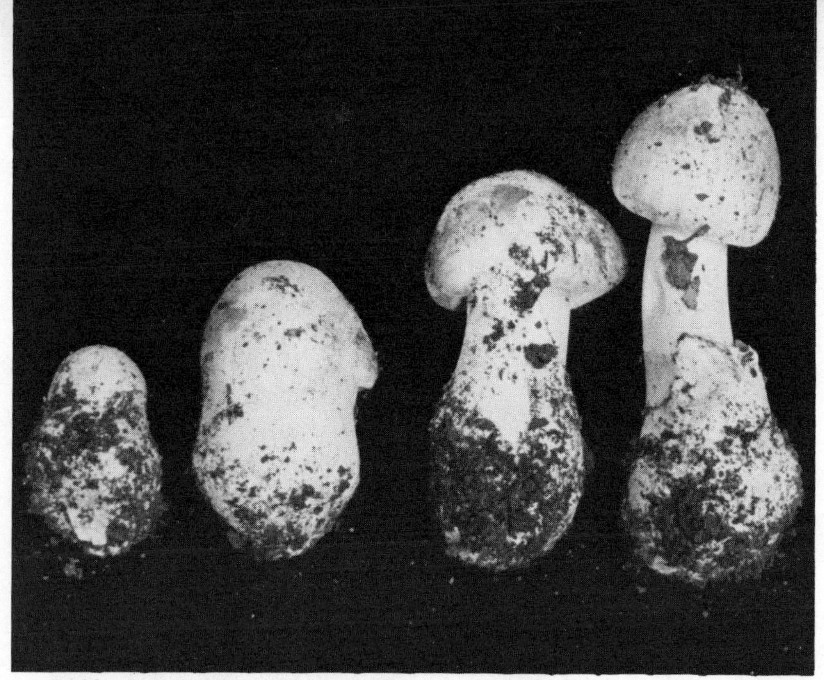

Fruiting body development in the deadly *Amanita phalloides*. At first it is enclosed in a volva; then the cap emerges as the stalk elongates. Finally the cap opens and the veil covering the gills breaks to form a ring on the stalk.

sometimes obliterated and the volva can be carelessly overlooked, so just to be safe, don't eat any mushroom with any two of these characteristics, unless you are absolutely certain of its identity. Remember, your life is at stake! The cap color (usually greenish but extremely variable), absence of warts or striations on the cap, pungent odor in age (it literally reeks of death), and association with live oak are good secondary fieldmarks.

Amanita ocreata (Death Angel; Destroying Angel)

CAP 5-15 cm broad, egg-shaped becoming convex and finally plane; surface viscid when moist, smooth, white, in age discoloring pinkish, buff, or yellowish-brownish, especially toward the center; sometimes with a very thin white volval patch; margin not striate. Flesh thick, firm, white, odor mild becoming disagreeable in old age. **GILLS** at first attached, then free, close, white. **STALK** to 15 cm long, rather thick with an enlarged base, white, powdery at apex. **VEIL** membranous, white, forming a very fragile superior or apical skirtlike ring, or shredding, or disappearing entirely. **VOLVA** membranous, saclike, sheathing the base of the stalk; typically large, white, loose, ample. **SPORE PRINT** white; spores 9-14 × 7-10 μm, broadly ellipsoid to ovoid, smooth, amyloid. Flesh and cap turning bright yellow in KOH.

Maturing specimens of *Amanita phalloides* show the veil (ring), volva (sack), and white gills that characterize the deadly Amanitas. Cap color is variable—usually some shade of green, yellow-green, or brown. These specimens have a thin white volval patch on the cap, but the cap is usually bald.

HABITAT: Solitary or in small groups in oak and oak-madrone woods, winter and spring; common, but seldom abundant. It is known only from California and is apparently associated with live oak. It normally appears in late January or February after *A. phalloides* has finished fruiting.

EDIBILITY: DEADLY POISONOUS! It doesn't enjoy the same notoriety as *A. phalloides* because it's not as common. However, recent studies have revealed the presence of amanita-toxins, so every mushroom hunter should be aware of it.

COMMENTS: This elegant, pristine-pure, lethal-looking *Amanita* is our only white mushroom with a veil and saclike volva. The species name *ocreata* (meaning "sheathed") refers to the voluminous volva, which may extend as much as half way up the stalk! The veil, however, is very fragile and does not always form a ring. *A. alba* (see *A. vaginata*) has a saclike volva and no veil, but the cap is markedly striate. *A. ocreata* differs from the deadly white Amanitas (destroying angels) of eastern North America (*A. virosa, A. verna,* and *A. bisporigera*) in its larger spores and tendency to discolor as it ages.

A small white *Amanita* with a very thin, saclike volva closely pressed against the stalk also occurs in our area. It appears to be undescribed

Amanita ocreata. This deadly white species is pure white when young but develops pinkish or brownish stains on the cap as it ages. Note the fragile ring, voluminous volva, and white gills. Another specimen is shown on p. 14.

and should definitely be considered poisonous. *A. bivolvata* is another pure white *Amanita* peculiar to California. It closely resembles *A. ocreata* but has a double volva (a free collar within the outer sack). It was originally described from Claremont, California, but I have found it in a drainage ditch in the Santa Cruz Mountains with live oak and knobcone pine in close proximity. Whether it is indeed distinct from *A. ocreata* or is merely an ecological variant is for the *Amanita*-authorities to decide.

Left: This elegant example of *Amanita ocreata* is more aptly called "Death Egret" than "Death Angel." **Right:** *Amanita silvicola* is white like *A. ocreata*, but has a cottony cap and lacks a sack at base of stalk.

Amanita silvicola (Sylvan Amanita)

CAP 5-10 cm broad, convex then plane; surface dry, white, covered with cottony or fluffy remains of the volva; margin often hung with veil remnants, not striate. Flesh firm, white, odor mild or slightly soapy. **GILLS** white, close, usually attached but sometimes free in age; edges finely powdered. **STALK** to 12 cm long but usually stocky in relation to cap, enlarged at base but not rooting; dry, white, powdered above. **VEIL** white, delicate, forming a slight ring or disappearing entirely. **VOLVA** circumscissile or indistinct—consisting of cottony white zones or patches at base of stalk which often disappear or remain in ground. **SPORE PRINT** white; spores 9-12 × 5-6 µm, ellipsoid, smooth, weakly amyloid.

HABITAT: Solitary or in small groups in mixed woods of tanoak, madrone, and Douglas-fir, near Boulder Creek. Rather rare, fruiting in fall and winter. Central California may be the southernmost limit of its range. It is common in the Pacific Northwest.

EDIBILITY: Unknown. Do not experiment.

COMMENTS: This attractive, pure white *Amanita* can be told at a glance by its cottony white cap and rather stocky stature. The cap is not warty as in *A. strobiliformis* and relatives, the volva is not saclike as in *A. ocreata*, and the stalk does not have a tapered, rooting base as in *A. baccata.* The attached gills and indistinct volva can lead to confusion with *Armillaria*, but the stalk is cleanly separable from the cap and it has that indescribable "*Amanita* aura."

Amanita baccata

CAP 5-10 cm broad, convex becoming plane; surface dry, white (but usually dirty), with obscure mealy or powdery warts or volval remnants which may disappear; margin often hung with veil remnants, not striate. Flesh white, firm, odor mild or slightly pungent. **GILLS** close, white, becoming dingy yellowish in old age, usually attached but sometimes free. **STALK** to 18 cm long, equal above with a long tapered rooting base and enlarged just above the "root"; dry, white, powdery-cottony or with delicate ragged scales. **VEIL** white, cottony, very fragile, disappearing or forming a thin, poorly defined superior ring. **VOLVA** indistinct or present as a scaly zone just above the rooting base; friable **SPORE PRINT** white; spores 10.5-14 × 4-6.5 µm, cylindrical, smooth amyloid.

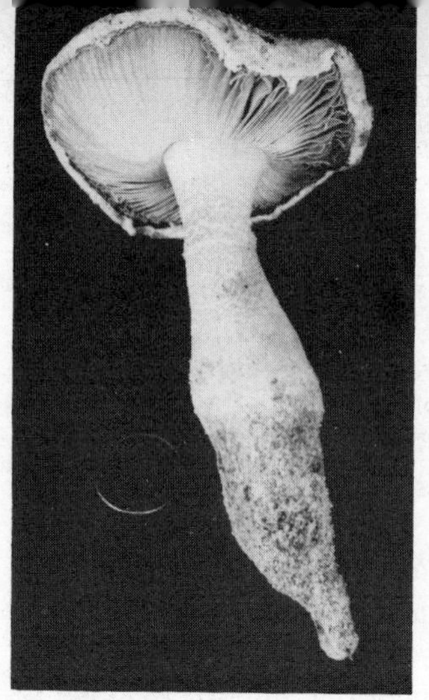

Left: *Amanita baccata.* This unusual whitish species has a tapered rooting base and grows almost exclusively in sand. The cap lacks prominent warts. **Right:** Top view of the warty cap in *Amanita strobiliformis.*

HABITAT: Solitary or in small groups on the ground (usually buried) in dry, open, sandy woods of oak and pine. Late fall and winter, uncommon. I have found it near Bonny Doon and Felton. It appears to be associated with live oak.

EDIBILITY: Unknown. Do not experiment!

COMMENTS: To my knowledge, this is the first published report of this odd, inelegant *Amanita* from North America. It occurs in similar habitats in southern Europe and northern Africa and has several pseudonyms, including *A. boudieri.* The tapered, rooting stem base, habitat in sand, cylindrical spores, and lack of prominent warts on the cap are the critical features. The cap is scarcely elevated above ground level and both the cap and rooting base are usually covered with dirt or sand. An unidentified, whitish *Amanita* with a large, broad bulb on the stalk and a short, tapered rooting base also occurs in our area. It is much stockier than *A. baccata*, has ellipsoid to ovoid spores and is not found in sandy soil. In fact, it is more reminiscent of *A. rubescens*, but doesn't stain reddish.

Amanita strobiliformis (Pine Cone Amanita)

CAP 5-30 cm broad, convex becoming plane; surface dry or slightly viscid when moist, white to creamy-white becoming yellowish-buff in old age (sometimes with darker stains), covered with erect, persistent, pyramidal or truncated warts which become flattened in age; margin usually with cottony veil remnants, not striate. Flesh thick, firm, white,

Amanita strobiliformis. An impressive whitish *Amanita* with prominent warts on the cap, a warty volva, and rooting stalk base.

odor mild or like chlorine or dirty socks. **GILLS** attached or free, very close, white or creamy, delicately powdered. **STALK** to 25 cm long, rooting in the ground, equal above, slightly enlarged below with the rooting portion tapering to a blunt point; white or with brownish-buff stains. **VEIL** membranous, white, forming a fragile, superior, skirtlike ring. **VOLVA** scaly, consisting of a series of concentrically arranged warts or scales at the base of the stalk, which darken somewhat in age. **SPORE PRINT** white; spores 9.5-15 × 5.5-10 μm, ovoid to ellipsoid, smooth, amyloid.

HABITAT: Solitary or in small groups under live oak and pine. Sporadically common in the fall and spring, less so in winter.

EDIBILITY: Unknown. Its edibility has been contested, but all white Amanitas should be avoided.

COMMENTS: One of our most spectacular mushrooms—the large, prominent warts on the cap set it apart, making it look like a white pine cone. There is doubt as to whether our variety is the true *A. strobiliformis*, but the above description will suffice for a complex group of warty white Amanitas with amyloid spores that have collectively passed under the names *A. solitaria* and *A. strobiliformis*. The name *A. chlorinosma* has been applied to any number of chlorine-smelling forms, while one large western species was recently christened

A. smithiana. At least two distinct varieties occur in our area: at one extreme is the common form with large, erect, inherent warts (interwoven with the cap surface); at the other extreme is a form with superficial warts (easily rubbed off). Needless to say, intermediates occur, and the situation is complicated by variation in spore size and odor. Until the situation is cleared up (or muddled further) by eminent amanitologists, there is no harm in nonchalantly referring to the pine cone-like variety as *A. strobiliformis* and the others as *A. solitaria* (or *A. smithiana*).

Amanita sp. (unidentified) (Anonymous Amanita)

CAP 2.5-8 cm broad (usually 3-5 cm), convex becoming plane; surface dry, grayish-white to gray or brownish-gray, covered with mealy or powdery warts which are easily obliterated; margin not striate. Flesh white, odor rather pungent in age. **GILLS** usually attached, close, creamy-white becoming dingy yellowish or yellowish-orange in old age. **STALK** to 7.5 cm long but usually much shorter, equal or tapering downward, sometimes with a short, rooting base, sometimes swollen slightly above the base; white and striate above the veil, dingy whitish or tinged cap color below and somewhat scaly. **VEIL** membranous but very fragile, disappearing or forming a superior, median, or even basal ring. **VOLVA** scaly or indistinct, friable, usually leaving obscure grayish scales or powdery-mealy warts over lower portion of stalk. **SPORE PRINT** white; spores 7-11 × 5-8.5 μm, ovoid to ellipsoid, smooth, amyloid.

Amanita sp. (unidentified). An odd, unimposing species that is locally abundant in pastures and open ground. Note the small size, stocky stature, and grayish warts on the cap. The fragile ring and volva are easily obliterated.

HABITAT: Scattered to densely gregarious in pastures, open fields, vacant lots, etc., fall and winter. Fairly common; overwhelmingly abundant during the soggy fall of 1977 in and around Santa Cruz. It usually grows in the open and is apparently not mycorrhizal. It sometimes mingles with *Agaricus campestris*, which it superficially resembles.

EDIBILITY: Unknown. Do not experiment!

COMMENTS: This anomalous, anonymous *Amanita* is quite unamanitalike with its short stem, compact mealy-warty grayish cap, and predilection for growing in pastures. The volva is so friable that it may disappear, but the warts on the cap signify *Amanita*. It belongs to a very complex group of white to grayish Amanitas (the "Lepidellas") with amyloid spores and friable volvas. In addition to *A. strobiliformis*, *A. silvicola*, and *A. baccata*, we have several members of this group that do not seem to fit any existing descriptions. This species is a prime example. *A. cinereoconia* is a somewhat similar but larger species found in eastern North America.

Amanita rubescens (Blushing Amanita; The Blusher)

CAP 5-15 cm broad, at first egg-shaped, soon convex, finally plane; surface viscid or dry, at first completely covered with mealy white warts, becoming sordid reddish, pinkish, reddish-brown, brown, or grayish-brown in age, the warts often wearing away; margin sometimes obscurely striate. Flesh white, slowly turning reddish when bruised, maggot tunnels also reddish; odor mild. **GILLS** attached when young, sometimes free in age, white or pallid, sometimes stained reddish, close. **STALK** to 15 cm long, equal above with an enlarged base, at first white or pallid, but soon stained reddish or pinkish (and often somewhat scaly) below the veil; powdery-white or tinged pinkish above. **VEIL** white, membranous, forming a fragile superior skirtlike ring. **VOLVA** friable, usually indistinct, when visible consisting of sordid reddish zones at base of stalk. **SPORE PRINT** white; spores 8-10 × 5-6 μm, ellipsoid, smooth, amyloid.

HABITAT: Solitary, scattered, or in groups under or near live oak. Fruiting throughout the mushroom season but normally common only in late winter and spring (Feb.-April); frequently found with *A. velosa* and *A. ocreata*. In 1977 there was a sizable crop after the first fall rains.

Amanita rubescens is an extremely variable species. These mature specimens show the warts on the cap, prominent ring, reddish-stained stalk, and indistinct volva.

EDIBILITY: Indigestible raw, edible when cooked. It is highly esteemed in Europe (chiefly France), but I'm not particularly fond of it, and the possibility of confusing it with poisonous Amanitas precludes me from recommending it.

COMMENTS: The "blushing" of the cap, stem, and flesh is the one infallible fieldmark of this fickle fungus. The blushing is slow, and is best seen on wounded areas or around the edges of larvae tunnels. In other respects it is an exasperatingly variable *Amanita.* Young specimens may be pure white while older individuals will usually develop strong reddish or brownish tones. The warts may be evenly disposed over the entire cap surface, or concentrated at the center, or more prevalent toward the margin, or completely absent (especially after it rains). Mature specimens are sometimes mistaken for *A. pantherina* (if they are brownish), or even *A. muscaria* (if they are reddish), but the indistinct volva, reddish stains, and amyloid spores separate it. Pure white buttons, on the other hand, can be confused with the *A. strobiliformis*-group, but lack the tapered, rooting base of those species. The attached gills and absence of a volva may lead one to look for it in *Armillaria,* but once again the reddish stains (usually most pronounced on the stem) are distinct.

There is a subtle disparity between our variety and the *A. rubescens* of eastern North America and Europe. The differences are difficult to pinpoint, but they may account for the discrepancy in flavor—at any rate, a critical comparison would be useful.

Amanita aspera. The form illustrated here has a dark brown to yellow-brown cap and is common under conifers. The warts are yellow becoming grayish in age. A form with a bright yellow cap is frequent under madrone. (Bill Everson)

Amanita aspera

CAP 5-15 cm broad, obtuse to convex, then plane; surface viscid when moist, dark brown to grayish-brown, yellow-brown, or yellow, covered with yellow mealy warts which become flattened and grayish to dingy buff in age, or occasionally disappear; margin not striate or faintly striate. Flesh white or tinged yellow, soft. **GILLS** white or creamy-yellowish, close, at first attached, then free. **STALK** to 24 cm long, tapering upward, the base usually enlarged, pallid to yellow above the ring, grayish to yellow, grayish-yellow, pallid, or brownish below. **VEIL** membranous, white or pale yellow above, bright yellow to grayish-yellow on the underside; forming a superior skirtlike ring. **VOLVA** scaly and easily obliterated, consisting of a series of soft, powdery concentric yellow to yellowish-gray scales at base of stalk. **SPORE PRINT** white; spores 8-10 × 6-7 μm, ellipsoid, smooth, amyloid.

HABITAT: Solitary, scattered, or in small groups in woods, often growing with *A. muscaria*, partial to pine and madrone. The fruiting pattern is like that of *A. vaginata*—instead of appearing in one large, spectacular burst, it is common throughout the season, but seldom abundant.

EDIBILITY: To be avoided. Chemical analysis has failed to reveal the presence of toxins found in other Amanitas, but this does *not* mean it is edible.

COMMENTS: The yellow volva and veil remnants distinguish this elegant *Amanita* from *A. pantherina* and *A. gemmata.* Also, the volva is powdery-scaly rather than circumscissile, and the spores are amyloid. The cap color ranges from bright yellow through dark brown, and is apt to bewilder the color-conscious beginner. In my experience the variety found with madrone is more highly colored than the one found with conifers—the two may even be distinct. Fresh specimens are among our most beautiful mushrooms.

Amanita muscaria (Fly Agaric; Fly Amanita)

CAP 7-35 cm broad, almost round when young, becoming convex and finally plane; surface viscid when moist, deep red to bright red, fading or washing out to orange, yellow-orange, or paler; at first covered with a dense coating of cottony or mealy white or yellow warts which are scattered and flattened in age or sometimes washed off by rain; margin striate. Flesh soft, thick, white, odor mild, taste nauseating. **GILLS** free or barely attached, white or creamy, close. **STALK** to 30 cm long, stout, equal with a bulb at the base, white or tinged creamy-yellowish, somewhat fibrillose. **VEIL** white or with yellowish patches, membranous, usually forming a thin, superior skirtlike ring. **VOLVA** friable, scaly, consisting of a series of concentric rings on or above the bulb. **SPORE PRINT** white; spores 8-11 × 6-8 μm, broadly ellipsoid, smooth, not amyloid.

HABITAT: Solitary, scattered, or gregarious in woods or at their edges, during cool weather, fall through early spring. Very common in pine forests, occasional under live oak and madrone. It is often found with *Boletus edulis*. In our area they both grow primarily with pine and secondarily with oak (one very large fairy ring of more than 100 fly agarics had three bulky *Boletus edulis* growing in the middle of it!). In the Rocky Mountains both are abundant at high elevations under spruce and less commonly under pine. In the Himalayas I found them side by side under fir. *Amanita muscaria* is also mycorrhizal with birch.

EDIBILITY: Poisonous and hallucinogenic. Esteemed both by maggots and magic mushroom hunters. Fatalities are extremely rare, but it is undoubtedly dangerous in large amounts. The effects vary from person to person and from mushroom to mushroom, and there is no way to determine in advance what your reaction will be. Too many people have had unpleasant experiences for me to recommend it. Tales of "getting off" by nibbling a piece of the veil and licking the "stars" off the cap are frivolous not to mention foolish. For an account of the

Amanita muscaria, immature and mature specimens. Cap is bright red, the stalk and warts are white (or occasionally yellow). Note the scaly volva, consisting of a series of concentric rings.

symptoms, see p. 633. The name "fly agaric," incidentally, comes from its use as a fly poison (it stuns flies but doesn't kill them). It is also remarkable for its ability to concentrate vanadium—a rare, malleable, ductile metal used to add tensile strength to steel.

Amanita muscaria. **Left:** A young button completely covered with white warts (the outer veil). **Right:** "Bloody mirror of the galaxy." This large button was frisbee-sized when fully expanded. (Joel Leivick)

COMMENTS: This brilliant red mushroom needs no introduction—it is known to every myopic middle-class mystic in America. Its caricature appears on key chains, incense holders, posters, candles, curtains, calling cards, and in children's books. Large plastic reproductions can be found on lawns and in display windows. The irony of it is that few people realize such a mushroom actually exists! The color, of course, is its outstanding fieldmark. The presence of a ring, volva, and warts on the cap separate it from other red mushrooms (notably Russulas), and unless you're color blind it is difficult to confuse it with any other native *Amanita.* The cap may fade as it ages, especially when growing in the open, but will usually retain faint vestiges of its original splendor.

Varieties with yellow-orange and grayish-white caps are also known. These color forms can be separated from *A. gemmata* by the structure of the volva, which consists of a series of concentric rings, the lowermost of which rims the bulb. Large specimens must be transported very carefully, as the stalk breaks easily near its juncture with the cap.

Amanita pantherina (Panther Amanita)

CAP 5-25 cm broad, convex becoming plane; surface viscid when moist, dark brown to light brown, tan, dull yellow, or yellow-brown, often paler at the margin; covered with whitish warts (sometimes sparse or washed off by rain); margin striate. Flesh firm, white, odor mild. **GILLS** at first reaching the stalk, then free; close, white. **STALK** to 18 cm long, equal with an enlarged base or bulb; dry, white, smooth above the ring, fibrillose below. **VEIL** white, membranous, forming a superior or median skirtlike ring, sometimes leaving tissue on cap margin also. **VOLVA** circumscissile, adhering to the bulb but with a free rim or collar and sometimes also with one or more ragged zones above the collar. **SPORE PRINT** white; spores 9-12 $\times$ 6.5-8 μm, elliptical, smooth, not amyloid.

HABITAT: Solitary, scattered, or gregarious in woods of all kinds, fall through spring, very common. The typical form, a characteristic component of northern coniferous forests, fruits in our area from November through February. A small, slender form with a toothed ring is common in winter and spring under hardwoods.

EDIBILITY: Poisonous/hallucinogenic. It contains the same toxins as *A. muscaria* but in higher concentrations. Large doses can be fatal.

COMMENTS: The brown to tan or dull yellowish cap with whitish warts and the free rim or collar at the top of the basal bulb are the key

Amanita pantherina, young button at right, mature specimen at left, intermediate stages between. Note the circumscissile volva (collared bulb at the stalk base).

characteristics. It resembles *A. muscaria* but does not have a red cap. As is often the case in *Amanita*, the cap color varies considerably, and even appears to intergrade with *A. gemmata. A. porphyria* is a somewhat similar species with a large basal bulb, grayish patches on the stem, and a grayish-brown cap sometimes tinted purplish. It is frequent under conifers farther north.

Amanita gemmata (Jonquil Amanita)

CAP 5-14 cm broad, convex to plane; surface viscid when moist (beneath the warts), yellow to pale yellow, creamy-yellow, or yellowish-buff, covered with large whitish warts (or sometimes a patch or patches); margin striate. Flesh white, soft, odor mild. **GILLS** at first attached, then free; close, white or creamy. **STALK** to 15 cm long, equal with an enlarged base or bulb, dry, white or whitish. **VEIL** membranous, white, forming a fragile superior ring or sometimes none at all. **VOLVA** circumscissile, adhering to the bulb with a free rim or collar, sometimes with ragged zones above the collar. **SPORE PRINT** white; spores 7.5-12 × 6-9 μm, ellipsoid, smooth, not amyloid.

HABITAT: Solitary or in small groups in woods, fall and winter. Fairly common, especially under oak.

EDIBILITY: To be avoided. Some *Amanita*-addicts claim it's edible, but the risk of confusing it with *A. pantherina* is great.

COMMENTS: The yellow to creamy-yellow cap distinguishes this species from typical *A. pantherina*. However, a confusing series of "hybrids" exist, whose cap color and toxicity is intermediate between the two. The ring and volva are not yellow as in *A. aspera*, and the volva is not saclike as in *A. calyptroderma*. In some cases the warts merge to form a volval patch. *A. junquillea* is very similar if not the same. A short, stocky version (*A. exannulata*) with a dense coating of volval material on the cap and no ring is occasionally encountered. *A. cothurnata* is a similar species with a ring and white or whitish cap.

Amanita calyptroderma (Coccora)

CAP 7-35 cm broad, egg-shaped becoming convex, finally plane; surface smooth, viscid when moist, orange to orange-brown, dark brown, or pale yellow, usually with a large, thick, cottony white patch of volval tissue; margin striate, usually yellow. Flesh thick, soft, white or yellowish, odor mild. **GILLS** adnate to free, white to creamy-yellowish, close. **STALK** up to 25 cm long, 2-3 cm thick, equal or enlarged below, smooth, pallid to creamy-yellowish, hollow, often filled with a cottony or jellylike substance. **VEIL** membranous, pallid or creamy-yellowish, forming a large but fragile superior skirtlike ring which is easily obliterated. **VOLVA** membranous, forming a large sack at base of stalk; thick, ample, felty or cottony, white, sometimes double (with a free collar inside the sack). **SPORE PRINT** white; spores 9-11 × 5-6 μm, ellipsoid, smooth, not amyloid.

Amanita calyptroderma, immature specimens. Note the large cottony white volval patch on the cap and the huge volva. An unexpanded button is shown on p. 527.

Amanita calyptroderma, mature specimens. Note the striate cap margin. The volval patch is not as thick and cottony as in young specimens. (Joel Leivick)

HABITAT: Solitary, scattered, or gregarious in woods, common in the fall after heavy rains, especially at higher elevations in the coastal mountains. Madrone is its favorite mycorrhizal associate, but it occasionally grows with conifers and oak. The fruiting behavior of the typical variety (with orange to brown cap) mimics that of *Boletus appendiculatus*—stupendous crops are sometimes produced in October or November, but if rains are delayed until December, it does not fruit at all. The variety with a pale yellow cap is fairly common in the winter, but never abundant. It is more prevalent in the Sierras. Both varieties are restricted to the west coast.

EDIBILITY: Edible and unsurpassed. Careful cooking is required to highlight its subtle, delicate flavor. Caps are superb stuffed and then broiled. The hollow stems can be sliced crosswise (to make rings) and marinated. Too many people eat and enjoy this *Amanita* for me not to recommend it—however, be *absolutely sure* of your identification, and review comments on p. 227. The soft flesh does not keep well, so use what you pick as soon as possible. Italian-Americans hunt it with a passion, undoubtedly due to its resemblance to the fabled *A. caesaria* of Italy. "Coccora" (or "Cocoli" or "Coconi") is derived from the Italian for "cocoon"—a very apt description of the large, soft, cottony "eggs."

COMMENTS: This magnificent mushroom is distinguished by (1) the large size (2) orange to brown (or pale yellow) cap (3) cottony white "skullcap" on the cap (4) striate cap margin (5) creamy-yellowish tints to the stalk and veil (6) thick, voluminous, saclike volva (7) non-amyloid spores. Even beginners have little trouble recognizing it once they've seen it several times. In the deadly *A. phalloides* the cap is usually (but not always) greenish, there is no volval patch or if one is present it is very thin, the cap margin is not striate, the spores are amyloid, and a pungent odor usually develops in age. Veteran toadstool-testers can differentiate them at a glance by their color, but beginners should not place undue emphasis on such a variable character.

A rare species, *A. calyptrata*, is a confusing compromise between the two. It has the greenish cap of *A. phalloides* and the thick volval patch, striate cap margin, and non-amyloid spores of *A. calyptroderma*. Many mycologists regard it as another color form of *A. calyptroderma*, and deem it unworthy of specific rank. I have found it only once, under a live oak, in January. It is undoubtedly edible but should *not* be eaten because of its resemblance to *A. phalloides*. Our other Amanitas with a thick volval patch (*A. velosa, A. "pachycolea,"* etc.) lack a ring and are differently colored. Occasionally the warts on *A. gemmata* or *A. pantherina* merge together to simulate a patch, but the volva in both species is circumscissile, not saclike.

Finally, no catalog of the Amanitas is complete without homage being paid to the coccora's close cousin—the splendid *A. caesaria* ("Caesar's Amanita"). This peerless prince of the Amanitas has a bright red to orange cap, yellow gills, and a voluminous white saclike volva. Judged by many to be the most delectable of all gilled fungi, it is found in the hardwood forests of southern Europe and eastern North America (especially in the South, where it sometimes forms enormous fairy rings), as well as in the mountain pine forests of Arizona, New Mexico, Mexico, and possibly southern California.

Amanita velosa (Springtime Amanita)

CAP up to 15 cm broad, at first egg-shaped, soon convex, finally plane; surface viscid when moist, smooth, pale orange to salmon-buff or pinkish-tan, fading in age (or sunlight) to tan, buff, beige, or even silvery-white; usually with a cottony white volval patch or several large, thick warts; margin striate. Flesh thick, white, odor rather pungent. **GILLS** attached or free, close, white, sometimes tinted sordid pinkish in old age. **STALK** to 12 cm long, more or less equal, white or tinged cap color, apex powdery, lower portion smooth or broken into scales; stuffed or hollow. **VEIL** (inner) absent, but a rudimentary ring sometimes present as a cottony-scaly zone. **VOLVA** saclike, usually buried,

Amanita velosa. This variable species may have a volval patch on the cap or a few large warts. Note the striate cap margin and absence of a ring. It fruits in late winter and spring.

sheathing the stalk base, membranous, white, ample but sometimes disintegrating. **SPORE PRINT** white or tinged very slightly pinkish; spores 8.5-11 × 6-10.5 μm,, nearly round to ovate, smooth, not amyloid.

HABITAT: Solitary, scattered, or gregarious in pastures and around their edges, in brushy areas, poor soil, and lawns—associated with live oak. Common, winter and spring. It usually grows in the open, but its mycorrhizal host (live oak, often stunted) will be found within fifty feet. It is endemic to the Pacific Coast and is more common in central and southern California than anywhere else. *A. velosa*, *A. rubescens*, and *A. ocreata* form a striking triumvirate of springtime Amanitas that are monogamous (in our area) with live oak.

EDIBILITY: Edible and good—I have tried it. It's especially useful because it fruits in the spring, when there is a paucity of edible mushrooms about, but it is definitely *not* a good mushroom for beginners. The danger of misidentification far outweighs the benefits reaped from eating it.

COMMENTS: The more or less pale orange to beige cap with a striate margin and volval patch (or warts), absence of a ring, saclike volva, and habit of fruiting in the open are the fallible fieldmarks of this handsome but variable fungus. Bleached-out caps bear little resemblance to fresh ones, but its fondness for growing in pastures is unusual for an *Amanita*. It is the last of its clan to appear—not showing up until late January or February—but, as if to make up for its tardiness, it lingers around until April or May.

Its closest relative is *A. calyptroderma*, which is larger, has a ring, and grows in the woods. However, *A. velosa* often has a rudimentary ring and one specimen I found had a full-fledged membranous veil that covered the gills when young and broke to form a ring. This lends credence to the recent trend of de-emphasizing gross anatomical (Friesian) features and paying more attention to chemical and microscopic similarities. The obsolete genus *Amanitopsis* (Amanitas without a ring) was incorporated into *Amanita* on just such a pretext. The trend may bode ill for the multitudes without microscopes, but it does at least reflect natural affinities more accurately.

Amanita "pachycolea" (Western Grisette)

CAP 7-20 cm broad, at first egg-shaped, then convex, finally plane or with a low, broad umbo; surface smooth, viscid when moist, dark brown to brown, usually darker at the center and paler toward the margin, sometimes washed out and much paler; occasionally with a thick white volval patch; margin conspicuously striate or furrowed. Flesh soft, white, odor mild. **GILLS** white when young, sometimes discolored slightly in age, close, adnexed becoming free. **STALK** 12-30 cm long or longer, rather slender, equal or tapering upward, usually covered with delicate grayish or brownish fibrillose scales; stuffed or hollow. **VEIL** (inner) absent. **VOLVA** saclike, membranous, white but often rusty-stained; large, thick, ample, sheathing the lower portion of stalk but attached only at the base. **SPORE PRINT** white; spores 11-14.5 × 8-10.5 μm, ovate to nearly round, smooth, not amyloid.

HABITAT: Solitary or in small groups in mixed woods and under conifers, fall and winter, fairly common. Like *A. vaginata*, it does not fruit in large numbers. Known only from the west coast.

EDIBILITY: Edible when cooked and fairly good; along with *A. vaginata,* it is the safest of the Amanitas for the table. See comments on p. 227 if you intend to eat it.

COMMENTS: This lofty *Amanita* is easily recognized by its brown deeply striate cap, large saclike volva, and absence of a ring. It is one of the most stunningly elegant of all mushrooms, differing from its close relative *A. vaginata* in its brown (rather than gray) cap, much longer stem, and frequent presence of rusty stains on the volva. The stalk in mature specimens is so long and fragile that transporting them home in one piece is difficult. The name *A. "pachycolea"* is placed in quotes be-

Amanita "pachycolea," mature specimens. This lofty, elegant *Amanita* has a large saclike volva, no ring, and a deeply striate dark brown cap.

cause the person who named it (N. Nakamura) never published it. It is tentative, pending a critical comparison with *A. umbrinolutea*, a European species with a dark brown ring around the inner edge of the cap striations. At least a few of our specimens exhibit this idiosyncrasy.

Amanita vaginata (Grisette)

CAP 5-15 cm broad, at first egg-shaped, then convex, finally plane or with a slight umbo; surface viscid when moist, smooth, gray to grayish-brown, sometimes with a white volval patch; margin deeply striate (furrowed). Flesh soft, white, odor mild. **GILLS** white or tinted slightly grayish, close, adnexed to free. **STALK** to 15 cm long, rather slender, equal or tapering upward, smooth and white or covered with delicate grayish or grayish-brown fibrillose scales. **VEIL** (inner) absent. **VOLVA** saclike, membranous, white, sheathing the stalk but attached only at base. **SPORE PRINT** white; spores 8-12 μm, more or less round, smooth, not amyloid.

HABITAT: Solitary, scattered, or in small groups on ground in woods of all kinds. Common, but seldom in large numbers, fall and winter, occasionally early spring.

EDIBILITY: Edible when cooked and fairly good. It is the safest of the edible Amanitas insofar as it is easy to identify, but see comments on p. 227 before eating it. It does not refrigerate well.

COMMENTS: The combination of deeply striate gray to brownish-gray cap, white gills, absence of a ring, and membranous sack at the base of the stem typifies a group of Amanitas collectively called *A. vaginata*. The group is especially complex in the West, and on the local level there are at least two varieties (in addition to *A. "pachycolea"* and *A. "constricta"*). In one the stem is smooth and silky white; in the other it is decorated with delicate grayish fibrillose scales. Both are smaller and grayer than *A. pachycolea* and don't have a rusty stained volva. Both differ from *A. inaurata* and *A. "constricta"* in their ample, saclike volva which is attached only to the very base of the stem.

In addition there are two species formerly considered color forms of *A. vaginata. A. fulva* has a reddish-brown to orange-brown (fulvous) cap. It is reported from southern California but I haven't seen it. *A. alba* is a very rare species with a white cap. I have found it once in Santa Cruz County and it is also recorded from San Mateo County. Both have the deeply striate cap and white saclike volva characteristic of *A. vaginata*, and both lack a ring. *A. alba* should not be eaten because of its superficial resemblance to the death angel, *A. ocreata*. Synonyms for *A. vaginata* include *Amanitopsis vaginata* and *Vaginata plumbea*.

Left: *Amanita vaginata*, mature specimens. Cap is gray to grayish-brown and markedly striate; volva is saclike, ring is absent. A developing button is shown on p. 51. **Right:** *Amanita "constricta"* (see *A. inaurata*). The volva is not truly saclike: below it is constricted around the stalk, above it flares outward. It is the most common member of the *A. vaginata* group in our area.

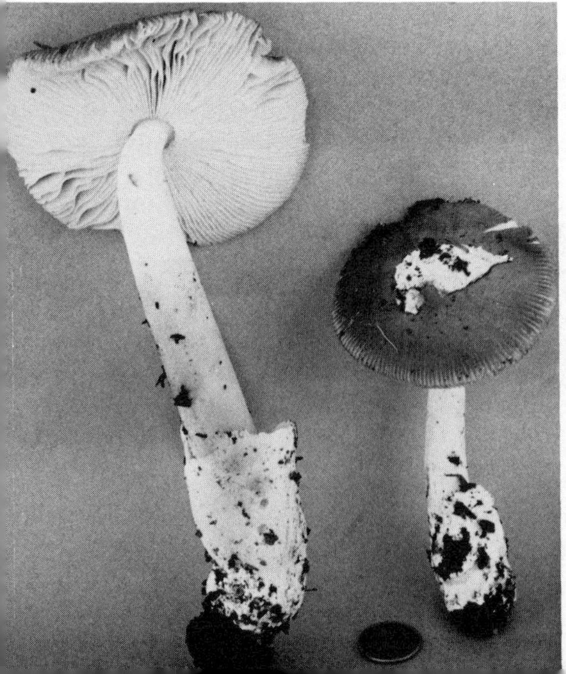

Amanita inaurata (Warty Grisette)

CAP 5-13 cm broad, egg-shaped to convex becoming plane; surface viscid when moist, brownish-black to grayish-brown or gray, covered with thick, grayish warts; margin conspicuously striate. Flesh thin, soft, white, odor mild. **GILLS** white or tinged grayish, close, slightly attached becoming free. **STALK** to 18 cm long, equal or tapering upward, hollow or stuffed, white with grayish patches, fibrils, or mealy scales. **VEIL** (inner) absent. **VOLVA** white or grayish, saclike but friable, usually crumbling and leaving behind only indistinct concentric zones at base of stalk. **SPORE PRINT** white; spores 11-15 × 9.5-13 μm, round or nearly round, smooth, not amyloid.

HABITAT: Solitary or in small groups in woods, fall through early spring. Rare, but *A. "constricta"* (see below) is the most common member of the *A. vaginata* group.

EDIBILITY: Edible with caution—be sure of your identification!

COMMENTS: Also known as *A. strangulata*, this showy species resembles *A. vaginata* but has a more friable volva which usually forms distinct warts or plaques on the cap and disintegrates (at least partially) around the base of the stem. It never forms the loose membranous sack characteristic of *A. vaginata* and *A. "pachycolea."* A very common species in which the lower half of the volva is constricted around the stalk and the upper portion flares abruptly outward has been tentatively christened *A. "constricta"* by Gary Breckon. The cap is grayish and often covered with a white or grayish patch of volval tissue which may break up into several pieces. The stalk is decorated with delicate grayish scales as in *A. inaurata*, but the spores are 9.5-13 × 8-10 μm. It appears to be intermediate between *A. inaurata* and *A. vaginata*, but never has the white, saclike volva of the latter. It is especially abundant in winter under hardwoods. Also occurring in California is *A. farinosa*, small, with a brownish-gray striate cap, no ring, and a powdery yellow volva.

LIMACELLA

Medium-sized terrestrial fungi. CAP *smooth; viscid or slimy.* GILLS *free or nearly free, close, white or pale yellowish.* STALK central, usually hollow or stuffed, cleanly separable from cap, dry or viscid. VEIL *present*, but sometimes evanescent. VOLVA *absent.* SPORE PRINT *white.* Spores smooth, not amyloid (rarely dextrinoid). Gill hyphae divergent, at least when young.

THE viscid cap, presence of a veil, free white gills, and absence of a volva typify this small, rare genus. Limacellas used to be placed in *Lepiota*, but the viscid cap and divergent gill hyphae suggest a closer relationship to *Amanita*. The stature of the fruiting body is similar to *Amanita*, but the volva is replaced by a layer of slime which coats the cap and often the stem.

About a dozen species are known. They are woodland fungi with whimsical fruiting habits. Generally they are rare but every so often there is a large, localized fruiting. I have found three species in our area.

Key to Limacella

1. Cap white or whitish .... *L. illinita*, p. 255
1. Cap yellow-brown to red-brown, at least at center 2

2. Stalk viscid or slimy .... *L. glischra*, below
2. Stalk dry .... *L. glioderma* (see *L. glischra*, below)

Limacella glischra (Brown Limacella)

CAP 5-10 cm broad, convex becoming plane with a broad, conspicuous umbo; surface smooth, slimy when wet, brown, dark brown to red-brown at the center, paler toward the margin, which may be hung with slimy veil remnants. Flesh soft, white, odor mild. **GILLS** close, free or narrowly attached, white becoming yellowish in old age. **STALK** to 10 cm long, slender, equal, often curved slightly, smooth, slimy or viscid, pallid above, colored more or less like cap below (darkest where slime is thickest). **VEIL** fibrillose beneath a layer of slime, evanescent, leaving no visible ring or at most a slight hairy zone. **SPORE PRINT** white; spores 4-5 μm, round or nearly round, smooth, not amyloid.

HABITAT: Scattered in woods in late fall and winter, uncommon. I have seen one luxuriant fruiting of this species under tanoak.

EDIBILITY: Unknown.

COMMENTS: The slimy-viscid brownish cap, slimy-viscid stalk, and free whitish gills distinguish this species. Our material differs slightly from most descriptions of *L. glischra*, which call for a uniformly yellow-brown to red-brown cap. In ours, the cap margin is nearly white and the center very dark. In other respects they appear to be the same. Perhaps an *ad hoc* committee should be appointed to investigate the problem. Another brownish-capped species, *L. glioderma*, also occurs. It is darker than *L. glischra* and has a dry stalk and hairy veil. I have found solitary specimens several times in mixed woods.

Limacella illinita (White Limacella)

CAP 3-7.5 cm broad, at first egg-shaped, soon convex, then plane or broadly umbonate; surface smooth, viscid or slimy, white or tinged yellowish at center, discoloring slightly in age; margin often hung with slimy veil remnants. Flesh thin, soft, white, odor mild. **GILLS** free, close, white. **STALK** to 13 cm long, slender, equal or tapering upward, white, dry and silky above the veil, slimy or viscid below. **VEIL** fibrillose beneath a layer of slime, evanescent, not forming a distinct ring. **SPORE PRINT** white; spores 5-6 × 4-5.5 μm, nearly round to broadly ellipsoid, smooth, not amyloid.

HABITAT: Scattered in mixed woods of Douglas-fir, live oak, and redwood, after a prolonged period of relentless fall rains. Not common.

EDIBILITY: Unknown.

COMMENTS: The slimy white cap and stem combine with the free white gills to set this slippery mushroom apart. The ivory waxy cap, *Hygrophorus eburneus*, is just as slippery but has adnate to decurrent gills. Also known from California is *L. solidipes*, a very rare white woodland waif with a dry stem and membranous veil. It superficially resembles *Lepiota naucina* but has a viscid cap.

spores

LEPIOTACEAE (THE LEPIOTAS)

Terrestrial mushrooms of variable size. CAP dry, usually scaly with a smooth center. GILLS *free*, close, *usually white or pallid to yellow*. STALK cleanly separable from cap, central, hollow or stuffed, base often enlarged. VEIL *present, usually forming a ring, or if not then stalk usually scaly below veil.* VOLVA *absent*. SPORE PRINT *white or dull green*. Spores smooth, usually dextrinoid. Gill hyphae parallel or interwoven.

THE Lepiotas resemble *Agaricus* but have white spores instead of chocolate-brown. Structurally they are similar: free gills, a veil, and no volva. Some taxonomists go so far as to place them in the same family. The Lepiotas also bear a superficial resemblance to the Amanitas, but lack a volva. In *Lepiota rachodes* the basal bulb on the stem may have a raised, cuplike rim. The cap, however, has brown scales (a feature found in many Lepiotas) rather than warts. There are also fundamental microscopic differences: the gill hyphae are parallel to interwoven in *Lepiota* (and *Agaricus*), divergent in *Amanita*. The spores are typically dextrinoid in *Lepiota*, whereas in *Amanita* they are frequently amyloid but never dextrinoid.

The family originally consisted of a single large and diverse genus, *Lepiota*. It has since been divided into several smaller genera, including *Chlorophyllum* (greenish spores), *Leucoagaricus* (thick-walled spores with an apical pore), *Leucocoprinus* (thick-walled spores with an apical pore and mealy, striate cap), and *Lepiota* (thin-walled spores). Another genus, *Macrolepiota*, is recognized by some. However, until one system of classification is firmly settled upon, it seems best, for the purposes of this book, to recognize only two genera—*Lepiota* and *Chlorophyllum*.

The original concept of *Lepiota* embraced two other genera: *Limacella*, with a smooth, slimy-viscid cap and divergent gill hyphae (now placed in the Amanitaceae), and *Cystoderma*, with gills attached to the stem (Tricholomataceae).

There are ecological factors linking *Lepiota* to *Agaricus* as well as morphological ones. Both are large genera centered in the tropics, and both fruit prolifically in moist, relatively warm weather. And, in contrast to *Amanita*, both are saprophytic rather than mycorrhizal. The larger Lepiotas frequent waste places, roadsides, lawns, gardens, and pastures. Many of the smaller species occur in the woods as well as in cultivated ground. Cypresses are unusually rich in Lepiotas (and *Agaricus*!), many of them unclassified. The mycelium of some Lepiotas is cultivated by ants as a perennial food source. It is not unusual to find *L. rachodes* growing out of anthills!

The large, white-spored Lepiotas are among our most delicious edible mushrooms. However, allergic reactions are reported for virtually every species and extreme care must be taken to identify them correctly. *L. rachodes* and *L. barssii* are the best of the local denizen; *L. naucina* is plentiful and popular. The dozens of smaller Lepiotas should be strictly avoided. Not only are they difficult to differentiate, but several have been shown to contain dangerous amanita-toxins! The green-spored *Chlorophyllum* and the powdery yellow greenhouse species, *L. lutea*, are also poisonous.

Over 50 *Lepiota* species are known from California, many of them awaiting categorization. I have recorded more than 30 for the Monterey Bay region, half of which are included here.

Key to the Lepiotaceae (Lepiota and Chlorophyllum)

1. Spore print greenish; gills greenish to greenish-gray in old age .... *Chlorophyllum molybdites*, p. 258
1. Spore print white to pale buff 2

2. Gills *and* cap surface bruising pink to reddish-orange .... *L. roseifolia* (see *L. flammeatincta*, p. 264)
2. Not as above 3

3. Cap surface and stalk quickly bruising scarlet *L. flammeatincta*, p. 264
3. Not as above 4

4. Fruiting body bright yellow or yellowish when fresh .. *L. lutea*, p. 272
4. Fruiting body not yellow 5

5. Veil typically forming a persistent ring on stalk (examine several specimens if possible); stalk usually smooth 6
5. Veil typically disappearing or forming a fibrillose zone on stalk; stalk often scaly below veil 14

6. Flesh in stalk staining orange or yellow-orange to reddish when cut; cap 5-18 cm broad; stalk with a large bulb .... *L. rachodes*, p. 259
6. Not as above 7

7. Cap conspicuously striate, more or less mealy-scaly, white to pinkish .. .. *L. cepaestipes*, p. 271
7. Not as above 8

8. Cap 5-15 cm broad, white or gray, sometimes tinged buff; without colored scales or fibrils; in lawns, pastures, cultivated areas *L. naucina*, p. 261
8. Not as above 9

9. Cap smooth, yellowish-tan at center, paler toward margin, less than 4 cm broad; in woods .... *L. sequoiarum*, p. 267
9. Not as above 10

10. Tall (at least 15 cm); stalk covered with concentric brown scales below ring; cap large .... *L. procera* (see *L. rachodes*, p. 259)
10. Not as above 11

11. Cap scales or fibrils brownish-gray to gray, greenish-gray, or black 12
11. Cap scales or fibrils dark brown to red, reddish-brown, pink, etc. .. 13

12. Center of cap black or dark gray; scales dark gray to greenish-gray; in woods .... *L. atrodisca*, p. 265
12. Scales or fibrils gray, grayish-brown, to cinnamon-gray; in cultivated ground .... *L. barssii*, p. 262

13. Cap 4-7.5 cm broad, typically with radiating fibrils *L. rubrotincta*, p. 263
13. Cap 5 cm broad or less; typically with small, scattered scales .... *L. cristata*, p. 266

14. Cap minute, less than 2.5 cm broad, white or tinged pinkish-cinnamon at center .... *L. seminuda*, p. 267
14. Not as above; usually larger 15

15. Cap covered with soft, erect warty scales which rub off *L. hispida*, p. 270
15. Not as above 16

16. Stalk scaly or cottony below veil 17
16. Stalk more or less smooth below veil .... *L. cristata*, p. 266

17. Fruiting body small, less than 5 cm tall; cap and stalk more or less ochraceous .... *L. castanea*, p. 269
17. Not as above 18

18. Stalk shaggy, ragged, or cottony, often yellowish; cap margin often ragged-cottony; spores 13-18 µm; in woods .... *L. clypeolaria*, p. 269
18. Stalk not shaggy, ragged, or cottony; spores less than 13 µm long; mostly in cultivated ground or under trees, including cypress *L. helveola*, p. 268

Chlorophyllum molybdites (Green-Spored Parasol)

CAP 5-30 cm broad, egg-shaped becoming convex, finally plane; surface dry, at first smooth but soon breaking up into light brown (occasionally pinkish-brown) scales on a white background, the center darker. Flesh thick, white. **GILLS** free, close, white for a long time, then finally turning greenish or grayish-olive; bruising dingy brownish or yellowish when pallid. **STALK** to 25 cm long, enlarged below, smooth, white or brownish-stained. **VEIL** membranous, white, forming a superior ring which becomes brownish beneath and may be movable in age. **SPORE PRINT** greenish; spores 8-13 × 6.5-8 µm, ellipsoid, smooth.

HABITAT: Typically in groups or rings on lawns and other grassy areas, occasionally in gardens. Not yet reported from the Monterey Bay region, but very common farther south in warm, moist weather. I have

Chlorophyllum molybdites. Buttons in foreground are shaped like drumsticks; the cap breaks into scales as it expands. The gills turn greenish-gray in old age, as shown at right.

seen enormous fruitings in spring and summer in Fresno and Los Angeles. It is also reported from Palo Alto.

EDIBILITY: Poisonous. Though some are not affected by it, others are made very ill. It is so large and tempting as to border on irresistible. After eating it several times without effect, I was made ill by some which sat in the refrigerator for two days.

COMMENTS: Every mushroom hunter should be aware of this aberrant warm weather species. It may eventually turn up in our area, just as *Amanita phalloides* has. It is widely distributed in the southern and eastern United States as well as in the tropics. It is often mistaken for *Lepiota rachodes*, especially in the button stage, but differs in its habitat, bruising reactions, and spore color. The gills, however, remain white or pallid for a very long time before turning greenish. Young buttons look like drumsticks when they first emerge from the ground, and may not show any white on the cap. Frisbee-sized adults are commonplace. *Lepiota morgani* and *L. molybdites* are synonyms.

Lepiota rachodes (Shaggy Parasol)

CAP 5-18 cm broad, egg-shaped becoming convex with a flattened top, then plane or slightly umbonate; surface dry, at first a uniform cinnamon-brown, brown, or reddish-gray, soon breaking up into large, coarse or shaggy scales as the cap expands, the center remaining smooth and dark; margin fringed or shaggy. Flesh thick, soft, white, bruising yellow-orange or orange when cut (especially in stalk), then pinkish-brown to reddish-brown, finally cinnamon-brown or darker. **GILLS** broad, free, white, close, sometimes dingy brownish in age or when handled. **STALK** 5-18 cm long, 1-2.5 cm thick, equal with a large bulb at the base, the bulb sometimes with a raised rim; white when young, developing brownish stains in age or upon handling; smooth, dry, interior staining bright orange or saffron and then reddish to dark brown. **VEIL** soft, membranous, white or with a brown, ragged margin; forming a large, thick, collarlike, superior ring which is often movable in age. **SPORE PRINT** white; spores 8.5-12 $\times$ 6.5-8.5 μm, ellipsoid, truncate, smooth, dextrinoid.

HABITAT: Partial to sandy soil (especially under cypress), but also found near stables, on ant hills, under bushes, hedges, and planted conifers, along roads and in other disturbed areas. Usually in groups, flourishing whenever conditions are favorable (mild and moist), mostly

Lepiota rachodes. **Left:** Buttons are nearly smooth on top, but as the cap expands, it breaks up into scales. **Right:** Mature specimens with scaly caps, and a young button with a smooth, brown cap. Gills are white through maturity.

in the fall. Infrequent, but often occurring in large quantities when it fruits. Two patches on my street produced over a dozen crops each during the soggy 1977-78 season. It has been found on Año Nuevo Island in sand and elephant seal dung and in the splash zone at Pebble Beach.

EDIBILITY: Edible and excellent, one of the very best. It has a strong, meaty flavor but the water content is high, especially in older specimens. For best results, cook quickly on high, dry heat in an open pan. Do *not* eat it raw—I know at least two people who are violently allergic to it.

COMMENTS: The outstanding features of this striking mushroom are the large brown scales on the cap, free white gills, prominent collarlike (not skirtlike as in *Amanita*!) ring, large bulb at the base of the stem, and bruising of the flesh to orange and then reddish. The latter is best seen by cutting the stem. The brightness and duration of the color changes vary according to the moisture content and age of the mushroom. The basal bulb may have a free, raised rim which can be mistaken for a volva. However, the brown cap scales and collarlike ring point to *Lepiota*. The poisonous *Chlorophyllum molybdites* looks very similar but has greenish spores and does *not* stain orange. *L. rachodes* can also be mistaken for an *Agaricus* (especially *A. augustus*), but has white spores.

The true parasol mushroom, *Lepiota procera*, is a lofty, imposing species apparently confined to eastern North America and Europe. It has a delicate coating of concentric scales on the stem below the veil, and does not stain orange. Reports of it occurring in southern California appear to be erroneous. It is prized by connoisseurs for its strong, meaty flavor. Both *L. procera* and *L. rachodes* (also spelled *rhacodes*) have been detached from *Lepiota* proper and placed in either *Leucoagaricus* or *Macrolepiota*, depending on which illustrious lepiotologist you choose to listen to.

Lepiota naucina (Smooth Lepiota; Woman On Motorcycle)

CAP 5-15 cm broad, obtusely egg-shaped when young, then convex, finally plane; surface dry, white, or whitish-buff to grayish, the center sometimes tinged pinkish-buff; smooth, but often becoming somewhat scaly in age, staining yellow-brown after prolonged handling. Flesh thick, white, not bruising. **GILLS** free, close, white becoming buff, pinkish, or grayish-pink in age, finally brownish upon drying or cooking. **STALK** 5-15 cm long, rather slender but with an enlarged base; dry, smooth, white, staining yellow to brownish with age or upon handling. **VEIL** membranous, white, forming a distinct persistent superior sleevelike or collarlike ring which is often movable in age. **SPORE PRINT** white or very faintly pinkish; spores 7-10 × 5-6.5 µm, ellipsoid to ovate, smooth, dextrinoid, with a germ pore.

HABITAT: Scattered to gregarious on lawns, in pastures, in iceplant along freeways, etc. Common, at times abundant, fall and early winter, occasionally in spring and summer as well.

EDIBILITY: Edible and tasty, with caution. Either some persons are sensitive to it or certain variants (perhaps the gray ones) are toxic. According to one source it is the most frequent cause of mushroom poisoning in the Pacific Northwest, yet is listed as "edible" in every mushroom

Lepiota naucina. Buttons at right are grayish, but can also be white. Mature specimens at left are white. Note free gills, ring, absence of volva, growth in grass. (Nancy Burnett)

book. A friend of mine (who had eaten it previously) was made quite ill by a cream-of-*L. naucina*-soup. There is also the more serious danger of carelessly confusing it with a deadly *Amanita*.

COMMENTS: The white to grayish cap, membranous ring, free gills, white spores, and habitat in grass are the hallmarks of this cosmopolitan mushroom. Its appearance on lawns and parkways marks the beginning of the fall mushroom season. A good way to become acquainted with it is to bicycle around town: there it will be—tall, white, stately, in scattered groups on lawns. Later it appears in pastures. It is a beautiful mushroom when young, the smooth unexpanded cap resembling a motorcycle helmet. The shape, though difficult to describe, is very distinctive (see illustration). Though the stalk base is usually enlarged, there is never a sack as in the deadly Amanitas, and the ring is not skirtlike. The cap is not viscid as in *Limacella.* The tendency of the cap and stem to become brownish or brownish-yellow after handling is an important fieldmark. However, the darkening of the gills to pink or brown in age leads to confusion with *Agaricus.* I have also seen young buttons of *Agaricus californicus* interspersed with *L. naucina* which were virtually indistinguishable. A final hint: if your "*L. naucina*" fails to turn brown when cooked, throw it out! You undoubtedly have something else! *Leucoagaricus naucinus* is a synonym.

Lepiota barssii (Barss's Lepiota)

CAP 4-13 cm broad, convex or almost round when young, becoming broadly convex to plane, the margin sometimes uplifted or splitting; surface dry, grayish, covered with flattened brownish-gray to cinnamon-gray or fuscous fibrils, the center often darker; sometimes becoming scaly in age or direct sunlight. Flesh fairly thick, white, grayish in age, not bruising. **GILLS** close, white, free. **STALK** to 10 cm long, up to 2 cm thick, equal or tapering above and below, the base *not* enlarged; smooth, white or stained brownish. **VEIL** membranous, white, forming a superior ring which may be movable (or drop off) at maturity. **SPORE PRINT** white; spores 7.5-9.5 $\times$ 5-6 μm, ellipsoid, smooth, dextrinoid.

HABITAT: In cultivated or composted soil, lawns, gardens, pastures, and plowed fields, usually in small groups. Fruiting mostly in summer and fall, not common.

EDIBILITY: Edible and choice—in my humble fungal opinion, better than its well-known cousin, *L. rachodes.* In Oregon (where it is common) it is very popular.

COMMENTS: The grayish fibrillose cap, membranous ring, free white gills, absence of a basal bulb, and habitat in cultivated ground are the telltale features of this fine fungus. The stalk is usually buried deep in the ground, especially if it is growing in mulch. The flesh does not stain noticeably when cut. The veil is persistent but may be obliterated if the mushroom pushes up through grass or hard-packed soil. In this case, the free gills are an important fieldmark. It is much stouter and paler than *L. atrodisca*, and does not grow in the woods. It is darker than *L. naucina.* It can also be confused with an unidentified *Amanita* (p. 238), which has warts on the cap, amyloid spores, and yellowish gills in old age. I have found the two growing in close proximity to each other.

Lepiota rubrotincta

CAP 4-7.5 cm broad, egg-shaped becoming convex, finally plane or broadly umbonate with an uplifted margin; surface dry, at first uniformly reddish or pinkish-brown, then breaking into flat, radially arranged fibrils or scales which vary in color from cinnamon-buff to pinkish-red, reddish, or pinkish-orange; center remaining smooth, darker (deep red to chestnut); margin often splitting in age. Flesh thin, white. **GILLS** free, white, close, not bruising. **STALK** to 20 cm long,

Lepiota rubrotincta. Cap has reddish-pink to reddish-brown scales and a smooth, dark center. Found commonly in wooded areas in the fall. (Joel Leivick)

slender, usually enlarged slightly below and extending fairly deep into humus; smooth, white, discoloring somewhat in age. **VEIL** membranous, white, forming a thin fragile but persistent ring at or above the middle of the stalk; typically sleevelike above and flaring below. **SPORE PRINT** white; spores 6.5-9.5 × 4-5 μm, ellipsoid, smooth, dextrinoid.

HABITAT: Solitary or scattered in humus. Sporadically common in the fall, in woods.

EDIBILITY: Like myself, not firmly established.

COMMENTS: One of the most common and attractive of our woodland Lepiotas. It is larger and taller than *L. cristata*, and has a more persistent ring. The cap color varies considerably but usually has a strong reddish tone. The smooth, dark center (umbo) on the cap is suggestive of a human breast. It usually appears in the fall, soon after the rains begin. It is placed by some investigators in *Leucoagaricus*. *Lepiota glatfelteri* has a vinaceous-brown fibrillose cap and is found in rich soil or under cypress. I have not seen it but large fruitings have been reported from Santa Barbara.

Lepiota flammeatincta (Flaming Lepiota)

CAP up to 7.5 cm broad, convex when young, then plane or with uplifted margin, sometimes broadly umbonate; surface dry, with nearly black to dark purple-brown to brown or reddish-brown fibrils or scales (sometimes very sparse); surface staining scarlet-red to scarlet-orange when bruised, then slowly turning dark brown or dark purple-brown. Flesh white, staining slightly pinkish to orange when bruised. **GILLS** free, close, white, not staining. **STALK** to 15 cm long, slender, white above the veil, scaly-fibrillose (like cap) below, bruising scarlet like cap surface, then discoloring dark brown. **VEIL** membranous, white, forming a distinct sleevelike ring. **SPORE PRINT** white; spores 6.5-8 × 4-5 μm, ellipsoid, smooth, dextrinoid.

HABITAT: Solitary or in small groups in woods and along trails. Fairly common but seldom in large numbers, fall and early winter.

EDIBILITY: Unknown.

COMMENTS: Our most striking *Lepiota*, instantly recognized by the spectacular scarlet-staining of the cap and stem. The dark brown to purple-brown color that wounded areas subsequently assume is also

Lepiota flammeatincta, mature specimens. Note how the surface of the cap and stalk stains reddish-orange when rubbed. Note also the free white gills and ring. The cap is rounded (convex) or oval when young. (Joel Leivick)

characteristic. *L. roseifolia* is a very similar species in which the gills turn pinkish when bruised. It is fairly common in the woods. *L. americana* is a rare species found in cultivated ground in which the gills bruise reddish-orange and the entire mushroom becomes reddish when dried.

Lepiota atrodisca

CAP to 6.5 cm broad, egg-shaped to convex, then broadly umbonate or plane, the margin sometimes uplifted in age; surface dry, white, covered with flattened black, gray, or greenish-gray scales or fibrils, the center darker. Flesh thin, white, not bruising. **GILLS** free, white or creamy, close. **STALK** to 10 cm long, usually slender but sometimes rather stout, enlarged somewhat at base; smooth, dry, white or discoloring slightly upon handling. **VEIL** membranous, white, forming a fragile ring at or above middle of stalk, sometimes disappearing. **SPORE PRINT** white; spores 6.5-8 $\times$ 3-5 μm, ellipsoid, smooth, dextrinoid.

HABITAT: Solitary or scattered on ground or woody debris in woods. Common, fall and winter, abundant during the dry winter of 1977. It is by far the most common *Lepiota* of mixed chaparral (oak and manzanita), but is by no means restricted to that habitat. Known only from the west coast.

EDIBILITY: Unknown. Too small to be of importance.

Lepiota atrodisca, mature specimens. This common woodland *Lepiota* has black to greenish-gray cap scales and a smooth stem. Note the free white gills and sleevelike ring.

COMMENTS: This attractive little woodland *Lepiota* is easily recognized by its unique grayish-black cap scales. A rare but widespread species, *L. felina*, has blackish scales on both the cap and stem, and an evanescent veil. It is reputedly poisonous, like *L. helveola* and *L. castanea*.

Lepiota cristata

CAP to 5 cm broad, convex becoming plane or broadly umbonate; surface dry, white with small tawny to russet or red-brown scales, the center smooth and darker (red-brown to dark brown). Flesh thin, white, not bruising. Odor often faintly sweet or farinaceous. **GILLS** free, white to buff, close. **STALK** slender, to 10 cm long, white to pinkish-buff, darker toward base, equal or enlarged below, more or less smooth, fragile. **VEIL** white, sometimes disappearing, at other times forming a

Lepiota cristata. This small, ubiquitous woodland *Lepiota* has reddish-brown cap scales and a smooth, deeply colored center. The veil forms a fragile ring or disappears.

thin, fragile ring. **SPORE PRINT** white to pale buff; spores 6-8 × 3-5 μm, bicornute (spurred at one end), smooth.

HABITAT: Scattered or in small groups in woods and under trees. Very common, especially under redwood and cypress, fall and winter.

EDIBILITY: To be avoided—perhaps poisonous.

COMMENTS: The chestnut to dark brown cap center, fragile ring, small size, and smooth stem characterize a number of Lepiotas which can, for most intents and purposes, be referred to *L. cristata*. *L. castaneidisca* has ellipsoid rather than bicornute spores but is otherwise identical. In my experience it is just as common as *L. cristata*. There are many other similar species too numerous to mention. They include: *L. decorata,* with reddish to pink scales, and *L. roseilivida,* with a purplish hue. In both of these the center of the cap is minutely hairy, a character best seen with a hand lens.

Lepiota sequoiarum

CAP up to 4 cm broad, egg-shaped becoming convex and then plane; surface dry, smooth, without distinct scales, yellowish-tan at the center, pallid toward the margin. Flesh thin, white. **GILLS** white, free, close. **STALK** to 10 cm long, slender, equal or enlarged below, white, smooth. **VEIL** membranous, white, forming a superior, collapsed ring. **SPORE PRINT** white; spores 7-9 × 3.5-4 μm, ellipsoid, smooth, dextrinoid.

HABITAT: Scattered or in small groups in woods, fall and winter. Endemic to California. I have found it several times under redwood.

EDIBILITY: Unknown. Do not experiment.

COMMENTS: The smooth cap, small size, membranous ring, free white gills, and woodland habitat are the decisive features of this lackluster *Lepiota*. The less said about it the better.

Lepiota seminuda (Lilliputian Lepiota)

CAP about 1.5 cm broad, conic or convex becoming plane; surface dry, white or tinged pinkish at center, smooth or minutely mealy; margin often with veil fragments. Flesh very thin, white. **GILLS** free, white to pale pinkish-buff, close. **STALK** to 5 cm long, very thin (about 2 mm), white, tinged cinnamon over lower portion. **VEIL** evanescent, leaving remnants on cap margin or disappearing entirely. **SPORE PRINT** white; spores 4-5 × 2-3 μm, ellipsoid, smooth.

Lepiota seminuda. Our smallest *Lepiota,* with a cap about the size of a penny. Note the free whitish gills and fragile veil that leaves remnants on the cap margin.

HABITAT: Solitary or scattered in needle duff under conifers, especially redwood; also in mixed woods. Fairly common in damp weather (fall and winter), but easily overlooked.

EDIBILITY: Unknown. Hardly worth troubling with.

COMMENTS: This is our smallest and most delicate *Lepiota.* Its lilliputian dimensions might lead to confusion with *Mycena* or *Collybia,* but it has free gills and a veil. It is smaller than *L. sequoiarum,* and has an evanescent rather than persistent veil. *L. sistrata* is an alias.

Lepiota helveola

CAP 2-4 cm broad, convex to plane, sometimes umbonate; surface dry, with pinkish-brown to reddish-brown scales, the center darker; rosy tints developing in age or upon drying. Flesh thin, pallid, odor faintly sweet, especially if several are left in a closed container. **GILLS** free, close, white to creamy, not staining. **STALK** to 7.5 cm long, slender, equal or enlarged at base, fibrillose-scaly (like cap) below veil. **VEIL** evanescent, *not* forming a distinct ring. **SPORE PRINT** white; spores 6.5-8 $\times$ 3.5-4.5 μm, ellipsoid, smooth, dextrinoid.

HABITAT: Solitary or in small groups in cultivated ground or under trees, including cypress. Fall through spring, not common.

EDIBILITY: Poisonous. Deadly amanita-toxins have been isolated in this species and several relatives. Fortunately, it is unlikely to be eaten because of its small size and infrequent occurrence.

COMMENTS: Though not common, I have included this petite *Lepiota* because of the threat it poses to those who sample mushrooms wantonly. It belongs to a large group of poorly-known Lepiotas with an evanescent veil and more or less scaly stem. A number of these occur under cypress and appear to be undescribed. (Whether or not the "true" *L. helveola* occurs here is moot). A related species, *L. felina*, has blackish scales on both the cap and stem, and also contains amanita-toxins.

Lepiota castanea

CAP up to 4 cm broad, convex-umbonate to nearly plane; surface dry, covered with mealy, rusty-ochraceous to rusty-chestnut scales on a yellow-brown or ochraceous background. Flesh very thin, yellowish-buff, odor sometimes faintly sweet. **GILLS** close, free, white to buff. **STALK** to 6.5 cm long, slender and fragile, equal above, enlarged slightly at base; smooth above the veil, covered with rusty-ochraceous scales (like on cap) below. **VEIL** evanescent, *not* forming a distinct ring, but sometimes leaving remnants on cap margin. **SPORE PRINT** white; spores 9-13 × 3.5-5 μm, ellipsoid-truncate, smooth, dextrinoid.

HABITAT: Solitary or scattered in rich humus in woods; fairly common, fall and winter, but never in large numbers.

EDIBILITY: Poisonous! Has been shown to contain amanita-toxins, along with *L. helveola* and *L. felina.*

COMMENTS: The ochraceous to rusty-ochraceous cap, scaly stem, free (or nearly free) gills, and lack of a distinct ring typify this small *Lepiota.* It might be mistaken for a *Cystoderma* because of the mealy scales, but the gills are free and the spores dextrinoid.

Lepiota clypeolaria (Ragged Lepiota)

CAP 2.5-8 cm broad, egg-shaped when young, becoming convex to nearly plane with a low, broad umbo; surface dry, breaking up into yellow-brown, red-brown, or brown scales except for the smooth, darker center; margin soft and ragged, hung with cottony veil remnants. Flesh white, odor sometimes pungent. **GILLS** free, close, white or creamy. **STALK** long (to 18 cm), slender, equal, fragile, covered with soft, ragged, cottony scales below the veil; usually yellow or colored like cap, but pallid in one form (see comments). **VEIL** cottony, leaving shaggy remnants on cap margin or a slight cottony-fibrillose ring. **SPORE PRINT** white; spores 13-18 × 4-6 μm, fusiform, smooth, dextrinoid.

Lepiota clypeolaria, mature specimens. The shaggy stalk plus the smooth dark cap center typify this beautiful woodland species. The cap is convex when young.

HABITAT: Solitary or in groups under conifers and in mixed woods, fall and winter. Our most common *Lepiota* of deep coniferous woods.

EDIBILITY: Edible according to some authorities, poisonous according to others. All woodland Lepiotas are best avoided.

COMMENTS: The ragged appearance of the cap margin and stalk, plus the absence of a distinct ring, free white gills, and long narrow spores are diagnostic. In prime condition it is one of the most beautiful and exquisitely adorned of all mushrooms. In age, however, it assumes a rather decrepit appearance—the stalk is weak and collapses easily. The cap color varies considerably, and in our area there seem to be at least two distinct forms. The typical form is shaggy-looking with pronounced yellow in the stem and imposing "eye" at the center of the cap. The second form, found by Hugo Sloane, is sometimes common under oak. It is not as shaggy, has a whitish stem, and more evenly colored cap. Because of the cookie-colored cap cuticle I have christened it variety *"nabiscodisca."*

Lepiota hispida (Sharp-Scaled Lepiota)

CAP 2-7.5 cm broad, egg-shaped or convex when young, broadly convex to plane at maturity; surface dry, white to buff, covered with distinct, erect, pyramidal, brown wartlike scales which are easily rubbed off. Flesh white, rather thin, not bruising. Odor sometimes faintly farinaceous. **GILLS** free, white to buff, close. **STALK** to 10 cm long, equal or enlarged slightly at base, dry, smooth above, covered with warty scales (like cap) below the veil. **VEIL** evanescent, *not* forming a membranous ring, but sometimes a fibrillose zone. **SPORE PRINT** white; spores 4-7 × 2-3 μm, ovate, smooth.

HABITAT: Solitary or scattered in woods and under cypress, fall and winter, not common.

EDIBILITY: Unknown.

COMMENTS: The powdery, pyramidal, brownish scales on the cap and stem are the outstanding feature of this *Lepiota.* The scales can be rubbed off rather easily. It can be mistaken for an *Amanita* but has no volva. A small form is occasionally encountered along streams. A related species, *L. acutesquamosa*, is listed in many mushroom books.

Lepiota cepaestipes

CAP 2-7.5 cm broad, conic to bell-shaped, expanding slowly in age, but eventually drooping or collapsing; surface dry, powdery or mealy becoming somewhat scaly; white to light pinkish, the granules sometimes slightly darker; margin conspicuously striate. Flesh thin, white, sometimes bruising yellowish. **GILLS** white, close, free. **STALK** to 10 cm long, equal with a small basal bulb or sometimes swollen slightly in the middle; slender, white, sometimes discoloring pinkish or yellowish, smooth or minutely powdery. **VEIL** thin, white, forming a superior, persistent but easily detachable ring. **SPORE PRINT** white; spores 7-10 × 5-8 μm, elliptical, truncate, smooth, faintly dextrinoid.

HABITAT: In groups or clusters in rich soil, wood chips, around old stumps, straw piles, gardens—in other words, in decomposing organic matter of almost any kind. Fruiting in summer and fall or during warm, moist weather. Not common.

EDIBILITY: Edible, but not recommended. I haven't tried it.

COMMENTS: The mealy white cap with striate margin sets this *Lepiota* apart. It is essentially a white version of *L. lutea.* In fact, they used to be considered color forms of the same species, and on two occasions I have found them growing together. *L. lutea*, however, is reportedly poisonous, and is typically an indoor species, whereas *L. cepaestipes* is supposed to be edible and usually fruits outdoors. Both may be of tropical origin. Because of their mealy, striate cap and thick-walled, truncate spores, they are now placed in *Leucocoprinus.* A yellow-staining form with a white cap and brownish center also occurs.

Lepiota lutea. Bright yellow color and striate cap set this greenhouse species apart. Buttons are illustrated at left; those at right have begun to shed spores. Eventually the cap spreads out and collapses.

Lepiota lutea (Yellow Lepiota)

CAP up to 5 cm broad or occasionally larger, egg-shaped or conical when young, slowly expanding to convex or plane, then drooping; surface dry, powdery or mealy or minutely scaly, striate, less powdery and more scaly in age; bright sulfur-yellow, golden-yellow, or greenish-yellow, the center sometimes tinged brown or buff; fading to pale yellowish. Flesh thin, yellow. **GILLS** free, close, yellow. **STALK** 2.5-10 cm long, slender, enlarged somewhat at base; dry, smooth or powdery like cap, yellow. **VEIL** yellow, forming a small, superior collarlike ring which sometimes disappears. **SPORE PRINT** white; spores 9.5-12 × 6.5-8 μm, ovoid to ellipsoid, truncate, smooth, dextrinoid.

HABITAT: Solitary or tufted in flower pots, greenhouses, planter boxes, gardens, etc. Fruiting indoors most anytime, outdoors in summer and early fall. The specimens photographed were growing in a planter box in front of the Bank of America in downtown Los Angeles, in August.

EDIBILITY: Reportedly poisonous.

COMMENTS: Now known as *Leucocoprinus luteus* (or *L. birnbaumii*), this brilliant yellow greenhouse species was once considered a color form of *L. cepaestipes*. It can be the cause of considerable trepidation for plantlovers when it pokes up overnight in their favorite flower pot. However, it won't hurt the plant (or you, unless you eat it!).

If one should appear, consider yourself lucky and take advantage of the situation—sprinkle it lightly as you would any other houseplant, and watch new individuals develop from tiny "pinheads" within a few days.

The bright yellow color and striate cap sets *Lepiota lutea* apart from other Lepiotas. In stature it resembles *Coprinus* but the spores are white and it doesn't deliquesce. *Bolbitius vitellinus* is another common yellow mushroom, but it has a slimy-viscid cap and rusty spores. *L. luteophylla* is a rare species with yellow gills and stem, known only from coastal California. It does not have a striate cap and grows mostly under cypress.

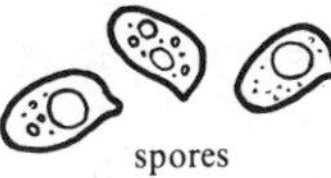

AGARICACEAE

Medium-sized to large terrestrial mushrooms. CAP smooth or scaly, not viscid. Flesh usually white. GILLS close, *free or nearly free,* pallid or pinkish when young, *chocolate-brown to blackish-brown at maturity.* STALK central, fleshy, cleanly separable from cap. VEIL *present, membranous or cottony, usually forming a ring.* VOLVA *absent* (except in *A. rodmani* and relatives). SPORE PRINT *chocolate-brown.* Spores smooth, mostly ellipsoid or almond-shaped.

AGARICUS (*Psalliota* of older texts) is the only common genus in this family. Familiar to most people as the cultivated mushroom sold in produce stands and supermarkets, it is a cinch to recognize: chocolate-brown spores, free gills, a veil, and no volva. *Stropharia* is somewhat similar but has a viscid cap and attached gills which are never pink.

This mature *Agaricus augustus* shows the three key fieldmarks of any *Agaricus*: presence of a veil (ring), and free gills which are chocolate-brown at maturity.

The principal characters used to differentiate *Agaricus* species are bruising reactions, chemical reactions, odor, and structure of the veil. Bruising reactions should be noted on the surface of the cap and stem, the flesh of the cap and the flesh in the *extreme* base of the stem. Only one chemical test is emphasized here: in many species, a drop of 10% potassium hydroxide (KOH) or sodium hydroxide (NaOH) will stain the cap surface bright yellow. It is especially useful for distinguishing the edible *A. campestris* from the inedible *A. californicus*. Draino (one teaspoon per 1/4 cup water) can be substituted. So can Lysol, but for obvious reasons, don't eat the tissue tested with these chemicals!

Three odors are common: mild (or "fungal") as in the commercial variety, *A. bisporus*; fragrant (like anise or almond extract) as in *A. augustus*; and phenolic, as in *A. xanthodermus*. The latter is an unpleasant chemical odor which resembles bleach, tar, creosote, library paste, ink, phenol, or carbolic acid.

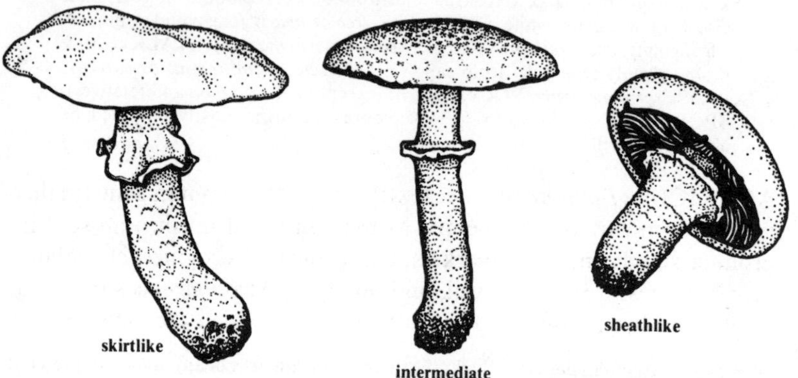

Different types of rings in *Agaricus*. Left to right: *A. silvicola, A. meleagris, A. rodmani.*

The type of ring is also significant. It may be skirtlike (**pendant**), sheathlike (**peronate**), or intermediate between the two. In many species, two distinct layers can be seen, the lower layer taking the form of flat patches on the underside of the upper layer (see p. 275).

From both an economic and edibility standpoint, *Agaricus* is the most important genus of gilled mushrooms. It contains many delicious edibles, the best known and most mediocre of which is the commercial mushroom, *A. bisporus*. The meadow mushroom, *A. campestris*, is also esteemed, but the best species are lesser known: *A. augustus, A. crocodilinus*, and *A. rodmani* are choice mushrooms if there are any; *A.*

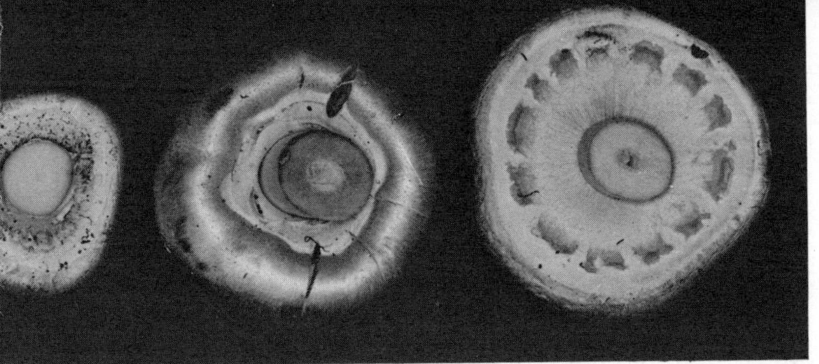

Veil detail in *Agaricus*. Left to right: *A. campestris*, with a cottony veil; *A. californicus*, with a membranous veil and inrolled, lobed cap margin; and *A. arvensis*, with a membranous veil that has patches on underside. (Ralph Buchsbaum)

arvensis, A. silvicola, and *A. subrutilescens* are also excellent. *Agaricus* is often characterized as a "safe" genus, implying that the various species can be eaten with impunity. This is certainly not the case. True, none are dangerously poisonous, but the phenol-smelling types can produce vomiting and diarrhea. In fact, *they are the most frequent cause of mushroom poisoning in California.* The phenol odor is not always evident in the field, but usually becomes pronounced in cooking. Also, the taste of these mushrooms may be astringent or metallic. Nevertheless, some people eat them regularly. Since allergies to even the edible species are not infrequent, each should be sampled cautiously to determine one's reaction to it.

Agaricus is also notable for its beauty. Some species rival the Amanitas for stateliness and elegance, others are robust and meaty like *Boletus*. It is a large genus centered in the tropics; hence one would expect to find more species in the southern United States than in the north. They are saprophytic fungi, and form a large portion of the mushrooms found in cultivated areas—pastures, lawns, roadsides, gardens, compost piles. It is not unusual for more than one species to grow in the same area, so be especially careful to examine each specimen closely. Several species are common in the woods, but comprise a much smaller percentage of the fungi found there. Few, if any, are mycorrhizal. It is interesting to note that cypresses are remarkably rich in endemic and unclassified *Agaricus* species.

Agaricus appears in profusion whenever conditions are favorable—that is, moist and mild. More than 30 species occur in our area, but they are difficult to separate, and their nomenclature is a mess. To facilitate identification, the species concepts presented here are broad. Anyone with a good nose and keen eye can at least learn to assign every *Agaricus* they find to a group or species "complex." Rare or unknown species do turn up, however, especially in habitats not normally searched by mycologists. Sixteen species are described here.

Key to the Agaricaceae (Agaricus)

1. Flesh in *extreme base* of stalk instantly staining *bright* yellow when cut 2
1. Not as above (base may stain faintly yellow) 3

2. Cap white becoming grayish or buff in age, margin usually staining bright yellow when rubbed .... *A. xanthodermus*, p. 290
2. Cap with inky gray to grayish-brown fibrils or scales *A. meleagris*, p. 289

3. Flesh (in cap or stem) turning orange, pink, or reddish when cut 4
3. Not as above, but rain may stain caps of many species reddish 8

4. Cap beige, scaly or cracked; flesh tough, with brinelike odor; growing in sandy or salty soil .... *A. bernardii* (see *A. rodmani*, p. 281)
4. Not as above 5

5. Cap and stalk quickly bruising reddish 6
5. Not as above 7

6. Cap with brown fibrils .... *A. haemorrhoidarius*, p. 284
6. Cap more or less white .... *A. benesi* (see *A. haemorrhoidarius*, p. 284)

7. Underside of veil purple-gray to brown .... *A. "annae"*, p. 283
7. Underside of veil white or pallid .... *A. bisporus*, p. 280

8. Cap white, but may discolor (yellow, buff, or grayish) when bruised or in age 9
8. Cap with colored fibrils or scales, at least at center 17

9. Ring double, the lower layer sheathing the stalk like a volva or both layers flaring outward to form a large, collarlike band (see pictures, p. 282); usually in hard-packed or sandy or disturbed soil *A. rodmani*, p. 281
9. Not as above 10

10. Found in woods 11
10. Found elsewhere 14

11. Cap surface bruising yellow; odor fragrant, aniselike (at least when young) 12
11. Not as above 13

12. Cap quickly bruising amber, young gills often bruising also; fruiting body stout, robust .... *A. albolutescens* (see *A. silvicola*, p. 293)
12. Not as above .... *A. silvicola*, p. 293

13. Ring large, thick, felty; cap reddish-gray in age, 5 cm broad or more; base of stalk noticeably enlarged .... *A. hondensis*, p. 286
13. Not as above .... *A. "californicus"*, p. 287

14. Small and slender (cap less than 4 cm broad, stalk less than 10 mm thick); odor aniselike; rare ..... *A. comptulus* (see *A. micromegathus*, p. 297)
14. Not as above 15

15. Medium-sized to massive, robust; *young* cap usually bruising yellow; odor when young often aniselike or almondy; unbroken veil with scaly patches on underside (these sometimes adhering to stalk) 16
15. Not as above; medium-sized; odor never aniselike 21

16. Cap with prominent warty scales .... *A. crocodilinus*, p. 294
16. Cap smooth or slightly scaly .... *A. arvensis*, p. 292

17. Cap small (less than 5 cm broad), stalk slender (less than 10 mm thick); veil thin and fragile; odor often (but not always) aniselike 18
17. Not as above; larger 19

18. Cap tinted amethyst or lilac, at least toward center; in woods .... *A. purpurellus*, p. 299
18. Cap with brownish fibrils, at least at center; in grass or woods, odor usually aniselike .... *A. micromegathus*, p. 297

19. Medium-sized to very large; odor and taste sweet, almondy; cap with tawny to dark brown fibrils or scales (often warty in dry weather), bruising yellow when young; stalk scaly below ring, base buried in ground .... *A. augustus*, p. 295
19. Not as above; odor never sweet or almondy 20

20. Growing in grass (lawns, pastures, fields, etc.) 21
20. Growing elsewhere (under trees, in woods, gardens, etc.) 22

21. Gills pallid in button stage (may be pink later); veil membranous, usually forming a persistent ring; stalk typically *not* tapered at base; odor often slightly phenolic (crush flesh!); young cap often lobed with margin tucked in; cap usually with brown fibrils or scales, at least at center, often with a metallic luster; stalk often staining yellowish, brown, or reddish-brown; cap surface yellow in KOH . *A. "californicus,"* p. 287
21. Gills pinkish in button stage; veil cottony, usually disappearing in age; stalk usually tapered at base; odor mild or mushroomy; cap white or with brown fibrils or scales; cap surface *not* yellow in KOH .... *A. campestris*, p. 278

22. Cap with wine-colored, purple-brown, or reddish-brown fibrils or scales; stalk cottony or scaly below ring, at least when young; growing in woods .... *A. subrutilescens*, p. 285
22. Not as above 23

23. Cap with pale pinkish-brown to fawn colored fibrils, darkening in age; ring large, thick, felty; stalk smooth, base enlarged; growing in woods .... *A. hondensis*, p. 286
23. Not as above 24

24. Gills pinkish in button stage; stalk usually stocky and stout; veil cottony; cap scales or fibrils brown to reddish-brown; odor of crushed flesh mild or mushroomy; found mostly in manure, compost, under cypress, and in stores; cap surface *not* yellow in KOH .... *A. bisporus*, p. 280
24. Gills pallid in button stage; stalk usually longer than width of cap; veil not cottony; cap scales or fibrils brown to inky-gray; odor of crushed flesh usually (but not always) phenolic; cap usually flattened on top when young with margin tucked in and often lobed; growing almost anywhere (including gardens and under cypress), but not growing in compost or manure; cap surface yellow in KOH 25

25. Medium-sized to large (mature cap at least 5 cm broad); cap with inky-gray to grayish-brown fibrils or scales; generally growing in woods .... *A. meleagris*, p. 289
25. Small to medium-sized (cap 8 cm broad or less); cap with scattered brown scales or fibrils, or smooth with a brownish center; growing mostly in towns and cultivated places .... *A. "californicus"*, p. 287

Agaricus campestris (Meadow Mushroom; Field Mushroom)

CAP 4-13 cm broad, convex when young, plane in age; surface dry, smooth or silky; typical form white with silky fibrils which may become brownish in age or break up into small scales (another form with brown, hairy surface from the very beginning); typically not bruising yellow but one form does slightly; margin usually hung with veil remnants, extending beyond gills. Flesh thick, white, unchanging, but sometimes discoloring brownish or reddish in age or wet weather (especially above gills); odor and taste mild. **GILLS** close, free, pale pink in button stage, then bright pink, becoming purple-brown, then chocolate-brown to blackish-brown. **STALK** to 10 cm long, but typically shorter than width of cap, usually tapered below, firm, white, more or less smooth. **VEIL** cottony, white, forming a thin, collapsed (never skirtlike) ring or disappearing entirely, or shredding on cap margin. **SPORE PRINT** chocolate-brown; spores 5.5-7.5 × 3.5-5 μm, ellipsoid, smooth. Basidia mostly 4-spored. Cap surface negative in KOH.

Agaricus campestris. Note pink gills in button stage, tendency of the veil to disappear, stocky stature, and growth in grass. Cap is pure white or has brown fibrillose scales.

Agaricus campestris, close-up of buttons. Specimen at left has bright pink gills. It is unusual for this species to grow in clumps, but pairs (left) are not uncommon.

HABITAT: As its name implies (*campestre*=field), this is a grassland species, occurring throughout the world from sea level to above timberline. It usually grows in groups or rings in grass: lawns, pastures and meadows, cemeteries, golf courses, baseball fields, etc. It fruits whenever conditions are favorable, but is most abundant in the fall and early winter, when stupendous crops are produced in our pastures. Thousands of pounds, in fact, go unpicked every year. Though they can often be seen from the road, fungophobic Americans drive right by them, some undoubtedly on the way to the store to buy mushrooms.

EDIBILITY: Edible and excellent, raw or cooked—the most widely picked mushroom in English-speaking countries, the "champignon" of France (it is also called the "Pink-Bottom"). Those who equate it with the commercial mushroom do it a gross injustice: its flavor is far superior. When the gills are bright pink and the cap pure white, it is as beautiful as it is delicious.

COMMENTS: The bright pink gills when young, evanescent cottony veil, tapered stem, stocky stature, chocolate spores, and habitat in grass are the principal fieldmarks of this universal favorite. The gills are pink even in the button stage. The cap is white or has scattered brownish fibrils, but a smaller, thinner, softer variety with a fuzzy or hairy (tomentose) brown cap is locally common. Whether it is distinct is for the experts to decide, but it tastes just as good. In most regions the meadow mushroom is perfectly safe for beginners. Unfortunately, in California it is frequently confused with the mildly poisonous, phenol-smelling *Agaricus* species. Compare it *very* carefully with *A. californicus,* and study the differences enumerated in the key (couplet

21). There is no single, infallible difference—only by using a *combination* of critical characteristics can beginners safely distinguish them.

A small, anonymous grayish *Amanita* (p. 238) sometimes grows with *A. campestris* and looks very similar from the top. However, its gills are white to yellow-orange, never pink or chocolate-brown. The name *A. campestris* has been misapplied to the commercial variety, *A. bisporus*, which has two-spored basidia and does *not* grow in grass.

Agaricus bisporus (Commercial Mushroom)

CAP 2.5-12 cm broad, convex when young, plane in age; surface dry, sometimes white but usually covered with flattened silky brown fibrils, sometimes scaly in age or dry weather; margin often extending beyond gills. Flesh thick, white, firm, discoloring slightly pinkish-brown to pinkish-orange or reddish when cut, or not at all; odor and taste mild. **GILLS** free, close, pinkish when young, chocolate-brown in age. **STALK** to 10 cm long but usually shorter, more or less equal, dry, white, stout, sometimes dingy brownish in age, smooth or slightly cottony-scaly below ring. **VEIL** cottony, white, two-layered; typically forming a delicate median to superior ring which may collapse against the stalk. **SPORE PRINT** chocolate-brown; spores 7-8.5 × 5-5.5 μm, ellipsoid, smooth; basidia mostly 2-spored. Cap surface negative in KOH.

HABITAT: Gregarious (sometimes in clumps) in compost and hard-packed soil, manured areas, gardens, and under cypress. Common in fall, winter, and spring but can be found year-round in markets and produce stands.

EDIBILITY: Edible. As with any mass-produced agricultural product, flavor has been sacrificed for appearance, keeping quality, yield, and disease resistance. Pesticides are used, of course, and the result is, in Valentina Wasson's felicitous phrase "a sickly simulacrum" of what a mushroom should be. The wild form is slightly better, especially the young, hard buttons.

COMMENTS: The commercial mushroom mimics the meadow mushroom, *A. campestris*, but differs in its two-spored basidia, more prominent ring, browner cap, and habitat. If you use mushroom compost in your garden or put old commercial mushrooms in your compost pile, you are likely to get some sooner or later. The largest fruitings I've seen have been around old compost piles and under

Agaricus bisporus looks like the commercial mushroom, which it is. Specimens at far right are mature; next to them is a button. Cap usually has brownish scales.

cypress. A four-spored form with reddening flesh is also common under cypress. *A. hortensis* and *A. brunnescens* are often listed as synonyms, though the former is sometimes applied only to the pure white strain. Care should be taken not to confuse *A. bisporus* with *A. californicus*, which is common in gardens as well as under cypress. The latter is more slender and smells like phenol, at least when cooked. Consult the key to *Agaricus* (couplet 24) for a more definitive comparison.

Agaricus rodmani (Banded Agaricus)

CAP 5-18 cm broad, broadly convex becoming plane; surface dry, smooth, often dirty; white, not bruising yellow but discoloring yellowish-tan or brownish in age; margin often extending beyond gills. Flesh thick, very firm, white, unchanging, odor and taste mild. **GILLS** close, free or nearly so, pallid pinkish to deep reddish-brown or purple-brown, chocolate-brown in age. **STALK** stout, up to 10 cm long and to 2.5 cm thick or more; smooth, white, equal or narrowed at base. **VEIL** membranous, white, double, upper surface usually striate; forming a persistent ring in which both layers flare outward or the lower layer sheathes the stem like a volva, or the two join to form a large, collarlike band. **SPORE PRINT** chocolate-brown; spores 4.5-6.5 × 4-5 μm, ellipsoid to almost round, smooth. Cap surface negative in KOH.

HABITAT: Solitary or in groups in hard-packed soil, sand, along roads and other disturbed areas, and under cypress. Fall, winter, and spring, not common. In colder regions long rows often appear in summer and fall along roads where salt was spread in the winter.

EDIBILITY: Edible and highly sought after. We may soon find it cultivated commercially because it is resistant to the mushroom virus disease that plagues *A. bisporus*. It is larger, firmer, and meatier than *A. bisporus* and *A. campestris*. One convert goes so far as to say: "Life is

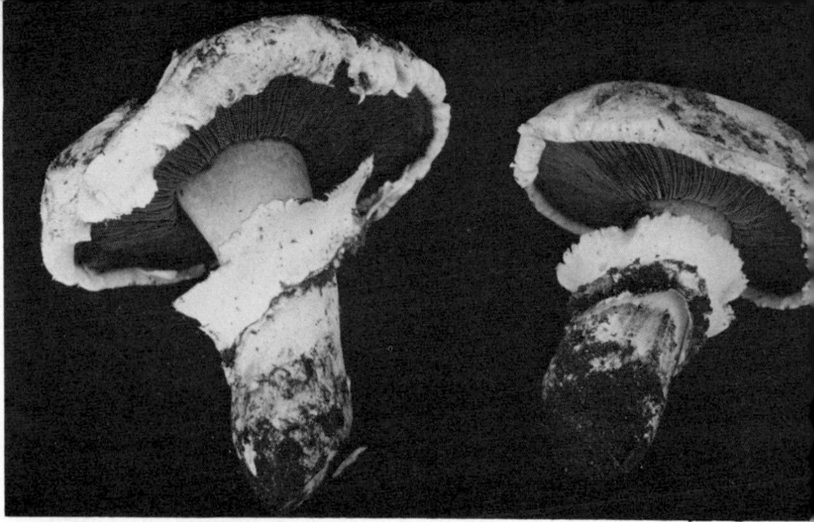

Agaricus rodmani, mature specimens. Note the large, prominent, flaring bandlike ring. The flesh is exceptionally firm, especially in the stalk. *A. bernardii* (not illustrated) is similar but stains orange to reddish when cut. It is common around San Francisco.

like an *Agaricus rodmani*—all good except for a few gills." Life may not be so consistently good, but *A. rodmani* certainly is.

COMMENTS: The white cap and double ring (which sheathes the stem like a volva or forms a prominent collarlike band) plus the firm flesh and habitat set this handsome fungus apart. There is no anise or phenol odor and it does not stain yellow. *A. bitorquis* and *A. edulis* are synonyms. We have several related species, some of them unclassified. *A. bernardii* is an inedible salt-loving species with a double, sheathlike veil. It has a cracked or scaly beige cap, brinelike odor, and flesh that turns reddish-orange when cut. I have encountered a form on lawns

Agaricus rodmani growing in disturbed ground. Note how the large bandlike ring can look just like a volva (specimens at top and far right). Cap is white but may discolor in age.

with a smooth cap and reddening flesh. Another variety has three-spored basidia, unchanging flesh, and a tendency to develop vinaceous tones in age. Still another, with a sheathlike veil and long, cordlike "root" at the base of the stem can be found under cypress.

Agaricus "annae"

CAP up to 12 cm broad, obtusely bell-shaped to convex when young, plane in age or with a slightly uplifted margin; surface dry, covered with brown to dark reddish-brown scales or fibrils. Flesh thick, white, firm under the disc, usually wormy, turning slightly yellowish-orange to pinkish-orange when cut (especially in the stem); odor and taste mild. **GILLS** pallid becoming pale brown, finally dark chocolate-brown, close, free or nearly so. **STALK** to 10 cm long, less than 2.5 cm thick, equal or slightly enlarged below, smooth or slightly scaly near base, white, discoloring somewhat in age. **VEIL** membranous, lower layer consisting of white felty patches which soon wear away, exposing a purplish-gray to purple-brown or brown scaly layer beneath, which eventually forms a persistent, superior, skirtlike, striate ring. **SPORE PRINT** chocolate-brown; spores 7-10 × 6-7 μm, ellipsoid, smooth. Cap surface negative in KOH.

HABITAT: Scattered to densely gregarious under cypress and cryptomeria (an exotic, bushy conifer); fall, winter, and spring. Generally uncommon, but abundant during the warm, wet winter of 1977-78. Under a single cypress I have seen more than 300 fruiting bodies, alongside dozens of *A. bisporus.*

Agaricus "annae." The outstanding feature is the purple-gray to purple-brown veil, as shown at left. It practically touches the gills and doesn't break until cap is fully expanded. Background is *not* their natural habitat.

EDIBILITY: Presumably edible, but rather tough.

COMMENTS: The most peculiar feature of this peculiar *Agaricus* is the brown to purplish-gray veil. Its overall appearance is distinctive but hard to describe: the stalk tends to be straight and cylindrical, the veil is close to the top of the stem and remains intact for a long time. Whether this is the true *A. annae* of Europe or a similar, undescribed species restricted to coastal California is uncertain. At any rate, if you hunt often under cypress, you will undoubtedly come across it.

Agaricus haemorrhoidarius (Bleeding Agaricus)

CAP 5-13 cm broad, convex becoming plane; surface dry, smooth, covered with brown to reddish-brown flattened silky fibrils. Flesh thick, white, quickly staining red when cut; odor and taste mild. **GILLS** close, free at maturity, pallid becoming pinkish, then reddish, finally chocolate-brown. **STALK** to 15 cm long, up to 2.5 cm thick, equal or enlarged below, smooth and white above the ring, sometimes with fine brownish fibrils below; red where bruised. **VEIL** membranous, white, forming a thin median to superior skirtlike ring. **SPORE PRINT** chocolate-brown; spores 5-7 × 3-4.5 μm, ellipsoid, smooth. Cap surface negative in KOH.

HABITAT: Solitary or in small groups in woods and brush, and under trees, particularly cypress. Fall and winter, uncommon.

Agaricus haemorrhoidarius. Note how the stalk and cap stain reddish when cut. These specimens were growing at Point Lobos under cypress. (Ralph Buchsbaum)

EDIBILITY: Edible. "Rich" according to Shalom Compost, who put it in a soup.

COMMENTS: This *Agaricus* is readily recognized by its "bleeding" flesh. Cypresses are particularly rich in species with reddening flesh. *A. benesi* also "bleeds" but has a white cap and stem. *A. pattersonae* is a large, stately species with brown cap scales and flesh that stains pink to orange-red. Its stem is much thicker than *A. haemorrhoidarius* (2.5 cm or more), and the ring often splits into two distinct layers. *A. annae* is still another member of the group (see description). All of these are edible. The reddening flesh should not be confused with the pinkish or reddish stains which appear on the caps of many *Agaricus* species in rainy weather.

Agaricus subrutilescens (Wine-Colored Agaricus)

CAP 5-15 cm broad, convex with a somewhat flattened top, becoming plane; surface dry, covered with purplish-brown to wine-colored fibrils or scales, sometimes only at the center. Flesh white, firm, unchanging, odor and taste mild. **GILLS** close, free at maturity, at first whitish and sometimes bruising rosy-pink when cut, darkening gradually to pinkish-brown and finally chocolate-brown. **STALK** 5-20 cm long,

Agaricus subrutilescens, immature specimens. Note the deeply colored (purple-brown) cap. This combined with the cottony white scales on the stalk (which do not show up well here) are the main fieldmarks. Mature specimens have chocolate gills. (Bill Everson)

equal with an enlarged base or tapering upward, smooth and white above the ring (or tinged cap color), covered with soft, cottony white scales or patches below, but sometimes nearly smooth in old age. **VEIL** membranous to somewhat cottony, white, forming a thin median to superior skirtlike ring. **SPORE PRINT** chocolate-brown; spores 5-6 × 3-3.5 μ, ellipsoid, smooth. Cap surface negative or slightly greenish in KOH.

HABITAT: Solitary or in small groups in woods, mostly with conifers. Common in fall and winter. Endemic to the west coast, and more common in California than anywhere else.

EDIBILITY: Edible and choice. Not as meaty as some species, but the buttons are excellent.

COMMENTS: The dark purple-brown cap and cottony white stem set this *Agaricus* apart. It tends to be tall and slender, but thick squat buttons are not uncommon. Along with *A. hondensis* it is the most prominent *Agaricus* of deep, undisturbed woods. The greenish KOH reaction is peculiar. Compare it closely with the poisonous *A. hondensis,* which has a smooth stalk and paler cap.

Agaricus hondensis (Felt-Ringed Agaricus)

CAP 5-18 cm broad, convex becoming plane; surface dry, smooth, white with very pale pinkish-brown to pinkish-gray to fawn-brown flattened, silky fibrils or fibrillose scales, at least at center; darkening in age to brown, reddish-brown, or reddish-gray. Flesh thick, white, bruising pale yellowish; odor of crushed flesh mild or faintly phenolic (especially in base of stalk), taste unpleasant. **GILLS** pale pinkish to pinkish-gray becoming chocolate-brown, close, free. **STALK** to 18 cm long, with a bulbous base, firm, smooth, without scales, white, bruising faintly yellowish, then discoloring pinkish-brown. **VEIL** membranous, white, very thick; forming a large, feltlike superior ring which usually flares outward instead of collapsing against the stalk. **SPORE PRINT** chocolate-brown; spores 4.5-5.5 × 3-3.5 μm, ellipsoid, smooth. Cap surface yellow in KOH.

HABITAT: In groups, troops, or rings, in woods of all kinds, particularly where there are thick accumulations of fallen branches and other debris. Common, at times abundant, late fall and winter. The main fruiting follows close on the heels of *A. meleagris.* In both the dry winter of 1977 and the wet winter of 1978 it was exceedingly common in

Agaricus hondensis. A common woodland species with a large, thick felty ring, smooth stem, and pale brown to pinkish-brown cap scales.

oak and tanoak woods. Like *A. subrutilescens* (which grows in similar habitats), it is endemic to the west coast. In fact, it was originally described from La Honda.

EDIBILITY: Mildly poisonous to many people, causing stomach distress. It's difficult to imagine a mushroom looking more delicious, but it has an unpleasant astringent-metallic taste.

COMMENTS: This handsome, alluring woodland *Agaricus* is distinguished by the pale cap fibrils which darken in age, the thick felty ring, smooth naked stalk, and chocolate spores. It is frequently mistaken for edible varieties, particularly *A. subrutilescens*, which has a darker cap and cottony stem. It has also been confused with *A. silvaticus*, a European species with slightly reddening flesh and mild odor and taste. An *Agaricus* meeting these specifications occurs in our area, but is rare.

Agaricus "californicus" (California Agaricus)

CAP 4-12 cm broad, at first convex with a somewhat flattened top, the margin tucked in and often somewhat lobed, then expanding to plane; surface dry, smooth or with small scales; color variable, most often brown at the center and pallid toward the margin, sometimes with brown or grayish-brown fibrils or scales throughout (often with a metallic luster), sometimes entirely white or grayish, usually darker in age, occasionally staining yellow when bruised, often becoming pinkish or reddish-stained in rainy weather; margin often extending beyond gills. Flesh thick, white, unchanging or slightly yellowish when crushed,

Agaricus "californicus" is often confused with *A. campestris*. Note how the cap often has a metallic luster. Gills are pallid in button stage and stalk often stains brownish. Note also the lobed cap of specimen at center (see close-up of veil on p. 275). (Ralph Buchsbaum)

or eventually discoloring sordid pinkish; odor and taste of crushed flesh phenolic, but not always detectable. **GILLS** close, free, pallid until the veil breaks, then bright pink to pinkish-brown, finally chocolate-brown. **STALK** up to 12 cm long, rather slender, equal or more often slightly enlarged at base; dry, smooth, without scales; dull white bruising or discoloring pale yellowish or pinkish-brown to dingy brown. **VEIL** membranous, white, with felty patches on underside which are sometimes obliterated; forming a persistent, superior to median ring. **SPORE PRINT** chocolate-brown; spores 4-6 $\times$ 3.5-5 μm, ellipsoid, smooth. Cap surface yellow in KOH.

HABITAT: Scattered to gregarious, growing anywhere and everywhere. Especially abundant in cultivated places: lawns, gardens, parks, under trees (rarely in pastures except under trees). Found year-round but most abundant in the fall, sometimes mingled with *A. campestris* and *Lepiota naucina.*

EDIBILITY: Mildly poisonous to some people; frequently mistaken for the meadow mushroom, *A. campestris,* with which it sometimes grows.

COMMENTS: This mushroom gives my students more trouble than any other, partly because it mimics the commercial mushroom (*A. bisporus*) and meadow mushroom (*A. campestris*), and partly because of the endless variation it exhibits. There is doubt as to which species the name *A. californicus* was originally applied; thus its use here should be regarded as tentative. Since it is the most ubiquitous *Agaricus* in coastal California (one quickly tires of finding it), the name is certainly appropriate. It is as variable as it is abundant. "Typical" forms (if they can be said to exist) do not stain bright yellow like *A. xanthodermus* but yellow slightly in cooking (in addition to giving off a phenol odor). The persistent membranous ring, modest size, rather long stalk, slight phenol odor (often not evident to those unfamiliar with it) and pallid gills in the button stage are the telltale traits. The cap varies tremendously in color and scaliness, but is usually brownish at least at the center and somewhat shiny. For a comparison with *A. campestris* and *A. bisporus*, see couplets 21 and 24 in the *Agaricus* key.

Agaricus meleagris (Flat-Topped Agaricus)

CAP 5-25 cm broad, at first convex with a flattened top, expanding to plane; surface dry, covered with flattened inky-gray to grayish-brown fibrils or scales, sparser toward the margin; developing pinkish or reddish stains in rainy weather, surface occasionally bruising yellow. Flesh thick, white, unchanging or bruising yellowish; odor and taste of crushed flesh unpleasant, phenolic (sometimes faintly so). **GILLS** close, free, at first pallid, then light pink to reddish-brown, finally chocolate-brown. **STALK** to 18 cm long, equal or enlarged below, or sometimes tapering to a point if growing in clusters; dry, smooth, without scales, dull white discoloring pinkish-brown or dingy brown, flesh in extreme base often bruising bright yellow. **VEIL** membranous, white, with thick, flat, felty patches on underside; forming a persistent superior ring. **SPORE PRINT** chocolate-brown; spores 4-6 × 3.5-4.5 μm, ellipsoid, smooth. Cap surface yellow in KOH.

Agaricus meleagris. The grayish scales on the cap, smooth stem, and phenol odor are characteristic of this large, handsome woodland species. These are large specimens.

HABITAT: Solitary or in groups or clusters in woods and under trees, sometimes in open. Common in fall, winter, and early spring, especially along paths and roads. The largest fruiting is usually in November.

EDIBILITY: Poisonous to many, causing vomiting and diarrhea. Some people eat it but the metallic taste does not please everyone. Like *A. hondensis*, it is a very tempting specimen.

COMMENTS: The inky to grayish-brown fibrils, smooth stem, and phenolic odor of the crushed flesh identify this handsome, omnipresent *Agaricus*. In addition, the base of the stalk often bruises bright yellow when nicked, as in *A. xanthodermus*. It is larger than *A. californicus*, and in fact its size and shape approach that of the prince, *A. augustus*. The stem is smooth, however, and the odor completely different. For a long time it has been called *A. placomyces*, an east coast species that differs in several minor respects.

Agaricus xanthodermus (Yellow-Staining Agaricus)

CAP 5-24 cm broad, nearly round to cylindrical or convex with a flattened top, expanding gradually to plane, margin at first tucked in and sometimes lobed; surface dry, smooth, white to gray, often buff or ochraceous-buff toward the center, discoloring brownish in old age and sometimes cracking into scales; usually bruising bright yellow, then sordid brownish. Flesh thick, firm, white, turning yellow when crushed; odor and taste unpleasant, phenolic. **GILLS** close, free, at first white, then pink or grayish-pink, finally chocolate-brown. **STALK** 5-18 cm long, equal or with enlarged base, smooth, white, usually bruising yellow; brownish-stained in age, flesh in very base turning bright yellow when cut. **VEIL** membranous, white or yellow-stained, with flat patches on underside; forming a large thick median to superior ring. **SPORE**

Agaricus xanthodermus, three mature individuals and one button. Note the yellow stains on the cap and the prominent veil.

Agaricus xanthodermus growing with *Alyssum* (the flowers) along a road. Note how the sliced specimen at far right is stained yellow at base of stalk. Cap is white when young, grayish to buff in age.

PRINT chocolate-brown; spores 5-6.5 × 3-4 µm, ellipsoid, smooth. Cap surface bright yellow in KOH.

HABITAT: Scattered to densely gregarious under trees and hedges, in yards, lawns, along roads and paths, in cultivated areas; also in woods, pastures, and under cypress. Common, at times abundant, fall through spring. I have seen enormous fruitings in an old olive orchard above Santa Cruz.

EDIBILITY: Poisonous to many people—causes headaches, nausea, vomiting, and diarrhea. It is a very tempting, meaty mushroom, but the unpleasant odor becomes unbearably obnoxious in cooking.

COMMENTS: The tendency of all parts to stain bright yellow, the phenolic odor, and the white to grayish cap are the trademarks of this common and variable species. The yellow-staining is usually most dramatic on the cap (especially the margin of young specimens), but some populations do *not* stain yellow on the cap and several other *Agaricus* species also stain yellow on the cap. However, in all variants I have encountered, the *extreme base* of the stalk turns brilliant yellow when nicked. This is perhaps the best fieldmark, since the only other *Agaricus* which displays this reaction is *A. meleagris* (and then only sometimes). *A. hondensis* stains faintly yellow in the base of the stem, but never bright yellow. The edible horse mushroom, *A. arvensis*, superficially resembles *A. xanthodermus*, but does *not* stain yellow at the base of the stem, and does not smell or taste like phenol.

Agaricus arvensis. Cap is white or yellowish, shape and size are variable. Large specimen at left is not unusual. Note how the unexpanded veil has starlike pattern of patches on its underside (see close-up of veil on p. 275). Odor is aniselike when young.

Agaricus arvensis (Horse Mushroom)

CAP 7-30 cm broad, convex becoming plane; surface smooth, dry, but sometimes cracking into small scales in age, especially at the center; pure white, discoloring buff or yellowish in age; usually bruising yellow when young, less so or not at all in age; margin sometimes hung with veil remnants. Flesh very thick, firm, white, unchanging or yellowing slightly; odor fragrant (like anise) when young, somewhat unpleasant or horsey in age; taste pleasant. **GILLS** close, free at maturity, pallid becoming grayish-pink, then deep chocolate-brown. **STALK** 5-16 cm long, equal or slightly enlarged below or more often swollen in the middle; smooth or with small cottony scales below the ring; white, sometimes bruising yellowish, but extreme base never bruising bright yellow. **VEIL** membranous, white or tinged yellow, with cottony toothlike patches on underside (often in a star-shaped pattern), these sometimes adhering to the stalk or obliterated; forming a fragile, skirtlike ring. **SPORE PRINT** chocolate-brown; spores 7-11 $\times$ 4.5-5.5 μm, ellipsoid, smooth. Cap surface yellow in KOH.

HABITAT: Scattered or in groups or rings in pastures, lawns, and manured areas. Common in the fall and spring. Often found with *A. campestris* (in the fall), and *Calvatia gigantea* (in the spring). The unusually warm, wet winter of 1977-78 brought it out in stupendous abundance. Bushels could have been gathered.

EDIBILITY: Edible and choice. Large buttons store well and have an excellent flavor—almost the equal of *A. augustus.*

COMMENTS: This magnificent mushroom is distinguished by its white to yellowish cap, thick firm flesh, anise odor when young, membranous veil, chocolate spores, and habitat in grass. The cap may bruise yellow but the flesh in the base of the stem does not. Pizza-sized caps are not uncommon—they have solid flesh more than one inch thick! The stature is generally more robust than *A. silvicola,* which grows in the woods and has smaller spores. The gills are never bright pink as in *A. campestris.* The cap is not as warty as *A. crocodilinus.* Compare it closely with *A. xanthodermus,* a large poisonous species that stains bright yellow in the base of the stem.

Agaricus silvicola (Woodland Agaricus)

CAP 5-15 cm broad, convex becoming plane; surface dry, smooth or silky-fibrillose, sometimes becoming fibrillose-scaly in age; white, usually aging yellowish and turning slightly yellow when bruised, especially at margin. Flesh firm, white, odor fragrant (like anise or almonds), taste pleasant. **GILLS** close, free, white becoming gray or pinkish-gray, finally chocolate-brown. **STALK** 5-25 cm long, usually rather slender and enlarged below; smooth or with small cottony scales below ring; white, aging or bruising yellowish but base *not* staining bright yellow when cut. **VEIL** membranous, white or stained yellow, with patches on underside; forming a prominent, superior skirtlike ring. **SPORE PRINT** chocolate-brown; spores 5-6.5 × 3-4.5 μm, ellipsoid, smooth. Cap surface yellow in KOH.

HABITAT: Solitary or in small groups in woods, fall and winter. Common, but never in great numbers (generally fruiting in twos and threes). The typical form is most common under oak, but see comments.

EDIBILITY: Edible and choice, with caution. Some people are allergic to it. Make sure there is no volva and the mature gills are not white—I have found it in the company of deadly Amanitas!

COMMENTS: *A. silvicola* (also spelled *A. sylvicola*) is a collective epithet—several very similar species have been masquerading under the same name. All have a white cap that bruises yellow, an anise odor, skirtlike ring, and chocolate spores. They are similar to the horse mushroom, *A. arvensis,* but grow in the woods, have smaller spores, and are not nearly as robust. Typical *A. silvicola,* with a flattened bulb

Agaricus silvicola, or to be more exact, a member of the *A. silvicola* complex. This is the large, stately form that seems to grow exclusively with tanoak. Cap is white and stains yellow. Odor is aniselike.

on the stem, is rather infrequent. A large, strikingly beautiful variety (see illustration) is common under tanoak. A third species (possibly *A. albolutescens*) has a large cap which stains amber (rather than yellow) when rubbed, and a strong fragrant odor. The cap eventually becomes entirely amber, and even the gills stain yellow quickly when immature. It is stockier and more robust than *A. silvicola*, and generally fruits in larger numbers. I have seen large fairy rings in mixed woods and under live oak. None of these stain yellow at the base like *A. xanthodermus*.

Agaricus crocodilinus (Crocodile Agaricus)

CAP large, 7-40 cm broad, convex becoming plane; surface dry, soon breaking into prominent pyramidal or truncated warty scales; white or pallid, aging pale yellowish or buff. Flesh very thick, firm, white, odor fragrant (somewhat aniselike) when young, mushroomy in age, somewhat unpleasant in old age. **GILLS** close, more or less free, pale grayish becoming grayish-pink and then deep chocolate-brown. **STALK** to 10 cm long, stout, thick (at least 2.5 cm), equal or thickest in the middle, colored like cap, smooth or somewhat scaly below ring. **VEIL** membranous, white, forming a median to basal ring, the lower layer sometimes adhering to stalk. **SPORE PRINT** chocolate-brown; spores 8-16 $\times$ 5.5-8 μm, ellipsoid, smooth. Cap surface yellow in KOH.

Agaricus crocodilinus, mature specimens. Note the warty scales on cap, large size, and squat stature. Each of these caps is nearly a foot across. (Bill Everson)

HABITAT: Scattered in pastures and grassy areas, fruiting mostly in spring, also fall. Distribution uncertain, but fairly common in coastal pastures north of San Francisco, where it can usually be spotted from the road.

EDIBILITY: Indisputably delicious—both fresh and dried. The flesh can be several inches thick. One good-sized specimen is enough for several people, and keeps well if refrigerated.

COMMENTS: A squat, massive mushroom, distinguished from *A. arvensis* by its warty cap (like a crocodile's skin?) and larger spores. *A. augustus* is occasionally warty but grows in the woods. The degree of wartiness depends somewhat on environmental conditions. In extreme cases the warts can be as large as those in *Amanita strobiliformis.* Specimens weighing ten pounds have been reported. A similar, large-spored European species, *Agaricus macrosporus (=A. villaticus)* has a smoother cap and, according to some authorities, flesh that stains slightly pinkish. The suggestive moniker *A. urinescens* has been bestowed upon one variant, a fitting tribute to the indiscreet odor that may develop in age.

Agaricus augustus (The Prince)

CAP large, 5-40 cm broad, at first convex with a flattened top, slowly expanding to plane or with an uplifted margin; surface dry, covered with numerous dark brown to tawny-brown fibrils or scales; surface bruising yellow when young, often developing golden tones in age;

Agaricus augustus, immature individuals at right and nearly mature specimen at left. Note the large size, brown cap scales, scaly stem, and flattened top when young. Odor is sweet and almondy. A mature specimen is shown on p. 273, and a large button on the frontispiece.

scales often warty in dry weather. Flesh thick, white, firm; odor and taste sweet, like almond extract, especially when young. **GILLS** close, free at maturity; remaining pallid for a long time, finally turning light brown or pinkish-brown, then chocolate-brown. **STALK** to 30 cm long, up to 4 cm thick, equal or enlarged slightly below, the base buried deep in the ground; smooth above the ring, cottony or scaly below (may be smooth in old age); white, aging or bruising yellowish-brown. **VEIL** membranous, with white to yellow-brown cottony scales or patches on underside (but these sometimes obliterated); forming a large, ample superior skirtlike ring. **SPORE PRINT** chocolate-brown; spores 8-11 × 5-6.5 μm, ellipsoid, smooth. Cap surface yellow in KOH.

HABITAT: Solitary, more often in groups or clumps under trees and in the woods, but almost always near roads, paths, clearings, and other places where the soil has been disturbed, occasionally in flower beds or compost. Common in spring, summer, and fall (winter if it is mild enough), showing a definite preference for warm weather. Several crops are produced each year, so visit your patches regularly. It is curious that such a large mushroom requires so little moisture to fruit. Fog is all that's necessary. It is probably more common in the Santa Cruz Mountains than anywhere else.

Agaricus augustus growing in the woods near a trail. That's a quarter in the center of the picture, so these specimens are quite hefty. Note the prominent veil. It fruits year-round.

EDIBILITY: Edible and one of the very best. Especially important since it fruits in the spring and summer, when edible fungi are scarce. It's like getting two mushrooms in one: sweet and almondy when young, strong and mushroomy at maturity. Unfortunately, maggots and sowbugs are crazy about it too.

COMMENTS: This prince of a mushroom is distinguished by its large size (caps of "LP" dimensions (one foot) are not uncommon), almond odor, yellow-staining cap with brown fibrils or scales, chocolate spores, and scaly stem usually buried in the ground. The cottony veil is large and exquisitely constructed. The flattened top of young specimens is also characteristic, though several other mushrooms (such as *A. meleagris* and *Lepiota rachodes*) have the same shape. The gills remain pallid for a long time, but the stature points to *Agaricus*. *A. meleagris* grows in the same habitat, but has grayish cap scales, a smooth stem, and a phenol odor. *A. augustus* has several close relatives, including *A. subrufescens*, with smaller spores 6-7.5×4-5 µm, and *A. perrarus*, more ochraceous in color, fairly common in the coastal spruce-fir forests of northern California. Unrecognized taxa also exist (I've found a strange one under acacia), but since all are equally edible, slight differences needn't concern you. At least, they don't concern me.

Agaricus micromegathus

CAP up to 7 cm broad but generally 2-4 cm, convex becoming plane, fragile; surface dry, with silky brownish or grayish-brown fibrils, at least at the center (sometimes very sparse), yellow or yellow-orange stains sometimes developing in age or from handling. Flesh thin, white, odor typically aniselike, taste pleasant. **GILLS** free or nearly so, close,

Agaricus micromegathus. A small, slender species with a distinct anise odor. Note the free gills in mature specimens at far left. *A. purpurellus* (not illustrated) has a similar stature.

pallid then pinkish, finally chocolate-brown. **STALK** to 7.5 cm but generally shorter, slender (about 6 mm), equal or with a small bulb at base, white or stained yellow, yellow-orange, or yellow-brown, smooth. **VEIL** thin, white, forming a fragile superior to median skirtlike ring or disappearing entirely. **SPORE PRINT** chocolate-brown; spores 4.5-6 × 3-4.5 µm, ellipsoid, smooth. Cap surface yellow in KOH.

HABITAT: Solitary or scattered in lawns, pastures, fields, under trees, occasionally in woods. Fairly common in mild weather, especially in the fall, often growing with *A. campestris*.

EDIBILITY: Edible but thin-fleshed. Its fragrance suggests that its flavor is good, but it doesn't often occur in sufficient quantity to merit collecting.

COMMENTS: A fragile *Agaricus* recognized by its small size, brownish cap fibrils, anise odor, and habitat (usually) in grass. It resembles *Stropharia coronilla*, which has attached gills, a slightly viscid cap, and mild odor. There are a number of small, poorly-known relatives, including: *A. comptulus*, with a white to yellowish cap and bright pink gills when young, mostly in grass; and *A. semotus*, with brown to reddish-brown fibrils, found mostly in woods. Both have an aniselike odor, and both are edible. Another small species, found rarely in greenhouses and rich soil, is *Melanophyllum echinatum*. This odd member of the Agaricaceae has a mealy cap, blood-red gills when young, an evanescent veil, and olive-gray to olive-brown spore print which becomes reddish-chocolate or dark brown as it dries. The latter feature has led investigators to place it in several unrelated genera, including *Agaricus, Lepiota, Cystoderma,* and *Inocybe*. Its edibility is unknown.

Agaricus purpurellus (Purple Agaricus)

CAP 2-4 cm broad, convex becoming plane; fragile, surface dry, covered with flattened purplish-pink to amethyst fibrils which become reddish-brown in age; margin paler (pinkish-buff to grayish-buff). Flesh thin, white, odor mild or faintly fragrant. **GILLS** close, free or nearly so, pinkish becoming chocolate-brown. **STALK** to 5 cm long, thin (about 6 mm), fragile, smooth, equal or with a small basal bulb, white or pallid, yellowish below the ring in age. **VEIL** membranous, thin, white, forming a fragile superior skirtlike ring which sometimes disappears. **SPORE PRINT** chocolate-brown; spores 4-5 × 2.5-4 μm, ellipsoid, smooth. Cap surface yellow in KOH.

HABITAT: Solitary or scattered in humus, uncommon. I have found it several times in late fall and winter, in mixed woods and under oak.

EDIBILITY: Presumably edible, but insubstantial. I haven't tried it.

COMMENTS: A petite *Agaricus*, distinguished by its soft amethyst-tinted cap. It belongs to a large group of small, mostly tropical species. *A. diminutivus* has reddish or pinkish cap fibrils; *A. lilaceps* is larger (cap 5-12 cm broad), with pronounced pink and lilac tints, and bruises yellow. I have not seen the latter, but it was originally described from Pacific Grove, in grass under pine.

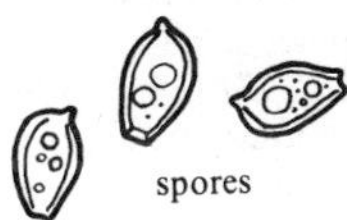
spores

STROPHARIACEAE

THIS is a medium-sized family of saprophytic mushrooms with purple-brown to black spores, attached gills, and a filamentous cap cuticle. A veil is usually present but does not necessarily form a ring. The gills are not decurrent as in the Gomphidiaceae, nor are they usually free as in the Agaricaceae. The gills do not deliquesce as in *Coprinus*, and the small, fragile species resembling *Psathyrella* and *Panaeolus* have a viscid and/or brightly colored cap. Their closest relatives belong to the brown-spored genus *Pholiota* of the Cortinariaceae.

The family is traditionally divided into three genera: *Stropharia*, *Naematoloma*, and *Psilocybe*. However, the differences between them are not clearcut, giving the "lumpers" a good excuse to combine them. At present they are delimited primarily on the basis of microscopic and chemical criteria, such as the presence or absence of special sterile cells (chrysocystidia) on the gills. However, using the combination of characteristics outlined in the key, they can usually be told in the field.

It is not an important family from an edibility standpoint, but it is *the* most significant group to magic mushroom hunters. Psilocybes are well known for their hallucinogenic properties, the active principles being psilocybin and psilocin (see p. 634 for details).

Key to the Strophariaceae

1. Stalk (especially base) *and/or* flesh in cap bruising blue or green .... *Psilocybe*, p. 307
1. Not as above 2
2. Cap some shade of brown or buff; growing on dung, or if not on dung, then cap narrowly conical .... *Psilocybe*, p. 307
2. Cap usually brightly colored (yellow, orange, green, white, etc.) 3
3. Veil typically evanescent; cap usually not viscid; usually growing on wood .... *Naematoloma*, p. 305
3. Veil typically persistent; cap viscid when moist; usually growing on ground .... *Stropharia*, below

STROPHARIA

Small to medium-sized saprophytic mushrooms. CAP *usually viscid when moist*, typically convex to plane, often brightly colored. GILLS *attached*, dark brown to gray or black at maturity. STALK fleshy but sometimes slender, central. VEIL *present, usually forming a ring*. VOLVA absent. SPORE PRINT *deep brown to purple-brown to black*. Spores typically elliptical, with germ pore. Chrysocystidia present on gills. Cap cuticle filamentous.

STROPHARIA is a rather small genus of brightly colored mushrooms with a viscid cap, persistent veil, attached gills, and dark spores. The cap is usually some shade of yellow, yellow-brown, orange, red, green, or white. In most cases the veil forms a ring, or at least leaves copious remnants on the cap margin.

Stropharia is sometimes confused with *Agaricus*, which has free gills (frequently pink when young) and chocolate-brown spores. *Agrocybe* is also similar, but has browner spores and a dry or only slightly viscid cap. *Stropharia* is separated with some difficulty from *Psilocybe*, but in the latter either the stalk bruises bluish-green or the veil is absent or evanescent. Most Stropharias are found in humus, grass, or dung. Those found in the woods might be mistaken for *Naematoloma*, but the veil is more persistent, and they rarely grow in clusters.

Many Stropharias are attractive, but none are outstanding edibility-wise. Some may actually be poisonous though there are conflicting opinions on this point. About 15 species are recorded from California, most of them uncommon. Four are described here. In addition, I have found a mysterious brownish-capped species growing on lawns.

Key to Stropharia

1. Cap white to yellow, tawny, or yellow-brown 2
1. Cap green, blue, orange, or red 6

2. Growing in woods, especially along streams .... *S. ambigua*, p. 303
2. Growing in grass, dung, cultivated places, etc. 3

3. Growing in dung or manure 4
3. Not as above 5

4. Cap more or less pale gray, bell-shaped to conical ....
   .... (see *Panaeolus separatus*, p. 335)
4. Cap yellowish; usually hemispherical or convex .. *S. semiglobata*, below

5. Ring persistent, its upper surface conspicuously grooved or striate; stalk not viscid .... *S. coronilla*, p. 302
5. Ring may or may not persist, its upper surface not grooved or striate; stalk usually viscid below veil .... *S. semiglobata*, below

6. Cap green to greenish-blue, at least when young ...... *S. aeruginosa*, p. 304
6. Cap orange to red .... *Naematoloma aurantiaca* (see *S. aeruginosa*, p. 304)

Stropharia semiglobata (Hemispherical Stropharia)

CAP 2-4 cm broad (rarely larger), hemispherical (rounded) or broadly bell-shaped becoming convex, rarely plane; surface smooth, viscid, light yellow to straw color, yellowish-buff, yellowish-tan, or yellow-brown. Flesh pale watery yellowish, thin. **GILLS** adnate, at first gray, then dark purple-brown or black. **STALK** to 13 cm long, slender, equal or slightly enlarged below, somewhat fibrillose above the veil, viscid below; white to yellowish. **VEIL** viscid, delicate, forming a fragile superior ring or fibrillose zone which is blackened by falling spores, or disappearing entirely. **SPORE PRINT** dark purple-brown to nearly black; spores 15-20 × 8.5-11 µm, ellipsoid, smooth.

HABITAT: Solitary, scattered, or in small groups on dung, manure, rich soil, straw, and grass. Common in fall, winter, and spring; occasional in summer.

EDIBILITY: Edible but of poor quality.

COMMENTS: Our most common and uninteresting *Stropharia.* The viscid or slimy yellowish cap, long slender viscid stem, and dark gills set it apart. The veil may or may not form a distinct ring. *Agrocybe* is similar but has brown spores. There are several closely related species, including: *S. albonitens*, terrestrial, with a creamy-yellowish to white cap and membranous but fragile veil; *S. stercoraria*, with a more or less yellow cap usually plane at maturity and slightly larger spores; and *S. siccipes*, with dry, rooting stalk and smaller spores. Since none are worth eating, distinguishing between them needn't concern you. At any rate, it doesn't concern me.

Stropharia coronilla

CAP 2-5 cm broad, convex to nearly plane; surface smooth, viscid when moist, golden-brown to yellow-brown to buffy-tan to nearly white. Flesh soft, white. **GILLS** adnate, close, grayish becoming purplish-black or grayish-black in age, close. **STALK** to 5 cm long, usually rather short, slender, equal, dry, white, minutely scaly or cottony above the ring, fibrillose below. **VEIL** membranous, white, forming a persistent median to superior ring which is conspicuously striate or grooved on upper surface. **SPORE PRINT** dark purple-brown to grayish-black; spores 7-9.5 × 4-5 μm, ellipsoid, smooth.

HABITAT: Scattered or in groups on lawns, baseball fields, even pastures. Fruiting year-round but mostly in the fall; often growing with *Agaricus campestris, A. micromegathus*, and *Panaeolus* species. Not uncommon.

Stropharia coronilla, various stages of development. This grass-inhabiting species resembles *Agaricus* but has attached gills and a striate (grooved) ring.

EDIBILITY: Dubious; hardly worth experimenting with.

COMMENTS: This attractive little *Stropharia* looks like a small *Agaricus* (especially *A. micromegathus*), but has attached gills and a grooved ring. It is shorter than *S. semiglobata*, the ring is more prominent, and the stalk is not viscid. Forms with a very deeply grooved ring have been called *S. bilamellata*, but they appear to intergrade with typical *S. coronilla*.

Stropharia ambigua (Questionable Stropharia)

CAP 4-13 cm broad, convex becoming plane; surface smooth, viscid or slimy when moist, bright yellow to yellowish-brown or yellowish-buff, sometimes nearly white; margin hung with cottony veil remnants. Flesh white, thick, soft. **GILLS** pale gray gradually darkening to purplish-black; close, typically adnate. **STALK** to 18 cm long, more or less equal, stuffed or hollow, silky white above the veil, covered with soft, delicate, dry white scales below, sometimes yellowish toward base in age. **VEIL** soft, white, leaving cottony shreds or strands on cap margin, sometimes a superior ring on stalk. **SPORE PRINT** dark purple-brown to nearly black; spores 11-14 × 6-7.5 µm, elliptical, smooth.

Stropharia ambigua. **Left:** Note the cottony stalk and veil remnants on cap margin. (Betty Barnhart). **Right:** Gill detail; note how ring has been darkened by falling spores.

HABITAT: Solitary or in scattered groups in rich, damp humus; fall through early spring, common. The best place to look for it is along streams or in gullies.

EDIBILITY: Edible, but mediocre. According to one authority, it tastes like old leaves. As I do not make a habit of chewing on old leaves, I cannot personally attest to the validity of this statement.

COMMENTS: There is nothing ambiguous about this graceful, stately *Stropharia*. At its best it is one of the most exquisite of all mushrooms, and is well worth seeking out. The soft, delicate white scales that cover the stem and the thin strands of veil tissue on the cap are very striking. The sticky yellow cap and grayish gills are also distinctive. Similar, but with a persistent, well-developed ring is *S. hornemanni*. I haven't seen it in our area, but it is found farther north.

Stropharia aeruginosa (Green Stropharia)

CAP 3-7 cm broad, broadly bell-shaped to convex, becoming plane; surface viscid, smooth or with a few whitish scales near margin, bright green to bluish-green when fresh, yellowish in age. Flesh soft, white or tinted blue. **GILLS** adnate, close, at first pallid, soon grayish, finally chocolate-brown. **STALK** to 7 cm long, equal, smooth and pallid above the ring, somewhat scaly below and colored like cap or paler, viscid. **VEIL** membranous, forming a superior ring, occasionally disappearing. **SPORE PRINT** dark brown or purple-brown; spores 7-10 × 4-5 μm, elliptical, smooth.

HABITAT: Solitary or in small groups in rich humus, gardens, even lawns. Fall, winter, and spring. Rare.

EDIBILITY: Questionable. Though eaten in Europe, it is best left alone.

COMMENTS: One of the most distinctive of all gilled mushrooms, instantly identified by its viscid, greenish cap and gray to chocolate-brown gills. But you are lucky indeed to find it. A very similar mushroom, *Pholiota subcaerulea*, is fairly common in the Pacific Northwest. The two are obviously closely related, but paradoxically, the system of classification utilized here places them not only in different genera, but different families—solely on the basis of their slightly different spore color! In contrast, the green-spored *Chlorophyllum molybdites* is grouped with the white-spored Lepiotaceae because of obvious morphological similarities.

Two other colorful but rare Strophariases are *S. (Naematoloma) aurantiaca* and *S. thrausta (S. squamosa* var. *thrausta).* The first has an orange to reddish-orange cap and smooth stem. I have found it in San Francisco. The second has a bright reddish cap and scaly stem. The true *S. squamosa* has an orange-brown to yellow-brown cap with scattered scales and a scaly stem.

NAEMATOLOMA

Small to medium-sized mushrooms *found mostly on wood.* CAP smooth, typically not viscid; *brightly colored.* GILLS attached, dark at maturity. STALK usually slender, more or less central. VEIL *typically evanescent.* VOLVA absent. SPORE PRINT *deep brown to purple-brown.* Spores typically elliptical with germ pore. Chrysocystidia present on gills. Cap cuticle filamentous.

THIS is a small group of dark-spored mushrooms with an orange, yellow, or greenish-yellow cap. The veil, if present, does not normally form a ring, and the cap is not usually viscid. These two features distinguish it from *Stropharia* and *Psilocybe. Psathyrella* is often confused with *Naematoloma,* and in fact many Psathyrellas were grouped with *Naematoloma* in the obsolete genus *Hypholoma.* But they differ from *Naematoloma* by their fragile flesh, white or pallid stem, brown to buff cap, and cellular cap cuticle.

Only two Naematolomas are common in our area, and neither is significant from an edibility standpoint. They usually grow in attractive clusters on logs, stumps, buried wood, or humus rich in lignin. Other species grow scattered on the ground, but never in dung or grass.

Key to Naematoloma

1. Gills yellow to green when young; taste bitter ..... *N. fasciculare,* below
1. Gills pale grayish when young; taste mild .... *N. capnoides,* p. 306

Naematoloma fasciculare (Clustered Woodlover)

CAP 2-7 cm broad, at first broadly conic or bell-shaped, soon becoming convex and finally plane; surface smooth, not viscid, orange at the center, yellow toward the margin, often with greenish tones, sometimes yellow throughout. Flesh thin, yellow, taste extremely bitter. **GILLS** close, typically adnate, at first sulfur-yellow, becoming greenish-yellow or olive-green, then dusted with purple-brown spores. **STALK** to 15 cm long, slender, tapering downward, pallid buff to tawny-yellow above,

Naematoloma fasciculare grows in clusters on wood. Caps on mature specimens at left have been darkened by spores. Gills of young specimens at right are yellow to greenish-yellow. (Ralph Buchsbaum)

often rusty-brownish toward base, darkening with age. **VEIL** evanescent, leaving slight vestiges on cap margin or an obscure hairy zone on stalk, which is subsequently darkened by falling spores. **SPORE PRINT** purple-brown; spores 6.5-8 × 3.5-4 μm, ellipsoid, smooth.

HABITAT: Gregarious, usually in clusters, on decaying wood of both hardwoods and conifers; sometimes growing from buried wood and appearing terrestrial. Extremely common, fall through spring. One of the first woodland mushrooms you are likely to encounter.

EDIBILITY: Poisonous, but so bitter that it's difficult to imagine anyone eating it.

COMMENTS: The greenish-yellow gills, purple-brown spores, bitter taste, and clustered growth habit are the principal fieldmarks of this attractive mushroom. There are several tall, slender Naematolomas that grow in groups (but not clusters) on the ground. They include *N. dispersum*, with pallid to dingy olive or purplish-brown gills and tawny-yellow to orange cap; and *N. olivaceotinctum*, with dull greenish cap and greenish-gray gills. Both have a mild taste and grow mostly under conifers. Neither is common.

Naematoloma capnoides

CAP 2-7 cm broad, convex then plane; surface smooth, not viscid, orange-brown at the center, yellow toward the margin. Flesh pallid, thin, taste mild. **GILLS** close, usually adnate but often seceding, at first pallid, then grayish, finally dark gray to purple-brown. **STALK** to 10 cm long, equal or tapering downward, dry, slender, yellowish above, rusty-brown to tan below. **VEIL** evanescent, sometimes leaving small patches on cap margin or obscure hairy zone on stem. **SPORE PRINT** purple-brown; spores 6-7.5 × 3.5-4.5 μm, elliptical, smooth.

HABITAT: Gregarious, usually in clusters, on decaying conifers. Occasional, fall and winter. The only place I've seen it in quantity is at Fall Creek, growing on rotting Douglas-fir in November.

EDIBILITY: Edible, but has little to recommend it.

COMMENTS: This nondescript *Naematoloma* resembles its ubiquitous relative, *N. fasciculare*, but has a mild taste and grayish rather than greenish-yellow gills. Several Pholiotas look similar but have brown or rusty spores.

PSILOCYBE

Small to medium-sized mushrooms found in variety of habitats. CAP smooth, *viscid when moist, usually some shade of brown or gray,* the skin easily separable (except in *P. cubensis, P. merdaria,* and *P. coprophila*). GILLS *attached,* dark at maturity. STALK usually slender, *often turning blue or green when handled.* VEIL present or absent. VOLVA absent. SPORE PRINT *purple-gray to purple-brown.* Spores mostly elliptical, with germ pore. Chrysocystidia absent on gills. Cap cuticle filamentous.

NOTORIOUS for their hallucinogenic properties, Psilocybes are among the most exalted and sought-after of all mushrooms. As a group, however, they are difficult to characterize. The majority are listless little brown mushrooms with a viscid cap and dark spores. The hallucinogenic species usually turn blue or greenish when bruised, especially on the stem. Almost any little brown mushroom can be mistaken carelessly for *Psilocybe*, with potentially disastrous results. A spore print will eliminate the brown-spored genera, many of which are poisonous (*Galerina, Inocybe, Conocybe*, etc.). Among the dark-spored genera, *Naematoloma* and *Stropharia* are usually brightly colored, while the cap color in *Psilocybe* (with the notable exception of *P. cubensis*) ranges from dark brown to grayish-brown to pale buff. The gills do not dissolve as in *Coprinus*. The viscid-capped *Panaeolus* species have black spores, while *Psathyrella* never stains blue.

Contrary to popular belief, Psilocybes do not grow exclusively on that brown stuff that sounds like a bell. Rather, they occur in a wide variety of habitats: in grass, gardens, landscaped areas, on wood or wood chips, humus, and moss. The hallucinogenic species are centered in two regions: the Pacific Northwest and southern Mexico. In California, alas, they are like solar eclipses—seemingly rare, but actually more common than any one person's experience would indicate. They are not something you can really *look* for—it is more a matter of geography, being in the right place at the right time. This situation may change, of course, as introduced species spread.

Since it was discovered that Native Americans in Oaxaca used Psilocybes as visionary agents, they have received an inordinate amount of attention in the American press. Newspapers and magazines are replete with frivolous articles on "getting off," and there is a glut of magic mushroom field guides on the market. As so often happens, it has become difficult to sort fact from fancy. Those wishing to pursue the subject seriously should invest in a *responsible* book on psilocybin mushrooms, and *use it in conjunction* with a general field guide.

Don't rely on shortcuts. Though most psilocybin-containing mushrooms exhibit a blueing reaction when bruised, the desirable dosage varies so much from species to species that indiscriminate sampling is dangerous. Furthermore, I have seen people confuse the blueing reaction with staining reactions in other mushrooms (for instance, the blackening of the flesh in *Hygrophorus conicus*). All the more reason to develop a general knowledge of mushrooms' habits and characteristics before venturing into the realm of little brown mushrooms. Four Psilocybes are described here, only one of which is common.

Key to Psilocybe

1. Some part of mushroom bruising green or blue (especially the base of the stalk or flesh of the cap) 2
1. No part of mushroom bruising green or blue 4

2. Ring present .... *P. cubensis*, p. 311
2. Ring absent 3

3. Cap narrowly conical to bell-shaped, expanding only very slightly .... *P. pelliculosa*, p. 309
3. Cap obtusely conical to bell-shaped, expanding to broadly convex or umbonate; margin often wavy or uplifted in age .... *P. baeocystis*, p. 310

4. Cap bell-shaped to convex or plane; usually growing on dung 5
4. Cap narrowly conical to bell-shaped; not on dung *P. pelliculosa*, p. 309

5. Cap some shade of brown; stalk dry; growing exclusively on dung .... *P. coprophila*, p. 309
5. Cap some shade of yellow; stalk viscid; on dung or ground .... (see *Stropharia semiglobata*, p. 301)

Psilocybe coprophila. Our most common dung-inhabiting agaric. Cap is brown, spore print is deep brown.

Psilocybe coprophila (Dung-Loving Psilocybe)

CAP less than 2.5 cm broad, convex or broadly bell-shaped; surface smooth, viscid when moist, cap orange-brown to reddish-brown or brown. Flesh thin, brown. **GILLS** attached, fairly well-spaced, grayish-brown becoming deep purple-brown, edges white. **STALK** to 6.5 cm long, thin, dry, equal, straight, yellowish or yellow-brown, darker in age. **VEIL** absent or rudimentary. **SPORE PRINT** purplish-brown; spores 11-15 × 6.5-9 μm, broadly elliptical, smooth.

HABITAT: Solitary or in colonies on dung and manure (especially cow pies), following rain or heavy fog, most any time. One of our most common coprophilous (dung-loving) fungi. Successive crops can be raised by bringing a cow pie home and keeping it moist.

EDIBILITY: Regarded as harmless, but sometimes containing enough psilocybin to be rewarded with the label "active." A large number would be needed to produce noticeable effects.

COMMENTS: The small size, convex brownish cap, and purplish-brown to dark brown spore print distinguish this diminutive dung addict. The cap is not yellow as in *Bolbitius* or *Stropharia.* Also found on dung is *P. merdaria,* with a cinnamon to brownish-yellow cap and slight ring on the stalk. Both of these Psilocybes are disdained by magic mushroom hunters, yet they add a great deal of beauty to the cow pies of this world, and play an important part in returning them to the soil.

Psilocybe pelliculosa (Liberty Cap)

CAP less than 2.5 cm broad, conical expanding slightly to bell-shaped with an umbo; surface smooth, viscid when wet, brown to dark dingy yellow-brown or gray-brown, often with olive tones, fading in age to pale brownish-yellow with greenish-gray tints. Flesh thin, watery brownish, bruising blue or green slightly. **GILLS** close, adnate but seceding in age, dull cinnamon-brown becoming gray-brown or purple-brown, edges pallid. **STALK** to 10 cm long, very thin, equal or with small, enlarged base, pallid to grayish, brownish below, darkening in age, usually bruising blue or greenish somewhat when handled, especially toward base. **VEIL** absent or rudimentary. **SPORE PRINT** purplish-brown; spores 9-13 × 5-7 μm, ellipsoid, smooth.

HABITAT: Scattered to gregarious in cool shady places in woods or along their margins, growing on conifer wood, debris, and humus rich in lignin. Found in Pacific Northwest and northern California. Whether it occurs south of San Francisco is uncertain.

EDIBILITY: Mildly hallucinogenic, 20-40 caps constituting an average dose. *P. semilanceata* (see below) is more potent. The two are often mistaken for each other.

COMMENTS: This is one of the smallest Psilocybes. The conical to bell-shaped cap, bruising reaction of the flesh and stem, and purple-brown spore print are diagnostic. The "true" liberty cap, *P. semilanceata*, is similar but has a paler, more narrowly conical cap and stem which may or may not bruise bluish. It grows in roadside pastures and tall grass. Both species resemble *Panaeolus* but are smaller, have viscid caps which peel easily, and purple-brown (rather than black) spores.

Psilocybe baeocystis

CAP 2-5 cm broad, obtusely conic or bell-shaped expanding somewhat in age to broadly convex or umbonate with an uplifted, wavy margin; surface smooth, viscid when moist, dark olive-brown fading to buffy-brown or grayish-brown with a darker center, the margin sometimes greenish; greenish-blue where bruised. Flesh thin, bruising greenish-blue. **GILLS** typically adnate, fairly close, brown to purplish-brown or purplish-gray, edges whitish. **STALK** to 7 cm long, thin, equal, whitish, dry, staining blue or greenish. **VEIL** evanescent or absent, not forming a distinct ring. **SPORE PRINT** lavender-gray; spores 11-13 × 7-9 μm, elliptical, smooth.

HABITAT: Scattered or in groups on moss, decaying wood, cones, wood chips, mulch, even lawns; fruiting in moist weather. Perhaps introduced adventitiously into California, it turns up occasionally in odd places, such as San Francisco.

EDIBILITY: Hallucinogenic when eaten raw and extremely potent—along with *P. cyanescens* (see comments), the most powerful west coast species. Though small, only one or two caps are needed to induce

Lactarius camphoratus (Candy Cap), p. 73

Russula emetica (Emetic Russula), p. 88

Ray Gipson

Hygrophorus coccineus, p. 100

Hygrophorus conicus (Witch's Hat), p. 104

Ray Gipson

Nancy Burnett

Omphalotus olivascens (Jack-O-Lantern Mushroom), p. 130

Lepista (= *Clitocybe*) *nuda* (Blewitt), p. 133

Nancy Burnett

Armillariella mellea (Honey Mushroom), p. 171

Marasmius oreades (Fairy Ring Mushroom), p. 185

Amanita phalloides (Death Cap), p. 231

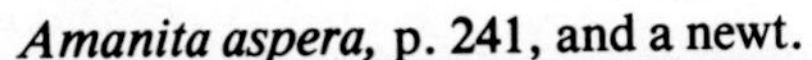

Amanita aspera, p. 241, and a newt.

Amanita muscaria (Fly Agaric), p. 242

Amanita calyptroderma (Coccora), p. 246

Amanita velosa (Springtime Amanita), p. 248

Lepiota (= *Leucocoprinus*) *lutea* (Yellow Lepiota), p. 272

Nancy Burnett

Agaricus subrutilescens (Wine-Colored Agaricus), p. 285

Agaricus arvensis (Horse Mushroom), p. 292

Coprinus lagopus, p. 321

Betty Barnhart

Stropharia ambigua
(Questionable Stropharia), p. 303

Coprinus comatus (Shaggy Mane), p. 316

Panaeolus sp.
(*P. subbalteatus* complex),
p. 332

Nancy Burnett

Gymnopilus spectabilis (Giant Gymnopilus), p. 373

Chroogomphus rutilus (Pine Mushroom), p. 398

Nancy Burnett

Boletus edulis (King Boletus), p. 424

Laetiporus sulphureus (Sulfur Shelf), p. 446

Coriolus versicolor (Many-Colored Polypore), p. 451

Herb Saylor

Hericium coralloides (Coral Hericium), p. 482

Ramaria araiospora (Red Coral), p. 509

Ray Gipson

Herb Saylor

Clavaria vermicularis (Fairy Fingers), p. 498

Herb Saylor

Gomphus floccosus (Woolly Chanterelle), p. 519

Cantharellus cibarius (Chanterelle), p. 520

Craterellus cornucopioides (Horn of Plenty), p. 523

Astreus hygrometricus (Hygrometric Earthstar), p. 549

Bob Tally

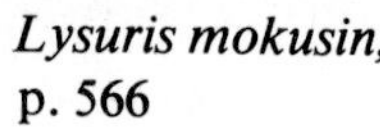

Lysuris mokusin, p. 566

Tremella mesenterica (Common Witch's Butter), p. 580

Aleuria aurantia (Orange Peel Fungus), p. 591

Nancy Burnett

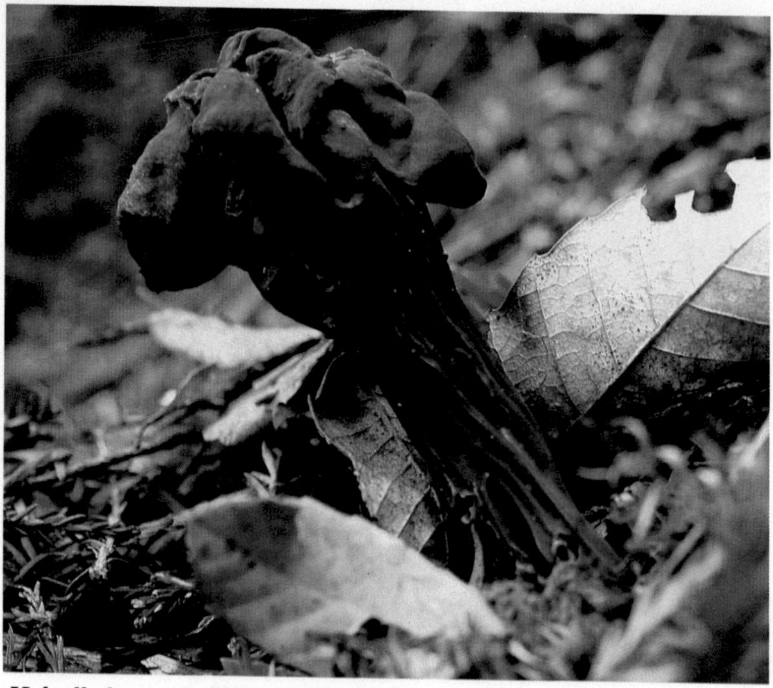

Ray Gipson

Helvella lacunosa (Black Elfin Saddle), p. 601

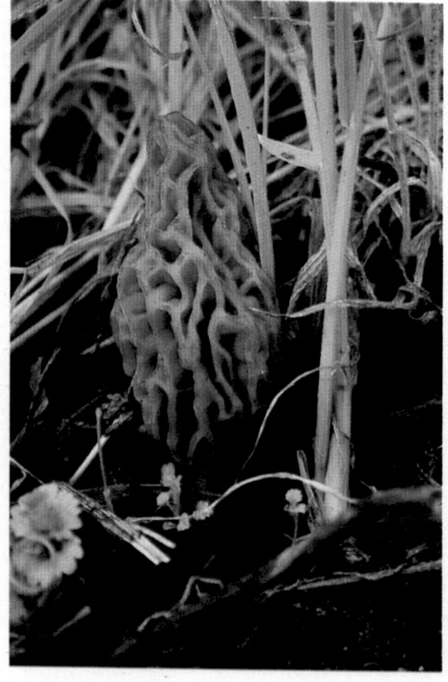

Nancy Burnett

Morchella conica (Conic Morel), p. 611

Psilocybe baeocystis. This powerful hallucinogenic species stains bluish-green when bruised. The cap is viscid, the spore print purple-gray. (Rick Kerrigan)

marked changes in perception and sensation. Psilocin is primarily responsible, with psilocybin and several related compounds contributing to the effects. Together they constitute 0.6% of the mushroom on a dry weight basis, substantially more than the better known *P. cubensis!* A six year old Washington boy died after ingesting an unknown quantity of *P. baeocystis* along with other unidentified mushrooms. Unusual side effects have not been noted in adults.

COMMENTS: The lavender-gray spores, viscid olive-brown to grayish-brown cap, absence of a ring, and blueing of the stem and flesh are the critical fieldmarks of this potent Psilocybe. There are a number of other Psilocybes that bruise bluish-green and lack a ring. One, *P. cyanescens*, is found in similar habitats, but has a caramel-brown cap fading to yellowish, and darker spores. Its mycelium is supposedly aggressive enough to be transplanted successfully. An exotic species with a yellow-brown to ochraceous cap, *P. mairei*, has been found in Golden Gate Park, probably introduced with plants. With all of these, a spore print should be taken to avoid confusion with deadly *Galerina* and *Conocybe* species.

Psilocybe cubensis

CAP 2.5-9 cm broad, broadly conic, egg-shaped, or bell-shaped with a distinct umbo when young, gradually expanding to convex with a broad umbo or plane; surface smooth, viscid when moist, nearly white to yellow, yellowish-buff, yellow-brown, or brownish-buff, blueing where bruised or in age, margin sometimes hung with veil remnants. Flesh firm, white, staining blue when bruised. **GILLS** close, adnate to adnexed, gray becoming deep purplish-gray to nearly black, edges white. **STALK** to 15 cm long, equal or thicker below, dry, white or discoloring yellowish-brown in age, bruising blue when handled or dried, usually striate above the ring and smooth below. **VEIL** membranous, white, usually forming a thin, fragile ring which is blackened by falling spores. **SPORE PRINT** dark purplish-brown to nearly black; spores 11-17 × 7-10 μm, elliptical to oval, smooth.

HABITAT: Solitary or in groups on dung and manure, widespread throughout the warmer parts of the northern hemisphere, including the southern United States, Mexico, and Colombia. Since it is being cultivated on a widespread basis in California, it may eventually appear of its own accord in the warmer areas of the state. It can be cultivated on a variety of simple substrates. However, temperature control and strict sterilization measures are necessary to induce fruiting and prevent contamination.

EDIBILITY: Hallucinogenic when eaten raw. Though not as powerful as *P. baeocystis*, it is larger, so the desirable dosage is about the same. It used to be that the demand for psilocybin mushrooms far outstripped the supply, the result being that most of the "psilocybin" mushrooms sold on the street proved to be commercial mushrooms laced with LSD or other substances (one specimen I examined proved to be a soggy piece of chanterelle soaked in ammonia!). Now that cultivation procedures have been refined, you're much more likely to get the real thing. It is usually sold dried, though this decreases its potency. Ironically, Oaxacans regard it as inferior—instead of using it themselves they sell it to consciousness-starved gringos. The mycelium is also potent.

COMMENTS: This is the largest, handsomest, and best known Psilocybe. The yellowish cap, membranous ring, and blueing of the stem identify it. It resembles the yellow-capped Stropharias so much that it is listed as *Stropharia cubensis* in many books. Its shape is similar to *Agrocybe praecox* (see photograph, p. 339), but the spore print is darker, and its "aura" is "cosmic" (or so I'm told by one confirmed fruitcake). A smaller species with a ring, *P. stuntzii*, is common in the Pacific Northwest.

COPRINACEAE

THESE are fragile mushrooms with purple-brown to black spores and a cartilaginous stem. The gills are not decurrent as in the Gomphidiaceae, and those with free gills have black spores (unlike the Agaricaceae). The cap cuticle is cellular—composed of round or pear-shaped cells—as opposed to filamentous as in the Strophariaceae. Since this distinction is microscopic, it is better to learn the characteristics of each genus than attempt to distinguish the families *in toto*. As a rule, however, the fragile white to brown species belong to the Coprinaceae, while those with a viscid *and/or* brightly colored cap belong to the Strophariaceae. Both families should be checked when in doubt. There are three common genera, keyed below.

Key to the Coprinaceae

1. Gills (and sometimes cap) digesting themselves at maturity, turning into an inky black fluid .... *Coprinus*, below
1. Gills not digesting themselves 2

2. Cap translucent-striate at maturity .... *Coprinus*, below
2. Not as above 3

3. Growing in grass, dung, or manure; cap usually bell-shaped to conical or hemispherical (but may expand in age) .... *Panaeolus*, p. 330
3. Growing in woods, humus, on stumps, etc.; *not* growing in dung and manure; if growing in grass, then cap broadly convex to plane .... *Psathyrella*, p. 325

COPRINUS (INKY CAPS)

Minute to medium-sized ephemeral saprophytic mushrooms. CAP at first egg-shaped, cylindrical, or conical, *translucent-striate at maturity in the smaller species*. GILLS free or attached, gray to black at maturity, *autodigesting into an inky black fluid in the larger species*. STALK hollow, cartilaginous, usually white. VEIL present or absent. VOLVA absent or rudimentary. SPORE PRINT *typically black*. Spores mostly elliptical, with germ pore; discoloring in concentrated sulfuric acid. Cap cuticle cellular.

MEMBERS of this genus are called inky caps because the gills (and sometimes the cap) digest themselves at maturity, turning into an inky black fluid that drips to the ground. The **autodigestion** or **deliquescing** of the gills plus the black spore print are the main diagnostic features. In *Bolbitius* the gills sometimes liquefy but the spore print is rusty.

Autodigestion in *Coprinus comatus.* **Left:** The gills have just begun to blacken and liquefy at the cap margin. **Right:** Dry weather has caused the autodigestion process to cease with a few rags of tissue left. Normally it continues until only the stalk remains. (Bill Everson)

The autodigestion process is a very sophisticated method of spore dispersal and should not be confused with the normal process of decay that occurs in most mushrooms. Rather then the spores maturing at an even rate, those near the margin of the cap mature first. Enzymes are then released which dissolve the surrounding tissue, causing the edge of the cap to spread out and curl back. This pulls the gills apart, enabling the spores to be discharged into the air. If you look at the gills of a shaggy mane *(Coprinus comatus)*, you'll see that they are crowded together like the pages of a book. If autodigestion did not occur, the spores would be discharged onto adjoining gills and their dissemination would be greatly impeded. Of course, many spores are trapped in the inky liquid that drips to the ground, but millions more are successfully discharged into the air.

In the larger inky caps, both the cap and gills dissolve, until there is nothing left but a few rags of black tissue stuck to the top of the stalk. This phenomenon was undoubtedly the inspiration for Shelley's memorable lines:

> Their mass rotted off them flake by flake
> Til the thick stalk stuck like a murderer's stake,
> Where rags of loose flesh yet tremble on high
> Infecting the winds that wander by.

In the smaller species, such as *C. radiatus*, an inky fluid is not necessarily formed. There is so little substance to the gills that they wither instead of liquefying, and the cap is **translucent-striate**—so thin that the gills can be seen through it as radiating lines.

Inky caps frequent areas inhabited by livestock and human beings, fruiting whenever it is moist. The smaller types are especially common on dung and manure, the larger ones in gardens, cellars, along roads, around stumps, in disturbed soil and humus. It is a difficult group to study because the life span of the fruiting bodies is so short (in some cases only a few hours), and because many species fruit where you don't think to look for mushrooms. As we alter the environment and create new niches, we can expect new species to evolve. One winter, following three weeks of rain, an unidentified *Coprinus* sprung from the orlon carpet on the floor of my '67 Rolls Canardly (it rolls down one hill and can hardly make it up the next). People naturally assumed it was the result of carrying around so many mushrooms in my car, yet it was a species I had never seen before!

The larger inky caps are edible and the shaggy mane, *C. comatus*, is a well-known favorite. The smaller species are too thin and insubstantial to merit collecting. The common inky cap, *C. atramentarius*, contains a compound which reacts with alcohol in the body, producing peculiar symptoms (see p. 635). Inky caps should be eaten before they deliquesce and will *not* keep overnight. They are among the most easily digestible of all fungi, but their high water content makes them unsuitable for certain dishes. As they frequently occur in large numbers, you may wish to preserve them for later use. This is best effected by marinating, drying, or sauteing and then freezing. The "ink" from the fleshier species can be diluted with a little water and used as an ink.

There are dozens of *Coprinus* species in California, but they have not been critically studied. The smaller ones are especially difficult to identify, even with the aid of a microscope. A few distinctive types are described here.

Key to Coprinus

1. Cap translucent-striate at maturity; typically 5 cm broad or less 2
1. Cap not translucent (but may be striate); 2 cm broad or more 6

2. Cap covered with white to gray hairs or silky patches when young 3
2. Hairs or patches absent 4

3. Cap minute, up to 15 mm broad; on dung, manure . *C. radiatus*, p. 321
3. Not as above; larger .... *C. lagopus*, p. 321

4. Growing on dung, manure .... *C. ephemerus* (see *C. plicatilis*, p. 323)
4. Not growing on dung or manure 5

5. Cap minute (5-10 mm broad), bell-shaped; growing in dense groups, not autodigesting .... *C. disseminatus*, p. 324
5. Not as above .... *C. plicatilis*, p. 323

6. Cap tall, cylindrical, shaggy, white with a brown center *C. comatus*, below
6. Not as above 7

7. Cap inky-gray to lead-gray or grayish-brown .. *C. atramentarius*, p. 317
7. Cap tan, yellow-brown, red-brown, to nearly white 8

8. Gills liquefying; cap white to pale tawny, at first covered with a silky white fibrillose coating .... *C. "domesticus,"* p. 320
8. Gills scarcely liquefying; cap some shade of brown, with glistening particles that soon disappear .... *C. micaceus*, p. 319

Coprinus comatus (Shaggy Mane)

CAP 5-25 cm tall, narrowly cylindrical or columnar, expanding somewhat at maturity until more or less bell-shaped; surface dry, white, with flattened scales which recurve in age; scales brown, at least at center; margin striate in age. Flesh soft, white. **GILLS** very crowded (like pages in a book), narrowly attached to free, white, then passing through delicate shades of pink, pinkish-red, wine color, and finally black; deliquescing from the bottom up. **STALK** 7-50 cm long, tapering upward or equal with an enlarged, more or less pointed base; dry, smooth, white, hollow, separable from cap. **VEIL** membranous, inferior, forming a small, white movable ring which is easily obliterated. **SPORE PRINT** black; spores 13-18 × 7-8 μm, elliptical, smooth.

HABITAT: Solitary, scattered, clustered, or in troops, on hard ground and grassy areas, disturbed soil, etc., especially along roads and paths. Common in the fall, occasional otherwise. "Shags" seem to gravitate toward asphalt and often burst up through it. They've been known to ruin tennis courts and one is reported to have lifted a 10 lb. slab of concrete in a heroic attempt to proliferate its species. I have seen them form a continuous column for one mile along a gravel road; Alexander Smith relates an instance of over 1000 appearing on a baseball field, extending in a line from first base to short left field.

EDIBILITY: Edible and choice; one of the best known and most popular of all mushrooms, as well as one of the safest. The flavor is a disappointment to some, and it is indeed delicate (let their juices boil off). The texture, however, is marvelous—not slimy as in okra, but succulent as in octopus. Use only young caps—darkened ones are mostly water. For a delicious snack, saute them in butter and serve on toast. In rare instances they may react with alcohol to produce a reaction similar to that of *C. atramentarius*, but I have cooked them in wine many times with no ill effects.

Coprinus comatus, immature specimens. The shaggy, cylindrical heads are common along roads. Deliquescing individuals are shown on p. 314; ring on the stem is shown in another picture of immature shaggy manes, p. 56.

COMMENTS: Shaggy manes are the soldiers among mushrooms, the sentinels of the roads. Their tall, shaggy, cylindrical heads are unmistakable, even in silhouette. Deliquescing individuals are usually found in the vicinity of young ones, leaving no doubt as to their identity. "Shags" are as pleasing to the eye as to the palate, especially in the delicate tints they assume as they mature. Their height varies according to the depth of the humus they must transcend. I have found stalks 60 cm (2 ft.) tall, but the normal height is 12-30 cm. "Shags" also possess a special spontaneity. They seem to miraculously pop up overnight after a rain, whereas most mushrooms fruit during the drying cycle, several days after. Don't pick more than you can eat in two meals—unless you plan to preserve them for later use. Extreme aridity may arrest development so that the spores never mature and the gills remain white.

Coprinus atramentarius (Inky Cap)

CAP 2-10 cm broad and tall, occasionally larger; egg-shaped or round, becoming bell-shaped or convex, often lobed or folded somewhat; surface dry, lead-gray to inky-gray or grayish-brown, at first overlaid with silvery-white silky fibrils, minutely scaly in dry weather; margin tattered in age, striate but not translucent. Flesh thin, watery, pallid or grayish. **GILLS** free or nearly so, crowded, at first pallid, soon gray and finally black, deliquescing at maturity into an inky black fluid. **STALK**

Coprinus atramentarius. **Left:** Immature individual, showing the oval cap. (Nancy Burnett) **Right:** A large cluster of young specimens.

to 25 cm long but usually much shorter, equal or base sometimes enlarged, sometimes narrowed; white and silky above, white and somewhat fibrillose below, dry, hollow. **VEIL** fibrillose, evanescent, or leaving a ragged ring or "volva" at or near base of stalk. **SPORE PRINT** black; spores 8-12 × 4.5-6.5 μm, elliptical, smooth.

HABITAT: Scattered, gregarious, or in large clumps in cultivated areas: lawns, gardens, roadsides, practically anywhere where there is organic matter (but not the woods). Common in fall, winter, and spring. Successive crops are normally produced. It used to be an unwanted intruder in cultivated mushroom beds.

EDIBILITY: Edible when young and fairly good, but sometimes reacting with alcohol to produce a peculiar type of poisoning (see p. 635). The dingy grayish-brown caps are hardly appetizing. Precisely for this reason it was the very first wild mushroom I ventured to eat. Inky cap and salami sandwiches were a staple item in my diet, until I discovered finer and more flavorful fungal foods, such as "Sparassis Sole" and "Agaricus Elegante."

COMMENTS: The inky-gray to gray-brown bell-shaped caps are a familiar if unappealing sight in vacant lots and gardens. At maturity, of course, they turn into an inky black mess, suitable for writing with, but not eating. They sometimes rival shaggy manes for size and abundance. In fact, the two often mix company. I have seen gigantic 10-lb. clusters in an old field. For an unexpected and titillating visual treat, examine the cross-section of a young, unexpanded button. *C. insignis* is a similar species with rough spores. It likes to grow from hardwood stumps such as maple, and is said to be poisonous. I have not seen it.

Coprinus micaceus. These small specimens were growing from a piece of buried wood. There are still a few glistening particles clinging to the caps.

Coprinus micaceus (Glistening Inky Cap)

CAP 2-5 cm broad, at first egg-shaped but soon bell-shaped, expanding to convex; surface yellowish-tan to yellow-brown, orange-brown, or reddish-brown, margin often paler; at first sprinkled with minute glistening white particles which soon disappear; sometimes entirely grayish in old age, margin conspicuously striate, usually tattered or torn at maturity. Flesh very thin, white or pallid, watery. **GILLS** crowded, attached narrowly to stem, pallid soon becoming gray, finally black, autodigesting somewhat, but not truly liquefying. **STALK** to 10 cm long, slender, more or less equal, smooth or slightly fibrillose, white or pallid, fragile, hollow. **VEIL** absent. **SPORE PRINT** dark brown to black; spores 7-10 × 4-5 μm, elliptical, smooth.

HABITAT: Gregarious or in dense clusters on wood and woody debris, around stumps, very commonly from buried roots (thus appearing terrestrial). Common after rains year-round, but especially in the fall.

EDIBILITY: Edible. Of fair flavor, but thin-fleshed and watery. Since it often occurs in large numbers, it is easy to gather enough for a meal. It does not digest itself completely, another point in its favor.

COMMENTS: The cap color of this ubiquitous *Coprinus* varies considerably, but is nearly always some shade of brown. It is striate, but not translucent. It might be mistaken for a *Psathyrella* because the gills do not dissolve, but old caps become very tattered as the margin gets eaten away. The micalike particles responsible for its name are not always evident.

Bountiful crops sprout periodically from the woodwork of a very popular cafe in downtown Santa Cruz. Its employees are divided on how to react: whether to advertise its presence as an advantageous and organic addition to the existing decor, or whether to mask its presence by squishing them every morning, for fear of alienating the more squeamish members of their clientele. *C. silvaticus* is a somewhat similar woodland species with a brownish cap, deliquescing gills, and rough spores.

Coprinus "domesticus" (Domestic Inky Cap)

CAP to 5 cm high, egg-shaped to bell-shaped, scarcely expanding; surface grayish-yellow to grayish-white, with a tawny or reddish-brown center, at first covered with silky white fibrils or scales, these becoming dispersed in age; conspicuously striate nearly to the center, margin often splitting in age. Flesh thin, pallid. **GILLS** crowded, free or narrowly attached, white becoming gray or reddish-gray, finally black, liquefying at maturity. **STALK** to 5 cm long, slender, white, finely striate, equal, hollow. **VEIL** evanescent, basal, sometimes forming a ragged zone or "volva" at stalk base. **SPORE PRINT** black; spores 14-17 × 7-10 μm, elliptical, smooth.

Coprinus "domesticus," immature specimens. Cap is grayish-buff to whitish and conspicuously striate. These were found on wood chips in a garden in Saratoga.

HABITAT: In small, scattered clumps on wood chips and vegetable debris in a large garden in Saratoga. Crops were produced continuously over a period of several months.

EDIBILITY: Presumably edible. I haven't tried it.

COMMENTS: The name *C. domesticus* has been applied to more than one species, so its application here must be regarded as very tentative. The above description is based on material I personally collected. It clashes with some interpretations of *C. domesticus* while jibing with others. It resembles *C. micaceus* but is larger, has silky white fibrils on the cap instead of glistening particles, deliquesces to a greater degree, and has larger spores.

Coprinus radiatus

CAP 2-15 mm broad, minute, at first egg-shaped or cylindrical, then bell-shaped finally expanding to plane or nearly so; surface deeply striate, translucent at maturity, pale brown to yellowish-brown, darker at the center, at first covered with a dense coating of long white hairs or fibrils. Flesh very thin, practically non-existent. **GILLS** narrow, well spaced, free or nearly free, at first pallid, but soon gray to black, shrivelling or autodigesting with cap. **STALK** to 5 cm long, very slender, fragile, hollow, equal, white, darkening somewhat in age, hairy at base. **VEIL** absent. **SPORE PRINT** black; spores 10-14 × 6-9 μm, elliptical, smooth.

HABITAT: Solitary on in troops on dung, compost, and manure. Common in wet weather.

EDIBILITY: Too small to be of value.

COMMENTS: This miniature version of *C. lagopus* is one of our commonest cow pie fungi. There are actually several minute, dung-inhabiting inky caps, but a microscope is needed to distinguish them. *C. radiatus* is the most prominent, along with *C. ephemerus*, a larger species with a yellow-brown to reddish-brown cap and no hairs. It looks like a *Mycena* but has black spores. *C. niveus* is a pure white species.

Coprinus lagopus

CAP 2-5 cm broad or tall; narrowly cylindrical or conical becoming broadly conical, the margin then splitting, curling back and in; surface grayish, at first covered with dense white powdery patches of hairs or

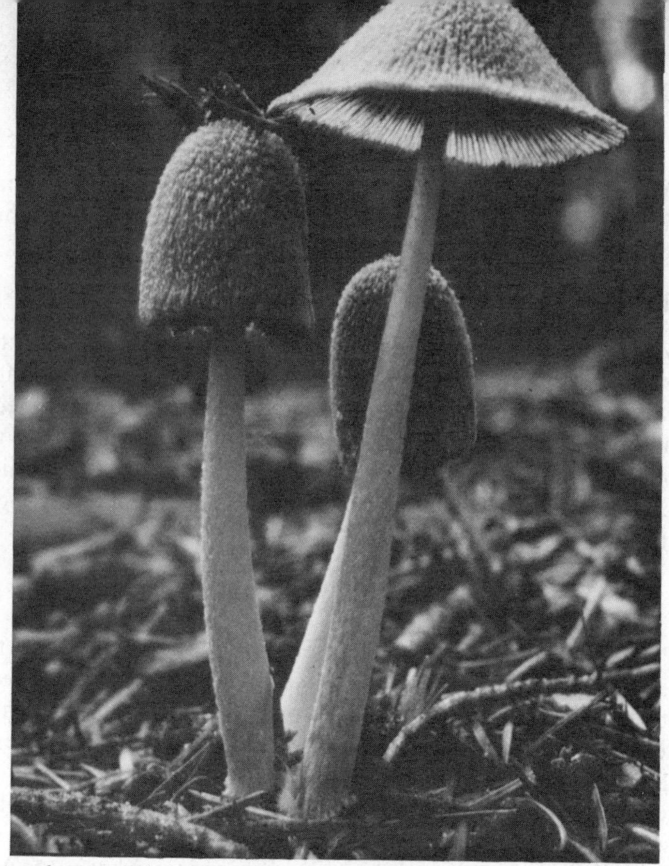

Coprinus lagopus. This beautiful woodland species is covered with delicate hairs when young, but the hairs wear away as the cap unfurls. The margin eventually turns up and in.

fibrils which become grayish in age or disappear; translucent-striate nearly to center at maturity. Flesh very thin, pallid grayish. **GILLS** free, narrow, fairly well-spaced, grayish then black, rapidly dissolving or withering. **STALK** to 20 cm long, slender, very fragile, white, hollow, equal or tapering upward, with minute whitish scales, hairy at base. **VEIL** absent or evanescent. **SPORE PRINT** black; spores 12-14 × 7-8 µm, elliptical, smooth.

HABITAT: Solitary, scattered, or in groups, in leaf litter and debris. Common in fall, occasional in winter and spring. Fruiting bodies only last a few hours.

EDIBILITY: Fleshless and flavorless.

COMMENTS: This common, exquisite woodland *Coprinus* can be told by its long, slender, fragile white stem and gray, translucent-striate cap at first covered with white hairs. There are many closely related variants which are one big headache for compulsive categorizers. They include *C. cinereus* (*C. fimetarius* of some authors), which grows in troops on dung, manure, and straw, *C. arenatus*, which grows in sand, and *C. "chevicola."* The latter appeared one day in the floor of my ramshackle '67 Chevy II Nova Supersport, and has shown up regularly ever since. It superficially resembles *C. lagopus* but differs in several key respects, not the least of which is its choice of abode.

Coprinus plicatilis

CAP up to 2.5 cm broad, at first conic, soon plane or with an upturned margin in age; surface gray to pale grayish-brown, the center usually brown; translucent-striate at maturity. Flesh very thin, fragile. **GILLS** free, attached to a collar around the stalk apex, well-spaced, gray to black, tending to shrivel rather than liquefy. **STALK** to 7.5 cm long, very thin, fragile, dry, smooth, white, hollow, equal or with small basal bulb. **VEIL** absent. **SPORE PRINT** black; spores 10-12 $\times$ 7.5-9.5 μm, broadly elliptical, smooth.

Coprinus plicatilis, mature specimens which have begun to deliquesce. Note the absence of scales or hairs on the cap. (Joel Leivick)

HABITAT: Scattered or in small groups in grassy areas, along paths and roads, exposed soil, etc. Fairly common, especially in the fall.

EDIBILITY: Inconsequential.

COMMENTS: The smooth, translucent-striate cap, small size, and terrestrial habit are characteristic. It is larger than *C. disseminatus* and not bell-shaped. It is smaller than *C. micaceus* and translucent at maturity. It lacks the white patches or hairs on the cap typical of the *C. lagopus* group. There are several similar species, including *C. ephemerus*, slightly smaller, growing on dung and manure, with a warm brown to yellow-brown cap. Another brownish species, *C. silvaticus,* grows in the woods.

Coprinus disseminatus

CAP 5-12 mm broad; egg-shaped becoming bell-shaped; surface at first pallid, then gray to grayish-brown, buff at the center, deeply striate to the very center, translucent at maturity, minutely scurfy when young. Flesh very thin, soft, pallid. **GILLS** attached, fairly well-spaced, narrow, at first white but soon gray, finally black, not deliquescing. **STALK** to 4 cm long, thin, hollow, white, equal, smooth, often curved. **VEIL** absent. **SPORE PRINT** black; spores 7-10 × 4-5 μm, elliptical, smooth.

HABITAT: Densely gregarious on ground or well-decayed wood and debris, fairly common, fall through spring.

Coprinus disseminatus. This minute, attractive species does not deliquesce. Note the striate bell-shaped cap and growth in clusters.

EDIBILITY: Too small to be of value.

COMMENTS: Because the gills do not deliquesce, the "splitters" have rewarded this dainty little fungus with a genus of its own, *Pseudocoprinus.* It is the same shape as *C. micaceus* but much smaller. The translucent cap separates it from *Psathyrella.* The bell-shaped cap is suggestive of *Mycena* but the spore print is black. *C. impatiens* is similar but has an ochraceous cap and usually occurs in smaller numbers—up to one dozen individuals.

PSATHYRELLA

Small to medium-sized mushrooms *found mostly on wood or in humus.* CAP conical to convex or plane, often hygrophanous, *typically some shade of brown, buff, or gray. Flesh markedly fragile.* GILLS dark brown to black at maturity, usually attached but not decurrent. STALK slender, cartilaginous, fragile, usually white or pallid. VEIL present or absent. VOLVA absent. SPORE PRINT *purple-brown to black.* Spores smooth or rough, with germ pore, discoloring in concentrated sulfuric acid. Cap cuticle cellular.

FEW fleshy fungi have less to offer the average mushroom hunter (not to mention the average human being) than the Psathyrellas. They constitute an immense, monotonous, and metagrobolizing multitude of dull whitish, buff, or brownish mushrooms with cartilaginous stem, fragile flesh, and purple-brown to black spores. Psathyrellas are so nondescript and unassuming that it's much easier to define what they aren't than what they are: the gills do not deliquesce as in *Coprinus*, nor is the cap translucent; the flesh never bruises blue as in *Psilocybe*; the cap is not colorful as in *Naematoloma* and *Stropharia*, and only rarely is it viscid; and they don't grow in dung like *Panaeolus.* Some Psathyrellas are quite attractive, however, and all have their indispensable "roles" to fulfill.

Though wood-inhabiting, Psathyrellas usually appear terrestrial because they feed on wood in the final stages of decay, after all the other wood-lovers have had their fill. A few, such as *P. hydrophila*, grow on or around stumps. *P. candolleana* is very common in lawns and gardens. The rest are partial to damp, shady situations, especially along trails or streambeds. A very good place to look for them is in willow-alder thickets, and a very good time to look for them is in the late fall or early winter, but I can't think of a very good *reason* to look for them.

Psathyrellas are listed in older books under two obsolete names, *Psathyra* and *Hypholoma.* A few are edible, but most have not been tested. Alexander Smith has authored an abstruse monograph in which he describes more than 400 North American species. The overwhelming majority can only be identified if one has a microscope and a special fondness for tedious undertakings. My advice is to leave the Psathyrellas to professional psathyrellologists, whose job it is to wrestle with such matters. A mere four species are described here.

Key to Psathyrella

1. Cap conspicuously fibrillose 2
1. Cap more or less smooth 3

2. Growing in burned-over areas .... *P. carbonicola* (see *P. velutina*, p. 329)
2. Not as above .... *P. velutina*, p. 329

3. Cap convex when young, nearly plane in age 4
3. Cap bell-shaped or conical when young, scarcely expanding 6

4. Growing on stumps or decayed wood; cap dark reddish-brown when moist, tan or brown when dry .... *P. hydrophila*, p. 327
4. Not as above; usually appearing terrestrial 5

5. Cap honey-colored when moist, whitish when dry; spore print deep brown .... *P. candolleana*, below
5. Not as above; in grass or manure; spore print black (see *Panaeolus*, p. 330)

6. Clustered or densely gregarious; cap margin markedly striate .... (see *Coprinus micaceus*, p. 319)
6. Not as above .... *P. longipes*, p. 328

Psathyrella candolleana (Common Psathyrella)

CAP 2.5-7.5 cm broad, convex when young, plane in age; surface smooth, with a few scattered patches of fibrils near the margin when young; hygrophanous, honey-colored when moist, fading quickly to whitish in age or upon drying. Flesh thin, fragile, same color as cap. **GILLS** close, at first whitish, soon grayish, finally dark brown or purple-brown. **STALK** to 10 cm long but usually shorter, slender, equal, hollow, fragile, white or whitish, fibrillose. **VEIL** white, evanescent, but usually leaving remnants on cap margin, rarely a fibrillose ring on stalk. **SPORE PRINT** purple-brown; spores 7-9 × 4-5 μm, elliptical, smooth.

HABITAT: Gregarious or tufted in gardens, on lawns, parkways, disturbed soil, sometimes in woods, often springing from old, buried stumps. Common year-round.

EDIBILITY: Described as delicious by some authors, but has little substance and is not particularly easy to identify.

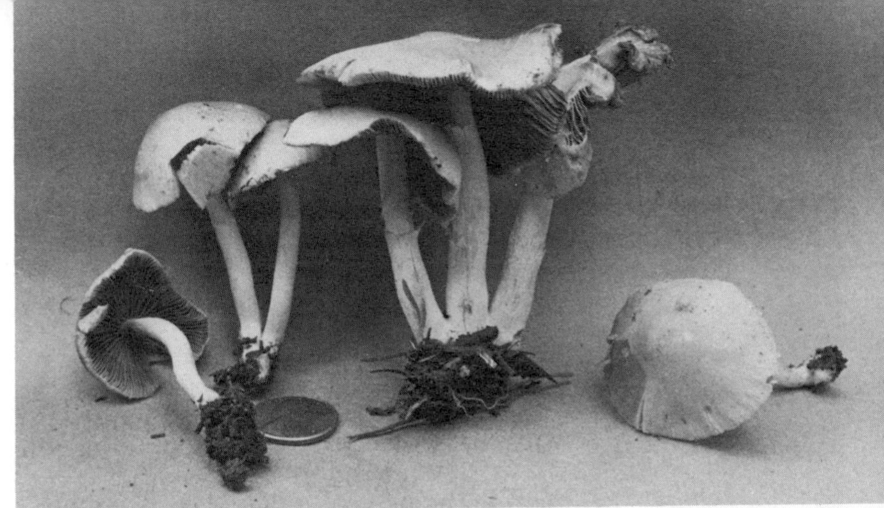

Psathyrella candolleana, mature specimens. These caps have already faded to whitish, but were honey-brown when moist. Note the shape: convex becoming plane. The flesh is extremely fragile, as evidenced by broken specimens.

COMMENTS: The fragile convex cap, honey-colored when fresh and whitish in age, plus the deep brown spores and habitat mark this ubiquitous species. The cap color is so variable that it is more of a hindrance to identification than a help. The situation is complicated by the presence of some very similar species: *P. hymenocephala* has a more cinnamon-colored cap when moist; *P. incerta* (formerly *Hypholoma incertum*, often listed as a synonym for *P. candolleana*) has smaller spores, 6-7.5 × 3.5-4 μm. All of these are remarkable for their extreme fragility. Transporting them home in one piece is a chore.

Psathyrella hydrophila (Clustered Psathyrella)

CAP 2-5 cm broad, obtusely conic to convex when young, expanding to nearly plane in age; surface smooth, hygrophanous, dark reddish-brown when moist, fading to pale tan when dry, often darker around the margin. Flesh watery brown to tan, thin, fragile. **GILLS** close, at first pale brown, then dark brown, attached. **STALK** to 7 cm long, slender, equal, hollow, white or slightly grayish, sometimes brownish in old age. **VEIL** fibrillose, white, leaving remnants on cap margin, sometimes an obscure zone on stalk. **SPORE PRINT** purple-brown; spores 4.5-5.5 × 3-3.5 μm, elliptical, smooth.

HABITAT: Gregarious, usually in large, dense clusters on hardwood stumps, logs, sometimes buried wood. Common, fall through spring.

EDIBILITY: To be avoided. It is harmless, but closely related species haven't been tested.

Psathyrella hydrophila. This mature cluster is growing at the base of a large oak stump (not visible). Note white stem, brown cap, growth in clusters. Spores are deep brown.

COMMENTS: This is one of several Psathyrellas that grow in large, attractive clusters on wood. The distinctive features of the group are the white stem, smooth hygrophanous cap, and dark purple-brown spores. *P. fuscofolia* is similar but lacks a veil.

Psathyrella longipes

CAP 2-5 cm broad, broadly conical to bell-shaped, expanding slightly in age; surface smooth, hygrophanous, yellow-brown when moist, darker brown when dry. Flesh very thin and fragile. **GILLS** close, adnate, at first whitish, soon darkening to dark brown or blackish. **STALK** long (up to 15 cm), slender, fragile, hollow, more or less equal, white. **VEIL** white, leaving cottony remnants on cap margin. **SPORE PRINT** dark purple-brown (almost black); spores 10-13 × 7-9 μm, elliptical but flattened, nearly angular, smooth.

HABITAT: Solitary or scattered in woods, especially hardwoods. Common, fall and winter.

EDIBILITY: Unknown.

COMMENTS: The broadly conical to bell-shaped cap, long white fragile stem, dark spores, and growth on the ground are characteristic, but there is a multiplicity of *Psathyrella* look-alikes. These include: *P. atrifolia*, with elliptical spores 8-10 μm long and little or no veil remnants on the cap margin; *P. subnuda*, slightly larger and more cinnamon-colored when moist; and *P. longistriata*, with a striate ring on the stem. A small, unidentified white-capped species is abundant at Fall Creek.

Psathyrella longipes, or a very similar species. Note the broadly conical cap, dark gills, and whitish veil remnants on cap margin.

Psathyrella velutina

CAP 2.5-10 cm broad, obtuse to convex or slightly umbonate, becoming nearly plane; surface densely fibrillose, sometimes fibrillose-scaly in age, dry, dull yellow-brown or tawny to dark brown; margin often paler, splitting in age. Flesh watery brown to yellowish, rather thick. **GILLS** adnate or notched to nearly free, pale yellowish becoming light brown, finally dark brown as spores mature; sides usually mottled, edges white and sometimes beaded with water droplets. **STALK** to 13 cm long, equal, fibrillose or fibrillose-scaly, dry, whitish above, light brown to dingy tawny below. **VEIL** fibrillose, usually leaving remnants on cap margin and an obscure, superior hairy zone on stalk. **SPORE PRINT** blackish-brown; spores 9-12 × 6-8 μm, elliptical, rough.

HABITAT: Solitary or in small groups in grassy places, roadsides, sawdust piles, gravelly ground, etc. Infrequent, fall through spring.

EDIBILITY: Edible, but not recommended.

COMMENTS: This species is unusually large and sturdy for a *Psathyrella*, and is likely to be looked for in another genus. The fibrillose cap, fibrillose stem with an obscure hairy ring, and blackish-brown spores are distinctive. It is also known as *Lacrymaria velutina*. *P. lacrymabunda* is often given as a synonym, but according to Smith it has smooth spores. *P. canoceps* is a small species with a coating of silky white fibrils on the cap. *P. carbonicola* also has whitish cap fibrils but grows in charred soil, often in the company of *Pholiota highlandensis*.

PANAEOLUS

Small, fragile *dung- or grass-inhabiting* mushrooms. CAP usually *hemispherical, bell-shaped, or conical when young*. GILLS attached, gray to deep brown to black when mature; *sides often mottled*. STALK thin, rigid, brittle, cartilaginous. VEIL present or absent. VOLVA absent. SPORE PRINT *black* (deep brown in *P. foenisecii*). Spores mostly elliptical, with germ pore, retaining color in concentrated sulfuric acid. Cap cuticle cellular.

THIS is a small genus of little brown mushrooms with a bell-shaped to conical cap and thin, brittle stalk. The sides (faces) of the gills often have a mottled appearance due to uneven maturation of the spores. They do not deliquesce as in *Coprinus*. Psathyrellas are similar but never grow in dung, and those that grow in grass have convex caps. *Psilocybe* and *Conocybe* are common in dung but do not have black spores.

Panaeolus is abundant in pastures, lawns, dung, and manure heaps, fruiting whenever it's moist. It often mixes company with other little brown mushrooms (*Conocybe, Stropharia, Agrocybe*, etc.), and like these it would rapidly be relegated to the ranks of fungal forgetability were it not for the fact that many of its members contain traces of psilocybin and other pupil-dilating (the term "mind-expanding" being open to debate) compounds. However, in their search for a more promising and less painful reality, people will stoop to anything, even if it grows on cow pies and is only two inches tall. Thus, after every rain, our pastures are marred by hordes of magic mushroom hunters, inevitable plastic bags in hand.

Actually, there is considerable confusion as to which ones are pupil-dilating. Traces of psilocybin have been isolated in virtually every species, but its presence and concentration is contingent on a number of genetic, geographic, and environmental factors. My own experience (with the *P. campanulatus-P. sphinctrinus* complex) indicates that a sizable quantity *may* produce mild hilarity or even a transitory state of pseudoerotic effervescence. More often, however, it will produce a queasy stomach and if gulped down too eagerly, hiccups. It hardly seems worth the effort to harvest and digest the necessary number of fungal fructifications (30-50), but some people will do anything to "alter" reality and it can be argued, I suppose, that doing anything is better than doing nothing.

Frivolous sampling of little brown mushrooms is foolish, of course, since some are poisonous. Seven *Panaeolus* species are keyed here.

Key to Panaeolus

1. Spore print deep brown or purple-brown; veil absent; growing on lawns ... . *P. foenisecii,* below
1. Spore print black; veil present or absent; usually growing in dung or manure, sometimes on lawns 2
2. Ring present on stalk .... *P. separatus*, p. 335
2. Ring absent 3
3. Fairly large, cap whitish to pale buff; stalk 5-15 mm thick, 8-20 cm long; .... *P. solidipes* (see *P. separatus*, p. 335)
3. Not as above; usually smaller 4
4. Cap bell-shaped to conical, scarcely expanding; margin usually (but not always) adorned with small toothlike veil remnants; very common .... *P. campanulatus*, p. 334
4. Not as above; veil absent; not particularly common 5
5. Stalk 4-10 mm thick; cap convex or slightly umbonate to plane, pallid to buff or brownish; gills brownish soon becoming gray and then black; growing in groups or small clumps in manure, compost, fertilized ground .... *Panaeolus* sp. (unidentified), p. 332
5. Stalk 2-5 mm thick; cap broadly conical to hemispherical, convex, or sometimes plane; gills gray to black; growing in groups (but not clumps), mostly in grass .... *P. papilionaceus*, p. 333

Panaeolus foenisecii (Haymaker's Panaeolus)

CAP up to 2.5 cm broad, obtusely conic or bell-shaped, expanding to convex, broadly umbonate, or nearly plane; surface smooth, moist, hygrophanous, red-brown to cinnamon-brown or dark brown when moist, often with a darker band around the margin, fading to dingy buff when dry. Flesh thin, fragile, watery brown. **GILLS** adnate, seceding slightly, fairly well-spaced, chocolate-brown or purple-brown, the sides often mottled, edges white. **STALK** to 10 cm long but typically shorter, thin, equal, brittle, pallid brownish-gray to dingy brown. **VEIL** absent. **SPORE PRINT** deep brown or purple-brown; spores 12-17 × 6-9 μm, elliptical, rough.

HABITAT: Scattered or in groups on lawns and other grassy places, very rarely in pastures, Fruiting year-round whenever moisture is sufficient.

EDIBILITY: Harmless. Chemical analysis has revealed traces of psilocybin in certain strains, but material I tested was inactive.

COMMENTS: This pixieish *Panaeolus* occurs throughout the northern hemisphere. It is one of the little brown mushrooms most

Panaeolus foenisecii is one of our most common lawn lovers. Cap is deep brown when moist, paler in age as it expands to nearly plane. Spores are deep brown, veil is absent.

likely to pop up on your front lawn (assuming you have one), especially in warm weather. It often mingles with *Marasmius oreades, Agrocybe pediades,* and *Conocybe lactea*. The small size, bell-shaped cap expanding in age, thin stem, and dark purple-brown spores are distinct. The spore print is not black as in other *Panaeolus* species. The "splitters" have erected a special genus for it, *Panaeolina*, whereas Alexander Smith dumps it in *Psathyrella* in his voluminous testament to that genus.

Panaeolus sp. (unidentified)

CAP 2-6 cm broad, convex or broadly conical or umbonate to plane; surface smooth or becoming fissured, buff to tan or brownish (or dusted black by spores), not viscid, sometimes with a dark brown marginal zone. Flesh thin, brownish. **GILLS** adnexed to adnate, at first pale watery brownish, darkening gradually to black; edges whitish. **STALK** to 7 cm long, rather thick (4-10 mm), equal or tapering downward or enlarged at base, pallid becoming brownish, fibrillose-striate, firm, hollow but not fragile. **VEIL** absent. **SPORE PRINT** black; spores 10-14 × 6-8 μm, elliptical, smooth.

HABITAT: Gregarious, often in small clumps, in fertilized soil. Fruiting year-round in mild weather, not common. I've seen several hundred specimens on mushroom compost (from a mushroom farm), in a garden.

EDIBILITY: Hallucinogenic. A middle-aged woman who mistook them for commercial mushrooms was hospitalized with hallucinations (a

Panaeolus sp. (unidentified). This hallucinogenic species is probably *P. subbalteatus*, but a careful comparison should be made. Note clustered growth habit and convex cap. These were growing in mushroom compost in a garden. (Ralph Buchsbaum)

frightening experience if you're unprepared for them). My own experience with them has been very pleasant, with 10-15 caps producing elation and visual wonders. No unusual side effects have been noted.

COMMENTS: This species is distinguished from *Psilocybe* by its non-viscid cap, black spores, and failure to stain blue, and from other *Panaeolus* species by its convex to umbonate or plane cap, pale brown gills when young, rather thick, firm stalk, absence of a veil, and tendency to grow in small clusters. Its closest relative appears to be *P. subbalteatus*, a consistently hallucinogenic species whose cap usually has a darker brown marginal zone. It is common in the Pacific Northwest. Like the above species, it grows in manure, compost, and straw, and has reddish-gray to brownish gills when young, a thicker stalk than most *Panaeolus* species, and lacks a veil. In fact, our species is probably just a local form of *P. subbalteatus*.

Panaeolus papilionaceus

CAP 1-4 cm broad, hemispherical becoming convex or even plane; surface dry, at first smooth but then cracking into fine scales, especially toward the margin; pallid to grayish, tan, or buff, sometimes blackish in age from spores. Flesh thin, whitish. **GILLS** attached, broad, close, pale grayish becoming black, sides often mottled, edges white. **STALK** 5-9 cm long, 2-5 mm thick, slender, cartilaginous, stiff, equal or tapering downward, smooth, whitish or pallid, often brownish toward base. **VEIL** absent or evanescent, not leaving remnants on cap margin. **SPORE PRINT** black; spores 15-18 × 8-11 μm, broadly elliptical, smooth.

HABITAT: Scattered or in groups in dung, manure, and grass in moist, mild weather. Fairly common in the summer, occasional otherwise. I have seen several large fruitings on lawns.

EDIBILITY: Mildly hallucinogenic, according to many sources. I haven't tried it.

COMMENTS: This attractive species is separated from *P. foenisecii* by its black spores and from *P. campanulatus* by its paler color and hemispherical to convex (rather than conical or bell-shaped) cap *without* veil remnants on the margin. It conforms to one popular concept of *P. papilionaceus*, but some *Panaeolus* pundits maintain that *P. papilionaceus* is just another name for *P. campanulatus*, in which case our species would need a new label. *P. acuminatus* also has black spores and no veil, but has a date-brown conical cap. *P. castaneifolius* lacks a veil and resembles *P. foenisecii*, but has deep violet-black spores.

Panaeolus campanulatus (Bell-Shaped Panaeolus)

CAP to 4 cm broad, conical or bell-shaped, scarcely expanding; surface smooth, dry, brown to gray-brown, smoky-gray, or olive-buff, fading as it dries to dingy tan, sometimes cracking into small scales; margin hung with small, white, toothlike veil fragments, at least when young. Flesh thin, watery. **GILLS** adnate, seceding slowly, fairly close, gray to black, the sides mottled unevenly, edges white. **STALK** to 15 cm long, very thin, equal, usually long in proportion to cap, rigid, brittle, brown to gray-brown. **VEIL** present, leaving whitish remnants on cap margin or disappearing. **SPORE PRINT** black; spores 13-18×9-13 μm, elliptical, smooth.

HABITAT: Scattered or in groups on or near dung or where animals have grazed, occasionally in compost or cultivated mushroom beds. One of the commonest mushrooms of our pastures, fruiting in fall, winter, and spring, sometimes in great numbers.

EDIBILITY: May have mild hallucinogenic effects when eaten raw; 30-50 caps are necessary, however. Psilocybin has been isolated in some races, but there appear to be other active compounds as well.

Panaeolus campanulatus. Bell-shaped cap is the trademark of this pastureland species. Note the toothlike veil remnants on cap margin. These often disappear in age. Stalk is long, thin, and very brittle. (Bill Everson)

COMMENTS: The gray to brown bell-shaped cap, long thin stiff stalk, mottled gray to black gills, veil remnants on the cap margin when young, and habitat in dung are characteristic of a group of closely related species: the *P. campanulatus-P. sphinctrinus* complex. Since experts cannot agree on the exact differences (if any) between these species, it would be presumptuous to attempt to differentiate them here. *P. retirugis* is a slightly smaller species with a wrinkled cap.

Panaeolus separatus (Black-Ringed Panaeolus)

CAP 3-6.5 cm broad and tall; conical or bell-shaped; surface viscid when moist, smooth, pale gray to grayish-white or buff. Flesh thin, pallid. **GILLS** adnate, close, gray becoming black, sides mottled, edges white. **STALK** to 18 cm long, relatively slender, equal, smooth below ring, finely striate above; whitish. **VEIL** membranous, forming a persistent median ring which is blackened by falling spores. **SPORE PRINT** black; spores 15-20 × 8-11 μm, elliptical, smooth.

HABITAT: Solitary or in small groups on manure, dung, and around stables, in wet weather. Mark Hildebrand reports luxuriant fruitings near Boulder Creek.

EDIBILITY: Harmless according to most sources, but some strains may contains traces of psilocybin. I haven't tried it.

COMMENTS: Also known as *P. semiovatus* and *Anellaria separata*, this *Panaeolus* is noteworthy for its large size, black ring, and pale cap that is slightly viscid when moist. A related species, *P. solidipes (=P. phalaenarum),* is even larger (to 20 cm tall), with a whitish cap and no ring. It is to be looked for in similar habitats.

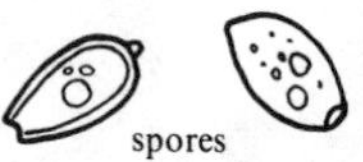

BOLBITIACEAE

TWO microscopic features separate this small brown-spored family from the Cortinariaceae: the cap cuticle is cellular rather than filamentous, and the spores are usually furnished with a germ pore. People not armed with a microscope are better off learning the three generic constituents of the Bolbitiaceae rather than trying to devise an unwieldy set of fieldmarks for distinguishing them as a unit.

Their closest relatives, the Coprinaceae, also have a cellular cap cuticle and spores with a germ pore, but the spore color is purple-brown to black. The Bolbitiaceae and Coprinaceae are mostly frail fungi saprophytic on dung, grass, decaying wood, and humus. In contrast, the bulk of the Cortinariaceae are mycorrhizal or wood-inhabiting and not noticeably fragile.

Owing to their fragile consistency, the Bolbitiaceae are of negligible food value. The three common genera are keyed below. If your little brown mushroom does not key out persuasively, check *Galerina* and *Tubaria* (p. 383)—particularly if it was found in or near the woods.

Key to the Bolbitiaceae

1. Cap viscid when moist, conspicuously striate (at least at maturity) .... *Bolbitius*, p. 342
1. Not as above (cap may be viscid or striate but not both) 2

2. Cap conical to bell-shaped; stalk thin, fragile .... *Conocybe*, p. 340
2. Cap convex to plane, stalk thick or thin .... *Agrocybe*, p. 337

AGROCYBE

Small to medium-sized mushrooms. CAP *convex to plane*, dry or slightly tacky, rarely striate. GILLS *attached*, brown to rusty-brown at maturity. STALK central, thick or thin but not markedly fragile. VEIL present or absent. VOLVA absent. SPORE PRINT *brown to dark brown*. Spores smooth, usually with a germ pore. Cap cuticle cellular.

AGROCYBE is a difficult genus to characterize. The two most common species are best recognized by their smooth or cracked (but not scaly) convex to plane cap, brown spores, and occurrence in grass or cultivated ground. In one species a membranous veil is present and in the other it is not. They resemble *Pholiota* and *Hebeloma* and have been keyed out in the Cortinariaceae for this reason. In fact, before the advent of the microscope, Agrocybes were placed in *Pholiota* and *Naucoria*.

All known species are edible, but extreme care must be taken not to confuse them with the metagrobolizing masses of nondescript brown-spored mushrooms, particularly the poisonous Hebelomas. Six species are reported from California, two of which are described here.

Key to Agrocybe

1. Veil absent or rudimentary; cap generally less than 4 cm broad; stalk thin .... *A. pediades*, below
1. Membranous veil present (check young specimens), forming a ring or disappearing; cap generally 3 cm broad or more 2

2. Growing on ground; common .... *A. praecox*, p. 338
2. Growing on or near wood; rare ... *A. acericola* (see *A. praecox*, p. 338)

Agrocybe pediades (Common Agrocybe)

CAP up to 5 cm broad, but usually about 2.5 cm; obtuse or convex becoming broadly convex or plane; surface dry or slightly viscid when moist, smooth, typically some shade of yellow-brown, tawny, dull yellow, or creamy-white, occasionally tinged reddish-brown; margin sometimes adorned with a few veil remnants, not striate. Flesh thin, pallid, odor mild or faintly farinaceous. **GILLS** adnate to adnexed but seceding, pallid becoming pale brown, then cinnamon-brown or dark brown, close. **STALK** to 7 cm long, slender, equal or tapering downward or with a slightly enlarged base, dry, smooth or fibrillose, colored like cap or paler. **VEIL** absent or rudimentary. **SPORE PRINT** brown; spores 11-14 × 7-8 μm, elliptical, smooth, with a germ pore.

Agrocybe pediades. This listless grass-inhabiting little brown mushroom has brown gills, brown spores, and a smooth convex cap. These specimens are slightly larger than normal.

HABITAT: Scattered to gregarious in lawns, pastures, and cultivated ground. Flourishing whenever conditions are conducive. Partial to warm weather, often mingling with *Marasmius oreades, Panaeolus foenisecii*, and *Conocybe lactea.*

EDIBILITY: Edible but hardly incredible. It is too small to be valuable and is easily confused with other little brown mushrooms.

COMMENTS: The yellowish cap, brown spores, absence of a ring, and small size typify this commonplace lawn lover. The cap is not conical as in *Conocybe* and *Panaeolus* and the spores are neither purple-brown as in *Stropharia*, nor white as in *Marasmius*. Small *Hebeloma* species are very similar, but have a filamentous cap cuticle and generally grow near trees or in the woods. *Agrocybe pediades* is listed in older books as *Naucoria semiorbicularis.*

Agrocybe praecox

CAP 3-10 cm broad, obtuse becoming convex and finally plane; surface dry or slightly tacky, light brown to tan, hazel-brown, or creamy, smooth when young, sometimes fissured in age or dry weather. Flesh soft, whitish or pale ochre, odor mild or faintly farinaceous, taste slightly bitter. **GILLS** close, adnate or notched, at first pallid, then light brown, finally dull dark brown. **STALK** to 13 cm long, fleshy, equal or enlarged below, white or pallid, becoming brownish below in age, fibrillose. **VEIL** thin, membranous, white, forming a fragile superior ring, or disappearing, or shredding on cap margin. **SPORE PRINT** rich brown; spores 8.5-10.5 × 5-7 µm, elliptical, smooth, with a germ pore.

Agrocybe praecox. Note the unbroken veil (left), the ring on center specimen, and absence of ring on mature individual (second from right). Gills are brown and cap is creamy to tan.

HABITAT: Solitary, scattered, or in groups in cultivated ground—gardens, roadsides, grass, etc. Abundant in early spring (February and March), but occurring year-round.

EDIBILITY: Edible, of fair quality. The slightly acidic taste disappears with thorough cooking, but be sure of your identification!

COMMENTS: The tan to hazel to creamy cap, membranous veil (check young specimens!), rich brown spores, and habitat are the telltale signs of this attractive mushroom. It is a common fungal feature of towns and cultivated areas. Specimens with a prominent veil are reminiscent of *Agaricus*, but have attached gills. Heavy spore deposits appear very dark, leading to confusion with *Stropharia*, which has purple-brown to black spores and a viscid cap. Specimens which have lost their veil are likely to be mistaken for *Hebeloma*, which also has a viscid cap. Confusion with *Pholiota* and *Rozites* is also possible, but the habitat and absence of fibrils or scales are characteristic. In older books it is listed as *Pholiota praecox*.

The form with pale, fissured cap and spores 11-13 μm long has been called *Agrocybe dura (=Pholiota vermiflua).* Other Agrocybes with a membranous veil include: *A. aegerita*, edible, in clusters on hardwood stumps (especially cottonwood); *A. acericola*, on rotten or buried wood, with white rootlike strands (rhizomorphs) penetrating the substrate; and *A. erebia*, terrestrial under cottonwood and poplar, with a radially grooved (striate) cap margin. None of these are common, and all were formerly placed in *Pholiota.*

CONOCYBE

Fragile little brown mushrooms *found in grass, dung, and moss.* CAP *sharply conical to bell-shaped, usually not viscid, not striate or only slightly so.* GILLS typically attached, sometimes free. STALK *thin, very fragile, cartilaginous, hollow.* VEIL present or absent. VOLVA absent. SPORE PRINT *rusty-brown to ochraceous.* Spores smooth or rough, with a germ pore. Cap cuticle cellular.

THIS is an obscure group of ephemeral *Mycena*-like mushrooms with conical cap, long thin stalk, and rusty spores. Galerinas are sometimes conical but, as a rule, Conocybes frequent cultivated ground while Galerinas favor moss, decaying wood, and humus. Also, Galerinas are often translucent-striate at maturity, a feature not typical of *Conocybe. Bolbitius* also resembles *Conocybe* but has a viscid, conspicuously striate cap.

Conocybes are partial to warm weather, and fruit in great abundance on watered lawns. Some (such as *C. lactea*) are so frail that they appear in the morning and shrivel up or deteriorate by late afternoon. They are much too small to be of food value, and at least one (*C. filaris*) is potentially dangerous. The California species are not well known. Three common types are described here.

Key to Conocybe

1. Membranous veil present, forming a fragile ring on stalk *C. filaris*, below
1. Veil absent 2

2. Cap white to pale cinnamon, often somewhat wrinkled *C. lactea*, p. 342
2. Cap some shade of brown, tan, or buff, more or less smooth .... *C. tenera*, p. 341

Conocybe filaris

CAP 5-15 mm broad, conical or bell-shaped, expanding slightly in age; surface smooth but not viscid, brown. Flesh thin, brown. **GILLS** pale brown becoming rusty-brown, close, attached (at least when young). **STALK** up to 6 cm long, very thin (1-3 mm), fragile, more or less equal, dry, colored like cap or paler, smooth. **VEIL** membranous, brown, forming a delicate median to superior ring. **SPORE PRINT** rusty-brown; spores 7.5-13 × 3.5-6.5 µm, elliptical, smooth, with a germ pore.

HABITAT: Scattered or in groups on lawns and other grassy places, also in moss or even on wood; infrequent. It can be found most any time, but the largest fruiting I've seen was in October.

EDIBILITY: Poisonous, potentially fatal! Analysis has revealed the presence of amanita-toxins; 20-30 caps are equivalent to one half of an *Amanita phalloides* cap—a compelling reason not to eat little brown mushrooms!

COMMENTS: The delicate brown membranous ring separates this dainty little brown mushroom from other Conocybes. Several Galerinas (also poisonous) have a ring, but usually grow on wood and have a viscid translucent-striate cap.

Conocybe tenera

CAP up to 2.5 cm broad and tall, conical becoming bell-shaped; surface smooth, dry, brown to yellow-brown, fading in age to buffy-brown; margin striate when moist. Flesh thin, watery brown. **GILLS** attached, sometimes free in age, pale brown becoming cinnamon-brown or rusty. **STALK** to 8 cm long, very thin, fragile, equal, rigid, smooth, cap color or paler. **VEIL** absent. **SPORE PRINT** rusty-brown; spores 7.5-12 × 5.5-7 μm, elliptical, smooth, with a germ pore.

HABITAT: Scattered or in groups in lawns, gardens, fields, and other cultivated areas. Fairly common, year-round. I've seen more than 100 fruiting bodies in a planterbox filled with lettuce seedlings.

Conocybe tenera. Note the conical brown cap and long thin stem. The much more common *C. lactea* (not illustrated) has a paler, slightly wrinkled or striate cap and is common on lawns in the summertime.

EDIBILITY: Unknown. Do not experiment.

COMMENTS: The conical brown cap and long, thin stem are reminiscent of *Panaeolus* (with which it sometimes grows), but the spore print is rusty-brown. The cap is not wrinkled as in *C. lactea*, nor viscid as in *Bolbitius*, and it is not as ephemeral as either of those fungi. Actually, *C. tenera* is a composite species to which many brownish Conocybes have been referred. I see no compelling reason to discontinue the trend, though we undoubtedly have more than one species passing under the same name. *C. angusticeps* is similar but has a semi-cylindrical cap with a pointed umbo when young. *C. coprophila* grows on dung.

Conocybe lactea (Dunce Cap)

CAP up to 2.5 cm broad and 4 cm tall; at first narrowly conical (like a dunce cap), then bell-shaped; surface usually dry, milky-white to pinkish-buff or pale cinnamon, the center often darker; sometimes wrinkled, margin striate when moist. Flesh very thin, whitish. **GILLS** attached sometimes becoming free, close, pale brown then cinnamon-brown. **STALK** to 10 cm long, very thin and fragile, longer than width or height of cap, equal or with a small basal bulb, dry, hollow, white or whitish, scurfy above. **VEIL** absent. **SPORE PRINT** reddish-brown or cinnamon; spores 11-14 × 6.5-9 μm, elliptical, smooth, with a germ pore.

HABITAT: Scattered or in troops on lawns, baseball fields, and other grassy areas. Common in mild, moist weather, particularly in the summer. Often prominent in the morning, but shrivelling up or collapsing by afternoon.

EDIBILITY: Unknown. To say it lacks substance is an understatement.

COMMENTS: This delicate species is easily recognized by its pale "dunce cap," long, thin fragile stem, and brief life span. The striate cap is not viscid, or only slightly so. It is never yellow or slimy as in *Bolbitius vitellinus*, and is paler than *C. tenera. C. lateritia* is a synonym.

BOLBITIUS

Small, rapidly-decaying fungi found on *dung, grass, or wood.* CAP *conspicuously striate at maturity, viscid when moist*, usually white, yellow, or purple-gray. GILLS typically free at maturity, *often liquefying in wet weather.* STALK *slender, fragile, cartilaginous, hollow.* VEIL and VOLVA *absent.*. SPORE PRINT *rusty-brown to ochraceous.* Spores smooth, with a germ pore. Cap cuticle cellular.

THIS small group of fragile, flaccid, putrescent fungi is reminiscent of *Coprinus* (particularly in the striate cap and tendency of the gills to liquefy), but has rusty-brown to ochraceous rather than black spores. The viscid cap separates *Bolbitius* from *Conocybe*. The cap is rarely brown as in *Galerina* and the habitat is quite different.

Bolbitius species are worthless as food. The most common types fruit during wet weather in dung, manure, straw, tall grass, and other vegetable matter. A few grow on wood. Two species are keyed below. *Pluteolus* is an obsolete generic alias.

Key to Bolbitius

1. Cap gray to purple-gray; growing on or near wood .... *B. reticulatus* (see *B. vitellinus*, below)
1. Not as above; in grass, dung, etc. 2

2. Cap narrowly conical when young, dry or very slightly viscid, white to pale cinnamon; gills *not* liquefying; on lawns (see *Conocybe lactea*, p. 342)
2. Cap egg-shaped to bell-shaped when young, viscid when moist, creamy to bright yellow; gills liquefying somewhat in wet weather; in dung, manure, straw, tall grass .... *B. vitellinus*, below

Bolbitius vitellinus

CAP up to 5 cm broad, conic, egg-shaped, or bell-shaped when young, expanding slightly in age; surface smooth, viscid or slimy when wet, bright yellow to pale yellow, slowly discoloring in age; margin striate, becoming striate-grooved nearly to the center in age. Flesh very thin, soft, yellowish. **GILLS** at first attached, free at maturity, soft, close, dull or light brown becoming rusty-ochre in age; dissolving somewhat in wet weather. **STALK** to 12 cm long, slender, equal or enlarged below, white or tinged cap color, fragile, hollow, powdery or minutely scaly above. **SPORE PRINT** bright rusty-orange to rusty-brown; spores 10-13 × 6-7.5 μm, elliptical, smooth, with a germ pore.

HABITAT: Solitary or in small groups in dung, cow pies, manure, straw, grass, etc. Common in wet weather. The most luxuriant fruiting I've seen was in a horse corral where dozens of large, robust specimens were interspersed with the common dung-inhabiting cup fungus, *Peziza vesiculosa*.

EDIBILITY: Harmless, fleshless, flavorless.

COMMENTS: The viscid yellow striate cap, rusty spores, soft fragile flesh, and habitat are the hallmarks of this habitual dung-lover. The

Bolbitius vitellinus. **Top:** Young, rounded, slimy specimens growing in straw. (Nancy Burnett) **Bottom:** Older, rather decrepit individuals found on dung. Gills are brown and liquefy somewhat in wet weather.

fruiting body tends to dissolve in wet weather and shrivel up in dry weather. The stature is rather tall and slender, but a robust form (perhaps distinct) also occurs. An even more fragile species with a small, creamy cap *(B. cremeus?)* is sometimes found. Another putrescent member of the genus, *B. reticulatus*, occurs on or near rotting wood. It has a viscid violet-gray cap, pallid gills becoming rusty-cinnamon in age, a white powdered stem, and rusty-brown spores. As the cap dries, it assumes a veined (reticulate) appearance.

CORTINARIACEAE

ALMOST every brown-spored mushroom you find will belong to the Cortinariaceae. Like their white-spored counterparts, the Tricholomataceae, they are a vast, diverse, and baffling group. There are fewer genera, but just as many (if not more) species. The gills are not deeply decurrent or poroid as in the Paxillaceae. Unlike the Bolbitiaceae, the cap cuticle is typically filamentous and the spores usually lack an apical pore. Though the latter characters are microscopic, with a little experience the two families can be distinguished in the field. The Cortinariaceae are primarily woodland fungi, a dominant feature of cool, temperate forests, whereas the Bolbitiaceae are warm-weather fungi found mostly in grass, gardens, and dung. Also, with the exception of *Galerina* and *Tubaria,* the Cortinariaceae tend to be larger, fleshier, and less fragile than the Bolbitiaceae.

As applied to the Cortinariaceae, the term "brown-spored" is somewhat misleading. The spore color actually ranges from bright rusty-orange (*Gymnopilus*) to rusty-brown (*Cortinarius*) to dull brown, ochre-brown, or yellow-brown. Mushrooms with a filamentous cap cuticle and deep brown ("purple-brown") spores are traditionally placed in the Strophariaceae. However, the difference between "brown" and "purple-brown" is not always clearcut, and some mycologists quite sensibly unite the two families.

There are very few esteemed edibles in the Cortinariaceae. Many types are very poisonous (particularly Galerinas, Inocybes, and Hebelomas) and many more have not been tested, in part due to difficulty in identification. Having access to a microscope does little to expedite the tedious and labyrinthine identification process—so many species are poorly known or unnamed. Several representatives from each genus are included in this book.

Key to the Cortinariaceae

1. Spore print bright orange to rusty-orange; gills yellow to rusty-orange; stalk fleshy; veil often present; usually (but not always) growing on wood .... *Gymnopilus,* p. 372
1. Spore print not rusty-orange; not as above 2
2. Stalk absent or lateral; growing shelflike on wood .... *Crepidotus,* p. 387
2. Not as above; if growing on wood, stalk more or less central 3

3. Terrestrial; stalk extending deep into humus, tapering to a point to form a long "tap root"; veil absent .... *Phaeocollybia,* p. 370
3. Not as above 4

4. Membranous veil present, forming persistent ring on stalk 5
4. Membranous veil absent (fibrillose or cobwebby veil often present) . 8

5. Stalk thin (about 2-5 mm), cartilaginous; brittle or fragile .... *Galerina* and *Tubaria,* p. 383
5. Not as above; stalk fleshy, though sometimes slender 6

6. Cap radially wrinkled and covered with a hoary sheen when young; spore print rusty-brown .... *Rozites,* p. 371
6. Not as above 7

7. Cap and stalk without colored scales; usually on ground in cultivated places, rarely on wood; cap dry or slightly viscid (see *Agrocybe,* p. 337)
7. Cap or stalk (or both) scaly or if not, then growing on wood and cap viscid .... *Pholiota,* p. 376

8. Cap silky, fibrillose, or minutely scaly, not viscid, usually umbonate; margin often splitting at maturity; odor occasionally sweet, usually unpleasant; spore print some shade of brown but not rusty-brown or cinnamon .... *Inocybe,* below
8. Not as above 9

9. Spore print rusty-brown to cinnamon; hairy or cobwebby veil present, at least when young, often leaving hairs on stalk; stalk fleshy, though sometimes slender .... *Cortinarius,* p. 356
9. Not as above 10

10. Stalk thin (about 2-5 mm), cartilaginous, usually brittle or fragile; cap small, generally less than 4 cm broad.. .... *Galerina* and *Tubaria,* p. 383
10. Stalk fleshy, though sometimes slender; cap 2.5 cm broad or more . 11

11. On ground; cap and stalk without scales (but stalk may be powdered at apex) .... *Hebeloma,* p. 352
11. On wood, or if on ground, then cap and/or stalk scaly .... *Pholiota,* p. 376

INOCYBE

Small to medium-sized fungi *found on ground* or very rotten wood. CAP *often umbonate or conical; surface typically dry; radially fibrillose, silky, or minutely scaly;* margin often splitting at maturity; *odor often unpleasant.* GILLS adnate to nearly free, more or less brown at maturity. STALK usually rather slender. VEIL absent or if present, fibrillose and more or less evanescent. VOLVA absent. SPORE PRINT some shade of brown. Spores smooth, warty, angular, or nodulose; without apical pore. Gills with cystidia, at least on edges. Cap cuticle filamentous.

INOCYBE is a large, listless, and lackluster assemblage of malodorous brown mushroms, of little interest to the average mushroom hunter except that many are poisonous. The best means of recognizing an *Inocybe* is by the characteristically silky, fibrillose, minutely scaly, or woolly cap, which is often umbonate and seldom viscid. The spore color is rather variable but is not rusty as in *Cortinarius*. Most Inocybes have a noticeable odor—usually unpleasant or spermatic, occasionally sweet or fruity and in the case of *Inocybe sororia,* like fresh green corn.

Like *Cortinarius,* Inocybes are a common and conspicuous fungal facet of temperate forests, but unlike *Cortinarius,* they are not the least bit colorful. They come in an endless, senseless procession of drab browns, sordid yellows, dismal grays, and wishy-washy whites, with only *Inocybe geophylla* var. *lilacina* (among the local species) deviating from the norm. Almost without exception it is necessary to know the size and shape of the spores and cystidia before an accurate identification can be made. Even then, unraveling them is a tedious task. Its futility is exceeded only by its pointlessness, and underscored by the sad fact that most Inocybes are poisonous. I would venture to guess, in fact, that *Inocybe* contains a higher percentage of poisonous mushrooms than any other mushroom genus, including *Amanita.* The toxin is muscarine, which can be fatal in large amounts (see p. 632). It is therefore advisable to avoid all Inocybes, even those rumored to be edible. Over 400 species are known from North America. A mere seven are described here.

Key to Inocybe

1. Cap white or lilac, more or less smooth, small, not staining reddish or pinkish in age .... *I. geophylla,* p. 350
1. Not as above 2

2. Cap with dark reddish to wine-colored fibrils .... *I. jurana,* p. 349
2. Not as above 3

3. Odor sweet or fruity .... *I. pyriodora,* p. 350
3. Odor may be strong, but not sweet 4

4. Cap sharply conical when young, pale yellow to straw color, yellow-brown, or sordid ochre-brown 5
4. Not as above 6

5. Odor typically of fresh green corn .... *I. sororia,* p. 348
5. Odor merely unpleasant or spermatic .... *I. fastigiata* (see *I. sororia,* p. 348)

6. Stalk (and usually cap) whitish, soon flushed pinkish-orange to reddish .... *I. pudica,* p. 351
6. Not as above 7

7. Center of cap covered with silky white fibrils or white patch .... *I. lanotodisca* (see *I. flocculosa,* p. 352)
7. Not as above 8
8. Cap small, less than 4 cm broad, more or less brownish, fibrillose to minutely scaly or hairy .... *I. flocculosa,* p. 352
8. Larger; cap 2.5 cm broad or more, dark brown, fibrillose .... *I. maculata,* p. 349

Inocybe sororia (Straw-Colored Inocybe)

CAP 2-8 cm broad, sharply conical when young, expanding somewhat but retaining a prominent umbo; surface dry, silky, radially fibrillose, pale yellowish to honey-yellow or straw color, somewhat darker or more sordid in age; margin usually upturned or splitting at maturity. Flesh thin, pallid or yellowish to greenish-yellow; odor usually distinct, like freshly husked green corn. **GILLS** close or crowded, pallid becoming yellow or yellowish, then olive-yellow, finally brownish-gold, attached at first, sometimes free in age. **STALK** 5-14 cm long, slender, equal or with a slightly bulbous base, white or tinged cap color, fibrillose or scurfy. **VEIL** absent. **SPORE PRINT** brown; spores 10-13 × 5-7 μm, bean-shaped, smooth. Cystidia only on gill edges, thin-walled.

HABITAT: Solitary or in small groups in woods, especially oak. Common, fall and winter.

Inocybe sororia. Conical cap, brown spores, and strong odor of fresh green corn typify this poisonous woodland species. It is especially common with oak.

EDIBILITY: Very poisonous; contains high concentrations of muscarine.

COMMENTS: A common and prominent *Inocybe,* easily recognized by its sharply conical, yellowish, fibrillose cap and odor of fresh green corn. The stem is often quite long and slender. *I. fastigiata* is very similar but smells unpleasant or spermatic, and is slightly more brownish (yellow-brown to brownish-ochre). *I. cookei* has a silky yellowish cap, small but prominent bulb at the base of the stem, and smaller spores, up to 10 μm long.

Inocybe jurana (Reddish Inocybe)

CAP 2.5-7.5 cm broad, conical or bell-shaped, expanding in age but retaining an umbo; surface dry, radially fibrillose, the fibrils reddish, carmine, or wine-colored, with small scales at the center; margin often splitting in age. Flesh tinged wine-color, especially beneath umbo, thin, odor mild or unpleasant. **GILLS** pallid, then grayish-brown, close, attached. **STALK** up to 7.5 cm long, equal or slightly enlarged at base, dry; white, flushed cap color below. **VEIL** absent. **SPORE PRINT** brown; spores 10-13 × 5.5-7 μm, bean-shaped, smooth. Cystidia on gills thin-walled.

HABITAT: Gregarious in leaf litter under live oak, uncommon, fall and winter. I have found it only once.

EDIBILITY: According to some sources edible, but it's foolish to tempt fate. Similar species are poisonous.

COMMENTS: The deep reddish cap fibrils are the hallmark of this illustrious *Inocybe.* Though not common, it is quite distinct.

Inocybe maculata (Large Brown Inocybe)

CAP up to 7.5 cm broad, conical when young, expanding in age to convex or plane with an obtuse umbo; surface fibrillose, with small scales at the center, the fibrils dark brown, margin often lobed or splitting. Flesh thin, whitish, odor mild or slightly aromatic. **GILLS** pale grayish becoming grayish-brown to brown; close, attached or free. **STALK** up to 10 cm long, stout, equal or with enlarged base, fibrillose-striate, pallid or tinged cap color, dry. **VEIL** absent, but outer veil may leave faint whitish spots on cap. **SPORE PRINT** brown; spores 9-11 × 4.5-6 μm, bean-shaped, smooth. Cystidia on gills thin-walled.

HABITAT: Solitary or in small groups in rich soil—in mixed woods and under oak. Occasional, fall and early winter.

EDIBILITY: Poisonous.

COMMENTS: Any large *Inocybe* with a dark brown fibrillose cap can be referred here and conveniently forgotten about. I have encountered forms with an obnoxious odor, others which were mild or slightly aromatic. Undoubtedly more than one species is involved.

Inocybe pyriodora (Sweet-Smelling Inocybe)

CAP 2-5 cm broad, bell-shaped or obtusely conical becoming umbonate; surface dry, at first silky-fibrillose, then fibrillose-scaly (especially the center); pallid soon becoming dingy ochraceous or brownish, sometimes with pinkish stains; margin splitting in age. Flesh thin, white, slowly staining pinkish when cut; odor sweet, fruity (like pears), becoming disagreeable in old age. **GILLS** notched, close, whitish becoming brown. **STALK** up to 7 cm long, more or less equal, white or pallid, flushed pinkish in age, smooth or finely fibrillose, dry. **VEIL** absent. **SPORE PRINT** brown; spores 8-10 × 5-6 μm, elliptical to bean-shaped, smooth. Cystidia abundant on gills.

HABITAT: Solitary or in small groups in woods, especially oak. Occasional, fall and winter.

EDIBILITY: To be avoided.

COMMENTS: This is one of several Inocybes with a sweet, fruity odor. *I. corydalina* has a whitish or brownish-white cap and smells sickeningly sweet, like rotting fruit. *I. godeyi* has a white to reddish cap, small bulb at the base of the stem, and fruity odor. None of these should be eaten.

Inocybe geophylla

CAP about 2.5 cm broad, obtusely conical to bell-shaped, slowly expanding or remaining umbonate; surface dry, silky, white (lilac in var. *lilacina*), finely fibrillose; margin sometimes upturned or split in age. Flesh thin, white, odor slightly disagreeable or spermatic. **GILLS** attached, close, at first pallid, then grayish, finally dull brown. **STALK** to 6.5 cm long, slender, equal, dry, white or grayish-white. **VEIL** fibrillose, whitish, evanescent or leaving slight hairy zone on stalk. **SPORE PRINT** brown; spores 7-10 × 4.5-6 μm, elliptical, smooth. Cystidia on gills club-shaped, thick-walled.

Inocybe geophylla. Note the whitish umbonate cap and brown gills. Specimen on right is a young button.

HABITAT: Scattered to gregarious on ground in woods of all kinds, very common, fall through early spring.

EDIBILITY: Poisonous; contains muscarine.

COMMENTS: The dry white umbonate cap, small size, and dull brown gills characterize this ubiquitous little *Inocybe*. It might be mistaken at first glance for a small *Hygrophorus* or *Mycena*. but the spores are brown and the gills brown at maturity. *Inocybe geophylla* var. *lilacina* (=*I. lilacina*) has a beautiful lilac cap but is otherwise identical. It is sporadically common under conifers in the winter.

Inocybe pudica (Blushing Inocybe)

CAP 2-5 cm broad, bell-shaped becoming umbonate or convex; surface dry or tacky, silky-fibrillose, whitish becoming stained with salmon-pink or red. Flesh thin, white, odor unpleasant. **GILLS** pallid or flushed pinkish, becoming dull brown in age, notched, close. **STALK** up to 6 cm long, rather stout, equal or enlarged at base, white, soon flushed salmon-pink or reddish, dry, silky. **VEIL** fibrillose, evanescent. **SPORE PRINT** brown; spores 7-9.5 × 4.5-5.5 μm, elliptical or bean-shaped, smooth. Cystidia on gills thick-walled with pear-shaped, thin-walled ones also present.

HABITAT: Scattered, or in groups, or troops, in brushy places under pine and Douglas-fir. Common, late fall and winter.

EDIBILITY: Poisonous; contains muscarine.

COMMENTS: This is one of the commonest Inocybes of western North America as well as one of the most readily recognized. The tendency of the whitish cap and stem to develop pinkish stains is the principal fieldmark. The cap may be tacky or slippery in wet weather but is not truly viscid.

Inocybe flocculosa

CAP up to 4 cm broad, bell-shaped to convex with an umbo; surface dry, brown, hairy or fibrillose becoming minutely scaly, especially at center, which may be tinged grayish; margin splitting at maturity. Flesh thin, whitish, odor spermatic. **GILLS** notched, close, dirty brown. **STALK** to 5 cm long, equal or slightly enlarged below, slender, apex powdery, smooth, at first white, then tinged salmon-buff or cap color. **VEIL** cobwebby, evanescent or leaving obscure remains on cap margin and stalk apex. **SPORE PRINT** brown; spores 8-11 × 5-6 μm, ovate, smooth. Cystidia on gills flask-shaped, thick-walled.

HABITAT: Scattered to gregarious on ground in woods, especially along paths and roads. Common, fall through spring.

EDIBILITY: Unknown, but should be considered poisonous.

COMMENTS: There are innumerable little brown Inocybes with hairy or minutely scaly caps. They are differentiated largely on microscopic characters such as the shape and size of cystidia and spores. Most have an unpleasant, more or less spermatic odor, and none should be eaten. Other species include *I. sindonia* and *I. lanotodisca,* with silky white hoariness on the cap, the former with cystidia on both the sides and edges of the gills, the latter with cystidia only on the gill edges; *I. calamistrata,* stem tinted greenish-blue below and spores smooth; *I. decipientoides,* cap brownish-ochraceous and spores angular-warty; *I. lacera,* cap brown to grayish and spores long, smooth, cylindrical (12-18 × 4-6 μm); and *I. lanuginosa,* found on ground or very rotten wood, with nodulose spores, rich brown cap, and thin, scaly or hairy stalk.

HEBELOMA

Small to medium-sized *terrestrial* fungi. CAP *viscid when moist, more or less smooth,* white to buff or brown. Odor often radishlike. GILLS *adnate or notched,* more or less *brown at maturity.* STALK *fleshy.* VEIL *usually absent; if present then fibrillose, evanescent.* VOLVA absent. SPORE PRINT *brown, rarely reddish-brown.* Spores more or less ellipsoid, smooth or rough, without apical pore. Cystidia present on gill edges. Cap cuticle filamentous.

THIS is yet another faceless and featureless assemblage of brown-spored mushrooms. The fruiting body has the stature of a *Tricholoma* or *Entoloma.* The smooth, slightly viscid cap separates *Hebeloma* from *Inocybe,* and the spores are not rusty as in *Cortinarius.* Agrocybes are similar, but tend to grow in grass or cultivated soil, whereas Hebelomas are usually associated with trees, though they sometimes show up in nurseries and gardens.

The colors in *Hebeloma* are subdued—whites, browns, tans, and buffs predominate, making identification based on color hopeless. More minute measures of individuality must be resorted to, such as the size and shape of cystidia and spores. Hebelomas should not be eaten. Some are definitely poisonous and the group as a whole is poorly known. Three familiar species are described here.

Key to Hebeloma

1. Veil present, forming a fibrillose zone on stalk .... *H. mesophaeum,* p. 355
1. Veil absent 2

2. Cap more or less white 3
2. Cap buff to brown (may be creamy-white when young) 4

3. Spore print reddish-brown .... *H. sarcophyllum* (see *H. crustuliniforme,* below)
3. Spore print brown .... *H. albidulum* (see *H. crustuliniforme,* below)

4. Stalk usually powdered at apex; odor of crushed flesh often radishlike; usually found in woods or with trees on lawns 5
4. Not as above; usually found in grass or cultivated places .... (see *Agrocybe,* p. 337)

5. Cap cinnamon-brown .... *H. sinapizans,* p. 354
5. Cap creamy-buff to pale tan or crust-brown .... *H. crustuliniforme,* below

Hebeloma crustuliniforme (Poison Pie)

CAP 4-10 cm broad, broadly convex with an inrolled margin, becoming plane or with slightly uplifted margin; surface viscid when moist, smooth, at first pale (creamy-white), gradually darkening to buff, pale tan, or crust-brown, the margin often paler. Flesh thick, white, odor radishlike. **GILLS** very close, adnate becoming notched, pallid when young, soon watery brown or dull brown, edges white and finely scalloped, beaded with water droplets in humid weather. **STALK** 5-13 cm long, equal or with enlarged base, fibrillose, white or whitish-buff, the apex densely powdered. **VEIL** absent. **SPORE PRINT** brown;

Hebeloma crustuliniforme. Creamy-tan cap, brown gills, and fleshy stem are the main features. Debris stuck to the cap indicates it's viscid.

spores 9-12 × 5.5-7.5 μm, almond-shaped, smooth or very minutely roughened.

HABITAT: Solitary, scattered, or in groups in woods and under planted trees, occasionally in gardens. Associated primarily with oak and pine, very common, fall through spring.

EDIBILITY: Poisonous; causes severe gastrointestinal distress.

COMMENTS: Despite my general disdain for Hebelomas, I must admit this is a most attractive mushroom when fresh. The smooth, pie-colored cap, more or less notched brown gills, absence of a veil, and radish odor (which may be very slight) are the important fieldmarks. You will undoubtedly encounter several subtly different species which fit the above description. Most of these cannot be differentiated without a microscope. One, *H. hiemale,* is smaller and lacks the radish odor. There are also several brown-spored, brown-gilled Hebelomas with white or whitish caps; *H. albidulum* is the most common. I have also found *H. sarcophyllum,* an unusual species with a chalk-white cap, deep flesh-colored gills, and reddish-brown spores. It resembles *Pluteus pellitus* but has attached gills and grows on the ground.

Hebeloma sinapizans

CAP 5-13 cm broad, broadly convex with an inrolled margin becoming plane or with uplifted margin; surface viscid, smooth, cinnamon-tan overlaid with a pallid sheen. Flesh thick, whitish, odor and taste radish-like. **GILLS** close, notched, pallid becoming pale brown to cinnamon-brown. **STALK** 5-13 cm long, up to 2.5 cm thick, rigid, equal or with enlarged base, white, powdery-scaly, especially at apex. **VEIL** absent. **SPORE PRINT** brown; spores 10-13×6-8 μm, almond-shaped, rough.

HABITAT: Scattered to gregarious in woods and under trees, mostly pine. Common, late fall and winter.

EDIBILITY: Poisonous.

COMMENTS: A characteristic feature of our coastal pine forests, this sturdy *Hebeloma* can be recognized by its smooth, viscid (when moist) cinnamon cap, dull brown notched gills, fleshy stem, absence of a veil, and radish odor. It is our largest *Hebeloma,* more robust than *H. crustuliniforme* and not nearly as attractive. It often grows with *Tricholoma imbricatum,* which has a brown cap, white gills, and white spores.

Hebeloma mesophaeum

CAP 2.5-6.5 cm broad, conical to umbonate when young, convex to broadly umbonate, or even plane in age; surface viscid when moist but soon dry, smooth, brown to dark reddish-brown at center, buff to whitish at margin, the margin sometimes hung with delicate veil remnants. Flesh watery brown or whitish, odor none or slightly radishlike, tasté slightly bitter. **GILLS** close, adnate becoming notched, whitish becoming pale brown to dull cinnamon. **STALK** up to 8 cm long, slender, more or less equal, apex powdered, silky-fibrillose below

Hebeloma mesophaeum. Cap is semi-conical when young, but soon expands. Gills are brown and the veil (not shown) is evanescent.

the veil; whitish, becoming dark grayish-brown in age. **VEIL** a fibrillose cortina, disappearing or forming hairy superior ring on stem. **SPORE PRINT** brown; spores 8-10 × 5-6 μm, ellipsoid, smooth.

HABITAT: Scattered to densely gregarious in woods, fall through early spring. Infrequent, but I have seen it fruit by the thousands in a willow swamp adjacent to a small reservoir.

EDIBILITY: Poisonous.

COMMENTS: The presence of a cortina distinguishes this *Hebeloma* from the more common members of the genus, but it likewise leads to confusion with *Cortinarius.* The spore print, however, is brown or dull ochre-brown, not rusty-brown.

CORTINARIUS

Terrestrial woodland fungi, mostly medium-sized. CAP viscid or dry. GILLS typically attached but rarely decurrent, variously colored when young, becoming *rusty-brown to cinnamon at maturity.* STALK fleshy, thick or slender. VEIL *present, hairy or cobwebby, disappearing or leaving a ring of hairs on stalk.* VOLVA absent. SPORE PRINT *rusty-brown to cinnamon;* spores round to elliptical, rough, without apical pore. Cystidia on gills usually absent. Cap cuticle filamentous.

CORTINARIUS is a large and bewildering genus, easier to recognize than it is to characterize. Young specimens can be told by the presence of a cobwebby veil **(cortina),** mature individuals by the typically rust-colored gills. Among the terrestrial brown-spored mushrooms, *Inocybe* and *Hebeloma* may have a cortina, but they have dull brown to ochre-brown spores. Terrestrial *Gymnopilus* species have rusty-orange spores and usually lack a veil.

The cortina, which is the hallmark of *Cortinarius,* is a special type of inner veil composed of silky or cobwebby fibers. As the cap expands the cortina disappears or forms a ring of collapsed hairs on the stem which subsequently turns rusty-cinnamon as it traps falling spores. In some species an outer veil is also present. It is often viscid and may leave remnants on the cap and stem.

Cortinarii are among our most colorful fungi. To make any headway in identification, it is absolutely essential to know the color of immature individuals, especially the color of the gills. Every imaginable hue can be found—blues, violets, yellows, browns, and oranges predominate, but reds, greens, and whites are not uncommon. As the spores mature, most species lose their individuality and assume a nondescript (but characteristic) rusty-brown look.

Cortinarius is the largest genus of fleshy fungi in North America, perhaps in the world. Between 600 and 1,000 species have been described, with many more awaiting classification. Most mycologists don't even attempt to name the Cortinarii they find—there are just too many puzzling variations to cope with. Because of its diversity and beauty, however, *Cortinarius* is an appealing group. Though you won't be able to name most of the species you find, you can still learn to recognize many of them on sight. Names, after all, are just a handy means of reference—you may even want to coin names of your own.

It is possible to short-circuit the long, tedious identification process to some extent by learning to place each species in one of the following natural groups (subgenera):

Myxacium—cap *and* stem viscid or slimy
Bulbopodium—cap viscid; stem dry, with a more or less abrupt basal bulb
Phlegmacium—cap viscid; stem dry, equal or club-shaped
Cortinarius (Dermocybe)—cap dry, not hygrophanous, often scaly or fibrillose; stem dry
Telamonia—cap dry, hygrophanous; stem dry

(These are raised to generic rank by a few authors.)

Cortinarius is one of the dominant features of our woodland fungal flora. Most species are mycorrhizal and practically all are terrestrial. They attain their maximum numbers and diversity in the northern coniferous forests of North America and Europe, but are also common under hardwoods. Their fruiting behavior is notoriously erratic. A few varieties are common every year, but most will be exceedingly abundant one year, then rare or absent for the next five or ten (or even twenty!) years. Sometimes there is one spectacular burst of Cortinarii (usually in December or January), at which time their numbers rival the Russulas; other years they fruit in a rather uninspired, desultory fashion throughout the rainy season.

In view of the vast number of poorly known species, it is best not to eat any *Cortinarius*. Many have an unpleasant or woody taste and a few (*C. orellanus* and relatives) are dangerously poisonous (see p. 636 for details). If you are adamant about experimenting, stick to the ones with viscid caps (none of which, *as yet,* is known to be poisonous). Around 200 species occur in California. Only a handful of species "complexes" can be included here.

Key to Cortinarius

1. Both cap *and* stalk slimy or viscid 2
1. Stalk not viscid; cap viscid or dry 3

2. Stalk with concentric belts or plaquelike scales ..... *C. collinitus,* p. 368
2. Stalk not as above .... *C. cylindripes,* p. 369

3. Stalk with several concentric bands or scaly belts .... *C. crocolitus* (see *C. collinitus,* p. 368)
3. Not as above 4

4. Cap viscid when moist 5
4. Cap dry, often finely fibrillose or scaly 11

5. Stalk with distinct bulb at base (bulb abrupt when young, less so in age) 6
5. Not as above 9

6. Cap covered with silky or hoary white outer veil remnants .... *C. calyptratus,* p. 366
6. Not as above 7

7. Gills blue, blue-gray, or violet when young .... *C. glaucopus,* p. 365
7. Gills not as above 8

8. Gills yellow to yellow-orange or tawny when young .... *C. fulmineus,* p. 367
8. Gills pallid to brown when young .... *C. multiformis,* p. 368

9. Cap and gills uniformly sooty-olive when young ... *C. infractus,* p. 364
9. Not as above 10

10. Stalk large, hard, at least 2 cm thick; cap also large .... *C. largus* (see *C. varius,* p. 365)
10. Smaller; stalk generally 2 cm thick or less .... *C. varius,* p. 365

11. Fruiting body deep violet to almost black .... *C. violaceus,* p. 360
11. Not as above 12

12. Cap and gills pale violet to silvery-violet when young .... *C. alboviolaceus,* p. 359
12. Not as above 13

13. Cap densely scaly .... *C. squamulosus,* p. 361
13. Cap smooth, silky, or finely fibrillose 14

14. Gills deep red to blood red when young .... *C. phoeniceus* var. *occidentalis,* p. 361
14. Not as above 15

15. Gills yellow to bright orange when young 16
15. Gills pallid or some shade of brown when young ..... *C. distans,* p. 363

16. Gills yellow to olive-yellow when young .... *C. cinnamomeus,* p. 362
16. Gills orange when young .... *C. croceofolius* (see *C. cinnamomeus,* p. 362)

Cortinarius alboviolaceus is a slender, silvery-violet species. Note the cobwebby veil remnants on specimen at right. It does not always grow in clusters.

Cortinarius alboviolaceus (Silvery-Violet Cortinarius)

CAP up to 7.5 cm broad, obtusely bell-shaped becoming convex or broadly umbonate; surface dry, smooth, silky, shining, pale silvery-violet, fading in age. Flesh pallid to pale violet. **GILLS** adnate or notched, fairly close, pale violet to ashy-violet, becoming rusty-brown in age; edges paler, eroded or serrate. **STALK** up to 10 cm long, rather slender, tapering upward, same color as cap, dry, silky, sometimes clothed with silky veil remnants. **VEIL** white, evanescent, rusty-stained in age. **SPORE PRINT** rusty-cinnamon. Spores 6.5-9 × 4-5 μm, elliptical, minutely roughened.

HABITAT: Solitary or in small groups under both hardwoods and conifers. Infrequent, fall and winter.

EDIBILITY: Reputedly edible; I haven't tried it.

COMMENTS: The pale silvery-violet color of the cap and stem is the outstanding feature of this beautiful species. The cap is not viscid and the stem lacks a basal bulb. The poisonous *Inocybe geophylla* var. *lilacina* is similarly colored but has a dull brown spore print. Other species include *C. traganus,* with a dry lilac cap and stem and faintly pungent odor, and *C. anomalus,* with a dry, brownish-violet to grayish-violet cap and gills violet-tinted when immature.

Cortinarius violaceus. Entire fruiting body is deep violet. This is a rather sorry specimen, but it is not a common species. The "swelling" on the stalk is just some debris.

Cortinarius violaceus (Violet Cortinarius)

CAP up to 12 cm broad, obtusely convex becoming broadly convex, plane, or slightly umbonate; surface dry, covered with erect tufts or small scales, fibrillose toward the margin, deep violet throughout, with a metallic luster in age, the margin often fringed or ragged. Flesh thick, deep violet becoming grayish-violet. odor and taste mild. **GILLS** adnate becoming adnexed or notched, fairly well spaced, deep violet or more or less cap color, then dusted with cinnamon spores. **STALK** up to 15 cm long, usually enlarged downward, same color as cap, dry, fibrillose. **VEIL** fibrillose, violet, soon disappearing, or leaving a few indistinct hairs on stalk. **SPORE PRINT** rusty-brown; spores 12-17 × 8-10 μm, broadly elliptical to oblong, minutely roughened.

HABITAT: Solitary or in twos and threes in mixed woods, usually next to rotting logs. Late fall and winter, rare. It occurs frequently in old coniferous forests, such as those in Olympic and Mt. Ranier national parks in Washington, but is becoming increasingly rare as areas are logged over. I have found it in Henry Cowell Redwood State Park and near Boulder Creek.

EDIBILITY: Edible and fairly good, but its main asset is its beauty.

COMMENTS: The intense deep violet color makes the violet Cortinarius as unique as it is unforgettable. The cap is dry and rough due to the presence of small scales or tufted fibrils. The color is at times so deep that it borders on black, making it difficult to pick out in the shade of the forest. Many Cortinarii are purple but none are so deeply colored. Even a color photograph cannot do it justice. Its only rival for intensity, *Entoloma nitidum,* is deep blue with pink spores.

Cortinarius squamulosus (Scaly-Capped Cortinarius)

CAP 5-13 cm broad, convex becoming broadly umbonate or plane; surface dry, densely fibrillose-scaly, soon breaking up into scales, brown to chocolate-brown. Flesh thick, pallid, odor somewhat spicy. **GILLS** adnate becoming deeply notched, close, dark grayish-purple becoming dark cinnamon or chocolate. **STALK** 7-15 cm long, stout, enlarged below, colored more or less like cap, dry, scaly or fibrillose. **VEIL** pallid to brownish, fibrillose, forming a bandlike ring near the top of the stalk. **SPORE PRINT** dark rusty-brown; spores 6.5-8.5 × 6-6.5 μm, broadly elliptical to nearly round, rough.

HABITAT: Solitary to gregarious in woods. Fall and winter, rare.

EDIBILITY: Said to be edible, but not recommended.

COMMENTS: I have not yet found this species, but an attractive, unidentified variety with yellow gills when young and a yellow-brown densely scaly cap is common in tanoak-madrone woods (often intermixed with *C. infractus* and *C. collinitus*). Both are typical of a large group of Cortinarii with dry, scaly caps.

Cortinarius phoeniceus var. **occidentalis**

CAP 2.5-8 cm broad, obtuse to broadly convex becoming plane or umbonate; surface dry, finely fibrillose, maroon-red or dark red. Flesh thin, reddish near cuticle, olive-brownish near gills; odor mild or slightly radishlike. **GILLS** deep red or blood-red, becoming rusty in age; adnate or notched, fairly close. **STALK** to 7.5 cm long, slender, more or less equal, yellowish, dry, fibrillose, sometimes brownish in old age. **VEIL** scanty, yellowish, disappearing or leaving a few hairs on stem. **SPORE PRINT** rusty-brown; spores 6-6.5 × 4-4.5 μm, oblong to ellipsoid, minutely roughened.

HABITAT: Solitary or in small groups under conifers and madrone. Not common, late fall and winter.

EDIBILITY: Probably edible, but not recommended; untested variants may be poisonous.

Cortinarius phoeniceus var. *occidentalis*, mature specimens. Dry red cap, red gills, and yellow stem are distinctive. Young specimens are conical or umbonate. (Ray Gipson)

COMMENTS: The deep red gills and maroon-red cap are set off nicely by the yellow stem, making this a most beautiful mushroom. Other species with dry cap and red gills are: *C. semisanguineus,* with yellow stem *and* yellow cap; *C. sanguineus* and *C. cinnabarinus,* both entirely blood-red or dark red, the first growing mostly with conifers, the second with oak; and *C. californicus,* with a *hygrophanous* rusty-reddish cap and dull orange (or paler) stem. None of these are common. All are excellent choices for dyeing (not dying!) if you can find enough.

Cortinarius cinnamomeus (Contrary Cortinarius)

CAP up to 5 cm broad, obtusely conical becoming convex or umbonate; surface dry, finely fibrillose, yellowish-tawny to yellow-brown or olive-brown, more cinnamon in age. Flesh thin, yellowish or olive-yellow. **GILLS** adnate to notched, close, bright yellow to olive-yellow, yellowish-cinnamon in age. **STALK** up to 10 cm long, slender, equal, often curved, dry, finely fibrillose, colored like gills above, like cap below (or duller), brownish in age. **VEIL** fibrillose, yellow-olive, leaving inconspicuous hairs on stem. **SPORE PRINT** rusty-brown; spores 6-8 $\times$ 4-5 μm, elliptical, rough.

HABITAT: Scattered to gregarious under conifers, mostly pine. Common but not abundant, late fall and winter.

EDIBILITY: Edible, but should be avoided. Related species (see comments) are dangerously poisonous.

COMMENTS: This contrary little *Cortinarius* is not cinnamon-colored at all. The yellowish cap and gills plus the slender stem and fibrillose veil are characteristic of a large complex of species which can only be differentiated with a microscope, and it may be that the "true" *C. cinnamomeus* does not occur here. Other species with dry, conical to

Cortinarius cinnamomeus, various stages of development. The umbo is not always as prominent as in these specimens. Gills are yellowish becoming rusty-cinnamon. *C. croceofolius* (not illustrated) looks similar but has orange gills.

convex or umbonate caps include *C. croceofolius*, with bright orange gills and a cinnamon-brown cap, associated with both hardwoods and conifers and just as common as *C. cinnamomeus*; and *C. aureifolius*, which grows buried in sand under pine. *C. orellanus* is a very poisonous European species with rusty-orange cap and gills. It hasn't been reported from California, which *doesn't* mean it doesn't occur. Species in this group with reddish gills are listed under *C. phoeniceus* var. *occidentalis*.

Cortinarius distans

CAP up to 8 cm broad, obtusely bell-shaped expanding somewhat to broadly umbonate; surface *not viscid,* minutely scaly, hygrophanous; cinnamon to reddish-brown or bay-brown when moist, tawny or orange-brown when dry, margin sometimes splitting in age. Flesh thin, brownish, odor mild or slightly spicy. **GILLS** adnate becoming notched, well spaced, brown becoming dark cinnamon. **STALK** up to 12 cm long, equal, tapered or enlarged below, fibrillose, watery brownish, outer veil often leaving a whitish zone near the top. **VEIL** whitish, fibrillose, disappearing or leaving hairs on stem. **SPORE PRINT** rusty-cinnamon; spores 6-8 × 5-6 μm, oval, rough.

HABITAT: In groups on ground in woods. Fairly common, fall and winter.

EDIBILITY: Unknown. To be avoided.

COMMENTS: There are innumerable Cortinarii with dry, brownish caps. In this one the cap is hygrophanous—changing color markedly as it dries. The color is subdued but the mushroom is still attractive. *C. decipiens* is a small, slender species (stem 4-7 mm thick) with a brownish, conical to umbonate, hygrophanous cap. *C. castaneus* has a chestnut cap and violet-tinted gills when young. All of these are distinguished from *Inocybe* by their rusty spores.

Cortinarius infractus (Sooty-Olive Cortinarius)

CAP 5-13 cm broad, convex becoming plane; surface smooth, viscid, uniformly dark olive or sooty-olive, becoming slightly browner in age; margin sometimes faintly zoned. Flesh thick, firm, pallid. **GILLS** notched or adnate, close, dark olive to sooty-olive, dark cinnamon-brown in old age. **STALK** up to 13 cm long, usually enlarged slightly below, solid, fibrillose, dry, pallid, sometimes slightly violaceous at apex. **VEIL** fibrillose, usually forming a hairy, rusty-cinnamon ring. **SPORE PRINT** rusty-cinnamon; spores 7-9.5 × 5-7 μm, oval to nearly round, rough.

HABITAT: Scattered to gregarious in mixed woods, especially tanoak-madrone. Common, fall and winter.

EDIBILITY: Unknown.

COMMENTS: A distinctive *Cortinarius,* recognized by its uniform sooty-olive color. The cap is viscid but there is no abrupt bulb at the base of the stem. It is a prominent fungal feature of the tanoak-madrone woods in the Santa Cruz mountains, often found in the company of *Entoloma rhodopolium* and *Cortinarius collinitus.*

Cortinarius infractus, mature specimens. This common inhabitant of our tanoak-madrone forests is identified by its sooty-olive color. Note veil remnants on stalk.

Cortinarius varius

CAP 5-10 cm broad, convex becoming plane or slightly depressed; surface smooth, viscid, some shade of tawny-yellow, the margin paler. Flesh white, thick, odor and taste mild. **GILLS** at first violaceous, at length cinnamon-ochre; notched to adnate, close. **STALK** up to 15 cm long, rather slender, slightly enlarged below; dry, nearly smooth, tinged violet above and ochre below. **VEIL** fibrillose, white, leaving hairs on stalk which become rusty-cinnamon. **SPORE PRINT** rusty-cinnamon; spores 10-12 × 5-6 μm, almond-shaped, rough.

HABITAT: Solitary or in small groups in woods; fall and winter. Common but never in large numbers.

EDIBILITY: Edible and good; however, there are too many similar, untested varieties for me to recommend it.

COMMENTS: This fairly common species is identified by its viscid, tawny cap and violaceous gills when young. There is no abrupt bulb at the base of the stem as in *C. glaucopus. C. largus* is a ponderous species with a hard stem up to 5 cm thick and 15 cm long, and viscid, ochraceous to brownish cap 8-20 cm broad. Like *C. varius,* the stem is not bulbous, and the gills are violaceous becoming cinnamon. I have found it several times in mixed woods and under oak.

Cortinarius glaucopus

CAP 5-15 cm broad, convex becoming plane, the margin sometimes wavy; surface smooth, viscid, rich greenish-brown to greenish-gray, streaked with yellowish-ochre fibrils, especially toward center, rusty-brown in old age. Flesh thick, firm, pallid, grayish or tinted violet-blue, ochraceous in base of stalk. **GILLS** close, adnexed or notched, at first bluish-violet, then bluish-gray or grayish, finally rusty-brown. **STALK** 5-10 cm long, up to 2.5 cm thick, more or less equal with a basal bulb, violet-blue above becoming brownish in age, variously colored below, dry. **VEIL** fibrillose, pallid or pale bluish-violet, leaving a ring of hairs on stalk which turns rusty from falling spores. **SPORE PRINT** rusty-brown; spores 8-10 × 4-5.5 μm, almond-shaped, slightly roughened.

HABITAT: Scattered to densely gregarious in troops, mostly under oak. Common, at times abundant, fall and early winter.

EDIBILITY: None of the species in this group (see comments) are worth eating. Some are bitter.

Cortinarius glaucopus is one of many species with violet-blue gills when young and a prominent bulb at the base of the stalk. Note the cobwebby veil in immature specimen at left, and notice how the bulb is less exaggerated in age (mature specimen on right).

COMMENTS: This is a colorful mushroom when young, but in age it resembles dozens of other rusty Cortinarii. There are many viscid-capped species with blue to purple immature gills and a bulb at the base of the stalk. *C. glaucopus* is the most common. Some others are: *C. cyanopus,* with more pronounced bluish tones, a bitter cap cuticle, and larger spores (10-13 × 6-7 μm); *C. caesiocyaneus,* entirely pale blue when young except for the large whitish bulb; *C. purpurascens* with flesh that turns purple when cut; and a common but unidentified species with pale lilac gills when young, a smooth brown (often violet-tinted at margin) cap, bitter taste, and very broad basal bulb. The cortina and rusty spores separate all of these from the blewitt, *Lepista nuda.*

Cortinarius calyptratus

CAP 5-10 cm broad, broadly convex becoming plane; surface viscid when moist, soon dry, grayish-violet becoming dark brownish, the center covered with whitish felty patch or silky hairs. Flesh thick, more or less cinnamon-buff. **GILLS** at first dull lavender, becoming brown, finally rusty-brown, close, attached. **STALK** up to 10 cm long, stout, equal above, with a large, broad bulb at base, more or less cap color. **VEIL** fibrillose, evanescent or leaving hairs on stalk which turn cinnamon from falling spores. **SPORE PRINT** rusty-brown; spores 7-9.5 × 4.5-6 μm, almond-shaped, rough.

HABITAT: Scattered or in groups in woods, fall and winter, rare (but see comments).

EDIBILITY: Unknown.

COMMENTS: The patchy white remnants of the outer veil on the cap is the outstanding feature of this robust member of the subgenus

Bulbopodium. The outer veil may also leave hairy remnants on the margin of the bulb. A similar species with brown gills when young is fairly common in our area, especially under oak.

Cortinarius fulmineus

CAP 5-13 cm broad, convex then plane; surface yellow to orange-yellow to tawny-fulvous, brownish-orange in age, viscid, smooth; margin at first incurved. Flesh thick, firm, yellowish or paler, odor mild. **GILLS** close, adnate or notched, yellow becoming tawny-yellow or yellow-orange, finally rusty-brown. **STALK** up to 10 cm long, equal above with a large basal bulb; dry, more or less cap color but paler, rusty-stained in age. **VEIL** fibrillose, pallid or yellowish, leaving hairs on stem which become rusty in age. **SPORE PRINT** rusty-brown; spores 8-10 × 4-5.5 μm, almond-shaped, rough.

HABITAT: Scattered or in groups in mixed woods and under oak. Fairly common but never in large numbers, fall and winter.

EDIBILITY: Unknown.

COMMENTS: This is one of several viscid-capped Cortinarii in which the gills are yellow to tawny when young. Another common, but unidentified species has yellow gills and a striking bright green or citrine cap. Still another, *C. percomis,* is entirely yellow with a strong, sweet, penetrating odor tantalizingly reminiscent of homemade taffy.

Cortinarius fulmineus, mature specimens. Cap is viscid, gills are yellow when young. Note veil remnants and bulbous stalk. Specimen in center is unusually small and slender.

Cortinarius multiformis

CAP 5-10 cm broad, convex becoming plane; surface viscid when moist, smooth, ochraceous-buff to tan becoming rusty-buff or orange-buff in age, silky-hoary when young. Flesh thick, firm, pallid. **GILLS** adnate or notched, close, at first pallid, then watery tan, finally cinnamon, edges eroded in age. **STALK** to 10 cm long and up to 2.5 cm thick, equal above, with a bulb at the base which is abrupt when young, becoming oval or obscure in old age; dry, whitish to tan. **VEIL** fibrillose, scanty, white, disappearing or leaving hairy zone which becomes rusty-cinnamon in age. **SPORE PRINT** pale cinnamon; spores 8-11 × 5.5-7.5 μm, elliptical, minutely roughened.

HABITAT: Solitary or in small groups in mixed woods and under oak. Fairly common, fall and early winter.

EDIBILITY: Unknown. Supposedly eaten in Europe, but caution is advisable.

COMMENTS: The viscid ochraceous-tan cap and watery tan gills when young are distinctive. The cap color is reminiscent of *Hebeloma* but the spores are rusty. The hoary white film on young caps is suggestive of the gypsy mushroom, *Rozites caperata,* but the veil is not membranous. There are several closely related species.

Cortinarius collinitus (Banded Cortinarius)

CAP up to 10 cm broad, convex becoming plane; surface smooth, slimy or viscid, color variable, usually yellowish to orange-yellow or orange-brown; the margin often paler. Flesh firm, whitish to yellowish-buff. **GILLS** close, attached, pallid or pale grayish-violet becoming brown, finally rusty-brown. **STALK** 7-15 cm long, equal or tapering downward, usually rooting somewhat, viscid or slimy, decorated with thick, irregular bands or patches (from the outer veil) which range in color from yellowish to rusty-cinnamon to violaceous. **VEIL** forming a collapsed fibrillose ring near the top of the stalk. **SPORE PRINT** rusty-cinnamon; spores 10-15 × 6-8.5 μm, almond-shaped, rough.

HABITAT: Scattered in mixed woods, especially tanoak-madrone. Common, late fall and winter.

EDIBILITY: Edible, but not choice.

COMMENTS: Also known as *C. mucifluus,* this is an easy species to recognize by virtue of the bandlike scales on the viscid stalk. Several

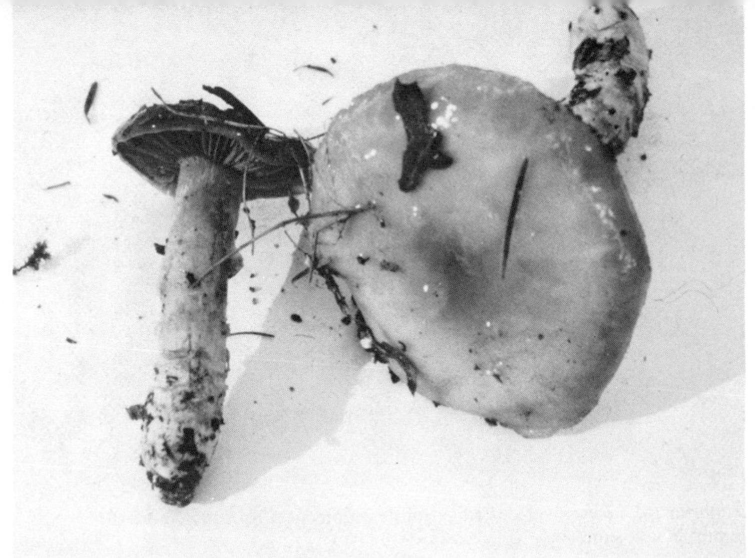

Cortinarius collinitus, mature specimens. The two outstanding features of this species are the slimy-viscid cap and viscid stem marked by scaly belts. The latter feature, unfortunately, is barely visible in this picture.

varieties have been named based on spore size and stem color. The common form in the Santa Cruz Mountains does not show violaceous shades on the stem. There are several superficially similar species: *C. elatior* has a viscid, radially wrinkled (or grooved) cap and viscid, scaly stem; *C. crocolitus* has a *dry* stem marked with brownish-yellow scaly belts. I have found it several times in mixed hardwood forests. *C. armillatus* is a delicious species with striking reddish bands on a dry stem. It is associated with birch and aspen and is to be looked for in the high Sierras.

Cortinarius cylindripes

CAP up to 10 cm broad, convex becoming plane; surface smooth, viscid, very slimy when wet, at first violet or lavender, slowly becoming yellowish, finally brownish-ochraceous. Flesh rather thin, violaceous becoming pallid. **GILLS** at first grayish-lavender, soon grayish-cinnamon, finally rusty-cinnamon, adnate or notched, close. **STALK** up to 15 cm long, more or less equal (cylindrical), viscid or slimy from remains of outer veil, violaceous to silvery-violaceous, fading somewhat. **VEIL** slimy, evanescent or leaving remains near top of stalk. **SPORE PRINT** dark cinnamon-brown; spores 12-15 × 6.5-9 μm, almond-shaped, rough.

HABITAT: Scattered to densely gregarious in mixed woods, late fall and winter; locally abundant. It fruits in profusion every year under manzanita, oak, and madrone in the Santa Cruz Mountains.

Cortinarius cylindripes, various stages of development. Cap and veil are slimy; stalk is pale purple and slimy.

EDIBILITY: Unknown; hardly appetizing because of its sliminess.

COMMENTS: This species may not be the most distinctive or desirable of our Cortinarii, but it unquestionably qualifies as the slimiest. The yellow to lavender cap, viscid lavender stalk, and slimy veil are diagnostic. *C. salor* is a similar species with smaller, round spores. Like *C. cylindripes,* it lacks the scaly bands on the stem characteristic of *C. collinitus. C. griseoviolaceus* is similar but has a club-shaped stalk. *C. vanduzerensis* has a slimy purple stem and chestnut-black to chestnut-brown cap.

PHAEOCOLLYBIA

Medium-sized terrestrial woodland fungi. CAP usually viscid when moist. GILLS attached to nearly free, usually rusty-cinnamon at maturity. STALK *rooting deeply in soil.* VEIL *absent.* VOLVA absent. SPORE PRINT *rusty-brown to cinnamon-brown;* spores ovate to ellipsoid, rough, without apical pore. Cystidia present at least on gill edges. Cap cuticle filamentous.

THE long "tap root" and absence of a veil distinguish this small genus from its closest relative, *Cortinarius,* while the Collybias with rooting stems have white spores. The "tap root" **(pseudorhiza)** is merely an extension of the stem rooted deeply in the humus. It gradually tapers to a point, becoming so thin and fragile that it can't be traced to its origin (possibly tree roots).

Phaeocollybias are rare in our area, but are common in the coniferous forests of southern Oregon and northern California. Perhaps they are a fungal remnant of the great redwood forests that dominated that area long ago. Little is known about their edibility. A dozen species occur in California. One is described here.

Phaeocollybia californica

CAP up to 6.5 cm broad, at first conical or convex, expanding in age to plane with an umbo; surface smooth, viscid when moist, brown, rusty as it matures. Flesh thin, pallid or cap color. **GILLS** attached to nearly free, same color as cap or paler, close. **STALK** to 25 cm long or more, rooting deeply, slender, cartilaginous, hollow, equal above, the "tap root" tapering gradually to a point; dry, same color as cap or darker (deep reddish-brown). **SPORE PRINT** rusty-brown; spores 8-10 × 5-6 μm, ovate, rough.

HABITAT: Densely gregarious in a large ring about 18 m (60 feet) in diameter, in mixed woods of Douglas-fir and redwood; fall and early winter, rare.

EDIBILITY: Unknown.

COMMENTS: The long "tap root," rusty spores, and rusty-cinnamon color are distinctive. *Collybia umbonata* has a "tap root" but the spores and gills are white. There are several closely related species distinguished primarily by differences in the sterile cells (cystidia) on the gills. Three radically different cousins found in northern California are: *P. olivacea,* with slimy olive cap and whitish gills when young; *P. fallax,* with slimy olive cap and lilac-tinted gills when young; and *P. kauffmanii,* with a large, viscid, liver-brown to reddish-cinnamon cap and thick stem.

ROZITES

THIS genus includes a single widespread edible species aptly characterized as "a *Cortinarius* with a membranous veil." It was once placed in *Pholiota,* but, like *Cortinarius,* has rough spores and is terrestrial.

Rozites caperata (Gypsy Mushroom)

CAP 5-13 cm broad, egg-shaped becoming broadly convex or obscurely umbonate; surface dry, uneven, radially wrinkled or corrugated, at first covered with a white hoary coating of silky fibrils; warm tan to cinnamon-buff to orange-brown, the margin usually paler. Flesh thick, white, firm. **GILLS** adnate becoming notched, close, at first pallid, soon brown, sometimes transversely banded with darker and lighter zones. **STALK** 5-13 cm long, less than 2.5 cm thick, equal, solid, white to pale

Rozites caperata. Note how the membranous veil forms a ring on the stalk. Spore print is rusty-brown; cap is warm tan. (Nancy Burnett)

tan, apex often striate or scurfy, base sometimes with an obscure volvalike zone. **VEIL** membranous, ample, forming a more or less median persistent ring. **SPORE PRINT** dark rusty-brown; spores 12-15 $\times$ 7-10 μm, almond-shaped, rough. Some cystidia present on gill edges. Cap cuticle filamentous.

HABITAT: Scattered or in groups on ground in old conifer forests. Sporadically common in northern California and the Sierras, late summer and fall.

EDIBILITY: Delectably delicious, one of the finest flavored of fleshy fungi, certainly the best of the Cortinariaceae. It is especially good with rice after a long, hard day of backpacking. The tough stems should be discarded.

COMMENTS: I have not found the gypsy mushroom in central California but include it here in hopes that it may turn up. It would most likely be found in old Douglas-fir or redwood forests. The warm brown wrinkled cap has a characteristic hoary sheen when young. The membranous ring and rusty-brown spores are also distinctive. *Agrocybe praecox* is somewhat similar but does not have a wrinkled cap and grows in cultivated ground.

GYMNOPILUS

Medium to large fungi found mostly on wood. CAP dry, smooth or scaly. GILLS notched to slightly decurrent, usually *yellow to rusty-orange.* STALK more or less *central, fleshy.* VEIL *usually (but not always) present,* persistent or evanescent. VOLVA absent. SPORE PRINT more or less *bright rusty-orange.* Spores typically ellipsoid, rough, without apical pore. Cystidia present at least on gill edges. Cap cuticle filamentous.

THIS is a distinctive group of rusty-orange spored mushrooms formerly placed in *Pholiota* and the defunct genus *Flammula.* The fruiting body is typically bright yellow to reddish-brown and a veil is often present. Though most species feed on wood, they may appear terrestrial. The few truly terrestrial types lack a veil. *Pholiota* is the genus most often confused with *Gymnopilus.* However, Pholiotas often have viscid caps and their spores, though sometimes rusty, lack the strong orange tint characteristic of *Gymnopilus.*

Gymnopilus is found primarily in the woods, but a few species, perhaps exotic, turn up in nursery flats and flower pots. Though common, *Gymnopilus* is never abundant to the extent that *Cortinarius, Inocybe,* and *Hebeloma* are.

About 75 species are known from North America. Several are quite striking but none have gastronomic value. Certain strains or geographical races of *G. spectabilis* and *G. aeruginosus* are said to be hallucinogenic. Three species are described here.

Key to Gymnopilus

1. Cap with greenish or bluish-green cast, at least when young .... *G. aeruginosus* (see *G. luteofolius,* p. 375)
1. Not as above 2
2. Cap with dark red to purple-red or reddish-brown fibrils or scales .... *G. luteofolius,* p. 375
2. Not as above 3
3. Cap with tawny to brown fibrillose scales .... *G. fulvosquamulosus* (see *G. luteofolius,* p. 375)
3. Cap uniformly colored (but may be somewhat fibrillose or scaly) 4
4. Medium-sized to very large; membranous veil present, usually forming a ring on stalk .... *G. spectabilis,* below
4. Not as above; veil if present fibrillose, evanescent .... *G. sapineus,* p. 376

Gymnopilus spectabilis (Giant Gymnopilus)

CAP 5-30 cm broad or more, convex becoming plane; surface dry, smooth or somewhat fibrillose, occasionally breaking into small scales; bright rusty-orange to yellow-orange or orange-brown; margin sometimes wavy, incurved at first. Flesh thick, firm, yellow, taste bitter. **GILLS** adnate to slightly decurrent, sometimes notched, close, yellow becoming cap color (more or less rusty-orange). **STALK** up to 24 cm long, to 4 cm thick, equal or thickened in middle or below, dry, solid, more or less cap color, fibrillose below ring. **VEIL** yellowish or rusty-

Gymnopilus spectabilis, mature specimens. Note how large this species is! The uniform yellow to rusty-orange color, presence of a veil, and clustered growth habit on wood are distinctive. Young specimens are much smaller and more compact, with very thick flesh. A mature cluster is shown on p. 636.

stained, membranous, forming a persistent superior ring which may collapse against the stalk or disappear in old age. **SPORE PRINT** bright rusty-orange; spores 7-10 × 4.5-6 μm, ellipsoid, rough.

HABITAT: Solitary, more often in clusters, on or around old conifer stumps (occasionally hardwoods), late fall and winter. Fairly common in coastal pine forests.

EDIBILITY: Inedible because of the bitter taste, but eastern strains are consistently hallucinogenic ("pupil-dilating"). An Ohio woman had an unforgettable experience after inadvertently nibbling on one. She found herself in an alien world of fantastic shapes and glorious colors, and while concerned friends were rushing her to the hospital, she was heard to mutter, "If this is the way you die from mushroom poisoning, then I'm all for it. . . ."

COMMENTS: Also known as *Pholiota spectabilis* and *Gymnopilus junonius*, this species is set apart by the bright rusty-orange color of the spores and fruiting body plus the membranous veil and growth on wood. One of our largest mushrooms, it is not unusual to find pizza-sized caps (more than one foot in diameter) and clusters weighing 10 pounds or more. Young specimens present an entirely different appearance: squat and compact with hard, thick yellow flesh and very narrow (shallow) gills. The jack-o-lantern mushroom, *Omphalotus olivascens*, is somewhat similar but is usually olive-toned, does not have rusty spores, and grows with hardwoods rather than conifers.

Gymnopilus luteofolius. These two clusters were growing in wood chips and debris. The cap is covered with dark reddish scales; gills are bright yellow; stalk has a ring.

Gymnopilus luteofolius

CAP 2.5-8 cm broad, convex or obtuse becoming nearly plane; surface dry, at first covered with dense dark red to purple-red or reddish-brown scales, these fading slowly to pinkish-red or yellowish-red, finally yellowish in old age. Flesh thick, reddish fading to yellowish, odor mild or pungent, taste bitter. **GILLS** notched to adnate or slightly decurrent, fairly close, yellow becoming bright rusty-orange. **STALK** up to 10 cm long, fleshy, equal or enlarged below, solid, dry, fibrillose, more or less yellowish becoming rusty-stained. **VEIL** fibrillose to fibrillose-membranous, yellowish, forming a hairy superior ring which may disappear. **SPORE PRINT** bright rusty-orange; spores 5.5-8.5 $\times$ 3.5-4.5 μm, ellipsoid, rough.

HABITAT: In groups or clusters on decaying coniferous wood, sawdust, etc. (rarely on hardwoods). Fall and winter, uncommon. I have seen one large fruiting—at New Brighton Beach State Park under pine, with *Pluteus cervinus* and large clusters of *Pholiota terrestris* and *Naematoloma fasciculare* also present (all are confirmed wood-lovers).

EDIBILITY: Unknown.

COMMENTS: This impressive species is easily distinguished by the dark red scales on the cap, yellow gills, rusty-orange spores, and presence of a veil. At first glance I mistook it for *Tricholomopsis rutilans,* which has white spores and no veil. A related species, *G. aeruginosus,* has a dry, greenish to bluish gray-green cap when young, fading to (or becoming variegated with) yellow, buff, or brownish. A third species, *G. fulvosquamulosus,* has tawny to brown scales on the cap.

Gymnopilus sapineus

CAP up to 8 cm broad but typically more or less 5 cm; convex, expanding slightly, sometimes obscurely umbonate; surface golden-yellow to tawny-orange, the margin sometimes paler; dry, smooth, more often with scattered patches of fibrils, sometimes cracking in age. Flesh thick, yellowish, firm, taste often bitter. **GILLS** attached (usually adnate), close, yellow becoming rusty-yellow in age. **STALK** 2.5-7.5 cm long, more or less equal, innately fibrillose, yellowish-buff becoming yellow-brown below in age. **VEIL** yellow, fibrillose, evanescent or leaving hairs on stem which stain rusty-orange from falling spores. **SPORE PRINT** rusty-orange to bright rusty-brown; spores 7-10 × 4-5.5 μm, elliptical, minutely roughened.

HABITAT: Solitary or in small groups on rotting logs and humus rich in lignin. Common but never abundant, fall and winter.

EDIBILITY: Unknown.

COMMENTS: There are several small to medium-sized *Gymnopilus* species that fit the above description. Most have a fibrillose or evanescent veil, some have no veil at all. They resemble *Cortinarius* but have oranger spores and usually grow on wood. *G. penetrans* is very similar but has a smooth cap and white veil. Another, unidentified species with a tawny to cinnamon cap shows up commonly in nursery flats. Still another species develops black or brownish-black stains in age, especially on the gills. None of these should be eaten.

PHOLIOTA

Medium-sized fungi found *mostly on wood or woody debris*. CAP viscid or scaly. GILLS attached, rarely decurrent. STALK *more or less central, fleshy* but frequently slender, *often scaly below veil*. VEIL *present;* membranous, slimy, or fibrillose, persistent or evanescent. VOLVA absent. SPORE PRINT *brown to rusty-brown*. Spores mostly ellipsoid, smooth, usually with an apical pore. Cystidia present on gills. Cap cuticle filamentous.

PHOLIOTA is a very large genus of wood-inhabiting agarics. The fruiting body is larger and fleshier than in *Galerina* and has a well-developed, more or less central stem, unlike *Crepidotus*. *Pholiota* intergrades somewhat with *Naematoloma, Stropharia,* and *Gymnopilus* but can usually be distinguished by its spore color. The presence of a veil and brown spores afford the best means of recognizing those species which do not grow directly on wood. The veil may be fibrillose, slimy, or membranous, and typically leaves visible remains on the stem. When it doesn't, the stem is usually decorated with small scales below the veil.

Most Pholiotas are edible but few are worth eating and some are mildly poisonous. Some of the edible species listed in older books have since been removed to other genera (e.g., *Rozites* and *Agrocybe*).

Pholiotas are quite abundant in coniferous slash in the West. In my experience, however, they are poorly represented in our region. Over 200 species are known from North America. Microscopic characters play an important part in their delineation, especially the types of sterile cells (cystidia) found on the gills. Of the seven species described here, only one, *Pholiota terrestris*, is common.

Key to Pholiota

1. Growing on charred ground or burnt wood .... *P. highlandensis* (see *P. spumosa*, p. 381)
1. Not as above 2

2. Growing on ground or humus 3
2. Growing on stumps or logs 6

3. Usually clustered; stalk scaly below veil; cap viscid or dry; common .... *P. terrestris*, p. 379
3. Not as above; not usually clustered; cap viscid 4

4. Cap bright rusty to ochraceous, without scales .... *P. ferrugineo-lutescens*, p. 380
4. Not as above (cap different color or with scales) 5

5. Veil slimy .... *P. velaglutinosa*, p. 382
5. Veil not slimy .... *P. spumosa*, p. 381

6. Cap bright yellow to ochraceous, with scales at least when young 7
6. Not as above; cap smooth or if scaly, then not brightly colored 8

7. Cap scales yellow; on conifers .... *P. flammans*, p. 378
7. Cap scales brown; on hardwoods .... *P. adiposa* (se *P. flammans*, p. 378)

8. Cap and stalk smooth, without scales; usually growing in clusters; spore print rusty .... *P. malicola*, p. 378
8. Not as above 9

9. Cap 2.5 cm broad or less; in clusters .... *P. scamba* (see *P. spumosa*, p. 381)
9. If growing in clusters, cap larger 10

10. Cap with prominent, erect scales, pallid to cinnamon-buff or pale tawny; in clusters .... *P. squarrosoides*, p. 379
10. Cap smooth or with scattered scales; solitary or in small clusters .... *P. spumosa*, p. 381

Pholiota malicola

CAP up to 10 cm broad, convex becoming plane or remaining slightly umbonate; surface viscid when moist, smooth, ochraceous-tawny or orange-buff or yellow, fading somewhat in age, margin often wavy. Flesh pallid or yellowish, taste mild. **GILLS** close, adnate or notched, yellow or same color as cap, rusty-brown in old age. **STALK** up to 15 cm long, equal, tapered or enlarged below, dry, solid, not scaly, pallid to yellowish above, darker below, becoming rusty-brown in age from falling spores. **VEIL** fibrillose, usually forming a faint zone of fibrils near the top of the stem. **SPORE PRINT** rusty; spores 7.5-11 × 4.5-5.5 μm, smooth, elliptical.

HABITAT: In groups or clusters on rotting logs or stumps, fall and winter, uncommon.

EDIBILITY: Unknown.

COMMENTS: This nondescript species is included here as a representative of a group of Pholiotas which resemble *Naematoloma* but have rusty spores. They also approach *Gymnopilus,* but the spore color is not as orange. *P. astragalina* is a beautiful northern species with a pink to ochraceous cap, bitter taste, bright yellow gills, and rusty spores.

Pholiota flammans (Flaming Pholiota)

CAP up to 7.5 cm broad, obtusely conic becoming broadly umbonate to nearly plane; surface brilliant yellow, covered with yellow fibrillose scales (sometimes nearly smooth in age), viscid when wet beneath the scales; margin usually fringed with veil remnants. Flesh firm, yellow. **GILLS** adnexed, bright yellow, close. **STALK** 5-10 cm long, equal or slightly enlarged at base, same color as cap, densely scaly below the veil. **VEIL** bright yellow, fibrillose, evanescent or forming a hairy superior zone on stem. **SPORE PRINT** brown; spores 4-5 × 2.5-3 μm, smooth, oblong to ellipsoid.

HABITAT: Solitary or in small clusters on conifer logs and stumps. Rare, fall and winter.

EDIBILITY: Edible, but not choice. *P. squarrosa-adiposa* (see comments) is said to taste "like marshmallows without sugar."

COMMENTS: The brilliant yellow color sets this striking species apart. It is one of our most beautiful mushrooms, but very rare. Slightly more common is the "Fat Pholiota," *P. adiposa.* Though not necessarily fat, it is definitely a *Pholiota.* It is also bright yellow, but the cap scales are brown, the stem viscid, and it occurs on hardwood logs. *P. aurivella* has an orange to tawny viscid cap which is scaly at first, a dry scaly stem, and spores 7-10 μm long. *P. squarroso-adiposa* has a viscid dark brown to ochraceous-tawny cap, dry scaly stem, and spores 6-7.5 μm long. All of these grow on stumps or logs, never on the ground.

Pholiota squarrosoides (Scaly Pholiota)

CAP 2.5-7.5 cm broad, convex or broadly umbonate to nearly plane; surface whitish to cinnamon-buff to pale tawny, covered with pointed, dry, erect tawny scales, sparser toward the margin; viscid when wet beneath the scales. Flesh whitish, thick. **GILLS** adnate or adnexed, close, whitish becoming slowly dull rusty-brown. **STALK** 5-10 cm long, equal, dry, covered with coarse tawny scales (like cap) below veil, otherwise pallid. **VEIL** pallid, evanescent or forming a fibrillose superior ring. **SPORE PRINT** brown; spores 4-6 × 2.5-3.5 μm, elliptical, smooth.

HABITAT: In large clusters on hardwood logs and stumps, mostly maple and alder. Uncommon, fall and winter. I have not found it in our area, but it is widely distributed and may well occur.

EDIBILITY: Edible; supposedly the best of the Pholiotas.

COMMENTS: The pointed, erect cinnamon-buff scales on the cap and stem and growth habit in dense clusters typify this widely distributed species. It is closely related to *P. terrestris* but has a scalier cap and grows on wood. Another well-known species, *P. squarrosa,* has a dry cap, greenish-tinted gills, and a frequent garlic odor. I have seen it on aspen in the Sierras. *P. destruens* is a large species with a whitish scaly cap, growing on cottonwood, poplar, and aspen.

Pholiota terrestris (Terrestrial Pholiota)

CAP up to 10 cm broad, obtusely conic becoming convex to plane or somewhat umbonate; surface usually covered with dry, fibrillose scales, but viscid in wet weather beneath the scales and at times slimy when the scales wear off; color variable, light brown to yellow-brown or tawny, the scales darker, margin often hung with veil remnants. Flesh watery yellowish-buff to brown. **GILLS** attached, close, at first pallid, finally

Pholiota terrestris almost always grows in groups or clusters on the ground. Note the scaly stem and scaly cap. The spore print is brown. (Joel Leivick)

cinnamon-brown. **STALK** up to 13 cm long, equal or narrowed below, slender, solid becoming hollow, dry, pallid to buff, brownish toward base, covered with dark brown scales or patches below the veil. **VEIL** fibrillose, usually forming a hairy superior ring, sometimes disappearing. **SPORE PRINT** dark cinnamon-brown; spores 4.5-7 $\times$ 3.5-4.5 μm, elliptical, smooth.

HABITAT: In groups or clusters on the ground, especially along roads, paths, and disturbed areas; also on lawns, lignin-rich debris, rarely on or around old stumps. Common, at times abundant, fall and winter. Single individuals are occasionally found.

EDIBILITY: Edible but thin-fleshed, insipid, and usually wormy to boot.

COMMENTS: Our most common *Pholiota,* the only brown-spored mushroom that commonly grows in large clusters on the ground. (Several dark-spored Psathyrellas also do.) The scaly stem and evanescent veil are good secondary fieldmarks, but the viscidity, degree of scaliness, and cap color vary considerably according to weather conditions. The veil does not form a prominent ring, but after collapsing, it traps falling spores, turning brown as in *Cortinarius.* I have seen fantastic fruitings around an old wood pile behind the ranger station at New Brighton Beach State Park.

Pholiota ferrugineo-lutescens

CAP 4-10 cm broad, convex becoming plane or slightly umbonate; surface viscid or slimy, smooth, bright rusty-orange to ochraceous-tawny, margin often hung with veil remnants. Flesh thick, pallid to watery yellow. **GILLS** attached, pallid, then dull brown, close. **STALK**

Pholiota ferrugineo-lutescens, mature specimens. Note the scaly stem and viscid cap (as evidenced by the debris stuck to it). The veil collapses on stalk and is darkened by falling spores (specimen at left).

to 10 cm long, more or less equal, white or whitish but developing yellowish stains, fibrillose below, becoming sordid rusty-brown in old age. **VEIL** fibrillose, ample, forming a hairy superior ring on stem. **SPORE PRINT** brown; spores 5.5-7 × 4-4.5 μm, elliptical, smooth.

HABITAT: Scattered to gregarious on debris in mixed woods and under conifers. Uncommon, fall and winter.

EDIBILITY: Unknown.

COMMENTS: The slimy-viscid bright rusty cap, brown gills, and pallid-yellowish stem set this impressive species apart. Since it grows on the ground it is likely to be looked for in *Stropharia.* The spores, however, are paler.

Pholiota spumosa

CAP 2.5-6.5 cm broad, obtusely conic becoming convex or umbonate, finally plane; surface smooth or appearing fibrillose, viscid or slimy, dingy-tawny to olive-brown, darker toward the center; margin often yellow, at least at maturity. Flesh yellow or greenish-yellow, thin, soft. **GILLS** adnate or notched, yellow to pale greenish-yellow, becoming tawny, finally cinnamon-brown, close. **STALK** up to 7.5 cm long, slender, equal, yellow to pale greenish-yellow above, becoming sordid brownish below, fibrillose. **VEIL** pallid yellowish-white, delicate, fibrillose, disappearing or leaving slight remains on cap margin and stem. **SPORE PRINT** dark cinnamon-brown; spores 5.5-8 × 4-4.5 μm, elliptical, smooth.

Pholiota spumosa, mature specimens. This small, tawny species has a viscid cap and hairy veil. *P. velaglutinosa* (not illustrated) is very similar but has a slimy-viscid veil.

HABITAT: Scattered or in small clusters on ground, or on buried or rotting wood, usually coniferous. Occasional, fall and winter.

EDIBILITY: Unknown.

COMMENTS: This species belongs to a complex group of Pholiotas with yellow to greenish-yellow flesh and gills, viscid to slimy cap, and evanescent veil. The veil is not slimy as in *P. velaglutinosa.* There are many other Pholiotas which grow on the ground or wood debris, including: *P. lenta,* cap whitish to gray with scattered scales; *P. decorata,* cap with radially arranged fibrils or scales, stem cottony-white; *P. albivelata,* with a persistent, membranous white ring; and *P. scamba,* with a pale to pinkish-cinnamon silky-fibrillose cap less than 2.5 cm broad, and a scaly stem. I have found the latter growing in small clusters on rotting conifers. There are also several Pholiotas which grow exclusively on burnt wood or charred ground. The most common is *P. highlandensis*, which often fruits in large numbers with *Psathyrella carbonicola*. It has a rusty cap, yellow veil, and rather slender stalk (6 mm thick or less); *Pholiota brunnescens* is similar but has a thicker stem, while *P. carbonaria* has a bright cinnamon veil. All of these were formerly placed in the defunct genus *Flammula.*

Pholiota velaglutinosa (Slimy-Veiled Pholiota)

CAP up to 6.5 cm broad, convex becoming plane, surface slimy or viscid, smooth or appearing streaked, bright to dingy brown, margin often decorated with veil remnants. Flesh thin, greenish-yellow becoming buff. **GILLS** attached, pale brown becoming dull, dark brown at maturity, close. **STALK** up to 7.5 cm long, slender, equal, hollow, greenish-yellow above, yellowish-buff below with concentric zones of small fibrillose patches or scales; rusty-stained where handled and dark brown below in age. **VEIL** slimy, collapsing against stem or leaving remnants on cap margin. **SPORE PRINT** brown; spores 6-7.5 × 3.5-4.5 µm, elliptical, smooth.

HABITAT: Scattered or in small groups on debris and duff under pine. Fairly common, late fall and winter, especially on the Monterey Peninsula. Known only from the west coast.

EDIBILITY: Unknown.

COMMENTS: The slimy cap and slimy veil, scaly stem, and growth on the ground are characteristic. The greenish-yellow flesh is reminiscent of *P. spumosa,* but the slimy veil distinguishes it from that species. The cap is not as brightly colored as that of *P. ferrugineo-lutescens.*

GALERINA and TUBARIA

Small or minute little brown mushrooms found on wood, moss, or ground. CAP smooth, brownish, usually translucent-striate toward margin when moist. GILLS *brown at maturity,* attached (slightly decurrent in *Tubaria*). STALK *thin (generally less than 4 mm thick), cartilaginous, fragile or brittle,* hollow, more or less central. VEIL absent or if present, fibrillose. VOLVA absent. SPORE PRINT *some shade of brown.* Spores rough or smooth, apical pore usually lacking. Cystidia present on gill edges. Cap cuticle usually filamentous.

GALERINA is a large genus of little brown mushrooms formerly split between *Pholiota* and the obsolete genus *Galera.* A veil is present in many species but does not always form a ring. Those without a veil can be recognized by their small size, smooth conical to convex cap, thin stem, and brown spores. *Mycena* and *Nolanea* are similar but have white and pinkish spores respectively. Conocybes are also similar but have more conical caps and are even more fragile.

About 200 species of *Galerina* are known from North America, the mundane majority of them indistinguishable in the field. They are found on rotting wood, in moss, occasionally on the ground or in wet grass. They are not prominent except during dry spells when other fungi are scarce. *Tubaria* is a small genus with slightly decurrent gills, a convex cap, and thin-walled spores. There are several other insignificant genera.

Several Galerinas contain deadly amanita-toxins, which is why all little brown mushrooms should be strictly avoided. Two Galerinas and one *Tubaria* are described here. If your mushroom does not key out convincingly, check the Bolbitiaceae, p. 336. For more comments on little brown mushrooms, see p. 34.

Key to Galerina and Tubaria

1. Veil present, forming a distinct but fragile ring on stalk 2
1. Veil absent or evanescent, not forming a distinct ring 3

2. Cap conical when young; ring membranous; in grass or moss .... (see *Conocybe filaris,* p. 340)
2. Cap convex, never conical; ring fibrillose or fibrillose-membranous; on rotting sticks, logs, stumps, buried wood .... *Galerina autumnalis,* below

3. Gills slightly decurrent .... *Tubaria furfuracea,* p. 386
3. Not as above 4

4. Cap conical to convex, translucent-striate when moist .... *Galerina heterocystis,* p. 385
4. Cap convex to plane, not striate .... (see *Agrocybe pediades,* p. 337)

Galerina autumnalis (Autumn Galerina)

CAP 2-5 cm broad, convex to nearly plane; surface smooth, viscid when moist, dark brown to yellow-brown, fading to tan or buff as it dries; margin translucent-striate when moist. Flesh thin, watery brown, odor mild or slightly farinaceous. **GILLS** attached, seceding in age, close, pale brown becoming rusty-brown or brown. **STALK** up to 7 cm long, thin, equal, dry, hollow, fibrillose below the veil; brown, darker below in age, the base often with white mycelium. **VEIL** fibrillose, usually forming a thin, superior white ring which is darkened by falling spores and easily obliterated. **SPORE PRINT** rusty-brown; spores 8.5-10.5 × 5-6.5 µm, elliptical, wrinkled.

HABITAT: In small groups or clusters on rotting wood and debris (both hardwoods and conifers). Fairly common, fall and winter, especially during relatively dry years.

Galerina autumnalis. This deadly little brown mushroom is identified by its small size, brown spores, growth on wood, and persistent veil which *usually* forms a thin ring. These are average-sized specimens, but in regions of high rainfall it grows larger.

EDIBILITY: DEADLY POISONOUS! Contains amanita-toxins (see p. 631 for details).

COMMENTS: Since this drab little brown mushroom is deadly poisonous, it is important to learn its distinguishing characteristics: (1) rusty-brown spores, (2) small size and thin stem, (3) veil usually (but not always) forming a thin whitish superior ring on stem, (4) habitat on wood (sometimes buried or very decayed). The ring may turn brown from falling spores (or disappear) so it is best to avoid any mushroom that is remotely similar. Other deadly poisonous species with a ring include *G. marginata,* with a moist but not viscid cap, on decaying conifers; and *G. venenata,* with a reddish-cinnamon cap, on buried wood (sometimes in grass), known only from Oregon and Washington. *Kuehneromyces (=Pholiota) mutabilis* is a somewhat similar mushroom with an even more markedly hygrophanous cap, and fine recurved scales on the stem (below the veil). It grows in large clusters on rotting logs and stumps. Though edible, the possibility of confusing it with *Galerina* precludes me from recommending it.

Galerina heterocystis

CAP less than 2.5 cm broad, obtusely conic becoming bell-shaped or convex, sometimes umbonate; surface smooth, hygrophanous, pale yellow to pale cinnamon to tawny and translucent-striate when moist, buff when dry. Flesh very thin, fragile. **GILLS** close, usually attached but not decurrent, pale yellowish becoming pale cinnamon-brown from spores. **STALK** up to 10 cm long, very thin (less than 3 mm), equal, tubular, fragile, pallid to pale yellowish darkening to brown or cinnamon, lower portion faintly fibrillose. **VEIL** absent or rudimentary. **SPORE PRINT** pale cinnamon-brown; spores 11-17×6.5-8.5 µm, more or less ellipsoid, rough to nearly smooth.

HABITAT: Gregarious in damp mossy or grassy places. Common, fall through spring, more prevalent in relatively dry years.

EDIBILITY: Unknown. Do not experiment!

COMMENTS: There are dozens of Galerinas that will more or less fit the above description. The veil is absent or evanescent and the cap usually translucent-striate when fresh. They are typically found in the woods or in grassy places at the edges of woods. *Conocybe* species are more sharply conical, not as translucent, and favor lawns or cultivated ground. Some other Galerinas are: *G. semilanceata,* with a fibrillose veil, usually found on ground; *G. cedretorum,* with a more or less convex cap, no veil, on humus and debris under conifers; *G. hypnorum,* with rudimentary veil, minute, on mossy logs; and *G. triscopa,* also minute, with sharply conic cap when young, on logs.

Tubaria furfuracea

CAP up to 2.5 cm broad or slightly larger; convex becoming plane or even slightly depressed; surface smooth or finely fibrillose, not viscid but hygrophanous: brown or cinnamon-brown when moist, buff or pinkish-buff when dry, sometimes with whitish flecks or patches from the veil; margin striate when moist. Flesh thin, watery brownish. **GILLS** close, adnate to slightly decurrent, more or less same color as cap. **STALK** to 4 cm long, thin, equal or with a slightly enlarged base, fibrillose, more or less cap color or slightly paler, sometimes with whitish flecks, hollow. **VEIL** whitish to pale buff, fibrillose, evanescent. **SPORE PRINT** brown; spores 7-9 × 4-5.5 μm, ellipsoid, smooth.

HABITAT: Scattered to gregarious on ground, sticks, and debris in wet places—woods, vacant lots, gardens, fields, etc. Common, fall through spring, especially during relatively dry weather.

EDIBILITY: Unknown.

COMMENTS: This little brown mushroom is as featureless as it is ubiquitous. The brown spores, adnate to decurrent gills, thin stalk, and whitish flecks on the cap and stem (when young) are the most reliable fieldmarks. *T. pellucida* is smaller, with spores 5.5-7 × 4-5 μm. Other miscellaneous little brown mushrooms include: *Macrocystidia cucumis,* a rather attractive species with dark brown conical to bell-

Tubaria furfuracea. A ubiquitous little brown mushroom with slightly decurrent gills (shown at right).

shaped cap, strong fishy-cucumber odor, and large lance-shaped cystidia on gills and stem; *Naucoria centencula,* cap olive-brown when fresh, gills adnate, olive-gray with finely scalloped edges, growing on hardwood logs (usually willow or alder) or in rich soil; and *N. carpophila,* minute, with tall, thin, densely mealy stalk, growing on leaves.

CREPIDOTUS

Small to medium-sized fungi *growing shelflike on wood.* CAP round to kidney-shaped in outline, surface smooth or hairy. Flesh soft, thin. GILLS brownish at maturity. STALK *absent or lateral.* VEIL and VOLVA absent. SPORE PRINT *brown or cinnamon.* Spores rough or smooth, lacking an apical pore. Cystidia often present on gills. Cap cuticle filamentous.

THIS is a common but undistinguished group of wood-inhabiting fungi with little or no stem. They superficially resemble the oyster mushrooms *(Pleurotus)* but have brown spores and are smaller. We have many species, drab in appearance and difficult to identify. *Phyllotopsis* and *Claudopus* are similar but have pinkish spores. Other brown-spored wood-inhabiting mushrooms have prominent stems and *Crepidotus* appears to be only distantly related.

Crepidotus species are worthless as food—they are small, thin-fleshed, and decay rapidly. Nevertheless, they are a prevalent group on decaying logs and branches, especially oak, cottonwood, and alder. Two representatives are described here.

Key to Crepidotus

1. Gills forking or with veins between, pale yellow to yellow-orange .... (see *Paxillus panuoides,* p. 391)
1. Not as above 2

2. Cap minute, white or whitish, not gelatinous .... *C. versutus,* p. 388.
2. Cap gelatinous in wet weather, often with small brown scales, pallid to tawny .... *C. mollis,* below.

Crepidotus mollis (Flabby Crepidotus)

CAP up to 5 cm broad, more or less shell-shaped; pallid to tawny with small scattered brown scales which wear away, gelatinous in wet weather, flaccid in age. Flesh soft, thin. **GILLS** close, pallid, then dull cinnamon, radiating from point of attachment. **STALK** absent or present as a short basal (lateral) plug of tissue. **SPORE PRINT** brown; spores 7-9 × 5-7 μm, elliptical, smooth.

Crepidotus mollis. These sorry specimens are nevertheless representative. The cap is very soft and flabby in age. It always grows on wood.

HABITAT: In groups on decaying logs and branches, also standing trees, especially oak. Common, fall through early spring.

EDIBILITY: Unknown.

COMMENTS: Our most prominent *Crepidotus,* recognized by its gelatinous cap in wet weather, brown gills, brown spores, and absence of a stem. In age it becomes flabby and is likely to attract your attention for this reason if for no other.

Crepidotus versutus

CAP minute, 8-18 mm broad, kidney-shaped to semicircular in outline; surface dry, white, covered with minute downy hairs. Flesh very thin, fragile. **GILLS** pallid, slowly becoming pale cinnamon; fairly well spaced, radiating from point of attachment. **STALK** more or less absent. **SPORE PRINT** brown; spores 9-10 $\times$ 6-7.5 μm, elliptical.

Crepidotus versutus is one of several minute white *Crepidotus* species common on sticks and small logs. The gills are whitish at first, pale brown in age.

HABITAT: In groups or troops on fallen branches, sticks, debris, etc. Common but easily overlooked, fall and winter.

EDIBILITY: Unknown. Hardly worth experimenting with.

COMMENTS: This is one of several minute members of the genus with hairy white caps. They can only be distinguished with a microscope. They resemble *Claudopus* but have brown spores. Their ranks include: *Crepidotus herbarum,* very minute with spores 6-7.5 × 3-4 μm; *C. variabilis,* with spores 5.5-6 × 3-3.5 μm; and *C. applanatus,* somewhat larger, with a smooth watery-white cap, crowded gills, and round spores.

spores

PAXILLACEAE

Fleshy, medium-sized fungi found on decaying wood or ground. CAP convex to depressed, usually brownish, margin sometimes strongly inrolled. GILLS *decurrent,* often forked or veined, usually yellow to orange; peeling easily from cap *(Paxillus).* STALK fleshy, central to lateral or practically absent. VEIL and VOLVA absent. SPORE PRINT *yellow-brown to brown* (white in *Hygrophoropsis*). Spores mostly elliptical, smooth.

THIS is a small family of medium-sized mushrooms with decurrent gills and (with one exception) yellow-brown to brown spores. The flesh is not dry, white, and brittle as in *Russula,* and there is no latex as in *Lactarius.* The spores are not rusty-orange as in *Gymnopilus,* and the stem is much fleshier than *Tubaria.* Other brown-spored agarics without a veil do not normally have decurrent gills.

In the central genus, *Paxillus,* the margin of the cap is frequently inrolled when young. The gills peel rather easily and are often veined or poroid near the stem. Like the black-spored Gomphidiaceae, *Paxillus* is thought to be related to the boletes.

Phylloporus includes one widespread species which, despite the presence of gills, is considered a true bolete by many mycologists. The gills are bright yellow and bruise slightly bluish—just like the tubes in many boletes. The third genus, *Hygrophoropsis,* is comprised of a single well-known species, the false chanterelle. Microscopically and morphologically it resembles *Paxillus,* but the spores have lost their pigmentation—the spore print is white instead of brown. Since *Hygrophoropsis* is traditionally placed in the Tricholomataceae, it is keyed out there.

The Paxillaceae are woodland fungi like the boletes, but are not as numerous or conspicuous (in South America the situation is reversed—*Paxillus* is a large and prominent group while the boletes are few and far between). None of the Paxillaceae are particularly good to eat; *Paxillus* and *Hygrophoropsis* may actually be poisonous. Five widespread species are keyed below.

Key to the Paxillaceae

1. Stalk covered with a dense coating of dark brown to blackish-brown velvety hairs .... *Paxillus atrotomentosus* (see *P. involutus*, below)
1. Not as above 2

2. Spore print white; gills usually orange, dichotomously forked (like this key!) .... *Hygrophoropsis aurantiacus*, p. 393
2. Spore print not white; gills rarely orange, may be veined but not repeatedly forked 3

3. Stalk lateral to absent; on wood or debris .. *Paxillus panuoides*, p. 391
3. Stalk more or less central; usually on ground 4

4. Cap margin strongly inrolled when young; gills close, staining brown ... . *Paxillus involutus*, below
4. Cap margin not strongly inrolled; gills well spaced, usually bruising blue or green (sometimes slowly), occasionally bruising brown .... *Phylloporus rhodoxanthus*, p. 392

Paxillus involutus (Inrolled Paxillus)

CAP 5-15 cm broad, at first convex with a strongly inrolled margin, eventually depressed with the margin unrolled; surface viscid when moist but soon dry, at first covered with soft, matted hairs, smooth in old age, dingy yellowish-brown, olive-brown, sometimes reddish-brown, often with darker spots or stains. Flesh thick, firm, buff to yellowish bruising brown. **GILLS** decurrent, close, pallid to pale yellowish becoming olive-yellow, bruising or stained brown, usually forking or poroid near the stalk. **STALK** to 10 cm long, usually shorter than width of cap, more or less central, dry, smooth, colored like cap or paler, often stained dingy brown. **SPORE PRINT** more or less yellowish-brown; spores 7-9 $\times$ 4-6 μm, elliptical, smooth.

HABITAT: Solitary or in groups on ground in woods, around stumps, on lawns under trees. Fairly common, especially in the fall. Widely distributed, in this region showing a special affinity for oak.

EDIBILITY: Potentially dangerous. Popular in Europe, but may cause hemolysis (destruction of red blood cells by antibodies) if eaten

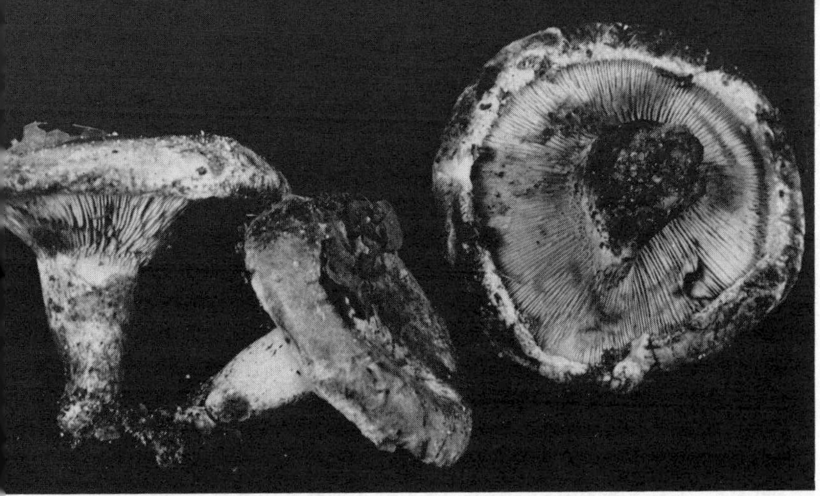

Paxillus involutus. Note the brownish-stained decurrent gills and inrolled cap margin of immature specimen at right. (Joel Leivick)

repeatedly. Apparently the human body develops a sensitivity to it. It is mediocre at best, so it's best avoided. Never eat it raw.

COMMENTS: The dingy brownish cap with inrolled margin and decurrent gills (veined near the stem and bruising brown) are the unappealing features of this unappealing fungus. Actually, its symmetry and compactness are quite intriguing, but its choice of color is downright disastrous—an unsavory blend of dingy browns and sordid yellows. The stature is reminiscent of *Lactarius* and *Russula*, but the gills do not exude a latex and the yellowish flesh is not noticeably dry or brittle. *P. atrotomentosus* is another widespread member of the genus. It has an off-center, velvety, brownish-black stalk, and grows on or around conifer stumps and logs. Its edibility is also suspect.

Paxillus panuoides (Fan Paxillus)

CAP to 7.5 cm broad, petal-shaped or fan-shaped, attached laterally to a stemlike base; surface dry, minutely hairy becoming smooth, brownish-yellow or olive-yellow, margin often lobed. Flesh thin, soft, whitish, odor mild. **GILLS** radiating from the base of the cap, close, pale or dingy yellowish, often forked or connected by veins. **STALK** absent or present as a small fleshy base attached to substrate. **SPORE PRINT** yellowish-buff; spores 4-6 $\times$ 3-4 μm, short elliptical, smooth.

HABITAT: Solitary or in groups (sometimes several arising from a common base) on logs, wood chips, and humus rich in lignin, late fall and winter, fairly common. I have found it in abundance only once—under pine at New Brighton Beach State Park.

EDIBILITY: Unknown.

Paxillus panuoides. These specimens were growing on wood chips. Note the lateral stalk, fan-shaped cap, and forking gills.

COMMENTS: The fan-shaped cap and absence of a stalk rescue this listless little brown mushroom from the obscurity it so richly deserves. It might be mistaken for a *Crepidotus* or *Phyllotopsis*, but the gills are usually forked or veined. It also resembles the false chanterelle, *Hygrophoropsis aurantiacus*, but has yellowish-buff spores and is not nearly so attractive.

Phylloporus rhodoxanthus (Gilled Bolete)

CAP 2-5 cm broad, convex to plane or with uplifted margin; surface dry, minutely velvety, dull brown to olive-brown or red-brown, sometimes cracked or fissured in age, pallid or yellow in the cracks. Flesh thick, buff or yellow. **GILLS** well spaced, thick, usually decurrent (occasionally adnate), bright yellow or golden-yellow, typically bruising greenish-blue slowly, sometimes staining brown. **STALK** to 6 cm long, tapering downward, yellow or yellowish-buff above, soon stained dingy brown or reddish-brown below; dry, smooth, solid. **SPORE PRINT** yellow-brown to olive-brown; spores 11-15 × 4.5-6 μm, spindle-shaped, smooth.

HABITAT: Solitary or in twos and threes, on ground in woods, late fall and winter; occasional. Like *Boletus subtomentosus*, it is most often found along roads and trails. Douglas-fir is one of its associates.

EDIBILITY: Edible, but rarely found in enough quantity to merit collecting. Some boletivores rate it highly, but I find it bland.

COMMENTS: This evolutionary oddity is an adamant nonconformist. The dry, velvety brown cap is an almost exact replica of *Boletus subtomentosus* and relatives, yet the underside of the cap has gills! These are thicker than the gills of most agarics, are bright yellow and bruise blue like the tubes of most boletes (it may take several minutes,

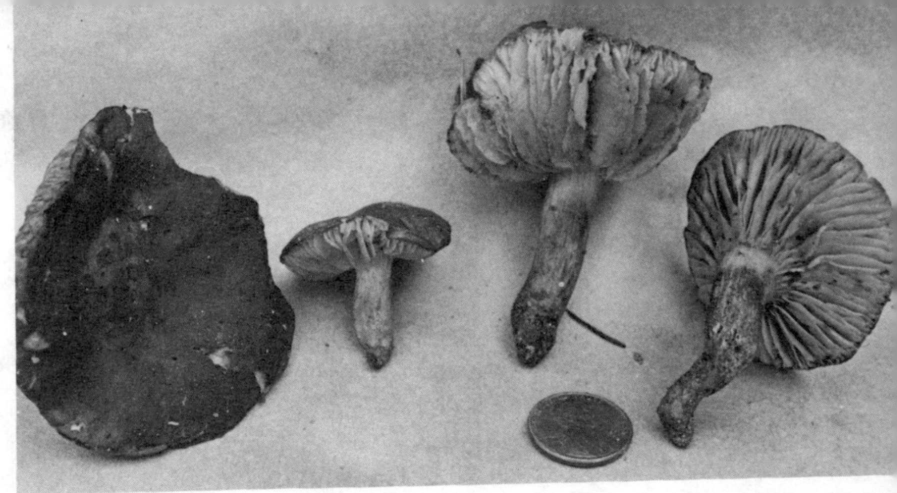

Phylloporus rhodoxanthus, mature specimens. Cap is brown; bright yellow gills are well-spaced, decurrent, and stain weakly bluish-green.

however, for the color change to manifest itself). What's more, the spores are "boletoid"—long, narrrow, and spindle-shaped. Because of its stubborn refusal to follow the rules, *Phylloporus* has been deprived of nomenclatural stability and is at the complete mercy of the taxonomist. Like baseball's itinerant tobacco-chewing utility infielders of southern rural origin, its group affiliation is in a constant state of flux as it is systematically shuttled back and forth between one "team" and another.

Hygrophoropsis aurantiacus (False Chanterelle)

CAP 2.5-10 cm broad, convex becoming plane or depressed; surface dry, somewhat velvety; color variable but typically some shade of brownish-orange, yellowish-orange, or yellowish-brown, occasionally whitish. Flesh thin, pallid or tinted cap color, odor mild. **GILLS** decurrent, close or crowded, thin, forking repeatedly (dichotomously), deep orange to pale orange, sometimes yellowish-orange, rarely pallid. **STALK** to 10 cm long, central or off-center, equal or enlarged toward base, often curved; dry, orange to orange-brown or colored like cap. **SPORE PRINT** white; spores 5-7 × 3-4 μm, elliptical, smooth, dextrinoid.

HABITAT: Solitary, scattered, or gregarious under conifers, fall through early spring; often common in dry weather when there are few fleshy fungi about. I have seen large fruitings under pine and redwood.

EDIBILITY: Based on my experience it is edible—but far from incredible. It is often listed as mildly poisonous.

Hygrophoropsis aurantiacus. **Left:** Mature specimen showing decurrent gills, which are usually bright orange. **Right:** Cap is usually yellow-brown and depressed at maturity. It is unusual for this species to grow in large numbers like these.

COMMENTS: Despite its name, the false chanterelle cannot be confused with the true chanterelle *(Cantharellus cibarius)* if the following feature is kept in mind: the gills are thin, crowded, and well developed (not thick, shallow, and foldlike), and are usually deeper orange. In other words, the false chanterelle has "true" gills while the true chanterelle has "false" gills. Also, *Hygrophoropsis* has thinner flesh, a browner cap, and is less robust. The gills are repeatedly forked but not connected by cross-veins. *Hygrophoropsis* is never olive-tinted like *Omphalotus olivascens* and only rarely grows in clusters. It was originally placed in *Cantharellus* and is listed in most modern mushroom books under *Clitocybe*. However, the forking gills, frequently off-center stem, and dextrinoid spores connote a closer kinship to *Paxillus*.

spores

GOMPHIDIACEAE

THIS is a small but prominent family with smoky-olive to black spores, fleshy stem, and decurrent gills. No other group of black-spored mushrooms has consistently decurrent gills. *Gomphos*, meaning "wooden peg," refers to the shape of the young mushrooms, which look like tent stakes, with their long stems and small, rounded to conical caps. The spores are "boletoid"—long, narrow, and spindle-shaped. The Gomphidiaceae, in fact, are thought to be more closely related to the boletes than to other gilled fungi. They are mycorrhizal with conifers and often occur with the bolete genus *Suillus*. This may be purely coincidental (since *Suillus* is also mycorrhizal with conifers), or it may be that the fungal mycelia are in some way associated with each other as well as with their host.

There are two common genera, *Chroogomphus* and *Gomphidius*. In older books both are listed under *Gomphidius*.

Key to the Gomphidiaceae

1. Flesh in the cap white to grayish; gills pallid (white to gray) when young .... *Gomphidius*, below
1. Flesh in the cap colored (yellow, orange, salmon-buff, reddish, etc.); gills colored when young .... *Chroogomphus*, p. 397

GOMPHIDIUS

Medium to large terrestrial mushrooms with soft flesh. CAP *viscid or slimy, flesh white to grayish,* not amyloid. GILLS *decurrent, waxy,* well spaced, pallid when young, blackening in age. STALK fleshy, more or less central, *flesh in base usually bright yellow.* VEIL present in local species, disappearing or collapsing on stem. VOLVA absent. SPORE PRINT *smoky-black.* Spores long and narrow, spindle-shaped. Cap tissue not amyloid.

THE soft waxy decurrent gills, pallid flesh, and smoky-black spores are the hallmarks of *Gomphidius. Hygrophorus* has waxy gills but the spores are white, while *Chroogomphus* has colored flesh.

In our area *Gomphidius* is associated exclusively with Douglas-fir, and commonly fruits with *Suillus caerulescens, S. ponderosus,* and *S. lakei.* Farther north, however, it occurs with a variety of conifers, including spruce, fir, larch, and hemlock. November rains usually mean *Gomphidius* galore—enormous numbers of fruiting bodies being produced, though not as many as *Chroogomphus.*

Gomphidius species are edible but not widely collected, perhaps because their flesh is soft and decays rapidly, darkens in cooking and becomes slimy. Some people relish them nonetheless. Four species are keyed here.

Key to Gomphidius

1. Usually growing in small clumps with base buried in ground, often with some small, aborted individuals; spores always less than 14µm long .. .. *G. oregonensis*, p. 396
1. Not as above; spores more than 14 µm long 2
2. Stalk with little or no yellow at base *G. smithii* (see *G. oregonensis*, p. 396)
2. Stalk yellow at least at base 3
3. Cap pink to rosy-red .... *G. subroseus*, p. 396
3. Cap not as above .... *G. glutinosus* (see *G. oregonensis*, p. 396)

Gomphidius subroseus (Rosy Gomphidius)

CAP 2.5-7.5 cm broad, convex becoming plane or with uplifted margin in old age; surface smooth, viscid or slimy, pink to rosy-red, spotted grayish in old age. Flesh thick, white becoming grayish, firm or soft. **GILLS** decurrent, soft, waxy, fairly well-spaced, white becoming smoky-gray to blackish in old age. **STALK** up to 7.5 cm long, rather slender, tapering slightly toward base, white or grayish above, pale yellow below, bright yellow at very base, smooth or fibrillose. **VEIL** slimy, thin, disappearing or forming a ring or sheath of slime on the stem which is blackened by falling spores. **SPORE PRINT** black; spores 15-21 × 4.5-7 μm, spindle-shaped, smooth.

HABITAT: Scattered or in small groups, associated with Douglas-fir. Common but seldom abundant, fall through early spring.

EDIBILITY: Edible. Peel off the slimy skin before cooking.

COMMENTS: The rosy-pink cap and small size separate this fungus from other *Gomphidius* species. It shows less yellow in the stem than either *G. oregonensis* or *G. glutinosus,* but more than *G. smithii*. It is easily the most attractive member of its clan.

Gomphidius oregonensis (Oregon Gomphidius)

CAP up to 18 cm broad, convex becoming plane; surface smooth, slimy or viscid, salmon-pink to reddish-brown or purple-gray, usually dingy or dirty, grayish-spotted in old age. Flesh thick, soft, white or grayish, tinted cap color under cuticle. **GILLS** decurrent, soft, waxy, fairly well spaced, white, blackening in age. **STALK** 5-15 cm long, stout, equal or base may be enlarged or tapered, smooth, white above, bright yellow below. **VEIL** slimy, forming a slimy superior ring which blackens from falling spores, or disappears entirely. **SPORE PRINT** black; spores 10-13 × 4.5-8 μm, spindle-shaped, smooth.

HABITAT: Solitary or scattered, usually in small clumps which originate deep in the ground, and which often include one or more aborted fruiting bodies. Common, fall through early spring, associated with Douglas-fir; often mingling with *Suillus* species *(S. caerulescens, S. lakei, S. ponderosus).*

EDIBILITY: Edible. Peel off the slimy skin before cooking.

COMMENTS: This species is easily recognized by the waxy decurrent gills that blacken in age, slimy cap, and brilliant yellow flesh in the lower

Gomphidius oregonensis. Cross-section reveals white flesh in the cap, bright yellow flesh in lower half of stalk. Gills are decurrent. Other *Gomphidius* species are similar but don't often grow in clumps like the one at left.

half of the stalk. The cap color varies according to weather conditions, exposure, and the age of the mushroom. The "Glutinous Gomphidius," *G. glutinosus*, is similar but has larger spores (15-21 μm) and does not normally grow in clumps. A third species, *G. smithii*, is occasionally encountered. It shows little or no yellow in the stalk.

CHROOGOMPHUS

Medium-sized terrestrial mushrooms. CAP convex or conical becoming plane; viscid or dry, often polished. Flesh *colored* (yellow-orange, salmon-buff, etc.). GILLS *usually decurrent*, thick, well-spaced, yellow-orange to ochraceous when young, blackening in age. STALK more or less central, fleshy, dry. VEIL present, fibrillose, usually disappearing. VOLVA absent. SPORE PRINT *smoky-olive to black*. Spores long and narrow, spindle-shaped. Gills with prominent cystidia. Cap tissue amyloid.

AN outstanding fungal feature of our coastal pine forests, *Chroogomphus* (crow-oh-góm-fus) is easily recognized by the thick, decurrent gills, yellow-orange to salmon-colored flesh, and smoky-olive to black spores. They are attractive fungi, brightly colored with a lean, clean look and a tendency to become reddish or wine-colored in old age. The gills and stem are orange-buff but the gills blacken as the spores mature.

Chroogomphus grows strictly with pine (at least in our region), usually in the company of slippery jacks *(Suillus pungens, S. fuscotomentosus*, etc. *)*. They fruit from the onset of the fall rains through the spring, and are especially abundant in dry years when other fungi are scarce. They do not decay as rapidly as *Gomphidius*, but are particularly susceptible to attack by a greenish mold.

Chroogomphus is an excellent genus for beginners, since all species are edible. They become slimy and purple when cooked, but drying gives them a pleasant, chewy texture that is perfect for tomato sauces. At least that is the gospel according to "Saint Ciro," a wondrously demented and exceptionally resourceful toadstool-tester of Sicilian extraction. With a large family to feed and an immense forest of unpicked *Chroogomphus* across the street, he isn't the least bit deterred by their lack of renown. Every year he gathers trunkloads and dries them for summer use. Five species are recorded from California, all of which are keyed below.

Key to Chroogomphus

1. Cap yellow-orange to ochraceous at maturity 2
1. Cap may be orange when young, but grayish-brown to reddish-brown or wine color at maturity 3

2. Cap dry, fibrillose .... *C. tomentosus* (see *C. rutilus*, below)
2. Cap viscid when moist, smooth .... *C. ochraceus* (see *C. rutilus*, below)

3. Stalk robust, patchy-fibrillose; cap soon dry; spore print olive-black .... *C. pseudovinicolor* (see *C. vinicolor*, p. 399)
3. Not as above; if stalk robust, then spore print smoky-black 4

4. Cap typically convex or umbonate to plane; cystidia thin-walled .... *C. rutilus*, below
4. Cap typically conical to broadly conical or convex; cystidia thick-walled .... *C. vinicolor*, p. 399

Chroogomphus rutilus (Pine Mushroom)

CAP 2.5-13 cm broad, convex, sometimes with a low umbo, expanding somewhat in age to plane or even slightly depressed; surface smooth, viscid when moist, glossy when dry; color variable: at first dark olive-brown to grayish-brown, becoming ochraceous, finally reddish-brown or wine-colored. Flesh thick, firm, pale salmon in cap, yellow or yellow-orange in stalk. **GILLS** thick, fairly well-spaced, adnate soon becoming decurrent, dull orange to ochraceous-buff to cinnamon, grayish to black in age. **STALK** up to 20 cm long, less than 2.5 cm thick, solid, tapering toward base, often curved; dry, slightly fibrillose; dull orange aging or stained wine color. **VEIL** dry, fibrillose, forming a hairy, apical zone on stalk or disappearing. **SPORE PRINT** smoky-gray to black; spores 14-22 × 6-7.5 μm, spindle-shaped, smooth. Cystidia on gills thin-walled.

Chroogomphus rutilus, young specimens at left, mature individuals at right. These are rather slender specimens. Note the veil which disappears in age. Decurrent gills are smoky-black at maturity. Flesh is colored, never white. (Ralph Buchsbaum)

HABITAT: Scattered to gregarious, associated with pine. Common to abundant, especially in sandy soil, fall through spring. The largest fruiting is usually in December or January.

EDIBILITY: Edible; excellent dried (see remarks under genus).

COMMENTS: Anyone who hunts pine forests will come across this common mushroom, especially when looking for *Boletus edulis.* It is also frequent in yards where pines have been planted. The colorful mixture of orange, gray, red, and brown, plus the decurrent gills and smoky-black spores make it as distinctive as it is attractive. Both slender and robust forms are common. *Gomphidius viscidus* is an older name for it. *C. ochraceus* is a similar species with a smooth orange to ochraceous cap. *C. tomentosus* has a dry, hairy or woolly orange cap. It is fairly common in the mixed coniferous forests of northern California, but I have not seen it south of San Francisco. For a comparison with *C. vinicolor*, see that species.

Chroogomphus vinicolor (Wine-Colored Pine Mushroom)

CAP 2.5-7.5 cm broad, almost conical when young, often with a central umbo, expanding somewhat in age; surface viscid when moist, shiny when dry, smooth, dull orange or ochraceous when young, becoming

Chroogomphus vinicolor is more slender than *C. rutilus*, with an orange cap when young becoming wine-colored in age. Note decurrent gills, which are smoky-black at maturity.

reddish-brown and then dark wine color. Flesh thick, firm, salmon-orange aging or staining wine-red. **GILLS** well spaced, thick, pale yellow-orange to dull orange, then dusted gray to black by spores, adnate soon becoming decurrent. **STALK** long and slender, to 20 cm long, solid, slightly fibrillose, dry, often curved, orange-buff to yellow-orange becoming wine-colored in age. **VEIL** dry, fibrillose, forming a hairy apical zone on stalk or disappearing. **SPORE PRINT** olive-black; spores 17-23 × 4.5-7.5 μm, spindle-shaped, smooth. Cystidia on gills thick-walled.

HABITAT: Scattered to gregarious under or near pine, fall through spring. Very common; more abundant than *C. rutilus*, at least in my experience.

EDIBILITY: Edible; good when dried (see comments under genus).

COMMENTS: Both *C. vinicolor* and *C. rutilus* undergo a confusing series of changes as they mature, making color distinctions between them difficult and rather arbitrary. In general, *C. vinicolor* tends to be more orange when young and more wine-colored in age, more conical and more slender. The most reliable difference, however, is microscopic—the protruding sterile cells (cystidia) on the gills are thick-walled in *C. vinicolor*, thin-walled in *C. rutilus*.

C. pseudovinicolor is a large, robust species with a smooth, dry, glossy cap and thick, scaly-fibrillose stem. I have found it several times with ponderosa pine, but never in large numbers. It is also edible.

Boletes

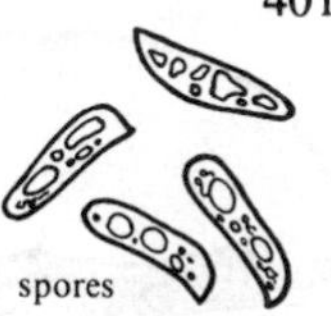

BOLETACEAE

BOLETES have a spongelike layer of tubes on the underside of the cap instead of gills. Otherwise they resemble agarics: medium to large terrestrial fungi with a fleshy cap and central stalk. Polypores also possess a tube layer, but are tough and leathery and grow on wood. The few fleshy, terrestrial polypores have an eccentric (off-center) stalk.

The boletes produce spores on basidia which line the inner surfaces of the tubes. These tubes are arranged vertically so that the spores, when discharged, drop into the air. The mouths of the tubes are known as the **pores**. They are sometimes stuffed with a pith when young, making the pore surface appear smooth. In some species the pores are arranged in rows which radiate from the stalk, giving a somewhat gill-like effect. This is carried to an extreme in *Phylloporus rhodoxanthus* (p. 392), a "bolete" with true gills, which serves to illustrate why boletes are thought to have more in common with gilled mushrooms than with, say, the corals or teeth fungi.

Boletes used to be lumped together in one giant, unwieldy genus, *Boletus*. Numerous genera are now recognized, the most prominent being *Suillus, Leccinum, Tylopilus,* and *Boletus*. The term "bolete," however, is applicable to any member of the Boletaceae, not just those still retained in *Boletus*.

The salient characters for identification are much the same as for agarics. It is especially important, however, to note color changes on the pore surface, cap, stalk, and flesh. Many boletes will stain blue or greenish-blue when bruised.

Another important feature is the type of ornamentation on the stalk (p. 402). In *Boletus* and *Tylopilus* the upper portion may be **reticulate** or "netted": covered with a network of fine veins. In *Leccinum* it is always **scabrous:** decorated with rough tufts or scales **(scabers)** which typically darken at maturity. In *Suillus* the stalk is frequently speckled with brown spots called **glandular dots**. These exude a resinous substance that will stain your fingers brown.

Spore color ranges from yellow to olive, brown, or reddish-brown. A spore print is easily obtained, but pigmentation in the tubes may stain the paper, making the spore color look brighter than it actually is. The spore shape is characteristically "boletoid": long and narrowly elliptical or spindle-shaped, inequilateral in profile. Viewed through the microscope, a bolete spore is an unusually large, handsome, and healthy-looking specimen, somewhat reminiscent of a surfer with a good tan.

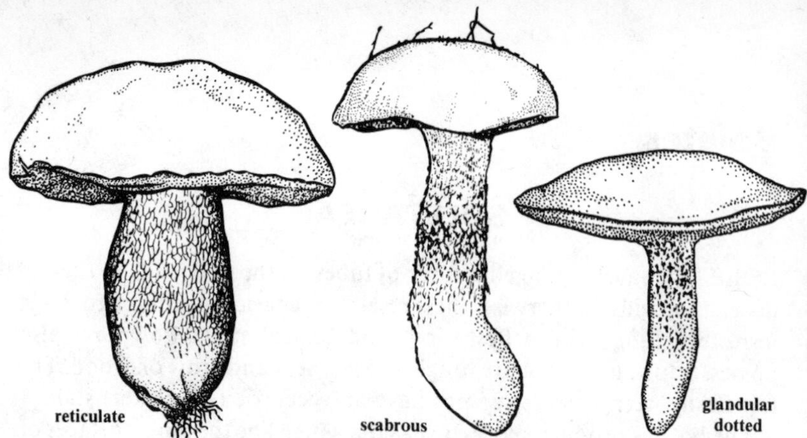

Stalk ornamentation in the boletes. Left to right: *Boletus edulis, Leccinum manzanitae, Suillus pungens.*

The boletes are one of the safest groups for the table, as well as one of the most substantial and rewarding. Only a few members of the genus *Boletus* are poisonous. Since they are large and fleshy, boletes are a popular picnicground for maggots. These may enter in the usual manner, via the stem, or surreptitiously, through the tubes. Always check for worms in the field, and cut away soggy or infested areas (assuming you already know the species) before popping them in your basket. That way you are less likely to have a maggot-infested mush two days later. Some people peel off the tubes as well—when old and spongy they are mostly water anyway. Also, boletes are vulnerable to attack by a variety of moldy-looking parasites. Discard any such individuals when picking for the table. For more on hunting boletes, see p. 434.

The boletes are a conspicuous and colorful component of our woodland fungi. The cap can be very hefty and the tubes are usually brightly colored. The vast majority are mycorrhizal. More than 80 species are known from California. Though not complete (what book is?) and more than a trifle expensive (what book isn't?), *California Mushrooms: A Field Guide to the Boletes* by Harry Thiers is a definitive must for the serious and self-respecting bolete buff.

Key to the Boletaceae

1. Tubes disoriented, not vertically arranged; spore print unobtainable; shape often irregular; usually buried in humus; rare .. *Gastroboletus*, p. 433
1. Tubes vertically arranged; spore print obtainable; usually above ground when mature; common 2

2. Veil present (check young specimens if possible) 3
2. Veil absent 4

3. Veil bright yellow, dry, cottony or powdery, covering cap when young; pores bruising greenish-blue; rare .... *Pulveroboletus*, p. 431
3. Not as above; common .... *Suillus*, p. 403

4. Stalk with rough scales or tufts (scabers) which are usually dark brown to black at maturity; pores rarely yellow .... *Leccinum*, p. 429
4. Not as above 5

5. Stalk more or less equal, with resinous glandular dots ... *Suillus*, p. 403
5. Glandular dots absent 6

6. Spore print pale yellow; stalk usually hollow at maturity; cap *and* stalk brown to orange-brown; rare .... *Gyroporus*, p. 432
6. Not as above; spore print not yellow 7

7. Spore print reddish-brown to reddish-chocolate to flesh color; uncommon .... *Tylopilus*, p. 427
7. Spore print olive to brown; common .... *Boletus*, p. 411

SUILLUS (SLIPPERY JACKS)

Medium to fairly large terrestrial boletes *associated with conifers.* CAP fleshy, *usually viscid or slimy.* PORES rarely bruising blue. STALK rarely bulbous or reticulate, *often with resinous brown glandular dots.* VEIL *often present.* SPORE PRINT *olive to brown.* Spores elliptical to spindle-shaped, smooth. Bundles of cystidia on inner surfaces of tubes staining dark brown to black in potassium hydroxide.

AS a rule slippery jacks have either a veil or a glandular-dotted stem or both. In addition, the cap is usually viscid or slimy. An exception is *S. brevipes,* with "invisible" glandular dots, no veil, and a slimy cap. A related genus, *Fuscoboletinus,* is also furnished with a veil, but has red-brown to chocolate spores and has not been found in California.

Ixocomus is a European synonym for *Suillus,* but all species will be found in older books under *Boletus.* It is probably the most primitive genus in the Boletaceae, leading to *Boletus* on the one hand and to the Gomphidiaceae (via *Fuscoboletinus*) on the other. *Suillus* splits nicely into two natural groups. In the first (genus *Boletinus* of some) a veil is present and the pores may be arranged radially. In our area this group occurs with Douglas-fir, often accompanied by species of *Gomphidius.* The second group has either a slimy cap, glandular-dotted stem, or both. In our area it grows exclusively with pine, often interspersed with *Chroogomphus.*

Suillus fruits throughout the mushroom season, from fall through early spring, often in mind-boggling abundance. It is a good group for the beginner since none are known to be poisonous. Only a few species are worth eating, however. *S. brevipes* and *S. pungens* are the best of the local varieties, but they dry poorly. About 25 species are known from

California, all mycorrhizal with various conifers. Seven are keyed below. Many more occur in the Sierras and northern California, where there is a greater diversity of conifers.

Key to Suillus

1. Veil present, or at least a roll of cottony tissue on the cap margin 2
1. Veil absent 6
2. Associated with Douglas-fir; lower portion of stalk usually staining blue or greenish when cut 3
2. Associated with pine; stalk never staining blue 5
3. Cap covered with pink to brick-red scales or fibrils ..... *S. lakei,* below
3. Not as above 4
4. Veil viscid, yellow to orange at least before breaking (check young specimens) .... *S. ponderosus* (see *S. caerulescens*, p. 405)
4. Not as above; veil pallid or white, moist .... *S. caerulescens*, p. 405
5. Cap white to olive-gray when young; ring absent ... *S. pungens,* p. 408
5. Cap more or less honey-colored; ring present but often obscure .... *S. pseudobrevipes*, p. 406
6. Glandular dots on stalk absent or very inconspicuous; pores pale yellow to olive-yellow .... *S. brevipes*, p. 410
6. Not as above 7
7. Cap smooth, slimy to viscid, white to olive-gray to cinnamon-orange, etc.; pores white when young, often with milky droplets .. *S. pungens*, p. 408
7. Cap usually fibrillose, dry to viscid, brownish; pores orange-buff when young; droplets sometimes present .... *S. fuscotomentosus*, p. 407

Suillus lakei (Lake's Suillus)

CAP 5-15 cm broad, convex to plane; surface dry or slightly viscid, covered with brick-red to reddish-brown to pinkish fibrils or scales on a yellowish-orange to brownish background. Flesh thick, yellow, discoloring pinkish. **PORES** large, yellow when young, darker in age, usually discoloring reddish or dingy reddish-brown where bruised, somewhat radially arranged. **STALK** to 8 cm long, more or less equal, dry, stout, solid, colored like the pores above and like the cap (or brownish) below; interior usually staining weakly blue-green near base. **VEIL** white, dry, forming a ring or ragged zone on stalk, sometimes leaving remnants on cap margin. **SPORE PRINT** olive-brown; spores 8-11 × 3-4 µm, spindle-shaped, smooth.

HABITAT: Usually in groups in woods, always with Douglas-fir nearby. Common, fall and winter. It prefers poor, exposed soil and is common on roadbanks.

Suillus lakei, mature specimens. Cap has reddish to reddish-brown scales. Note the ring on stalk and veil remnants on cap margin.

EDIBILITY: Edible but of poor quality.

COMMENTS: This is one *Suillus* that does not have a viscid cap (except in wet weather). The dark reddish cap scales, presence of a ring, and association with Douglas-fir set it apart. When young it is quite attractive, the scales being often more pink than red. Heavy rain will wash them off, however, and gelatinize the cap surface. Then the yellow to orange-brown background color predominates, making it look like *S. caerulescens.*

Suillus caerulescens (Blue-Staining Suillus)

CAP 5-18 cm broad, convex to plane; surface viscid, with scattered fibrils, scales, or streaks, usually dull reddish-brown toward the center and orange-brown to yellowish near the margin, but color quite variable, may even develop greenish stains in cold weather. Flesh thick, pale yellow, sometimes discoloring pinkish. **PORES** yellow when young, darkening with age, discoloring dingy brown. **STALK** to 10 cm long, stout, equal or tapering downward, solid, dry, same color as pores above ring, dingier and fibrillose below; interior usually staining blue or green when cut near base. **VEIL** moist, white or pallid, forming a distinct ring, or leaving remnants on cap margin. **SPORE PRINT** dingy cinnamon-brown; spores 8-11 × 3-5 μm, spindle-shaped, smooth.

HABITAT: Scattered to gregarious in woods, associated with Douglas-fir. Sporadically abundant from the onset of the rains through early spring. The largest fruiting is usually in late November.

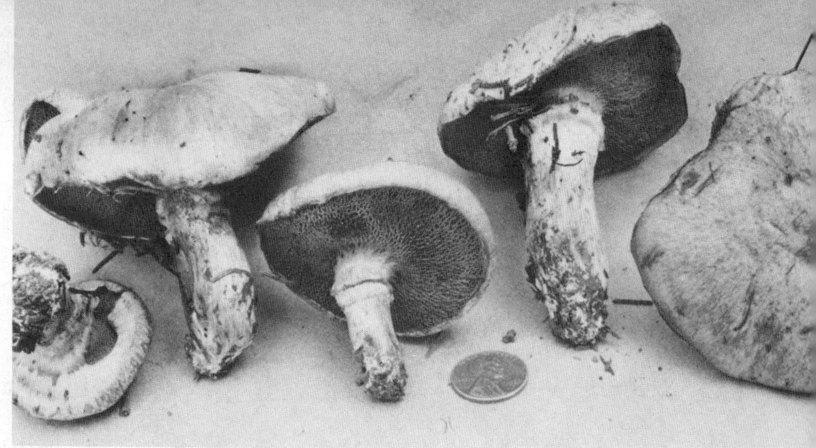

Suillus ponderosus (see *S. caerulescens*). Note the veil, which forms a ring, and the nearly smooth cap. *S. caerulescens* is very similar. Both grow with Douglas-fir.

EDIBILITY: Edible, but far from incredible.

COMMENTS: This is a very common species; indeed, you will soon tire of finding it if you hunt Douglas-fir woods often. The orange-brown to yellowish cap, presence of a veil, and association with Douglas-fir are the key characteristics. *S. ponderosus* is equally common in our area, and is an equally mediocre addition to a meal. It differs by its viscid yellow to orange veil (before breaking) and smoother cap, which is often more yellow. Its name refers to its size, which is sometimes gigantic (ponderous) and not to the fact that it isn't associated with ponderosa pine. In fact, it is associated with Douglas-fir just like *S. caerulescens,* and the two often mix company.

Suillus pseudobrevipes

CAP 5-15 cm broad, convex to plane; surface slimy or viscid, smooth, often appearing streaked, honey-colored to yellow-brown, darker in age; margin usually hung with veil remnants. Flesh thick, white to pale yellow, not bruising, odor mild. **PORES** yellow, darker in age, not bruising. **STALK** to 7.5 cm long but usually much shorter, relatively thick, equal, dry, white when young, then yellow, glandular dots obscure, darkening slowly with age. **VEIL** white to dingy lavender, usually forming a collapsed ring on stalk or a sheath over the base, sometimes only remnants on cap margin. **SPORE PRINT** pale brown; spores 7-9 × 2.5-3.5 μm, spindle-shaped, smooth.

HABITAT: Scattered under ponderosa pine, fall and winter; fruiting every year at Henry Cowell Redwoods State Park but otherwise uncommon.

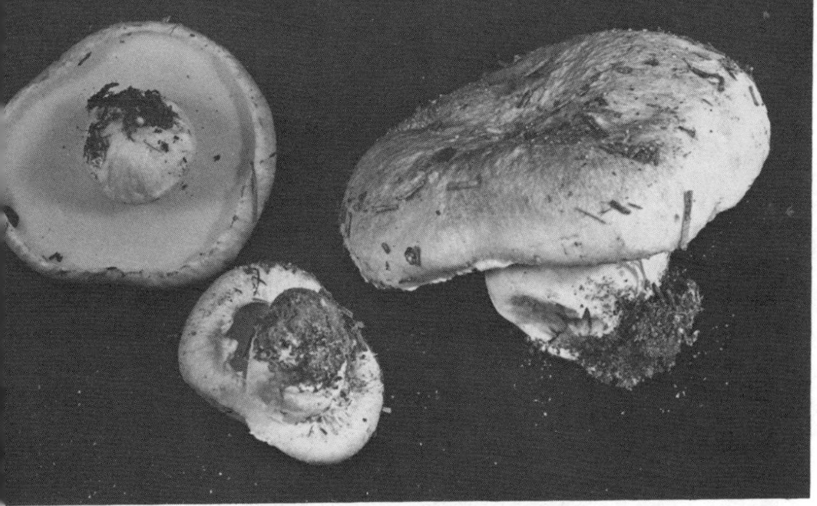

Suillus pseudobrevipes. The veil is breaking in button (center) and has practically disappeared in specimen at left, but veil remnants cling to cap margin. (Joel Leivick)

EDIBILITY: Presumably edible. I haven't tried it.

COMMENTS: This species has a short, stocky stem like its namesake, *S. brevipes,* but the presence of a veil and paler cap color distinguish it. Sometimes the veil persists as a roll of cottony tissue on the cap margin instead of forming a ring. On the Monterey Peninsula where there are stands of bishop pine, you may find *S. glandulosipes.* It also has a cottony roll of tissue on the cap margin, but as its name implies, the stem is prominently glandular-dotted. The remote stands of sugar pine in Los Padres National Forest near Cone Peak may harbor *S. brunnescens,* which has a smooth, white cap becoming chocolate in age, and an evanescent veil. Common in northern California under pine is *S. umbonatus.* It has a viscid, umbonate, olive-buff cap, sticky-gelatinous bandlike ring (veil), and slender stalk with obscure glandular dots.

Suillus fuscotomentosus

CAP 4-15 cm broad, convex to nearly plane; surface viscid when wet, otherwise dry, olive-brown to cinnamon with darker (fuscous) fibrils or small scales, often appearing streaked in age. Flesh thick, yellow to orange-buff, not bruising, taste rather unpleasant. **PORES** orange-buff when young, yellowish-buff to olive in old age, not changing when bruised. **STALK** to 12 cm long, equal, solid, smooth, yellow to brownish-buff, often pinkish-orange or orange toward base; glandular dots usually conspicuous. **VEIL** absent. **SPORE PRINT** olive-brown; spores 9-12 × 3-4 μm, spindle-shaped, smooth.

HABITAT: Scattered to gregarious, often in large numbers, associated with pine. Common to abundant in fall and winter, especially in sandy

Suillus fuscotomentosus. This abundant species has fibrillose brownish cap scales, no veil, and glandular dots (not visible in picture) on stalk. It usually grows with knobcone and ponderosa pine.

soil. It shows a preference for knobcone and ponderosa pine while *S. pungens* is partial to Monterey pine.

EDIBILITY: Edible, but not choice. Like the color term "fuscous," it leaves a lot to the imagination.

COMMENTS: This common bolete was originally described from Santa Cruz County. The pores are never white as in *S. pungens,* and the brownish or grayish-brown cap fibrils are also distinctive. It is more abundant inland than *S. pungens,* and correspondingly less common along the coast. *S. acerbus* is a very similar species with a viscid, less fibrillose cap, supposedly associated with Monterey pine. However, I often encounter individuals which could be referred to either species. A third species with a fibrillose cap, *S. tomentosus,* is more distinct—its flesh and pores bruise bluish. It is rare in our area but common farther north.

Suillus pungens (Pungent Slippery Jack)

CAP to 18 cm broad, convex to nearly plane; surface smooth, slimy or viscid, white when very young, soon olive-gray, then yellow, tawny-cinnamon, orange-brown, or red-brown, often streaked with a combination of these colors; margin sometimes with a slight roll of cottony tissue when young. Flesh thick, white becoming lemon-yellow, soft, not bruising; odor pungent. **PORES** white when young with milky white droplets in wet weather, becoming yellow and finally dark yellow-brown, not bruising. **STALK** to 13 cm long, equal, dry, smooth, with

Suillus pungens. Note glandular dots on stem, slimy cap, whitish droplets on pores, and pine needles. It always grows with pine. (Nancy Burnett)

conspicuous brown glandular dots; white when young, yellow in age. **VEIL** absent. **SPORE PRINT** brown; spores 9-10 × 3-3.5 μm, spindle-shaped, smooth.

HABITAT: Scattered to densely gregarious, sometimes in clusters, associated with pine. Usually abundant in fall and winter but can be found other times as well. It is said to be restricted to Monterey and knobcone pine, but I have found it fruiting with *Chroogomphus pseudovinicolor* under a large, solitary ponderosa pine. It is endemic to the central California coast.

EDIBILITY: Edible. Disdained by some mycologists due to its "harsh, unpleasant, subnauseous" taste. Apparently they haven't cooked it properly because I know people who pronounce it delicious. Its soft flesh is a bigger drawback than its flavor. Since it occurs in such quantity, it is definitely worth experimenting with. To remove the slime, simply peel off the skin.

Suillus pungens. Note variation in cap color. Cap is slimy, white becoming grayish-olive, then yellow to cinnamon. Pores are beaded with whitish droplets when young. Glandular dots are visible on specimen at left. (Joel Leivick)

COMMENTS: This is our most prolific bolete, appearing in colossal quantities wherever there are pines. The remarkable series of color changes it undergoes is apt to baffle the beginner; at the same time, when several individuals are present it affords an instantaneous means of recognition. The milky white droplets on the pore surface of young specimens are also distinctive.

S. pungens vies with the glutinous gomphidius (*Gomphidius* spp.) and the ivory waxy cap (*Hygrophorus eburneus*) for the title of "slipperiest and slimiest fungus among us." An organic version of hockey (or caroms) can be played on a wet surface, using the cap of a young *S. pungens* for a puck. Overmature individuals, on the other hand, are more aptly called *S. "spongens"* than *S. pungens.* They literally seethe with fat, agitated maggots and sag with so much excess water they positively demand to be wrung out like a sponge. A related edible species, *S. granulatus,* has a cinnamon cap that is never white or olive-gray. It has a worldwide distribution but is supplanted in our area by *S. pungens.*

Suillus brevipes (Short-Stemmed Slippery Jack)

CAP 5-13 cm broad, convex to plane; surface smooth, slimy or viscid, dark vinaceous-brown when young, fading in age to red-brown or cinnamon-brown, sometimes appearing streaked. Flesh thick, white, yellow in age, not bruising; odor mild. **PORES** yellow when young, olive-yellow in old age, not bruising. **STALK** to 7 cm long but typically shorter; equal, dry, white to pale yellow, glandular dots absent or barely visible. **VEIL** absent. **SPORE PRINT** brown; spores 7-10 × 3-4 μm, spindle-shaped, smooth.

Suillus brevipes. Note dark brown slimy-viscid cap, relatively short stem, absence of both glandular dots and a veil. It always grows with pine.

HABITAT: In groups or troops under pine, fall and winter. Widely distributed but rare in Santa Cruz County; more common on the Monterey Peninsula, abundant in northern California.

EDIBILITY: Edible and good, the best of the local slippery jacks. Peel the slimy pellicle before cooking.

COMMENTS: This is perhaps the most common *Suillus* in California, but is largely replaced in our area by *S. pungens* (due to the presence of Monterey and knobcone pine). *S. brevipes* never shows the olive-gray color characteristic of young *S. pungens* and lacks the glandular dots. The smooth, dark slimy cap and more or less equal stem separate it from *Boletus*. The epithet *brevipes* is apt: it means "short-stemmed."

BOLETUS

Medium to large terrestrial boletes. CAP fleshy, *usually dry*, sometimes fissured or cracked. PORES typically white, yellow, or red, often bruising blue. STALK fleshy, bulbous or equal, thick or slender, *often reticulate*, neither glandular-dotted nor scabrous. VEIL *absent*. SPORE PRINT *brown to olive-brown*. Spores elliptical to spindle-shaped, smooth.

IF your bolete is not a *Suillus, Leccinum, Tylopilus, Gyroporus, Pulveroboletus,* or *Gastroboletus*, then chances are it's a *Boletus*. In other words, it is much easier to characterize what *Boletus* isn't than what it is. There is neither a veil nor glandular dots as in *Suillus*, and the stem is not scabrous as in *Leccinum*. The spore print is neither yellow as in *Gyroporus*, nor reddish as in *Tylopilus*.

Boletus splits neatly into two natural groups. The first includes the large, heavy forms like *B. edulis*. The stem is thick and usually reticulate, the pores small, the different kinds relatively easy to recognize. They are fairly finicky as to mycorrhizal associates and have exceedingly erratic fruiting habits. Heavy rains in October or November may elicit a bumper crop of nearly every species, but if the rain is delayed until December, they may not fruit at all.

Species belonging to the second group (genus *Xerocomus* of some authors) are smaller, with a dry, minutely velvety (**subtomentose**) cap which often cracks in age, exposing the flesh beneath. The pores are usually large and the stem relatively slender. They are cosmopolitan, have a much longer growing season, but rarely fruit in large numbers. Identification is sometimes difficult without chemicals and a microscope.

Boletus boasts among its ranks some of the finest and most flavorful of fleshy fungi. First and foremost, of course, is that fabulous fungus cherished by the Europeans above all others—the king boletus or cep, *B. edulis*. The butter boletus *(B. appendiculatus)* is also excellent. On the other hand, some species are toxic and poisoning from *B. satanas* may even require hospitalization. A general rule of thumb is to avoid all those whose pores bruise blue. But this eliminates some very good species (such as *B. appendiculatus*), and in California it can be amended to: avoid those blue-staining species with pink, red, or orange pores. This does *not* mean to munch on them indiscriminately, however—the edibility of some species has yet to be established and even raw *B. edulis* can cause trouble.

The oak-madrone woodlands of the Santa Cruz Mountains support a unique and bountiful *Boletus* flora. Prominent species include *B. satanas, B. erythropus, B. appendiculatus, B. aereus,* and *B. flaviporus* (along with *Leccinum manzanitae*). Pine forests, on the other hand, are favored by *B. edulis*.

When conditions are favorable, *Boletus* species can be harvested by the bushel, and are easily preserved by slicing and drying. But remember: if you should stumble into a "*Boletus* bonanza," take only as many as you can use. This will allow others to share your luck and aside from the good social practice it builds, it will test your will power to its limits!

Even in its modern sense *Boletus* is a large and complex genus. More than 30 species are known from California, 13 of which are described here.

Key to Boletus

1. Small (cap 5 cm broad or less); taste peppery .... *B. piperatus*, p. 414
1. Size variable; taste may be distinctive, but not peppery 2

2. Pore surface red, pink, or orange when fresh, turning blue or bluish-black when bruised 3
2. Not as above 6

3. Stalk reticulate above, often bulbous 4
3. Stalk not reticulate, not bulbous 5

4. Stalk large and bulbous; cap gray to pinkish-gray ... *B. satanas*, p. 422
4. Stalk not bulbous; cap red-brown *B. pulcherrimus* (see *B. satanas*, p. 422)

5. Cap pink to purple-red ...... *B. amygdalinus* (see *B. erythropus*, p. 424)
5. Cap some shade of brown .... *B. erythropus*, p. 424

6. Pores typically staining blue or blue-green when bruised (sometimes weakly) 7
6. Pores not staining blue or blue-green when bruised 15

7. Medium-sized to large; pores minute, typically less than 1 mm in diameter; stalk typically 2 cm thick or more 8
7. Small to medium-sized; pores typically 1 mm or more in diameter; stalk typically 2 cm thick or less 11

8. Stalk finely reticulate above; taste mild 9
8. Stalk not reticulate; taste mild or bitter 10

9. Cap red to pink, occasionally fading to yellow .... *B. regius* (see *B. appendiculatus*, p. 420)
9. Cap some shade of brown or reddish-brown *B. appendiculatus*, p. 420

10. Cap reddish to red-brown; taste typically mild ... *B. dryophilus*, p. 418
10. Cap not reddish; taste latently bitter .... *B. "marshii"*, p. 421

11. Stalk with reddish tints, at least in age 12
11. Stalk yellow to buff, no red present .... *B. subtomentosus*, p. 415

12. Cap reddish to red-brown; stalk relatively short and often pinched at base; associated with oak; uncommon .... *B. dryophilus*, p. 418
12. Not as above; cap olive-gray to brown or nearly black 13

13. Cap dark olive-gray to black, with a frosted appearance when young; often reddish (at least toward margin) in age; surface not usually cracking . ... *B. zelleri*, p. 417
13. Not as above; surface of cap usually cracking conspicuously 14

14. Fissures in cap usually pinkish or reddish-tinted, at least toward margin; spores not truncate .... *B. chrysenteron*, p. 416
14. Cracks rarely pinkish-tinted; spores truncate .... *B. truncatus* (see *B. chrysenteron*, p. 416)

15. Pores pinkish-flesh to dark brown, staining darker brown when bruised; spore print flesh color .... (see *Tylopilus indecisus*, p. 428)
15. Not as above 16

16. Medium-sized to large; pores white when young, dull yellow to olive or even brownish in old age; stalk reticulate, thick 17
16. Not as above 18

17. Cap dark brown to nearly black; associated with oak *B. aereus*, p. 426
17. Cap red-brown to brown, pale brown, or nearly white; associated mostly with pine, occasionally oak .... *B. edulis*, p. 424

18. Cap viscid to slimy 19
18. Cap not viscid 20

19. Associated with pine; cap dark brown when young, dull cinnamon in age; pores not brilliant yellow .... (see *Suillus brevipes*, p. 410)
19. Associated with hardwoods; cap reddish to cinnamon; pores brilliant yellow .... *B. flaviporus*, p. 419

20. Cap dull brown to dark brown or black 21
20. Cap red to purplish .... *B. coccyginus* (see *B. citriniporus*, p. 418)

21. Stalk with reddish granules or entirely red .... *B. zelleri*, p. 417
21. Stalk without any red 22

22. Cap dull brown to yellow-brown, olive-brown, occasionally reddish-brown or cinnamon-brown .... *B. subtomentosus*, p. 415
22. Cap dark brown to nearly black .... *B. citriniporus*, p. 418

Boletus piperatus (Peppery Boletus)

CAP 2.5-5 cm broad, convex to plane; surface slightly viscid when moist, smooth, yellow-brown to cinnamon or reddish-brown. Flesh thin, yellowish-buff to pinkish, taste very peppery. **PORES** reddish-brown or reddish-copper, not bruising blue; tubes tawny-yellow to reddish-yellow. **STALK** to 7 cm long, slender, equal or tapering downward, dry, smooth, colored like cap or more yellowish, base usually brighter yellow with yellow mycelium. **SPORE PRINT** cinnamon-brown; spores 8-12 × 3-4 μm, spindle-shaped, smooth.

HABITAT: Scattered under conifers, mostly fruiting in the fall. I have found it under Douglas-fir and pine in the Santa Cruz Mountains, but it becomes increasingly rare southward.

EDIBILITY: Uncertain. Not as bitter as the peppery *Russula* and *Lactarius* species, possibly useful as a spice. According to one source, however, the peppery taste is lost when cooked and according to another it is mildly poisonous.

COMMENTS: Our smallest bolete, suggestive of a *Suillus,* but lacking a veil or glandular dots. It is viewed by some mycologists as a possible "missing link" between *Suillus* and *Boletus.* If you have any doubt as to its identity, just chew a small piece of the cap for a couple minutes!

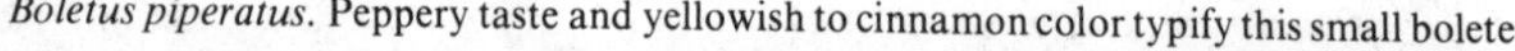

Boletus piperatus. Peppery taste and yellowish to cinnamon color typify this small bolete.

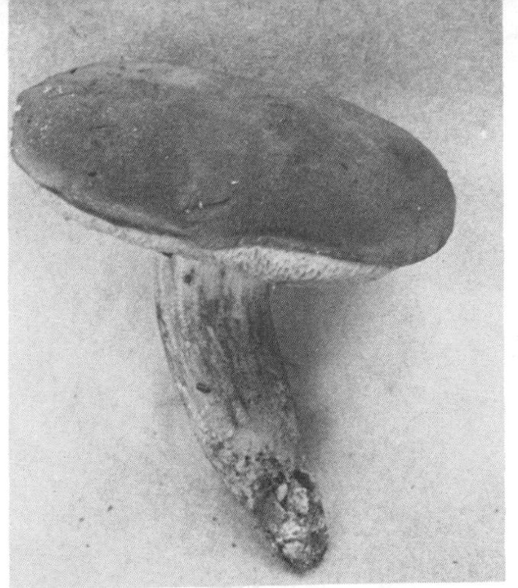
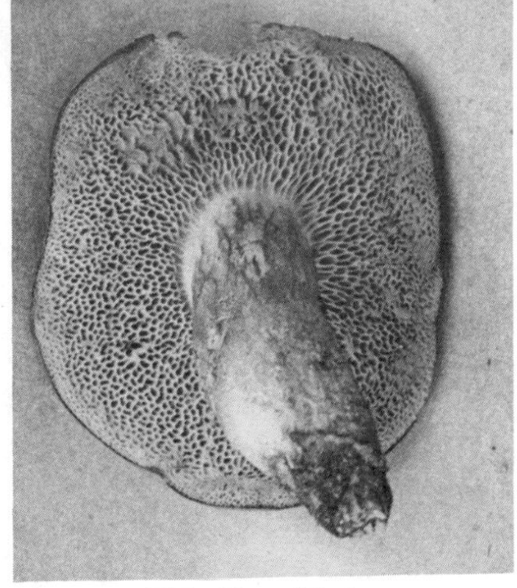

Boletus subtomentosus. **Left:** View of the dry, dull brown cap. **Right:** View of the large yellow pores which may or may not bruise bluish.

Boletus subtomentosus

CAP to 12 cm broad but usually smaller, convex to plane; surface dry, minutely velvety (subtomentose), sometimes cracking near the margin, yellow or pallid in the cracks; color variable: dull yellow-brown to drab olive-brown, darker in age, sometimes reddish in wet weather. Flesh white to pale yellow, sometimes blueing slightly when exposed. **PORES** large (1-2 mm in diameter), bright yellow, changing weakly to blue or green when injured or not changing at all. **STALK** to 14 cm long, relatively slender, more or less equal, smooth, dry, yellow above, often darker below. **SPORE PRINT** olive-brown; spores $11.5\text{-}16 \times 3.5\text{-}5\ \mu m$, spindle-shaped, smooth.

HABITAT: Solitary or in small groups in woods, showing a preference for poor soil (e.g., along road cuts). Common, fall through early spring, but never abundant.

EDIBILITY: Edible but not choice. For some reason I've never been inspired to try it.

COMMENTS: This uninteresting but ubiquitous bolete does not show red on either the cap or stem, in contrast to *B. chrysenteron.* In addition the cap doesn't crack so much. *B. spadiceus* is an equally uninteresting and ubiquitous bolete. It grows in the same places, at the same time, and has the same general appearance. True, the cap tends to be more reddish-brown and the pores may blue more readily, but the only way to separate it with certainty is to apply a drop of ammonium hydroxide to the cap surface. If it gives a fleeting blue-green to blue-black reaction, it is *B. spadiceus;* if not, then *B. subtomentosus.* Since neither is worth eating, the distinction is academic. Inundating little brown boletes with ammonium hydroxide may be your idea of fun, but it's not mine.

Boletus chrysenteron. The cap cuticle of this species and its relative *B. truncatus* cracks conspicuously in age. In *B. chrysenteron* the cracks reveal pinkish-tinted flesh near cap margin. Note how the pores bruise blue.

Boletus chrysenteron (Red-Cracked Boletus)

CAP 4-10 cm broad, convex to plane; surface dry, minutely velvety when young, conspicuously cracked or fissured in age, at least near margin; dark brown to dark grayish-olive to dull grayish-brown, paler in age, pinkish tints often visible in the cracks along margin. Flesh fairly thick, yellowish, sometimes bruising blue. **PORES** rather large, yellow to greenish-yellow or dingy brownish, bruising blue or greenish (but sometimes weakly). **STALK** to 13 cm long, equal or tapering downward, smooth, dry, longitudinally ridged or striate, color variable, but typically a mixture of yellow and red (yellow with reddish fibrils or yellow above and red below). **SPORE PRINT** olive-brown; spores 12-13.5 × 5-6 µm, spindle-shaped, smooth.

HABITAT: Solitary or in groups in wooded areas, often near trails. Common and ubiquitous, fall through spring.

EDIBILITY: Edible, but mediocre.

COMMENTS: The conspicuously fissured cap with pinkish tints near the margin and yellow pores usually bruising blue are the hallmarks of this cosmopolitan bolete. It is sometimes confused with *B. zelleri* which does not normally develop cracks on the cap.

There are several related species which are difficult to differentiate, including *B. truncatus* (=*B. porosporus* var. *americanus*), a common species with truncate spores and pallid to yellow (rarely pinkish) flesh in the cracks on the cap; and *Tylopilus amylosporus,* uncommon, with dark reddish-brown, erratically amyloid spores and pallid flesh in the cracks. Since they're not worth eating, it hardly matters whether you identify them correctly, unless you aspire to be a professional boletologist. All of the above are prone to attack by a bright yellow parasitic fungus (*Sepedonium chrysospermum,* p. 624), which eventually engulfs the entire fruiting body, making it look like a very sick puffball.

Boletus zelleri (Zeller's Boletus)

CAP 2.5-13 cm broad, convex to plane; surface dry, with a somewhat frosted or powdered appearance when young; black, dark gray, or fuscous, reddening somewhat in age, especially toward margin; surface not usually cracking. Flesh thick, white to pale yellow, sometimes blueing, odor and taste mild. **PORES** olive-yellow to dark yellow, usually (but not always) blueing when bruised. **STALK** to 10 cm long, equal or swollen toward base, dry, yellow with delicate red granules when young, dark red throughout in age. **SPORE PRINT** olive-brown; spores 12-16 × 4-5.5 μm, spindle-shaped, smooth.

HABITAT: Scattered or in groups in woods of all kinds. Common in fall and winter, even spring. One of the few boletes with a tolerance for redwood. I have even found it growing on a redwood stump!

EDIBILITY: Edible. Several books rate it highly. In my experience, however, it cooks up slimy and tasteless.

COMMENTS: The sensational combination of black, yellow, blue, and red makes this our most colorful bolete. *B. chrysenteron* and *B.*

Boletus zelleri. Red stem, yellow pores that usually bruise blue, and dark gray to black or reddish-black cap set apart this beautiful bolete. Specimen at left center has debris clinging to its stem.

truncatus are not so highly colored and have more cracks on the cap. *B. citriniporus* does not have a red stem. The largest fruiting I have seen was at Forest of Nisene Marks State Park.

Boletus dryophilus (Oak-Loving Boletus)

CAP to 10 cm broad, convex to plane; surface dry, minutely velvety when young, often cracking in age; reddish-brown to dark red, but sometimes masked with a coating of minute olive-brown hairs. Flesh thick, yellow, erratically blueing when exposed. **PORES** olive-yellow, blueing when bruised. **STALK** to 7 cm long, rather short, often pinched at base but otherwise equal; dry, yellow above, reddish below, darker in age. **SPORE PRINT** brown; spores 12-16 × 5.5-8 μm, spindle-shaped, smooth.

HABITAT: Solitary or in small groups in humus under live oak, fall and winter, not common. Known only from coastal California south of San Francisco. I have collected it in Santa Cruz and Carmel.

EDIBILITY: Unknown.

COMMENTS: An infrequently encountered member of the *B. chrysenteron-B. subtomentosus* group, this species tends to be stouter than its relatives and has so far been found only with oak. The dark reddish-brown cap color is unusual. *B. smithii* also has a reddish-brown cap and is common in coniferous woods north of San Francisco. Its stalk may be narrowed at the base, but there is usually a bright red band around the apex.

Boletus citriniporus

CAP to 7.5 cm broad, convex to plane; surface dry, smooth, usually minutely velvety, dark brown to nearly black. Flesh white or pallid, not bruising blue. **PORES** small, brilliant yellow, not staining blue when injured. **STALK** to 7.5 cm long, rather slender, equal or enlarged below with a pinched base; dry, smooth, reticulate only at very apex or not at all; white or pallid, yellow at apex. **SPORE PRINT** olive-brown; spores 11-13.5 × 3.5-4.5 μm, spindle-shaped, smooth.

HABITAT: Solitary or in small groups in mixed woods and under oak. Infrequent, fall and winter.

EDIBILITY: Unknown, but probably harmless.

COMMENTS: The brilliant yellow unchanging pores, dark brown cap, and pallid stem (with no traces of red) are characteristic. The cap is neither viscid nor reddish as in *B. flaviporus.* An unidentified species with a dark brown cap and bright yellow, unchanging pores also occurs. It is larger than *B. citriniporus,* and has a yellow, reticulate stalk. I have collected it repeatedly under a live oak near Santa Cruz, but have found it nowhere else. It is edible and delicious.

Other species with a dry cap and unchanging yellow pores include *B. coccyginus,* cap red to purple-red, rare; and *B. mirabilis* ("Admirable Boletus"), a tall stately species with a dark maroon cap. It is fairly common north of Mendocino, where its favorite habitat is on rotting hemlock logs. It is as edible as it is admirable.

Boletus flaviporus (Yellow-Pored Boletus)

CAP to 13 cm broad, convex to plane; surface viscid or slimy when wet, smooth or fibrillose, reddish-brown to cinnamon-brown, not cracking into scales. Flesh thick, white to pale pink, not staining when bruised. **PORES** brilliant yellow, slightly greenish-yellow in age, not bruising blue. **STALK** to 15 cm long, equal or with a short tapering rootlike base, smooth, viscid when wet, otherwise dry; typically yellow above and pallid to reddish-brown below but color variable. **SPORE PRINT** dark olive-brown; spores 11-15 × 4-6 μm, spindle-shaped, smooth.

Boletus flaviporus has a viscid cap and brilliant yellow pores that do *not* stain blue. Stalk lacks glandular dots. It grows under hardwoods.

HABITAT: Solitary or scattered in mixed woods and under hardwoods. Sporadically common in the fall, occasional in winter and spring, never in large numbers. Apparently endemic to our oak, madrone, and manzanita woods.

EDIBILITY: Edible but mediocre.

COMMENTS: This is our only *Boletus* with a distinctly viscid cap and intense yellow pores that do *not* stain blue. It might be taken for a *Suillus* but it isn't associated with conifers and has neither glandular dots nor a veil. The stem is not consistently reticulate like *Boletus edulis,* and the pores are not whitish when young.

Boletus appendiculatus (Butter Boletus)

CAP 5-25 cm broad, convex to nearly plane; surface smooth, usually dry, yellow to yellow-brown, cinnamon-brown, or brown, frequently stained rusty-reddish. Flesh thick, dense, yellow, changing slowly to blue or not at all. **PORES** small, bright butter-yellow, blueing immediately when bruised, olive-yellow in old age. **STALK** thick, usually bulbous, to 13 cm long, solid, dry, butter-yellow or brownish-stained in age (especially below); finely reticulate above. **SPORE PRINT** dark olive-brown; spores 12-14 × 4-5 µm, spindle-shaped, smooth.

HABITAT: Solitary to gregarious in hardwood forests, especially oak and oak-madrone, mostly in fall. Occurrence sporadic— abundant some years, absent others. Often found growing with *B. satanas.*

EDIBILITY: Edible and choice. It lacks the nuttiness of *B. edulis* but is a fine fungus in its own right. It is remarkable for its density—a joy to find as well as to eat, something you can really sink your teeth into. When cooked it turns blue, then grayish, then back to yellow.

COMMENTS: The butter boletus is easily recognized by its heaviness, butter-yellow color, reticulate stalk, and pores that bruise blue. Don't be misled by the variation in cap color. Growing in the same habitat is *B. regius,* a very similar edible species with a rose-red to pink cap sometimes fading to yellow with pinkish spots. Intermediate color forms are frequent, and there is doubt in my mind whether the two are indeed distinct. *B. "marshii"* differs from both species by its bitter taste and nonreticulate stem.

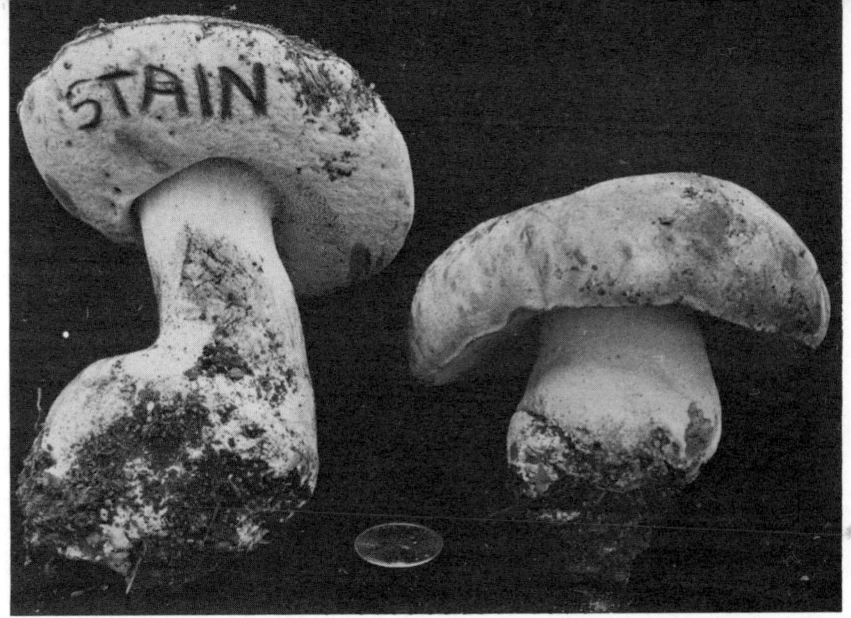

Boletus appendiculatus. These modest-sized specimens have bright yellow pores that bruise blue, a yellow stalk, and brown cap. Fine reticulation on upper portion of stalk is not visible in this picture.

Boletus "marshii" (Ben's Bitter Boletus)

CAP 5-25 cm broad, convex to nearly plane or somewhat irregular; surface dry, smooth, cracking in age, pale grayish-white to grayish-brown or buff when young, becoming dull brownish and developing darker brown stains in age or upon handling; margin even or wavy. Flesh thick, dense, white or grayish, turning blue to bluish-gray erratically when exposed; taste bitter, at least latently. **PORES** pale yellow becoming olive-yellow, bruising blue immediately then eventually turning dingy brown. **STALK** up to 15 cm long and 2-5 cm thick at apex, enlarged below but sometimes tapered at base, smooth, not reticulate, yellow above (sometimes with a very slight reddish zone), dingy brown below, darker brown throughout in age; bruising blue. **SPORE PRINT** olive-brown; spores 11-13.5 $\times$ 4.5-6 μm, spindle-shaped, smooth.

HABITAT: Scattered to gregarious in humus under live oak, summer and early fall. Known only from the Santa Cruz area, common only on the UC Santa Cruz campus.

EDIBILITY: Sauteed delicately in butter with a pinch of pepper and a clove of garlic, served steaming hot on toast with cream cheese and celery, broiled belligerently on a skewer with spiced lamb and bell peppers, or layered lovingly in a casserole with parmesan cheese, egg noodles, and onions, *Boletus "marshii"* is still inedible.

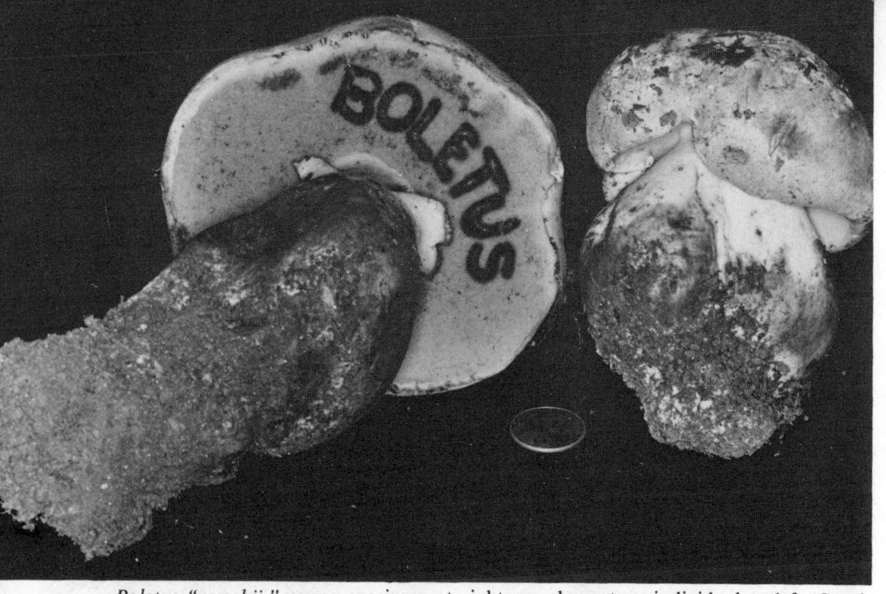

Boletus "marshii," young specimen at right, nearly mature individual at left. Cap is grayish-buff to pale brown; pores stain blue instantly when cut. Taste is latently bitter. (Ralph Buchsbaum)

COMMENTS: This bulky bolete with the bitter taste appears to be unnamed. However, it is known to local yokels as *B. "marshii"* due to the uncanny resemblance it bears to its discoverer, Ben Marsh, who is also dense, bulky, bitter, and bulbous, and who spent many fruitless hours (and ruined many otherwise marvelous meals) in a highly commendable if ill-conceived attempt to make it palatable.

It is easily distinguished from *B. appendiculatus* by its paler cap, bitter taste, and nonreticulate stem. Its habit of fruiting *before* the onset of the rainy season is odd indeed. Two other bitter boletes occur in California, but I have not found them here: the infamous *B. calopus* may also be massive, but the stalk is distinctly reticulate; the more slender *B. rubripes* has a dark reddish stem at maturity.

Boletus satanas (Satan's Boletus)

CAP 7-30 cm broad, convex, often massive; surface dry, smooth, sometimes cracked in age, gray or grayish becoming suffused with pink (yellowish if slug-eaten). Flesh white or yellow, blueing when bruised, especially near tubes. **PORES** deep red becoming red, orange, or even yellow-orange in age, turning blue or blue-black when bruised; tubes yellow to greenish. **STALK** up to 15 cm long and 2-5 cm thick at apex, massive, abruptly bulbous when young, the bulb less pronounced in age; dry, reticulate above; more or less cap color except that pink tones predominate when young and disappear in age. **SPORE PRINT** brown; spores 12-15 × 4-6 μm, spindle-shaped, smooth.

Boletus satanas, young specimens. Individual at left is turned upside down to show the deep red pore surface. Note enormous, bulbous stalk. Pores and flesh quickly bruise blue.

HABITAT: Solitary or in groups in humus under live oak (often at the edges of pastures); fruiting in the fall. Not particularly common but occasionally and locally abundant in October and November. One of the first boletes to appear.

EDIBILITY: Poisonous, at least when raw, causing vomiting, diarrhea, and severe cramps. Thorough cooking reputedly destroys the toxins, and some people eat it regularly. Its voluminous avoirdupois is certainly tempting—but when so many more delectable and less dangerous mushrooms abound, why tempt fate?

COMMENTS: The red pores, grayish cap, and bulbous, reticulate stem are diagnostic. Young specimens can be told by their obesity alone—the bulb may measure up to 15 cm broad, often larger than the cap and just as round! The red color of the pores sometimes fades in old age but the pronounced bulb and blue-staining tubes signify *B. satanas.* I found one specimen at the edge of a meadow that weighed six pounds, and half of it had been eaten by a cow! *B. pulcherrimus* (formerly *B. eastwoodiae*) is the only other red-pored bolete in coastal California that has a reticulate stem. It, too, is large and impressive, but the cap is red-brown and the stem equal or club-shaped, never with an exaggerated bulb. It is said to frequent mixed or coniferous woods, but I have yet to find it south of San Francisco. Like *B. satanas,* it is poisonous.

Boletus erythropus

CAP 5-15 cm broad, convex to nearly plane; surface dry, minutely velvety, yellow-brown to cinnamon-brown or dark brown, sometimes red-brown; immediately staining blue-black when bruised. Flesh thick, yellowish, blueing instantly upon exposure to air. **PORES** brick-red to orange, blueing when bruised; tubes yellow to greenish-yellow. **STALK** to 12 cm long, equal or thicker below, but never bulbous; dry, yellow with a coating of delicate red granules, dingier in age, not reticulate. **SPORE PRINT** ochraceous-brown; spores 13-16 × 5-5.5 μm, spindle-shaped, smooth.

HABITAT: Solitary or in small groups in hardwood forests (probably associated with live oak), fall and early winter, infrequent. I have seen it in abundance only once—about thirty fructifications under a decrepit "live" oak. If you hunt regularly in oak-madrone woods you are likely to run across it once or twice every year.

EDIBILITY: Poisonous to some—to be avoided. Two books which list *B. satanas* as poisonous state flatly that *B. erythropus* is edible. However, Bill Everson (an intrepid Santa Cruz toadstool-tester who was unaffected by cooked *B. satanas*) ate a small portion and vomited soon after—an explicit example of why you should be cautious when trying any mushroom for the first time, even a so-called "edible" one.

COMMENTS: The red to orange pores, nonreticulate stem, and brown cap typify this beautiful bolete. It certainly has substance, but is puny in comparison to the bulky hulk (hulking bulk?) of *B. satanas.* It bruises blue so rapidly that a few minutes' frenzied handling will render it unrecognizable. A red-pored bolete unique to our area, *B. amygdalinus,* occasionally lurks under manzanita and madrone, where it is often concealed by fallen leaves. It differs in having a red to rose-colored cap and larger spores. Its edibility is unknown. *B. erythropus,* incidentally, is an excellent choice for dyeing (not dying!): it imparts a rich, warm olive-gold color to yarn.

Boletus edulis (King Boletus, Cep, Steinpilz, etc.)

CAP 5-30 cm broad, convex to plane; surface smooth, dry or viscid, color variable: whitish, buff, pale crust-brown to cinnamon-brown to dark reddish (often white tinted pinkish while still under the duff). Flesh thick, firm, white, sometimes yellowish in age, occasionally blueing slightly near tubes; odor pleasant. **PORES** white when young,

Boletus edulis, young specimens in which pores are still white. Stalks have been trimmed in a few of these to check for maggots. Growth in pairs as shown is *not* typical. Reticulation on stalk is visible in upper specimens if you look closely. (Joel Leivick)

becoming yellow, finally olive-yellow or even dingy reddish-brown; not bruising blue. **STALK** to 25 cm long and up to 5 cm thick, usually large or elongated in relation to cap; equal or enlarged below, white to pale brown; reticulate above. **SPORE PRINT** dark olive-brown; spores 13-18 × 4-7 μm, spindle-shaped, smooth.

HABITAT: Solitary, scattered, or gregarious in woods. Associated mostly with pine, but also oak. Common in fall, sporadic in winter, spring, and even summer. There is normally one large fruiting in November or December.

EDIBILITY: One of the finest of fleshy fungi, certainly the best-loved and most sought-after in Europe, where it has more common names than there are languages. If any mushroom deserves the dubious title of "king," this is the one. It is magnificent—a consummate creation, the peerless epitome of earthbound substance, a bald bulbous pillar of thick white flesh—the one aristocrat the peasantry can eat.

Both the cap and stalk are excellent fresh, and even the tubes if they're firm. It is delicious raw, but difficult to digest, so play it safe and cook it. The odor and taste of dried *B. edulis* is marvelous—nutty, earthy, and meaty. But you have to find them before you can eat them and it isn't always easy. You can't just casually look for them—you have to sniff them out, hunt them down, root them up from under the duff before they're visible to others. Timing is of paramount importance, because

Boletus edulis, mature specimens. The one at left is 25 cm (10 inches) broad. Cap is brown to reddish-brown; pores are dingy olive or brownish in old age. Note presence of pine needles. (Nancy Burnett)

you face formidable competition from both maggots and boletivores (see p. 434). Of course, you can always resort to the dried, imported version found in delicatessens.

COMMENTS: This magnificent mushroom boasts at least two distinct forms in our area. The first has a moist to viscid, brown to dark red cap, often with a yellow margin. It occurs mostly with pine. The second form is associated with live oak and in my experience is not common. It has a much paler cap (crust-brown to nearly white) that is rarely viscid. Both forms are safe for beginners. Remember: buff to red-brown cap, pores white when young and not bruising blue, and thick reticulate stalk. No mushroom is more substantial and satisfying to find!

Boletus aereus

CAP 5-20 cm broad, convex to plane; surface dry or moist but not viscid, smooth, dark brown to almost black, paler in age, covered with a fine white bloom when young. Flesh thick, white, odor pleasant. **PORES** white when young, yellow in age, not blueing when bruised. **STALK** to 13 cm long, at least 2 cm thick, equal or enlarged below, solid, dry, white when young, darker in age, reticulate above. **SPORE PRINT** dark olive-brown; spores 12-14 $\times$ 4-5 μm, spindle-shaped, smooth.

HABITAT: Solitary or scattered under hardwoods (live oak, tanoak, madrone); fall and early winter, rare. I have found it only once, near Bonny Doon. It is said to be fairly common in the live oak woodlands of San Mateo County.

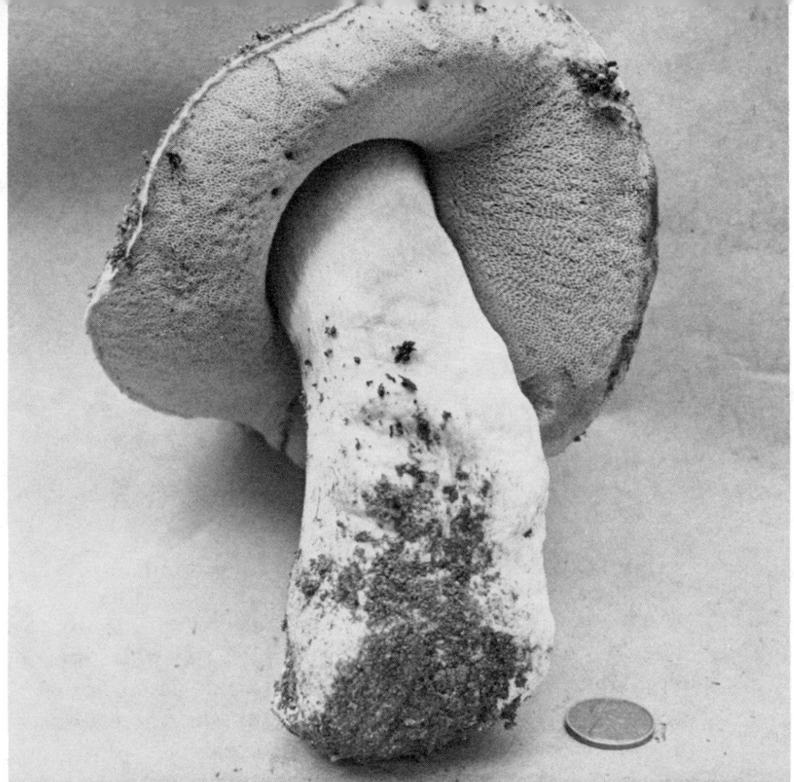

Boletus aereus. The underside is shown here because the cap color in this specimen was much paler than normal, due to it being hidden under the humus.

EDIBILITY: As good as *B. edulis*. Highly prized in Europe—the *bourdeaux cepe* of France.

COMMENTS: Previously known only from southern Europe, this handsome bolete was recently discovered in California. It grows in the same habitat as *B. appendiculatus* but the pores are white when young and do not stain blue. The dark cap separates it from *B. edulis*. The whitish bloom on young caps is also distinctive.

TYLOPILUS

Medium to large fleshy terrestrial boletes. CAP not viscid. PORES *pallid to pinkish to brown* (except *T. amylosporus*). STALK rarely bulbous, *often reticulate*. VEIL absent. SPORE PRINT *flesh color to reddish-brown or reddish-chocolate*. Spores more or less spindle-shaped, smooth.

TYLOPILUS resembles *Boletus* but has redder spores, ranging from flesh color to reddish-chocolate. It is a prominent group in eastern North America but infrequent here. Many of the species are bitter but ours are exceptions. Six species are reported from California; three are keyed below.

Key to Tylopilus

1. Pores yellow (but often with reddish discolorations .... *T. amylosporus* (see *T. indecisus,* below)
1. Pores not yellow 2
2. Pores dark brown to nearly black; spore print dark reddish-brown .... *T. pseudoscaber* (see *T. indecisus,* below)
2. Pores flesh-colored to brown; spore print flesh color .... *T. indecisus,* below

Tylopilus indecisus (Indecisive Tylopilus)

CAP 5-15 cm broad; convex to plane; surface dry, smooth, dark brown when young, paler brown in age, staining darker brown where bruised. Flesh thick, white, taste mild. **PORES** pink to pale flesh color when young, darkening with age, staining dark brown where bruised. **STALK** 5-10 cm long; rather thick, equal or enlarged below, dry, reticulate over upper portion; buff to brown, darker brown where bruised. **SPORE PRINT** flesh color; spores 10.5-13 × 3-5 μm, spindle-shaped, smooth.

HABITAT: Solitary or in small groups, in mixed woods and under oak, rare. I have seen it on three occasions, in late fall and early winter.

EDIBILITY: Edible according to the literature. I haven't tried it.

COMMENTS: There is nothing particularly indecisive about this bashful bolete—but then there is nothing particularly decisive about it either. The brown cap and reticulate stalk are suggestive of *Boletus edulis,* but the pores are never white or olive-yellow and the spores are flesh-colored. The other *Tylopilus* in our area, *T. amylosporus,* is radically different. It has yellow pores that bruise greenish, and looks very much like *Boletus chrysenteron* and *B. truncatus,* with a dull olive-brown to grayish-brown cap that cracks in age. However, the spores are reddish-chocolate, truncate, and usually amyloid. A third species, *T. pseudoscaber,* is daringly decisive, with dark brown cap and pores, chestnut-brown spores, and flesh turning blue to dark brown when injured. When wrapped in waxed paper, it stains the paper bluish-green. It is not uncommon north of San Francisco and may show up farther south.

LECCINUM

Medium to large fleshy terrestrial boletes. CAP *usually some shade of orange, brown, or red;* viscid or dry, often rimmed with a flap of sterile tissue when young. PORES usually pallid, *neither yellow nor bruising blue* (in California species). STALK thick, fleshy, *tough,* not reticulate, *with scabers which usually darken at maturity.* VEIL absent. SPORE PRINT *brown to dark brown.* Spores spindle-shaped, smooth.

LECCINUM is distinct by virtue of the rough tufted scales **(scabers)** on the stem. The scabers are pallid when young but usually darken to brown or black at maturity. They should not be confused with the resinous brown glandular dots found in *Suillus.*

Like most boletes, Leccinums are mycorrhizal, their favorite hosts being aspen and birch. But in coastal California, where these trees are absent, they invariably link up with manzanita and madrone. Commonly called "manzanita boletes," these endemic Leccinums are prized by boletivores, second only to *Boletus edulis.*

Leccinums are important from an edibility standpoint for two reasons: all are edible, and most have the same general appearance—they are readily recognized and thus can be eaten practically anywhere in the world! They are easily dried and the local species are less apt to be riddled with maggots than other boletes.

All Leccinums used to belong to *Boletus* and are still listed as such in many mushroom books. *Krombholzia* is a European synonym. Three coastal species are keyed below. Several others occur in the Sierras with aspen and pine.

Key to Leccinum

1. Cap dark red to orange or brown .... *L. manzanitae*, below
1. Cap paler (pink to apricot-buff) 2

2. Scabers dark brown at maturity .... *L. constans* (see *L. manzanitae*, below)
2. Scabers remaining pallid through maturity .... *L. armeniacum* (see *L. manzanitae*, below)

Leccinum manzanitae (Manzanita Bolete)

CAP 7-30 cm broad, convex to plane; surface viscid when wet, smooth or fibrillose, dark red to reddish-brown, orange, or brown; margin with a sterile flap of tissue when young which breaks up into segments and then disappears. Flesh thick, soft, white, sometimes bruising fuscous or

Leccinum manzanitae, mature specimens. Buttons are much more compact; old specimens have a much broader cap. Note the dark, rough scales (scabers) on the stalk. Cap is reddish-orange to reddish-brown and viscid.

vinaceous-fuscous. **PORES** pallid when young, soon grayish or grayish-olive, finally olive-buff, not bruising blue but often discoloring brownish. **STALK** to 20 cm long, equal or thicker below, tough, hard, dry, solid; whitish covered with rough, protruding scabers which darken to brownish-black at maturity; lower portion often bruising bright blue. **SPORE PRINT** brown; spores 13-17 $\times$ 4.5-5 μm, spindle-shaped, smooth.

HABITAT: Solitary, scattered, or in small groups in madrone woods and manzanita thickets. Common, fall and winter, but seldom in large numbers.

EDIBILITY: Edible and choice, prized by boletivores nearly as much as *Boletus edulis*. Mature or waterlogged specimens should be dried to concentrate their flavor. Otherwise they tend to be watery and bland. Most Leccinums blacken when cooked or dried. If this intimidates you, that's fine with me—I'll be more than happy to take them off your hands!

COMMENTS: This large, impressive bolete is easily identified by its red-brown cap, dark scabers, and hard, tough stem. The staining reaction of the flesh varies considerably. *L. arbuticola* has been found with madrone in the Sierras and may occur here as well. Its flesh bruises reddish. *L. armeniacum* has a pale apricot to pinkish cap and scabers remaining pallid through maturity. I have found it near Felton. Another local species, *L. constans,* is similarly colored but has dark scabers, and flesh not changing color when bruised. A striking variety with orange scabers has been found near Boulder Creek. All are edible and pass under the collective label "manzanita bolete"—a reference to their fondness for manzanita and madrone. *L. aurantiacum,* the species most often pictured in mushroom books, has flesh that bruises reddish. It and *L. insigne* (with flesh bruising fuscous) are addicted to aspen and occur in the Sierras.

PULVEROBOLETUS

THERE is an awesome total of one species in this genus. *Pulvero-* is derived from pulverulent, which means "powdery." It refers to the powdery or cottony consistency of the bright yellow veil which covers the cap and stalk of the young fruiting body, a unique feature among the boletes.

Pulveroboletus ravenelii

CAP 5-12 cm broad, convex or nearly round when young, plane in age; surface dry and powdery-cottony, slightly viscid if wet; bright yellow, with reddish or brown tones developing in age, especially near the center; margin often covered with veil remnants. Flesh thick, white to yellow, changing slowly to blue when exposed and then to dingy brown or dull yellow. **PORES** bright yellow, darkening with age, bruising greenish-blue and then sometimes turning dark brownish. **STALK** to 10 cm long, rather slender, dry, equal, bright yellow, the lower part usually powdery or cottony. **VEIL** brilliant yellow, powdery or cottony, covering the cap when young, usually leaving remains on the stalk but rarely a distinct ring. **SPORE PRINT** dark olive-brown; spores 8-11 × 4-6.5 μm, spindle-shaped or elliptical, smooth.

HABITAT: I have stumbled on this species only once, at Henry Cowell Redwoods State Park, in mixed woods of oak and pine, in late November. It is probably mycorrhizal with oak.

EDIBILITY: Like myself, not firmly established.

COMMENTS: I was dumbfounded by the sight of my first *Pulveroboletus.* It is such an odd sort of creature, a gaudy misfit, an audacious anomaly. The bright yellow powdery-cottony veil which covers the cap when young plus the red and yellow colors set it apart from other boletes. Though rare, it is included here because it is so bizarre—if you should be (un)fortunate enough to fall on top of one, as I did, I would like you to know what it was.

GYROPORUS

Small to medium-sized terrestrial boletes. CAP dry. PORES pallid when young. STALK not bulbous, not reticulate, *hollow at maturity*. VEIL usually absent. SPORE PRINT *pale yellow*. Spores ellipsoid, smooth.

THIS is a small genus and only one species is known from California. The pale yellow spore print and hollow stem are distinctive.

Gyroporus castaneus

CAP 2.5-6 cm broad, convex to plane or shallowly depressed; surface dry, minutely hairy, brown to pinkish-brown, orange-brown, or chestnut-brown. Flesh thick, white, not bruising. **PORES** white to pale yellowish, small, not staining blue. **STALK** to 5 cm long, rather slender, more or less equal, hollow at maturity (at least in lower portion), dry, surface often uneven, colored like cap. **SPORE PRINT** pale yellow; spores 8-12 $\times$ 4.5-6 μm, elliptical-oblong, smooth.

HABITAT: Solitary or in small groups under oak, extremely rare. I have found it only once, under a large live oak in late October.

EDIBILITY: Edible and choice, but, alas, hard to come by. Highly esteemed in Europe, where it is common. One day I was picking fairy ring mushrooms *(Marasmius oreades)* on a lawn. A round Polish woman came out and said the mushrooms I was picking were no good. Then she invited me inside, where she proceeded to stuff me with sour cream cookies (she thought I was too skinny). She showed me a picture of her son, who was in the navy. Then she gave me a necklace of dried *Gyroporus castaneus.* They were her last ones, she said, and they came from "the old country, where everything tastes better." They made a fabulous soup. So did the *Marasmius.*

COMMENTS: Unlikely to be confused with anything, as it is unlikely to be found.

GASTROBOLETUS (GASTROID BOLETES)

Small to medium-sized boletes *usually buried in humus.* CAP convex to irregular. TUBES irregularly arranged, *not vertically oriented.* STALK short, poorly developed, sometimes off-center. SPORE PRINT *unobtainable.* Spores ellipsoid to spindle-shaped, smooth, brown under microscope.

THESE funky fungi have been modified or "reduced" from normal, everyday, upright boletes to abnormal, underground, "decadent" ones. They resemble puffballs in that they do not forcibly discharge their spores, yet they retain a modicum of respectability in the form of a definite tube layer, arranged haphazardly within the misshapen cap.

None are known to be poisonous, yet none are known to be edible, since none are known to have been tried. Only one coastal species is recorded so a key hardly seems necessary. Several others have been found in the high Sierras.

Gastroboletus turbinatus (Bogus Boletus)

CAP 2-5 cm broad, convex, but often highly irregular in outline; surface dry, often pitted or wrinkled, bright yellow with red to brown spots and stains. Flesh soft, yellow, bruising blue quickly. **PORES** yellow to greenish-yellow or pinkish, bruising blue immediately; tubes disoriented, irregular and sinuous, arranged at different angles, not truly vertical. **STALK** to 4 cm long, more or less equal, usually protruding only a short distance below the tubes; dry, yellow or colored like cap. **SPORE PRINT** unobtainable; spores 13.5-15.5 $\times$ 7.5-8.5 μm, spindle-shaped, smooth, brown.

Gastroboletus turbinatus, mature specimens found underground. In this photograph they don't look like much, but they don't in nature either. Specimen at far right stained dark blue as soon as it was sectioned. Stalk is poorly developed.

HABITAT: Gregarious in humus, buried or barely visible at maturity. I have found it under live oak, in early October, following a heavy thunderstorm, growing with *Boletus "marshii."* It is hard to say whether it is rare in this region, since it is so easy to overlook. Elsewhere it grows with conifers.

EDIBILITY: Like myself, unknown and likely to remain so.

COMMENTS: A curiously wrought fungal afterthought, instantaneously recognized by its grotesque shape, underground growth habit, and disoriented tubes. Since the spores are not forcibly discharged, there is no need to elevate the cap above the ground. Just how the spores are spread is a mystery—perhaps with the help of boletivorous bipeds such as I. Many agarics have been "reduced" to gastroid habits (see Hymenogastrales, p. 571); this is one instance in which a bolete has. I was surprised to find it growing under live oak, as it is generally thought to associate exclusively with conifers. The material I collected differed slightly from typical *G. turbinatus* in the yellow, not pinkish, pores and absence of brown on the cap. In all other respects, however, it was the same.

BOLETIVORES

AS their name suggests, these curious creatures are a major predator of *Boletus edulis.* Since they are likely to be encountered by anyone who looks for mushrooms, it seems appropriate to include a few observations on their habits.

Boletivores put in their appearance shortly after the onset of the fall rains, not coincidentally, at the same time *Boletus edulis* appears. As a group, they share a number of common traits which the experienced eye learns to discern at a glance. Their overall appearance is rather dingy and disheveled, the colors drab. The cap is quite variable, ranging from deflated and depressed to inflated and ecstatic; its surface may be dry and distinctly tomentose, or smooth and somewhat viscid. The flesh is pallid, becoming blue when bruised and exuding a red latex when cut, but it is most often obscured by a ragged woolly cuticle which is typically appressed above and baggy below. The stalk may be fleshy or cartilaginous, and more often than not, bent. The odor varies considerably from individual to individual; the taste is unpleasant. A spore print is not obtainable, at least with normal methods. Boletivores are strictly terrestrial, and are invariably equipped with a long pointed stick, rapacious eye, and capacious bucket. At least two species occur in our area; these are keyed below.

Key to the Boletivores

1. Retreating furtively when approached .. *Boletivorus clandestinus,* below
1. Advancing boldly when approached ..... *Boletivorus brutalosipes,* below

Boletivorus clandestinus is the more common of the two. In addition to its secretive nature, it can be recognized (if you can get close enough) by its tough, wizened stalk with a persistent, even permanent, stoop. The gait is highly distinctive: curiously hitched and truncated, marvelously efficient, yet flailing and disjointed. The overall impression is that of a creature completely immersed in, yet not designed for, its element—like a kayaker trying to negotiate a rapids without wetting his back. When one is crept up on unawares, it can be heard alternately cooing to and swearing at its prospective prey in a vaguely familiar, yet unintelligible, tongue. It occurs solitary to scattered in the woods, but always near roads. There is usually a rusty pick-up, shabby station wagon, or '65 Dodge Dart nearby, parked on the side of the road. Near the vehicle will be found one or more telltale "middens"—neat piles of discarded tubes and wormy stalks. These resemble the feathers that remain from a freshly and systematically decapitated bird—positive proof of the boletivore's singular lust and unbridled craving for its quarry.

Boletivorus brutalosipes (the "Brutal-Footed Boletivore") can be instantly recognized by its inquisitiveness, its bold advance and cavalier stance. In addition, the stalk is more fleshy than that of *Boletivorus*

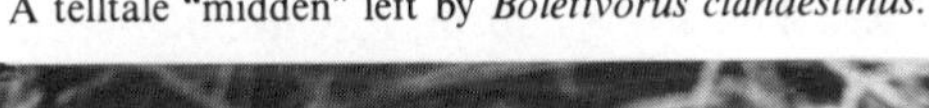
A telltale "midden" left by *Boletivorus clandestinus.*

clandestinus—often swollen in the middle or even bulbous. The gait is decidedly compact, the stride purposeful, yet completely arbitrary. When one comes rushing toward you, the net effect is that of a rapids intent upon wetting *your* back. Its insatiable greed for *Boletus edulis* may be cleverly disguised by an amicable disposition and disarmingly friendly, fibrillose smile. But it will stop at nothing to achieve its ends. Never leave your basket unattended in the woods! If it has *Boletus edulis* in it, they will be gone; if it contains other species, they will be stepped on, masticated and regurgitated, or otherwise obliterated. Trampled fly agarics *(Amanita muscaria)* are also a sure sign that brutal-footed boletivores are in the vicinity. *Boletivorus brutalosipes* is found in roughly the same habitats as *Boletivorus clandestinus.* Invariably there is a rusty pick-up, shabby station wagon, or '65 Dodge Dart nearby, parked in the middle of the road.

Boletivorus clandestinus is probably harmless, though I haven't been able to get close enough to find out. *Boletivorus brutalosipes,* on the other hand, has a well-deserved reputation for unprovoked acts of aggression. If you have some *Boletus edulis* in your basket, watch out!

Between these extremes, as might be expected, "hybrids" occur, in addition to possibly autonomous species (I have even seen a skinny, blonde, bare-footed variety). However, further study (and preferably, a critical comparison with European specimens) is necessary before a definitive and natural classification can be worked out. Both species are common throughout the range of *Boletus edulis* and *Leccinum manzanitae.* On weekends they are notably abundant on lower Empire Grade, above Santa Cruz, where their crafty cousin, *Pseudoboletivorus incognitus,* is also in evidence. The latter closely mimics *Boletivorus clandestinus,* but only *pretends* to be stalking *Boletus edulis*—the object of its desires really being *Amanita calyptroderma.*

As a final note, I might add that what boletivores do during the summer is a mystery. It has been suggested by one colleague of mine that they hibernate in the trunks of their cars. Another possibility is that they follow the mushroom season up and down the coast. A third is that they migrate east (or west). But perhaps the most reasonable hypothesis is that they are like squirrels—they stash away what they gather in hedges, holes, nests, or sheds, for when the hunting is good, they have neither the time nor inclination to eat. Then, in the summer, when they have nothing but time, they do nothing but eat.

Polypores and Bracket Fungi

spores

POLYPORACEAE and Relatives

Tough, leathery, corky, or woody (occasionally fleshy) fungi *growing mostly on wood.* FRUITING BODY variously shaped but most *often bracketlike,* SPORE-PRODUCING SURFACE *usually with minute pores.* STALK *absent* or *if present, typically off-center to lateral.* VEIL and VOLVA absent (except in *Cryptoporus).* SPORE PRINT white to brown (occasionally some other color), but frequently unobtainable. Spores usually smooth. Hyphae monomitic, dimitic, or trimitic.

THIS large and exceedingly diverse group comes in a mind-boggling multiplicity of shapes and sizes and a pleasing array of gay decorator colors. As the term "bracket fungi" implies, the fruiting body is most often bracketlike. Polypore (meaning "many-pored") refers to the spore-producing tube layer which lines the underside of the cap. However, the tube mouths or **pores** are sometimes so minute that they're virtually invisible, and in some bracket fungi there are no pores—the spore-producing surface being smooth, warty, or even gilled. The boletes also come equipped with tubes, but they are rapidly-decaying, terrestrial fungi with a soft, fleshy cap and central stem.

Polypores, in contrast, grow mostly on wood. The most familiar types fruit on logs and stumps in dense, shelving masses (or in ascending tiers if the tree is still standing). Others, called **conks,** are those hard, woody hooflike growths you see on living trees. Still others are **resupinate:** with neither cap nor stem, they lie flat on the wood or incrust it. Those that grow on the ground usually originate from roots or buried wood. They have a stem, but only rarely is it central.

Polypores are usually described as tough, leathery, or woody. This is certainly true of old specimens, but some, such as *Phaeolus schweinitzii* are so soft and watery (when fresh) they can be wrung out like a sponge. Others, like the beefsteak fungus *(Fistulina hepatica)* and the sulfur shelf *(Laetiporus sulphureus)* "weep" in wet weather, exuding colored water droplets. In contrast, *Fomes* and *Ganoderma* are woodier than the wood they feed on!

Like most fungi, polypores fruit during the rainy season. However, mature fruiting bodies are so tough they tend to dry out instead of decaying. They may persist for months, even years. Some (notably *Ganoderma, Fomes,* and *Phellinus)* are actually perennial: rather than going to the trouble of manufacturing new fruiting bodies every year, they quite sensibly make use of existing resources by adding a new growth layer onto the old one. In this manner they may attain gargantuan proportions—a 5 ft. × 3 ft. specimen from the Pacific Northwest weighed 300 pounds, undoubtedly a record for fleshy fungal fructifications!

There is much more to polypores than their fruiting bodies, however. One cannot fully appreciate them without appreciating their work—that is, the chemical and structural changes they produce in their hosts. Bracket fungi are absolutely indispensable to the forests of this world. They are *the* major group of wood-rotting fungi. Though of great economic importance because of the havoc they wreak (15-20% of all standing timber in this country is defective or unusable because of fungal decay, more than 90% of it caused by bracket fungi, and structural timber is also destroyed—in ships, mines, houses, bridges, etc.) the polypores should not be seen as enemies. Without them there would be no logging industry in the first place; every cut stump, felled log, and lopped-off limb would lie indefinitely on the forest floor, the woods would quickly become impenetrable, and new trees would have no room to grow.

In living trees the dead wood (heartwood) in the center of the trunk is more susceptible to attack than the living wood (sapwood) beneath the bark. Trees infected by **heart rot** may look outwardly sound, even when they are completely hollowed out inside. Sometimes the only clue to the pernicious presence of the rot is the fruiting body of the fungus! Since heartwood is dead, heart rot fungi are not technically parasites, but they *can* be deleterious—the infected trees are steadily weakened until they come crashing down at the slightest provocation. (Remember not to breathe too hard when picking polypores from a standing tree!) A few, such as *Fomes annosus,* are virulent parasites, destroying both the sapwood and the heartwood.

Spores generally gain access to living trees through wounds in the bark. Trees bruised or battered by wind, nearby construction, careless machinery, or mindless vandalism ("Jody loves Judy") are especially vulnerable. Sometimes spores enter through holes bored by grubs or beetles; these insects may in turn munch on the mycelium growing in their tunnels.

Heart rot continues after the tree dies, and **sap rot** sets in. On fallen logs and branches you will find large clusters of colorful bracket fungi (such as *Coriolus versicolor* and *Stereum hirsutum)* which are digesting the sapwood. Several varieties may simultaneously or successively inhabit the same log. Recently felled timber is also susceptible to attack; only complete immersion in water will prevent infection.

Wood is composed of dead, empty cells from which the fungus extracts nutrients by digesting the cell walls. These walls are composed largely of cellulose compounds (which make the wood soft and tough) and lignin compounds (which make the wood hard and brittle). Cellulose-dissolving fungi are called **carbonizing decays** or **brown rots** because they leave the lignin behind, rendering the wood dry, brittle, and darker than normal wood. Lignin-dissolving fungi are called **delignifying decays** or **white rots** because they leave the cellulose behind, making the wood soft, spongy, and whiter than normal wood. Some species remove both cellulose and lignin, completely hollowing out the trunk or producing small, hollow pockets called **pocket rot.** The mycelial threads of bracket fungi can often be seen if the wood is broken open and examined closely. But if more than one species inhabits the same piece of wood, interpretation and diagnosis become complicated. Only repeated observation can tell you which ones produce which types of rot.

The part of the tree infected should also be noted. **Butt rots** such as *Phaeolus schweinitzii* are confined to the roots and base of the tree and the fruiting bodies are often found on the ground. **Trunk rots** like *Phellinus pini* infect the entire trunk, white **top rots** such as *Fomes roseus* inhabit the top of the trunk.

Polypores were originally lumped together in one giant genus, *Polyporus.* Dozens of families and genera have subsequently been proposed in a laudable effort to break the group down. As usual, however, there are widely divergent opinions on exactly how the task should be accomplished. The result is scholarly chaos, precisely the opposite of what scientific nomenclature is supposed to accomplish. The confusion is slowly being dispelled, but be forewarned—each book uses a different set of names based on a different set of criteria (e.g., *Polyporus versicolor, Trametes versicolor, Polystictus versicolor,* and *Coriolus versicolor* are all names for the same fungus). Following is a synopsis of the more important genera recognized here:

Fomes, Phellinus, and *Ganoderma* (called "conks") have hard, knobby, hooflike to fan-shaped fruiting bodies with a hard surface crust which may appear shellacked. They are perennial, new tubes being added each year. If the tubes are arranged in stratified layers the age of the fruiting body can be determined, just like counting growth rings on a felled tree. Ages of 50 to 70 years have been recorded. In *Ganoderma* the spores are brown, minutely spiny, and truncate. *Fomes* and *Phel-*

Most polypores grows shelflike or bracketlike on wood. This is a close-up of a log completely covered with *Coriolus versicolor*, a very common and attractive species.

linus are responsible for most important timber rots, with *Phellinus pini, Fomes officinalis,* and *F. annosus* being especially destructive.

Albatrellus and *Polyporus* (used here in a fairly restricted sense) have a tough to fleshy-tough fruiting body with a cap and stem. The few central-stemmed, terrestrial species are readily distinguished from the boletes by their tougher flesh, decurrent pores, and pale (never olive-brown) spores.

Bondarzewia and *Polypilus (Grifola)* have compound fruiting bodies in which several or many caps arise from a single stalk or branched framework. *Laetiporus* includes a single, well-known yellow-pored species which is large, fleshy, and shelflike.

Coriolus is one of several genera with thin, tough fruiting bodies commonly found in shelving masses on logs and stumps. The cap is often exquisitely zoned with different colors and velvety to the touch. *Tyromyces* is similar but soft and watery when fresh. *Lenzites* looks like *Coriolus* but has platelike gills on the underside of the cap. Many smaller bracket fungi resemble *Coriolus*, but have a smooth spore-producing surface. *Stereum* is the most prominent of these.

In *Cryptoporus* the pore surface is covered by a tough, volva-like membrane. The fruiting body in *Poria* is entirely resupinate, a simple tube layer without cap or stem. *Merulius* and *Serpula* are somewhat similar but the pore surface has a veined or honeycombed appearance.

The vast majority of bracket fungi are too tough or too bitter to eat. A few (such as *Phaeolus schweinitzii)* may actually be poisonous and even the edible species are indigestible unless cooked well. One happy exception is the sulfur shelf *(Laetiporus sulphureus),* a delectable and unmistakable treat. The beefsteak fungus *(Fistulina hepatica)* is also excellent.

Several hundred bracket fungi are known from North America, almost half of which occur in California. Obviously, only a fraction can be included here— the most common species plus several unusually striking ones. Many of the distinctions between genera are microscopic (spore ornamentation, type of hyphae, etc.), so they are keyed together here.

Since so few bracket fungi are edible, they are shunned by most people and barely mentioned in mushroom books. As I am also shunned by most people (and have yet to be mentioned in any kind of book), I feel I have something in common with these indispensable organisms. A fairly extensive (but by no means comprehensive) treatment is presented here in hopes that people will at least learn to acknowledge their presence, if not identify them.

Key to the Polyporaceae and Relatives

1. Fruiting body smooth, more or less round (like a ball) to oval, 7 cm broad or less; hollow, the pore surface hidden (inside the "ball"); on conifers .... *Cryptoporus volvatus,* p. 456
1. Not as above 2

2. Fruiting body knoblike, hooflike, bracketlike, shelflike, or crustlike; stalk absent or lateral; growing on wood 3
2. Fruiting body with a cap (or caps) and stalk; stalk off-center to central (rarely lateral); usually growing on ground 30

3. Fruiting body typically resupinate (lying flat on wood or incrusting it), consisting of a simple layer of spore-producing tissue (without a cap) 4
3. Fruiting body with a cap (upper surface) and underside (but occasionally resupinate if growing on undersides of logs) 7

4. Spore-producing surface veined to form large, shallow honeycomb-like pores .... *Serpula lacrymans,* p. 475
4. Not as above 5

5. Fruiting body a simple layer of tubes .... *Poria corticola,* p. 474
5. Tubes absent; spore-producing surface smooth or warty 6

6. Spore-producing surface veined or warty *Phlebia merismoides,* p. 476
6. Spore-producing surface more or less smooth .... *Corticium* and *Peniophora* (see *Phlebia merismoides* p. 476)

7. Spore-producing surface (underside) more or less smooth, without pores; fruiting body small 8
7. Spore-producing surface with pores (sometimes very minute) or gills; fruiting body small to very large 9

8. Growing on herbaceous stems; fruiting body purple-brown to chocolate or dark grayish-brown .... *Thelephora terrestris* p. 478
8. Growing on wood; differently colored .... *Stereum hirsutum,* p. 476

9. Fruiting body perennial, medium-sized to very large, thick; punky or woody with a hard surface crust, pore surface white or pallid (but may be brownish in very old specimens) 10
9. Not with above combination of characteristics 12

10. Cap rusty-brown to blackish, the margin sometimes brighter (dark red to yellow); pore surface *not* turning brown when scratched .... *Fomes pinicola,* p. 458
10. Not as above; pore surface usually turning brown when scratched .. 11

11. Cap shiny or appearing varnished, dark reddish to mahogany; on conifers .... *Ganoderma oregonense,* p. 458
11. Cap not varnished, gray to brown, usually on hardwoods; very common .... *Ganoderma applanatum* p. 456

12. Cap reddish to liver-colored; flesh meatlike, streaked with white and red, exuding bloodlike droplets when fresh .... *Fistulina hepatica,* p. 445
12. Not as above 13

13. Pore surface red, pink, rosy, or violet-tinted 14
13. Spore-producing surface some other color 15

14. Cap small, white to grayish, hairy; pores violet-tinted when fresh .... *Hirschioporus abietinus,* p. 450
14. Cap pinkish-brown to red-brown or darker; pores rosy-pink to red-brown .... *Fomes subroseus,* p. 460

15. Pore surface sulfur-yellow when fresh; fruiting body large, fleshy, shelflike; cap bright orange to yellow, fading to whitish .... *Laetiporus sulphureus,* p. 446
15. Not as above; spore-producing surface not yellow 16

16. Underside of cap with gills *or* greatly elongated, meandering, mazelike pores 17
16. Underside of cap with pores (but pores may be somewhat sinuous or irregular) 20

17. Gills present 18
17. Gills absent; pores meandering and greatly elongated 19

18. Cap grayish to white, hairy; gills appearing longitudinally split or grooved .... *Schizophyllum commune,* p. 455
18. Not as above; cap more or less zoned, variously colored .... *Lenzites betulina,* p. 454

19. Perennial; growing on conifers; common .... *Phellinus pini,* p. 460
19. Usually annual, mostly on hardwoods; uncommon .... *Daedalea confragosa* (see *Lenzites betulina,* p. 454)

20. Perennial *or* pore surface brown, ochraceous-brown, rusty-brown to greenish-yellow *or* both; flesh yellow-brown to brown 21
20. Not as above 23

21. Growing on dead hardwoods; cap or at least the growing margin ochraceous to yellow .... *Phellinus gilvus,* p. 462
21. On conifers 22

22. Annual; pores greenish-yellow to brown; cap velvety when fresh; growing near the ground on stumps and trees .... *Phaeolus schweinitzii,* p. 462
22. Perennial; pores never greenish-yellow; growing on all parts of trunk .... *Phellinus pini,* p. 460

23. Fruiting body soft, spongy, watery, or cheesy when fresh 24
23. Fruiting body thin, tough, and leathery, even when fresh 28

24. Cap dark brown to black, velvety or hairy .... *Ishnoderma resinosum* (see *Tyromyces caesius,* p. 449)
24. Not as above; cap pallid, at least before handling 25

25. Fruiting body turning yellowish to rusty-reddish when handled .... *Tyromyces fragilis,* p. 449
25. Not as above 26

26. Blue-gray tones usually present; spore print bluish-tinted .... *Tyromyces caesius,* p. 449
26. Not as above 27

27. Growing shelflike on wood; stalk absent .... *Tyromyces albellus,* p. 448
27. Cap usually with a stalklike extension; cap small, less than 2.5 cm broad .... *Tyromyces floriformis* (see *T. albellus,* p. 448)

28. Pore surface gray to black .... *Bjerkandera adusta,* p. 450
28. Pore surface pallid, at least when fresh 29

29. Cap conspicuously zoned with contrasting colors; very common .... *Coriolus versicolor,* p. 451
29. Cap not zoned, or if zoned, then colors not contrasting .... *Coriolus hirsutus,* p. 452

30. Spore-producing surface smooth, without pores 31
30. Spore-producing surface with pores (sometimes very minute) 33

31. Fruiting body erect, branched (like a coral mushroom) .... *Thelephora palmata,* p. 479
31. Not as above 32

32. Fruiting body chocolate-brown to purple-brown or very dark grayish-brown .... *Thelephora terrestris,* p. 478
32. Fruiting body paler (hazel to buff or even whitish) .... *Stereum "burtianum,"* p. 477

33. Fruiting body usually distorted with almost entire surface covered with pores; white to tan .... *Polyporus biennis,* p. 467
33. Not as above 34

34. Pores greenish-yellow to mustard-yellow to brown, bruising darker when fresh; cap fuzzy or velvety, soft or spongy when fresh, tough in age; cap yellow to orange-brown, rusty, or dark brown; medium to large, common on ground near conifers .... *Phaeolus schweinitzii,* p. 462
34. Not as above 35

35. Fruiting body typically compound; several to many caps arising from a common stalk or base .... *Bondarzewia berkeleyi,* p. 470
35. Fruiting body typically simple, but several caps arising from different stalks may fuse together 36

36. Stalk or lower half of stalk soon black; growing on rotting wood ... 37
36. Not as above; usually on ground 38

37. Cap more or less chestnut-brown; entire stalk usually black .... *Polyporus picipes,* p. 465
37. Cap more or less tan; only lower half of stalk black .... *Polyporus elegans,* p. 464

38. Pores yellow-brown to brown; flesh very thin (less than 2 mm); cap velvety or silky, often zoned .... *Coltrichia cinnamomeus,* p. 464
38. Not as above; pores usually pallid 39

39. Cap blue to greenish-blue, ochraceous-stained in age .... *Albatrellus flettii,* p. 471
39. Cap some other color, never blue 40

40. Cap and pores becoming lemon-yellow; cap without fibrils; growing on ground .... *Albatrellus ovinus,* p. 472
40. Not as above 41

41. Cap tinted violet-gray to pinkish-gray ... *Albatrellus avellaneus,* p. 473
41. Not as above 42

42. Cap white to grayish 43
42. Cap some other color 44

43. On wood; stalk off-center to lateral; cap small .... *Tyromyces floriformis* (see *T. albellus,* p. 448)
43. On ground; stalk more or less central .... *Boletopsis griseus* (see *Albatrellus avellaneus,* p. 473)

44. Stalk arising from an underground "tuber" which is black and rubbery when fresh, rock-hard when dry .... *Polyporus tuberaster,* p. 469
44. Not as above, but stalk may be attached to buried wood 45

45. Pores *not* decurrent; stalk central; spore print pale yellow .... (see *Gyroporus castaneus,* p. 432)
45. Pores typically decurrent; not as above 46

46. Cap (or cap scales) greenish-yellow to yellow-brown or orange-brown 47
46. Cap brown to reddish-brown 48

47. Cap with greenish-yellow to yellow-brown scales, usually occurring with conifers .... *Polyporus ellissii* (see *P. pescaprae,* p. 466)
47. Cap with orange-brown to yellow-brown scales, usually occurring with hardwoods .... *Polyporus decurrens,* p. 466

48. Cap covered with tiny, stiff hairs; taste bitter *Polyporus hirtus,* p. 468
48. Cap plushlike to fibrillose or scaly; taste not bitter .... *Polyporus pescaprae,* p. 466

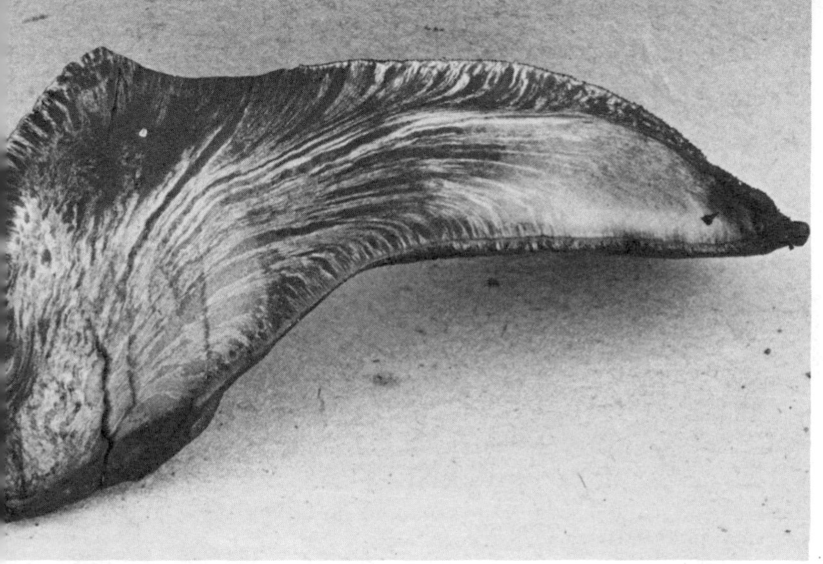

Fistulina hepatica. This cross-section shows the meatlike flesh streaked with dark red and white. It even exudes a bloodlike juice when cut.

Fistulina hepatica (Beefsteak Fungus; Ox-Tongue)

FRUITING BODY resembling an ox-tongue. **CAP** 7-30 cm broad or long, up to 6.5 cm thick; emerging knoblike, becoming tongue-shaped, or sometimes shelflike or hooflike; nearly flat when mature; surface roughened, velvety when dry, gelatinous when wet, reddish-orange becoming dark red or liver-colored; margin rather thin, sometimes lobed. Flesh thick, soft, juicy, dark red with paler, horizontal veins or streaks, oozing with dark reddish juice when fresh; taste rather strong, acidulous. **PORES** about 1 per mm, pallid to yellowish-buff, becoming flesh colored, reddish, or reddish-brown; tubes same color or darker, close to each other but discrete, separable. **STALK** (if present) lateral, rather short, up to 7 cm long, continuous with and colored like cap. **SPORE PRINT** pinkish to pale rusty-brown; spores 4-6 × 3-4 μm, ovoid to nearly round, smooth.

HABITAT: Solitary or several on hardwood trees and stumps, rare. I have found it only twice, in the fall. It is fairly common in southeastern North America and Europe on chestnut and oak, but in California it favors chinquapin (a close relative of chestnut). It produces a serious carbonizing decay—the rich, warm brown hue it imparts to the wood was once prized by cabinetmakers.

EDIBILITY: Edible. The strong, acidulous taste is displeasing to some, esteemed by others. Most sources recommend parboiling, which removes the taste, as well as the nutrients (it is rich in vitamin C). One source suggests eating it raw with salad greens! I haven't tried it.

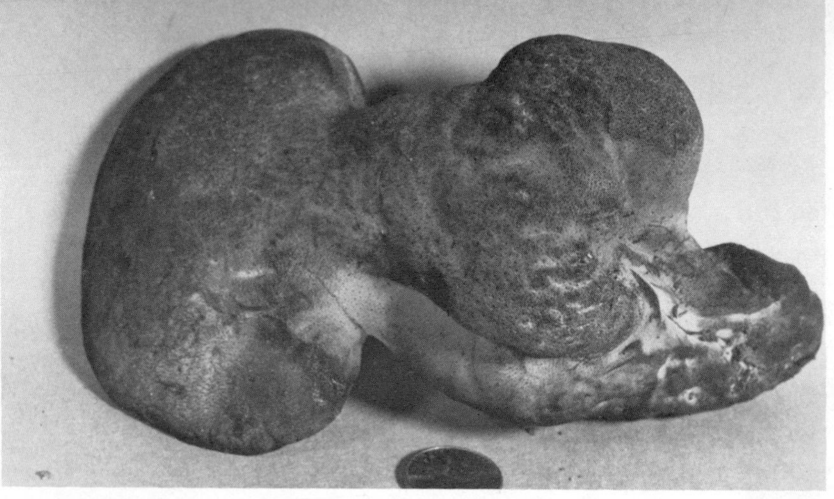

Fistulina hepatica, a young specimen viewed from the top. It's easy to see why it is sometimes called "Ox Tongue."

COMMENTS: This highly distinctive fungus does indeed resemble a slab of steak when sliced, especially in the way it oozes "blood." The streaked or veined flesh is also unique. It is not a true polypore because the tubes, though close together, are discrete, individual units, arranged like bristles in a brush; thus *Fistulina* is placed in a family of its own. This character is best seen with a hand lens.

Laetiporus sulphureus (Sulfur Shelf; Chicken of the Woods)

FRUITING BODY shelflike or in a rosette. **CAP** up to 60 cm broad, soft and fleshy when young, tough and brittle when dry; tongue-shaped or knobby, becoming fan-shaped; surface smooth but uneven, dry, deep orange to bright yellow or with pinkish-salmon tints, margin usually yellow; fading slowly in age to yellowish and finally dull white; margin at first thick and blunt. Flesh pale yellow or salmon-orange, occasionally white; thick, succulent, and juicy when fresh (reminiscent of uncooked chicken), often exuding colored water droplets; tough or punky when mature, taste somewhat sour or acidulous, becoming strong and unpleasant in age. **PORES** minute, 3-4 per mm, bright sulfur-yellow fading slowly in age; tubes shallow; pore surface when young appearing smooth. **STALK** absent or present as a narrowed point of attachment. **SPORE PRINT** white; spores 5-7 $\times$ 3.5-5 μm, ovoid to nearly round, smooth.

HABITAT: Solitary or in shelving masses on dead stumps and logs, sometimes on living trees, sometimes growing in rosettes from roots or buried wood; fruiting from the same stump year after year. Fairly common, late summer and fall, but old faded fruiting bodies may persist

Laetiporus sulphureus. This large yellow-orange polypore is unmistakable. This one is growing on a poison-oak-covered eucalyptus stump. It is nearly mature. Young specimens are much blunter (more rounded).

for a year or more. It grows on a wide range of hardwoods and conifers, but here its favorite hosts are eucalyptus (September-October, ushering in the new mushroom season) and Douglas-fir (November-December). It causes a destructive red-brown carbonizing heart rot that eventually hollows out the tree, producing cracks in the wood in which thin sheets of white mycelium appear. It is said to have caused considerable damage in British sailing vessels.

EDIBILITY: Delectable, with a hearty, meaty flavor. There have been several cases of sulfur shelf poisoning on the west coast, so try it cautiously and never eat it raw. Unless it is just emerging, use only the tender, rapidly growing margin (about 5 cm). You can trim it off and return later to harvest more! Mature specimens are tough and their flavor is overpowering. When young, the succulent flesh cooks to the consistency of tofu and retains its color (which is reminiscent of "candy corn"), making it especially attractive (and delicious) in omelets. In my experience, the form growing on eucalyptus is more tender than the one found on Douglas-fir.

COMMENTS: One of the "foolproof four"—the brilliant yellow-orange shelving masses are unmistakable. Actually, nothing is foolproof, but the sulfur shelf is certainly intelligence-proof, and I trust no one reading this book is a fool. There is always an element of disbelief involved in stumbling onto a large cluster—it looks like

Laetiporus sulphureus, young specimens just emerging from a eucalyptus stump. In this stage they are delectable.

something out of a Jacques Cousteau movie. You would no more expect to find it on an aging eucalyptus stump by the railroad tracks than you would expect to find a freight train at the bottom of the sea.

Fresh specimens weigh far more than their appearance suggests. It is strange that a fungus so large and full of water requires so little moisture to fruit. The cap color ranges from deep orange to yellow but the pores, when fresh, are a uniform sulfur-yellow. A variety with white pores is known, but very rare. *Polyporus sulphureus* and *Grifola sulphurea* are synonyms.

Tyromyces albellus

FRUITING BODY shelflike or bracketlike. **CAP** more or less fan-shaped, up to 10 cm broad; soft, watery, and somewhat flexible when fresh, rigid when dry; surface white to buff, yellowish-buff, or watery gray; smooth or slightly hairy. Flesh white, odor fragrant when fresh. **PORES** angular, 3-4 per mm, white to yellowish. **STALK** absent. **SPORE PRINT** white; spores minute, 3.5-5 × 1-2 μm, cylindric or sausage-shaped, smooth. Hyphae in flesh branched.

HABITAT: Solitary or in groups on dead hardwoods, occasionally conifers. Fairly common, fall and winter. Produces a wet, stringy delignifying decay of the sapwood.

EDIBILITY: Unknown.

COMMENTS: The pale color, soft texture when fresh, modest size, fragrant odor, and absence of staining reactions are the key characteristics. *T. tephroleucus* is very similar but has unbranched hyphae and a mild odor. *T. floriformis* is a small (less than 2.5 cm broad) whitish species with a narrowed, stemlike base and bitter taste. I have found it several times on rotting conifers. Another whitish species, *T. anceps,* grows on conifers, has a bitter taste, but no stalk.

Tyromyces caesius

FRUITING BODY shelflike or bracketlike. **CAP** to 7 cm broad; soft, spongy or watery (not rigid) when fresh, tougher when dry; surface white to gray, usually tinged bluish, especially toward margin; covered with soft whitish hairs, not zoned. Flesh white, odor sometimes sweetish. **PORES** angular or elongated, 2-4 per mm; white or colored like cap. **STALK** absent. **SPORE PRINT** pale ashy-blue; spores minute, 3-5 × 1-1.5 μm, cylindric or sausage-shaped, smooth.

HABITAT: Solitary or in small groups on decaying wood (both hardwoods and conifers). Occasional, fall and winter. Usually associated with a brown carbonizing decay.

EDIBILITY: Unknown.

COMMENTS: The delicate bluish-gray tint to the cap and soft texture when fresh distinguish this unassuming polypore. *Tyromyces* embraces several other small, fleshy bracketlike species. *Leptoporus* is a generic synonym. *Ishnoderma resinosum* is a widely distributed, fleshy shelflike fungus with a dark brown to blackish hairy cap and pallid pores. It grows on hardwoods, especially elm, occasionally on conifers. The infected wood may have an unmistakable anise odor. *Inonotus hispidus* has a densely hairy yellow to rusty-reddish cap and grows on hardwoods.

Tyromyces fragilis

FRUITING BODY shelflike or bracketlike. **CAP** up to 7 cm broad, soft and watery when fresh, rigid and brittle when dry; at first white, discoloring yellowish and then rusty-reddish when handled or upon drying; surface covered with soft white hairs that become matted in age. Flesh soft, white, discoloring like cap; taste mild. **PORES** 2-4 per mm, easily visible; pure white bruising yellowish or rusty-reddish. **STALK** absent. **SPORE PRINT** white; spores 4-5 × 1-1.5 μm, sausage-shaped, smooth.

HABITAT: Solitary or several on rotting conifers, especially Douglas-fir. Occasional, fall and winter. Produces a brown, carbonizing decay.

EDIBILITY: Unknown.

COMMENTS: The tendency of all parts, especially the pores, to stain rusty-reddish when handled is the one noteworthy feature of this unnoteworthy polypore. *T. mollis* is similar but stains directly to rusty-reddish and has a smoother cap. *T. guttulatus* may also stain but has a very bitter taste.

Bjerkandera adusta

FRUITING BODY shelflike or bracketlike. **CAP** up to 7 cm broad but usually smaller, tough to corky when fresh, rigid when dry; surface white to smoky-gray, gray-brown, or pale tan, often zoned, finely hairy or velvety to nearly smooth, the margin at first whitish, then darker. Flesh white, then grayish to brown, thin, pliable, tough; odor mild. **PORES** very minute, scarcely visible, 5-7 per mm, at first whitish (darker where bruised), soon gray or smoky, finally black; tubes shallow. **STALK** absent. **SPORE PRINT** white or pale yellow; spores 4-6 × 2-3.5 μm, ellipsoid, smooth.

HABITAT: On dead hardwood trees, logs, stumps (rarely on conifers), usually in dense, overlapping clusters; fairly common but not abundant, fall through spring. Produces a general delignifying decay of the sapwood, giving it a whitish-flecked appearance.

EDIBILITY: Indisputably inedible.

COMMENTS: The gray to black pore surface is the principal field mark of this small, tough bracket fungus. *Gloeoporus adustus* is a synonym. *Bjerkandera fumosa* is very similar but somewhat thicker and larger with slightly larger pale gray to smoky-brown (rarely black) pores, larger spores, and stronger odor (aniselike to unpleasant). A thin, dark line separates the pores and flesh in both species, especially the latter. Intermediate forms occur, however, so it is questionable whether the two are distinct.

Hirschioporus abietinus (Violet-Pored Bracket Fungus)

FRUITING BODY shelflike or bracketlike. **CAP** small, leathery and tough when fresh, drying rigid, up to 4 cm broad; surface white to grayish, covered with hairs. Flesh very thin (1 mm or less), tough, pallid gray or brownish. **PORES** 2-4 per mm; angular becoming torn or

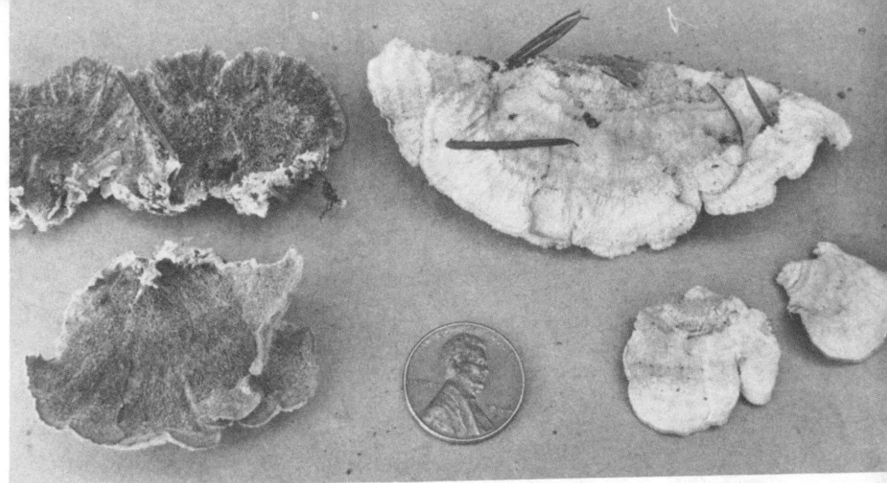

Hirschioporus abietinus. Violet-tinted pore surface is shown in specimens at left; grayish-white hairy cap is shown at right. It is common on rotting conifers.

toothlike; white to brownish but typically tinted violet when fresh. **STALK** absent. **SPORE PRINT** white; spores 4-6 × 1.5-2.5 μm, cylindric or sausage-shaped, smooth.

HABITAT: In groups on decaying conifers, especially Douglas-fir. Common year-round—the most important delignifier of conifer sapwood.

EDIBILITY: Inedible, but can be eaten in a pinch. For cooking suggestions, see *Coriolus versicolor.*

COMMENTS: *H. abietinus* is to rotting conifers what *Coriolus versicolor* and *Lenzites betulina* are to rotting hardwoods—overwhelmingly abundant. The violet-tinted pore surface when fresh separates this species from other small polypores. The cap is not multicolored as in *Coriolus versicolor.* A slightly larger species with violet-tinted pores, growing on hardwoods, is *Hirschioporus pergamenus. Fomes subroseus* has rose-tinted pores, but is much thicker and fleshier.

Coriolus versicolor (Many-Colored Polypore)

FRUITING BODY shelflike or bracketlike, fan-shaped, or in circular rosettes. **CAP** up to 7 cm broad, thin and leathery when fresh, rigid or slightly flexible when dry, reviving; surface velvety, covered with silky hairs, multicolored, strongly zoned with narrow concentric bands of contrasting colors (but more uniformly colored when growing in sheltered situations); colors extremely variable: a mixture of white, gray, yellow, brown, blue-gray, reddish-brown, green, or black; margin often wavy. Flesh very thin (1 mm), white, tough. **PORES** usually white

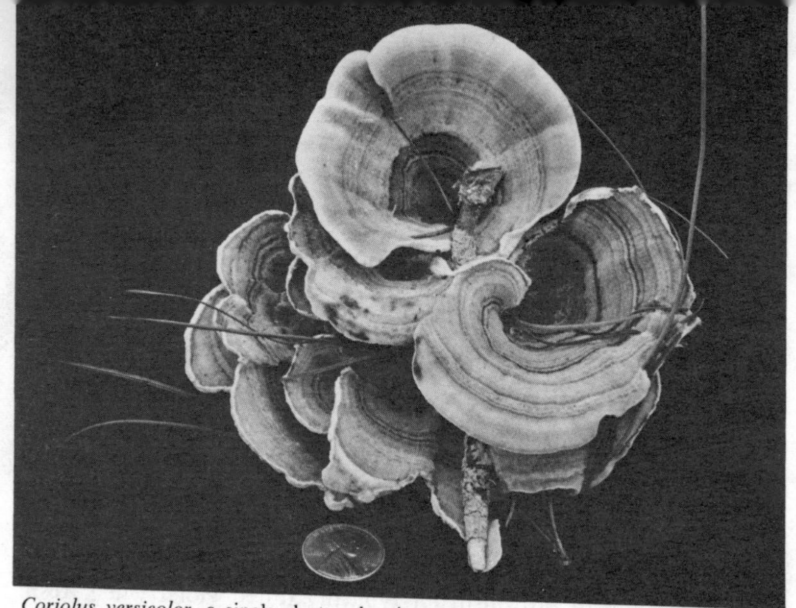

Coriolus versicolor, a single cluster showing delicately zoned, leathery cap. Though intergrown with pine needles, it was growing on dead oak. It is also pictured on p. 440.

but visible, 3-5 per mm. **STALK** usually absent. **SPORE PRINT** white; spores 4-7 × 1.5-3 μm, cylindric or sausage-shaped, smooth.

HABITAT: On logs, stumps, and fallen branches of live oak, eucalyptus, and other hardwoods, sometimes on wounds in living trees, rarely on conifers. Abundant year-round but fruiting in the fall and winter—can be seen on almost any jaunt through the woods. It causes a general delignifying decay of the sapwood, and is occasionally a parasite on peach trees.

EDIBILITY: Boil for 62 hours, squeeze thoroughly, and serve forth.

COMMENTS: Our most common polypore, this species is well known to everyone who loves the woods—at least by sight if not by name. The multicolored, concentrically zoned caps do not decay readily, making excellent ornaments, brooch clips, earrings, and necklaces. The multiplicity of colors is both its most bewildering and most distinctive characteristic—no two are alike. Our other small, tough polypores are less radically colored. *C. versicolor* is listed in many books under *Polystictus* and *Trametes,* in addition, of course, to *Polyporus.*

Coriolus hirsutus

FRUITING BODY shelflike or bracketlike or in circular rosettes. **CAP** 2.5-15 cm broad, leathery when fresh, fairly rigid when dry, reviving somewhat; surface more or less uniformly grayish to yellowish or grayish-brown (the margin often darker, hazel-brown to dark brown); conspicuously hairy or woolly to coarsely velvety, usually concentrically zoned or furrowed, but the colors of each zone not sharply contrasting. Flesh tough, white. **PORES** 3-4 per mm, minute, white to yellowish or yellowish-gray. **STALK** usually absent. **SPORE PRINT** white; spores 5-8 × 2-3 μm, cylindric or sausage-shaped, smooth.

HABITAT: In groups on dead hardwoods (especially oak), rarely on conifers. Not as common as *C. versicolor;* fruiting in the fall and winter but persisting through the spring. It causes a general delignifying decay of the sapwood.

EDIBILITY: Inedible (but see *C. versicolor* for cooking suggestions).

COMMENTS: This lesser known cousin of *C. versicolor* is larger but not as brightly colored. Also, the hairs on the cap are longer and woollier. The specimens illustrated are unusually large and attractive. I have had them for two years and they show no signs of decay. *C. pubescens* is a smaller species with a white to grayish-yellow silky-hairy cap, a radially striate margin, and a somewhat fleshier texture when fresh. It is fairly common on dead hardwoods but never abundant. *C. basilaris* is a grayish species that produces a brown carbonizing heart rot in cypress. *C. biformis* is a rare hardwood species with a white to tan cap and large pores (1-2 per mm).

Coriolus hirsutus is larger and duller than *C. versicolor.* The cap is actually quite similar to *Lenzites betulina.*

Lenzites betulina. Cap (at left) is usually zoned and resembles *Coriolus* species. However, underside is furnished with thick gills as shown at right. (Ralph Buchsbaum)

Lenzites betulina (Gilled Polypore)

FRUITING BODY shelflike or bracketlike. **CAP** 2-13 cm broad, tough and leathery; surface velvety or hairy, multicolored, with narrow, concentric zones of gray, brown, yellow-brown, etc. (often covered with green algae in old age). Flesh thin, tough, white. **GILLS** thick, platelike, often branching toward the margin, even poroid in places (especially when young); white or whitish, drying darker, often wavy in age. **STALK** absent. **SPORE PRINT** white; spores 4-7 × 1.5-3 μm, cylindric, smooth.

HABITAT: In rows, columns, and shelving masses on rotting hardwood logs and stumps; exceedingly common throughout the year, often sharing logs with *Coriolus versicolor.* It produces a delignifying decay of the sapwood.

EDIBILITY: Inedible, but dries nicely. If you are adamant about trying it, see *Coriolus versicolor* for cooking suggestions.

COMMENTS: *Lenzites* is an excellent example of convergent evolution—a gilled fungus which is not an agaric. In all respects, save the gills, it is a typical bracket fungus or polypore; the multicolored, velvety, zoned cap bears an uncanny resemblance to *Coriolus versicolor.* In fact, sometimes they can't be separated without examining the underside of the cap. The genus *Daedalea* neatly plugs the gap between *Coriolus* and *Lenzites:* the pores are elongated, meandering or mazelike, and it is easy to see how the ridges between the pores gradually became "gills" and the pores became the spaces between the gills. *Lenzites* and *Daedalea* encompass only a handful of species, of which *Lenzites betulina* is by far the most common. Others include *Daedalea confragosa* and *D. unicolor,* usually on hardwoods; *Lenzites* (=*Gloeophyllum*) *trabea,* and *L. saepiaria,* both with brown gills, the first on hardwoods and conifers, the second on conifers.

Schizophyllum commune (Split-Gill)

FRUITING BODY shelflike. **CAP** up to 4 cm broad, more or less fan-shaped; tough; surface white to grayish-white (brownish-gray when moist), densely hairy, margin often lobed. Flesh tough, leathery, thin, gray. **GILLS** radiating from point of attachment, white to grayish, well separated, edges appearing split or grooved longitudinally, rolled back when dry, cuplike in cross-section. **STALK** absent. **SPORE PRINT** white; spores 3-4 × 1-1.5 μm, cylindrical, smooth.

HABITAT: On hardwood sticks, stumps, and logs, usually in groups or rows, common practically year-round. It shrivels up in dry weather but revives when moistened. Distribution worldwide.

EDIBILITY: Too small and tough to be of value. However, natives in Madagascar are said to chew them, for reasons unknown.

COMMENTS: This unorthodox but attractive little fungus appears to have no close relatives. The peculiar manner in which the gills seem to split longitudinally is unique. The hairy white cap is reminiscent of *Hirschioporus abietinus,* a common bracket polypore. The "splitting" gills are actually two adjacent plates which separate upon drying. Specimens sealed in a tube in 1911, then moistened 50 years later, unrolled their gills and began shedding spores! *Schizophyllum* has been widely used in genetic studies because it fruits readily in the laboratory.

Schizophyllum commune. This small widespread species has a hairy whitish cap like a polypore, but boasts longitudinally split grayish gills underneath.

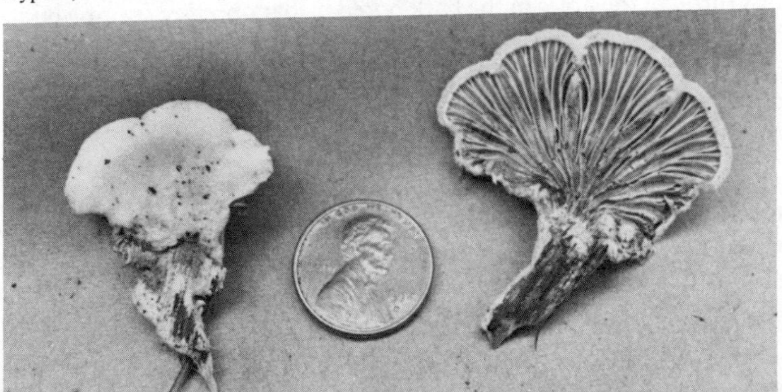

Cryptoporus volvatus is a unique polypore that looks something like a puffball (right), but reveals a tube layer and hollow interior when cross-sectioned (left). It is common on conifers, especially pine.

Cryptoporus volvatus (Cryptic Globe Fungus)

FRUITING BODY more or less round to oval or slightly compressed, interior hollow; up to 7 cm broad; upper surface with a thin, smooth resinous crust, whitish to warm tan, drying ochraceous or darker, extending down and under, forming a "volva" or "veil" which completely covers the pore surface until old age, when it is perforated by one or two holes. Flesh very thin. **PORES** hidden until old age; minute (3-4 per mm), white becoming brownish. **STALK** absent. **SPORE PRINT** pinkish or flesh-colored; spores collecting in a heap on the "floor" or "volva" of fresh specimens, 8-12 × 3-5 μm, smooth, cylindric or ellipsoid.

HABITAT: Solitary, more often in groups, on dead (occasionally living) conifers, especially pine. Fruiting in fall, winter, and spring; possibly parasitic.

EDIBILITY: Inedible. Smith says that worms found inside it can be used as fishbait; so can worms found outside it.

COMMENTS: This bizarre evolutionary anomaly looks like a cross between a confused puffball and a bemused oak gall. The smooth, warmly tanned exterior is quite attractive; most of the interior is hollow, unlike a puffball, and the tube layer can be seen when it is sliced in half. Working on the trapdoor principle, the "volva" eventually ruptures, dumping the spore heap into the outside world. Tiny fungus beetles which feed on it also help to spread the spores. Spores gain access to the host through the holes in the bark bored by bark beetles; fruiting bodies later emerge through the same holes.

Ganoderma applanatum (Artist's Fungus)

FRUITING BODY emerging whitish and knoblike, becoming hooflike, shelflike, fan-shaped or somewhat irregular. **CAP** up to 60 cm broad and 20 cm thick; upper surface crustlike, very hard, often

Ganoderma applanatum. This common perennial conk grows on practically any kind of hardwood. Note how the white spore-producing surface turns brown when scratched. This specimen is several years old, judging by its height. Thinner shelflike fruiting bodies are also common. The tree in this picture is an elm.

cracked, furrowed, ridged, or warty; gray to gray-brown or brown, but often covered with a brown or reddish-brown spore powder. Flesh punky or corky, brown, odor fungal. **PORES** barely visible, 4-6 per mm; white or whitish when fresh, instantly brown when scratched; tube layer distinctly stratified, each layer 4-12 mm thick and separated by thin layer of chocolate-brown tissue. **STALK** absent. **SPORE PRINT** reddish-brown or brown; spores 6-9 × 4.5-6 µm, slightly truncate at apex, ovoid, minutely spiny.

HABITAT: Solitary or in groups on hardwood logs, stumps, and wounds in living trees; perennial, very common. Its hosts include virtually every hardwood found in North America. In our region it is partial to bay laurel, but it can also be found on oak, magnolia, pepper trees, acacia, eucalyptus, elm, and even Douglas-fir. The only place it doesn't occur is in deserts or prairies—where there aren't any trees. Though it usually attacks dead or dying trees, it can be parasitic. It produces a whitish, delignifying decay of the sapwood and heartwood; infected trees are blown over easily.

EDIBILITY: Inedible, but sturdy specimens can be made into stools.

COMMENTS: This is the hard, woody growth you see so often on bay laurel. Since the bruising reaction to brown on the pore surface is reasonably permanent, it makes an excellent medium for etching (or better yet, for leaving cryptic messages in the woods)—hence its name, artist's fungus. It's been calculated that a large specimen (one I found weighed 18 lbs.) liberates 30 billion spores a day, 6 months a year—or over 5,000,000,000,000 (5 trillion) spores annually! Millions of these are borne aloft by air currents and deposited on *top* of the cap, turning it brown. Two closely related species restricted to California are *G. brownii,* with a pale yellow to gray pore surface, and *G. annularis,* with unstratified tubes and no flesh. Both have larger spores, 9-12 × 6-9 μm.

Ganoderma oregonense

FRUITING BODY emerging knoblike and white, soon hooflike or fan-shaped, hard and woody. **CAP** to 30 cm broad (sometimes much larger), and to 10 cm thick; surface hard, crusty, more or less shellacked, smooth or with ridges, furrows, and cracks; uniformly reddish-mahogany aging blackish-mahogany, the margin sometimes paler. Flesh white to brownish, soft and punky, tough. **PORES** minute, 2-4 per mm, white discoloring brownish in age or where wounded, tubes up to 2.5 cm deep. **STALK** absent or present as a lateral, narrowed point of attachment, continuous with and colored like cap. **SPORE PRINT** brown; spores 10-16 × 7.5-9 μm, ovoid with truncate apex, minutely spiny.

HABITAT: Solitary or in small groups on dead conifers, producing a wet, whitish carbonizing rot. Perennial, uncommon. Known only from western North America.

EDIBILITY: Inedible.

COMMENTS: The shiny, mahogany-colored surface crust is characteristic of this species and its close relatives. It is shinier than *G. applanatum* and lacks the brightly colored margin of *Fomes pinicola. Ganoderma tsugae* and *G. lucidum* are two widespread, shellacked species. They are similar to *G. oregonense* but brighter. They are used for ornamental purposes and even worshipped by some cultures. *G. lucidum* occurs in California on hardwoods, including bay laurel, willow, oak, and citrus trees.

Fomes pinicola (Belted Wood Conk)

FRUITING BODY emerging as a whitish, pale yellow, or lilac-tinted knob, becoming hoof-shaped, convex, or shelflike. **CAP** 5-40 cm broad, up to 20 cm thick, hard, woody; surface soon crustlike, resinous, hard, often concentrically furrowed, more or less zoned when mature; typically rusty or blackish-brown near the center and dark reddish otherwise, the growing margin rounded and blunt, usually brightly

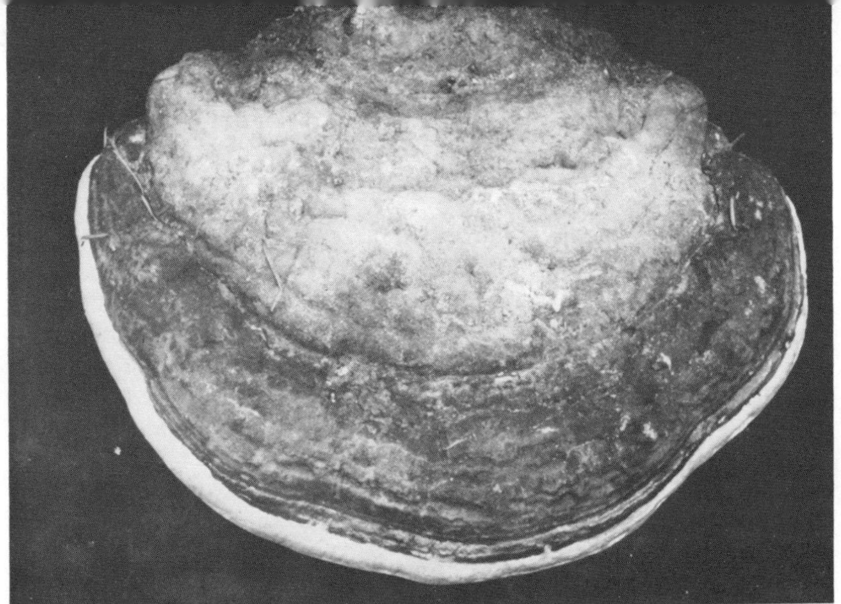

Fomes pinicola, mature shelflike specimen. The pallid spore-producing surface of this conifer-loving conk does *not* turn brown when scratched. Cap is rusty to reddish or reddish-black.

colored (white, yellow, ochraceous, or reddish). Flesh corky or woody, very tough, white to pinkish-buff or lemon-yellow when young, pale brownish in age, bruising pinkish when young; odor when fresh rather strong and fungal. **PORES** minute, 3-5 per mm, white or pale yellow, brownish in old age but not turning brown when scratched (may turn yellowish or lilac); tube layers distinctly stratified, each 3-5 mm deep. **STALK** absent. **SPORE PRINT** white or pale yellowish; spores 5-7 × 4-5 μm, ovoid to nearly round, smooth.

HABITAT: One or several on dead wood (usually conifers): logs, stumps, and standing trees, rarely on living trees. In our area occurring primarily on Douglas-fir and redwood. Perennial, common. It attacks both the heartwood and sapwood, producing a slow, carbonizing rot which fractures the wood and turns it brown ("brown crumbly rot"). Large mycelial mats can often be seen.

EDIBILITY: Inedible, unless you are fond of wood.

COMMENTS: This beautiful species is a major destroyer of dead timber. The reddish cap with brightly colored margin and pores which do not bruise brown are good fieldmarks. *Ungulina marginata* is a synonym. Other woody species with whitish flesh and pores include: *F. annosus,* often parasitic, gray-brown to brown, on conifers (Douglas-fir, pine, cypress), occasionally hardwoods; and *F. officinalis* (quinine fungus), hoof-shaped with chalky white, extremely bitter flesh, on conifers.

Fomes subroseus (Rosy Conk)

FRUITING BODY shelflike or bracketlike. **CAP** 2.5-13 cm broad, usually less than 2.5 cm thick; tough; surface covered with fine hairs, nearly smooth in age, not crustlike; more or less zoned pinkish-red, pinkish-brown, grayish-brown, or even black; margin generally thin, acute. Flesh rosy-pink to pinkish-cinnamon or pinkish-brown, soft-corky. **PORES** minute, 4-5 per mm; rosy (pinkish-red to pinkish-brown), reddish-brown in age; tube layers shallow, not stratified. **STALK** absent. **SPORE PRINT** whitish; spores 4-7 × 1.5-2 μm, cylindric, slightly curved, smooth.

HABITAT: In colonies on dead conifers, especially Douglas-fir. Also reported on madrone and various fruit trees. Fairly common, usually perennial. I find it most often on the cut ends of recently felled logs. It produces a carbonizing brown pocket rot but is of minor economic importance.

EDIBILITY: Inedible.

COMMENTS: The beautiful rosy pore surface is the outstanding feature of this outstanding polypore. The upper surface is not as hard and crusty as in many types of *Fomes;* therefore it is apt to be looked for in another genus. *Trametes carnea* is an obsolete synonym. *Fomes roseus* is identical but with broader spores (5-7×2.5-3.5 μm), paler flesh (silvery-pink to pale rose), and surface slightly incrusted in old specimens. It also occurs on conifers, especially at the tops of dead trees.

Phellinus pini (Pine Conk)

FRUITING BODY hoof-shaped, convex, fan-shaped, or shelflike. **CAP** up to 20 cm broad and 15 cm thick but usually much smaller; very tough; surface hard, crusty but not shiny, rough or cracked; at first tawny or rusty, then brown to brownish-black, minutely hairy becoming smooth. Flesh thin, tough, woody, tawny to rusty-reddish. **PORES** 2-5 per mm, often sinuous and irregular (daedeloid), ochraceous-orange to rusty-brown or brown. **STALK** absent. **SPORE PRINT** brown; spores 4-6 × 3.5-5 μm, round or nearly round, smooth. Large, pointed brown sterile cells (setae) intermingled with basidia. All parts turning black in KOH.

HABITAT: In vertical columns up and down living or dead conifers, infecting all important species except cypress and cedar. Perennial,

Phellinus pini. A common parasite on conifers, particularly pine. The tough fruiting bodies often line the entire trunk. Note the mazelike, sinuous pores.

widely distributed and common; in our area mostly on knobcone pine. It attacks the heartwood (and sometimes the sapwood) in living trees, producing a delignifying pocket rot known as "conch rot." It causes more timber loss than any other fungus.

EDIBILITY: Inedible.

COMMENTS: The rough unpolished cap, ochraceous to rusty pores and flesh, sinuous pores, and habitat on conifers are characteristic of this destructive fungus, better known as *Fomes pini.* The presence of brown setae and the black potassium hydroxide reaction have led modern investigators to transfer it to *Phellinus.* It has also been placed in *Trametes* and *Cryptoderma.*

Other perennial polypores with yellow-brown to rusty-brown flesh include: *Phellinus (Fomes) robustus,* large, woody but not incrusted, gray-brown to grayish-black, with bright yellow-brown flesh and stratified tubes, mostly on hardwoods including eucalyptus, pittosporum, and walnut (also on cactus!); *Phellinus (Fomes) igniarius,* similar but with duller flesh and tubes not stratified, on hardwoods, especially aspen and birch, also madrone, manzanita, chinquapin, willow, and apple; *Phellinus (Fomes) tenuis,* usually resupinate, *Poria*-like, rusty-brown to blackish, on both hardwoods and conifers; *Phellinus (Fomes) pomaceus,* causing serious heart rot in fruit trees *(Prunus); Fomes rimosus,* with rich brown cap and yellow-brown to dark brown pores, on locust, acacia, and other legumes; and *F. fomentarius,* gray to grayish-brown with a hard surface crust, on hardwoods.

Phellinus gilvus (Oak Conk)

FRUITING BODY bracketlike, shelflike, or fan-shaped. **CAP** up to 20 cm broad and 2.5 cm thick; leathery-tough or corky when fresh, rigid when dry; surface bright rusty-yellow to ochraceous when young, becoming yellowish-brown, and then dark rusty-brown, blackish in old age; not incrusted, at first velvety (just the growing margin if perennial), wearing away and becoming rough or somewhat zoned at maturity. Flesh tough, bright ochraceous to dark yellow-brown to cap color. **PORES** minute, 5-8 per mm, grayish-brown becoming reddish-brown or dark brown; tubes in 1-5 layers, gray within. **STALK** absent. **SPORE PRINT** white; spores rarely found, 4-5 × 2.5-3.5 μm, oblong-ellipsoid, smooth. Large brown sterile cells (setae) abundant. Flesh black in KOH.

HABITAT: In colonies on dead (occasionally living) hardwoods, especially oak and tanoak, rarely on conifers; perennial or fruiting in fall and winter. The most common large polypore on dead hardwoods, it produces a general delignifying rot of the sapwood, eventually rendering it whitish and very brittle.

EDIBILITY: Unknown.

COMMENTS: The dark rusty-brown color and velvety yellow-ochraceous growing margin are good fieldmarks. The upper surface is not crusty as in many conks. The color and texture are reminiscent of old *Phaeolus schweinitzii,* which grows with conifers, usually on the ground. For similar perennial polypores growing on hardwoods, see comments under *Phellinus pini.*

Phaeolus schweinitzii (Red-Brown Butt Rot)

FRUITING BODY usually compound, composed of several fused caps arising in tiers from a common base, but sometimes simple or sometimes shelflike on wood. **CAP** 5-30 cm broad or more; soft, spongy and watery when fresh; tough or corky, rigid and brittle when dry; plane or depressed; surface covered with a dense felty mat of hairs, with a knobby appearance when actively growing; orange to ochraceous to yellowish or greenish-yellow when growing, becoming rusty-brown, dark brown, or stained blackish in age, sometimes zoned with all of these colors. Flesh yellowish becoming rusty-brown. **PORES** irregular, 1-3 per mm or fused together to form larger pores; mustard-yellow to greenish, brownish to brownish-black where bruised or in age,

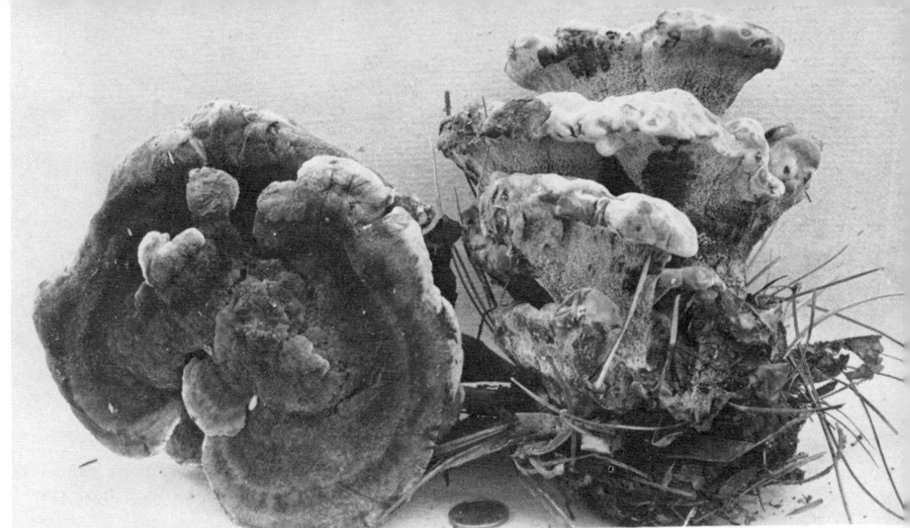

Phaeolus schweinitzii usually grows on the ground under conifers. Note how fruiting body is compound—several "caps" arising from a common base. Pores are greenish-yellow to brown; cap is spongy when young, tough or woody in age.

decurrent. **STALK** if present up to 5 cm long, central or off-center, same color and texture as cap and pores. **SPORE PRINT** white or tinted green; spores 5.5-8 × 4-5 μm, ellipsoid, smooth. All parts black (or cherry-red, then black) in KOH.

HABITAT: Scattered or in groups on or around dead or living conifers, particularly pine and Douglas-fir; usually, but not always, terrestrial (originating from roots). Fruiting in fall and winter, but persisting for a long time, common. It attacks the roots and heartwood of living trees, causing a serious, carbonizing decay known as "red-brown butt rot." It fractures the wood into cubical blocks (as high as fifteen feet up the trunk) so that the tree is blown over easily. There is one report of it growing on eucalyptus.

EDIBILITY: Unknown. It contains a stimulant found in the roots of the kava kava plant, but may contain poisons as well. It is too tough and hairy to be of food value anyway.

COMMENTS: One of the most common and impressive of the larger polypores, this species can be recognized by its hairy orange to rusty-brown cap (greenish-yellow when young), greenish-yellow pores, and habitat (usually) on the ground. It grows very quickly, engulfing pine needles, sticks, and other debris in the process. There is one similar species, *Polystictus tomentosus,* with a tan to ochraceous cap, hoary to dark brown pores, smaller spores, and pointed brown sterile cells (setae) among the basidia. It is a weak parasite on conifers throughout California and is not uncommon in our area. Like *Phaeolus schweinitzii,* it grows on the ground or close to ground level on the trunk, and stains black in potassium hydroxide. *Hydnellum* species are superficially similar but have short, blunt teeth instead of pores.

Coltrichia cinnamomeus. Note the small size, silky-fibrillose cap, more or less central stalk, and growth on the ground. Flesh is very tough. *C. perennis* (not illustrated) is similar but larger.

Coltrichia cinnamomeus (Fairy Stool)

CAP up to 5 cm broad, pliant and leathery when fresh, rigid when dry, convex to plane, depressed, or umbilicate; surface bright reddish-cinnamon to amber-brown, yellow-brown, or darker, with shining silky striations and narrow or inconspicuous concentric zones; margin often fringed or torn. Flesh very thin (less than 1 mm), rusty-brown. **PORES** 2-3 per mm, shallow, yellow-brown to brown, reddish-brown, or cinnamon, not decurrent. **STALK** to 5 cm long, thin, equal, more or less central, reddish-brown, velvety. **SPORE PRINT** yellowish-brown; spores 6-8 $\times$ 4.5-6 μm, ellipsoid, smooth. Pore surface black in KOH.

HABITAT: Solitary or in small groups on ground in woods and chaparral, typically along well-beaten paths, roadbanks, and in clearings; rarely on rotten wood. Occasional, late fall through spring.

EDIBILITY: Inedible.

COMMENTS: This beautiful little polypore is sometimes dried and used as an intriguing addition to flower and seedpod arrangements. It is identified by its thin, silky-shining cinnamon cap, brown pores, and reddish-brown (never black) stem. In similar habitats but not as common is its elegant cousin, *C. perennis.* It is larger, with a conspicuously zoned, finely velvety (rather than silky) pale cinnamon cap and pores sometimes decurrent on the stem. A small grayish form of *C. perennis* occurs on charred ground.

Polyporus elegans (Elegant Polypore)

CAP leathery-tough when fresh, rigid when dry, up to 7.5 cm broad but usually about 2.5 cm; convex becoming depressed or umbilicate; surface smooth, pale tan to dull tan, sometimes weathering to nearly

Polyporus elegans. Cap is pale tan and lower half of stalk is black in this common wood-inhabiting polypore. *P. picipes* (not illustrated) is similar but has an entirely black stem and chesnut-brown cap, and is sometimes much larger.

white. Flesh thin, pallid to pale cinnamon. **PORES** angular, 4-5 per mm; pallid when very fresh, soon becoming grayish to light brownish, decurrent; tubes shallow. **STALK** to 5 cm long, central or off-center, never lateral; pallid above, becoming black below; smooth or minutely powdery. **SPORE PRINT** white; spores 6-10 × 2.5-3.5 μm, cylindric, smooth.

HABITAT: Solitary or several on decaying hardwoods, rarely conifers, late fall through spring. Fairly common, especially on willow, alder, and oak, but never in large numbers.

EDIBILITY: Too tough to eat, but dries nicely.

COMMENTS: This dainty polypore is easily recognized by the tan cap, small size, and black lower half of the stem. *P. varius* is similar, but larger, with radially streaked or flecked cap, and stem sometimes entirely black.

Polyporus picipes (Black-Footed Polypore)

CAP up to 18 cm broad but usually much smaller (3-4 cm); leathery-tough when fresh, rigid when dry; convex becoming depressed or umbilicate; surface smooth, dry, chestnut-brown to dark red-brown, sometimes becoming blackish when old; margin often paler, wavy. Flesh thin, pallid, becoming pale brown. **PORES** minute, 5-7 per mm, somewhat decurrent, white to brownish; tubes shallow. **STALK** 6 cm long, central or off-center, pallid above and black below or more frequently black throughout, smooth. **SPORE PRINT** white; spores 6-8 × 3-4 μm, cylindric to ellipsoid, smooth.

HABITAT: Solitary or in groups on rotting hardwood stumps and logs, occasionally on conifers. Fairly common, late fall through spring.

EDIBILITY: Too tough to eat.

COMMENTS: This species is close to *P. elegans* but the cap is darker and the entire stem is usually black. Both of these are retained in *Polyporus* as defined in its narrowest sense.

Polyporus decurrens

CAP 5-7.5 cm broad, fleshy-tough when fresh, drying fairly rigid; convex to slightly depressed; surface dry, orange-brown to yellow-brown or even reddish-brown, with erect fibrillose scales which become flattened in age. Flesh white, tough. **PORES** angular, 1-2 per mm; decurrent, white but discoloring when dried. **STALK** central or off-center, to 5 cm long and less than 2.5 cm thick, equal, solid, white to somewhat brownish; reticulate above from the decurrent pores. **SPORE PRINT** white; spores 10-18 $\times$ 4-6 μm, cylindric, smooth.

HABITAT: Solitary or several on ground in woods (usually hardwoods), occasionally on dead wood. Fall and winter, uncommon. Known only from California. I have found it in Pasadena.

EDIBILITY: Unknown.

COMMENTS: The orange-brown to yellow-brown scaly cap with whitish decurrent pores distinguishes this species from *P. pescaprae* and others. *P. McMurphyi* is probably the same.

Polyporus pescaprae

CAP to 15 cm broad, sometimes larger; fleshy but tough when fresh, rigid when dry; convex to plane or somewhat irregular; surface dry, plushlike, or with fine fibrils or small scales, pinkish-brown to dark reddish-brown or dingy brown; margin sometimes deeply indented on one side. Flesh thick, white, bruising pinkish, taste mild. **PORES** large, 1-2 mm each in diameter, angular; white to dingy yellowish, sometimes becoming pinkish, decurrent. **STALK** up to 7.5 cm long and about 2.5 cm thick; usually enlarged below, sometimes several arising from a common base, usually central or off-center, if lateral then more or less perpendicular to cap; color usually dull, pallid to yellowish toward base or colored like cap or pores. **SPORE PRINT** whitish; spores 8-11 $\times$ 5-6 μm, ovoid, smooth, apiculate.

HABITAT: Solitary or several on ground in woods. Occasional, fall

Polyporus pescaprae. A terrestrial polypore with a well-developed stalk, pallid pores, and brown scaly cap. The pine needles in background are *not* its natural habitat.

and winter. I have found it several times in oak-madrone-tanoak woods near Boulder Creek and Bonny Doon.

EDIBILITY: According to European sources, young caps are quite tasty (and not too tough) when cooked thoroughly. I haven't tried it.

COMMENTS: The reddish-brown to brown fibrillose-scaly cap, large whitish pores, and fleshy stem distinguish this terrestrial polypore. It is quite attractive when fresh. *P. ellissii* is similar but with a greenish-yellow scaly cap. I have seen it in the Pacific Northwest and it is reported from California. It is also found on the ground, usually under conifers. Both are sometimes placed in the genus *Scutiger*.

Polyporus biennis

FRUITING BODY arising from a poorly developed stalk or fleshy base, several caps often fused together or overlapping; often distorted with most of the surface covered with pores. **CAP** up to 15 cm broad when well developed but usually much smaller, tough when fresh, surface woolly-hairy, white to tan. Flesh duplex, white or pinkish, tough. **PORES** large, 1-3 per mm, often irregular, meandering, or becoming toothlike; sometimes discoloring reddish, dingy in age, decurrent. **STALK** central to off-center, poorly developed or even absent, continuous with and colored like cap. **SPORE PRINT** white; spores 5-8 $\times$ 3-5 μm, ellipsoid, smooth.

HABITAT: Usually gregarious, on ground around hardwood stumps and trees, occasionally under conifers. Fall and winter, not common.

EDIBILITY: Unknown.

COMMENTS: Distorted fruiting bodies are usually found with pores covering almost the entire surface; this is the best fieldmark of this unimposing, profoundly forgettable, pitiful excuse for a polypore. The growth habit is sometimes reminiscent of *Phaeolus schweinitzii.*

Polyporus hirtus (Bitter Polypore)

CAP 5-18 cm broad, convex or somewhat irregular, fleshy when fresh, rigid when dry; surface dry, uniformly grayish-brown to dark brown, covered with fine, short, stiff, erect hairs (hispid). Flesh thick, white, taste decidedly bitter (but sometimes latently so). **PORES** 1-2 per mm, white to creamy, drying yellowish, usually decurrent; tubes rather deep. **STALK** to 13 cm long and to 2.5 cm thick, central, off-center, or even lateral, sometimes irregular, equal or tapering downward, surface similar to cap. **SPORE PRINT** white; spores 10-17 × 4.5-6 μm, fusiform, smooth.

HABITAT: Solitary or in groups on ground, around old stumps and trees (usually conifers), probably originating from buried wood or roots. Fall through early spring, regarded as rare but fairly common in our area. I have seen large fruitings at Big Basin State Park.

EDIBILITY: Inedible. If you boil it for several hours and change the water frequently, you might remove the bitterness, but you would remove everything else as well.

Polyporus hirtus. This terrestrial polypore has a brown cap, brown stem, white pores, and very bitter taste.

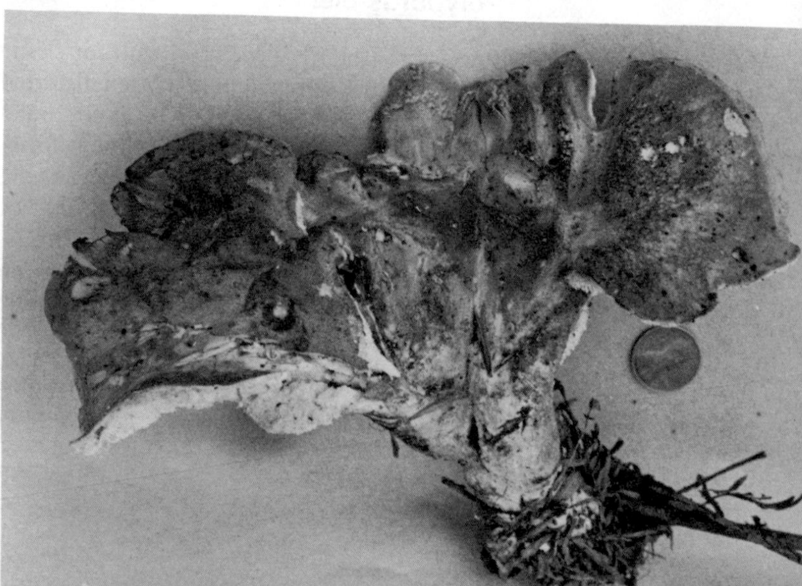

COMMENTS: The evenly colored brown hispid cap, white pores, bitter taste, and presence of a stem are good fieldmarks. *Bondarzewia* species are somewhat similar but have amyloid spores and are not bitter. It is tougher than *Boletus* and the pores are usually decurrent.

Polyporus tuberaster (Tuckahoe)

CAP 4-15 cm broad, fleshy-tough when fresh, rigid when dry, convex to plane with a depressed or umbilicate center; surface tan to ochraceous-tan, darkening in age, with scattered, radially arranged darker brown fibrils or scales; margin sometimes wavy or lobed. Flesh thin, tough, pallid. **PORES** 1-3 per mm; angular or circular; white to pale tan, decurrent. **STALK** more or less central, to 10 cm long, less than 2.5 cm thick, equal, brown or colored like cap, surface sometimes uneven; arising from a large, black underground "tuber" (sclerotium), which is

Polyporus tuberaster. This terrestrial polypore arises from an underground sclerotium ("tuber"), which is black and covered with dirt.

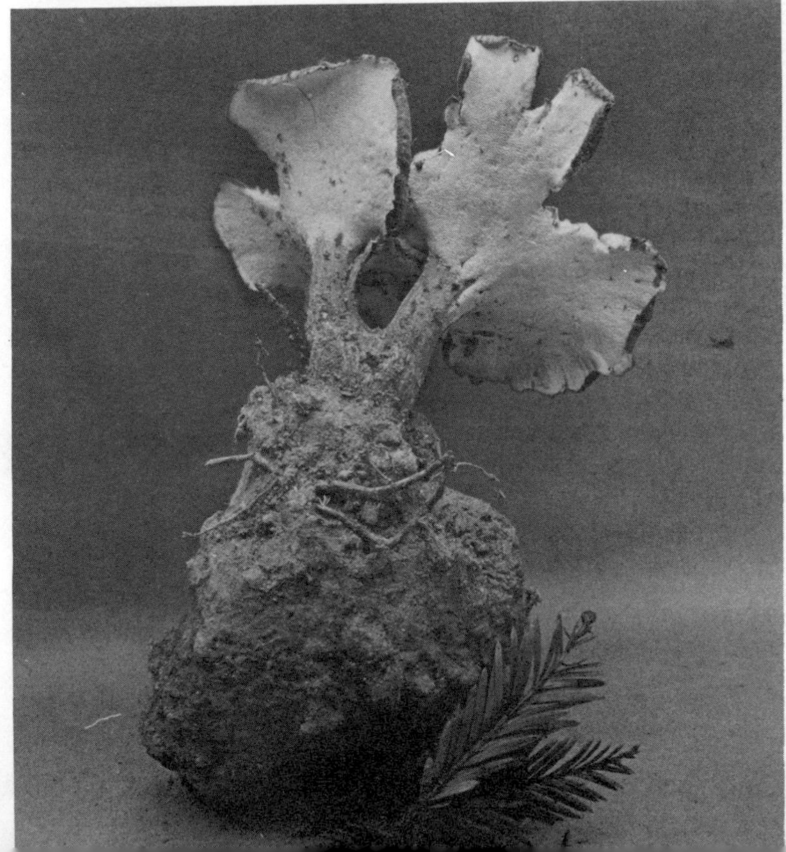

rubbery when fresh and rock-hard when dry. Exterior of sclerotium rough and irregular, interior usually containing dirt and debris. **SPORE PRINT** white; spores 10-16 × 4-6 μm, cylindric, smooth.

HABITAT: Solitary or in twos and threes on ground in mixed woods and under hardwoods. Occasional, fall through early spring.

EDIBILITY: Apparently edible; at least Native Americans valued it. Whether they ate the sclerotium (as once thought) or the fruiting body, or both, is unclear. The sclerotium is scarcely appetizing: black, full of dirt, and rock-hard when dry. But I've seen "Unnative" Americans eat stranger things—Spam, for instance, or Jujubes.

COMMENTS: The black "tuber" at the base of the stem immediately identifies this polypore. *Bondarzewia berkeleyi* may have a thick, rooting stem, but is much larger. The sclerotium might be mistaken for a piece of buried wood or a parasitized potato, but the rubbery texture when fresh is distinctive. It is thought to be a resting stage of the fungus, a secret storage compartment. If brought into the laboratory and moistened regularly, the sclerotium will produce one or more fruiting bodies. The North American version of this species is sometimes called (quite appropriately) *Polyporus tuckahoe.*

Bondarzewia berkeleyi (Berkeley's Bondarzewia)

FRUITING BODY massive, usually compound, up to 1 m (3 ft) broad; arising from a gnarled, usually rooting stalk. **INDIVIDUAL CAP(s)** 6-30 cm broad, fleshy-tough when fresh, rigid when dry; convex becoming centrally depressed; surface pale buff to grayish or yellowish-tan, finely hairy becoming smooth, sometimes with a fibrillose or pitted appearance. Flesh white, tough. **PORES** fairly large, 0.5-2 per mm; white or whitish, discoloring upon drying, decurrent. **STALK** short and thick, 5-13 cm long, and 2-5 cm thick above the ground, tapering to a gnarled, rooting underground base. **SPORE PRINT** white; spores 6-8 μm, round, with amyloid spines.

HABITAT: On ground around oaks or oak stumps, sometimes other hardwoods. Rare. It causes a serious delignifying butt rot of the heartwood in living trees ("string and ray rot").

EDIBILITY: Unknown. Too tough to be worthwhile but its mass makes experimentation tempting.

COMMENTS: The immense (usually) compound fruiting body and thick, gnarled rooting base set this species apart. The spiny, amyloid spores are diagnostic for the genus *Bondarzewia. B. montanus* has a dark tan to brown cap and grows around conifer stumps; it is also rare. A better-known species, *Polypilus frondosus,* strikes a very different pose: many small (less than 5 cm), crowded, overlapping spatula-shaped caps arising from a compact, branching framework. The overall appearance suggests a hen in her nest, hence its fanciful nickname, "Hen of the Woods." It grows at the base of hardwood stumps, and is a prize find—said to be the most delectable of all polypores, though it requires long, slow cooking. If it occurs in our area, it is rare indeed.

Albatrellus flettii (Blue-Capped Polypore)

CAP 7-25 cm broad, fleshy when fresh, tough when dry; convex becoming plane or with a depressed center, or somewhat irregular; surface dry, smooth, blue to dull blue-gray to greenish-blue when young, ochraceous-stained in age, margin usually paler, often wavy. Flesh thick, white, firm but tough. **PORES** small, 1-4 per mm, white, drying salmon, decurrent. **STALK** to 15 cm long and 4 cm thick, central or off-center, white, solid, smooth, drying dingy ochraceous. **SPORE PRINT** white; spores 3.5-4 × 2.5-3 μm, ellipsoid to nearly round, smooth.

Albatrellus flettii. The blue-gray to bluish-green cap, minute white pores, and prominent stalk distinguish this beautiful, unusual species. (Ralph Buchsbaum).

HABITAT: Gregarious or clustered on ground under knobcone pine, Henry Cowell Redwoods State Park, fall and winter. I have only seen it in the one locality but it may be more common than my own experience indicates. It is apparently endemic to the coniferous forests of the West.

EDIBILITY: Presumably edible and similar to *A. ovinus.* I haven't tried it.

COMMENTS: The blue cap and white pores contrast nicely to set this beautiful polypore apart. Dingy ochraceous or rusty-ochraceous stains develop on the cap in age but there are almost always vestiges of green or blue. The stature is similar to *A. ovinus,* perhaps not quite as compact.

Albatrellus ovinus

CAP 5-15 cm broad unless several are fused together; fleshy when fresh, tough when dry; convex becoming plane or sometimes irregular with a wavy margin; surface dry, unpolished, smooth at first but often cracking into scales in age, whitish becoming yellow, often developing olive or brownish tones in age. Flesh thick, white or yellowish, firm and tough. **PORES** minute, 2-4 per mm, white becoming lemon-yellow throughout or when bruised, usually decurrent. **STALK** to 10 cm long and 4 cm thick, central or slightly off-center, equal or enlarged below with a narrowed base, same color as cap or paler, solid, smooth, dry. **SPORE PRINT** white; spores 3-4.5 × 2.5-3.5 μm, ellipsoid to nearly round, smooth.

HABITAT: Solitary, scattered, or in fused masses, on ground under conifers, widely distributed but rather rare in our region; fall and winter.

EDIBILITY: Edible when cooked well. According to European sources it is fairly good. Large quantities can have a laxative effect, however. Material I tested in New Mexico was rather slimy ("okraceous") when cooked.

COMMENTS: This well-known and widespread *Albatrellus* is largely supplanted in our area by *A. flettii* and *A. avellaneus.* The colors are quite variable but there is usually a strong yellowish tint in age. A yellow pore surface (at maturity) is found in another species, *A. confluens,* which has a tan cap when young, tinted pinkish-cinnamon in age.

Albatrellus avellaneus. The pinkish-gray to purplish-gray cap (shown at center) distinguishes this terrestrial polypore. Pores are minute, pallid, and decurrent. Note tanoak leaves in background.

Albatrellus avellaneus

CAP 5-15 cm broad, fleshy when fresh, tough when dry; broadly convex to nearly plane, the margin often wavy and at first incurved; surface smooth, dry, violaceous-gray or with vinaceous to pinkish tones, typically more violaceous at the center and grayish on the margin. Flesh thick, firm, white. **PORES** minute, 2-4 per mm, decurrent, white or tinged gray to vinaceous-buff, shallow. **STALK** to 13 cm long, about 2 cm thick, central or slightly off-center, solid, dry, smooth, pallid or tinged cap color, sometimes rooting slightly, more or less equal or with a narrowed base. **SPORE PRINT** white; spores 3.5-4.5 $\times$ 2.5-4 μm, ellipsoid to nearly round, smooth.

HABITAT: Solitary or scattered in humus under tanoak and madrone, fall and winter; also said to grow under conifers. Fairly common near Bonny Doon, but usually visible only as a low hump ("mushrump") in the humus.

EDIBILITY: Presumably like *A. ovinus.* I haven't tried it.

COMMENTS: The delicate violaceous-gray to vinaceous-gray tones on the cap distinguish this attractive polypore from *A. ovinus.* Some treat it as a color form of that species. In our region the two are distinct insofar as they neither grow together nor intergrade. *Boletopsis griseus* is a bolete-like species with a white to grayish (often streaked) cap and short, thick stalk. It is found under both hardwoods and conifers but is partial to coastal sand dunes under pine. The white spores are warty and somewhat angular—a unique feature that sets it apart from all other polypores. It is edible but bitter.

A member of the *Poria corticola* group. Note the absence of both cap and stem. Most Porias consist solely of a layer of tubes.

Poria corticola (Poria)

FRUITING BODY resupinate, without a cap or stalk, but sometimes with a free margin. Flesh thin, white. **PORES** white, discoloring slightly in drying, 1-3 per mm; tubes rather soft, drying rigid, up to 10 mm long. **SPORE PRINT** white; spores 6-8 × 3-5 μm, ellipsoid, smooth.

HABITAT: In rows or confluent masses on rotting hardwood logs and branches; common, fall through spring. It produces a white rot. Several species are found on rotting conifers; a few are perennial.

EDIBILITY: The entire group is worthless from an edibility standpoint.

COMMENTS: Porias are among the most lackadaisical of fleshy fungi—they just lie there on their logs, listless and limpetlike, unobtrusively going about their business while boletivores and boletes blatantly go about theirs. The fruiting body may have a free margin or be entirely resupinate: a simple layer of tubes devoid of cap or stem. They generally grow on the undersides of logs, branches, and other dead wood. A few are serious pests of structural timber, especially in mines, where they find the abysmal, inhumane working conditions to their liking.

Like *Polyporus, Poria* has now been split, with the aid of the microscope, into several smaller genera. *P. corticola* is one of a half dozen species I have identified (there are dozens more I haven't). More than 150 species are known from North America. Even with a microscope, identification is a time-consuming and tedious (not to mention pointless) task. The fruiting body can be resupinate in several other genera, notably *Fomes* and *Trametes. Trametes (Coriollelus) serialis* has whitish tubes and a gray to brownish margin (or cap if present). It grows on dead conifers, occasionally on oak and madrone. *T. heteromorpha* is whitish to yellowish with large, irregular pores 1-2 mm in diameter. *T. carbonaria* is grayish to dark brown and grows on charred redwood. *T. sepium* should also be mentioned.

Serpula lacrymans (Dry Rot Fungus)

FRUITING BODY widely spreading, lying flat on horizontal substrate, sometimes bracketlike on vertical substrate; soft or spongy, 5 cm-1m (3 ft) broad; upper surface (or free margin) silvery-white to gray, hairy. Flesh thin, dingy yellowish; odor often unpleasant, musty. **PORES** olive-yellow, brownish-yellow, rusty-brown, orange-brown, or cinnamon; very shallow, large (1-3 mm broad), formed by a honeycomblike network of folds or ridges. **STALK** absent, but white or grayish mycelial strands (by which it spreads) often present. **SPORE PRINT** orange-brown to orange-yellow; spores 8-10 × 5-6 μm, ellipsoid, smooth.

HABITAT: A serious pest of structural wood (old houses, buildings, ships, etc.), developing in damp, poorly ventilated situations, often hiding under floorboards. Bulging wood and a musty odor are telltale signs of its presence. Common in Europe, where the ventilation in many houses was sealed off during the war; uncommon in North America. It is called dry rot because it extracts water from the wood and cracks it into cubical blocks, eventually reducing it to a fine, dark powder. Related species, such as *Merulius tremellosus,* occur in the wild—on rotten stumps, logs, and debris.

EDIBILITY: Utterly and indisputably inedible.

COMMENTS: One of the few fleshy fungi that lives up to the label *fungus* in its most pejorative sense—odious, insidious, obnoxious, downright abominable. Once it gains a foothold it is hard to eradicate because the often gigantic, padlike fruiting bodies exude great quantities of water, stimulating further fungal growth. The mycelial strands spread with astonishing rapidity. They feed only on wood, but like a horde of hungry army ants, they will overrun anything and everything in their way: bricks, stones, tiles, plaster, drain pipes, wires, leather boots, concrete floors, books, tea kettles, even corpses. For a fascinating account (and pictures) of some of its more heroic feats, see Ramsbottom's mycological masterpiece *Mushrooms and Toadstools.* The veined or honeycombed network of large, irregular, shallow pores is characteristic of *Serpula* (colored spores) and *Merulius* (colorless spores). They are now relegated, quite rightfully, to a family of their own.

Phlebia merismoides

FRUITING BODY resupinate, without cap or stalk the margin sometimes free; soft when fresh but soon tough; consisting of a layer of tissue forming continuous patches 2-30 cm long or more; upper surface flesh color to orange, fading to whitish in old age, covered with radiating warty veins or ridges; underside of margin (if free) with white woolly hairs. Flesh very thin. **SPORES** produced on surface, 4-6 $\times$ 1.5-2.5 μm, white, sausage-shaped, smooth.

HABITAT: On fallen logs and branches, especially oak, fall and winter, fairly common.

EDIBILITY: Inedible. It looks as if it has already been eaten (see below).

COMMENTS: The resupinate orange-flesh fruiting body with radiating veins is unique. Its overall appearance is somewhat reminiscent of regurgitated dog food. A similar species, *Radulum orbiculare,* has an irregularly warty spore-producing surface and is *distinctly* reminiscent of regurgitated dog food. There are many other resupinate fungi with a smooth spore surface (*Corticium, Peniophora,* etc). These are overlooked by amateurs and ignored by professionals, yet they play an integral role in forest decay. They can be found almost anywhere, at any time. Some "whitewash" sticks and branches, or cause dark discolorations on the surfaces of trees and stumps. Others are found on muddy soil or grasses, on old bridges and rotting rafters. None are edible.

Stereum hirsutum (Hairy Stereum)

FRUITING BODY usually bracketlike; pliant when fresh, rigid when dry, several often joined together; sometimes resupinate with a free margin. **CAP** up to 4 cm broad but usually smaller, upper surface somewhat concentrically zoned; grayish-buff or darker, covered with hairs, margin often golden-orange. Flesh thin, tough. **UNDERSIDE** smooth or somewhat uneven, orange-tawny fading to pinkish-buff, buff, or grayish, often brighter toward margin. **STALK** absent. **SPORE PRINT** white; spores 5-7 $\times$ 2.5-3.5 μm, oblong, smooth.

HABITAT: Gregarious in rows or overlapping clusters on hardwood stumps, logs, fallen branches, rarely on living trees. Exceedingly abundant in fall and winter, especially on live oak, but shriveled

Stereum hirsutum is one of our most common bracket fungi. It usually grows in large rows or columns on rotting hardwoods. The cap is usually zoned; the underside (second from right) is smooth—that is, it lacks pores.

specimens can be found almost any time. *Coriolus, Lenzites,* and *Tremella* often co-inhabit the same log.

EDIBILITY: Too thin and tough to be edible.

COMMENTS: This omnipresent little bracket fungus resembles *Coriolus versicolor* but has a smooth underside. It is the most common member of the genus. There are many other *Stereum*s. Like myself, they are too tough and thin to be edible. Unlike myself, they content themselves with unambitious undertakings—branches, sticks, and lopped-off limbs—leaving the stumps, logs, and living trees to the true polypores.

Because of the smooth pore surface, *Stereum,* though related to the polypores, is sequestered in a separate family, the Corticiaceae. Other species include: *S. fasciatum,* cap covered with soft hairs and underside buff, sometimes tinged violet, growing on oak; *S. rameale,* growing on hardwoods, smaller and thinner than *S. hirsutum,* cinnamon-buff to hazel with a golden margin; *S. ochraceoflavum,* a common species with miniscule, somewhat conical, hairy white cap and yellowish to buff underside, growing on hardwoods; *S. sanguinolentum* and *S. gausapatum,* exuding a red juice when cut, the first growing on conifers, the second on hardwoods; *S. purpureum,* parasitizing plum trees, causing silver-leaf disease; and *Hymenochaete rubiginosa,* velvety, zoned, cap chestnut-colored with golden margin, underside rusty-brown, growing on oak.

Stereum "burtianum"

CAP less than 2.5 cm broad, funnel-shaped, very thin, tough, often split or incised on one side; surface dry, with fine radiating silky fibrils, buff to hazel-brown. **UNDERSIDE** smooth or somewhat uneven, yellowish-ochre to buff or cap color. **STALK** to 2.5 cm long, more or less central, thin (less than 2 mm), solid, smooth, colored more or less like cap or underside. **SPORE PRINT** white; spores 5-6 × 3-4 μm, broadly elliptical to nearly round, smooth.

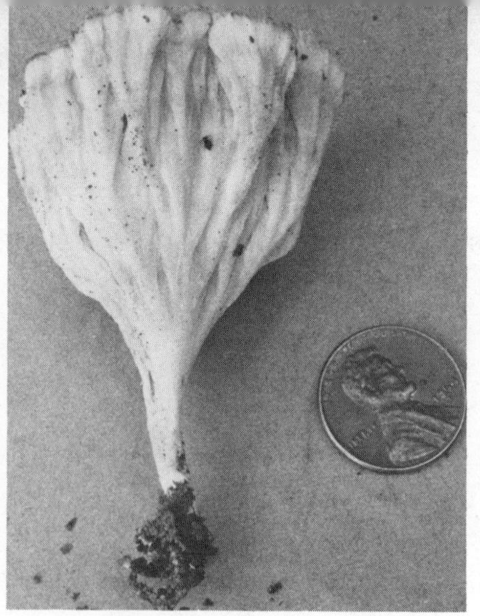

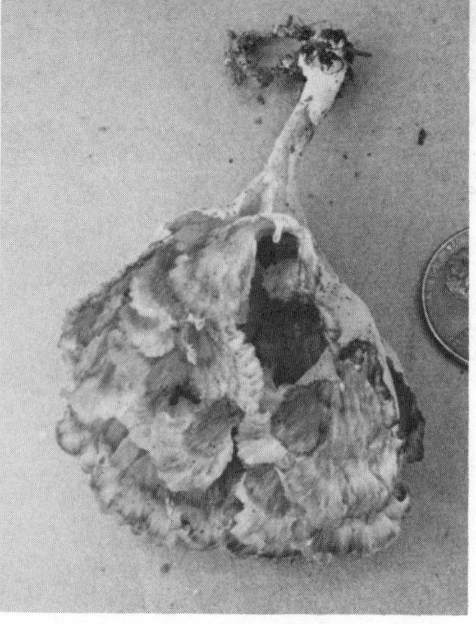

Stereum "burtianum" is a common terrestrial species with very thin, tough flesh and a smooth underside. **Left:** Close-up of underside. **Right:** Top view of the funnel-shaped cap, which in this specimen is compound.

HABITAT: Solitary or in groups in woods, among humus and debris; fall and winter, common.

EDIBILITY: A worthless, miniscule morsel.

COMMENTS: There are several discrepancies between our variety and the true *S. burtianum* but the above description will suffice for both. The presence of a stem separates it from other Stereums, while the pale hazel to buff color and white spores distinguish it from *Thelephora terrestris.* A similar whitish species, *S. diaphanum,* also occurs.

Thelephora terrestris

FRUITING BODY tough; usually funnel-shaped to fan-shaped, typically clustered or confluent, sometimes shelflike on plant stems; clusters up to 7.5 cm broad but usually smaller; surface with radiating silky fibrils, chocolate to brown to fuscous, margin usually fringed or split and often paler. Flesh very thin, tough. **UNDERSIDE** smooth or somewhat uneven, fuscous to fawn-colored to cap color. **STALK** when present thin and tough, colored like cap or paler, smooth. **SPORE PRINT** purplish-brown; spores 6-9 $\times$ 6-7 μm, angular, warted.

HABITAT: Usually clustered, occasionally solitary, in humus and decomposing vegetable matter, sometimes climbing herbaceous stems. Fairly common, fall through spring, but easily overlooked.

EDIBILITY: Unknown.

COMMENTS: The size and shape of this species is fairly variable but the color is quite constant (quite variable? fairly constant?). When growing on the ground in small, erect clusters it might be mistaken for an emaciated *Craterellus.* When growing on herbaceous stems it looks more like a *Stereum. Thelephora* belongs to the Thelephoraceae, a family which formerly included all the bracketlike and resupinate fungi with a smooth spore-producing surface (such as *Stereum*). There are several related species. *Thelephora laciniata* is a synonym.

Thelephora palmata

FRUITING BODY erect, branching; up to 10 cm high and broad; purplish-brown to chocolate-brown throughout, the numerous branches flattened with paler tips. Flesh leathery, odor garliclike becoming fetid or unpleasant. **STALK** usually present as a slender trunk below the branches, colored like branches. **SPORE PRINT** dark reddish-brown; spores 8-11 $\times$ 7-8 μm, angular, spiny.

HABITAT: Solitary or in groups on moist ground in woods. It usually grows along paths but blends uncannily into its surroundings. Fairly common, late fall and winter.

EDIBILITY: Unknown.

COMMENTS: This mushroom looks like a coral fungus and is keyed out there. Microscopically, however, it is closer to *Thelephora terrestris.* The flattened, purplish-chocolate branches and fetid garlic odor are diagnostic.

Thelephora palmata looks like a coral mushroom but has flattened branches and a fetid garlic odor.

Teeth Fungi

HYDNACEAE

AS their name implies, the teeth fungi produce their spores on pendant **spines** or "teeth." The fruiting body is usually stipitate (equipped with a cap and stem), with the spines lining the underside of the cap. *Hericium,* however, grows on wood and has teeth which hang like icicles from a rooting base or network of branches.

The teeth fungi include some stunningly beautiful mushrooms. They are common in heavily forested regions like the Pacific Northwest, but rather infrequent here. *Hericium* and *Dentinum* are excellent eating; the rest are too bitter or tough.

Just as the boletes were once lumped together in *Boletus,* so all the teeth fungi were originally placed in a single genus, *Hydnum.* Several families and genera are now recognized, delimited primarily by the shape and texture of the fruiting body and the color and ornamentation of the spores. For ease of identification, the six genera presented here have been retained in a single family.

Key to the Hydnaceae

1. Fruiting body with a cap and stalk; spines on underside of cap; growing on ground or on rotting conifer cones 2
1. Fruiting body a branched or unbranched mass of tissue from which icicle-like spines are suspended; growing on wood .. *Hericium,* p. 481

2. Fruiting body rubbery, small (5 cm broad or less), translucent white to watery gray; stalk lateral ... (see *Pseudohydnum gelatinosum,* p. 577)
2. Not as above 3

3. Small; stalk slender, attached to side of cap; growing on decaying cones of conifers .... *Auriscalpium,* p. 492
3. Not as above 4

4. Fruiting body fleshy or brittle 5
4. Fruiting body tough, fibrous (but may be spongy when young) 6

5. Spore print white; spines creamy-white to orange ..... *Dentinum,* p. 484
5. Spore print brown; spines usually dark (brown, violet, black, etc.) .... *Hydnum,* p. 486

6. Spore print white; individual caps small (5 cm broad or less), thin-fleshed .... *Phellodon,* p. 491
6. Spore print brown; individual caps medium-sized or large (4 cm broad or more) .... *Hydnellum,* p. 489

HERICIUM

Medium to large fleshy fungi *growing on wood.* FRUITING BODY *usually white; branched or unbranched, with clusters or rows of soft, delicate hanging spines.* SPORE PRINT white; spores more or less round, smooth, amyloid.

A pristine, full-grown *Hericium* is a breathtaking sight, one you are not likely to forget. The fruiting body is unmistakable: a mass of soft, fragile "icicles" suspended from a delicate framework of branches (or in the case of *H. erinaceus,* from an unbranched basal plug of tissue).

Hericiums grow exclusively on wood. This combined with the amyloid spores and novel fruiting body has led modern mycologists to reward them with a family of their own. They are sometimes abundant in the coniferous forests of the Pacific Northwest, but are rather rare in California. You are fortunate indeed to find one.

Hericiums are as delectable as they are beautiful—if you can bear to pick them in the first place. They are excellent fresh as well as marinated or pickled. Three species are described here.

Key to Hericium

1. Fruiting body unbranched; consisting of a tough, basal plug of tissue from which the long spines hang .... *H. erinaceus,* below
1. Fruiting body branched; spines hanging from branches 2
2. Branching open, delicate; spines 3-10 mm long, lining entire length of branches .... *H. ramosum,* p. 483
2. Branching compact until mature; spines 5-40 mm long, mostly clustered at branch tips .... *H. coralloides,* p. 482

Hericium erinaceus (Bear's Head Hericium)

FRUITING BODY unbranched, compact, to 30 cm in diameter; consisting of numerous long, slender spines hanging from a tough, solid, rooting plug of tissue; entirely white when fresh, aging or discoloring yellowish to dingy brownish. Flesh white. **SPINES** up to 7 cm long (usually 2-5 cm), soft. **SPORE PRINT** white; spores 5-6.5 × 4-5.5 µm, nearly round, smooth, amyloid.

HABITAT: Solitary or in groups, growing from wounds on living hardwoods or on the cut ends of recently felled logs; especially fond of live oak and tanoak. Fruiting in fall, winter, and early spring, rare.

EDIBILITY: Edible. I haven't tried it. The rooting base is so tough that it's difficult to remove from the log without a knife. Slow cooking is called for.

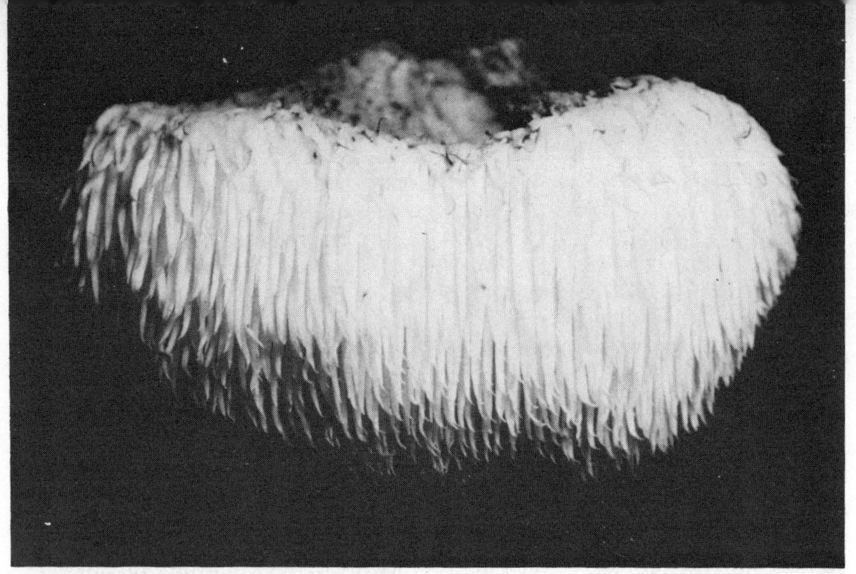

Hericium erinaceus. The fruiting body is unbranched, with long spines suspended from a tough, rooting base. It grows on hardwoods.

COMMENTS: The unbranched fruiting body and long, slender spines distinguish this impressive fungus from its relatives. Though not common, it is found just as often as the branched Hericiums.

Hericium coralloides (Coral Hericium)

FRUITING BODY up to 60 cm in diameter but usually smaller; comprised of a system of branches arising from a thick, tough, rooting base; large clusters of long spines hanging downward from branch tips; compact when young, more open in age; color pure white throughout when fresh, aging or discoloring yellowish to buff. Flesh white. **SPINES** up to 40 mm long but typically about 25 mm; soft. **SPORE PRINT** white; spores 5-6 $\times$ 4.5-5.5 μm, almost round, smooth, amyloid.

HABITAT: Solitary or several on stumps and logs of both conifers and hardwoods, fall and winter. Rare, but fruiting year after year from the same log.

EDIBILITY: Eminently edible, delectably delicious. This species and its relatives are among the best (as well as most beautiful) of all fungi. The cooked flesh has the texture of fish, and is excellent sauteed, curried, or marinated.

COMMENTS: This fantastic fungus is easily recognized by its branching fruiting body with terminal clusters of long, white spines. It is such an astonishing sight that one hesitates to pick it. *H. caput-ursi* is a synonym. Another large, fleshy species, *H. abietis (=H. weirii)* is known from the Pacific Northwest. It differs in having salmon-buff to yellowish or ochraceous spines.

Hericium coralloides. In this beautiful species the spines hang in clusters from the tips of the branches. This is the most common *Hericium* in northern California and the Pacific Northwest. (Herb Saylor)

Hericium ramosum (Delicate Hericium)

FRUITING BODY up to 30 cm broad but usually much smaller; comprised of an open, delicate system of branches arising from a small, tough "root"; pure white throughout when fresh, discoloring buff or yellowish-buff in old age. Flesh white. **SPINES** along entire length of

Hericium ramosum has spines lining entire length of branches instead of being clustered at branch tips.

branches, rather short (3-10 mm long), thin. **SPORE PRINT** white; spores 4-5.5 × 3.5-4 µm, almost round, smooth, amyloid.

HABITAT: Solitary or several on fallen hardwood branches, logs, and stumps (mostly live oak). Uncommon, fall and winter.

EDIBILITY: Edible and choice, but not as fleshy as the other Hericiums.

COMMENTS: This lovely species is smaller and more delicate than *H. coralloides.* The branching is more open and the spines occur along the entire length of the branches. Also, the spines are shorter and the spores slightly smaller. *H. laciniatum* is a synonym.

DENTINUM (HEDGEHOG MUSHROOMS)

Medium-sized *terrestrial* fungi with cap and stalk. CAP *fleshy,* not conspicuously scaly. SPINES soft, brittle, *white to pale orange.* STALK central or off-center, well developed, *fleshy.* SPORE PRINT *white.* Spores smooth, not amyloid.

THE most common and best-known of the teeth fungi, hedgehog mushrooms are easily recognized by their agaric-like fruiting body, fleshy texture, white to orange spines, and smooth white spores. *Phellodon* has white spores but is tough and thin-fleshed. *Hydnum* is fleshy but has brown, warted spores and darker spines.

Despite there being little doubt as to what a hedgehog mushroom *is,* there is (as usual) considerable controversy as to what a hedgehog mushroom should be *called. Dentinum* is the most popular candidate, but some mycologists steadfastly campaign for *Hydnum* and go so far as to erect another genus, *Sarcodon,* to account for the Hydnums of this book. A "correct" classification of the teeth fungi may not be essential to your well-being (it certainly isn't to mine), but please bear in mind that the exacting specialists owe their livelihood to the resolution of such matters—and that they are doing their best. Giving even tacit approval to one system of classification at the expense of another is thus transformed into an act of great importance, with one's professional reputation at stake. Why people can't arrive at a consensus is anyone's guess—I for one find them as mystifying as mushrooms!

Dentinums are excellent eating, a good choice for beginners since nothing poisonous remotely resembles them. They are woodland fungi, but their fruiting pattern is extremely erratic. In February of 1975 they were outrageously abundant on the poison-oak-shrouded hillsides of our coastal pine forests. While barely denting the crop I managed to harvest and can over 200 pounds, which I am still enjoying today! Since then, however, they've been practically absent, even during the waterlogged winter of 1978. Only a few species are known. Two are keyed below.

Key to Dentinum

1. Cap convex, plane, or depressed; stalk stout, generally 1 cm thick or more .... *D. repandum,* below
1. Cap umbilicate (with a navellike depression); stalk generally less than 1 cm thick .... *D. umbilicatum* (see *D. repandum,* below)

Dentinum repandum (Hedgehog Mushroom)

CAP up to 15 cm broad, convex becoming plane or depressed, the margin often wavy or indented; surface smooth or sometimes cracked at the center into scales; salmon-buff to orange-brown, reddish-tan, or cinnamon, sometimes nearly white. Flesh thick, firm, brittle, pallid, odor mild, taste mild or slightly peppery. **SPINES** 3-7 mm long, creamy-white to salmon-buff or pale orange, bruising or aging dark orange to ochraceous; slender, brittle, soft. **STALK** up to 10 cm long, solid, thick, central or off-center, colored like cap or paler, equal or enlarged below (occasionally tapered below), smooth. **SPORE PRINT** white; spores 6-8 × 5-6 μm, nearly round, smooth.

HABITAT: Scattered or in troops in woods, winter and spring. Common some years, practically absent during others. It grows with

Dentinum repandum. **Left:** This delicious edible species looks like an agaric from the top. Cap color varies from rufous-salmon to nearly white. **Right:** Underside of cap is lined with whitish to pale orange spines. (Ray Gipson)

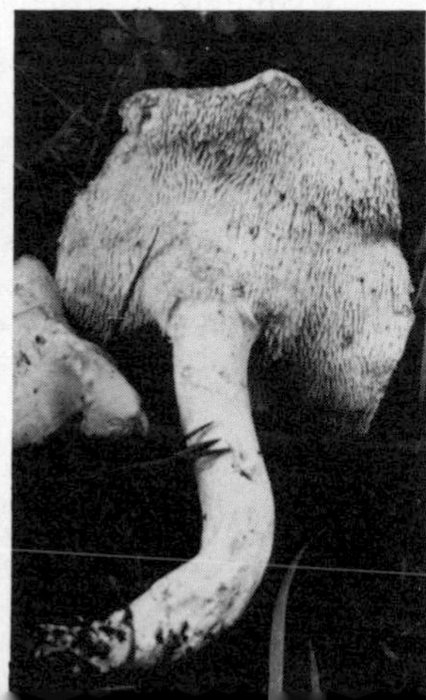

both hardwoods and conifers but in our region shows a definite preference for coastal pine forests in thickets of poison oak. Generous winter or spring rains will often elicit a bumper crop.

EDIBILITY: Edible and choice, comparable to the chanterelle in color and texture, but with a far superior flavor. The peppery taste (if present) disappears in cooking. It's superb in casseroles, tomato sauces, or sauteed in sour cream. Be careful to keep the spines clean while harvesting.

COMMENTS: This late bloomer superficially resembles the chanterelle *(Cantharellus cibarius)* but has white to pale orange spines under the cap. This alone should be enough to identify it. The cap color, though variable, is typically some shade of orange-buff to reddish-tan (with wounded areas darker orange), but a white form is sometimes found. *D. umbilicatum* is a smaller, equally edible hedgehog mushroom with a slightly darker umbilicate cap, slimmer (less than 1 cm) stalk, and larger spores (7.5-9 × 6-7.5 µm). It is partial to boggy areas under conifers.

HYDNUM

Medium-sized to large *terrestrial fungi* with cap and stalk. CAP *fleshy, often coarsely scaly*. SPINES soft, brittle, *usually dark* (brown, violet, black, etc.). STALK central or off-center, well developed, solid. SPORE PRINT *brown;* spores rough or warted.

HYDNUM as defined here embraces a large number of fleshy, terrestrial teeth fungi with brown spores. The fruiting body is not tough or woody as in the other brown-spored genus, *Hydnellum.* The spines are not white to pale orange as in *Dentinum,* and the cap is usually scaly. *Sarcodon* is a generic synonym (see comments under *Dentinum*).

Hydnums are strictly woodland fungi that fruit in the fall and winter. The edibility of many species is unknown, while others are bitter. I have found only two species in our area, keyed below.

Key to Hydnum

1. Cap, flesh, and spines deep violet when fresh, violet-black or bluish-black in age .... *H. fuscoindicum,* p. 488
1. Cap brown with darker brown scales; spines also brown .... *H. imbricatum,* p. 487

Hydnum imbricatum. Note the large brown scales on the cap. Specimen at left is turned over to show the layer of brown spines.

Hydnum imbricatum (Shingled Hydnum)

CAP 5-20 cm broad, convex with the center becoming depressed in age; surface dry, light brown with large, coarse, raised darker brown scales, becoming darker brown throughout in age. Flesh thick, firm, rather tough but not woody, pallid becoming brownish, odor mild, aromatic when drying, taste mild or more often somewhat bitter. **SPINES** pale brown becoming dark brown, 5-15 mm long, soft, brittle, decurrent. **STALK** to 10 cm long, about 2.5 cm thick, central or off-center, equal or enlarged below, smooth, more or less cap color. **SPORE PRINT** brown; spores 6-8 $\times$ 5-7 μm, nearly round, warted.

HABITAT: Solitary or in twos and threes in woods, fall and winter, widely distributed but infrequent in our area. I find it once or twice a year, usually under hardwoods.

EDIBILITY: Edible, but of poor quality. Bitter forms must be parboiled. Nevertheless, it is eaten in Europe and even marketed.

COMMENTS: The brown spines and coarse brown scales on the cap are the fallible fieldmarks of this arresting *Hydnum.* There are a number of similar species. One, *H. fennicum,* has a scaly brown cap, but the base of the stem is bluish-green to blackish-olive, the odor mealy (farinaceous), and the taste extremely bitter.

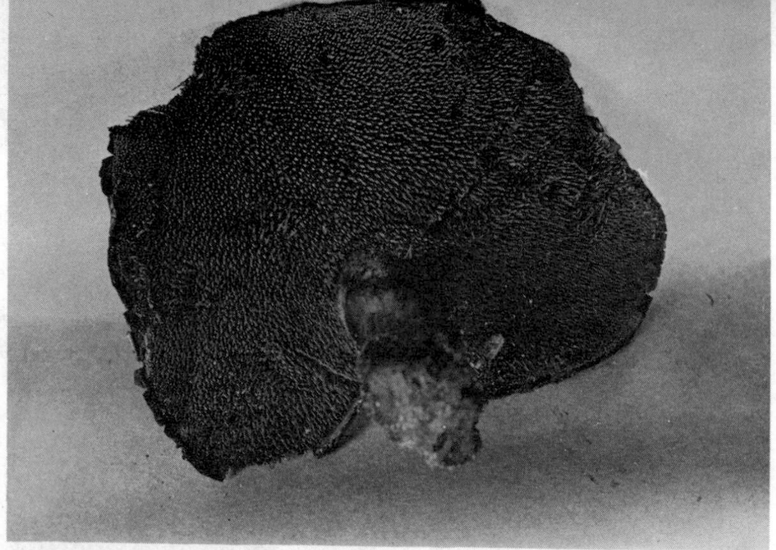

Hydnum fuscoindicum. Entire fruiting body, including the spines, is deep blue-black to violet-black. This specimen was found under tanoak and madrone.

Hydnum fuscoindicum (Violet-Black Hydnum)

CAP 5-18 cm broad, convex with a depressed center, expanding somewhat in age, the margin often undulating or wavy; surface dry, becoming coarsely scaly, deep violet becoming violet-black, bluish-black, or black. Flesh thick, firm, rather tough but not woody, odor and taste mild. **SPINES** deep violet to deep bluish-violet, tips paler, soft, brittle, decurrent, 4-15 mm long. **STALK** up to 8 cm long, stout, tapering downward, central or off-center, solid, firm, smooth, colored more or less like spines. **SPORE PRINT** brown; spores 5-6.5 × 4.5-5 μm, nearly round, warted.

HABITAT: Scattered to gregarious on ground in mixed woods of tanoak-madrone, fall and winter. Rare, but occurring in large quantities when it fruits.

EDIBILITY: Unknown. The taste is not bitter and none of its relatives are known to be poisonous, so it might be worth trying, if cooked well. It would also be interesting to see what colors it yields as a dye.

COMMENTS: The striking deep violet color sets this attractive *Hydnum* apart. There are several bluish-black Hydnellums, but they are much tougher. The cap is hard to pick out against the gloomy backdrop of the forest floor. Even the eagle-eyed *Hydnum*-hound is likely to pass it over, because from a distance it looks like an old, blackened *Russula.* I did not find it until just prior to the publication of this book, when it fruited in great abundance in a single locality near Bonny Doon. This illustrates why no mushroom field guide should make even a pretense of being complete—there is a direct correlation between the documented distribution of the lesser-known mushrooms and the undocumented distribution of the better-known mycologists—and so much depends on their being in the right place at the right time.

HYDNELLUM

Medium-sized to large *terrestrial* fungi with cap and stalk, growing singly or in compound rosettes. CAP *tough, fibrous or woody,* surface usually fibrillose, velvety, or warty. Flesh often duplex. SPINES typically short and blunt, variously colored. STALK central or off-center, sometimes nearly absent, continuous with cap, *tough.* SPORE PRINT *brown;* spores rough or warty.

THIS is a well-defined group of terrestrial teeth fungi found primarily in coniferous woods. The tough, fibrous or woody texture separates it from *Hydnum,* while the brown spore print distinguishes it from *Phellodon.* The cap may be spongy when fresh, with the aspect of a polypore (e.g., *Phaeolus schweinitzii*), but a closer look reveals the presence of spines on the underside instead of pores. The spines are shorter and blunter than in other teeth fungi, so that at times they look more like warts. Several Hydnellums and Hydnums, in fact, have polypore look-alikes, which suggests they had common ancestors. The flesh is often **duplex** (composed of two zones of somewhat different texture), and the surface of the cap is sometimes beaded with brightly colored droplets.

Hydnellums grow rapidly, engulfing needles and twigs in the process; several individuals often fuse together to form larger (confluent) masses. They are much too tough to eat, and often bitter besides.

Hydnellum is a sizable genus. Like *Hydnum* and *Phellodon,* it is common in the Pacific Northwest and northern California, but infrequent south of San Francisco. Two species are keyed below.

Key to Hydnellum

1. Cap white when actively growing, becoming orange to rusty-cinnamon; red water droplets absent .... *H. aurantiacum,* below
1. Cap white when actively growing, becoming cinnamon to reddish or blackish-red; surface often beaded with red to pink droplets .... *H. scrobiculatum* (see *H. aurantiacum,* below)

Hydnellum aurantiacum

CAP 4-15 cm broad; plane or depressed; surface rough (with knobs and lumps) when mature, finely velvety; white when rapidly growing, becoming orange to rusty-cinnamon, all of these colors often present;

Hydnellum aurantiacum resembles a polypore when seen from above (specimen at right). However, underside is lined with short, blunt "teeth" (specimen at left). Note how fruiting body engulfs debris as it grows.

darker in age. Flesh duplex (zoned); orange to rusty-cinnamon, thick, very tough; odor mild, taste bitter. **SPINES** short and blunt, 3-4 mm long, whitish becoming brown with pale tips. **STALK** to 5 cm long, less than 2.5 cm thick, very tough, continuous with cap, equal or enlarged below, orange to bright rusty-cinnamon, darker in age, with a large mat of pine needles and debris usually stuck to the base. **SPORE PRINT** brown; spores 5.5-7.5 × 5-6 μm, nearly round, warted.

HABITAT: Scattered or in groups (sometimes fused together), under pine and other conifers, late fall and winter, occasional. It is common throughout North America but seldom fruits in large numbers.

EDIBILITY: Irrefutably inedible.

COMMENTS: The tough texture, knobby or lumpy cap surface, and orange to rusty-cinnamon color at maturity are the key characteristics. It is more likely to be mistaken for a polypore than for a *Hydnum* or *Dentinum*. Another species, *Hydnellum scrobiculatum,* has a cinnamon to blackish-red cap usually beaded with red droplets. It is common in the coastal pine forests of northern California. Very similar is *H. diabolus,* with a marked sweetish-pungent odor. There are also several bluish species, including *H. cyanopodium,* with a bluish-vinaceous cap, brown spines, and a fragrant odor; and *H. caeruleum,* with a purple-tinted cap becoming whitish and then brown, flesh zoned with brown and blue or purple, and mild odor.

PHELLODON

Small to medium-sized *terrestrial* fungi with cap and stem, growing singly or in fused masses. CAP *tough or fibrous;* surface usually rough, hairy or felty. Flesh often duplex, odor usually fragrant. SPINES delicate, pale, becoming light brown to gray. STALK central or off-center, *tough,* well developed, often with mycelium at base. SPORE PRINT *white.* Spores spiny, not amyloid.

THIS is a small genus, similar to *Hydnellum* but with white spores and a smaller, thinner fruiting body. It can be separated from *Dentinum* by its tougher texture, thinner flesh, and different color. Like *Hydnellum,* the fruiting bodies often fuse together in rosettes and the flesh is frequently duplex.

There are several widely distributed Phellodons but I have yet to find any south of San Francisco. This means very little, however, since even the "common" teeth fungi have very erratic fruiting habits. Three species are keyed below, in the expectation that they may turn up, just as *Hydnum fuscoindicum* did. All are too tough to eat.

Key to Phellodon

1. Cap bluish-black .... *P. atratus* (see *P. tomentosus,* below)
1. Not as above 2

2. Mature cap zoned with yellow-brown and dark cinnamon, the margin usually white .... *P. tomentosus,* below
2. Cap grayish or brownish .... *P. niger* (see *P. tomentosus,* below)

Phellodon tomentosus

CAP less than 5 cm broad, plane to depressed; surface dry, zoned at maturity with yellow-brown and dark cinnamon; margin white, felty to the touch when young, brownish when rubbed. Flesh thin, tough, odor fragrant, taste faintly bitter. **SPINES** delicate, short (up to 2 mm long), pale fawn or pale brown at maturity, the tips white. **STALK** to 6 cm long, rather slender, continuous with cap, tapering downward, arising from spongy pads of mycelium, more or less cap color. **SPORE PRINT** white; spores 3.5-4.5 μm, round, minutely spiny.

HABITAT: Scattered to gregarious (sometimes fused together but stalks usually separate), on ground under conifers, fall and winter. I have found it in northern California; just how far south it occurs is uncertain.

EDIBILITY: Unknown. Too small and tough to be of value.

COMMENTS: The beautifully zoned yellow-brown-cinnamon cap, fragrant odor, and slender stem are good fieldmarks. It bears a striking resemblance to *Coltrichia perennis* (a polypore)—indicating a possible relationship between the two. There are several other Phellodons, including *P. atratus,* with a bluish-black cap, and *P. niger,* with a grayish cap. Both are rather small (individual caps usually less than 5 cm broad), and grow under conifers.

AURISCALPIUM

THIS genus contains a single odd species with a worldwide distribution. Microscopic characteristics indicate a closer relationship to the agaric genus *Lentinellus* than to other teeth fungi.

Auriscalpium vulgare (Ear Pick Fungus)

CAP less than 5 cm broad, broadly convex to plane or somewhat depressed; surface dry, covered with dense dark brown fibrils or hairs, sometimes blackish in age, margin often fringed and paler. Flesh firm, thin, pliant, tough, white to light brown. **SPINES** flesh-colored to brown or purple-brown, very fine, 2-3 mm long. **STALK** to 7 cm long, 1-3 mm thick, attached to side of cap, densely hairy (especially toward base), equal or slightly enlarged below, more or less cap color. **SPORE PRINT** white; spores 5-6 × 4-5 μm, round or nearly round, smooth becoming minutely spiny, amyloid.

Auriscalpium vulgare. This diminutive little tooth fungus grows only on decaying cones (in this case, Douglas-fir). Note the long, slender hairy stem attached to side of cap.

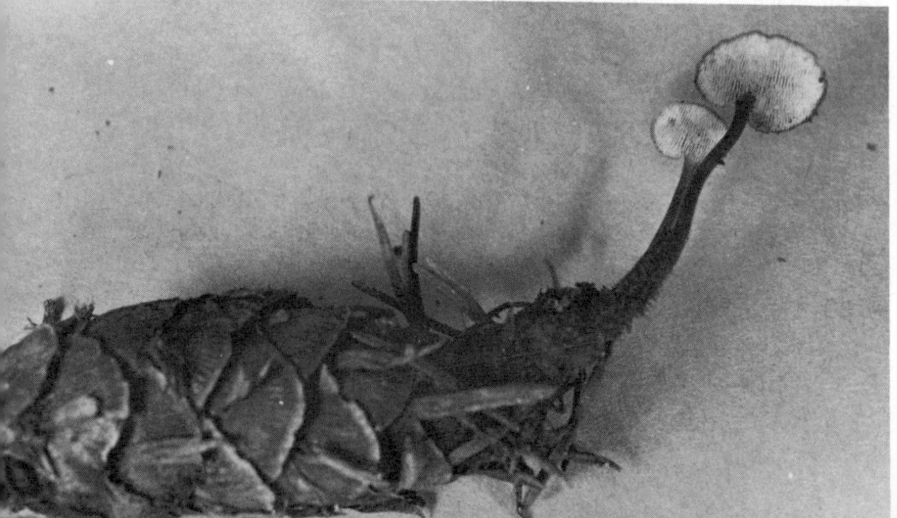

HABITAT: Solitary or in small groups on rotting (often buried) cones of conifers, or sometimes on thick mats of debris made up in part by decaying cones. Rare in our area; I have found it in winter near Boulder Creek on rotting Douglas-fir cones.

EDIBILITY: Too small and tough to be of value.

COMMENTS: The small size, thin hairy lateral stem, amyloid spores, and habitat on cones distinguish this petite tooth fungus. The stem, though lateral, may occasionally appear central. It is usually longer than the width of the cap and far thinner than that of any other tooth fungus.

Coral and Club Fungi

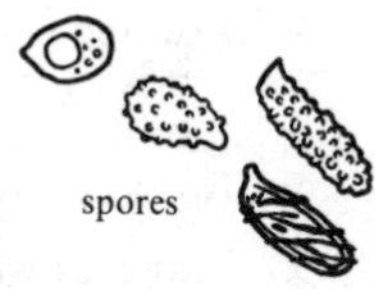

CLAVARIACEAE

This large and lovely group of fleshy fungi includes simple, unbranched, upright clubs and fleshy, intricately branched coral-like forms. With the exception of *Clavariadelphus,* the fruiting body is *not* differentiated into an upper sterile surface (or cap) and fertile underside. Instead the spores are produced on basidia which line the smooth to occasionally wrinkled surfaces of the upright clubs or branches. In many species, however, a sterile fleshy base (stalk or trunk) is present.

Coral fungi are a conspicuous and colorful component of our woodland fungi. They come in every imaginable color, and some of the larger branched forms (notably *Sparassis*) are edible. It is a difficult group from a taxonomic standpoint, however. All corals were originally lumped together in one unwieldy genus, *Clavaria.* Since the advent of the microscope, *Clavaria* has been split into more than 30 genera, only a few of which are treated here. Among them is *Ramaria,* which is microscopically similar to *Gomphus* of the Cantharellaceae, and is thought to have evolved from a common ancestor (the two are placed in the family Gomphaceae by some taxonomists). Microscopic and chemical characteristics have assumed great importance in identification, but a more traditional classification scheme is offered here. To facilitate identification in the field, the family has been divided into five groups, keyed below.

Key to the Clavariaceae

1. Fruiting body unbranched or very sparingly branched; solitary or in tufts or clusters 2
1. Fruiting body profusely branched from a common base 4
2. Fruiting body entirely black *or* black with white branch tips *or* parasitic on insects and truffles *or* entirely green to blue-green .... (see **Ascomycetes,** p. 583)
2. Not as above 3
3. Fruiting body with tough flesh, usually club-shaped or enlarged at apex, usually 7 mm thick or more .... *Clavariadelphus,* below
3. Fruiting body typically small and fragile, usually less than 7 mm thick .... *Clavaria* and *Clavulinopsis,* p. 496
4. Fruiting body with conspicuously flattened, wavy, or ribbonlike branches arising from a tough, rooting base; white to yellowish-buff or cinnamon-buff .... *Sparassis,* p. 514
4. Not as above 5
5. Branches white to gray or lavender-gray; spore print white* .... *Clavulina* and *Ramariopsis,* p. 500
5. Branches some other color (including violet); spore print yellowish to tan or ochraceous .... *Ramaria,* p. 503

* A spore print can be obtained in the usual manner, by laying the fruiting body on a piece of white paper and covering it with a glass or bowl.

CLAVARIADELPHUS (CLUB CORALS)

Medium-sized terrestrial woodland fungi. FRUITING BODY *erect, unbranched, more or less club-shaped; 7 mm thick or more,* surface usually wrinkled. *Flesh rather tough.* SPORE PRINT white to pale ochraceous; spores typically smooth, elliptical.

THESE are rather tough, club-shaped fungi with a smooth or wrinkled spore-producing surface. They are larger and thicker than the Clavarias and not nearly so fragile. In *C. truncatus* the apex of the club is very broad, flat, and sterile—in other words, a rudimentary cap.

Clavariadelphus species are too tough to be edible. They are confined to the woods and fruit mostly in the winter. Two widespread species are described here. If your "club coral" is small and irregularly shaped, check the earth tongues (Geoglossaceae), p. 614.

Key to Clavariadelphus

1. Apex broad, truncate (flattened to shallowly depressed); associated with conifers .... *C. truncatus,* p. 496
1. Apex obtuse to rounded or bluntly pointed; associated mostly with hardwoods .... *C. pistillaris,* p. 495

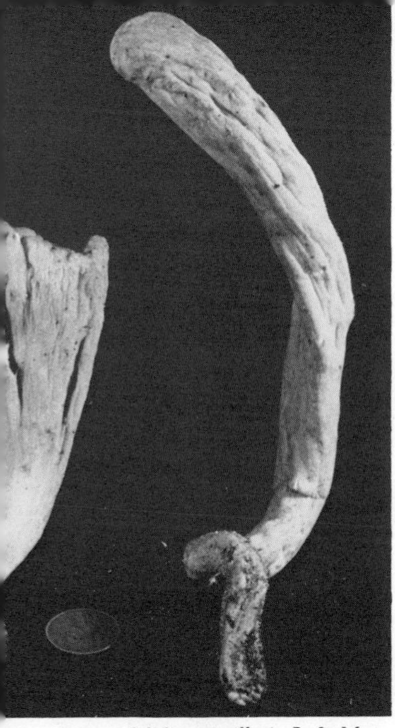
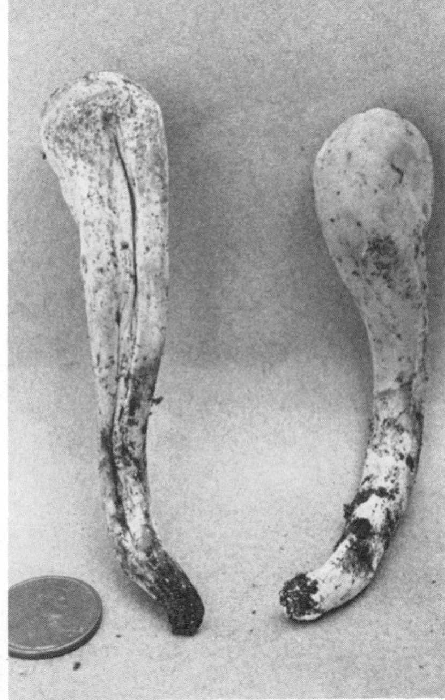

Clavariadelphus pistillaris. **Left:** Mature specimens showing variation in shape. Truncate individual on left resembles *C. truncatus.* **Right:** Typical club-shaped specimens.

Clavariadelphus pistillaris (Common Club Coral)

FRUITING BODY simple, erect, unbranched (occasionally forked), club-shaped or tapering downward, more or less hollow, apex rounded or somewhat flattened but not depressed; 7-20 cm high and 1-4 cm thick; surface longitudinally wrinkled or grooved (rugose), at first pallid, soon dull pinkish-brown to ochraceous or ochraceous-brown, darker brown when handled; apex at first yellowish but soon colored like rest of fruiting body. Flesh tough, fibrous, whitish, taste mild or bitter. **SPORE PRINT** white; spores $9\text{-}15 \times 5\text{-}9\ \mu m$, elliptical, smooth.

HABITAT: Scattered to gregarious on ground under hardwoods and in mixed woods. Late fall and winter, common, especially under oak, tanoak, and madrone.

EDIBILITY: Harmless. The taste and texture are reminiscent of stale rope.

COMMENTS: The yellow-orange to brown club-shaped fruiting body is characteristic of this cosmopolitan club coral. It is the commonest *Clavariadelphus* in our area, the only one I have found under hardwoods. *C. subfastigiatus* is a brownish-orange species common under conifers in northern California. It does not discolor as much when handled but turns bright green in potassium hydroxide.. *C. ligula* is a widespread species that fruits in dense carpets on needle duff under conifers. It is smaller, thinner, and paler (salmon to orange-buff) and has pale yellowish spores. None of these has the flagrantly flattened top of *C. truncatus.*

Clavariadelphus truncatus (Truncate Club Coral)

FRUITING BODY simple, erect, unbranched (rarely forked), club-shaped with a broadly flattened apex, hollow, up to 18 cm high and 8 cm broad at apex. Surface of apex (top) bright yellow to golden-yellow or yellow-orange, sometimes depressed somewhat in age; remainder of fruiting body more or less pinkish-brown with white hairs at base; usually wrinkled or veined near apex. Flesh thin, white, taste bittersweet. **SPORE PRINT** pale ochraceous; spores 9-13 $\times$ 5-7 μm, elliptical, smooth.

HABITAT: Scattered to gregarious in duff under conifers, especially Douglas-fir and pine, late fall and winter. I have seen it at Big Basin but it is not common.

EDIBILITY: Edible. I haven't tried it.

COMMENTS: The broad, golden-yellow flattened top distinguishes this species from its common cousin, *C. pistillaris.* Its color and shape are vaguely reminiscent of a chanterelle *(Cantharellus* or *Gomphus),* but the fruiting body is hollow. *Clavariadelphus borealis* is a white-spored version of *C. truncatus.*

CLAVARIA and CLAVULINOPSIS
(FAIRY CLUBS)

Small, fragile fungi found on wood or ground. FRUITING BODY erect, *unbranched or sparingly branched,* usually finger-shaped or club-shaped and *slender, often clustered. Flesh usually fragile.* SPORE PRINT *white;* spores typically smooth. Basidia typically 4-spored. Clamp connections absent *(Clavaria),* present *(Clavulinopsis).*

THESE are primitive fungi with an erect, undifferentiated fruiting body. The most common forms are unbranched and smaller, slimmer, and frailer than *Clavariadelphus.* They often grow in clumps, but the individual clubs do not arise from a fleshy base as in the branched corals (*Clavulina, Ramaria,* etc.). They are sometimes confused with earth tongues—which are tougher, usually flattened, and often velvety—and belong to an entirely different group of fungi, the Ascomycetes.

Fairy clubs are too small and fragile to have food value, but they are an attractive addition to our wintertime woods. They are saprophytic on humus, soil, or occasionally grass and decaying wood, and fruit (as do most coral fungi) from late fall through early spring. Four common species are described here.

Key to Clavaria and Clavulinopsis

1. Fruiting body bright yellow to yellow-orange 2
1. Fruiting body some other color 3

2. Fruiting body viscid, often sparingly branched; on wood .... (see *Calocera viscosa,* p. 581)
2. Fruiting body not viscid; unbranched; usually on ground .... *Clavulinopsis laeticolor,* p. 499

3. Fruiting body purple or purple-tinted .... *Clavaria purpurea* (see *C. fumosa,* p. 499)
3. Fruiting body some other color 4

4. Fruiting body very thin (1-2 mm), brown to yellowish-buff or paler .... *Clavaria juncea,* below
4. Not as above, thicker 5

5. Fruiting body slender, very fragile, white or stained yellow; surface smooth .... *Clavaria vermicularis,* p. 498
5. Fruiting body not white, or if white, then not exceedingly fragile, and surface wrinkled 6

6. Fruiting body yellowish-gray to gray, usually growing in clusters .... *Clavaria fumosa,* p. 499
6. Fruiting body white or whitish, sometimes sparingly branched; often gregarious but generally not in clusters .... (see *Clavulina* and *Ramariopsis,* p. 500)

Clavaria juncea

FRUITING BODY simple, unbranched, erect, very thin (1-2 mm), up to 10 cm high, tapering upward to an acute apex; leather-brown to yellowish-buff or paler, smooth. Base somewhat fibrillose and often creeping horizontally, with large white mycelial strands (rhizomorphs). Flesh very thin, brittle. **SPORE PRINT** white; spores 7-11 × 3.5-5.5 μm, broadly ovate, smooth.

HABITAT: Scattered to gregarious on oak and tanoak leaves or redwood needles in mixed woods, particularly along streams and other damp places. Fall and winter, fairly common but easily overlooked.

EDIBILITY: Utterly irrelevant.

Clavaria juncea. Fruiting body is only 1-2 mm wide; it grows on redwood needles and tanoak leaves. (Herb Saylor)

COMMENTS: This species is so thin that it can be mistaken for the bare stem of an herbaceous plant or a small agaric which has lost its cap. Its generic disposition is problematic, and it is placed in *Clavaria* only as a matter of convenience. *Typhula* species are very similar but arise from a small, beadlike body (sclerotium). It has also been classified as a *Clavariadelphus,* but may eventually merit a genus of its own.

Clavaria vermicularis (Fairy Fingers)

FRUITING BODY simple, unbranched or rarely forked at tip, erect, slender, up to 12 cm tall and 3-5 mm thick; pure white to translucent white or yellow with age from apex downward; smooth, usually tapered toward tip; cylindrical to flattened, soon withering. Flesh thin, white, exceedingly fragile. **SPORE PRINT** white; spores 5-7 × 3-4 μm, elliptical to nearly round, smooth.

HABITAT: On ground in tufts, clusters, or carpets, often with solitary fruiting bodies interspersed. In humus, moss, grassy places near woods, etc., fall and winter, common. Distribution worldwide.

EDIBILITY: Edible but insubstantial. The watery flesh dissolves when chewed.

COMMENTS: The distinctive clumps of slender white "fingers" make this species most attractive. It is by far our most common *Clavaria,* growing wherever moisture is sufficient. The fruiting body is not deeply wrinkled as in *C. fumosa* and *Clavulina rugosa,* and it crumbles

Clavaria vermicularis, mature specimens. This common, clustered white species has extremely fragile flesh.

seemingly without provocation. *Multiclavula mucida* is a minute (more or less 1 cm tall) white or whitish species that grows on mossy banks or algae-laden logs.

Clavaria fumosa (Grayish Fairy Club)

FRUITING BODY simple, unbranched, erect, up to 12 cm tall, 1.5-6 mm thick; yellowish-gray to mouse-gray, grooved or wrinkled longitudinally, often flattened, becoming hollow; tip blunt, sometimes brownish. Flesh fragile, whitish. **SPORE PRINT** white; spores 6-8 × 3-4 μm, ellipsoid, smooth.

HABITAT: In tufts or clusters on ground in woods and grass, late fall and winter, infrequent. I have found it several times in oak-madrone woods.

EDIBILITY: Harmless, fleshless, flavorless.

COMMENTS: The gray to yellowish-gray color and wrinkled surface typify this forgettable fairy club. It almost always grows in clusters. *C. purpurea* is a similar species that is purple when fresh, but fades in age to lavender-buff or smoky-brownish. Like *C. fumosa,* it grows on the ground in clusters and is not worth eating.

Clavulinopsis laeticolor (Golden Fairy Club)

FRUITING BODY simple, unbranched, erect, small, usually flattened, sometimes twisted, up to 5 cm tall but typically about 2.5 cm; bright orange to bright yellow-orange, sometimes yellow below, extreme base whitish. Flesh thin, somewhat pliant, pallid or yellowish. **SPORE**

Left: *Clavulinopsis laeticolor* is bright yellow-orange, does *not* often grow in clusters.
Right: *Clavulinopsis fusiformis* (see *C. laeticolor*) is taller and always clustered.

PRINT white; spores 4.5-7 × 3.5-5.5 μm, broadly ellipsoid to nearly round, smooth, apiculate.

HABITAT: Solitary, scattered, or in small groups on mossy banks, exposed soil, and humus in woods. Fairly common, fall and winter.

EDIBILITY: Inconsequential.

COMMENTS: The bright golden-orange color sets this dainty fairy club apart. *Clavaria laeticolor* and *C. pulchra* are synonyms. It can conceivably be confused with the viscid, coral-like jelly fungi *(Calocera),* which grows on wood. Three additional species of *Clavulinopsis* are found in California: *C. fusiformis* is a slender, unbranched, clustered, bright yellow to brownish-yellow species, 5-14 cm high; *C. corniculata* is a small branched species with an ochraceous base and yellow-orange to clear yellow branches. It is common in northern California, while Herb Saylor has found a striking bright reddish-orange, unbranched, clustered species, *Clavulinopsis aurantio-cinnabarina,* in Sonoma County.

CLAVULINA and RAMARIOPSIS

Small to medium-sized *coral-like* fungi found on ground or wood. FRUITING BODY *branched,* sometimes with a fleshy base. BRANCHES mostly erect, *usually white to gray or lavender-gray,* never ribbonlike. SPORE PRINT *white;* spores smooth *(Clavulina),* rough *(Ramariopsis);* basidia 2-spored *(Clavulina).*

THESE are white to grayish coral fungi of moderate size. The pale color and white spores distinguish them from *Ramaria,* while the branched fruiting body separates them from most Clavarias. In *Clavulina* the spores are smooth and the basidia 2-spored. In *Ramariopsis* the spores are rough and the basidia 4-spored. A third white-spored genus, *Clavicorona,* grows on wood and has crownlike branch tips and smooth, amyloid spores.

This group is harmless, but their small size and fragile consistency make them unsuitable for the table. They fruit in the late fall and winter, mostly in the woods. Five species are keyed below.

Key to Clavulina and Ramariopsis

1. Growing on wood; branch tips crownlike .... *Clavicorona pyxidata* (see *Clavulina cristata,* below)
1. Not as above 2
2. Mature fruiting body ashy-gray to lavender-gray .... *Clavulina cinerea* (see *C. cristata,* below)
2. Fruiting body white or whitish 3
3. Fruiting body unbranched or very sparingly branched; surface extensively wrinkled .... *Clavulina rugosa* (see *C. cristata,* below)
3. Fruiting body branched; not as above 4
4. Fruiting body very fragile, crumbling easily, usually branched profusely .... *Ramariopsis kunzei,* p. 502
4. Fruiting body not noticeably fragile; usually rather sparingly branched . ... *Clavulina cristata,* below

Clavulina cristata (Crested White Coral)

FRUITING BODY erect, branched, up to 10 cm high and 5 cm wide; usually rather sparingly branched. **BRANCHES** white, occasionally tinged yellowish in age; dainty and delicate, tips fine, sometimes crested. **STALK** up to 5 cm long but usually much shorter, rather slender, often somewhat flattened, white or whitish. Flesh brittle but somewhat tough, not noticeably fragile; white. **SPORE PRINT** white; spores 7-10 × 6-9 μm, round or nearly so, smooth.

HABITAT: Scattered to gregarious in woods of all kinds, along paths and streams, etc. Fairly common, fall and winter.

EDIBILITY: Edible.

COMMENTS: This is one of two common white branched coral fungi. The other *(Ramariopsis kunzei)* crumbles easily and is more profusely branched. Unbranched or sparingly branched forms with a longitudinally wrinkled (rugose) surface are usually called *Clavulina rugosa.* A closely related ashy-gray to lavender-gray branched species, *C. cinerea,* is common in northern coniferous forests. All three Clavulinas

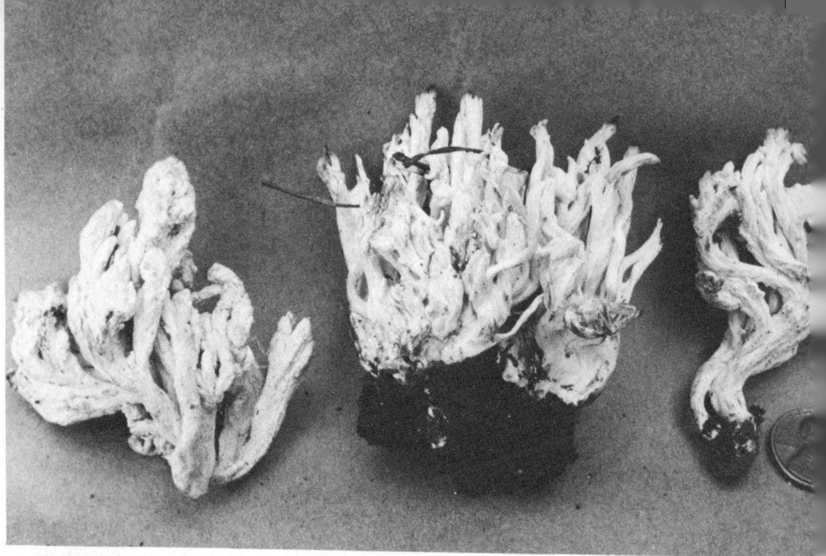

Clavulina cristata, or a form intermediate between *C. cristata* and *C. rugosa*. The fruiting body is whitish, sparingly branched, and often wrinkled as shown at left. *Ramariopsis kunzei* (not illustrated) is more elaborately branched and exceedingly fragile.

intergrade to some extent, and are separated from *Ramaria* by their paler color and white spores. *Clavicorona pyxidata* is a white to pale yellow species with crownlike branch tips and smooth, white amyloid spores. It grows on decaying logs, especially poplar and willow.

Ramariopsis kunzei (White Coral)

FRUITING BODY erect, branched, up to 10 cm tall and about as wide. **BRANCHES** white to creamy-white, sometimes tinged pinkish near base at maturity, unpolished, smooth, erect or spreading, rarely compact; tips blunt or pointed. **STALK** absent or present only as a short, fragile base. Flesh white, exceedingly fragile. **SPORE PRINT** white; spores 3-4 $\times$ 2.5-4.5 μm, round or nearly round, minutely spiny.

HABITAT: Scattered to densely gregarious in mixed woods and under conifers, frequently hidden in the duff. Usually abundant in our coastal pine forests from late fall through early spring, but not restricted to that habitat.

EDIBILITY: Harmless, fleshless, flavorless.

COMMENTS: This ubiquitous branched white coral mushroom is best recognized in the field by its extreme fragility. It is more profusely branched than typical *Clavulina cristata* (our other branched white coral), and has ornamented spores. Like *Clavaria vermicularis*, mature fruiting bodies crumble at the slightest provocation.

RAMARIA (CORAL MUSHROOMS)

Medium to large *coral-like* fungi found on wood or ground. FRUITING BODY *profusely branched, usually with a fleshy base.* BRANCHES mostly erect, smooth, never ribbonlike, *often brightly colored, rarely white or gray.* SPORE PRINT *yellowish to tan or ochraceous;* spores usually ornamented, produced on surfaces of branches.

THESE are fleshy or pliant fungi with intricately branched fruiting bodies. They represent an evolutionary advancement over the simple corals or fairy clubs *(Clavaria)* insofar as branching greatly increases the surface area on which spores are produced. The same principle is found in the teeth fungi (Hydnaceae), except the "branches" hang downward and are called spines.

Ramaria is distinguished from other branched corals *(Clavulina, Ramariopsis,* etc.) by its colorful fruiting body and tan to ochraceous spores which are usually ornamented with minute warts, spines, or ridges. Virtually every hue is represented, with yellow, orange, red, and tan predominating. It is the most attractive and prominent group of coral fungi, and never fails to attract the attention of the collector. However, it is also the largest and most complex group, with over 30 species reported from California.

To facilitate identification, *Ramaria* can be divided roughly into three groups: terrestrial species with a large, fleshy brittle fruiting body (such as *R. botrytis*); terrestrial species with a slender, tough or pliant fruiting body and abundant white mycelium (such as *R. myceliosa*); and wood-inhabiting species with a pliant-tough fruiting body (such as *R. stricta*). Pinpointing the exact identity of a *Ramaria* is a difficult task, however, even for the specialist. In part this is due to the nature of the fruiting body—aside from color, texture, and branching pattern, there are few criteria by which to identify species in the field. As a result, certain names have been applied indiscriminately to a slew of similar—but autonomous—species. Any attempt to correct this trend short of an exhaustive study of California Ramarias would only contribute to the confusion. Therefore, the descriptions offered here are very broad. This may not satisfy *Ramaria* researchers, but it will enable collectors to refer the Ramarias they find to a species "complex" without resorting to detailed microscopic study and special chemical tests. Besides, it is not necessary to know the exact identities of these coral fungi to appreciate their beauty. The manner in which they arise from the murky depths of the forest is indeed reminiscent of corals.

Ramarias are a popular group for the table since they are so distinctive. None are dangerously poisonous, but only the large fleshy species are worth collecting. Some are bitter and all are maggot-prone and hard to clean. A few (notably *R. formosa* and *R. gelatinosa*) are mildly poisonous, and even the edible species have laxative effects on certain individuals. Therefore it is best to test each type cautiously and not overindulge.

Ramarias are woodland fungi. The slender, pliant forms are saprophytic on humus and decaying wood, and are especially common under conifers. The large, fleshy types are usually terrestrial. In the Pacific Northwest they are partial to hemlock and in our area they favor tanoak, but are by no means restricted to those habitats. Ten species are described here.

Key to Ramaria

1. Growing directly on wood 2
1. Growing on ground 3

2. Branches pale yellow to tawny-buff or pinkish-tan with yellow tips .... *R. stricta,* p. 505
2. Branches dull buffy-tan or darker, sometimes tinted bluish-green or green .... *R. apiculata* (see *R. stricta,* p. 505)

3. Fruiting body tough to pliant, rarely larger than 10 cm high, stalk or trunk short to almost absent, often with conspicuous white mycelial mat permeating substrate 4
3. Fruiting body fleshy, brittle or gelatinous, generally 10 cm high or more at maturity; white mycelial mat absent 6

4. Branches flattened, dark brown to purple-brown, odor garliclike becoming fetid .... (see *Thelephora palmata,* p. 479)
4. Not as above 5

5. Fruiting body (especially lower branches) bruising or aging blue-green to olive-green .... *R. ochraceovirens,* p. 507
5. Not as above .... *R. myceliosa,* p. 506

6. Fruiting body tinted purple or violet at apex of stalk when fresh, or colored violet throughout 7
6. Not as above 8

7. Branches entirely violet .... *R. fumigata,* p. 509
7. Branches olive-gray to yellow-brown, with violet tints usually present on lower branches or upper portion of stalk .... *R. fennica,* p. 508

8. Branches deep red to coral-red, fading in age .... *R. araiospora,* p. 509
8. Not as above 9

9. Branches white or pallid with pink, red, purple or dull orange tips, becoming entirely tan or ochraceous in old age .... *R. botrytis,* p. 513
9. Branches yellow to orange or pinkish-orange when fresh 10

10. Branches pale yellow to bright yellow, yellow-orange, or pale orange when fresh 11
10. Branches pinkish, pinkish-orange, salmon, or paler when fresh .... *R. formosa* p. 510

11. Stalk bruising dark red or vinaceous when bruised .... *R. sanguinea,* p. 512
11. Not as above .... *R. rasilispora,* p. 511

Ramaria stricta (Strict Coral)

FRUITING BODY profusely branched from a poorly developed base (stalk); up to 10 cm high and 7 cm broad. **BRANCHES** erect, slender, mostly parallel, compact, sometimes grooved or flattened slightly; pale yellow becoming pinkish-tan or tawny-buff, slowly staining vinaceous-brown when bruised; branch tips fine, light yellow to light greenish-yellow. **STALK** rudimentary or practically absent, not fleshy. Flesh tough, pliant, taste somewhat bitter or metallic. **SPORE PRINT** cinnamon-buff; spores 7.5-10 × 3.5-5 µm, subellipsoid to narrowly ovoid, minutely roughened.

HABITAT: Solitary or in tufts on rotting logs and branches (mostly hardwood). Common, late fall and winter, but seldom in large numbers.

EDIBILITY: Inedible. There is very little flesh and the flavor is not pleasing.

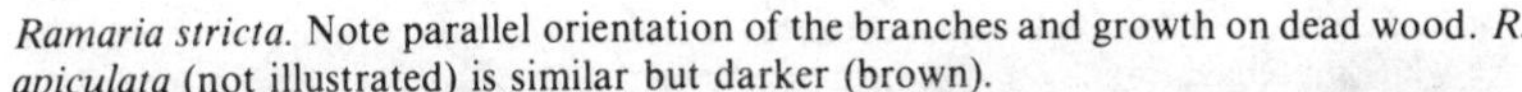
Ramaria stricta. Note parallel orientation of the branches and growth on dead wood. *R. apiculata* (not illustrated) is similar but darker (brown).

COMMENTS: This is one of several Ramarias that grow directly on wood ("log lines" are sometimes formed by Ramarias which appear terrestrial but actually originate from extremely decomposed logs). The erect, parallel orientation of the branches, yellow branch tips, and slender, graceful stature are distinct. *R. apiculata* grows on wood but is dull buffy-tan, bruising reddish-brown, and in one form exhibits green to blue-green tints on the branch tips or stalk base. *R.* (=*Lentaria*) *pinicola* grows on conifer logs and has smooth spores. *R. gracilis* grows in coniferous duff like *R. myceliosa,* but has roughened spores like *R. stricta. R. acris* grows on logs and has an acrid taste.

Ramaria myceliosa

FRUITING BODY abruptly branched from a slender base (stalk), up to 8 cm high and wide. **BRANCHES** slender, spreading, pliant, dull yellow-orange to ochraceous to olive-ochraceous to drab cinnamon-buff or orange-buff; tips same color. **STALK** slender, pliant, not fleshy, same color as branches, with abundant white mycelial strands (rhizomorphs) attached to base and permeating surrounding humus. Flesh thin, white, pliant, taste usually bitter. **SPORE PRINT** pale ochraceous; spores 3.5-6 × 2.4 μm, ovate to nearly round, minutely spiny.

HABITAT: In groups or carpets under conifers, especially redwood. Extremely common, fall and winter.

Ramaria myceliosa is a small ochraceous coral that is very common under redwood. Note the white mycelial strands on specimen at left.

EDIBILITY: Unknown. Hardly worth experimenting with.

COMMENTS: This is one of several small (less than 10 cm high), dull, pliant, terrestrial Ramarias with a conspicuous white mycelial mat and minutely spiny spores. It does not stain green or bluish-green like *R. ochraceovirens. R. pusilla* may or may not be a synonym. Other members of the club include: *R. invalii,* with golden-yellow branches and spores 6-8.5 × 4-6 µm; and *R. flaccida,* pale creamy-ochraceous with paler tips, and spores 5-8 × 3-4 µm. None of these grow on wood like *R. stricta* and relatives.

Ramaria ochraceovirens (Green-Staining Coral)

FRUITING BODY profusely branched from a slender base (stalk), 3-10 cm high and wide, usually rather small. **BRANCHES** pliant, ochraceous to pale cinnamon becoming olive-brown to dingy brown in age, slowly staining greenish or blue-green when bruised (or in age), especially the lower branches. **STALK** up to 2.5 cm long, slender, white to ochraceous or colored like branches, with white mycelial matter at base. Flesh pliant, discoloring dark brown slightly, taste bitter. **SPORE PRINT** pale yellowish-tan; spores 6-8 × 3-4.5 µm, ellipsoid, minutely spiny.

HABITAT: Scattered or in groups in duff under conifers (particularly redwood), rarely hardwoods. Fairly common, fall and winter.

Ramaria ochraceovirens. This tough, dingy terrestrial species bruises greenish on the lower branches and stalk.

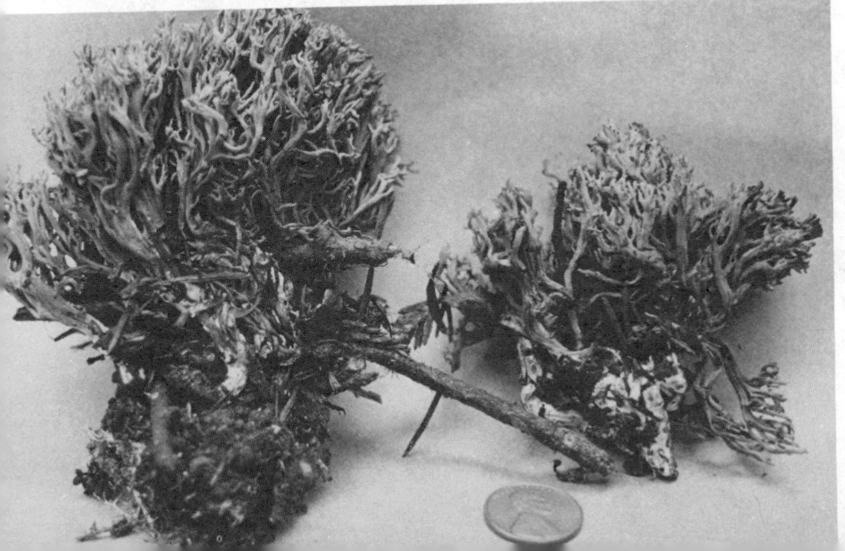

EDIBILITY: Too tough and bitter to be edible.

COMMENTS: The greenish-staining branches distinguish this species from the throngs of other small, pliant, dingy-ochraceous Ramarias (see *R. myceliosa*). In some books it is listed as *R. abietina,* an ambiguous species. The staining is enhanced by cold weather, which can be duplicated by placing the fruiting body in a freezer.

Ramaria fennica

FRUITING BODY typically with two to four large primary branches arising from a common base (stalk) and many smaller, secondary branches arising from primary ones; up to 18 cm high and 12 cm wide. **BRANCHES** smooth, erect, olive-gray to olive-umber or smoky-yellowish, in age becoming dingy yellow-brown; basal (primary) branches dark olive-brown or tinted violet; tips olive-yellow to dingy buff. **STALK** large, fleshy, white below, tinted violet above. Flesh white, firm, taste bitterish. **SPORE PRINT** pale ochraceous; spores 8.5-12 × 3.5-5 μm, ellipsoid, rough.

HABITAT: Solitary or in groups in humus under hardwoods and

Ramaria fennica is a large, attractive coral with smoky-olive branches and purple tints at the top of the trunk. Note the relatively long trunk and somewhat parallel orientation of the branches.

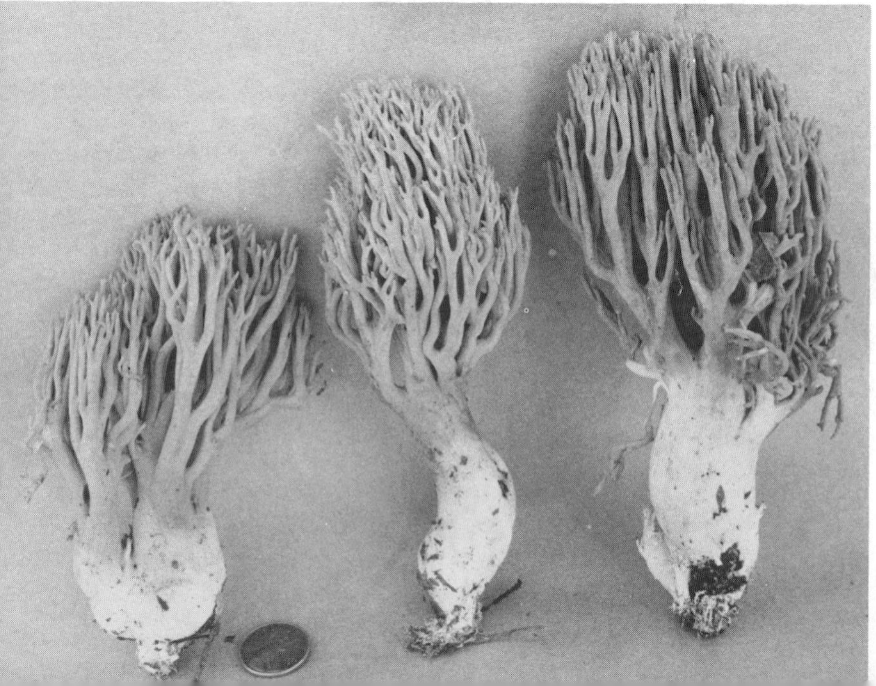

conifers. Infrequent most years, but abundant at Big Basin in the fall of 1977. Its favorite associate appears to be tanoak.

EDIBILITY: Unknown. The bitter taste is a deterrent.

COMMENTS: The subtle violet tints on the lower branches and top of the trunk plus the overall smoky-olive color are the telltale traits of this attractive species. In contrast to many Ramarias, it is typically taller than it is wide. *R. fennica* var. *violaceibrunnea* is a more precise name for our form.

Ramaria fumigata (Violet Coral)

FRUITING BODY typically with two to four large primary branches arising from a common base (stalk), and many smaller secondary branches arising from primary ones; 5-12 cm high and up to 12 cm wide. **BRANCHES** smooth, violet or lilac, slowly discoloring dingy yellowish in old age; tips also violet. **STALK** distinct as a white fleshy base below the main branches. Flesh white, firm, slightly bitter or acrid. **SPORE PRINT** pale ochraceous; spores 8.5-11 $\times$ 3-4 μm, ellipsoid, rough.

HABITAT: Solitary or in small groups in woods; fall and winter, rare. I have found it only once, near Boulder Creek, under tanoak and Douglas-fir.

EDIBILITY: Unknown.

COMMENTS: The violet branches and branch tips make this beautiful coral mushroom unmistakable. It is closely allied to *R. fennica* but is smaller and lacks the smoky-olive shades of that species. *Clavaria purpurea* is purple but unbranched.

Ramaria araiospora (Red Coral)

FRUITING BODY branching from a fleshy base (stalk), 5-13 cm high and 5-10 cm wide. **BRANCHES** deep red to coral-red, fading to light red or paler in age; tips red or yellow, fading slightly in age. **STALK** usually rather short, white or whitish at base, colored like branches (or paler) above. Flesh brittle, taste mild or slightly krautlike. **SPORE PRINT** pale ochraceous; spores 8-13 $\times$ 3-4.5 μm, elliptical to cylindrical, rough.

HABITAT: Solitary or scattered on ground in woods, fall and winter, uncommon. I have found it several times under tanoak, often in the company of other Ramarias.

Ramaria araiospora is bright coral-red with yellow tips (or in one variety, coral-red throughout). A very similar species, *R. subbotrytis*, has not been found in California.

EDIBILITY: Presumably edible; not as fleshy as *R. botrytis.*

COMMENTS: The brilliant coral-red color makes this gorgeous species unmistakable. It belongs to a group of red to coral-pink species known as the "*R. subbotrytis*-complex." There are two varieties of *R. araiospora:* var. *araiospora* has yellow branch tips, while var. *rubella* has red branch tips. As in other Ramarias, the color fades with age, and old specimens barely hint at their former splendor.

Ramaria formosa (Salmon Coral)

FRUITING BODY profusely branched from a fleshy base (stalk), 5-18 cm tall and wide. **BRANCHES** smooth, mostly erect; pinkish, pinkish-orange, or salmon, fading to tan or dingy ochraceous in age; tips bright yellow. **STALK** fleshy, tapering downward, white below and colored like branches (or paler) above. Flesh brittle, whitish, taste usually bitter or astringent. **SPORE PRINT** pale ochraceous; spores 9.5-12.5 $\times$ 3.5-5 μm, long elliptical, minutely roughened.

HABITAT: Solitary, scattered, or in groups or rings in mixed woods and under hardwoods (particularly tanoak). Common, fall and winter.

EDIBILITY: Said to have cathartic effects on many individuals. Until the identity of our variety (or varieties) is definitely established, it is best left alone.

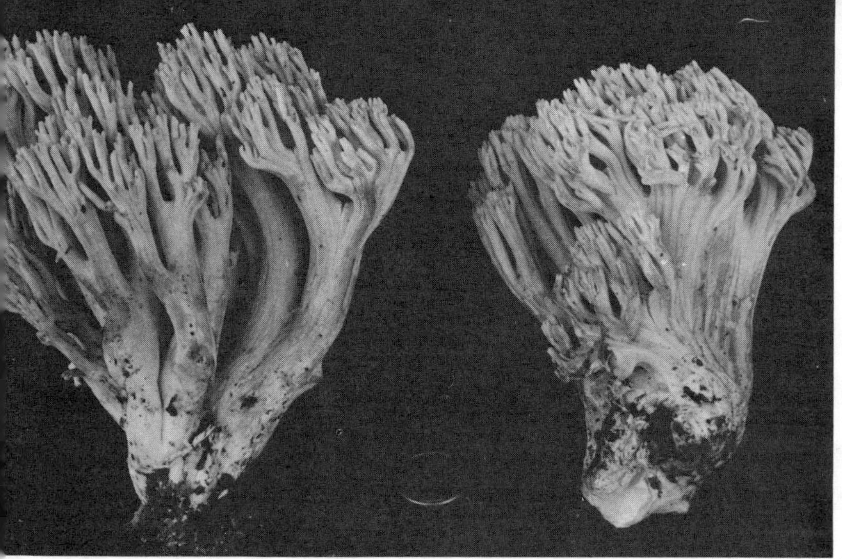

Ramaria formosa. Branches are pale orange to pinkish-orange and the stalk is not as fleshy as in some Ramarias. Branch tips are yellow.

COMMENTS: The pinkish to pinkish-orange branches with yellow tips are characteristic of this species. The "true" *R. formosa* is said to stain cinnamon to vinaceous-brown when bruised, whereas our variety does not. *R. gelatinosa* is a poisonous creamy-white to pinkish-flesh species with translucent, gelatinous flesh in the trunk. *R. cartilaginea* has light yellow to yellowish-tan branches with yellowish-brown branch tips and brittle to somewhat gelatinous flesh. *R. conjunctipes* has salmon to yellowish-orange branches with yellow tips, but rarely reaches 5 cm in height and has a hollow stem. None of these is as yellow as *R. flavagelatinosa* and *R. rasilispora.*

Ramaria rasilispora (Yellow Coral)

FRUITING BODY abundantly branched from a fleshy base (stalk), 5-16 cm high, 8-18 cm wide. **BRANCHES** smooth, mostly erect, pale yellow to yellow-orange or pale orange, tips yellow or same color as branches, sometimes darkening to brown. **STALK** fleshy, tapering to a point or rooting, white or whitish. Flesh fibrous, white with watery areas, taste mild. **SPORE PRINT** pale ochraceous or orange-yellow; spores 8-12 $\times$ 3-4.5 μm, cylindrical, smooth or slightly roughened.

HABITAT: Scattered or in groups or rings on ground in woods. Common, fall and winter, in mixed woods and under tanoak. Also common in the spring in the Sierras, under conifers and oak.

EDIBILITY: Edible. Said to be good raw in salads or candied like grapefruit rinds. Some people are adversely affected by it.

Ramaria rasilispora, mature specimens. This common coral has bright yellow branches. Young specimens are much more compact. Specimen at right shows branch tips as seen from above.

COMMENTS: The fleshy, terrestrial yellow and orange Ramarias do not lend themselves well to clearcut categorization. The names *R. flava, R. aurea,* and *R. formosa* (all European species) have enjoyed widespread use in this country, but do not adequately cover the many variants on the west coast. *R. rasilispora* is our most common species. The base does not bruise wine-red like *R. sanguinea* and the "true" *R. flava,* and there are no pinkish or pinkish-salmon tints as in *R. formosa.* Two varieties of *R. rasilispora* are recognized in California: var. *rasilispora,* with pale orange to yellow-orange branches and tips darkening to brown in age; and var. *scatesiana,* with yellow to pale yellow branches and tips. *R. flavagelatinosa* is a similar species with yellow branches and tips that occasionally bruise violet, and watery, gelatinous flesh. It is common in northern California and the Sierras.

Ramaria sanguinea (Bleeding Coral)

FRUITING BODY profusely branched from a fleshy base (stalk), 5-17 cm high and wide. **BRANCHES** smooth, mostly erect; pale, clear yellow, the lower (primary) branches turning dark red when bruised; tips slightly brighter yellow. **STALK** fleshy, tapered below, often very short, white or whitish, staining dark red or wine-red when bruised. Flesh white or yellowish, brittle, taste mild. **SPORE PRINT** pale ochraceous, spores 8.5-12 × 3.5-4 μm, oblong or long elliptical, rough.

HABITAT: Solitary or in groups in woods, late fall and early winter, not common. I have found it at Big Basin State Park in December, in dense forest made up mostly of tanoak.

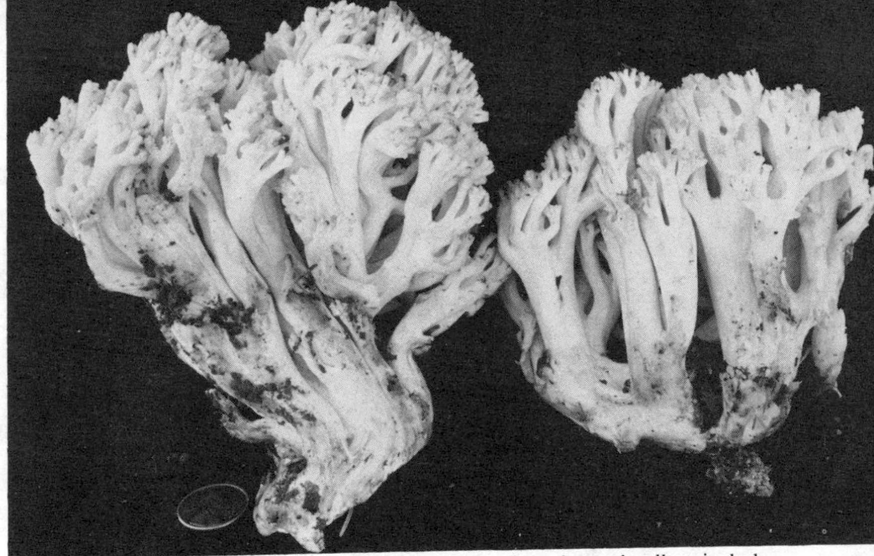

Ramaria sanguinea has pale, clear yellow branches. Lower branches and stalk stain dark red when bruised.

EDIBILITY: Presumably edible. I haven't tried it.

COMMENTS: The pale, clear yellow branches, red-staining trunk, and mild taste are the telltale traits of this lovely coral mushroom. Two very similar species are *R. synaptopoda,* smaller, with small spots of oxblood-red near base; and *R. vinosimaculans,* somewhat larger, with both base and branches staining reddish to violet-brown.

Ramaria botrytis (Pink-Tipped Coral)

FRUITING BODY profusely branched from a fleshy base (stalk); sometimes massive, 7-20 cm high and 6-30 cm broad when mature, very compact when young, less so in age. **BRANCHES** white or pallid when young, becoming buff to ochraceous-buff or tan in age; tips short, clefted, blunt, pink to purple or red when fresh, fading in age. **STALK** thick, fleshy, the base rounded, often swollen at or above ground level, white or whitish when fresh, tan to ochraceous in old age. Flesh firm, white, brittle, taste mild in some forms, bitter in others. **SPORE PRINT** pale ochraceous; spores 11-16 $\times$ 4-6 μm, long elliptical, longitudinally striate.

HABITAT: Solitary or in groups or rings on ground in woods. Common, fall and winter, often partially buried in the humus. It occurs in a variety of habitats, but I find it most often with tanoak.

EDIBILITY: Edible and choice, according to some, but it has laxative effects on certain individuals. It is our largest and fleshiest *Ramaria,* so it may be worth trying. Bitter or acrid forms should be discarded.

Ramaria botrytis, fairly young specimens. Note the large, compact fruiting body with dark (pink to purple-red) tips. In age the branches expand and become ochraceous-tan.

COMMENTS: This handsome, compact coral mushroom looks like a cauliflower—more so, in fact, than the cauliflower mushroom (*Sparassis*). The stubby branches with pink to reddish-purple tips afford an easy means by which to recognize it. The longitudinally striate spores are also distinctive. In old age the branches elongate and discolor and it is easily confused with other Ramarias. A related species, *R. strasseri,* has a tapered, rooting stalk, dull orange to brownish branch tips, and striate spores. An unidentified whitish species with bright pink branch tips and an exceedingly bitter-acrid taste also occurs. Despite its uncanny resemblance to *R. botrytis,* it has nonstriate spores, which places it in the *R. subbotrytis-R. araiospora* group.

SPARASSIS (CAULIFLOWER MUSHROOMS)

Medium to very large fungi *parasitic on the roots of trees.* FRUITING BODY *compact, branched.* BRANCHES *flattened, ribbonlike, wavy,* horizontal and vertical, *arising from a tough, rooting, fleshy base.* SPORE PRINT white; spores smooth.

THE wavy, flattened, ribbonlike branches set *Sparassis* apart from other coral fungi. Despite its name, it looks more like a giant brain than a cauliflower. It fruits at the bases of trees (another distinctive feature), and appears year after year in the same spot.

From an edibility standpoint, *Sparassis* is indisputably the king of the corals. It is highly esteemed for its fragrance, flavor, substance, and keeping quality. I found it to be a staple item in the monsoon diet of Himalayan villagers. It is a small genus, boasting only one common species in California.

Sparassis radicata. This large, impressive coral mushroom has flattened ribbonlike branches (**inset**). It grows at the bases of conifers. (Ralph Buchsbaum)

Sparassis radicata (Cauliflower Mushroom)

FRUITING BODY compactly branched from a fleshy, rooting base (stalk), up to 60 cm high and broad but usually somewhat smaller. **BRANCHES** horizontal and vertical, flattened, wavy, compact, smooth, white becoming creamy-yellowish to cinnamon-buff in age, sometimes with brown stains on edges. **STALK** fleshy, tough, buried deep in ground, colored like branches. Flesh firm, white, fairly tough or elastic, odor spicy or fragrant. **SPORE PRINT** white; spores 5-6.5 × 3-4 μm, broadly ellipsoid, smooth.

HABITAT: Parasitic on the roots of conifers, usually growing solitary at the base of the trunk. Fruiting once (rarely twice) a year, in late fall or winter. It is a prominent fungal feature of the pine forests on the Monterey Peninsula, but infrequent elsewhere. The best place to look for it is in old-growth forests where there are plenty of mature trees. The mycelium produces a brown or yellow carbonizing rot.

EDIBILITY: Edible and exceptional—the perfect mushroom for a special occasion. It is as elegant as it looks intelligent. Thorough cooking is necessary, however, to render it tender. Baking or stewing are best. Fresh specimens can be stored for one or two weeks in a cool, dry place, but be sure to check for maggots!

COMMENTS: Contrary to its name, this fantastic fungus looks more like a sea sponge or bouquet of egg noodles than a cauliflower. The flattened, compact, ribbonlike branches and tough, rooting base distinguish it from other coral fungi. The spicy odor is distinctive but hard to characterize. In the Pacific Northwest, 20 to 30 (or even 50!) pound specimens are not unheard of, but in our area the size range is generally 1-5 pounds, or about as large as a human head. (A cross-section reveals brainlike convolutions or "canals".) A cup fungus, *Peziza proteana* f. *sparassoides,* sometimes mimics the cauliflower mushroom but is brown or lilac-tinted. It is edible also.

Chanterelles

CANTHARELLACEAE

Medium-sized terrestrial woodland fungi. FRUITING BODY *with a cap and stalk.* CAP typically depressed, vase-shaped, or trumpet-shaped at maturity, not viscid. UNDERSIDE *smooth, wrinkled, veined, or with primitive foldlike, forking, decurrent gills.* STALK fleshy or hollow, continuous with cap. VEIL and VOLVA absent. SPORE PRINT *white to buff, tan, or yellowish.* Spores smooth or rough, not amyloid. Basidia long and narrow.

THIS is a colorful and conspicuous group with a more or less vase-shaped fruiting body differentiated into an upper or inner sterile surface (the cap) and lower or outer spore-producing surface (the hymenium). The latter may be smooth, wrinkled, veined, or gilled. The gills when present are foldlike (thick, shallow, blunt, and usually joined by connecting veins) rather than platelike (thin, broad, and sharp-edged) as in the true agarics.

The long, narrow basidia and relatively unspecialized hymenium suggest a close kinship between the chanterelles and coral fungi. In fact, if the apex of a club coral *(Clavariadelphus)* were broadened into a cap and the wrinkles on its sides amplified, you would essentially have a chanterelle!

The three principal genera are treated together here. In *Craterellus* the fruiting body is trumpet-shaped and dark grayish-brown to black. In *Cantharellus* it is convex to vase-shaped and often brightly colored, with foldlike gills. In *Gomphus* it is clublike to vase-shaped with a veined or wrinkled hymenium.

The Cantharellaceae are of paramount importance to the mycophagist. With the exception of the *Gomphus floccosus* group, all are edible.

The best (and most plentiful!) of our species are the renowned chanterelle *(Cantharellus cibarius)* and the unheralded (but far tastier) horn of plenty *(Craterellus cornucopioides).* Neither is attacked by maggots and both refrigerate well. Since large crops are commonplace, they can be preserved for summer use. The horn of plenty is excellent dried. Chanterelles dry miserably (they become as tough as leather) but can be pickled, canned, or sauteed and frozen.

The chanterelles are woodland fungi, saprophytic or mycorrhizal with a broad range of hosts. It is not a large group but is nevertheless fairly prevalent. Four local species are keyed below, plus three commonly found in northern California.

Key to the Cantharellaceae

1. Fruiting body a *Russula* or *Lactarius* engulfed by a pimpled layer of (usually) colored tissue (a parasite); overall shape more or less like an inverted pyramid; flesh crisp, brittle, usually white; spores produced in asci .... (see *Hypomyces lactifluorum,* p. 623)
1. Not as above 2

2. Underside smooth to slightly wrinkled or uneven 3
2. Underside with veins, folds, or gills 4

3. Fruiting body 5-15 cm high, more or less trumpet-shaped (clusters sometimes with a lacy appearance); fleshy-tough; black to dark gray-brown or gray, hollow to base of stalk .... *Craterellus cornucopioides,* p. 523
3. Not as above; very thin and tough; smaller, differently colored .... (see **Polyporaceae and relatives,** p. 437)

4. Fruiting body blue-gray to black or dark gray-brown .... *Craterellus cinereus,* p. 522
4. Fruiting body some other color 5

5. Underside purple to purplish-tan, veined or almost poroid; fruiting body club-shaped with a flattened top .... *Gomphus clavatus,* p. 518
5. Not as above; underside some other color 6

6. Fruiting body club-shaped or inflated above; hollow inside .... (see *Clavariadelphus,* p. 494)
6. Not as above 7

7. Fruiting body vase-shaped with hollow center; cap scaly, underside buff to yellowish or pallid; common north of San Francisco .... *Gomphus floccosus,* p. 519
7. Not as above 8

8. Cap small, brown; gills grayish-yellow; stalk yellowish, slender .... *Cantharellus infundibuliformis* (see *Craterellus cinereus,* p. 522)
8. Not as above; medium-sized to large 9

9. Fruiting body yellow-orange to orange (cap may fade in sunlight); common .... *Cantharellus cibarius,* p. 520
9. Fruiting body dull white, bruising or aging yellowish-orange; uncommon .... *Cantharellus subalbidus,* p. 521

Gomphus clavatus (Pig's Ears)

CAP to 10 cm broad, club-shaped with a flattened or slightly depressed top; surface moist or dry but not viscid, smooth or minutely scaly, light purplish to purplish-tan fading to liver-brown, olive-brown, or tan, margin usually lobed. Flesh thick, white or tinged buff, firm. **UNDERSIDE** with numerous blunt, forking veins which extend down the stalk, pale purple to purplish-tan. **STALK** to 10 cm long, continuous with cap, often compound (several fused together), equal or narrowed at base if solitary, more or less color of underside. **SPORE PRINT** pale tan; spores 10-13 × 5-6 μm, elliptical, wrinkled.

HABITAT: Solitary, scattered, or gregarious, usually in fused clusters, under conifers, fall and winter. Common in northern California, may possibly turn up south of San Francisco in areas of high rainfall (such as the Santa Cruz Mountains). *G. pseudoclavatus* (see below) occurs under hardwoods.

EDIBILITY: Edible, considered choice by some. I am not particularly fond of it. Unlike the chanterelle and horn of plenty, it is a popular picnicground for maggots.

COMMENTS: Also known as *Cantharellus clavatus*, the purplish-tan color, veined underside, and growth habit in fused clusters are distinctive. *G. pseudoclavatus* is a very similar species with smooth spores.

Gomphus clavatus is reminiscent of a club coral but has a flattened cap and veined, purplish spore-producing surface. (Ray Gipson)

Gomphus floccosus. Vaselike fruiting body with hollow, scaly center is distinctive. Cap scales are red to orange, underside is pallid. (Nancy Burnett)

Gomphus floccosus (Woolly Chanterelle)

CAP 5-15 cm broad and high; depressed to funnel-shaped or trumpetlike when mature; surface dry, with coarse woolly scales, orange-yellow to reddish-orange, the scales becoming recurved in age. Flesh fibrous, whitish, odor mild. **UNDERSIDE** creamy-buff to yellowish, with frequently forking low, blunt, foldlike decurrent ridges or "gills," sometimes with a somewhat poroid appearance in age. **STALK** continuous with the cap, to 5 cm long, same color as underside, hollow in age. **SPORE PRINT** ochraceous; spores 12-16 × 6-7.5 μm, elliptical, slightly wrinkled.

HABITAT: Scattered to gregarious under conifers, common in northern California in the fall.

EDIBILITY: Edible for some people and not for others. Try it cautiously if at all. I am not particularly fond of it.

COMMENTS: Also known as *Cantharellus floccosus,* this striking species is easily recognized by its hollow, vaselike fruiting body with coarse woolly orange scales. It is rare south of San Francisco, but is included here because it is so prominent in other parts of the state. Related species include *G. bonari,* orange to orange-buff, often growing in small clusters with aborted fruiting bodies nearby, common in the Sierras; and *G. kauffmanii,* a large species with brown to ochraceous-tawny scales. Like *G. floccosus,* these are mildly poisonous to some people.

Cantharellus cibarius (Chanterelle)

CAP up to 20 cm broad, broadly obtuse or rounded when young, becoming plane or depressed (vase-shaped) in age; surface more or less smooth, not viscid, orange to golden-orange or egg yellow, margin at first somewhat incurved, wavy in age. Flesh firm, thick, light yellowish or yellowish-orange, odor fruity (like pumpkins or apricots), taste slightly bitter. **UNDERSIDE** with thick, well-spaced, shallow, blunt, decurrent, foldlike "gills," usually forked or cross-veined, colored like cap or paler (brighter if the cap is faded); developing orange-brown stains in old age. **STALK** to 10 cm long and up to 3 cm thick, equal or tapering downward, stout, solid, dry, smooth, colored like cap or paler. **SPORE PRINT** yellowish; spores 8-11 × 4-5.5 μm, elliptical, smooth.

HABITAT: Scattered to gregarious in woods or organic food stores; common throughout California in fall, winter, and spring. It is associated primarily with conifers but in central California shows a definite preference for live oak, especially those at the edges of pastures. It has a long growing season and is a joy to find—brilliant splashes of gold against a subdued backdrop of decaying leaves. If you see one, probe around and you'll probably discover more, for they frequently hide under the humus. If rainfall is sufficient, successive crops are produced, so check your patches regularly.

EDIBILITY: Edible and choice, the most popular wild mushroom in our area. Chanterelles should always be cooked as they are somewhat bitter raw. They have a high water content and are best in simple dishes that highlight their delicate fruity fragrance and flavor. Cream of chanterelle soup is a traditional favorite. Mix them in with a bunch of vegetables and you won't be able to taste them. Chanterelles are virtually worm-free, a quality keenly appreciated by those who hunt *Boletus edulis* and *Agaricus augustus*. If your "chanterelles" are wormy, they're probably not chanterelles! They are low in protein but rich in vitamin A. Pick selectively—firm specimens will keep in the refrigerator for a week, whereas waterlogged individuals will decompose rapidly and cook up slimy and tasteless. Imported chanterelles can be purchased in small tins at delicatessens (for an outrageous price, of course). Attempts to cultivate them commercially have failed.

COMMENTS: *Cantharellus cibarius* is the proud possessor of a plethora of popular pseudonyms—more than any other mushroom with the possible exception of *Boletus edulis*. The best known are "chanterelle" and "girolle" (both French) and "pfifferling" (German). It

Cantharellus cibarius commonly grows with oak, but these were found under pine. Note shallow, blunt, veined gills. Cap is depressed in mature specimens, but convex when very young. A close-up of gills can be found on p. 37. (Nancy Burnett)

is an easy mushroom to identify if you remember that the gills are foldlike rather than platelike: thick, blunt, shallow, well spaced, decurrent, and forked or cross-veined (true chanterelles have "false" gills while false chanterelles have "true" gills). The fruity odor, golden-orange color, firm flesh, and wavy cap margin (at maturity) are also characteristic. In direct sunlight the cap surface may crack and fade to grayish-white (sometimes with greenish stains caused by algae), but the gills normally retain their color.

Mushrooms most likely to be mistaken for the chanterelle include the false chanterelle *(Hygrophoropsis aurantiacus), Hygrophorus* species (especially *H. pratensis*), *Hypomyces lactifluorum, Lactarius insulsus, Leucopaxillus albissimus,* and the jack-o-lantern mushroom *(Omphalotus olivascens).* Only the latter is poisonous, but it has thin, crowded, well-developed gills, usually grows in clusters, lacks a fruity odor, and develops olive tones in age. The other species also have platelike ("true") gills.

Cantharellus subalbidus (White Chanterelle)

CAP to 14 cm broad, plane to broadly depressed; surface smooth or slightly scaly, moist or dry but not viscid, dull white bruising yellowish-orange, margin wavy. Flesh thick, firm, white, odor mild. **UNDERSIDE** with thick, well-spaced, shallow, blunt, foldlike "gills," usually forked or veined between; dull white becoming yellowish in age or when bruised, decurrent. **STALK** to 7 cm long, up to 2.5 cm thick, equal or tapering downward, dull whitish discoloring yellowish-orange to brownish, stout, solid, firm, smooth, dry. **SPORE PRINT** white; spores 7-9 × 5-5.5 μm, elliptical, smooth.

HABITAT: Solitary or scattered in woods, fall and winter, usually concealed by leaves and needles; uncommon. I find it once or twice a year in mixed woods of tanoak, live oak, madrone, and pine.

EDIBILITY: Edible and choice, as good as *C. cibarius*. In the Pacific Northwest, where it is common, the buttons are heavy, firm, and compact—ideal for marinating or prolonged refrigeration. Unfortunately, it is not nearly so common here and the fruiting bodies, when found, are often waterlogged and overripe.

COMMENTS: The white chanterelle differs from the common chanterelle in its dull white to dingy yellowish color, mild odor, and white spores. It can be mistaken for a *Clitocybe* or *Hygrophorus* but the gills are "chanterellesque": thick, shallow, blunt, and usually veined.

Craterellus cinereus (Black Chanterelle)

CAP up to 5 cm broad and high; deeply depressed or funnel-shaped to shallowly depressed with a wavy margin; surface smooth or minutely scaly, dry, black becoming dark grayish-brown in age. Flesh thin, tough, more or less cap color. **UNDERSIDE** with thick, widely spaced, shallow, blunt, foldlike "gills" which fork frequently near the margin; bluish-black becoming bluish-gray or dark gray as the spores mature. **STALK** to 5 cm long; tapering downward, continuous with cap, thin, tough, hollow except at very base, dry, colored like cap or underside. **SPORE PRINT** white; spores 8-11 × 5-6 μm, elliptical, smooth.

Craterellus cinereus has a black cap and gray to bluish-gray gills. These are rather small specimens.

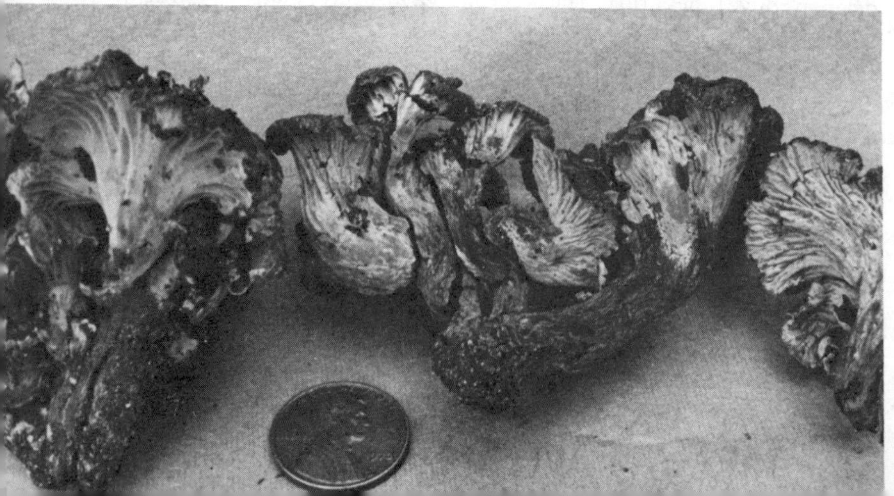

HABITAT: Scattered, in groups or small clusters, in mixed woods and under live oak, sometimes interspersed with *C. cornucopioides.* Fruiting in the winter, uncommon.

EDIBILITY: Edible and choice, as good or better than *C. cornucopioides;* delicious sauteed in butter.

COMMENTS: Also known as *Cantharellus cinereus,* the bluish-gray "gills" separate this species from its common cousin, *Craterellus cornucopioides,* which it mimics closely. Of similar size and shape but with a brownish cap, grayish-yellow "gills," and yellowish-tan stalk is *Cantharellus infundibuliformis.* It is sporadically abundant in the cold, damp coniferous forests of northern California.

Craterellus cornucopioides (Horn of Plenty)

CAP to 7 cm broad and 10 cm high, at first funnel-shaped or trumpet-shaped with a wavy margin, the margin splitting or lacerated in age (sometimes with a lacy appearance or convoluted to form small "suction cups"); surface not viscid, grayish-black to black when moist, dark brown to dark grayish-brown and minutely scaly when dry. Flesh thin, tough, dingy gray-brown or dark brown. **UNDERSIDE** smooth, uneven or slightly wrinkled, black to dark gray-brown, paler gray in age as it becomes dusted with spores. **STALK** to 7 cm long, continuous with cap, hollow to very base, thin, tough, often twisted, tapering downward, colored like cap or underside. **SPORE PRINT** pale buff; spores 8-11 × 5-6 μm, smooth, elliptical.

HABITAT: In scattered groups, clumps, or lacy clusters under hardwoods—especially live oak, but also manzanita, madrone, and tanoak. Common in winter; south of San Francisco it seldom appears before January. Though terrestrial, it often fruits near fallen branches, small shrubs, or manzanita burls.

EDIBILITY: One of the finest and most flavorful of fleshy fungal fructifications—a personal favorite. Like myself, it is thin, tough, and dark, and like myself it goes largely unappreciated. It is consistently passed up in favor of the larger, fleshier, more colorful and impressive types, yet its flavor is superb and its potential unlimited. Alas, it is partly to blame for this sad state of affairs, for its appearance is admittedly unassuming and somber. It shuns attention, unobtrusively blending into the dark, secretive situations where it thrives.

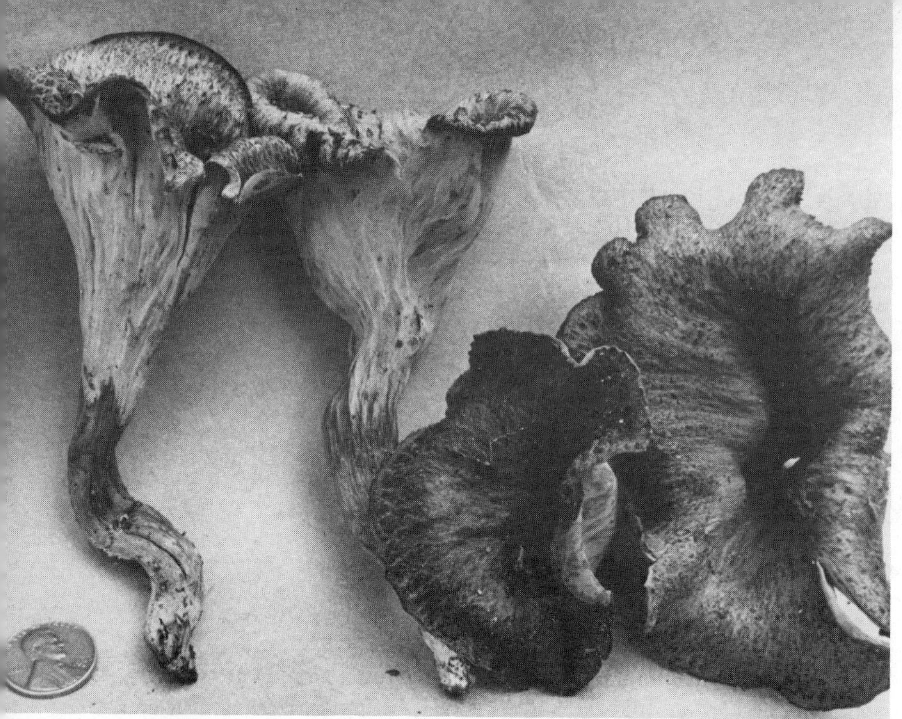

Craterellus cornucopioides. This delicious species is easily recognized by its gray-brown to black trumpetlike fruiting body. These unusually large specimens were growing singly, but dense lacy clusters are also common. Note the absence of gills on underside.

Though it takes an accomplished eye to detect its presence in the woods (from the top it looks like a black hole in the ground), it doesn't take an accomplished eye to detect its presence in a dish—for it cooks up black, announcing itself with unmistakable earthy authenticity. It can play any culinary position with equal finesse, from first base to second fiddle, enhancing practically any dish, be it soup, souffle, or sauce. Like its popular cousin the chanterelle, it is not attacked by maggots. Dried and powdered it has a cheesy odor and is known, quite appropriately, as "Poor People's Truffle."

COMMENTS: Aside from the equally edible *C. cinereus,* there is little this delectable fungus can be confused with. The dark trumpet-shaped fruiting body with smooth or slightly wrinkled underside (exterior) is unique. Several Ascomycetes are black, but never trumpet-shaped (*Plectania* and *Pseudoplectania* are cup-shaped). A terrestrial bracket fungus, *Thelephora terrestris,* is sometimes funnel-shaped but is thinner, smaller, and purple-brown rather than gray or black. The horn of plenty generally occurs in large groups. It is hard to pick out in the forest gloom but once you locate one, you're bound to find more. It is sometimes called the "Trumpet of Death," a tribute to its somber appearance, not its edibility. Actually, it is quite lovely when fresh—more like a black petunia than anything else. Clusters often have a lacy look.

GASTEROMYCETES

THIS large division of the Basidiomycetes includes those fungi better known as puffballs, earthstars, stinkhorns, bird's nest fungi, and false truffles. *Gastero-* (meaning "stomach") describes the manner in which the spores are produced— *internally,* rather than externally as in other Basidiomycetes. The other unique feature of the Gasteromycetes is that the spores are not forcibly discharged. Instead the basidia disintegrate and the leftover spore mass is dispersed by wind, rain, animals, or insects.

The most familiar fungi in this group—puffballs and earthstars—produce their spores in a round to oval "stomach" or **spore sac.** The mature spore mass is powdery and easily dispersed. The false truffles are similar but the spore mass remains intact and does not become powdery. The stinkhorns strike a decidedly different pose—they have a slimy spore mass at first enclosed by a membrane (which breaks to form a volva), then later elevated on a stalk, arms, or latticed ball. Last and least, there are the bird's nest fungi, which look like tiny nests with the spores encased in the "eggs" or **peridioles.**

Though every bit as diverse as the Hymenomycetes (agarics, polypores, etc.), Gasteromycetes are not as abundant. They are notable more for their variety of fantastic shapes and forms than for their colors or culinary qualities (only the puffballs are of importance to the mushroom eater). They are also interesting from an evolutionary standpoint and for the many marvelous methods they have developed for disseminating their spores. The major groups are keyed below.

Key to the Gasteromycetes

1. Fruiting body minute (12 mm high or less), consisting of a "nest" (cup, vase, or bowl) with one or more "eggs" (peridioles) ..... **Nidulariales,** p. 567
1. Larger; not as above 2

2. Fruiting body protruding from ground like a dusty stump; spores produced in lentil-like bodies (peridioles) imbedded in fruiting body, but peridioles soon disintegrating .... *Pisolithus* **(Lycoperdales),** p. 559
2. Not as above 3

3. Fruiting body at first enclosed in a membrane (which breaks to form a volva), then emerging as a cylindrical, phallic, tentacled, or latticed structure; spore mass slimy, with an offensive odor at maturity ... **Phallales,** p. 560
3. Not as above; spores produced in a spore sac or "stomach," which may split open or disintegrate in age 4

4. Spore sac eventually rupturing; spore mass solid when young, cottony or powdery *at maturity,* not remaining intact; mature fruiting body usually above the ground .... **Lycoperdales,** below
4. Spore sac scarcely rupturing; spore mass hard, spongy, or rubbery (rarely slimy or powdery) at maturity, remaining intact for a long time; fruiting body usually buried or partially buried, even at maturity .... **Hymenogastrales,** p. 571

Puffballs and Earthstars

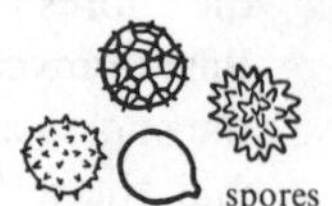

LYCOPERDALES

MOST people don't think of puffballs as mushrooms. Indeed, they have very little in common with the cap-and-stem commodity you buy at the store. The fruiting body is quite simple, consisting of a round to oval spore sac (in which the spores are produced), and in some cases, a stalk. The skin of the spore sac **(peridium)** is usually composed of two distinct layers **(exoperidium** and **endoperidium).** In the earthstars, the outer skin separates completely from the inner layer and splits into several starlike rays.

The interior of the puffball is called the spore mass or **gleba.** The spores are minute, usually round, often warted or spiny like sea urchins, sometimes with a "tail" **(pedicel)** attached. They bounce around like furry bon-bons under the microscope. Usually intermingled with the spores are microscopic filamentous cells called **capillitium.** These are the remains of the hyphae on which the basidia were formed. Their shape and branching pattern are of importance to the taxonomist, but are not emphasized here.

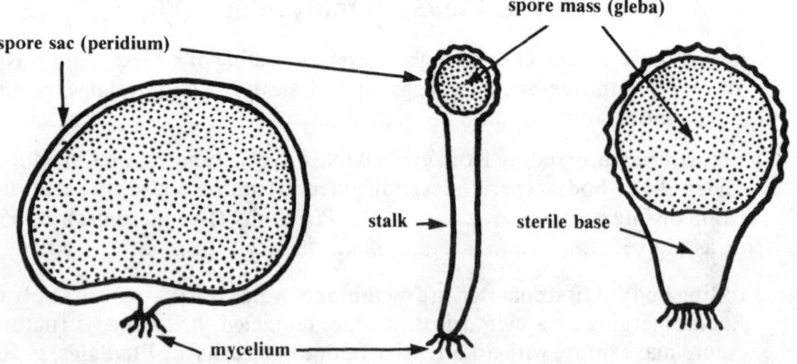

Cross-sections of three puffballs. Left to right: *Calvatia* (stalk and sterile base absent), *Tulostoma* (stalk present), *Lycoperdon* (sterile base present).

The spore mass is at first firm and white, but gradually darkens as the spores mature, becoming mushy as moisture is released, then powdery or cottony as the moisture evaporates. The spore sac eventually ruptures or disintegrates, exposing the mature spore mass to the wind and rain. The spore color corresponds to that of the mature spore mass.

The word "puffball" is a derivative of "puckfist," which in turn was derived from "pixie fart." All of these testify to the puffballs' method of spore dispersal. If a mature specimen is squeezed, poked, tapped, or kicked (thereby duplicating the action of a raindrop), a "puff" of spore dust will emerge.

In many puffballs there is a sterile region beneath the spore mass known, quite appropriately, as the **sterile base.** Composed of minute compartments that give it a somewhat spongy appearance, its presence is best ascertained by slicing the fruiting body lengthwise. The sterile base may be as large as the spore mass, and is often narrowed to form a "stem." Only the stalked puffballs (*Tulostoma* and *Battaraea*), however, possess a true stem.

Most puffballs are safe to eat so long as they're firm and white inside. However, some have purgative effects on certain people and others don't taste good. Once picked, they must be refrigerated or they will ripen rapidly. Any showing the slightest traces of color (usually yellow or green) should be discarded—they become bitter and indigestible. True puffballs are solid and homogenous within ("No gleba, no good") whereas a deadly poisonous Amanita "egg" reveals *the outline of cap, gills, and stalk,* and a stinkhorn "egg" is gelatinous within. False truffles are sometimes mistaken for puffballs, but they usually grow

Cross-section of an *Amanita* "egg" (*A. calyptroderma*) shows outline of cap, gills, and stalk. A puffball, on the other hand, is homogeneous (solid) within. As can be seen, this *Amanita* button could be carelessly mistaken for a puffball before the cap emerges.

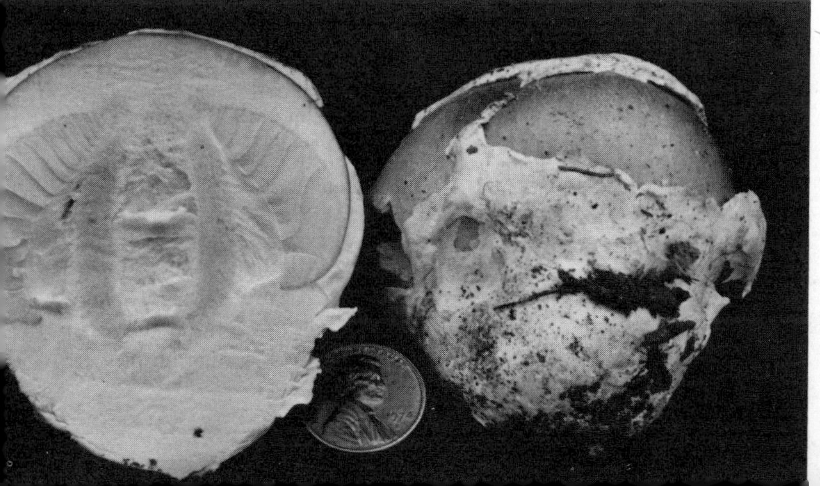

underground and do not have a powdery spore mass at maturity.

Though puffballs are unmistakable as a group, identifying the different species can be difficult because it is necessary to know the characteristics of both immature and mature fruiting bodies. But since indiscriminate sampling of any mushrooms (even puffballs) is poor practice, you should at least make an attempt to key out each type you find, even if you only have young (or old) specimens at hand. The principal genera are keyed below.

Key to the Lycoperdales

1. Outer layer(s) of skin splitting into starlike rays which fold out (and sometimes under) to expose the inner layer (spore sac) .... *Geastrum* and *Astreus*, p. 544
1. Not as above (skin may rupture in starlike fashion, but there is no separate spore sac within) 2

2. Spore sac mounted on a distinct, well-developed stalk which is usually longer than width of spore sac .... *Tulostoma* and *Battaraea,* p. 551
2. Not as above (rudimentary stalk may be present in the form of an elongated, narrowed sterile base or a bundle or rootlike fibers) 3

3. Spore sac (both mature and immature) hard, tough, rindlike; spore mass soon colored (purple-black to dark brown) .... *Scleroderma,* p. 553
3. Spore sac thin and brittle when mature (but may be thick when young); spore mass at first white, colored only in age 4

4. Sterile base absent; fruiting body small, more or less round; exterior usually smooth; *mature* spore sac papery .... *Bovista,* p. 543
4. Not as above 5

5. Medium-sized to very large; spore sac disintegrating or rupturing irregularly at maturity .... *Calvatia,* below
5. Small to medium-sized, rarely larger than a baseball; spore sac rupturing through an apical pore, mouth, or slit .... *Lycoperdon,* p. 537

CALVATIA (GIANT PUFFBALLS)

Medium to very large terrestrial puffballs. FRUITING BODY round to top-shaped or somewhat flattened; spore sac two-layered, *disintegrating or rupturing irregularly at maturity;* exterior smooth or warty. SPORE MASS firm and white when immature, olive-brown to dark brown at maturity (purple in *C. cyathiformis*), becoming powdery or cottony. STERILE BASE present or absent. SPORES more or less round, smooth or warted. Capillitium present.

THESE are baseball- to basketball-sized puffballs in which the spore sac disintegrates at maturity. A distinct apical pore is not formed as in *Lycoperdon.* The outer layer of the spore sac often takes the form of large warts or plates, but in some cases it is smooth, and it may adhere to the inner layer so that the two are indistinguishable. The skin is quite thick in the larger species, but (with the exception of *Calvatia pachyderma*) it is not hard and rindlike at maturity, as in *Scleroderma* or *Mycenastrum*. The texture of the mature spore mass (whether cottony or powdery) is an important feature in the identification of Calvatias.

Giant puffballs are among the most prolific of living organisms. It has been calculated that an average-sized (30 cm) specimen of *Calvatia gigantea* contains 7,000,000,000,000 (7 trillion) spores! In these days of rampant inflation, this may not sound like much, but consider this: if all 7 trillion spores (each one measuring 1/200 of a millimeter) were lined up in a row, they would circle the earth's equator! If each spore produced a 30 cm offspring, the resulting puffballs would stretch from the earth to the sun and back, and if their spores were equally successful, the formidable puffball mass would weigh 800 times as much as the earth! Each spore is theoretically capable of germinating, yet very few (obviously!) do. It would be interesting to know why so many don't, or conversely, why such a surplus of spores is (needlessly?) produced.

Giant puffballs are eaten by people who don't know a gill from a gall. None are poisonous but since the edible species have purgative effects on some people, they should be tested cautiously and eaten in moderation. *C. gigantea* and *C. cyathiformis* are the best of the local varieties.

Calvatias are partial to arid climates—curiously ironic considering that the fruiting bodies are so large. It is a large and complex genus in the West, where many varieties are endemic to the sagebrush deserts and high mountains. I have found several odd species which I have been unable to identify. A handful of the more common types are described here.

Key to Calvatia

1. Mature spore mass purple; fruiting body 4-15 cm high when mature; top of young specimens often pinkish or purplish-tinted and broken into small scales .... *C. cyathiformis*, p. 532
1. Mature spore mass not purple 2

2. Sterile base present, usually conspicuous 3
2. Sterile base absent or rudimentary 5

3. Fruiting body small, 5 cm high or less; common on lawns and other grassy places .... (see *Vascellum depressum*, p. 537)
3. Larger; not as above 4

4. Growing only at high elevations in mountains; exterior with large, prominent warts or pointed scales .... *C. sculpta,* p. 534
4. Not as above; exterior granular, scaly, to somewhat warty; common along coast .... *C. bovista,* p. 533

5. Mature spore mass cottony, remaining intact for a long time; fruiting body baseball-sized or smaller .... *C. lycoperdoides,* p. 535
5. Mature spore mass powdery; baseball- to basketball-sized or larger 6

6. Outer layer of skin a thick, white felty coat which wears away in patches, exposing hard, thick (2 mm) inner layer; fruiting body seldom larger than 15 cm broad; uncommon ...... (see *Mycenastrum corium,* p. 535)
6. Not as above; skin thick (2-4 mm), but inner layer thin, and fragile at maturity; fruiting body generally larger than 12 cm broad at maturity; common .... *C. gigantea,* below

Calvatia gigantea (Giant Puffball)

FRUITING BODY large, softball to basketball size (8-50 cm or more in diameter), occasionally somewhat flattened on top in age; skin thick when young (2-4 mm). Exterior at first smooth, dull white or brownish-stained, breaking up into flat scales or plates which eventually flake off, exposing the thin olive-brown inner layer, which soon disintegrates, or both layers falling off together. **STERILE BASE** absent or rudimentary, but a cordlike "root" sometimes present. **SPORE MASS** at first white, firm or cheesy, becoming greenish-yellow and mushy with

Calvatia gigantea, immature specimens. Note large size (skillet in foreground is 1 foot in diameter). Like all puffballs, it eventually ruptures and disintegrates. (Bill Everson)

Calvatia gigantea. A casual jaunt through a "puffball pasture" can yield quite a haul, as shown here. Note solid white interior and absence of sterile base. Many of these puffballs are starting to mature and break into scales. Each weighs at least a pound. (Joel Leivick)

an unpleasant odor (like old urine), finally deep olive-brown and powdery. Spores 4-6 × 3.5-5.5 μm, round or nearly round, practically smooth, apiculate.

HABITAT: Solitary, scattered, or in large circles in fields, pastures, cemeteries, on exposed hillsides, along roads, and in ditches. Fruiting after the first fall rains and again in the spring; common. When conditions are favorable, it is not unusual to find 30-40 pounds on a casual jaunt through a "puffball pasture." Because of their preference for open hillsides, they can often be spotted from the road. Large specimens, in fact, have been mistaken by passersby for herds of grazing sheep! (Mushroom hunters, on the other hand, are more likely to mistake grazing sheep for giant puffballs.) Dried specimens found under houses have been mistaken for bleached skulls, while a sinister-looking specimen found in England during the war was used for propaganda purposes—it was labeled "Hitler's Secret Weapon" at an exhibition to raise war funds!

EDIBILITY: Edible and choice when the flesh is firm and white, but has purgative effects on some people. It can be sliced and fried like pancakes, or dried quickly and reconstituted in soups. The tough outer skin should be peeled. Individuals which have begun to ripen should be discarded. Size is not necessarily an indication of maturity, so slice them open in the field. This will also enable you to check for maggots, which are fanatically fond of them. Infested areas can be cut away and the solid portions carried home. Dried puffballs have been used as sponges, tinder (before matches were invented), and dyes. They were burned under beehives to stupefy bees and used to squelch bleeding.

COMMENTS: The giant puffball is one of the best-known and most familiar of fleshy fungi. And it *is* fleshy—5 ft, 50 lb specimens have been recorded! The largest one I've found weighed "only" seven pounds. But the identity of our local giant puffball, strangely enough, is a minor mystery. It does not seem to be either *C. gigantea (=Lycoperdon giganteum, Langermannia gigantea)* of eastern North America and Europe, nor *C. booniana,* a sagebrush species of western North America. The former is smoother and whiter than our variety, while the latter is wartier.

To most people, however, it's "true" identity is academic, a problem best left to the puffball pundits, who are paid to pore over such matters—after all, any large puffball is a giant puffball and any giant puffball is a giant meal. We also have several slightly smaller Calvatias whose identities are unresolved, plus *C. pachyderma*, which has a hard, rindlike skin at maturity, and round to ellipsoid spores. All of these lack a sterile base, in contrast to *C. bovista* and *C. cyathiformis.*

Calvatia cyathiformis (Purple-Spored Puffball)

FRUITING BODY 5-15 cm high and broad; nearly round when young, becoming top-shaped or pear-shaped, or round with a flattened top and narrowed base. Exterior smooth at first, but soon cracking into small, flat scales or patches, at least on top; white to pinkish-tan becoming purplish or purple-brown; inner layer of skin dark purple, smooth, thin and delicate; both layers flaking off in old age. **STERILE BASE** usually present, chambered; white to dingy yellow or darker, persisting as a cuplike structure after the spores have dispersed. **SPORE MASS** firm and white when young, becoming yellowish, finally purplish and powdery. Spores 4.5-6 μm, round, spiny or warty to nearly smooth.

HABITAT: Scattered, in groups or rings in pastures and grassy places. Common in the fall, occasional otherwise.

EDIBILITY: Edible and choice when firm and white inside. Not as tasty as the giant puffball, but not as rich either.

COMMENTS: The striking purple color of the mature spore mass sets this *Calvatia* apart. It frequents the same habitats as *C. gigantea* and *C.*

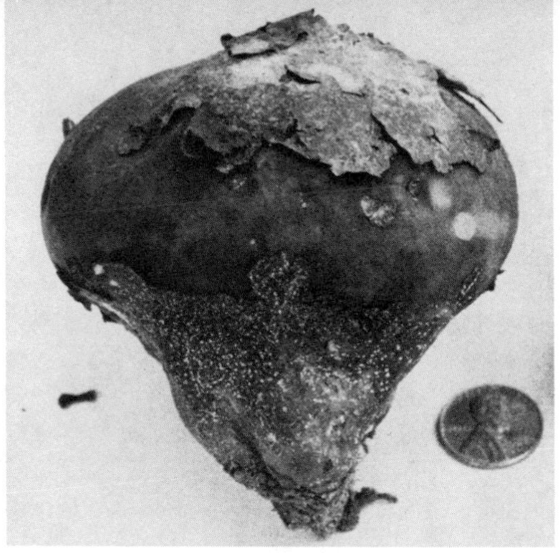

Calvatia cyathiformis. **Left:** Immature specimens below and an old, ruptured specimen above, filled with purple spore powder. **Right:** Mature specimen in which the outer layer of spore sac disintegrates, leaving a large bowl filled with dusty spores.

bovista, but there is normally only one major fruiting—in the fall. It is smaller and firmer than *C. bovista,* which also has a sterile base. The age of fairy rings growing in Colorado prairies has been estimated at 420 years—older than most trees! *C. cyathiformis* form *fragilis (=C. fragilis)* has only a rudimentary sterile base. It is also common.

Calvatia bovista

FRUITING BODY large, up to 25 cm high and 20 cm broad, top-shaped or pear-shaped with a broad, depressed top and large, prominent stemlike sterile base. Exterior white, grayish, or yellowish-brown, covered with pointed warts or soft particles, slowly breaking up into flat scales, then disintegrating. **STERILE BASE** very large, constituting more or less one half of the total height of fruiting body; chambered, exterior white, then brownish, smooth; persisting long after the spore sac has decomposed. **SPORE MASS** white and cheesy, then yellow or olive, finally olive-gold to dark brown and powdery. Spores 4-6 μm, round, smooth.

HABITAT: Solitary, scattered, or in groups in pastures, exposed soil, and open woods. Common, fall through spring, sometimes mingling with *Calvatia gigantea.*

EDIBILITY: Edible when immature, and supposedly good. The flesh is not as firm as in other Calvatias and I haven't been inclined to try it.

COMMENTS: This is the second largest of our puffballs, easily recognized by the flattened top and large sterile base. It looks something

Calvatia bovista, immature specimens. Note large size and prominent sterile base, which persists in old age as a "spore bowl." Specimen in center is seen from above.

like a gigantic *Lycoperdon perlatum* but does not form an apical pore. The bowl-shaped base persists long after the rest of the fruiting body has disintegrated. Bowls are often found filled with rainwater, mosquito larvae, and spores, or they may be windblown and completely empty. In this condition they may fool you, but don't let that faze you—a special genus *Hippoperdon* was once erected based on these empty bowls! This species is also known as *Calvatia caelata* and *C. utriformis*. *C. excipuliformis* is somewhat similar, but slightly smaller, with a cottony mature spore mass and warted spores.

Calvatia sculpta (Sculptured Puffball; Sierran Puffball)

FRUITING BODY more or less egg-shaped, pear-shaped, or irregular, 7-18 cm high. Exterior covered with long, pointed, white pyramidal warts (up to 2.5 cm long), erect or bent and joined at the tips; warts arising from angular plaques which crack and fall away. **STERILE BASE** present, white to yellowish in age. **SPORE MASS** white and firm, turning yellow and then deep olive-brown as it ripens; eventually powdery. Spores 3.5-6.5 μm, nearly round, minutely spiny.

HABITAT: Solitary or in small groups at high elevations, usually under conifers. Fairly common in the mountains of California in late spring, summer, and fall.

EDIBILITY: Like all puffballs, edible when immature.

COMMENTS: Though not coastal, I couldn't resist including this, the most spectacular of all puffballs. When fresh, the white pyramidal "peaks" make it look like a cross between a geodesic dome and a giant glob of meringue. *Calbovista subsculpta* is a grapefruit-sized mountain puffball with less prominent, more or less flattened warts. It used to be placed in *Calvatia,* but its capillitium have thornlike branches. This may not sound like much, but it is a momentous enough difference in the eyes of the puffball specialist to merit sequestering it in a genus of its own. In their unassuming little book on southern California mushrooms, the Orrs unfortunately confuse these two species.

Calvatia lycoperdoides

FRUITING BODY up to 5 cm high and broad, more or less round; surface with soft granules or spines, sometimes with small warts on top; breaking into large flakes at maturity, pallid becoming brownish in age. **STERILE BASE** absent. **SPORE MASS** firm and white when young, dark olive-brown at maturity, remaining intact for a long time, texture cottony. Spores 4-6.5 µm, round, warted.

HABITAT: Solitary or in small groups in woods and under trees, fall and winter, occasional.

EDIBILITY: Presumably edible when immature. I have not tried it.

COMMENTS: This is one of several Calvatias with a cottony (instead of powdery) mature spore mass and no sterile base. Others include: *C. umbrina,* dark brown to blackish; *C. diguettii,* ochraceous, on sandy soil along the coast; and *C. rubroflava,* with a greenish-orange mature spore mass and exterior quickly staining yellow when injured, mostly in cultivated soil.

MYCENASTRUM

THIS distinctive genus contains a single widespread, thick-skinned puffball, described below. Both *Mycenastrum* and its closest relative, *Calbovista* (see *Calvatia sculpta*) have capillitium with thornlike branches.

Mycenastrum corium

FRUITING BODY 5-18 cm broad, round to somewhat pear-shaped when young, eventually rupturing in irregular fissures to form rays or plates which may bend back in a somewhat star-shaped pattern. Outer layer of skin a thick, white felty coat which separates into blocklike areas, forming thin, grayish, fibrillose patches which eventually wear away, exposing the tough, hard, persistent, smooth inner layer, which is deep brown to purple-brown, and about 2 mm thick. **STERILE BASE**

Mycenastrum corium, immature specimens. These were found in a horse corral, a favorite haunt of this species. Note the thick skin and white felty material on exterior.

absent. **SPORE MASS** at first firm and white, becoming olive-yellow to olive-brown, finally purple-brown and powdery. Spores 8-12 μm, round, densely warted or reticulate. Capillitium branched, thorny.

HABITAT: Scattered to gregarious in horse corrals, composted soil, and fields where livestock have been grazing (sometimes partially buried); fruiting in fall and winter, but the tough spore sacs persist for months, sometimes breaking loose and blowing about in the wind. I have found it only twice, but it is probably quite common.

EDIBILITY: Presumably edible when firm and white inside.

COMMENTS: This peculiar puffball is easy to recognize but difficult to describe. The thick, tough inner skin distinguishes it from *Calvatia,* while the white, felty outer layer separates it from *Scleroderma.* The presence of capillitium in the spore mass indicates a much closer relationship to the other true puffballs than to the thick-skinned earthballs *(Scleroderma).* Its tendency to fruit in localities where livestock loiter is another helpful (but fallible) fieldmark.

VASCELLUM

Small grassland puffballs. FRUITING BODY more or less pear-shaped to top-shaped, spore sac two-layered, *upper portion disintegrating at maturity.* SPORE MASS powdery and dark olive-brown. STERILE BASE *present, with a thin membrane separating it from spore mass.* SPORES more or less round, minutely roughened. Capillitium present.

VASCELLUM is a small genus intermediate between *Calvatia* and *Lycoperdon.* A sterile base is present, unlike *Bovista.* The upper part of the spore sac disintegrates, while the lower portion and sterile base remain intact, forming a small bowl or urn.

Vascellum used to be included in *Lycoperdon,* but an apical pore or slit is not formed. The one species described here is exceedingly common in lawns and pastures.

Vascellum depressum is a small grassland puffball with a conspicuous sterile base. Specimens at left are immature. Note how the old individual on the right is bowl-shaped.

Vascellum depressum (Depressed Puffball)

FRUITING BODY up to 5 cm tall, typically more or less top-shaped (broader above), often wrinkled somewhat below. Outer layer of skin consisting of soft, scurfy particles or fine spines (especially on top) which disappear, exposing the inner layer. Color white when young, yellowish-tan to metallic brown in age, rupturing at the top, but the lower portion of the spore case remaining intact to form a bowl or urn. **STERILE BASE** well developed, prominent, chambered, white, separated from the spore mass by a thin membrane; brownish in age. **SPORE MASS** white but rather soft when young, then greenish-yellow, finally olive-brown and powdery. Spores 3-5 μm, round, almost smooth, more or less apiculate.

HABITAT: Scattered or in groups in grassy places—lawns, golf courses, pastures, etc. Very common in the fall and early winter, occasional otherwise.

EDIBILITY: Edible when immature; of mediocre quality.

COMMENTS: Formerly known as *Lycoperdon hiemale,* this undistinguished grassland puffball is distinguished by its small size, soft deciduous spines or granules, presence of a sterile base, and the bowl- or urnlike remains of ruptured specimens. It is often found in the company of *Bovista plumbea. Vascellum lloydianum* may be a better name for our fungus.

LYCOPERDON (COMMON PUFFBALLS)

Small to medium-sized puffballs, found mostly in woods. FRUITING BODY round to pear-shaped or top-shaped; spore sac two-layered, *rupturing through an apical pore.* SPORE MASS firm and white becoming powdery, olive-brown to purple-brown. STERILE BASE *usually present.* SPORES more or less round, usually warted or spiny. Capillitium present.

THESE are small to medium-sized puffballs rarely exceeding 10 cm (4 inches) in diameter. In contrast to *Calvatia* and *Scleroderma,* the spores are released through a hole, mouth, or slit **(apical pore)** at the top of the spore sac. The outer layer of the spore sac consists of spines, warts, or fine particles which fall away to expose the inner layer. A sterile base is usually present and at times may form a "stem."

Lycoperdons are our most common woodland puffballs. Old weathered specimens can be found at any time, but the major fruiting is in the fall. All species are edible when firm and white inside, but some taste better than others. As always, it is a good practice to identify each type before eating it, even though Lycoperdons are rather difficult to distinguish. Only four common species are described here.

Key to Lycoperdon

1. Sterile base absent; fruiting body small .... *L. pusillum* (see *Bovista plumbea,* p. 543)
1. Sterile base present 2
2. Exterior covered with very dark brown to black spines *when young;* yellow tones often developing in age .... *L. foetidium,* p. 541
2. Not as above (may be dark brown in old age) 3
3. Growing on or near wood (sometimes buried); exterior without spines, or spines if present not prominent; conspicuous white "roots" (rhizomorphs) attached to base .... *L. pyriforme,* p. 539
3. Not as above 4
4. Outer layer of spore sac peeling away in sheets at maturity; young spore sac often pinkish-tinted and often broader than it is tall .... *L. marginatum,* p. 542
4. Not as above 5
5. Exterior with cone-shaped spines which leave pockmarks behind after falling off; mature spore mass dark olive-brown; very common in woods .... *L. perlatum,* p. 540
5. Not as above 6
6. Up to 5 cm high; white when young; rupturing to form a bowl- or urn-shaped structure; very common in fields, lawns, pastures .... (see *Vascellum depressum,* p. 537)
6. Not as above 7
7. Fruiting body with a rooting base; spines on exterior often joined at the tips to form tufts or warts; mature spore mass brown .... *Bovistella radicata* (see *L. perlatum,* p. 540)
7. Not with above combination of characteristics 8
8. Exterior spines 2-6 mm long when young; often joined at tips to form "snowflakes" .... *L. echinatum* (see *L. perlatum,* p. 540)
8. Spines shorter, not as above ...... *L. umbrinum* (see *L. perlatum,* p. 540)

Lycoperdon pyriforme, immature specimens. Note the absence of prominent spines, narrow sterile base, clustered growth habit, and white mycelial strands.

Lycoperdon pyriforme (Pear-Shaped Puffball)

FRUITING BODY pear-shaped to nearly round, usually with a stemlike sterile base; 2.5-4 cm high, and almost as broad in widest part. Exterior pallid to pale brown when young, dark rusty-brown in age, sometimes yellowish; at first smooth or with a few small, scattered spines on top; becoming finely cracked to form minute granules (making it rough to the touch), this rough outer layer eventually falling away to expose the smooth inner layer in which an apical pore or tear is very slow to form. **STERILE BASE** well developed, occupying the stemlike base (if a base is present); chambers very small; conspicuous white "roots" (rhizomorphs) radiating from the base, and connected to others. **SPORE MASS** at first firm and white; then yellow to olive, finally deep olive-brown and powdery. Spores 3-3.5 μm, round, smooth.

HABITAT: Scattered or gregarious, on woody material—stumps, rotting logs, buried wood. Fairly common, fall and winter. It sometimes forms dense clusters as large as a loaf of bread.

EDIBILITY: Edible when young. In my fickle fungal opinion it is one of the best of the puffballs, but some forms are bitter.

COMMENTS: Most books emphasize the habitat on wood as an important identifying feature of this species; however, it may grow from buried wood or humus rich in lignin, thus appearing terrestrial. The white "roots" at the base and the absence of prominent spines are good secondary fieldmarks. It is one of the few smaller puffballs that occurs in sufficient quantity to collect for the table.

Lycoperdon perlatum, immature specimens. Note small cone-shaped spines and pear-shaped fruiting body. When spines fall off they leave small pockmarks behind. *L. umbrinum* (not illustrated) is similar but lacks pockmarks.

Lycoperdon perlatum (Common Puffball)

FRUITING BODY pear-shaped or top-shaped (broadest above); often wrinkled below, with a stemlike sterile base; up to 7.5 cm broad and high (occasionally larger). Outer layer of skin consisting of slender, cone-shaped spines (white, gray, or brownish in color, and interspersed with smaller granules) which leave pockmarks when they fall off. Inner layer may eventually become smooth; tan to yellowish-brown or grayish-brown in old age, eventually rupturing through an apical pore. **STERILE BASE** large, well developed, chambered, forming a stalklike base beneath the spore mass; at first white, then yellow, olive, or chocolate-colored. **SPORE MASS** firm and white, soon soft, becoming yellow, olive, finally dark olive-brown and powdery. Spores 3.5-4.5 μm, round, minutely spiny.

HABITAT: Solitary, scattered, or gregarious on ground in woods and under trees. Very common, fall through spring. The most abundant woodland puffball in North America—our region is no exception.

EDIBILITY: Edible when firm and white; specimens showing the slightest trace of yellow should not be eaten. It occasionally occurs in enough quantity to make collecting worthwhile.

COMMENTS: Also known as *L. gemmatum,* the slender cone-shaped spines which leave pockmarks behind is one distinctive feature of this cosmopolitan species. (The pockmarks, however, may eventually disappear.) The sterile base, dark olive-brown mature spore mass, and ubiquitousness also help to identify it. Very large specimens are occasionally found. It is one of the most variable of the puffballs, especially in its color. There are several similar puffballs with a dark purple-brown mature spore mass: *L. umbrinum (=L. molle),* common, has spines which do not leave pockmarks; *L. echinatum* and *L. pulcherrimum* have long (2-6 mm), thin white spines with tips often fused to form delicate "snowflakes"; in the former the spines usually leave marks behind when they fall off; in the latter they do not. Both have white "roots" (rhizomorphs) at the base, and are smaller than *L. perlatum.*

Finally, there is *Bovistella radicata,* a fairly large species (up to 12 cm) with a thick, rooting base. The exterior is composed of scurfy material intermingled with slender spines, typically joined at their tips. A large apical slit or tear forms at maturity. Its elaborately branched capillitium are characteristic of *Bovistella,* a small and infrequently encountered genus.

Lycoperdon foetidum (Black Puffball)

FRUITING BODY pear-shaped to nearly round, up to 4 cm broad. Outer layer of skin composed of fine, pointed black to dark-brown spines interspersed with granular material, these eventually falling away to reveal the smooth grayish-tan to yellowish inner layer; apical pore forming at maturity. **STERILE BASE** well developed, chambered, exterior usually paler than rest of fruiting body, at least when young. **SPORE MASS** white, becoming yellow, finally dull cinnamon-brown to dark brown and powdery. Spores 4-5 μm, round, minutely spiny.

HABITAT: Scattered to gregarious in deep woods. Common in the Santa Cruz mountains in fall and winter, but easily overlooked because of its color.

Lycoperdon foetidum, immature specimens. Note the dark brown to black color—its principal fieldmark.

EDIBILITY: Presumably edible when firm and white inside. I haven't tried it.

COMMENTS: This attractive puffball is the only one with dark brown to black spines *when immature.* These contrast nicely with the white flesh. Several Lycoperdons may be quite dark in age (see *L. perlatum*). *L. nigrescens* is a synonym.

Lycoperdon marginatum (Peeling Puffball)

FRUITING BODY at first more or less round, at maturity usually broader than it is tall; less than 5 cm in diameter, underside usually wrinkled, at least in age; sometimes with a short, rooting base. Outer layer of skin white or tinged pinkish when young, composed of short, erect warts or spines which peel off *in sheets,* exposing the smooth inner layer, which is pale to dark olive-brown, smooth or slightly scurfy. Apical pore eventually forming. **STERILE BASE** chambered, usually well developed, basal. **SPORE MASS** white and firm, then olive to grayish-brown, becoming powdery. Spores 3.5-4.5 μm, round, minutely ornamented.

HABITAT: In groups or clusters on ground, late fall and winter. I have found it in large quantities on sandy soil in mixed hardwood forest-chaparral.

EDIBILITY: Edible when firm and white inside. In Mexico, this species and *L. miztecorum* are used to induce auditory hallucinations. It is known as "gi-i-sa-wa," meaning "fungus of second quality" (*L. miztecorum* being the fungus of first quality). However, no intoxicating substances were found when these puffballs were analyzed.

COMMENTS: The peculiar manner in which the outer layer separates completely from the inner layer and peels off in sheets is the hallmark of this pleasing puffball. *L. candidum* is similar, if not the same.

Lycoperdon marginatum, maturing specimens. Note how the outer layer of the spore sac peels away in sheets. Exterior is white or pinkish-tinted when immature.

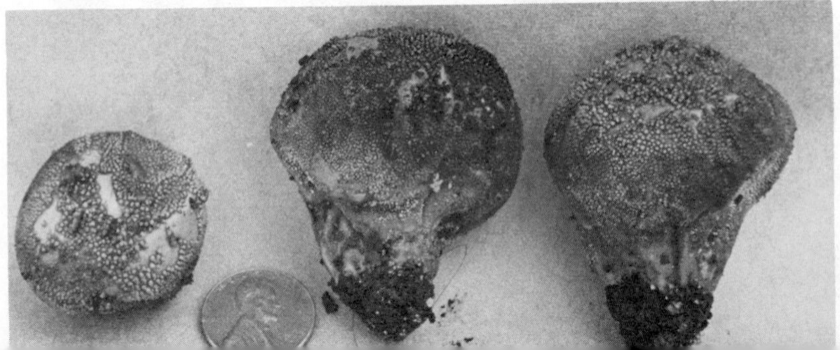

BOVISTA

Small puffballs found mostly in grass. FRUITING BODY more or less round. Spore sac two-layered, rupturing to form a large mouth in age. *Inner layer very thin, papery.* Exterior usually smooth. SPORE MASS firm and white becoming powdery at maturity. STERILE BASE *absent.* SPORES more or less round, minutely warty or spiny, pedicellate. Capillitium present, branched.

THESE are small (marble- to baseball-sized) puffballs without a sterile base. The mature spore sac is paper thin with a metallic luster, and so light that it is often blown about by the wind.

Bovistas are the most common puffballs of lawns and pastures. They also grow on poor or exposed soil. Though edible when firm and white inside, they don't amount to much. It is a small genus. Two species are keyed below.

Key to Bovista

1. Attached to ground by a small patch of fibers; spore sac purplish-brown to bluish-gray when mature; very common in grass .. *B. plumbea,* below
1. Attached to ground by a small cordlike root; spore sac brown or bronze when mature; not common 2

2. Typically 2.5 cm or more in diameter .. *B. pila* (see *B. plumbea,* below)
2. Typically less than 2.5 cm in diameter .... *Lycoperdon pusillum* (see *B. plumbea,* below)

Bovista plumbea (Paltry Puffball)

FRUITING BODY round or slightly flattened; up to 4 cm in diameter, with a small patch of dirt (held together by fibers) at the base. Outer layer of skin smooth, white, peeling away or shriveling up in age to reveal the smooth, papery inner layer which is bluish-gray to purplish-brown, with a metallic luster; large circular mouth forming at the top in age. **STERILE BASE** absent. **SPORE MASS** white and firm, then yellow-olive, finally deep chocolate-brown and powdery. Spores 5-7 $\times$ 5-6 μm, oval to nearly round, minutely spiny to nearly smooth with long, pointed pedicel ("tail") 8-14 μm long.

HABITAT: Scattered to gregarious in grassy places; very common. It fruits in the fall and winter in pastures, year-round on lawns and cultivated ground. The thin, papery, windblown spore sacs can be found most any time.

EDIBILITY: Edible when immature; the flavor is very mild and a great many are needed for a meal.

Bovista plumbea, immature specimens. This common, small round puffball of lawns and pastures lacks a sterile base. Mature specimens are purple-brown to purple-gray with a large mouth at the top.

COMMENTS: This small, round puffball is a common inhabitant of our pastures. In the immature stage the smooth white skin and absence of a sterile base are diagnostic. It is often found in the company of *Vascellum depressum. B. pila,* a slightly larger species, is attached to the ground by a small cord or "root," and has a dark brown to bronze mature spore sac. *B. minor* is a rare species with a trash-covered spore sac. It grows in poor soil, usually somewhat buried. Our smallest puffball, *Lycoperdon pusillum,* is marble-sized, round above and pinched below to a cordlike root. It too lacks a sterile base and the spores are not pedicellate. It so closely resembles *Bovista* that it is placed in that genus by some puffball scholars. *Disciseda* is a rare genus that grows in poor, exposed, or sandy soil. Several species are reported from southern California; they have a papery endoperidium (like *Bovista*), a dark brown to black exoperidium, and little or no sterile base.

GEASTRUM and ASTREUS (EARTHSTARS)

Small to medium-sized mostly terrestrial fungi. FRUITING BODY round or flattened when young, *at maturity consisting of a spore sac surrounded by (or mounted on) starlike rays.* SPORE SAC smooth or roughened, usually rupturing through an apical pore. SPORE MASS soon powdery, brown. STALK and STERILE BASE absent. SPORES round, warted or smooth. Capillitium present, branched (*Astreus*), unbranched (*Geastrum*).

EARTHSTARS are modified puffballs in which the thick outer (and middle) skin splits into starlike rays which slowly recurve, exposing the inner skin (spore sac) to the elements. Some puffballs and earthballs rupture in starlike fashion (e.g., *Scleroderma geaster*), but only in the earthstars is there a discrete, intact spore sac within.

Some earthstars are **hygroscopic**: the rays open in wet weather to expose the sac and close up in dry weather to protect it. This phenomenon can be recreated at home by placing a closed-up earthstar in a shallow bowl of water. If hygroscopic it will open up in a few minutes. Earthstars are also accomplished acrobats. They never cease

Immature earthstars resemble puffballs. However, the outer layer of the spore sac ruptures to form rays or arms, as shown in this picture of *Geastrum fornicatum.*

to amaze in the varied assortment of unorthodox and extraordinary poses they strike. *Geastrum fornicatum* in particular is a prodigious contortionist.

The principal genera, *Geastrum (=Geaster)* and *Astreus,* belong to two separate families but are grouped together here because they resemble each other closely. *Geastrum* embraces a sizable number of small earthstars (generally less than 5 cm in diameter) with small spores (less than 7 μm broad) and unbranched capillitium. *Astreus* is comprised of two hygroscopic species (one quite large) with larger spores and branched capillitium. Closely related to *Geastrum* is a third genus, *Myriostoma,* in which the spore sac is perforated by many holes (like a salt shaker) instead of a single apical pore or rupture. It has a wide distribution but is very rare.

Several types of earthstars occur in our area—under trees, in the woods, sandy fields, pastures, vacant lots, and waste places. Many more occur in the desert.

Though earthstars are real crowdpleasers, they have no culinary value. They are rarely found before they mature and the rays are too tough to eat. Five species are described here.

Key to Geastrum and Astreus

1. Spore sac seated in a saucerlike base .... *Geastrum triplex,* p. 548
1. Not as above 2

2. Fruiting body 5-15 cm broad when expanded, hygroscopic; upper (inner) surface of rays transversely checked (like a crooked crossword puzzle); spore sac rupturing irregularly .... *Astreus pteridis,* p. 550
2. Not as above 3

3. Fruiting body hygroscopic 4
3. Fruiting body not hygroscopic 5

4. Fruiting body generally less than 2.5 cm broad when expanded; spore sac smooth; spores less than 5 μm broad .... *Geastrum floriforme* (see *Astreus hygrometricus,* p. 549)
4. Fruiting body generally more than 2.5 cm broad when expanded; spore sac roughened by minute particles; spores more than 7 μm broad .... *Astreus hygrometricus,* p. 549

5. *Mature* fruiting body poised on the tips of its rays; spore sac mounted on a short stalk or pedicel 6
5. Not as above; spore sac not mounted on a stalk .... *Geastrum saccatum,* p. 547

6. Mature fruiting body typically less than 4 cm high; spore sac roughened with minute glistening particles .... *Geastrum coronatum* (see *G. fornicatum,* below)
6. Usually larger; not as above .... *Geastrum fornicatum,* below

Geastrum fornicatum

FRUITING BODY round or flattened when young and covered with debris, the outer skin splitting into 3-6 (usually 4) rays which peel back and eventually recurve under the spore sac; mature fruiting body 5-10 cm high and broad, poised on the pointed tips of the rays, which are usually joined to a mycelial "cup" or mat which is grayish on the inside, covered with trash on the outside. Underside (exterior) of rays smooth, tan to brown. Upper (inner) surface chocolate-brown to dark brown, peeling off patches to reveal the paler brown, smooth surface beneath. **SPORE SAC** mounted on a short stalk (pedicel), up to 2.5 cm wide, round or somewhat flattened, often with a compressed collar underneath; dark brown to chocolate-brown, surface finely velvety; rupturing through a large, irregularly torn or lacerated pore. **SPORE MASS** powdery when mature, chocolate-brown or blackish-brown. Spores 3.5-4.5 μm, round, warted.

HABITAT: Densely gregarious (several hundred, representing all stages of development) on rubbish and debris near a stable, in an area where horses are washed. Fruiting in fall, but persisting for months. I have collected it many times from the single locality described above. It is considered rare in North America.

EDIBILITY: Inedible. However, they are easily dried, making extraordinary ornaments or conversation pieces.

COMMENTS: One of the most distinctive of all fleshy fungi, a true pleasure to find. Mature individuals defy description, but look something like a cross between a flat tire and a ballet dancer. The

Geastrum fornicatum, mature specimens in which rays are poised on their tips to elevate spore sac. Note how rays peel in patches. Specimens at left are firmly attached to a cuplike mat of mycelium and debris. Immature specimens are pictured on p. 545.

tendency of the rays to straighten out and stand on their tips (like a ballet dancer) plus the membranous mycelial cup ("flat tire") to which they're attached are the principal fieldmarks. Because of its likeness to a human figure, it was named *Fungus anthropomorphus* when first described in 1688. Specimens are sometimes found with only one or two "arms" extended, as if they were putting out tentative "feelers" before committing themselves completely (and irrevocably) to exposure. *G. coronatum (=G. quadrifidum)* is a smaller (half as large) and more petite version found mostly under conifers, especially cypress. The spore sac is usually taller than it is wide, is covered with minute glistening particles, and has a neatly defined mouth at maturity.

Geastrum saccatum

FRUITING BODY round or flattened when young; up to 5 cm broad when fully expanded, with 4-8 rays which bend under sac at maturity. Outer (under) surface of rays relatively clean, buff to pale tan; inner (upper) surface fleshy, pallid becoming pale tan or pinkish-buff, sometimes cracking. **SPORE SAC** round or nearly round, less than 2.5 cm broad, smooth, dull, grayish to brownish, papery. Apical pore paler than rest of sac, well defined, fibrillose. **SPORE MASS** powdery when mature, coffee-brown. Spores 3.5-4.5 μm, round, roughened.

HABITAT: Solitary or in small groups in humus under trees (especially redwood), fall and winter. This species and its relatives are the most common Geastrums in our region.

EDIBILITY: Inedible.

COMMENTS: The spore sac in this species has neither stalk (as in *G. fornicatum*) nor saucer (as in *G. triplex*). There are several similar species, including *G. fimbriatum,* slightly darker, with a poorly defined, torn or fimbriate (fringed) apical pore.

Left: *Geastrum saccatum*, mature specimen. Note absence of "saucer." **Right:** *Geastrum triplex*, mature specimen. "Saucer" around spore sac distinguishes this species.

Geastrum triplex

FRUITING BODY more or less round or flattened when young, to 10 cm broad when expanded; with 5-8 rays that bend under sac at maturity. Outer (under) surface of rays usually free of adhering debris, dull yellowish-brown; upper (inner) surface of rays fleshy, rather thick, tan to brown, cracking into patches, the central region breaking loose to form a broad cup or saucer around the spore sac. **SPORE SAC** up to 2.5 cm broad, round but somewhat flattened, pale to dark tan; apical pore paler, raised (conic), radially fibrillose. **SPORE MASS** powdery when mature, deep brown to smoky-brown. Spores 3.5-4.5 μm, round, warted.

HABITAT: Solitary or in groups in humus; I have found it in mixed woods and under oak. Occasional, fall and winter.

EDIBILITY: Supposedly edible when young, but I have never found it when the spore mass was white.

COMMENTS: This attractive species is recognized by the shallow cup which surrounds the base of the spore case. The extent to which the upper surface of the rays cracks varies considerably.

Astreus hygrometricus, mature specimens. Ten minutes before this picture was taken, the fully expanded individuals were curled up like the one in foreground. However, immersion in water caused them to open. Note the roughened surface of spore sac.

Astreus hygrometricus (Hygrometric Earthstar)

FRUITING BODY round to somewhat flattened when young, 2.5-7 cm broad when expanded, the outer skin splitting into 6-15 pointed, tough rays which open in wet weather, close over the spore sac in dry weather. Upper (inner) surface of rays soon cracking, pale tan, darkening in age. Underside (exterior) fibrillose with adhering sand or sometimes with black hairlike strands (rhizomorphs) attached to the base. **SPORE SAC** pallid grayish, up to 2.5 cm broad, round or somewhat flattened, roughened by particles, rupturing through an irregular apical pore or slit. **SPORE MASS** powdery when mature, cocoa-brown. Spores 7-10.5 μm, round, warted.

HABITAT: Scattered to gregarious in old fields, sandy soil, pastures, exposed ground, etc. Fruiting in the fall but the fructifications persist for months. Weathered, blackened outer skins (which look like old tire patches) are often found, without the spore sac attached. It has a worldwide distribution and grows virtually anywhere—from sea level to above timberline, from verdant pastures to harsh deserts.

EDIBILITY: Inedible.

COMMENTS: This veritable barometer is the most theatrical of the earthstars. A few minutes submersion in water will open up old, dried specimens that seem as tight as clenched fists. The surface of the rays may be cracked, but not nearly as much as in *A. pteridis*. *Geastrum campestre* is very similar but has smaller spores (6-7.5 μm) and unbranched capillitium. It is widely distributed but I have yet to find it here. However, I have found a small hygroscopic species, *G. floriforme,* that is rarely more than 2.5 cm broad. It has 6-10 thin, pointed rays which rapidly close up in dry weather, and a more or less smooth spore sac. Similar species occur in the desert.

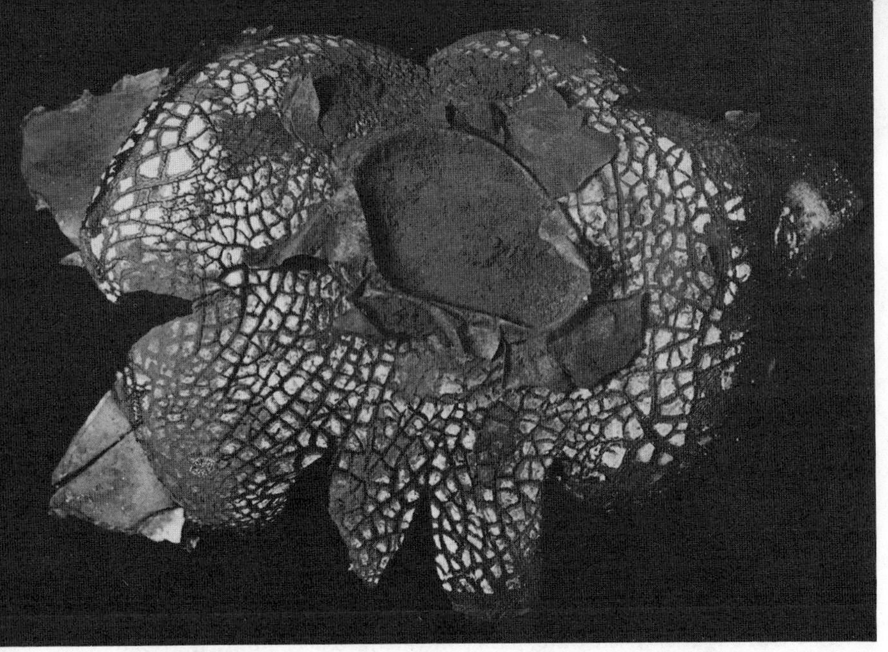

Astreus pteridis, mature specimen. About twice as large as *A. hygrometricus*, this species is easily recognized by the crazy checkerboard pattern on its rays. Note how spore sac disintegrates instead of forming a pore. (Joel Leivick)

Astreus pteridis (Giant Earthstar)

FRUITING BODY round or somewhat flattened when young, 5-15 cm broad when expanded, with 6 or more thick, hygroscopic rays (3-6 mm thick), which are woody when dry. Upper (inner) surface of rays conspicuously cracked or fissured transversely to form a checked pattern; tan, dark brown in the cracks. Underside (exterior) with a thin coating of matted brownish fibrils which may or may not wear away. **SPORE SAC** 2.5-5 cm broad, round or somewhat flattened, grayish-brown to brown; rupturing irregularly in old age; distinct apical pore not formed. **SPORE MASS** powdery when mature, dark brown. Spores 8-12 μm, round, warted.

HABITAT: Solitary or in small groups in humus, exposed soil, waste places, and along roads through the woods. Fall and winter, common.

EDIBILITY: Inedible.

COMMENTS: The checked rays (like a crooked crossword puzzle), large size, and irregular rupturing of the spore sac distinguish this impressive species from its more mundane cousin, *A. hygrometricus*. For some inexplicable reason, the fructifications remind me of "tribbles"—those lovable but ruthlessly prolific creatures of Star Trek renown.

TULOSTOMA and BATTARAEA

(STALKED PUFFBALLS)

Small to medium-sized puffballs growing in poor, exposed, or sandy soil. FRUITING BODY *with a spore sac mounted on a well-developed stalk.* SPORE SAC more or less round, two-layered, rupturing around the periphery or thru an apical pore. STERILE BASE absent. STALK *tough, woody, fibrillose.* VOLVA present or absent. SPORE MASS powdery at maturity, rusty-salmon to dark brown. Spores more or less round, smooth or ornamented. Capillitium present, well developed.

THESE are puffballs with a clearly defined, well-developed stalk. As in other puffballs, the mature spore mass is powdery and the skin is composed of two layers. In *Battaraea,* the outer layer at first envelops the fruiting body and ruptures to form a volva. The inner layer (spore sac) splits around its rim to release the spores. *Tulostoma* species are smaller, lack a volva, and release their spores through an apical pore.

Stalked puffballs are adapted to habitats unfavorable to most fungi—sand, poor soil, waste places, etc. Many grow in the desert, where they are sometimes abundant after cloudbursts. None are known to be poisonous, but none are considered edible either—they are invariably found after the spore mass is mature and the stalks are much too tough to eat, unless you're starving. Even then you're better off chewing on your shoe.

Key to Tulostoma and Battaraea

1. Cap cylindrical or egg-shaped, like a shaggy mane (not a true spore sac); growing in desert .... *Podaxis pistillaris* (see *Battaraea phalloides,* p. 552)
1. Spore sac present; not as above 2

2. Volva present; spore sac rupturing around periphery .... *Battaraea phalloides,* p. 552
2. Volva absent; spore sac rupturing through an apical pore .... *Tulostoma brumale,* below

Tulostoma brumale (Common Stalked Puffball)

FRUITING BODY consisting of a small spore sac mounted on a slender stalk. **SPORE SAC** round or flattened, about 1 cm broad, the underside shrinking in drying and pulling away from the stalk to form a collar. Outer layer brownish, dirty, covered with sand and debris, peeling away to reveal the inner layer except around the base. Inner skin smooth or with minute particles, tan to pinkish-buff, fading to gray.

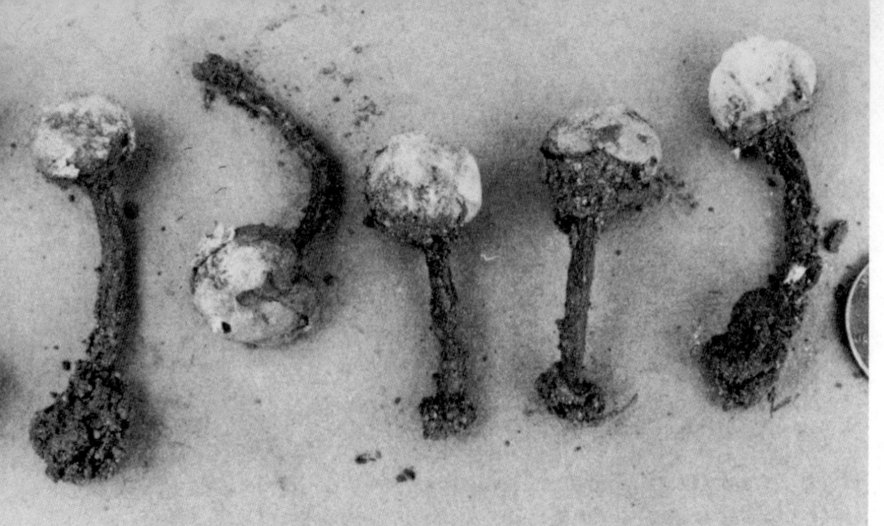

Tulostoma brumale, mature specimens. All Tulostomas have the same general appearance: a small spore sac mounted on a slender stalk.

Apical pore developing at maturity, usually well defined as a small raised tube or collar. **STALK** 1-5 cm long, 2-3 mm thick, equal with a small bulb at the base; tough, covered at first with brown to rusty-brown fibrils, smoother and paler in age, longitudinally striate. **VOLVA** absent. **SPORE MASS** rusty-salmon and powdery at maturity. Spores 3-5 µm, more or less round, minutely warted.

HABITAT: Scattered or in groups in sand, sandy soil, grass, and other waste places. Fruiting in fall and winter but persisting for a long time, usually buried so only the spore sac is visible. Common but easily overlooked. Related species occur in the desert.

EDIBILITY: Inedible.

COMMENTS: Tulostomas are easily recognized by their slender stalk, small spore sac, and rusty-salmon spores. There are several closely related species which will more or less fit the above description, all partial to sandy soil. These include *T. simulans,* which has larger spores and a spore sac remaining covered with sand for a long time, and *T. striatum,* with ridged spores.

Battaraea phalloides

FRUITING BODY at first enclosed by a membrane, the stalk then bursting through and elevating the spore sac. **SPORE SAC** up to 5 cm broad but usually smaller, more or less oval with the underside usually flattened; exterior smooth, cream-colored, splitting around the periphery to release the spores, the basal portion falling away or

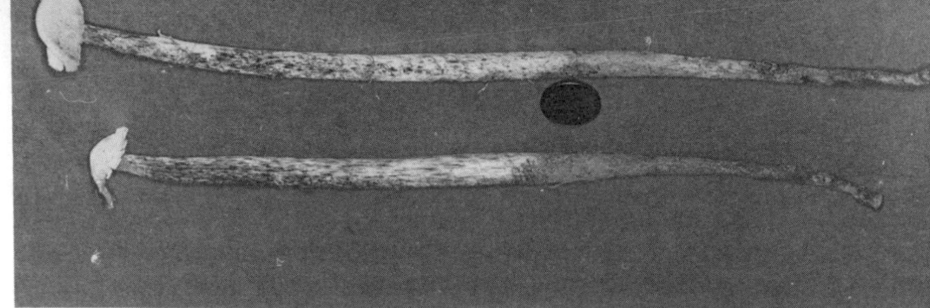

Battaraea phalloides, old weathered specimens in which the spore sac has ruptured and all the spores have been dispersed. Only the upper shell of the spore sac is left. The volva at the stalk base is also gone—and the woody stalk that remains is as light as straw.

sometimes forming a ring on the stalk, the upper portion persisting. **STALK** 15-40 cm long, slender, equal or tapering downward, woody, covered with coarse hairy or shaggy scales; brown. **VOLVA** at the base of the stalk in the form of a cup, easily left in ground. **SPORE MASS** mucilaginous in the egg stage, a sticky dark brown powder when mature. Spores 4-8 μm, more or less round, warty. Capillitium of two types: simple hyphae and elators (elongated cells with internal spirals).

HABITAT: Solitary to gregarious in sandy soil along the coast, also in deserts. Rather rare here, more common in southern California. It has been found in Pacific Grove, and at Moss Landing in an old field, in fall and winter.

EDIBILITY: Inconsequential.

COMMENTS: The long scaly stalk, presence of a volva, and curious manner in which the spore sac ruptures sets *Battaraea* apart. The dried stalks are remarkably light and not the least bit suggestive of "fungus." The spore sac eventually disintegrates except for the membrane on top, which persists as a thin "cap" with a torn or fringed margin. Similar species occur in the desert, where another distinctive fungus, *Podaxis pistillaris,* is common. Its cylindrical cap is reminiscent of an immature shaggy mane *(Coprinus comatus),* with a chambered or gill-like interior. The spore mass is pallid at first, then reddish-brown, finally blackish and powdery. There is no volva. It is not actually a stalked puffball but is likely to be mistaken for one.

SCLERODERMA (EARTHBALLS)

Medium-sized to large fungi found in soil or on rotten wood. FRUITING BODY more or less round to oval, sometimes star-shaped at maturity. Spore sac (skin) *one-layered, typically thick, tough, hard, rigid;* rupturing irregularly or in lobes (apical pore not formed); exterior smooth, rough or with fine scales, rarely white. SPORE MASS solid, *soon colored brown to purple-black,* often marbled with paler veins; powdery at maturity. STERILE BASE absent but a stalklike base of mycelial fibers often present. SPORES more or less round; warted, spiny, or reticulate. Capillitium absent or rudimentary.

EARTHBALLS can be identified by their hard, tough, rigid skin and dark brown to purple-black interior. Whereas immature puffballs are white inside, the spore mass in an earthball is soon colored. Though often called "thick-skinned puffballs," earthballs differ from puffballs in two fundamental respects: the skin (peridium) is composed of one layer only and there are no specialized filamentous cells (capillitium) in the spore mass. This has led many modern taxonomists to divorce *Scleroderma* from the puffballs proper (Lycoperdales) and place them (along with the stalked puffballs and the earthstar genus, *Astreus*) in a separate order, Sclerodermatales.

There are other differences as well. In *Scleroderma* the exterior of the spore sac lacks the spines or soft particles characteristic of so many puffballs. There is no sterile base. Instead, a stalklike or rootlike base of tough, mycelial fibers may be present. As their name implies, earthballs are often buried or partially buried before maturity, leading to possible confusion with false truffles (Hymenogastrales). However, the spore mass is powdery when mature and the hard, rigid spore sac is distinctive.

Scleroderma is not a large genus, but the California species are poorly known. They are very common—in gardens, under hedges, on exposed hillsides, along roads, in sand and asphalt, around old stumps, etc. They occur year-round, even in the summer.

Earthballs do not enjoy a good culinary reputation. Some are bitter and others are reportedly poisonous. They are not likely to be eaten, however, since they are rarely found when white inside. Four representative species are described here.

Key to Scleroderma

1. Skin very thick (3-10 mm), splitting into coarse lobes which curve back to form a "star"; large .... *S. geaster,* p. 555
1. Not as above (may split into lobes, but skin not nearly so thick); small to medium-sized 2

2. Spore sac covered with a white, felty layer when young; mature spore sac dark brown to purple-brown; spore mass white, then yellow-olive, finally dark brown .... (see *Mycenastrum corium,* p. 535)
2. Not as above 3

3. Exterior slowly staining wine-red when rubbed, especially underneath .... *S. cepa,* p. 557
3. Not as above 4

4. Skin two-layered, the outer layer thin and rindlike, white to brownish, peeling from inner layer in patches; spore mass white when young .... (see *Calvatia,* p. 528)
4. Not as above 5

5. Exterior with distinct scales; spore sac wall staining pinkish when cross-sectioned (if fresh) .... *S. citrinum,* p. 558
5. Not as above 6
6. Mature spore sac splitting into lobes which curve back to form a "star"; in sand or sandy soil .... *S. flavidum* (see *S. geaster,* p. 555)
6. Mature spore sac may or may not split into lobes, but lobes do *not* curve back .... *S. bovista,* p. 556

Scleroderma geaster (Dead Man's Hand)

FRUITING BODY 5-15 cm broad when closed, up to 30 cm broad when expanded; at first irregularly round, flattened, or lobed, and buried in the soil, then becoming exposed as skin splits into several coarse, irregular rays which curl back in starlike fashion to expose the spore mass; attached to soil by a mycelial "root" or strands. Skin hard and rigid, very thick (3-10 mm); exterior whitish to dull yellowish-clay, roughened, fissured, or somewhat hairy, then more or less cracked into scales; interior blackened and empty in old age. **SPORE MASS** dark brown to purple-brown when mature, solid becoming powdery. Spores 6-11 μm, round, warted.

HABITAT: Buried or half-buried in poor soils: on hillsides, in gardens, along roads, in asphalt, gravel, drainage ditches, etc. Solitary or in groups, common. Normally fruiting in the fall, but the old skins may persist for months.

Scleroderma geaster, mature specimens which have ruptured in a starlike pattern. Traces of the powdery spore mass remain inside.

EDIBILITY: Unknown. This is one fleshy fungus that I've never been tempted to eat.

COMMENTS: The large size and thick skin which splits into starlike rays are the extraordinary features of this extraordinary fungus. That dusty monstrosity *Pisolithus tinctorius* is its only rival for grotesqueness. The two, in fact, thrive in similar milieu (asphalt, sand, poor soil, and other inhospitable places), and make a well-matched if unsightly pair. A synonym for *S. geaster* is *S. polyrhizon*. It might be mistaken for a large cup fungus *(Sarcosphaera),* but there are usually traces of the spore mass inside. *Scleroderma flavidum* also splits in starlike fashion, but is smaller, with a much thinner (about 1 mm thick) skin. It has a smooth tawny surface, yellow-brown to dark brown spore mass, and grows in sandy soil. It may or may not have a stemlike base composed of mycelial fibers. *S. geaster* can also be confused with *Mycenastrum corium,* a puffball with a thick white felty outer skin and smooth purple-brown inner skin which splits into lobes at maturity.

Scleroderma bovista (Smooth Earthball)

FRUITING BODY more or less round or somewhat flattened above, 2.5-5 cm broad, usually attached to the ground by a stemlike or rootlike mass of mycelial fibers; skin hard, rigid, more or less 1 mm thick, white in cross-section and *not* staining pink, splitting irregularly or in lobes at the top in age. Exterior buff to yellowish or straw color, darkening to sordid brown, often becoming spotted blackish in old age, especially on top; smooth when young, sometimes cracking into small scales on top in

A member of the *Scleroderma bovista* group. Note the nearly smooth skin and "stalk" composed of tough mycelial fibers. Spore mass is dark brown.

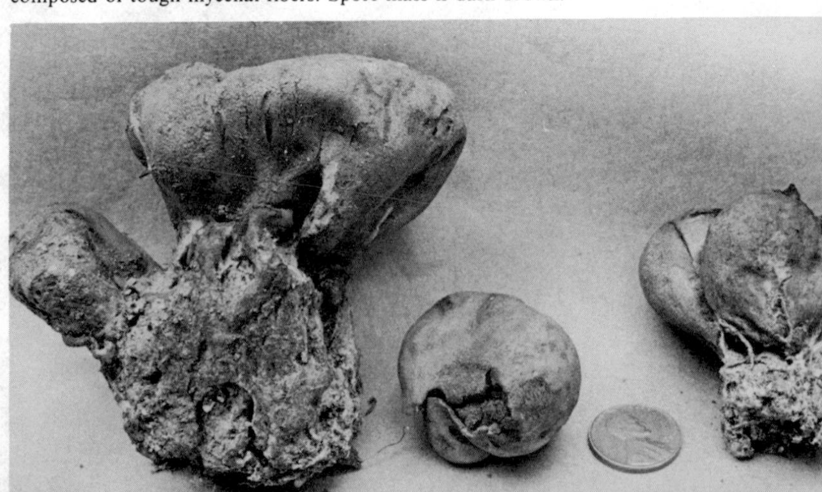

age. **SPORE MASS** soon brown to black (marbled with yellowish veins when young), solid when young, powdery at maturity. Spores 9-15.5 μm, round, warted.

HABITAT: Solitary or in groups in gardens, under trees and hedges, in vacant lots and waste places, etc. This species and its relatives (see below) are very common and fruit year-round.

EDIBILITY: None of these Sclerodermas (see below) are worth eating; some may actually be poisonous.

COMMENTS: We have several Sclerodermas with a more or less smooth, rigid, yellowish-brown spore sac. They are common as a group, but difficult to differentiate. *S. arenicola* is very similar but does not blacken on top and has larger, spiny, reticulate spores (15-22 μm). I have found it several times in sandy and poor soils. *S. furfurellum* has a scurfy exterior (with small branlike scales), a black spore mass marbled with pale veins, and slightly roughened spores (10-12.5 μm). *S. lycoperdoides* is a small species with fine, spotlike scales and a well-developed "stalk" of mycelial fibers. *S. verrucosum,* a species often illustrated in European books, is very similar, if not the same.

Scleroderma cepa

FRUITING BODY more or less round to somewhat flattened or lobed, 1.5-7 cm broad; usually attached to the ground by a mass of rootlike fibers. Skin hard, tough, 1-2 mm thick, turning pinkish to wine color when cut, eventually splitting irregularly into lobes which do not bend outward. Exterior pallid becoming grayish, buff, straw color, or brownish; slowly staining wine-red when rubbed (especially underneath), then discoloring brownish; smooth when young, often cracking

Scleroderma cepa. Note the thick skin, purple-black spore mass, and reddish-staining exterior. Specimen on right has cracked in scales, probably because of dry weather.

into scales on top as it ages. **SPORE MASS** solid when young, watery white soon becoming black or purple-black, eventually powdery in old age and fading somewhat to dark brown. Spores 7-12 µm, round, spiny.

HABITAT: Scattered to gregarious in cultivated or disturbed ground, occasionally in open woods. Flourishing whenever conditions are favorable. The specimens photographed were found along an asphalt road in July.

EDIBILITY: Inedible; according to some reports, poisonous.

COMMENTS: The tendency of the exterior to turn wine-red when rubbed or handled separates this attractive earthball from *S. bovista* and the other smooth-skinned earthballs. The spore sac wall in *S. citrinum* also turns pinkish when cross-sectioned, but the exterior in that species is embossed with scales and does not normally bruise reddish.

Scleroderma citrinum (Common Earthball)

FRUITING BODY round or depressed above, 2-7.5 cm broad, underside often with a ridged, stemlike base composed of mycelial fibers and adhering debris. Skin hard and rigid, 1-2 mm thick, white in cross-section but bruising pink when cut (if fresh), at maturity cracking into irregular lobes which do *not* bend outward. Exterior some shade of yellowish-brown, cracked into distinct, inherent scales which often have a smaller, central wart. **SPORE MASS** white when very young, soon gray with whitish lines running through it, then dark purple-gray to black, solid when young, eventually powdery. Spores 8-13 µm, round, strongly warted, reticulate.

HABITAT: The most common member of the genus in North America, but infrequent in our area. It usually grows on rotten wood or around stumps (especially in northern coniferous forests), but I have found it in a garden, in October.

EDIBILITY: Inedible; reportedly used by unscrupulous individuals to adulterate truffles. It is difficult to find specimens which are still white inside, and there are several reports of poisoning by this species.

COMMENTS: The prominent scales which often look embossed, and the tendency of the spore sac wall to stain pinkish when cut combine with the purple-black spore mass to render this well-known species distinct. *S. vulgare* and *S. aurantium* are synonyms.

PISOLITHUS

THIS aberrant genus is easily recognized by the hundreds of small, spore-containing, lentil-like chambers **(peridioles)** imbedded in the fruiting body. These are best seen by making a lengthwise cross-section. The mature fruiting body protrudes from the ground like a dusty, half-rotted stump or root. There is only one species, found throughout the world.

Pisolithus tinctorius (Dead Man's Foot)

FRUITING BODY up to 30 cm high and 12 cm broad, at first round to pear-shaped or club-shaped with a stalk or rooting base; breaking up in age and taking on the appearance of a large, dusty root. Outer skin thin, brittle, variously colored (usually yellowish or purplish to brown) with a metallic luster, soon flaking away. Upper half of interior containing many small oval to circular lentil-like chambers (peridioles) which disintegrate from the top of the fruiting body downward, releasing the dusty brown spores. Peridioles whitish, greenish-yellow, or brownish, imbedded in a sticky substance which becomes dry and brittle at maturity. Lower half of fruiting body a fibrous, stalklike rooting base; sterile, persistent, with coarse greenish-yellow mycelial fibers often attached. Odor aromatic to unpleasant depending on age. **SPORE MASS** dark brown to cinnamon-brown, powdery. Spores 8-12 μm, round, warty or spiny. Capillitium absent.

HABITAT: Solitary or scattered on or along roads and in poor soil; mycorrhizal with a wide variety of trees. Fruiting chiefly in fall and winter but persisting, as it slowly disintegrates, for weeks. Common and widespread.

EDIBILITY: Questionable. In Europe it is known as the "Bohemian Truffle" and used as an aromatic seasoning when unripe. But it is scarcely appetizing, and should be tried very cautiously, if at all. The name *tinctorius* reflects its use as a dye. A variety of rich colors (mostly browns and golds, but also blacks and dark blues) can be obtained, depending on the mordants used and the type of soil in which it is found.

COMMENTS: This large, dusty monstrosity is unquestionably among the most memorable of all fungi. To me it is also one of the most enthralling. When fresh, it stains anything and everything it comes in contact with, and the dry spore dust covers everything in the vicinity. It has a penchant for adversity, inevitably fruiting in poor soil, dry

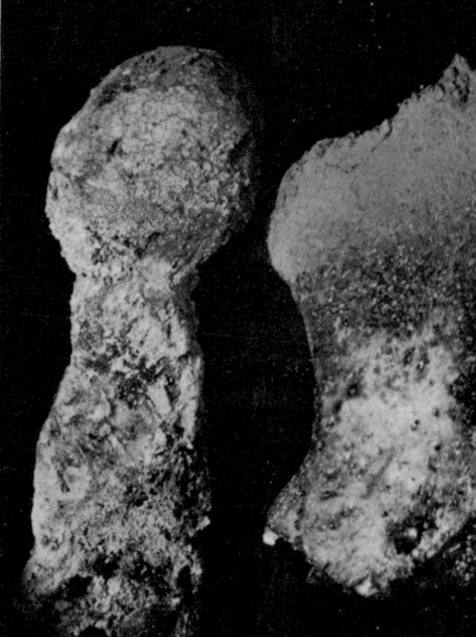

Pisolithus tinctorius. **Left:** Mature specimen sticking out of the ground like a half-rotted stump. **Right:** Younger specimens are roughly club-shaped. Specimen at right has been cut in half, but tiny lentil-like spore chambers have disintegrated. (Joel Leivick)

chaparral, on road cuts, even in asphalt. One specimen I cut open barely qualified as a fungus—it consisted mostly of tar, dotted here and there with token peridioles! Predictably, it is described by many authors with ill-disguised disdain ("It is the most objectionable of all fungi"; "This ugly, stinky fungus," etc.). I call it "Dead Man's Foot," not to demean it, but because it looks like one. It has several aliases, the most common of which is *P. arenarius*. Its closest relative, *Dictyocephalus*, has a tough, woody stalk. It has been found in southern California deserts, but is rare.

Stinkhorns

spores

PHALLALES

Medium-sized *foul-smelling* fungi found on ground or very rotten wood. FRUITING BODY *round to oval in egg stage, cylindrical or branched at maturity*. STALK *usually present as a column by which the spore mass is elevated*. VEIL usually absent. VOLVA *present as a sack at base of stalk*. SPORE MASS *slimy*, coating head or branches of mature fruiting body. Spores smooth, more or less oblong; capillitium absent.

STINKHORNS are among the most fascinating and highly specialized of the fleshy fungi. In the immature "egg" stage they resemble puffballs or unexpanded Amanitas—the slimy spore mass is completely enclosed in a volva. However, the resemblance to puffballs is rudely dispelled when the stalk which supports the spore mass elongates rapidly, bursting out of the volva and into the world.

In the common stinkhorns *(Phallus)* the mature fruiting body is explicitly phallic, with the slimy spore mass at the apex or "head." In *Anthurus* and *Lysurus* the fruiting body is branched and in *Clathrus* it is ornately latticed. In all cases the ruptured volva forms a sack at the base, much as in *Amanita*. The stinkhorns' most outlandish feature, however, is the unpleasant and provocative odor of the mature spore mass, which has been variously characterized as "foul," "fetid," "evil," "odious," "obnoxious," "cadaverous," "putrid," "maddening," "aggravating," "filthy," "vile," "disgusting," "spermatic," "garbageous," "nauseating," "like rotting carrion," "like spent incense," "like the damp earthy smell we meet with in some of our churches on Sundays," "enough to cause one to think that all the bad smells in the world had been turned loose," and most apt and understated of all: "indiscreet." Lured by the stench, flies come to feast on the slime and if the day is hot, roll around in it. With their eventual, reluctant departure, spore dispersal is accomplished. All in all, it is a relatively sophisticated process more characteristic of the so-called "higher" plants than of the "lowly" fungi.

As might be expected with unorthodox organisms of this sort, there is a veritable mother lode of stinkhorn lore. German hunters called them *Hirschbrunst* because they believed they grew where stags had rutted. They've been used in countless ointments and potions as a cure for gout, epilepsy, and gangrenous ulcers. They've been both blamed for cancer and prescribed as a sure-fire remedy. And of course, they've been employed as aphrodisiacs, and are still given to cattle for that purpose in parts of Europe. Alexander Smith tells of a remarkable encounter with an old man in the woods who carried a mammoth specimen under his hat in the fervent belief that it would cure his rheumatism. And, in an otherwise tedious book of Victorian reminiscences by Gwen Raverat, there is this astonishing passage:

> In our native woods there grows a kind of toadstool, called in the vernacular The Stinkhorn, though in Latin it bears a grosser name. This name is justified, for the fungus can be hunted by the scent alone; and this was Aunt Etty's greatest invention: armed with a basket and a pointed stick, and wearing special hunting cloak and gloves, she would sniff her way round the wood, pausing here and there, her nostrils twitching, when she caught a whiff of her prey; then at last, with a deadly pounce, she would fall upon her victim, and then poke his putrid carcass into her basket. At the end of the day's sport, the catch was brought back and burnt in the deepest secrecy on the drawing-room fire, with the door locked, *because of the morals of the maids.*

One wonders how such a splendid, vigorous organism could be so ruthlessly and unjustly maligned. This particularly perverse brand of fungophobia should perhaps be rechristened *phallophobia*. "Aunt Etty," incidentally, was Charles Darwin's daughter!

Times change, however, and at long last the stinkhorn's impetuosity and virtuosity are beginning to be appreciated. Mycological literature is replete with wonderfully provocative accounts of close encounters (of the casual kind) with stinkhorns—as riddled with them, in fact, as a *Russula cyanoxantha* is with maggots. When the stinkhorn is discussed, the language makes a startling and unprecedented qualitative leap, from monotonous minutiae to half-baked hyperbole, as if the authors were suddenly taking an interest in what they were saying. They are unstinted in their praise as they tread the fine line between double-entendre and forthright fungal fact: "The mischief-maker is a handsome specimen, as its plate shows" . . . "This is a highly specialized type of fungus fruiting body" . . . "Never have I seen such intricate lacework as on a *Phallus*" . . . "It is one of the seven unnatural wonders of the natural world" . . . "It undoubtedly emerges from the depths for a single noble and grand purpose—that of disseminating its spores. All of its parts have been developed to accomplish this function in the most effectual manner possible" . . . "It is a glorious fungus—an admirable specimen of herculean proportions pokes up periodically in my front yard."

Opinions on the edibility of stinkhorns run the gamut from ill-disguised disgust to idle speculation to passionate praise. The intolerable odor of mature specimens would seem to be enough to discourage even the most ardent and confirmed toadstool-tester from sampling it. However, it is reported that in 1929, a young English girl of twenty-two, "having eaten a morsel, was seized with violent convulsions, lost the use of her speech, and ultimately fell into a stupor which lasted forty-eight hours; prompt attention was given to her, but it appears to have been some months before she was perfectly cured." On the other hand, in parts of Europe stinkhorn eggs are considered a delicacy—they are pickled raw and even sold in markets.

Stinkhorns attain their maximum diversity in the tropics. Most of our species were probably introduced adventitiously. They are especially fond of populated areas, where they lurk in gardens, flower beds, along roads, in ditches, under bushes, hedges and porches, in the vicinity of churches and lumberyards, trash heaps and old sawdust piles. They fruit whenever conditions are conducive to development—that is, warm and moist. Of the six species keyed below, only *Phallus impudicus* is common.

Key to the Phallales

1. Fruiting body simple, unbranched 2
1. Fruiting body branched, with arms or a latticelike framework 3

2. Stalk white with a large, pitted "head" .... *Phallus impudicus,* below
2. Stalk slender, pinkish-red with smooth, narrowed "head" .... *Mutinus caninus* (see *Phallus impudicus,* below)

3. Stalk absent or much shorter than length of arms 4
3. Stalk present, generally longer than length of arms 5

4. Fruiting body more or less round to oval, forming an intricate closed latticework (like a whiffle ball) .... *Clathrus cancellatus,* p. 566
4. Fruiting body with tentacle-like arms usually free from each other at maturity ..... *Anthurus aseroiformis* (see *Clathrus cancellatus,* p. 566)

5. Arms bright pink to red .... *Lysurus mokusin* (see *Anthurus borealis,* p. 565)
5. Arms pale flesh color .... *Anthurus borealis,* p. 565

Phallus impudicus (Common Stinkhorn)

FRUITING BODY beginning as an "egg," completely enclosed in a white to lurid pinkish-purple membrane, with one or more cords (rhizomorphs) attached to the base; cross-section revealing a jellylike substance (the spore mass) in which is imbedded a compact "head" and stalk. Stalk then bursting out of the membrane and elongating rapidly, thrusting the slimy head upwards. Mature fruiting body 5-25 cm tall, roughly cylindrical, consisting of a more or less conical head mounted on a stalk. Surface of head pitted (reticulate), with a hole at the top; covered with a putrid, copious, olive-green spore-containing slime which eventually drips off or is carried or washed away. Odor of slimy spore mass offensive (see p. 561). **STALK** 1.5-3 cm thick; equal or tapered at both ends, white, somewhat spongy or honeycombed, hollow. **VEIL** absent. **VOLVA** present at the base of the stalk as a loose sack; pieces may also cling to the head. **SPORES** minute, 3.5-4.5 $\times$ 1.5-2 μm, ellipsoid to oblong, smooth.

HABITAT: In cultivated or disturbed soil; solitary, more often in groups, fruiting whenever conditions are favorable. Inconspicuous when unexpanded, unlikely to be noticed by anyone who is not looking for it. When fully elongated, however, it is pointedly, inescapably prominent. If the "eggs" are carried home and transplanted in cool, moist earth, more often than not they will continue to develop so that the fascinating elongation process can be observed firsthand.

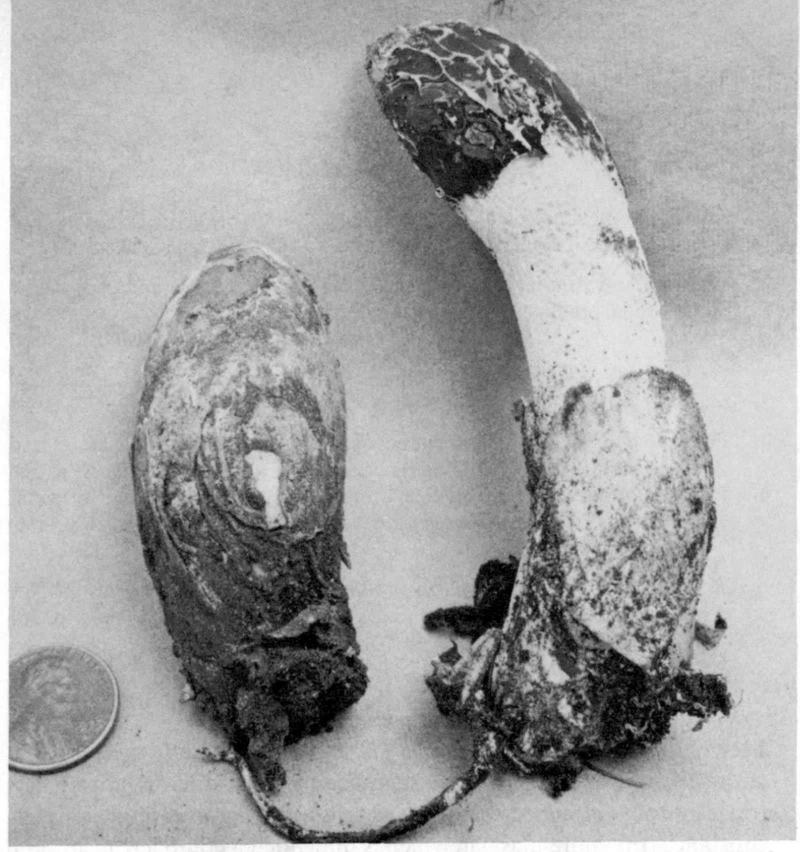

Phallus impudicus, immature specimen at left is still enclosed within membrane. Apex of mature specimen at right is covered with a foul-smelling slimy spore mass. Eventually the spore mass is removed, revealing a whitish, pitted head. Note cordlike "roots" at base of stalk. These are rather small specimens.

EDIBILITY: Nonpoisonous, but see comments on p. 562. According to mycophilic madman Charles McIlvaine, the *plenipotentiary extraordinaire* of toadstool-testers, "(the eggs) are semigelatinous, tenacious and elastic, like bubbles of some thick substance. In this condition, they demand to be eaten . . . Cut in slices and fried or stewed, they make a most tender, agreeable food."

COMMENTS: The stinkhorn is truly unmistakable. In shape it resembles nothing so much as a slimy cigar, leaky pipe, malodorous thumb, deformed horn, hollow baton, exotic candle, or putrescent pencil. But the most attractive thing about stinkhorns is their utter spontaneity. You never know when one is going to pop up right in front of you, so fast you can actually see it growing. And there is no way to predict or control them. It's the one thing in the world you can't push or hurry. They also have a highly appropriate sense of poetic justice. One "going strong" is said to have appeared in the concrete floor of the newly built house greeting a newly married couple. To accomplish this instructive feat, the mycelial cords had to force their way into the foundation from an old stump in the garden!

McIlvaine says: "Its favorite abode is in kitchen yards and under wooden steps where, when mature, it will compel the household to seek it out in self-defense. The distracted housewife searches in vain for a solution to the difficulty and the odor disappears as mysteriously as it came. If she is one of the initiated, however, she will search until she finds the haunt of the offender and then destroy it on the spot to avoid further repetition of the nuisance."

The stinkhorn is sometimes mistaken inexplicably for an old morel. There is a superficial resemblance, to be sure, but the "indiscreet" odor, slimy spore mass, and presence of a volva leave no doubt as to its identity. *Ithyphallus impudicus* is an obsolete synonym. Related stinkhorns include *Phallus ravenelii* with a smooth instead of pitted head; *Dictyophora duplicata,* with an intricately latticed skirtlike veil (indusium) on the stalk; and the dog stinkhorn, *Mutinus caninus,* which more than lives up to its name. It has a slim pink to orange-red stalk, with olive-green slime at the top. As all of these are common in eastern North America, they may at one time or another turn up here, in rich soil or humus. A white *Mutinus* occurs in Oregon.

Anthurus borealis

FRUITING BODY beginning as an "egg," completely enclosed in a white membrane, with one or more cords (rhizomorphs) attached to base. Stalk then bursting through the membrane and elongating rapidly. Mature fruiting body up to 13 cm tall, branched at apex into 4-6 erect arms with the slimy olive-brown spore mass on the wrinkled, inner surfaces. Arms hollow, up to 2.5 cm long, outer surfaces pale flesh color, longitudinally grooved; arms at first incurved (tips touching each other but not fused), later spreading apart. Odor of mature spore mass somewhat unpleasant. **STALK** more or less 1 cm thick, tapering downward, faintly striate, white or slightly yellowish, hollow. **VEIL** absent. **VOLVA** white, membranous, forming a loose, well-developed sack at base of stalk. **SPORES** 3-4 × 1-2 μm, ellipsoid to oblong, smooth. Basidia constricted at irregular intervals like a string of beads.

HABITAT: Solitary or in groups, sometimes clustered—in mulch, wood debris, rich soil, gardens, cultivated ground, etc. Not uncommon in southern half of the state, fruiting whenever moisture is sufficient.

EDIBILITY: Nonpoisonous. See comments on p. 562.

Left: *Anthurus borealis.* Found in the "egg" stage, these specimens were transplanted in a flower pot, where they continued to develop. Note slime-covered arms at top of stalk and large volva at base. (Bob Tally). **Right:** *Lysurus mokusin* (see *Anthurus borealis*) has bright red to pink arms and is common in southern California. (Bob Tally)

COMMENTS: This curious stinkhorn is easily recognized by the pale flesh-colored arms. The odor is not nearly as "indiscreet" as that of *Phallus impudicus. Lysurus borealis* is a synonym. *L. mokusin* is a slim, trim species with 4-7 bright pink to red arms at the top of the stalk. These are usually (but not always) united at their tips. It is found year-round in lawns and gardens in the warmer parts of California. I have seen it several times in southern California.

Clathrus cancellatus (Latticed Stinkhorn)

FRUITING BODY at first egg-shaped, completely enclosed by thick, white membrane with cords (rhizomorphs) attached to base. Mature fruiting body 5-14 cm high and broad, a round to oval latticed ball or netlike framework with large, polygonal meshes. Branches of framework pink to red to bright reddish-orange, flattened, hollow. Interior covered with slimy greenish-brown spore mass. Odor of mature specimens intolerable, cadaverous. **STALK** more or less absent. **VEIL** absent. **VOLVA** membranous, white, forming a sack at base. **SPORES** 5-6 × 2-3 μm, oblong, smooth.

HABITAT: Solitary or in small groups in cultivated soil, gardens, under trees and hedges, etc. Fruiting whenever conditions are favorable; rare. Has been found at De Anza College and Golden Gate Park.

EDIBILITY: Nonpoisonous. See comments on p. 562.

COMMENTS: The most spectacular of all stinkhorns, this species looks like a bright red whiffle ball (a sketch can be found at top of p. 54). It is not native to California but is to be expected in parks and botanical gardens where exotic trees and shrubs have been planted. *Anthurus aseroiformis (=A. archeri)* has 5-7 long "tentacles" arising almost directly from the volva; these are joined at first but later unfold like the petals of a flower. It has been found in damp soil under a bridge at Henry Cowell Redwoods State Park.

Bird's Nest Fungi

spores

NIDULARIALES

Minute fungi found on soil, wood, or dung. FRUITING BODY tough, round to cylindrical, *becoming cup-shaped or vase-shaped at maturity, with peridioles ("eggs") enclosed.* Peridium one to four layered. PERIDIOLES usually flattened, lens-shaped, white to gray, brown, or black. STALK absent. SPORES typically smooth, hyaline. Capillitium absent.

TRUE to their name, these minute Gasteromycetes look like miniature bird's nests. The fruiting body consists of a tiny vase or "nest" **(peridium)** furnished with spore balls or "eggs" **(peridioles).** In most cases a membranous "lid" **(epiphragm)** covers the nest when young. There is very little bird's nest fungi can be confused with. Empty nests can be mistaken for cup fungi but are much smaller and tougher. Three genera are known from California. In *Cyathus* and *Crucibulum* the eggs are attached to the nest by a thin cord **(funiculus).** In *Nidula* the eggs are imbedded in a sticky mucilage.

Spores are dispersed with the aid of raindrops and animals. The force of a single raindrop will splash the eggs out of the nest, as much as seven feet away. Both the cord and mucilage are devices for anchoring the splashed eggs to whatever they land on. The outer wall of the egg then either decays or is eaten by insects. Whereas most fungi produce millions of spores, the bird's nest fungi need only a few—each egg contains the correct mating strains, so a fertile secondary (dikaryotic) mycelium develops directly, obviating the need for large masses of spores.

Also included here is a dynamic relative of the bird's nest fungi, the cannon fungus, *Sphaerobolus.* It features only one "egg," which is shot out with terrific force, accompanied by an audible *pop* (*Sphaerobolus* literally means "sphere-thrower"). Taxonomists now place it in a separate order, Sphaerobolales.

Bird's nest fungi are found on various types of organic matter—rotting sticks, herbaceous stems, manure, humus, and dung. (Dung-inhabiting individuals result from "eggs" being ingested by grazing animals.) They are gregarious creatures, occurring in droves. Their small size, however, makes them difficult to see. None are large enough to be valuable as food. Six species are reported from California. These and *Sphaerobolus* are keyed below.

Key to the Nidulariales

1. Mature fruiting body star-shaped with a bright orange interior and only one egg; minute .... *Sphaerobolus stellatus*, p. 570
1. Mature fruiting body cup-shaped to vase-shaped; more than one egg normally present (unless all but one are expelled) 2

2. Eggs brownish to gray, without cords attached, imbedded in a jellylike substance which eventually dries out 3
2. Eggs white, gray, or black, often (but not always) with a small cord attached; jellylike substance absent 4

3. Exterior of nest shaggy, white .... *Nidula niveotomentosa* (see *N. candida,* below)
3. Exterior of nest not white .... *Nidula candida,* below

4. Eggs white or whitish; nest one-layered .... *Crucibulum levis* (see *Cyathus stercoreus,* p. 569)
4. Eggs gray to black; nest three-layered 5

5. Interior of nest striate or fluted .... *Cyathus striatus* (see *C. stercoreus,* p. 569)
5. Interior of nest smooth 6

6. Exterior of nest shaggy, at least when young *Cyathus stercoreus,* p. 569
6. Exterior of nest not shaggy ...... *Cyathus olla* (see *C. stercoreus,* p. 569)

Nidula candida

FRUITING BODY cylindrical becoming vase-shaped, tiny, 5-20 mm high and 3-8 mm broad; new ones sometimes developing inside old ones. Top at first covered with a lid; exterior whitish with dull cinnamon scurf over basal portion and lid; interior white to yellowish-brown. Flesh thin, tough. **EGGS** several, pallid to brownish, pill-shaped (flattened), 1-2 mm broad, imbedded in a mucilage or gel which dries out in age; no cords attached. **SPORES** 6-10 × 4-8 μm, round to ellipsoid, smooth, hyaline.

HABITAT: In groups on rotting wood, berry canes, and herbaceous

Top: *Nidula candida*, mature specimens in which the "eggs" are clearly visible within the nest. It usually grows on sticks or buried wood. **Bottom:** *Nidula niveotomentosa* (see *N. candida*), young specimens in which the "eggs" are covered by a "lid." Shaggy white exterior separates this species from *N. candida.* (Herb Saylor)

debris—in gardens, woods, along streams, etc. Fruiting mostly in fall and winter but the empty nests may persist for months. Common.

EDIBILITY: Far too small and tough to be edible.

COMMENTS: A common but frequently overlooked little fungus. The jellylike substance in which the eggs are imbedded plus the presence of a "lid" in young specimens is diagnostic for the genus *Nidula.* The name *candida* (meaning "shining white") is something of a misnomer since the fruiting body is neither white nor shining. However, a species with a shaggy white exterior, *N. niveotomentosa,* is also common in California. The genus *Nidularia* (rare in North America) also has a mucilage but the nest is very thin and lacks a lid.

Cyathus stercoreus

FRUITING BODY tiny, goblet-shaped or vase-shaped, 5-10 mm tall and 4-6 mm broad; top at first covered with a lid that soon disappears; exterior hairy or shaggy, becoming nearly smooth in old age, tan to gray-brown, or whitish below, sometimes with a basal pad of brownish mycelium. Interior smooth, dark gray-brown to black. Flesh tough, three-layered. **EGGS** several, dark gray to black, 1-2 mm broad, flattened, hard, smooth, sometimes with cords attached (especially the lower ones). **SPORES** large, 22-35 × 18-30 μm, size and shape variable, mostly round to oval, thick-walled, smooth, hyaline or nearly hyaline.

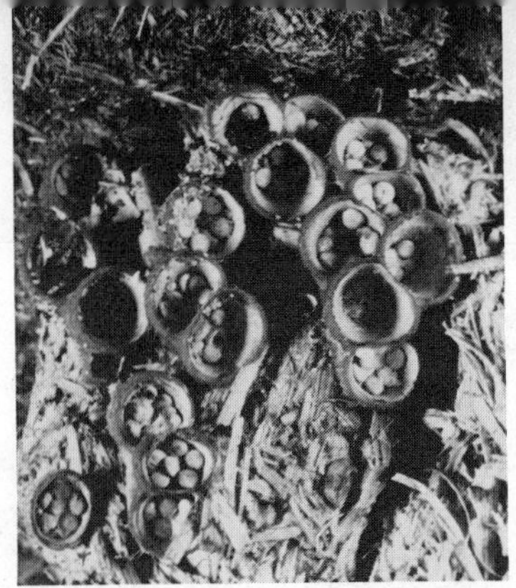
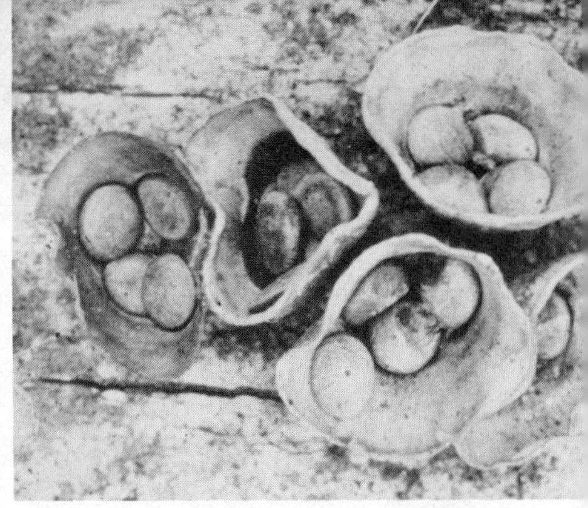

Left: *Cyathus stercoreus* growing on a cow pie. The "eggs" are darker (grayish-black) than they appear in this picture. **Right:** *Crucibulum levis* (see *Cyathus stercoreus*). A distinctive species with a broad "nest" and whitish "eggs." It usually grows on wood. (Nancy Burnett)

HABITAT: Densely gregarious on dung, manure, and organic debris. Fruiting mostly in fall and winter, common. I have seen large numbers on a well-manured lawn.

EDIBILITY: A meager morsel, much too small to be of value.

COMMENTS: The dark gray to black eggs and smooth cup interior are the fieldmarks of this petite bird's nest fungus. The cords by which the eggs are attached to the cup are not always evident, at least in my experience. Other common species are *C. olla,* not shaggy, with smaller spores only 8-12 × 5-8 µm, and *C. striatus,* with a delicately fluted or striate interior. *Crucibulum levis (=C. laeve, C. vulgare)* has whitish eggs with cords attached and a more or less cylindrical nest composed of one layer only. It is also fairly common.

Sphaerobolus stellatus (Cannon Fungus; Sphere Thrower)

FRUITING BODY minute, 2-3 mm broad, at first more or less round, dull ochraceous to white, then opening up into 5-8 bright orange starlike lobes or teeth, exposing the single spore-containing ball (egg), which is then shot out like a cannonball as the entire structure turns inside out. **EGG** (spore ball) dark chestnut-brown to olive-black, smooth, sticky or slippery, more or less round. **SPORES** 7-10 × 3.5-5 µm, oblong, smooth, hyaline.

HABITAT: Gregarious on rotting wood, sawdust, and plant debris, also on dung. Common and widely distributed, but easily overlooked, fruiting whenever moisture is sufficient. I have seen it several times in nursery flats.

EDIBILITY: Too miniscule to be of value.

COMMENTS: This remote relative of the bird's nest fungi is easily recognized by its diminutive dimensions, bright orange star-shaped "catapult," and single "egg" or spore ball. It makes a marvelous (albeit Lilliputian) laboratory pet—a small *"pop"* accompanies the ejection of the spore ball, which sticks to whatever it lands on. Its flight path has been measured at 14 ft. high and 17 ft. long (more than 1000 times the size of the fruiting body!). To equal such a herculean feat, we puny humans would have to throw a discus over one mile high and far! There must be a sufficient supply of water and light for the "cannon" to operate.

False Truffles and Related Fungi

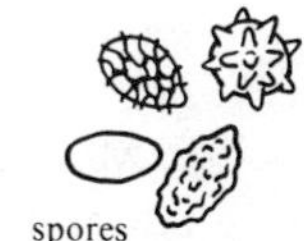

HYMENOGASTRALES

Medium-sized fungi *usually buried or partially buried in humus.* FRUITING BODY variously shaped but most often more or less round. SPORE MASS *remaining intact, rarely powdery.* STALK usually absent; if present often rudimentary. VOLVA usually absent. SPORES *not forcibly discharged,* variously shaped and ornamented. Capillitium absent.

THESE unimposing fungi are neither edible, nor attractive, nor conspicuous, nor easy to identify. They *are* rather interesting from an evolutionary standpoint, however, for they form a baffling series of sequential and inconsequential bridges between the Gasteromycetes and Hymenomycetes. For the purposes of this book, they can be roughly divided into two groups: false truffles and reduced agarics.

False truffles are primitive Gasteromycetes, the most common example of which is *Rhizopogon.* The fruiting body is round to oval to somewhat irregular. It lacks a stem and grows underground, like a truffle. (The true truffles are Ascomycetes with a marbled or channeled interior.) The spore mass is rubbery, spongy, cartilaginous, or hard (rarely slimy) and is usually minutely chambered. It is never powdery as in the puffballs and it remains intact. False truffles rely on rodents, insects, and rain to spread their spores. They often have strong odors to attract animals. Several smell like marzipan and one unidentified species I found reeked of gasoline.

In contrast, reduced agarics have more in common with agarics than with other Gasteromycetes. Most resemble unopened gilled mushrooms. Those that grow above the ground have a stalk; those without a stalk may have a sterile base or rudimentary stem **(columella)** penetrating the interior. They are thought to be agarics which, through a process of specialization, have lost the ability (or necessity) to forcibly discharge their spores—hence the unflattering moniker "reduced agarics." *Podaxis pistillaris,* a common desert and tropical fungus, is a good example. It resembles a shaggy mane *(Coprinus comatus)* but the cap never expands (protecting the spores from the desert heat) and the spores are thick-walled to prevent moisture loss. Similarly, *Endoptychum* resembles *Agaricus, Nivatogastrium* is close to *Pholiota,* and *Setchelliogaster* is related to the Bolbitiaceae. *Gastroboletus* (p. 433) and *Truncocolumella* are close to the boletes, while several genera *(Zelleromyces, Arcangeliella, Macowanites, Gymnomyces, Elasmomyces, Martellia)* resemble *Russula* and *Lactarius* (the first two even possess a latex!)

Most of the false truffles and practically all the reduced agarics are adapted to adverse conditions too extreme for most fungi—high mountains, for instance, or deserts. Naturally, the West is incomparably rich in endemic species, many of them reported from only a single locality. Some occur in more favorable habitats, however, such as the forests of coastal California.

Most false truffles are mycorrhizal and fruit during the rainy season. Rhizopogons are the most common, but even they are unlikely to be found unless you seek them out. The best way is to take a handrake or small shovel and sift gently through the humus or needle duff, paying close attention to places where squirrels or deer have been digging.

From an edibility standpoint this group has little to offer—their taste and texture are not particularly pleasing, at least to humans. Identification is difficult, regrettably requiring a microscope and chemical tests. (It is only recently that mycologists have begun to look at these fungi, and new species are being found constantly.)

Since my own experience with them is limited, a very meager treatment is presented here. A generic key is included (though it calls for the use of a microscope), and only the genus *Rhizopogon* is described.

Key to the Hymenogastrales and Relatives

1. Stalk present 2
1. Stalk absent 11

2. Spores produced in tubes (which usually bruise blue) .... (see *Gastroboletus,* p. 433)
2. Spores not produced in tubes 3

3. Fruiting body pale greenish-yellow; stalk stumplike, branched inside spore mass .... *Truncocolumella*
3. Not as above 4

4. Growing on coniferous wood in mountains .... *Nivatogastrium*
4. Not as above, typically on or in ground 5

5. Mature spore mass pallid to yellow; spore ornamentation amyloid ... 6
5. Mature spore mass brown to black 8

6. Latex present (cut apex of stalk) .... *Arcangeliella*
6. Latex absent 7

7. Sphaerocysts present in spore mass plates; fruiting body with a *Russula*-like appearance .... *Macowanites*
7. Sphaerocysts absent .... *Elasmomyces*

8. Cap oval to cylindrical, with a shaggy-mane-like appearance; stalk woody, scaly; in desert .... *Podaxis*
8. Not as above 9

9. Mature spore mass ochraceous-brown .... *Setchelliogaster*
9. Mature spore mass dark brown to black 10

10. Volva present; cap practically nonexistent; in desert .... *Montagnea*
10. Volva absent; cap present .... *Endoptychum*

11. Spore mass slimy at maturity 12
11. Spore mass not slimy 13

12. Skin readily cracking and coming away from the spore mass; columella distinct; odor offensive at maturity .... *Hysterangium*
12. Not as above; columella absent or rudimentary ... *Rhizopogon*, p. 574

13. Spore mass marbled with whitish or pallid veins; spore mass chambers often filled with a gel 14
13. Not as above 15

14. Spore mass more or less brownish; spore mass chambers soon filled with a gel .... *Alpova* (see *Rhizopogon ochraceorubens*, p. 574)
14. Spore mass black, marbled with white veins .... *Melanogaster*

15. Spores smooth, not amyloid; very common .... *Rhizopogon*, p. 574
15. Spores not smooth; ornamentation may or may not be amyloid; not common 16

16. Spores more or less round, with conelike spines; not amyloid, columella absent .... *Hydnangium*
16. Not as above 17

17. Spores rusty-brown under microscope, with coarse, nonamyloid warts or ridges 18
17. Not as above; ornamentation usually amyloid 19

18. Spores warted .... *Hymenogaster*
18. Spores longitudinally ridged .... *Gautieria*

19. Spore ornamentation not amyloid .... *Octavianina*
19. Spore ornamentation at least partially amyloid 20

20. Latex present (cut apex of columella) .... *Zelleromyces*
20. Latex absent 21

21. Sphaerocysts present in spore mass plates .... *Gymnomyces*
21. Sphaerocysts absent .... *Martellia*

RHIZOPOGON

Small to medium-sized fungi *growing mostly underground.* FRUITING BODY *round to oval to somewhat irregular.* Skin one-layered, but exterior often overlaid with rhizomorphs. SPORE MASS (interior) minutely *chambered;* spongy, rubbery, slimy, rock-hard, or tough *but never powdery.* STALK *absent* (rudimentary columella rarely present). SPORES hyaline to ochraceous or brown under microscope; usually smooth. Capillitium absent.

RHIZOPOGONS are by far the most common false truffles. Most look like rocks, tubers, or marbles. Though typically subterranean, they often develop close to the surface or are dug up by animals. The spore mass **(gleba)** is composed of tiny chambers which are best seen with a hand lens. The spores are produced on the inner walls of these chambers, an arrangement reminiscent of the tubes in boletes. Rhizopogons can be mistaken excitedly for truffles, which are Ascomycetes with a marbled, channeled, or coarsely chambered interior.

The edibility of most species is unknown. They are associated mostly with conifers, but other types of false truffles (see key to the Hymenogastrales, pp. 572-573) are common under hardwoods, especially oak. *Rhizopogon* is a large genus, with over 200 species known from western North America. Many are known only from a single locality. Identification is difficult and some of our species are undoubtedly new to science. Only two representatives are described here.

Key to Rhizopogon

1. Outer surface quickly bruising red or pink when handled .... *R. rubescens,* p. 575
1. Outer surface not bruising red or pink, but may bruise rusty-brown slightly .... *R. ochraceorubens,* below

Rhizopogon ochraceorubens

FRUITING BODY up to 4 cm broad, round to oval to somewhat flattened or irregular. Exterior mottled yellow, reddish, and ochraceous, overlaid with conspicuous brown rhizomorphs, not staining red but may bruise rusty-brown. **SPORE MASS** (interior) pallid to grayish becoming olive or olive-brown; chambered; spongy or rubbery becoming tough. Odor mild. **STALK** or columella absent. **SPORES** 6-8 × 2-3 μm, oblong, smooth.

Rhizopogon ochraceorubens. Specimen at left has been cross-sectioned to reveal the homogeneous interior composed of minute chambers. Note the mycelial strands (rhizomorphs) on exterior of specimens at right.

HABITAT: Scattered to gregarious in duff or soil under pine. Fairly common, fall and winter. Usually buried or half-buried.

EDIBILITY: Unknown.

COMMENTS: The conspicuous brown rhizomorphs (rootlike strands) covering the exterior are a good fieldmark, though certainly not unique to this species. There are many other Rhizopogons, too numerous to mention. One that is not too numerous to mention is a small, unidentified species with a bright orange exterior and an *overpowering* odor of turpentine or gasoline. *Alpova trappei* is a bright yellow false truffle with gel-filled chambers inside, separated by pallid meandering veins. It is mycorrhizal with conifers, particularly Douglas-fir.

Rhizopogon rubescens (Blushing False Truffle)

FRUITING BODY up to 5 cm broad, round to oval or somewhat irregular; exterior white becoming yellow or greenish-yellow, stained or bruising red or pinkish-red; smooth or overlaid with rhizomorphs. **SPORE MASS** (interior) chambered; spongy or rubbery, tough when dry, white (staining pink when cut) becoming tawny-olive to olive-buff to cinnamon-brown. Odor mild. **STALK** or columella absent. **SPORES** 5-10 × 3-4.5 μm, elliptical to oblong, smooth, tinged yellow under microscope.

HABITAT: Scattered to gregarious in duff or soil under conifers, especially pine and Douglas-fir. Usually buried or half-buried. Common, fall and winter.

EDIBILITY: Unknown.

COMMENTS: The red-staining peridium (skin) is the outstanding feature of this widespread *Rhizopogon.* Animals are fond of it.

Jelly Fungi

HETEROBASIDIOMYCETES

Small to medium-sized fungi *found mostly on decaying wood.* FRUITING BODY *gelatinous or rubbery when fresh;* variously shaped but most often lobed, convoluted, or brainlike. SPORE SURFACE smooth, warty, or with small spines, covering upper or lower surface of fruiting body. SPORE PRINT difficult to obtain. Spores usually white to yellow in mass; smooth. Basidia septate or forked.

JELLY fungi are easily recognized by their gelatinous or rubbery texture. The most familiar types (collectively called "Witch's Butter") have lobed or convoluted fruiting bodies that at times resemble amorphous masses of melting butter. Other jelly fungi have a cap and stalk, still others are cup-shaped or coral-like.

Jelly fungi are set off by a more fundamental character than their jellylike consistency—the basidia are either partitioned **(septate)** or forked. All the other Basidiomycetes in this book have simple basidia. The rust and smut fungi have partitioned basidia, but are not considered mushrooms.

The structure of the basidium also forms the basis for dividing the jelly fungi into three major groups: the Tremellales have longitudinally or obliquely septate basidia; the Auriculariales have transversely septate basidia, while the Dacrymycetales have forked (Y-shaped) basidia.

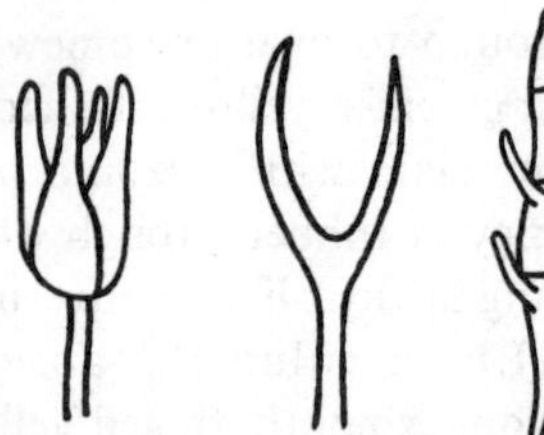

Different types of basidia in the jelly fungi. Left to right: longitudinally septate (Tremellales), Y-shaped (Dacrymycetales), and transversely septate (Auriculariales).

Jelly fungi thrive in cool wet weather, and are sometimes quite abundant on rotting stumps and logs. In dry weather they shrink down to almost nothing, but swell up again as soon as it rains. Only the yellow-orange witch's butter, *Tremella mesenterica,* is common. I know of no poisonous species, but they have little substance and are too watery and tasteless for most people's palates. They are sometimes pickled, candied, or eaten raw, however, and *Auricularia* is commonly used in Oriental cooking. Six representatives are presented here.

Key to the Heterobasidiomycetes

1. Fruiting body translucent white to watery gray or dingy brown; with a cap and short lateral stalk; underside of cap lined with tiny spines .... *Pseudohydnum gelatinosum,* below
1. Not as above 2

2. Fruiting body yellow, orange, or red 3
2. Fruiting body brown to black 7

3. Fruiting body spatula-shaped to funnel-shaped, pink to orange-red; growing on ground or rotting wood .... *Phlogiotis helvelloides* (see *Pseudohydnum gelatinosum,* below)
3. Not as above 4

4. Fruiting body growing upright; simple or branched (finger-shaped or antlerlike) 5
4. Not as above; fruiting body lobed, convoluted, or amorphous 6

5. Fruiting body branched, up to 5 cm high .... *Calocera viscosa,* p. 581
5. Fruiting body rarely branched; up to 12 mm high .... *Calocera cornea* (see *C. viscosa,* p. 581)

6. Typically on decaying hardwoods; lobed or convoluted, at least when fresh, bone-hard when dry .... *Tremella mesenterica,* p. 580
6. Typically on decaying conifers; somewhat lobed to droplike, collapsing when dry .... *Dacrymyces palmatus* (see *Tremella mesenterica,* p. 580)

7. Fruiting body shallow cup-shaped or ear-shaped, up to 12 cm broad .... *Auricularia auricula,* p. 582
7. Not as above 8

8. Fruiting body more or less top-shaped (occasionally cup-shaped with a gelatinous interior); common on hardwood logs .... (see *Phaeobulgaria inquinans,* p. 587)
8. Not as above 9

9. Fruiting body brown; lobed, convoluted, or brainlike; surface smooth .... *Tremella foliacea,* p. 579
9. Fruiting body usually black; small, variously shaped (round, cushion-shaped, etc.), often in confluent masses; fertile surface minutely warted .... *Exidia glandulosa,* p. 578

Pseudohydnum gelatinosum (Toothed Jelly Fungus)

FRUITING BODY rubbery-gelatinous, more or less tongue-shaped, with a short, lateral stalk; translucent white to watery gray throughout, sometimes dingy brownish in old age. **CAP** up to 5 cm broad but usually 2-3 cm; surface smooth; underside lined with small spines or teeth 2-5 mm long. **STALK** lateral, small, same texture as cap. **SPORES** produced on teeth, white in mass, 5-7 μm, nearly round, smooth. Basidia ellipsoid to nearly round, longitudinally septate.

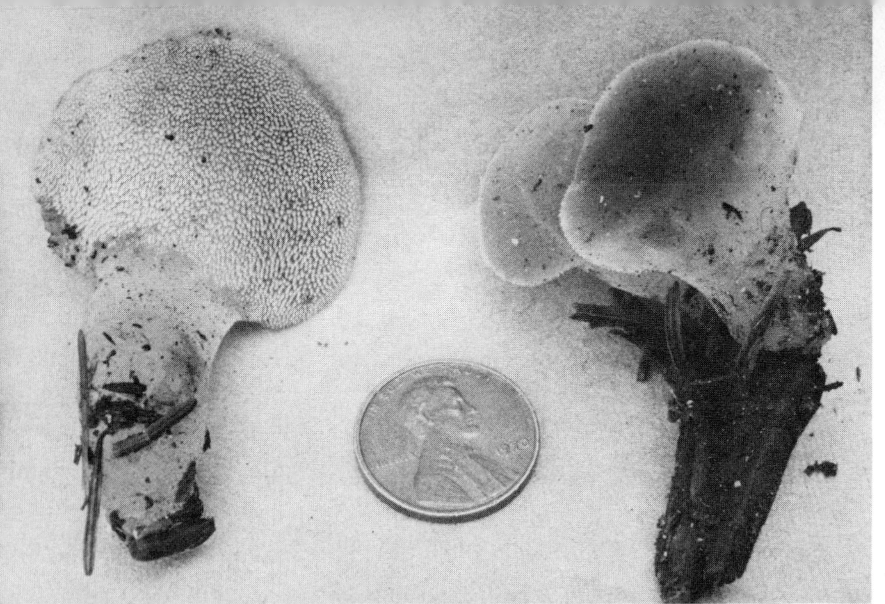

Pseudohydnum gelatinosum. Underside (left) is lined with tiny "teeth." Cap (right) is grayish to brown. Entire fruiting body is rubbery-gelatinous.

HABITAT: Solitary or scattered in damp humus, on twigs, rotting logs, etc. Sporadically common following heavy rains in fall and winter, especially under Douglas-fir.

EDIBILITY: Edible. Said to be fairly good with honey and cream (what isn't?); can also be marinated for use in salads. It has an interesting texture but little flavor.

COMMENTS: This is one of my fifty "five favorite fleshy fungal fructifications." The rubbery, resilient tongue-shaped fruiting bodies with small "teeth" on the underside are funnier than they are fungal. In fact, it is hard to take them seriously. The small teeth are reminiscent of the hydnums (teeth fungi); hence the name *Pseudohydnum,* meaning "false hydnum." *Tremellodon gelatinosum* is a synonym. Another striking jelly fungus, *Phlogiotis helvelloides,* is quite common in northern California and the Sierras. It is tongue-shaped, varying to spatula-shaped or funnellike, and stands upright on a small stalk. It is rubbery-gelatinous, rose-pink to orange-red, and has no teeth. It can be pickled or candied, and is reputedly the most flavorful of the jelly fungi (which is hardly a glowing recommendation). It grows in small groups on the ground or on rotting wood, under conifers.

Exidia glandulosa (Black Witch's Butter)

FRUITING BODIES in rows or masses up to 50 cm long, cushion-shaped, contorted or irregular, lying flat on substrate; soft, gelatinous, olive-black to jet-black, fertile (upper) surface rough or warty. **SPORES** white in mass, 8-16 × 3-5 μm, sausage-shaped, smooth. Basidia longitudinally septate.

HABITAT: Densely gregarious in rows or confluent masses on rotting hardwood logs and branches; fairly common, fall and winter.

EDIBILITY: Unknown, and like myself, likely to remain so.

COMMENTS: The minutely warted spore-producing surface and sausage-shaped spores distinguish *Exidia* from *Tremella.* The individual fruiting bodies are small, but occur in rows or masses which look like black jelly or slime. There are a number of similar species.

Tremella foliacea (Brown Witch's Butter)

FRUITING BODY gelatinous when moist, bone-hard when dry; up to 12 cm broad or more, consisting of a mass of leaflike folds, lobes, or convolutions, reddish-cinnamon to brown or brown tinted purple, paler when waterlogged. **SPORES** produced on upright lobes, 7-9 × 6-9 μm, round to ovate, smooth, white in mass.

HABITAT: Solitary or in small groups on hardwood stumps, logs, and fallen branches, perhaps on conifers as well. Fairly common, but easily overlooked, fall and winter.

EDIBILITY: Harmless, fleshless, flavorless.

A large specimen of *Tremella foliacea* in prime condition. Note the leaflike folds. Fruiting body is brown and gelatinous.

COMMENTS: This brown version of *T. mesenterica* is our largest *Tremella,* and quite striking when fresh. It is never cuplike or earlike, like *Auricularia auricula,* and is much more gelatinous. *Tremella encephala* is a flesh-colored to brownish species with larger spores (10-12 × 7.5-9 μm). It is sometimes parasitic on *Stereum,* a wood-inhabiting bracket-fungus; all the Tremellas, in fact, are frequently found with *Stereum.* Their names reflect their brainlike, lobed, or contorted fruiting bodies: *mesenterica* means "middle intestine"; *foliacea* means "leaflike"; and *encephala* means "brainlike."

Tremella mesenterica (Common Witch's Butter)

FRUITING BODY gelatinous when fresh, bone-hard and shriveled up when dry; up to 7 cm broad, consisting of a convoluted or contorted mass of brainlike lobes and folds, but amorphous in age or wet weather; bright yellow-orange to golden-yellow, paler (to nearly colorless) when old and waterlogged. **SPORES** produced on upright lobes, white in mass, 8-14 × 5.5-9 μm, elliptical, smooth. Basidia longitudinally septate.

HABITAT: Very common in wet weather on hardwood sticks, logs, and dead branches, especially live oak. Fall through early spring, often found on the same branches as *Stereum* species. Shriveled-up specimens tend to revive in wet weather.

Tremella mesenterica. **Top:** Large golden-yellow specimens. **Bottom:** A row of smaller yellow-orange specimens on a log. Fruiting body is gelatinous and nearly shapeless in wet weather. (Ray Gipson)

EDIBILITY: Harmless, fleshless, flavorless. The one time I attempted to saute it, it practically disappeared.

COMMENTS: This species is a familiar sight on logs and branches in rainy weather. It is easily recognized by its yellow-orange color and jellylike consistency. *T. lutescens* is very similar and it is debatable whether the two are distinct. Since neither is important from an edibility standpoint, this needn't concern you—at least, it doesn't concern me. A somewhat deeper orange jelly fungus, *Dacrymyces palmatus,* is found on decaying conifers. It is usually smaller, bloblike or cushion-shaped, and tends to occur in rows or masses. Its resemblance to *Tremella* is quite superficial because the basidia are Y-shaped and the long, narrow spores become septate. Related to *Dacrymyces* is *Guepiniopsis alpinus,* a small more or less cup-shaped yellow to orange-red species. It grows on rotting wood near melting snow, is abundant in the Sierras and may conceivably occur at high elevations in the coast range.

Calocera viscosa (Staghorn Jelly Fungus)

FRUITING BODY erect, branched, antler-shaped or coral-like, up to 5 cm tall (but usually smaller); viscid, pliant, bright yellow to yellow-orange, with a more or less rooting base. **SPORES** produced on branches, dirty-yellowish in mass, 9-14 × 3.5-4.5 μm, more or less sausage-shaped, smooth, septate at maturity. Basidia Y-shaped.

HABITAT: Solitary or several on rotting coniferous logs, stumps, and debris. Uncommon, fall and winter. I have found it several times, never in quantity.

Calocera viscosa. This small golden-orange jelly fungus looks like a coral mushroom, but has a distinctly gelatinous texture. These were growing from a buried stick. (Ray Gipson)

EDIBILITY: Inconsequential.

COMMENTS: This dainty little jelly fungus looks like a small coral mushroom, but is viscid, grows on wood, and has Y-shaped basidia. A slightly more common species, *C. cornea,* is smaller (up to 12 mm high), yellow, and unbranched. It grows on both hardwoods and conifers. The forked basidia place *Calocera* in the Dacrymycetales.

Auricularia auricula (Wood Ear)

FRUITING BODY up to 12 cm broad, rubbery or slightly gelatinous when fresh, bone-hard when dry, cup-shaped or ear-shaped, sometimes with several thick, earlike lobes originating from a central point of attachment. Upper surface sterile, covered with tiny hairs, pale brown to brown or liver-brown, blackish when dried. Underside somewhat gelatinous when moist; smooth, veined, or wrinkled, purplish-brown to liver-brown, black when dried. **SPORES** produced on underside, white in mass, 12-16 × 4-6 μm, sausage-shaped, smooth. Basidia transversely septate.

HABITAT: Attached centrally or laterally to dead wood, solitary or in groups, fall and winter. Common and widely distributed, but rather rare in this region, at least in my experience.

EDIBILITY: Edible. I haven't tried it. A related species, *A. polytricha,* is used in Oriental cooking and can be purchased (dried) in many stores. Along with the shiitake, it is the mushroom served most often in Chinese restaurants. In China it is called Yung Ngo or Muk Ngo.

COMMENTS: This species can be mistaken for a cup fungus (Ascomycete), but it produces spores on basidia lining the underside of the fruiting body, and its texture is rubbery-gelatinous. I have found individuals which looked more like pieces of seaweed than anything else. Dried specimens (both *A. auricula* and *A. polytricha*) undergo a startling transformation when soaked in warm water; they billow up like clouds, unabashedly showing off their intricate curves and convolutions. Another name for this fungus is "Jew's Ear," a corruption of "Judas' Ear." It was once believed that when Judas hanged himself on an elder tree, these ear-shaped excrescences were thereafter condemned to appear on elder trees. *Hirneola auricula-judae* is a sinister-sounding synonym.

ASCOMYCETES

THE Ascomycetes are the largest class of fungi, with over 15,000 species known. In Bisby's immortal words, they pose a challenge to "an army" of students. In form they are exceedingly diverse, ranging from the single-celled yeasts to the powdery mildews and common molds like *Penicillium* to the prized "sponge mushrooms" (morels) and elusive truffles. Their common bond is fundamental but microscopic: the spores are formed inside saclike mother cells called **asci** (singular: **ascus**). The fusion and division of parent nuclei normally takes place within the ascus, and in this sense it is analogous to the basidium of the Basidiomycetes.

Only a small fraction of the Ascomycetes have fruiting bodies large enough to qualify as "mushrooms." In the field they can be distinguished from the Basidiomycetes by a simple process of elimination—i.e., if your fleshy fungal fructification does not fit one of the major categories of Basidiomycetes (agarics, boletes, puffballs, etc.—see pictorial key, pp. 52-55), then chances are it's an Ascomycete.

The fleshy Ascomycetes treated in this book fall into two categories. In the Discomycetes, the asci line the exposed surface of the fruiting body much as the basidia line the surfaces of gills in the agarics. This palisade of asci is called the **hymenium,** and the fruiting body of a Discomycete is sometimes termed the **apothecium.** Morels, false morels, cup fungi, earth tongues, and truffles are all Discomycetes. Truffles, however, fruit underground and their hymenium is internalized.

The second group of Ascomycetes, the Pyrenomycetes, bear asci in flasklike "nests" called **perithecia** (singular: **perithecium**). They are discussed in more detail on p. 622. A field key to the major groups of Ascomycetes can be found on the next page.

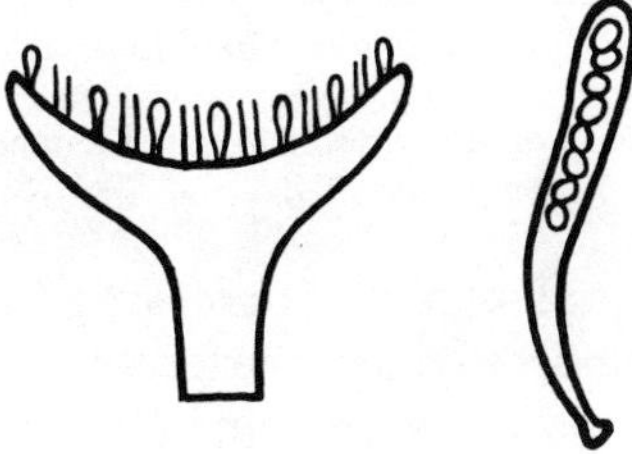

Left: Fruiting body of a cup fungus, showing paraphyses (sterile cells) and asci, arranged in a palisade on the upper (inner) surface. In reality there are thousands more asci than shown here. **Right:** An ascus containing 8 spores (the most common number).

Key to the Ascomycetes

1. Growing underground; interior with channels, veins, or one or more cavities .... **Tuberales,** p. 618
1. Growing above ground; not as above 2
2. Fruiting body parasitizing or engulfing other mushrooms, consisting of a pimpled or powdery layer of tissue .... **Pyrenomycetes,** p. 622
2. Not as above 3
3. Parasitic; fruiting body arising from insect larvae, pupae, or even adults, *or* from underground trufflelike Ascomycetes ..... **Pyrenomycetes,** p. 622
3. Not as above 4
4. Fruiting body black, tough or charcoal-like, surface minutely pimpled; growing on wood .... **Pyrenomycetes,** p. 622
4. Not with above combination of characteristics 5
5. Fruiting body cup-shaped to ear-shaped, spoon-shaped, or flattened (disc-like); stalk absent or short and continuous with cup .... **Pezizaceae and relatives,** below
5. Not as above; fruiting body with prominent stalk and usually a cap ... 6
6. Fruiting body cylindrical or branched (antlerlike); black below and white above; tough, growing on wood .... **Pyrenomycetes,** p. 622
6. Not as above 7
7. Fruiting body medium-sized to large, with a well-defined cap and stalk; stalk usually 8 mm thick or more; cap brainlike, saddle-shaped, pitted, honeycombed, conical, or even cuplike .... **Helvellaceae,** p. 597
7. Fruiting body usually small, sometimes with a well-defined cap; stalk generally 7 mm thick or less; cap when present wrinkled, smooth, knobby, fanlike, or spatula-shaped .... **Geoglossaceae,** p. 614

Cup Fungi

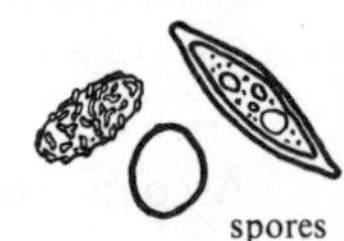
spores

PEZIZACEAE and Relatives

Small to medium-sized saprophytic fungi. FRUITING BODY *typically cup-shaped to disc-shaped or ear-shaped.* Flesh *usually brittle* (except *Phaeobulgaria*). STALK *absent or if present, continuous with cup and neither well developed nor deeply ribbed.* SPORES mostly ellipsoid to round, smooth or roughened at maturity. Asci mostly 8-spored, operculate.

AS their name implies, most cup fungi are cuplike. Spores are produced in asci which line the fruiting body's upper (or inner) surface, which may be smooth or somewhat veined. The spores are shot out of the asci with terrific force, usually in synchrony at some mysterious signal. Thus when cup fungi are picked or otherwise disturbed, they will often spew out white clouds of spores.

Some cup fungi, such as the common orange peel fungus *(Aleuria aurantia)*, are colorful, but the majority are brown or black. The largest genus, *Peziza*, includes many brown species with the same general appearance. If careful attention is paid to habitat, however, they can be differentiated. *P. domiciliana* is the most obvious—for it grows almost exclusively indoors. Several, such as *P. proteana*, show up in burned-over areas, while *P. vesiculosa* and *P. fimeti* fruit on dung and manure. Others fruit on rotten logs while still others occur on bare soil, in sand, and, of course, in humus.

None of the cup fungi are particularly good eating. They are thin-fleshed, brittle, and do not often occur in sufficient quantity to merit collecting. *Aleuria aurantia* is sometimes eaten raw in salads, but other cup fungi should be cooked. *Disciotis venosa* is said to be poisonous.

With the exception of *Aleuria*, most cup fungi don't appear until well into winter. Only the larger, more distinctive types are described here. Minute forms (only a few millimeters broad) abound, but are too miniscule to interest the average mushroom hunter. Several of the cup fungi described do not belong to the Pezizaceae in its strictest sense, but are grouped here because of their superficial resemblance.

Key to the Pezizaceae and Relatives

1. Fruiting body rubbery or semigelatinous; growing on wood 2
1. Fruiting body fleshy, rigid, or brittle 3

2. Fruiting body 2.5-15 cm broad, shaped like a shallow cup or with earlike lobes, often ribbed beneath; not common .... (see *Auricularia auricula*, p. 582)
2. Not as above; fruiting body top-shaped or cylindrical to cup-shaped, generally less than 4 cm broad; common .... *Phaeobulgaria inquinans*, p. 587

3. Interior (upper surface) bright orange to red 4
3. Interior some other color 6

4. Margin lined with black or dark brown hairs .... *Scutellinia scutellata*, p. 590
4. Not as above 5

5. Interior (upper surface) bright orange to golden-orange .... *Aleuria aurantia*, p. 591
5. Interior red fading to orange-red .... *Sarcoscypha coccinea*, p. 589

6. Fruiting body minute, blue to blue-green .... *Chlorosplenium aeruginascens*, p. 587
6. Not as above 7

7. Fruiting bodies more or less spoon-shaped, growing in large clusters; rare .... *Peziza proteana* form *sparassoides*, p. 595
7. Not as above 8

8. Fruiting body standing erect on end, somewhat cylindrical to ear-shaped .... *Otidea onotica*, p. 592
8. Not as above 9

9. Fruiting body buried at first and nearly spherical, then splitting into several lobes or rays as it expands; mostly in sandy soil 10
9. Not as above 12

10. Exterior covered with brown hairs .... *Sepultaria arenicola* (see *Sarcosphaera eximia*, p. 596)
10. Exterior not hairy 11

11. Interior tinted lilac or pinkish; in woods . *Sarcosphaera eximia*, p. 596
11. Interior pallid; in sand or sand dunes .... *Sarcosphaera ammophila* (see *S. eximia*, p. 596)

12. Growing on burnt ground or charcoal, etc. .... *Peziza violacea* (see *P. proteana*, p. 595)
12. Not as above 13

13. Growing in houses, cellars, etc. .... *Peziza domiciliana* (see *P. repanda*, p. 593)
13. Not as above 14

14. Growing on wood (logs, sticks, etc.) 15
14. Growing on ground or dung 17

15. Fruiting body black .... *Plectania melastoma*, p. 588
15. Fruiting body not black 16

16. Margin fringed with hairs .... *Humaria hemisphaerica* (see *Scutellinia scutellata*, p. 590)
16. Margin not fringed with hairs .... *Peziza repanda*, p. 593

17. Growing on dung and manure 18
17. Growing on ground (humus, soil, etc.) 20

18. Fruiting body minute (2 mm or less) .... *Ascobolus furfuraceus* (see *Peziza vesiculosa*, p. 594)
18. Fruiting body larger 19

19. Usually growing in clusters on dung or manure (including cow pies) .... *Peziza vesiculosa*, p. 594
19. Usually growing on cow pies, often solitary .... *Peziza fimeti* (see *P. vesiculosa*, p. 594)

20. Fruiting body typically with a stalk; lower or upper surface of fruiting body veined 21
20. Stalk absent 22

21. Stalk conspicuously ribbed, fluted, or veined .... (see *Helvella acetabulum*, p. 599)
21. Stalk short, thick, smooth; upper surface of fruiting body veined but stalk *not* veined .... *Discina perlata*, p. 597

22. Fruiting body small (less than 2.5 cm broad), soon disclike (flattened) .... *Peziza brunneoatra,* p. 593
22. Fruiting body larger, usually cup-shaped 23
23. Interior (upper surface) conspicuously veined or reticulate .... *Disciotis venosa* (see *Peziza badia,* p. 592)
23. Interior more or less smooth 24
24. Exterior (underside) brown .... *Peziza badia,* p. 592
24. Exterior pallid .... *Peziza sylvestris* (see *P. badia,* p. 592)

Chlorosplenium aeruginascens

FRUITING BODY 2-6 mm broad, at first cup-shaped, becoming flat or disclike with a slightly elevated margin. Interior (upper surface) bright blue-green to turquoise-blue (sometimes tinted yellowish in old age), smooth or slightly wrinkled; exterior (underside) similarly colored. Flesh thin. **STALK** usually present as a short, narrowed base, 1-2 mm thick and up to 3 mm long; colored like rest of fruiting body. **SPORES** 5-7 × 2-2.5 μm, ellipsoid, smooth.

HABITAT: Gregarious on dead wood (primarily oak), fruiting mostly in the winter, fairly common.

EDIBILITY: Indisputably inconsequential.

COMMENTS: This diminutive Ascomycete merits mention in this book because of its brilliant blue-green color. It is not a true cup fungus, but is included here because of its superficial resemblance. Its presence can be detected even when there are no fruiting bodies, because the mycelium stains its host blue-green. The stained wood was once used in the manufacture of inlaid wooden objects known as "Turnbridge Ware."

Phaeobulgaria inquinans

FRUITING BODY to 4 cm wide but usually smaller; at first round, then cylindrical or cup-shaped with a somewhat gelatinous or shiny interior, finally becoming top-shaped or stalked with a flabby cap. Interior (upper surface) black to blackish-brown; exterior (underside) rough, dark to dull brown. Flesh rubbery-pliant, not brittle. **STALK** sometimes present at maturity, continuous with cap. **SPORES** 12-14 × 6-7 μm, ellipsoid, smooth, brown; asci inoperculate.

HABITAT: Scattered to gregarious, often in rows, on hardwood logs and branches, especially tanoak and live oak. Common in the Santa

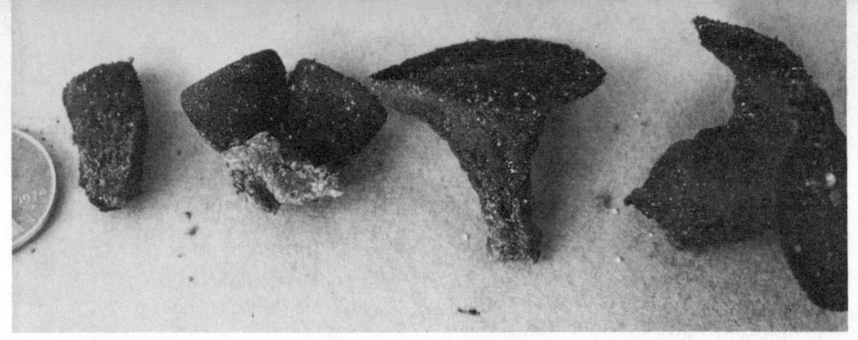

Phaeobulgaria inquinans. Young specimens at left are cup-shaped, while mature specimens at right are top-shaped. Fruiting bodies are rubbery and blackish-brown. They grow on dead hardwoods.

Cruz Mountains, fall through spring. I have seen luxuriant fruitings in March at Big Basin State Park.

EDIBILITY: Unknown.

COMMENTS: Also known as *Bulgaria inquinans,* the blackish-brown rubbery fruiting bodies of this species are a common sight on any wintertime hike through the woods. Its flesh is not brittle as that of other cup fungi, and in fact it is only distantly related. The texture is reminiscent of india rubber, also of the jelly fungus *Pseudohydnum gelatinosum.* Another jelly fungus, *Auricularia auricula,* is vaguely similar but is never black, is not as rubbery, differently shaped, and produces its spores on basidia. Other rubbery-gelatinous cup fungi include: *Bulgaria (=Sarcosoma) mexicana,* fruiting body urn-shaped at maturity with a short, thick, ribbed stalk, interior smoky-brown to dull brown, exterior blackish, on old sticks and woody debris of conifers, rare; *Sarcosoma globosa,* globose becoming flattened on top in age, with a thick, watery-gelatinous base, blackish, found under conifers, rare; and *Coryne sarcoides,* more or less top-shaped, reddish-flesh to dark purplish, found on rotting wood.

Plectania melastoma (Black Cup Fungus)

FRUITING BODY up to 2.5 cm broad and 3 cm high, at first nearly round or with a stemlike base, then opening slowly at the top, eventually expanding to become more or less cup-shaped, the margin remaining incurved for a long time. Interior (upper surface) smooth, shiny when wet, black or deep brownish-black. Exterior (underside) tough, cartilaginous (with a semigelatinous inner layer when wet), black, minutely hairy, strongly wrinkled. Flesh thin, tough, not brittle. **STALK** if present short and stout, black, with black mycelium extending into substrate. **SPORES** 20-26 × 9-12 μm, ellipsoid, smooth, hyaline.

Plectania melastoma. This small black cup fungus grows on rotting sticks. Note the wrinkled underside (exterior).

HABITAT: Solitary or more often in small groups or clusters on decaying hardwood sticks (especially oak). Common, winter and spring, but easily overlooked.

EDIBILITY: Unknown.

COMMENTS: There are several black cup fungi—this attractive species is by far the most common. The strongly wrinkled underside (exterior) and tough (rather than brittle) texture are good fieldmarks. It is not rubbery like *Phaeobulgaria.* It used to be placed in *Bulgaria* because of the semigelatinous internal layer, but the gelatinous quality is rarely evident in our specimens. I usually find it when I'm foraging for *Craterellus cornucopioides,* perhaps because both are black. Otherwise one is likely to overlook it. Other nongelatinous black cup fungi include: *Plectania nannfeldtii,* shallow cup-shaped with a well-developed stem, and elliptical spores 30-35 µm long, on rotting conifer wood; and *Pseudoplectania nigrella,* also on rotting conifers, with no stem and round spores 12-14 µm in diameter.

Sarcoscypha coccinea (Scarlet Cup Fungus)

FRUITING BODY up to 5 cm broad but usually about 2.5 cm; cup-shaped, the margin usually incurved. Interior bright red fading to orange-red, smooth, dry; exterior whitish, dry, covered with minute hairs. Flesh thin, brittle. **STALK** usually present, up to 4 cm long, minutely hairy, tapering downward, sometimes nearly absent. **SPORES** 24-40 × 10-14 µm, elliptical, smooth.

HABITAT: Solitary or in small groups on buried or partially buried hardwood sticks and branches, winter and spring, infrequent. I have found it in abundance along Scott Creek under willow, alder, buckeye, and cottonwood.

EDIBILITY: According to most sources, edible. I have not tried it.

Sarcoscypha coccinea. These specimens are attached to the stick, but their stems are not visible. Their bright red color makes them unique.

COMMENTS: The bright red color sets apart this exquisite cup fungus. The margin is not fringed with hairs as in *Scutellinia scutellata.* The length of the stem seems dependent upon how deep the stick from which it is growing is buried. It is a very attractive, striking species, unlikely to be confused with anything else. It used to be placed in the genus *Plectania.*

Scutellinia scutellata (Ciliate Cup Fungus)

FRUITING BODY up to 2 cm broad; at first round (globose), soon expanding to cup-shaped and then disc-shaped. Interior (upper surface) bright scarlet fading to orange, the margin fringed with dark brown or black hairs (cilia). Exterior (underside) also covered with hairs. Flesh very thin. **STALK** absent. **SPORES** 20-24 $\times$ 12-15 μm, elliptical, minutely warty.

HABITAT: Gregarious on decaying wood and soil in damp areas. Fairly common, winter and spring.

EDIBILITY: Unknown. Much too insubstantial to be of importance.

COMMENTS: This is another easily recognized cup fungus. The bright red to orange spore-producing surface and ciliate margin are good field characters. *Humaria (=Scutellinia) hemisphaerica* is a rare cup-shaped species with brownish-black cilia on the margin and exterior, and a white to grayish interior.

Scutellinia scutellata. This minute reddish-orange disclike species usually grows in dense groups as shown. Note the black (and hairy) margin of the disc. (Ray Gipson)

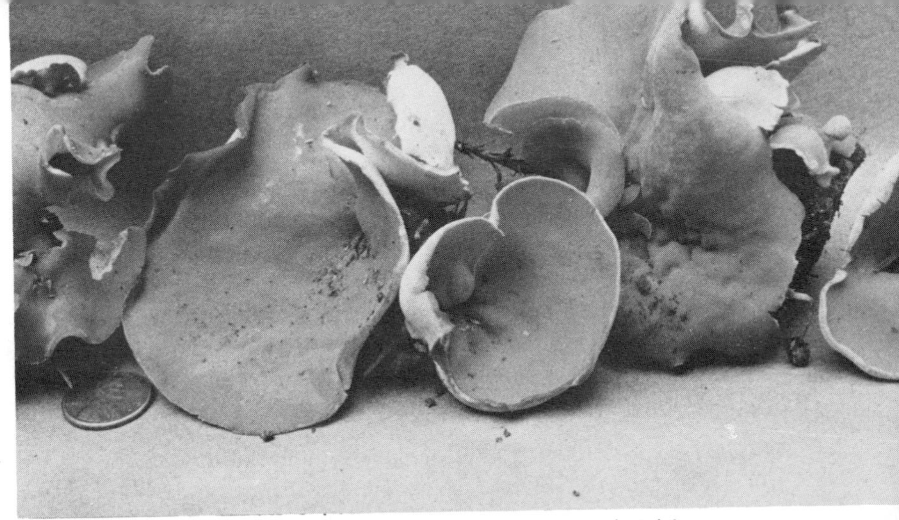

Aleuria aurantia is our most common cup fungus, easily recognized by its bright orange to golden-orange color. These are rather large specimens.

Aleuria aurantia (Orange Peel Fungus)

FRUITING BODY up to 10 cm broad; at first round (globose) but soon cup-shaped, saucer-shaped, or flattened, if clustered then often irregularly contorted from mutual pressure. Interior (upper surface) bright orange to golden-orange, fading somewhat in age, smooth. Exterior pallid, dry. Flesh thin, brittle. **STALK** absent. **SPORES** 18-22 × 9-10 μm, elliptical, reticulate-ridged.

HABITAT: Scattered to gregarious on ground, sometimes in fused clusters; common, fall, winter, and early spring. Partial to exposed soil along roads and paths through the woods, and sandy soil in grass or moss.

EDIBILITY: Edible, but thin-fleshed; rated highly by one European authority. Some sources suggest using it raw in salads. However, it's safer to cook it the first time.

COMMENTS: The orange peel fungus (or golden fairy cup, as it is sometimes called) can be mistaken at a glance for one of the old orange peels you frequently find in the woods. It is more brittle, however, and less common. The brilliant orange color renders it unique. The size and shape vary considerably according to environmental conditions. Some *Otidea* species are yellowish-orange, but they stand erect (on one end) instead of lying flat. A variety with smaller spores, 13-14.5 × 6.5-8 μm also occurs in our area. *Aleuria rhenana* is also orange but is much smaller and has a well-developed stem. It grows mostly in coniferous woods. *Caloscypha fulgens* is a small yellow-orange species with bluish-green stains commonly found under conifers in the spring at higher elevations.

Otidea onotica (Ear Cup Fungus)

FRUITING BODY to 7.5 cm high, and 5 cm broad, elongate ear-shaped, standing erect on one end, margin at first inrolled, expanding somewhat in age. Interior yellow-brown to orange-brown to orange-buff, often with a pinkish tint; exterior similar but without pinkish tint. Flesh thin, brittle. **STALK** absent. **SPORES** 12-14 × 6-8 μm, narrowly ellipsoid, smooth.

HABITAT: Usually in groups or clusters in woods, arising from a mass of mycelial debris. Infrequent, winter and spring.

EDIBILITY: Edible, but I have no information on related species.

COMMENTS: The erect growth habit separates *Otidea* from most other cup fungi. Other species include: *O. leporina,* tan to brown, with hooked paraphyses (sterile cells); *O. smithii,* more or less red-brown, with spores 18-24 × 12-14 μm; and *O. alutacea,* interior gray-brown, exterior dull brown to yellowish, growing in dense clusters.

Peziza badia (Large Brown Cup Fungus)

FRUITING BODY to 7.5 cm broad, at first round (globose), soon expanding to deeply cup-shaped, shallower in age. Interior (upper surface) smooth, dark brown to brown; exterior same color or slightly paler, minutely warty. Flesh brownish, brittle. **STALK** absent. **SPORES** 17-23 × 8-12 μm, elliptical, reticulate (roughened) at maturity.

Left: *Peziza badia*, a young unexpanded specimen. Eventually it will form a shallow cup. Note dark brown exterior. **Right:** *Peziza sylvestris* (see *P. badia*), young specimens. Note the whitish exterior.

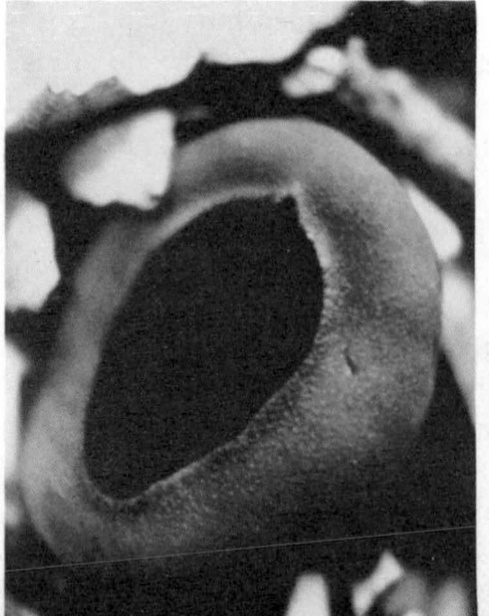

HABITAT: Solitary, scattered, or in small clusters on the ground in woods and along streams and roads. Common, but never abundant, winter and spring. It occasionally occurs (along with its relatives) in nurseries or gardens where humus and wood chips are added to the soil.

EDIBILITY: Edible, according to most books. I have not tried it.

COMMENTS: This is the first brown cup fungus you are likely to find in the woods. It is recognized by its deeply concave shape, brown exterior, and growth on the ground. There are several similar species with a whitish to golden-yellow exterior, including *P. sylvestris*, a common terrestrial species with smooth spores 15-20 μm long; *P. emileia,* on ground or wood, with rough spores 16-18 μm long; *P. succosa,* with flesh turning golden-yellow when broken; *P. melaleucoides,* brownish-black with rough spores 13-15 μm long; and *Disciotis (=Peziza) venosa,* a large reddish-brown terrestrial species with a deeply wrinkled or veined inner (upper) surface. The latter is said to be poisonous.

Peziza brunneoatra (Small Brown Cup Fungus)

FRUITING BODY less than 2.5 cm broad, disc-shaped to shallow cup-shaped. Interior (upper surface) brownish-black to brown, sometimes olive-tinted, smooth; exterior (underside) same color or slightly paler. Flesh thin, brownish, brittle. **STALK** absent or present as a very short base. **SPORES** 16-22 × 9-11 μm, elliptical, smooth or slightly roughened.

HABITAT: Scattered or gregarious on damp soil along paths and roads through the woods, near streams, etc. Common, winter and spring.

EDIBILITY: Unquestionably inconsequential.

COMMENTS: The small size is characteristic of this species. The average diameter is about 2 cm. It is a "cup fungus" in name only—mature specimens are usually disclike or even slightly convex.

Peziza repanda

FRUITING BODY to 13 cm broad, at first shallowly cup-shaped, expanding in age to flat or wavy. Interior (upper surface) pale brown or tan, darker in age, smooth to somewhat wrinkled or convoluted at the center; exterior (underside) pallid. Flesh fairly brittle. **STALK** absent

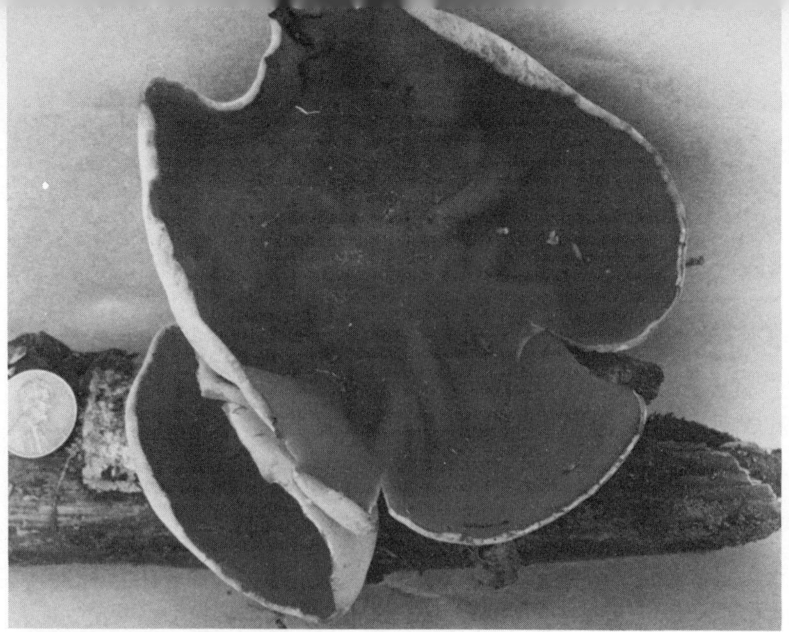

Peziza repanda, a large fresh specimen. Note its growth on wood. In age it flattens out. *P. domiciliana* (not illustrated) is very similar but slightly smaller and grows indoors.

or present only as a short basal attachment to the substrate. **SPORES** 15-17 × 8-10 μm, ellipsoid, smooth.

HABITAT: Solitary or several on rotten hardwood logs and branches. Occasional, winter and spring.

EDIBILITY: Edible.

COMMENTS: The salient features of this brown cup fungus are its large size, habitat on wood, and smooth spores. There are several other wood-inhabiting species. One, *P. clypeata,* is a smaller disc-shaped to shallowly concave species that grows on spongy hardwood logs. The upper surface is dark reddish-brown becoming greenish-black, the spores smooth, 25-27 × 12-14 μm. Another, *P. domiciliana,* is of special interest due to its penchant for growing indoors—either singly or in clusters—on lumber, plaster, sand, gravel, and coal dust. Hugo Sloane, Santa Cruz County's incorrigible *enfant terrible*-in-residence, has had solitary specimens grow out of the wall above his bathtub—in two separate houses! It also occurs in basements, greenhouses, shower stalls, in the vicinity of waterbeds, and under refrigerators.

Peziza vesiculosa (Dung Cup Fungus)

FRUITING BODY to 7.5 cm broad but usually smaller, at first round (globose), soon opening to become cup-shaped (crimped or convoluted if clustered). Interior (upper surface) pale brown, smooth. Exterior (underside) whitish or pallid, minutely warty. Flesh thin, brittle. **STALK** absent or present only as a short basal point of attachment. **SPORES** 20-23 × 10-13 μm, ellipsoid, smooth.

HABITAT: Gregarious, sometimes in large fused clusters (occasionally solitary) on manure, dung, in corrals, around stables and other heavily fertilized areas. Common in wet weather, fall through spring. I have seen massive clusters growing with *Bolbitius vitellinus* in a horse corral.

EDIBILITY: Unknown.

COMMENTS: This is one of our characteristic dung-inhabiting fungi. The habitat separates it from most other Pezizas. *P. fimeti* is a slightly smaller species usually found on cow pies. It does not normally grow in clusters and has smaller spores (less than 18 μm long). It was abundant in pastures in the waterlogged winter of 1978. *Ascobolus furfuraceus,* a pale yellow-green species, is one of a multitude of miniscule cup fungi that are less than 1 mm broad and grow exclusively on dung.

Peziza proteana form **sparassoides** (False Sparassis)

FRUITING BODY a dense clump of spoon-shaped, lopsided cups fused at the base; up to 25 cm wide. Interior of cups lilac to pinkish-tan to light brown, fading in age, smooth or wrinkled. Exterior same color or slightly darker, paler at base. Flesh thin, brittle. **STALK** absent. **SPORES** 10-13 × 5-7 μm, oblong, minutely warted.

Left: *Peziza vesiculosa* growing on dung. In background is *Psilocybe coprophila.* **Right:** *Peziza proteana* form *sparassoides* , top view of a typical cluster. Note how the "cups" are distorted by mutual pressure so as to resemble *Sparassis.* (Ray Gipson)

HABITAT: Clustered in lignin-rich humus. Sometimes at the base of a tree (like *Sparassis*). Rare, winter and spring.

EDIBILITY: According to one source, the large clusters are edible and fairly good.

COMMENTS: Form *sparassoides* is easily distinguished from other woodland cup fungi by its densely clustered growth habit. It superficially resembles the cauliflower mushroom, *Sparassis radicata.* The typical form of *Peziza proteana* looks like any other brown cup fungus, but likes to grow in burned-over areas. Other inhabitants of burnt ground and charcoal include: *P. pustulata,* with an ochraceous-brown interior and warty (pustulate) exterior; *P. violacea,* with a violet interior becoming blackish in old age; and *Rhizina undulata (=R. inflata),* with a flattened amorphous brownish-black fruiting body attached to the ground by a mass of rootlike fibers.

Sarcosphaera eximia (Crown Fungus)

FRUITING BODY 5-15 cm broad; at first a deep round cup, then splitting in crownlike fashion to form six to ten rays. Interior at first pallid, then grayish-lilac to pink, smooth; exterior pallid, more or less smooth. Flesh thick, not noticeably brittle. **STALK** if present short and thick. **SPORES** 15-19 × 8-9 μm, elliptical with flattened ends, smooth.

HABITAT: Solitary or scattered in woods, at first buried in the soil but visible at maturity; winter and spring, not common. The best place to look for it is in sandy soil under conifers, particularly ponderosa pine.

EDIBILITY: Problematic. One mycologist pronounces it edible and good, while another proclaims it poisonous. It is difficult to clean and should be cooked thoroughly.

COMMENTS: The crownlike fruiting body with grayish-lilac interior is unique. *S. crassa* and *S. coronaria* are synonyms. *S. ammophila* is a smaller species with an umber-brown interior, found buried in sand and sand dunes. A third crownlike species, *Sepultaria arenicola,* is known as the "Hole in the Ground," because it looks like one. It is strictly subterranean (hypogeous), up to 4 cm broad, cup-shaped at first but then splitting into lobes, with a pallid interior. It differs from *Sarcosphaera* in having a densely hairy brown exterior. It, too, grows in sandy soil. Since all three of these species split stellately they might be confused with certain Gasteromycetes like *Scleroderma geaster.* In the latter, however, traces of spore powder (gleba) are usually found adhering to the interior.

Discina perlata

FRUITING BODY up to 13 cm broad, at first flat, the margin then turning down and the center becoming depressed. Interior (upper surface) dark brown to dull cinnamon or tan, usually veined or convoluted. Exterior pallid-whitish. Flesh thin, brittle. **STALK** usually present, short and stout, 1-2 cm thick, sometimes ribbed. **SPORES** 30-35 × 12-14 μm, fusoid (elongated) with pointed ends, minutely warty.

HABITAT: Solitary or scattered in humus under conifers, sometimes on rotten wood, late winter and spring. A prominent member of the western mountain "snowbank" flora, but rare along the coast.

EDIBILITY: Edible. According to some, quite good.

COMMENTS: The shape of the spores is the most distinctive feature of this cup fungus. However, it can be recognized in the field by its flattened shape, convoluted upper surface, and frequent presence of a short, thick stalk.

Morels and False Morels

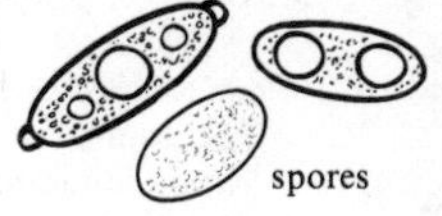

HELVELLACEAE

THESE medium to large fleshy Ascomycetes are furnished with a stem and cap (or "head"). In the morels *(Morchella)* the cap is pitted or honeycombed. The spore-containing asci line the surfaces of the pits while the ridges that separate the pits are sterile. In *Verpa, Gyromitra,* and *Helvella* (collectively called the false morels), the cap is smooth, wrinkled, brainlike, saddle-shaped, or even cuplike, but never pitted. The asci cover the exterior of the cap or the interior of the cup, and there are no sterile ridges.

As in the cup fungi, the mature spores are forcibly expelled from the asci through tiny "lids," causing the fruiting bodies to "smoke" when picked, jarred, or breathed on. The Helvellaceae, in fact, are closely allied to certain cup fungi (Pezizaceae), and are incorporated in that family by some taxonomists. They are separated here, however, to expedite identification.

The Helvellaceae fruit chiefly in the winter and spring, after most of the agarics, boletes, and other Basidiomycetes have departed from the scene. The morels are renowned for their marvellous flavor and texture, but some of the false morels (notably *Gyromitra*) are very poisonous and can even be fatal. There is little danger in confusing them if you remember that morels have a pitted head and hollow interior. Nevertheless, proceed with caution and for safety's sake *always cook what you eat*—even morels.

Key to the Helvellaceae

1. Cap composed of honeycomblike chambers (pits) separated by raised ridges; interior hollow; lower margin of cap attached to stalk .... *Morchella,* p. 608
1. Not as above 2

2. Cap smooth or wrinkled, more or less conical to bell-shaped; lower margin of cap free from stalk; stalk smooth, hollow, fragile .... *Verpa,* p. 607
2. Not as above; cap not conical; cap margin free or attached 3

3. Cap cup-shaped to more or less saddle-shaped .... *Helvella,* below
3. Cap irregularly lobed, convoluted, or brainlike 4

4. Cap some shade of brown .... *Gyromitra,* p. 604
4. Cap not brown .... *Helvella,* below

HELVELLA (ELFIN SADDLES)

Medium-sized terrestrial fungi. FRUITING BODY *with a cap and stalk.* CAP *cuplike to saddle-shaped or irregularly lobed,* white to brown or black; margin usually free from stalk (except *H. lacunosa*). Flesh rather brittle. STALK *well developed,* smooth or ribbed or deeply fluted and pitted; fragile or tough. SPORES typically ellipsoid, smooth. Asci typically 8-spored, operculate.

ELFIN saddles are the most prominent group of Ascomycetes in coastal California. They take their name from their frequently saddle-shaped cap. The cap can also be cuplike or irregularly lobed, but is not brainlike as in *Gyromitra,* nor pitted as in *Morchella,* nor conical as in *Verpa.*

Helvella (also spelled *Elvela*) splits neatly into three groups: those with a cuplike cap (e.g., *H. acetabulum*); those with a saddle-shaped cap and smooth stalk which is more or less circular in cross-section (e.g., *H. elastica*); and those with a saddle-shaped to irregularly lobed cap and deeply ridged, fluted, or pitted stalk which is chambered in cross-section (*H. lacunosa, H. maculata, H. crispa*).

Helvellas are very attractive (or grotesque, depending on your disposition), but as a rule should not be eaten because of their resemblance to the poisonous false morels *(Gyromitra)*. However, the black elfin saddle *(H. lacunosa)* is apparently harmless when cooked, and fairly good. It is the only one that occurs in sufficient quantity to eat.

Helvellas fruit mostly in the winter and early spring (before morels appear), in the woods or under trees. A dozen species occur in California, five of which are described here.

Key to Helvella

1. Cap cuplike (concave) 2
1. Cap saddle-shaped to irregularly lobed 3

2. Cup with branching ribs on underside which extend nearly to the margin .... *H. acetabulum,* below
2. Not as above .... *H. leucomelaena* (see *H. acetabulum,* below)

3. Stalk smooth or indistinctly grooved at base, more or less round in cross-section 4
3. Stalk deeply ridged or fluted (and often pitted), chambered or convoluted in cross-section 6

4. Cap saddle-shaped to irregularly lobed, reddish-brown to dark bay-brown (occasionally yellow-brown); often (but not always) growing on rotten wood .... (see *Gyromitra infula,* p. 606)
4. Not as above; cap saddle-shaped to nearly circular in side view, pale tan to brown or grayish-brown 5

5. Underside of cap smooth .... *H. elastica,* p. 603
5. Underside of cap pubescent (minutely hairy) .... *H. compressa* (see *H. elastica,* p. 603)

6. Cap white to buff or tinged yellowish .... *H. crispa,* p. 602
6. Cap darker (but may be covered with a whitish parasitic fungus) 7

7. Cap gray to black .... *H. lacunosa,* p. 601
7. Cap brown to grayish-brown 8

8. Cap 6-25 cm broad, spreading or undulating, underside with ribs extending nearly to margin .... *H. californica* (see *H. maculata,* p. 600)
8. Cap 2-6 cm broad, grayish-brown, often mottled; ribs on underside not extending nearly to margin .... *H. maculata,* p. 600

Helvella acetabulum (Elfin Cup)

CAP 2-6 cm broad and up to 3 cm deep, cup-shaped or bowl-shaped; surface (interior) some shade of brown, darker in age, smooth. Exterior (underside) somewhat paler, minutely hairy, conspicuously ribbed nearly to margin, the ribs pallid, branching. Flesh thin, rather brittle. **STALK** short but prominent, 1-5 cm long, continuous with cup, deeply

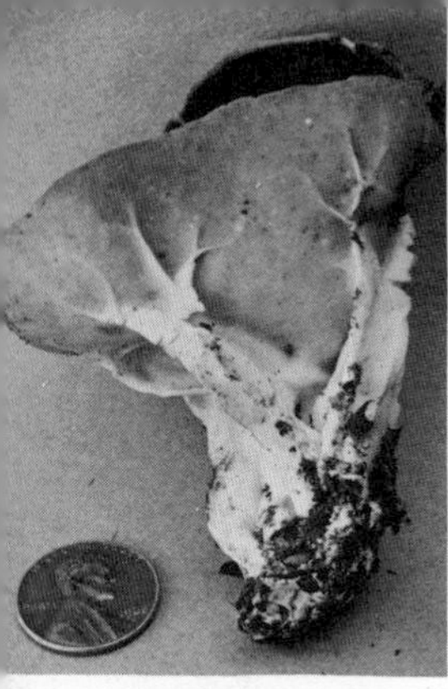
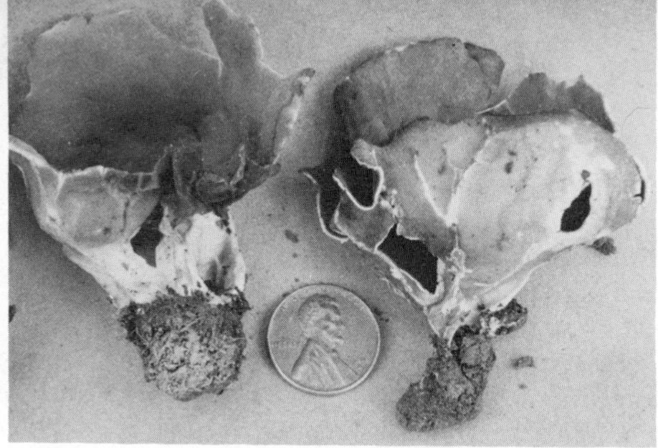

Helvella acetabulum. **Left:** Note branching ribs and ribbed stalk on this young specimen. **Right:** Two mature specimens, showing brown cup and white stalk.

ribbed or fluted, equal or thickened at base, whitish below; convoluted or chambered in cross-section. **SPORES** 18-22 × 12-14 μm, ellipsoid, smooth.

HABITAT: Solitary or scattered in woods, winter and early spring, not uncommon. I find it once or twice a year, usually under oak.

EDIBILITY: Unknown; best avoided.

COMMENTS: Formerly known as *Paxina acetabulum,* this species looks like a cross between a cup fungus and an elfin saddle, for it has the ribbed stalk of a *Helvella* and the brown cup of a *Peziza.* In fact, if the cup were inverted, you'd have a bonafide elfin saddle! There are several other Helvellas with a more or less cuplike cap and well-developed stalk. These include: *H. leucomelaena (=H. leucomelas),* with interior of cup brown to brownish-black, stalk short and thick, and ribs extending only to base of the cup; *H. queletii,* similar to *H. leucomelaena* but with a longer stalk and paler cup (interior brownish to grayish-brown, exterior yellowish-gray to tan); and *H. villosa,* with a smooth stalk (more or less round in cross-section), and grayish cup with a finely hairy exterior that often splits into lobes at maturity.

Helvella maculata (Brown Elfin Saddle)

CAP up to 5 cm high and 6 cm broad, irregularly saddle-shaped; surface mottled with various shades of grayish-brown, smooth or slightly wrinkled; margin rolled in (up) at first, unfurling with age and sometimes splitting, not attached to stalk. Underside creamy becoming buff or yellowish-gray, covered with minute soft hairs, sometimes with a few ribs extending a little way from the stalk. Flesh thin, brittle. **STALK** 2-10 cm long, up to 3 cm thick, deeply ribbed or fluted, white to pale buff, sometimes stained grayish in age, equal or tapering upward; convoluted or chambered in cross-section. **SPORES** 20-23 × 12-13.5 μm, bluntly ellipsoid, smooth.

Helvella maculata. Note the saddle-shaped brown cap and deeply fluted white stalk. Specimen at right is contorted so that only the pale underside of the cap is showing.

HABITAT: Scattered to gregarious in mixed woods and under conifers, winter and early spring, occasional. I have seen large fruitings under redwood in February. It is apparently endemic to western North America.

EDIBILITY: Unknown; best avoided.

COMMENTS: This showy elfin saddle can be identified by its grayish-brown mottled cap and deeply fluted stalk. It is darker than *H. crispa* and paler than *H. lacunosa. H. (=Gyromitra) californica* is a larger species with a strongly spreading (6-25 cm), undulating, paper-thin brown cap. The underside of the cap has ribs extending to the margin (as in *H. acetabulum*), and the fluted stalk usually stains wine-red at the base. As its name implies, it occurs in California (mostly at higher elevations), but I have yet to find it in our area. It is said to be poisonous.

Helvella lacunosa (Black Elfin Saddle)

CAP up to 10 cm high and broad but usually 5 cm or less; saddle-shaped to irregularly lobed; surface smooth or wrinkled, black or grayish-black fading to gray; margin often attached to stalk in places, incurved (toward stalk) at first. Underside pale gray to grayish-brown or black, smooth, *not* hairy. Flesh thin, rather brittle. **STALK** 2-8 cm long, 1-4 cm thick, deeply furrowed or fluted, with deep pits, equal or tapering

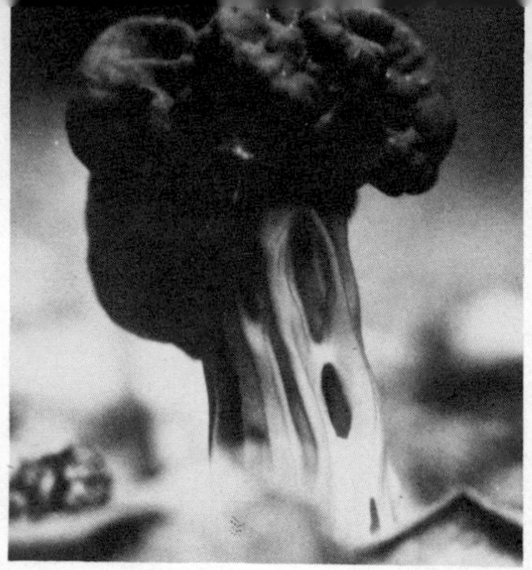

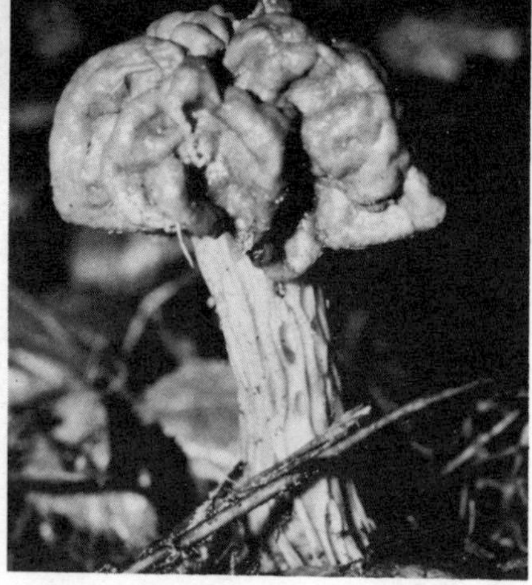

Helvella lacunosa. **Left:** Young specimen showing black cap and deeply fluted, pitted white stalk. (Rick Kerrigan) **Right:** An old specimen, showing how the cap and stalk become grayish. (Ray Gipson)

upward, white becoming dark gray as it ages, convoluted or chambered in cross-section; ribs sharp, sometimes double-edged. **SPORES** 15-20 × 9-13 μm, ellipsoid, smooth.

HABITAT: Solitary, scattered, or gregarious in woods (especially pine and oak), late fall through early spring. It is usually abundant in January and February in pine plantations or yards where Monterey pine has been planted.

EDIBILITY: Edible when cooked and fairly good, though chewy. The tough stems require longer cooking than the caps, and are best discarded. Eat only young, fresh specimens (in which the stalk is still white). It is sometimes dried and powdered.

COMMENTS: The black to gray irregularly lobed cap and deeply fluted stem make this elfin saddle unmistakable. It is by far the most common and gregarious of our Helvellas, often appearing in large groups or even troops, after heavy winter rains. It is frequently attacked by a white, moldy-looking parasite—leading to possible confusion with *H. crispa,* which has a whitish cap. Parasitized individuals should not be eaten. *H. mitra* is an obsolete synonym.

Helvella crispa (White Elfin Saddle)

CAP 2-5 cm broad and high, saddle-shaped to somewhat irregular; surface white to creamy-buff or tinged yellowish, smooth or wrinkled; margin at first rolled in (up), then expanding. Underside white to grayish, finely hairy (pubescent). Flesh thin, brittle. **STALK** 3-8 cm long, up to 3 cm thick, deeply ribbed or fluted, equal or tapering upward, white, darkening slightly in age; convoluted or chambered in cross-section. **SPORES** 17-23 × 10-14 μm, ellipsoid, smooth.

HABITAT: Solitary or in small groups in woods, widespread but not common. I have found it in October under redwood and tanoak. It undoubtedly fruits in the winter and spring as well.

EDIBILITY: Said to be edible when cooked. I haven't tried it.

COMMENTS: The creamy-white to buff cap identifies this beautiful elfin saddle. It resembles *H. lacunosa,* but is much paler.

Left: *Helvella crispa.* Note fluted stalk and whitish cap. **Right:** *Helvella elastica.* Cleft in saddle is so slight that cap appears circular in outline. Note long, smooth slender stalk.

Helvella elastica (Smooth-Stemmed Elfin Saddle)

CAP 1-3.5 cm broad and high, saddle-shaped to nearly circular in side view; surface pale brown to tan or buff, smooth, margin straight or somewhat incurved (toward stalk), free from stalk. Underside whitish to buff, smooth, *not* hairy. Flesh thin, brittle. **STALK** 3-14 cm long, slender, equal, sometimes curved; smooth or indistinctly grooved at base, whitish to pale yellowish-buff; more or less round in cross-section. **SPORES** 18-21 × 11-13.5 μm, ellipsoid, smooth.

HABITAT: Scattered or in groups in woods, winter and spring, occasionally in fall as well. Fairly common, but never abundant.

EDIBILITY: I can find no information on it.

COMMENTS: The long, smooth, slender stem and pale brown saddle-shaped cap are the hallmarks of this distinctive elfin saddle. The cleft (sinus) in the saddle is often so shallow that the cap appears circular in side view (see illustration). The stalk is not nearly as tough as that of other elfin saddles. There are a number of similar species, including: *H. leucopus,* with a dark brownish to black saddle and deeper sinus; *H. compressa,* slightly larger, with a brown to grayish-brown saddle and minutely hairy (pubescent) underside; and *H. stevensii,* with a tan to buff saddle and finely hairy underside. *Gyromitra infula* resembles all of these but is larger, darker brown, and not as consistently saddle-shaped.

GYROMITRA (BRAIN MUSHROOMS)

Medium-sized to large fungi found on ground or rotting wood. FRUITING BODY *with a cap and stalk.* CAP *usually contorted, lobed, wrinkled, or brainlike* (saddle-shaped in *G. infula*), *some shade of brown;* margin free from stalk or attached. Flesh rather brittle. STALK *well developed,* usually smooth and hollow (but sometimes ribbed). SPORES typically ellipsoid, smooth or rough. Asci typically 8-spored, operculate.

THESE small but dangerous brainlike mushrooms are also known as lorchels or false morels. The cap is neither conical as in the early morels (*Verpa*) nor pitted as in the true morels (*Morchella*). *Gyromitra* is most likely to be confused with *Helvella,* and in fact even the experts cannot agree on the exact differences between them. As a rule, however, forms with a brown brainlike cap belong to *Gyromitra,* and those with a differently colored and/or saddle-shaped cap (with the exception of *G. infula*) are placed in *Helvella.*

Gyromitra is not common in coastal California, but is quite prominent in mountainous regions during the spring, and in coniferous forests farther north. Though avidly collected by many people, several species (notably *G. esculenta*) are dangerously poisonous, *and should never be eaten raw.* The toxin, monomethylhydrazine (MMH) is normally destroyed by cooking or drying, but my advice is to avoid all Gyromitras (with the possible exception of *G. gigas,* a safe species found near melting snow). MMH, incidentally, is used as a rocket fuel (for more details, see p. 632), and inhalation of its vapors while cooking Gyromitras can be dangerous. Two species are described here.

Key to Gyromitra

1. Cap more or less saddle-shaped; stalk not ribbed .... *G. infula,* p. 606
1. Cap brainlike to convoluted or wrinkled 2

2. Stalk smooth or grooved but not ribbed, with one or two hollows in cross-section .... *G. esculenta,* below
2. Stalk usually ribbed, with inferior folds in cross-section .... *G. gigas* (see *G. esculenta,* below)

Gyromitra esculenta (Brain Mushroom; False Morel)

CAP 3-10 cm broad, brainlike to irregularly wrinkled, knobby, or convoluted; surface yellow-brown to brown, chestnut-brown, or dark brown, wrinkled. Interior hollow, whitish. Flesh thin, somewhat waxy, brittle. **STALK** rather short, 2-5 cm long, 1-2.5 cm thick, whitish to yellowish or pinkish, minutely powdered; smooth or grooved or somewhat compressed; with one or two narrow hollows in cross-section. **SPORES** 17-24 × 7-11 μm, ellipsoid, smooth.

HABITAT: Solitary or scattered on ground under conifers; widespread, but rare in our area, more common farther north. It fruits chiefly in the spring and is sometimes found with *G. gigas* (see below).

EDIBILITY: Poisonous! This species has caused numerous deaths (especially in Europe), but is still eaten by many people and even sold commercially in Europe. The poison (MMH) is volatile, and breaks down in the process of cooking or drying. If you must try it, parboil it and throw out the water, and *never* eat a large amount. Certain geographical races appear to be more dangerous than others. Its popularity is evidenced by its plethora of fanciful nicknames ("Lorchel," "Elephant Ears," "Beefsteak Morel," "False Morel," and "Brain Mushroom"), but my advice is to leave it alone. MMH is also carcinogenic.

COMMENTS: The brown, cerebral cap and smooth stalk are the hallmarks of this infamous fungus. Despite the moniker "false morel," it can scarcely be confused with true morels, for the cap is never pitted. Two related false morels reveal several interior folds or chambers when the stalk base is viewed in cross-section: the snow mushroom, *G. (=Neogyromitra) gigas,* has a short, massive, irregular stalk and broad, compact brown head. It is strictly a montane species, found near melting snow in the spring. It is delectable when cooked, but extreme care must be taken to identify it correctly. *G. caroliniana* has a deeply convoluted to irregularly pitted brown to brownish-black cap (vaguely suggestive of a morel), a longer stalk, and ornamented spores. It is said to prefer hardwoods and is recorded from California. I have not seen it.

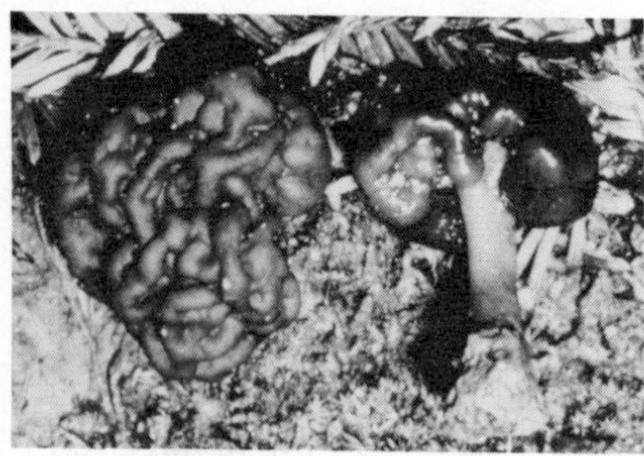

Top: *Gyromitra esculenta.* Note the brainlike brown cap and smooth stem. **Right:** *Gyromitra infula.* This specimen is bay-brown with a distinctly saddle-shaped cap, but the color varies to yellow-brown and shape can be quite irregular—but not truly brainlike.

Gyromitra infula

CAP 3-12 cm broad and high, saddle-shaped to irregularly folded or contorted, but not usually brainlike; surface reddish-brown to dark brown, occasionally yellow-brown, finely wrinkled, margin usually incurved (toward stalk). Underside hidden, whitish, minutely velvety. Flesh thin, brittle. **STALK** to 8 cm long and to 2 cm thick, equal or tapering upward, smooth or grooved but *not* ribbed; same color as cap or paler (even whitish); hollow in cross-section (not chambered). **SPORES** 15-18 × 6-7.5 μm, ellipsoid, smooth.

HABITAT: Solitary or scattered on rotting wood and in humus, fruiting mostly in winter and early spring. Widespread, but not particularly common.

EDIBILITY: Poisonous. Contains MMH. Never eat it raw!

COMMENTS: The irregularly saddle-shaped cap, dark reddish-brown to bay-brown color, and more or less smooth stem distinguish this false morel. Its penchant for growing on very rotten wood is also distinctive. Saddle-shaped specimens can be confused with *Helvella,* and it is listed under that genus in some books. It is sometimes folded and contorted, but never brainlike (cerebriform) as in *G. esculenta. G. ambigua* is a nearly identical species in which the spores have short projections at both ends.

VERPA (EARLY MORELS)

Medium-sized terrestrial fungi. FRUITING BODY *with a cap and stalk.* CAP *roughly conical or bell-shaped, wrinkled or smooth; margin free from stalk.* Flesh thin, fragile. STALK *well developed,* smooth, hollow. SPORES ellipsoid, smooth. Asci 8-spored or 2-spored, operculate.

THIS is a small genus intermediate between the false morels and true morels. The cap is roughly conical as in the latter, but the cap is not pitted and the margin is not attached to the stalk.

There are two widespread species, one with a smooth cap and one with a wrinkled cap. They are edible for most people, but fragile and rather bland. They grow in stream valleys and rich soil, and generally fruit in the spring, just before deciduous trees put out their leaves, and a week or two before other morels appear—hence they are sometimes called "early morels."

Key to Verpa

1. Cap conspicuously wrinkled; asci 2-spored .... *V. bohemica*, below
1. Cap more or less smooth; asci 8-spored *V. conica* (see *V. bohemica*, below)

Verpa bohemica (Early Morel)

CAP 1-3 cm broad and slightly higher, more or less obtusely conic or bell-shaped; surface pale to dark yellow-brown or brown, wrinkled by branching ribs or folds; attached to stalk only at the apex, the sides hanging down like a skirt with the margin free and sometimes turned up. Underside whitish. Flesh thin, fragile. **STALK** 6-14 cm long, more or less equal, hollow or stuffed with a loose pith, whitish becoming pale tan, smooth or minutely granulose; round in cross-section. **SPORES** 60-80 × 15-18 μm, elongated, smooth. Asci 2-spored.

HABITAT: Scattered to gregarious in woods, thickets, and rich soil, especially along streams. Fruiting in the spring, usually before the true morels appear. I have seen large numbers in April under cottonwood and alder along a creek.

Verpa conica (see *V. bohemica*). Smooth conical to bell-shaped cap and fragile, hollow stalk are distinctive. *V. bohemica* is very similar but has wrinkled cap. (Ray Gipson)

EDIBILITY: Edible for most people, and fairly good, though certainly not on a par with the true morels. When eaten in large amounts (or on several successive days), it can produce a loss of muscular coordination. Always cook it.

COMMENTS: This *Verpa* is easily recognized by its conspicuously wrinkled, more or less conical cap and smooth, hollow, whitish stem. The cap is occasionally pitted, but the free margin separates it from the true morels *(Morchella). Verpa conica* has the same general appearance, but its cap is smooth or only slightly wrinkled, and its asci are 8-spored. I have found it under redwood, but it is not common. Intermediate between *Verpa* and *Morchella* is *Morchella semilibera (=M. hybrida* or *Mitrophora hybrida),* which has the pitted, ridged cap of a *Morchella* and the free margin of a *Verpa.* It has a wide distribution and has been reported from Oregon. Both *Verpa conica* and *Morchella semilibera* are edible, with caution. On the basis of its 2-spored asci, the "splitters" have rewarded *V. bohemica* with a genus of its own—*Ptychoverpa.*

MORCHELLA (MORELS)

Medium to large terrestrial fungi. FRUITING BODY *with a cap and stalk.* CAP *honeycombed with raised ridges and deep pits or chambers; lower margin attached to the stalk* (except in *M. semilibera*). *Interior hollow.* STALK *well developed,* smooth or wrinkled below, hollow. SPORES typically ellipsoid, smooth. Asci 8-spored, operculate.

THESE prized delicacies are the best-known wild mushrooms in North America. And so esteemed are they in Europe that people used to set fire to their own woods in hopes of eliciting a bountiful morel crop the next spring! Luckily, morels are among the safest of all fungi—unmistakable by virtue of their hollow fruiting body with a pitted or honeycombed head (they are also known as "sponge mushrooms"). False morels *(Gyromitra)* are vaguely similar, but have a wrinkled or convoluted (not pitted) cap, while early morels *(Verpa)* have a free cap margin and smooth or wrinkled cap. Morels have also been inexplicably confused with stinkhorns *(Phallus),* which have a slimy head, cadaverous stench, and saclike volva (*Morchella esculenta* was originally classified as a *Phallus* by Linnaeus!).

It is difficult to pinpoint where morels are likely to be found. They grow under both hardwoods and conifers, in abandoned orchards, gardens, grassy ground, under hedges, on roadcuts, near melting snow, and in sandy soil along streams (in other words, wherever they please!). The best place to look for them, however, is on burnt ground in the wake of forest fires, where they sometimes fruit in awesome amounts. Numerous assaults have been made on morels' integrity—that is, there have been many unsuccessful attempts to raise them commercially. The spores germinate readily in culture and the mycelium also grows, but getting them to fruit has been the major stumbling block.

Morels are associated almost universally with spring ("May is morel month in Michigan"). In the Midwest, where they are particularly

Pitted cap and hollow interior are the hallmarks of morels. This particular specimen appears to be *Morchella conica*, with a little *M. esculenta* "mixed in."

abundant, the various species fruit in a definite succession, and the annual morel festivals are a major tourist attraction. In coastal California they fruit most any time, but, alas, are not nearly as common as one would wish. Finding them is largely a matter of luck—being in the right place at the right time. However, large quantities can be collected in the Sierras, where *M. angusticeps* appears every spring soon after the snow melts. Timing is of utmost importance since the season there is relatively short.

Though *Morchella* is unerringly distinct, the disposition of species is largely a matter of opinion. Many have been described, based on differences in color, shape, and orientation of the pits and ridges. However, each seems to intergrade with the next, leading many mycologists to recognize only two species. To most people, however, it's academic, since all morels are edible—and incredible.

Stuffed morels are a traditional favorite because the interior is hollow. However, they're also delicious sauteed, providing you don't drown them in butter. Split them lengthwise and clean the interior carefully, and to be on the safe side, *always* cook them. If you should stumble on a large batch, get them while you can (or better yet, show me where they're growing)! They are easily preserved by canning or they can be strung up on necklaces and dried.

Five *Morchella* "species" are keyed below. As I am meticulously mapping their variation and distribution, readers are requested to deliver any and all morels they find to my doorstep. While I am savoring the superb flavor of *croutes aux morilles a la normande,* you can bask in the altruistic satisfaction of having contributed to a noble cause.*

Key to Morchella

1. Fruiting body rather small; ridges white or whitish ... *M. deliciosa,* p. 612
1. Not as above ... 2

2. Pits elongated; ridges more or less longitudinally oriented and blackening in age; cap more or less conical (but often bluntly so) ... 3
2. Not as above; ridges not blackening ... 4

3. Found mostly in sandy soil along the coast ... *M. conica,* p. 611
3. Found mostly in mountains or coniferous forests ... *M. angusticeps* (see *M. conica,* p. 611)

4. Pits large and shallow; stalk enlarged at base; fruiting body medium-sized to large ... *M. crassipes* (see *M. esculenta,* p. 613)
4. Not as above; stalk base not enlarged or only slightly so; fruiting body small to medium-sized ... *M. esculenta,* p. 613

* The least you can do is invite me over for dinner.

Morchella conica. **Left:** Young specimen with brown ridges. (Nancy Burnett). **Right:** Mature individual with blackish ridges. Cap is not always so conical. (Ray Gipson)

Morchella conica (Conic Morel)

CAP 2-4 cm broad and 3-10 cm high (sometimes much larger), elongated or conical with the apex often acute; with elongated pits and more or less longitudinally arranged ridges. Ridges pallid becoming brown or brownish-black in age, branching or connected by cross-veins. Pits yellowish to yellow-brown becoming brownish-olive or darker. Flesh rather thin. Interior hollow. **STALK** 5-8 cm long and up to 4 cm thick (sometimes much larger), apex almost as broad (or even broader) than cap; equal or tapering downward; smooth above, usually wrinkled or grooved below, minutely scurfy, hollow, whitish to yellowish aging pale brown. **SPORES** 20-24 × 12-14 μm, ellipsoid, smooth.

HABITAT: Solitary or in small groups in iceplant, gardens, nurseries, along streams, at edges of woods, etc. Fruiting year-round but chiefly in the spring—the most common morel of coastal California. It shows a definite preference for sandy soil—I've even found it growing out of old sandbags.

EDIBILITY: Edible and choice, but some people are allergic to *M. angusticeps* (see below). Like all morels, it should be cooked.

COMMENTS: The more or less conical cap with radially (longitudinally) arranged ridges distinguishes this species from *M. esculenta.* However, I often encounter what appear to be "hybrids." The common morel of the Sierras, *M. angusticeps* ("Black Morel") has ridges that blacken in age. It is similar to *M. conica* and is sometimes considered a form of the same species. *M. angusticeps* is abundant in the spring after the snow melts, especially in the wake of forest fires. Certain localities are renowned for their bountiful crops, but to divulge them here would be imprudent. It is also abundant in Washington, Oregon, and Idaho. The morel monstrosities illustrated on the back cover appear to be a giant form of *M. conica* (*M. crassistipa*?). They fruit sporadically in the fern grotto of a large nursery.

Morchella deliciosa (White Morel)

CAP 1-4 cm high and 1-2 cm broad, more or less obtusely conic with elongated pits and longitudinal but irregularly branching ridges. Ridges whitish, darkening slightly in age, edges blunt. Pits gray to grayish-brown, sometimes brownish or brownish-black in old age. Flesh thin. Interior hollow. **STALK** 1-5 cm long and up to 1.5 cm thick, white to yellowish, base often enlarged; smooth above, often wrinkled somewhat at base; hollow. **SPORES** 19-22 × 10-12 μm, ellipsoid, smooth.

HABITAT: Solitary or in small groups in gardens, cultivated ground, rich soil, at the edges of woods, etc. Fruiting mainly in the spring. The

As pointed out, morels do not submit handily to categorization. The white ridges of young specimens in foreground suggest *Morchella deliciosa*, but the conical brown cap of mature specimens in background is reminiscent of *M. conica*.

largest fruiting I've seen was under a plum tree, on Christmas Day, in Santa Cruz. It is not common.

EDIBILITY: Eminently edible. This is one *deliciosa* that lives up to its name.

COMMENTS: Our smallest morel, best recognized by its whitish ridges and dark pits. The color scheme, in fact, is the precise opposite of *M. angusticeps* and *M. conica,* which have dark ridges (at least at maturity) and paler pits.

Morchella esculenta (Common Morel)

CAP 2-9 cm high and 2-6 cm wide, round to elongated or obtusely conic with a rounded apex; with somewhat elongated pits and branching ridges which are *not* longitudinally disposed. Ridges pallid to grayish, yellow-brown, or pale cinnamon (typically paler than pits), edges blunt. Pits yellowish to yellow-brown or light brown. Flesh rather thin. Interior hollow. **STALK** typically stout (about 1/2-2/3 as thick as the cap), up to 6 cm long, base often enlarged slightly and irregularly wrinkled, equal above; whitish to yellowish (paler than cap), browner in age, minutely scurfy. **SPORES** 18-25 × 12-14 μm, ellipsoid, smooth.

HABITAT: Solitary, scattered, or in small groups on ground in rich soil, gardens, orchards, under hardwoods, hedges, lightly burned grassy

Morchella esculenta. Note the rounded cap and irregularly arranged pits. (Bob Short)

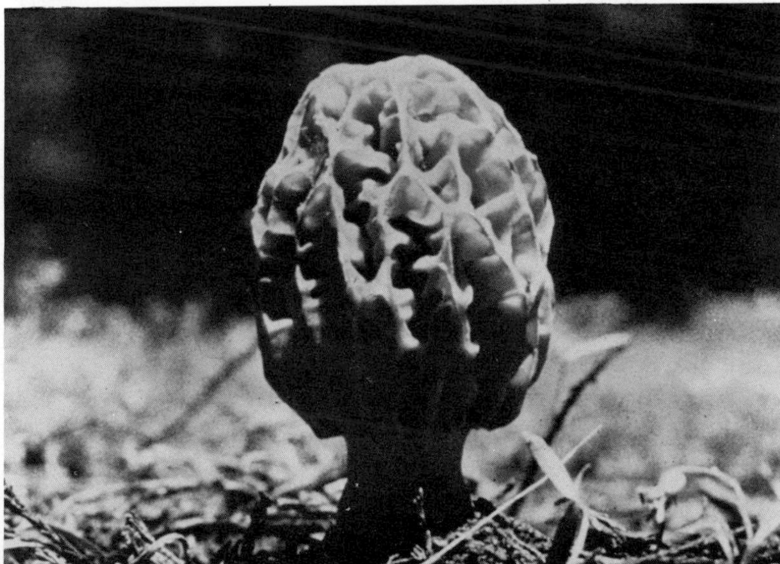

ground, swampy areas, etc. Widely distributed, but not common in California.

EDIBILITY: Edible and unsurpassed. Generally considered, along with *M. crassipes* (see below) to be the best of the morels. Always cook it.

COMMENTS: This fabulous fungus needs no introduction to foragers from eastern North America—the yellow-brown pitted cap is one of the highlights of spring. The ridges are not radially arranged as in *M. conica,* and are not as white as in *M. deliciosa.* Intermediate forms abound, however. A larger version (10-23 cm high) with a distinctly enlarged base has been dubbed *M. crassipes.* It is to be looked for in stream valleys under hardwoods.

Earth Tongues

spores

GEOGLOSSACEAE

Small fungi found on ground or rotten wood. FRUITING BODY upright, *mostly cylindrical to club-shaped or with a fan-shaped, spatula-shaped, tongue-shaped to knobby or wrinkled cap.* STALK smooth or velvety, *slender (usually 6 mm thick or less).* SPORES usually elongated or cylindrical, usually septate. Asci most often 8-spored, not operculate.

THESE attractive little Ascomycetes resemble the unbranched coral fungi (Clavariaceae), but in most cases are differentiated into a fertile "head" lined with asci and a sterile stem. The "head" or cap is often flattened, wrinkled, or twisted, but is never as large as the cap of an elfin saddle or false morel (Helvellaceae). The most common forms, which are black and velvety (*Trichoglossum* and *Geoglossum*), can scarcely be confused with anything else. Microscopically the earth tongues offer several features of interest. The spores are often very long (up to 250 μm!), and usually partitioned **(septate)**. In *Trichoglossum,* the most common earth tongue, there are long brown lance-shaped sterile cells **(setae)** interspersed with the asci.

These are woodland fungi that fruit chiefly in the winter and spring. I can find no instances of poisoning attributed to them, but their small size and tough or slimy texture make them barely palatable. Three species are described here.

Key to the Geoglossaceae

1. Fruiting body black 2
1. Fruiting body not black 3

2. Stalk velvety .... *Trichoglossum hirsutum*, below
2. Stalk not velvety .... *Geoglossum nigritum* (see *Trichoglossum hirsutum*, below)

3. Fruiting body slimy-viscid 4
3. Fruiting body not slimy-viscid 5

4. Stalk white or whitish .... *Leotia viscosa*, p. 617
4. Stalk colored (yellow-orange, orange, buff, etc.) .... *Leotia lubrica* (see *L. viscosa*, p. 617)

5. Fruiting body green or greenish-tinted .... *Microglossum viride* (see *Trichoglossum hirsutum*, below)
5. Not as above 6

6. Fruiting body with a flattened fan-shaped to spatula-shaped cap whose lower margin extends down the stalk on opposite sides .... *Spathularia flavida*, p. 616
6. Not as above 7

7. Fruiting body with a well-defined cap or "head" 8
7. Fruiting body irregular and extremely variable in shape (cylindrical, clublike, lobed, etc.); yellow .... *Mitrula irregularis* (see *Spathularia flavida*, p. 616)

8. Cap typically broader than it is tall .... *Cudonia circinans* (see *Leotia viscosa*, p. 617)
8. Cap typically taller than it is wide .... *Mitrula abietis* (see *Spathularia flavida*, p. 616)

Trichoglossum hirsutum (Common Earth Tongue)

FRUITING BODY 2-8 cm high, cylindrical to club-shaped or tongue-shaped or with a broad, flattened cap or "head" (more or less shaped like the tongue of a bell). **CAP** when distinct usually flattened, oval to arrow-shaped; surface dry, black, sometimes wrinkled. Flesh thin, rather tough. **STALK** slender (2-4 mm thick), more or less equal, black, densely velvety, sometimes twisted or curved. **SPORES** brown under microscope, 80-180 × 5-7 μm, greatly elongated, smooth, 15-septate at maturity. Asci 8-spored, interspersed with long brown setae (sterile cells).

HABITAT: Solitary to scattered or densely gregarious in woods—on ground or rotting wood; common, winter and spring. It was the single most abundant Ascomycete in the soggy 1977-78 season. Like the other

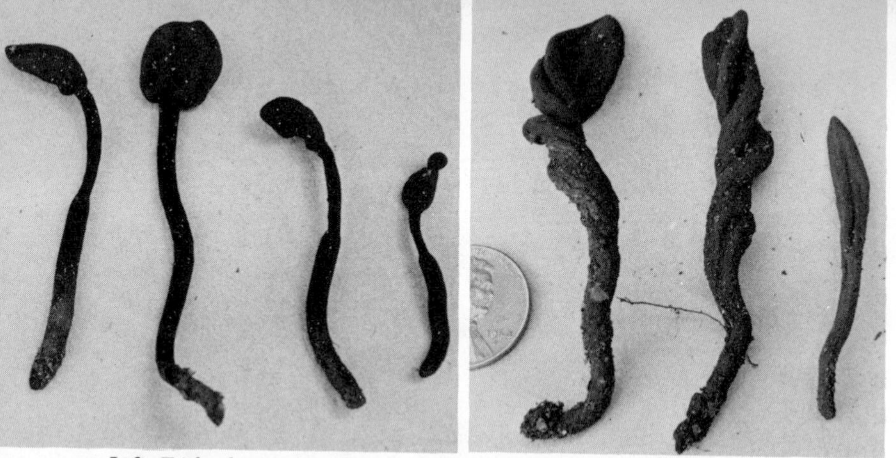

Left: *Trichoglossum hirsutum* is our most common black earth tongue. Note how cap is usually distinct from stem. Surface is velvety to touch. **Right:** *Geoglossum nigritum* (see *Trichoglossum hirsutum*) is also black, but cap is not as distinct and surface isn't velvety.

black fungi with which it often grows *(Craterellus cornucopioides, Plectania melastoma),* it is easily overlooked.

EDIBILITY: Edible but rather tough and flavorless.

COMMENTS: This dainty earth tongue is easily recognized by its black, velvety fruiting body. The fertile portion is usually (but not always) distinct from the stem as a thickened or flattened head. For the meticulous few with a microscope, the following black earth tongues can also be found, though not nearly so often: *Geoglossum nigritum,* not very velvety, with a poorly defined "head," brown spores 30-90 μm long and mostly 7-septate, and paraphyses (clear sterile cells) curved above; *G. glabrum,* similar to *G. nigritum,* but with paraphyses not curved; *G. fallax,* with some spores brown and others clear and 0-13 septate; and *G. glutinosum,* with a viscid fruiting body. All of these lack the brown setae found in *Trichoglossum.* Two greenish earth tongues should also be mentioned: *Microglossum viride,* with a pea-green to dark green fruiting body, and *M. olivaceum,* with an olive to greenish-brown fruiting body.

Spathularia flavida

FRUITING BODY with a cap and stalk. **CAP** up to 3 cm broad and at least as tall, greatly compressed (flattened), more-or less fan-shaped to spatula-shaped, running down the stalk on opposite sides; surface smooth or slightly wrinkled, pallid becoming pale yellow to light brown, not viscid. Flesh thin, pallid. **STALK** up to 5 cm long, hollow, whitish becoming yellow or brownish, sometimes with fluffy white to yellowish mycelium at base; equal or swollen at base; round or somewhat flattened in cross-section. **SPORES** 30-95 × 1.5-3 μm, elongated, smooth, usually multiseptate.

HABITAT: Scattered or in groups or rings on ground under conifers, late fall through spring. I have not seen it south of San Francisco, but it and its relatives (see below) have a wide distribution.

EDIBILITY: Inconsequential.

COMMENTS: The flattened fan-shaped or spatula-like cap and pale yellow to buff color render this curious earth tongue distinct. *S. clavata* is a synonym. *S. spathulata* is a similar species known only from California. It is darker and has smaller spores (18-26 μm long). *Mitrula* species are also somewhat similar but their cap is not as flattened and doesn't run down the stalk on opposite sides. The most common species, *M. abietis,* has a light brown to pinkish-buff cap, brownish stalk, and grows under conifers. *M. paludosa* has a light orange to yellow head and white stalk, and grows on leaves in boggy areas or puddles. *M. (=Spragueola) irregularis* is a spontaneous anomaly with an irregular (clublike, lobed, branched, twisted, etc.) yellow fruiting body. It is likely to be mistaken for a fairy club *(Clavaria)* but produces spores in asci, and can usually be distinguished by the diversity of shape within a single population. It grows gregariously under conifers.

Leotia viscosa

FRUITING BODY with a cap ("head") and stalk. **CAP** 1-3 cm broad, convex to convex-knobby, smooth or slightly wrinkled, margin incurved toward stalk; surface viscid-gelatinous, olive-green to dark green. Underside whitish. Flesh thin, soft. **STALK** 2-8 cm long, 5-10 mm thick, equal or tapering slightly upward, hollow, smooth, viscid, white or occasionally tinted orange, often dotted with minute greenish granules, especially above; round in cross-section. **SPORES** 16-28 × 4-6 μm, elongated, smooth, at least 5-septate at maturity.

HABITAT: Scattered, gregarious, or in small clusters in humus or woody debris. Sometimes common in the winter under oak, tanoak, manzanita, and madrone.

EDIBILITY: Harmless, but slimy.

COMMENTS: This slimy Ascomycete with the green head and whitish stem can hardly be confused with any other. The species pictured in most mushroom books, *L. lubrica,* has an ochraceous to yellow-buff or olive fruiting body in which the stalk is not white. It also occurs chiefly under hardwoods, but in my experience is not as common as *L. viscosa.*

Leotia viscosa. Slimy-viscid fruiting body with a greenish cap is distinctive. "Two-headed" specimen on right is unusual.

Cudonia species resemble *Leotia* but do not have a slimy-viscid fruiting body. The most common type, *C. circinans,* has a creamy to brown cap and brownish stem, while *C. monticola* has a pinkish-cinnamon to pinkish-buff cap. Both grow in groups or clusters, usually under conifers. For other nonviscid earth tongues with a well-defined cap, see *Spathularia flavida.*

Truffles

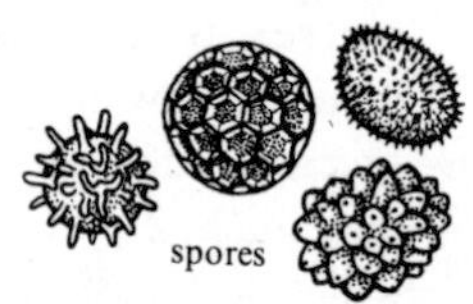

TUBERALES

Small to medium-sized *underground* fungi. FRUITING BODY *more or less round (globose) to irregularly warty, lobed, or bowl-shaped. Interior marbled with canals, veins, or cavities; fleshy or hard at maturity.* Odor often aromatic. STALK *absent.* SPORES usually sculptured (ornamented), sometimes smooth. Asci usually 8-spored, inoperculate.

THESE modified Discomycetes are seldom seen because they grow exclusively underground. They look like strange tubers ("earth nuts") until they are sliced open—at which point they reveal a system of canals, veins, or cavities that is their hallmark. The asci line the edges of the veins or cavities, and the spores are presumably spread with the help of various truffle-loving mammals and insects (many truffles have a powerful odor which enables predators to locate them). The only fungi

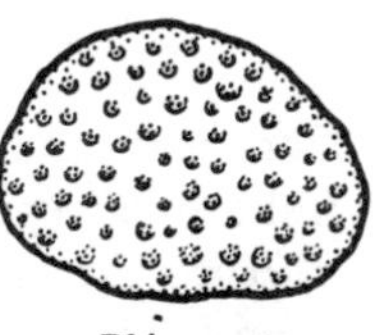

Cross-sections of three truffles, showing channeled or veined interior, and a false truffle (*Rhizopogon*), showing absence of channels or veins.

that remotely resemble truffles are the aptly called false truffles (Hymenogastrales), which bear their spores on basidia and do *not* have a marbled, veined, or channeled interior.

Truffles have been eaten for centuries. Unfortunately, the fabled truffles of France and Italy are now a luxury reserved solely for the rich. Due to their rarity (or the difficulty in finding them), they are sold in tiny tins for as much as $200 a pound! Their flavor and aroma are so strong, however, that a little goes a long way.

Since truffles grow underground, we humans, with our inferior sense of smell, have no means of detecting their presence. Goats have been used to track down truffles in Sardinia and bear cubs have been employed in Russia, but pigs and dogs are the most accomplished "truffle-hounds." Pigs have a natural nose (and appetite) for truffles, and require little or no training. However, they must be physically restrained from devouring their quarry, and are difficult to control even when there are no truffles about. Acorns are sometimes given as nutritional recompense (a pitiful substitute, if you ask me), or the pig is muzzled and pulled away just as it begins to dig up the truffle with its exceptional snout. Another problem with pigs is that they tire easily, and must be carted to and from the truffle grounds if they are distant.

Dogs, on the other hand, are tireless, devoted, and do not devour truffles as greedily. However, they must be trained to seek them out. There are special schools in Italy explicitly for this purpose, and a seasoned truffle hound commands a steep price. Both pigs and dogs can detect truffles from as far away as 50 yards, and there is one case on record of a dog that jumped a hedge, crossed a field, and "secured his prize" under a beech tree, at least 100 yards away!

Truffles are more common in California than anywhere else in North America. Alas, the fabled European species *(Tuber magnatum, T. melanosporum,* and *T. aestivum)* do not seem to occur, though special truffle hounds have been imported from Italy to look for them. Most of our native truffles are too tough or rare to eat. Some are edible, and I am told, quite flavorful, but they do not compare with their expensive

European counterparts. There are more than a dozen genera in California, representing various evolutionary stages of development. *Tuber* is the largest and most common. They are found in the woods from fall through early spring, and usually mature slowly. They favor hardwoods (especially oak), whereas the false truffles (Hymenogastrales) prefer conifers.

The odds against casually encountering a truffle are great—they can be found only by systematically digging through forest humus (a potentially destructive practice), or looking carefully for "truffle signs"—holes made by animals digging for them, or small cracks in the soil caused by those developing near the surface. Occasionally their odor is strong enough for seasoned trufflers to detect.

I have had little firsthand experience with truffles, having come across two paltry specimens in the course of my methodical meanderings; thus a comprehensive treatment is not attempted here. A generic key is included for serious trufflers, but it unavoidably calls for the use of a microscope. One representative *Tuber* is then described. As with the false truffles, unrecognized taxa undoubtedly exist.

Key to the Tuberales

1. Spore mass (interior) powdery at maturity; asci round .... (see *Elaphomyces,* under *Tuber candidum,* p. 621)
1. Interior fleshy or hard at maturity; asci not often round 2

2. Fruiting body hollow or convoluted into projections which separate canals or chambers; asci arranged in a distinct palisade 3
2. Not as above; asci irregularly arranged; interior with canals, cavities, or sterile veins 11

3. Interior cavities empty, at least at maturity 4
3. Interior cavities filled with hyphae 9

4. Paraphyses (sterile cells) in palisade projecting beyond asci and fused to form a secondary layer 5
4. Not as above 6

5. Spores more or less smooth .... *Petchiomyces*
5. Spores sculptured .... *Genea* (see *Tuber candidum,* p. 621)

6. Spores smooth 7
6. Spores sculptured .... *Hydnonytra*

7. Interior cavity simple, closed or with one opening to surface .... *Hydnocystis*
7. Interior cavity partitioned into chambers or canals, or with several openings 8

8. Interior canals converging at one conspicuous opening to surface .... *Barssia*
8. Not as above .... *Geopora* (see *Tuber candidum,* p. 621)

9. Interior cavities converging at apex .... *Pachyphloeus* (see *Tuber candidum,* below)
9. Cavities not converging 10

10. Cavities forming canals opening to surface .... *Choiromyces*
10. Not as above .... *Piersonia*

11. Fruiting body containing empty canals, chambers, or veinlike plates 12
11. Fruiting body divided by sterile veins into "nests" of asci 14

12. Spores smooth .... *Pseudobalsamia* (see *Tuber candidum,* below)
12. Spores sculptured 13

13. Interior usually marbled with dark and light veins (at maturity) .... *Tuber* (see *Tuber candidum,* below)
13. Not as above .... *Hydnobolites* (see *Tuber candidum,* below)

14. Asci 8-spored .... *Terfezia*
14. Asci 1-5-spored .... *Delastria*

Tuber candidum (American Truffle)

FRUITING BODY 1-2.5 cm broad, roughly round (globose), often with one or more furrows, the furrows sometimes uniting in circles to form "eyes." Exterior light brown to reddish-brown, the "eyes" when present often pinkish; smooth or divided into polygonal areas. **INTERIOR** marbled with large whitish veins, fleshy-hard. **SPORES** 28-48 × 22-32 μm, round to ellipsoid-ovoid, often more pointed at one end, spiny.

HABITAT: Solitary or in small groups in woods, buried in soil or humus. Fall through early spring, not common.

EDIBILITY: I can find no information on it.

COMMENTS: This is an extremely variable truffle best recognized by its spiny spores. It is the most common and widespread *Tuber* in North America. Other truffles in California include: *T. citrinum,* pale yellow; *T. argenteum,* silvery-white with a brownish interior marbled with white branching veins; *T. gibbosum,* brownish-buff with whitish veins visible on exterior, and interior brown to brick-red with shining white veins; *T. californicum,* whitish to ochraceous, much lobed, with a pubescent exterior, brown interior marbled with pale veins, and round spores; and *T. separans,* earth-brown with inconspicuous veins. Also found are: *Hydnobolites californicus,* dirty white becoming brownish, irregularly folded, with labyrinthine canals; *Pachyphloeus citrinus,* bright orange to brown, the exterior with low pyramidal polygons;

Pseudobalsamia magnata, orange to reddish-brown, with warty exterior and smooth spores; *Geopora harknessii,* exterior brown and densely hairy; and *Genea arenaria,* brown and coarsely lobed or folded, with a large, irregular internal cavity.

Finally, there is the genus *Elaphomyces*—trufflelike Ascomycetes belonging to an entirely different group, the Plectomycetes. They have a dark powdery marbled interior at maturity, a conspicuously warty exterior, and are sometimes parasitized by the Ascomycete *Cordyceps.*

Flask Fungi

spores

PYRENOMYCETES

Small to medium-sized fungi of various shapes. FRUITING BODY either *arising from insects, insect pupae, or other mushrooms, or fruiting body black or partially black, very tough, and growing on wood. Surface of fruiting body usually minutely pimpled.* SPORES produced in asci borne in perithecia.

THIS motley group of fungi bears asci in flask-shaped nests **(perithecia)** imbedded in the fruiting body. In this respect they differ fundamentally from the Discomycetes (morels, cup fungi, earth tongues, truffles, etc.).

The most common flask fungi *(Xylaria* and *Daldinia)* are black or partially black, very tough or charcoal-like, and grow on wood. A second group, *Cordyceps,* has an erect, clublike fruiting body and is parasitic on insects, insect pupae, and subterranean trufflelike Ascomycetes. A related genus, *Claviceps* (not treated here), is parasitic on plants. LSD was derived from wheat ergot *(Claviceps purpurea).* Finally, there are some very common flask fungi (typified by *Hypomyces*) that parasitize other mushrooms, engulfing the host and turning it into a pimpled or powdery mass of tissue.

With the exception of *Hypomyces lactifluorum,* the flask fungi are unpalatable. They fruit in moist weather, but some have fruiting bodies which persist year-round. Four of the more distinctive species are described here.

Key to the Pyrenomycetes

1. Growing on wood; fruiting body black or black and white 2
1. Not as above 4

2. Fruiting body erect, branched or unbranched 3
2. Fruiting body hemispherical to nearly round or lobed; charcoal-like .... *Daldinia grandis,* p. 624

3. Fruiting body usually branched; upper portion white when young .... *Xylaria hypoxylon*, p. 625
3. Fruiting body usually unbranched; entirely black .... *Xylaria polymorpha* (see *X. hypoxylon*, p. 625)
4. Fruiting body parasitic on insects, insect larvae, or underground trufflelike fungi; erect, unbranched, club-shaped, or with a small "head" .... *Cordyceps militaris*, below
4. Fruiting body parasitic on other mushrooms; not as above 5
5. Parasitic on boletes, reducing them to a bright yellow powdery mass .... *Sepedonium chrysospermum* (see *Hypomyces lactifluorum*, below)
5. Parasitic mostly on gilled mushrooms, covering them with a pimply layer of tissue .... *Hypomyces lactifluorum*, below

Cordyceps militaris

FRUITING BODY erect, cylindrical to club-shaped, 1.5-5 cm tall, minutely pimpled above, reddish-orange to orange, tapered below and arising from an insect pupa or larva. **SPORES** 3-6.5 × 1-1.5 μm, somewhat barrel-shaped (actually the segments of larger spores).

HABITAT: Solitary or in groups of two to five, parasitic on the larvae and pupae (often buried) of moths and butterflies. Fall through spring, rare.

EDIBILITY: Unknown.

COMMENTS: The simple, unbranched fruiting body of this fascinating fungus is reminiscent of the fairy clubs (Clavariaceae), but its habit of parasitizing immature insects is unique (see sketch at bottom of p. 55). *Cordyceps* has a number of parasitic species but none are common. Several grow on the subterranean trufflelike Ascomycetes *Elaphomyces*, including *C. capitata*, brown to olive-black with an abruptly enlarged fertile "head," and *C. ophioglossoides*, reddish-brown to olive-brown, club-shaped with a poorly defined "head."

Hypomyces lactifluorum

FRUITING BODY growing on and eventually engulfing the gills, stalk, and cap of a gilled mushroom, forming a more or less inverted pyramid structure; surface bright orange to yellow-orange or orange-red, pimply. Flesh (of the host) crisp, white. **SPORES** 30-40 × 6-8 μm, spindle-shaped or shaped like caraway seeds, roughened.

A *Russula* parasitized by *Hypomyces lactifluorum*. Entire fruiting body is covered with a minutely pimpled layer of tissue. Note how gills are reduced to mere ridges. (Herb Saylor)

HABITAT: Solitary to gregarious in woods, on fruiting bodies of *Russula* and *Lactarius*. Widespread and common in some regions, but rare in our area. Related species, however, are quite common.

EDIBILITY: Eaten by many people and sold at markets in Mexico. There is no absolute assurance that the host species is edible, but I haven't heard of any poisonings from it. Material I sampled was of fair quality.

COMMENTS: The genus *Hypomyces* is parasitic on mushrooms, and is easily recognized by the pimpled surface and manner in which it reduces the gills on the host to blunt ridges or engulfs them completely. The pimpled appearance is caused by numerous perithecia. Apparently the mycelium infects the host at a very early stage. The bright orange color of *H. lactifluorum* (reminiscent of the chanterelle, *Cantharellus cibarius*) makes it the most spectacular member of its clan. *H. luteovirens* is a greenish species also found on *Russula* and *Lactarius*. *Sepedonium chrysospermum* is a very common parasite on boletes, eventually reducing them to a bright yellow powdery mass of asexual spores.

Daldinia grandis (Crampball)

FRUITING BODY hemispherical to nearly round or somewhat irregular, 1-5 cm broad; surface black, roughened by minute pores or pimples. Flesh concentrically zoned in cross-section, grayish to black, somewhat silky-looking, carbonaceous. **SPORES** 11-17 × 6-9 μm, lance-shaped, smooth, dark brown to black.

HABITAT: Gregarious or in rows on rotting hardwood logs and branches, especially oak. Abundant year-round.

Left: *Daldinia grandis.* Black charcoal-like growths are very common on dead hardwoods. **Right:** *Xylaria hypoxylon* is also common on wood. Fruiting bodies may be branched like these or simple (unbranched). They are white above and black below.

EDIBILITY: Unequivocally inedible; perhaps useful as tinder.

COMMENTS: The charcoal-like fruiting bodies of this fungus can be found on almost any walk through the woods. Its common name is attributed to the old folk belief that carrying one around under your armpit cures cramps. The pimpled surface of mature specimens is caused by the openings of the perithecia (flasks). Since the fruiting body persists year-round, it does not always contain spores. Like *Xylaria,* it is sometimes coated with conidia (asexual spores). No other fungus remotely resembles it.

Xylaria hypoxylon (Candlesnuff Fungus)

FRUITING BODY 2-6 cm high, erect, slender, usually antlerlike (forked or branched at tip), sometimes unbranched (cylindrical). Upper portion or tips at first white and powdery, eventually black and minutely roughened; lower portion (stalk) hairy or velvety, black. Flesh tough, pallid. **SPORES** 10-14 $\times$ 4-6 μm, elongated, bean-shaped, smooth, black.

HABITAT: Gregarious on rotting logs, stumps, etc. (occasionally appearing terrestrial). Found practically year-round, but fruiting mostly in the fall and winter. Common and widely distributed.

EDIBILITY: Too tough to be of value.

COMMENTS: The candlesnuff fungus is easily recognized by its black and white antlerlike fruiting body. The powdered appearance of young specimens is caused by masses of asexual spores (conidia), which form directly on hyphae instead of in asci. Like *Daldinia,* mature fruiting bodies are roughened by the presence of pores through which the perithecia open. *Xylosphaera hypoxylon* is a synonym. *X. polymorpha* ("Dead Man's Fingers") is a large (4-8 cm tall), black, irregularly fingerlike species that grows in clusters on rotting wood. It is rarely branched and does not have white tips. I have yet to find it in our area.

MUSHROOM COOKERY

The abundance boneless
Without husk or scale or thorn,
Granting us a festival of all-embracing freshness

Pablo Neruda's tribute to the tomato is also a tribute to immediacy and vitality, that incomparable freshness that distinguishes a homegrown tomato or cucumber (or wild mushroom) from its flavorless, mass-produced counterpart. The challenge in cooking wild mushrooms is to maximize their freshness and earthy essence, while highlighting their individuality. After all, they are not one vegetable, but many, a pleasant surprise to people who are conditioned to mushrooms smelling and tasting "mushroomy." The major constraint is that you must make do with what you have. Obviously, you can't cook boletus broth when you have a basketful of blewitts, but you *can* make blewitt burgers, or blewitt biscuits, or a three-bean blewitt salad.

The most important thing to remember is that you can't expect wild mushrooms to be special unless you take the time to make them special. They are ephemeral, temperamental, delicate. It is a relatively simple task to render even the most marvelous mushroom tasteless. Likewise, many "mediocre" mushrooms are delightful when cooked with care and imagination. If you make a concerted effort to seek out, gather, identify, and eat wild mushrooms, it only makes sense to do them justice in the kitchen. Don't just throw them into the pot with a bunch of other vegetables—unless, of course, you want them to taste like a bunch of other vegetables. Different mushrooms call for different treatment—only then will they respond with their full measure of flavor.

With each type you will go through a period of discovery and experimentation—succulent successes and forgettable failures—followed by a process of adjustment and subtle refinement. Each mushroom will gradually acquire its own culinary identity, and cease to be a mushroom except in the botanical sense that broccoli is a plant. After all, when you're having broccoli, you don't say, "We're having steamed plants for dinner." Similarly, it will no longer be "mushrooms" for dinner, but "chanterelles," or "poor people's truffle," or in the case of the commercial mushroom, *"Agaricus bisporus"* (to be pronounced with a subtle insinuation of distaste).

Strive for a marriage (but not a compromise!) between elegance and simplicity. Successful mushroom cookery doesn't require exotic foods, or a bottomless bank account, or idle afternoons, or a degree in

"What was desire in the hills becomes fulfillment in the kitchen."—Angelo Pellegrini. At left is fresh *Agaricus campestris*. At right, a delicious cream sauce with white onions and sliced *A. campestris*.

gastronomical mechanics. It *does* require patience, sensitivity, enthusiasm, and imagination. There are no rigorous rules, but some basic do's and don'ts are outlined here.

HELPFUL HINTS

1. *Don't* eat a mushroom unless you're absolutely sure it's edible.
2. You wouldn't eat a rotten egg, so *don't* eat a rotten mushroom. Food poisoning is a frequent cause of so-called "mushroom poisoning."
3. You wouldn't eat five pounds of asparagus, so *don't* eat five pounds of mushrooms. Overindulgence is another common cause of so-called "mushroom poisoning," particularly for those who don't eat mushrooms regularly. On the other hand, don't be unnecessarily stingy—most wild mushrooms cook down more than the commercial variety, so use them generously.
4. When trying a species for the first time, eat only a small amount. Then wait for a few hours to see if you have an adverse reaction. Just as some people are allergic to eggs or chocolate or strawberries, so some people are adversely affected by certain kinds of mushrooms. Species to which many people are "allergic" (such as *Lepiota naucina*) should *not* be served to large groups.
5. If you do have an "allergy," you'll want to pinpoint the culprit, so *don't* mix two or more species together unless you've eaten them before.

6. As a rule, maggot-riddled mushrooms *should not* be eaten, especially when uninfested specimens are available. However, in the case of certain choice species (like *Agaricus augustus*), you may wish to remove the maggots with a knife (if there are only a few), or even leave them in (they're just a little extra protein). Use your own judgment on this matter.
7. Use as little water as possible when cleaning mushrooms. They absorb it so readily that it dilutes their flavor and causes them to cook up slimy. If you wash them, drain them on a paper towel before cooking. The best place to clean mushrooms *is in the field,* providing you're already familiar with them. Trim away all dirt with a knife or toothbrush, and don't mix dirty specimens with clean ones. Also remove maggots so they don't spread.
8. Use mushrooms as soon as possible after picking them. Prolonged refrigeration deprives all vegetables (including mushrooms) of their freshness and flavor. *Coprinus* species should be eaten the day they're picked. There's an old saying to the effect that you should boil the water before husking the corn. Well, it's not a bad idea to melt the butter before picking the shaggy manes!
9. During periods of heavy rainfall, most mushrooms will be waterlogged. These are apt to be insipid, but can be sliced and dried for later use (thereby concentrating their flavor).
10. *Never* steam or pressure-cook mushrooms. The object is to get rid of excess moisture, not add to it. Pressure-cooked mushrooms bear an uncanny resemblance to slugs.
11. *Don't* drown mushrooms with spices, butter, salt, garlic, or olive oil. All of these complement mushrooms nicely when used in moderation. Mushrooms and onions, for instance, are practically made for each other, but the mushrooms must always dominate (in quantity) because their flavor is more delicate.
12. If you don't like a "choice" mushroom, give it a second and third chance—after all, a lot depends on how you cook it and in what condition it was found. No one agrees on which ones are best, but a species does not acquire a widespread reputation unless it has something special to offer. On the other hand, some relatively unknown mushrooms (such as *Chroogomphus*) are quite good. Improvise!

PRESERVING MUSHROOMS FOR CONSUMPTION

Most mushrooms have erratic fruiting habits—they fruit in large numbers for one or two weeks, then are practically absent the rest of the year. To take advantage of their fleeting abundance, you have to harvest them while you can and then preserve them for later use.

Dried mushrooms make a marvelous addition to sauces, soups, and gravies. They should be stored in airtight jars to protect them from insects. This array of dehydrated delicacies includes *Agaricus, Boletus, Chroogomphus, Craterellus, Lepista,* and *Marasmius.*

DRYING

Drying is the easiest and most satisfactory method of preservation. Fleshy types like *Boletus* must be cut in thin slices; smaller species like *Marasmius* can be dried whole. *Don't* use an oven. Circulation is more important than heat—you want moisture to be carried away. Spread them out on screens using a light bulb or hot plate as a source (it's usually too wet to sun-dry them). Or string them up on thread and hang them in a warm, dry place. Remove all maggots before drying mushrooms, and brush away (but *don't* wash) dirt. If necessary, they can be cleaned before use by placing them in a strainer and scalding them with water.

When thoroughly dried (brittle), store them in an airtight jar to protect them from insects and mold. They will keep for months (or even years) in this state. They can also be pulverized or powdered and used as condiment. Certain mushrooms, such as *Cantharellus* and *Laetiporus,* do *not* dry well (they become too tough and leathery). Others, like *Marasmius, Boletus, Leccinum, Craterellus, Chroogomphus,* and *Agaricus,* are excellent.

There are several methods for reconstituting dried mushrooms, depending on the type of mushroom and kind of dish. They can be crumbled directly into soups or sauces, but should be soaked first if they're to be put in drier foods. An excellent method is to place dried pieces between wet paper towels overnight. This allows them to absorb moisture gradually while retaining their flavor.

CANNING

Canned mushrooms retain their flavor well, but canning is a big undertaking, and is only worthwhile if you have an enormous amount of mushrooms. A pressure canner, mason jars, and lids are required. Wash the mushrooms thoroughly and let them cook in their own juices for a while. Then pack them in sterilized pint jars, cover with boiling water, seal, and process at 10-15 pounds pressure for 30 minutes. A little ascorbic acid (vitamin C) can be added to retain color. They will keep for years like this, but failure to observe sterile procedures may result in botulism. *Dentinum, Cantharellus, Tricholoma, Boletus, Agaricus* buttons, and *Hericium* can well.

PICKLING

Pickling is just marinating on a larger and more elaborate scale. In Europe mushrooms are often preserved under oil and vinegar. It is a fairly simple procedure, but obviously, the mushroom flavor is masked. Jars should be sterilized, but pressure cooking isn't necessary. I have successfully pickled *Cantharellus, Lepista nuda,* and *Amanita calyptroderma.*

FREEZING

Mushrooms retain their flavor for a month or so when sauteed and frozen. Mushroom sauces and stock can also be frozen for later use. This method works with practically any mushroom (store in an airtight container). Don't freeze mushrooms raw—they will decompose as soon as they thaw.

MUSHROOM TOXINS

MOST CASES of "mushroom poisoning" are the result of allergies* (idiosyncratic reactions or hypersensitivity), overindulgence (especially of raw mushrooms), or food poisoning (ingestion of rotten mushrooms). All three usually result in nausea, vomiting, and/or diarrhea. Another common type of "mushroom poisoning" is imaginary—people who have lingering doubts about the safety of their meal are likely to experience discomfort whether there is a physiological basis for it or not. All the more reason not to eat a mushroom unless you're absolutely certain it's edible!

The two most common causes of mushroom poisoning are carelessness and ignorance. Despite what people say, mushroom experts do not die from mushroom poisoning. But of course, it is much more sensational for newspapers to say they do. Relatively few species are poisonous but some of the most dangerous ones are exceedingly common, and almost any poisonous mushroom can be fatal to a small child. Therefore it is useful to learn about the different kinds of mushroom poisoning, should you or a friend experience discomfort. Following is a brief rundown of the major groups of mushroom toxins. "Mushroom toxin" as defined here is a compound which produces an abnormal effect on the human body. This definition encompasses mind-altering drugs such as psilocybin, whether they are ingested deliberately or not.

* In this book the term "allergy" is used loosely to describe an adverse reaction to a normally harmless mushroom even though it may not be a genuine hypersensitivity.

As with any kind of poisoning, the two most important things to do are to seek immediate medical attention and identify the agent responsible. Idiosyncratic reactions to edible mushrooms are generally not serious enough to warrant a trip to the hospital, but if there is any doubt, consult a physician.

AMANITA-TOXINS

Mushrooms: *Amanita phalloides, A. ocreata, A. verna, A. virosa, A. bisporigera; Galerina autumnalis, G. marginata, G. venenata; Conocybe filaris;* and several small *Lepiota* species.

Poisoning by amanita-toxins is extremely serious, with a fatality rate of at least 50%. It is doubly dangerous because the symptoms are delayed—not appearing for from 6-24 hours after ingestion of the mushroom, by which time the toxins have been absorbed by the body.

There are several groups of amanita-toxins, at least in the Amanitas. Phallolysin was the first toxin discovered. It destroys red blood cells when injected into rats and has a very high mortality rate. However, it is unstable and apparently destroyed by cooking and/or the human digestive tract. A group of complex cyclic polypeptides called phallotoxins comprise the second group. They are also fatal when injected intravenously (they attack the liver), but are apparently destroyed by the digestive tract. It is another group of polypeptides, the amanitins, that are the culprits. They are twenty times more lethal than the phallotoxins. Their concentration varies tremendously from individual mushroom to individual mushroom, but an average fatal dosage is about 2 ounces (fresh weight) of *Amanita phalloides.*

All mushroom-induced fatalities in California in recent years have been caused by *Amanita phalloides* (and possibly *A. ocreata*). Both are large, handsome, tempting mushrooms, whereas the other deadly types (such as *Galerina*) are small, nondescript, and much less likely to be eaten. Of course, there is no excuse for eating *any* of these mushrooms if you take the time to learn about them.

Symptoms and Treatment

Amanitin poisoning usually manifests itself in four stages: (1) a latency period of 6-24 hours after ingestion, during which time the toxins are actively working on the liver and kidneys, but the victim experiences no discomfort; (2) a period of about one day characterized by violent vomiting, bloody diarrhea, and severe abdominal cramps; (3) a period of about one day during which the victim appears to be recovering (if hospitalized, the patient is sometimes released!); (4) a relapse, during which liver and kidney failure often leads to death. There is sometimes more than one remission or relapse.

Though their effects are centered on the liver and kidneys, amanitins damage tissue throughout the body by inhibiting RNA synthesis in cells. To make matters worse, the kidneys are apparently unable to eliminate amanitins from the body. The pancreas, adrenal glands, heart, lungs, muscles, intestines, and brain may be adversely affected, not only by the amanitins themselves, but indirectly because of liver and kidney failure. It is a slow and painful way to die.

There is no known antidote to amanitin-poisoning, but thioctic acid has met with some success when used promptly. Treatment is largely supportive and symptomatic—maintaining blood sugar and salts, eliminating urea by dialysis, etc. If you have any reason to suspect someone has eaten a deadly *Amanita* (or amanitin-containing mushroom), *don't wait for the symptoms to appear!* If the person is taken to the hospital soon after ingesting the mushrooms, at least some of the toxins can be removed.

GYROMITRIN

Mushrooms: Several *Gyromitra* and *Helvella* species, particularly *Gyromitra esculenta.*

Gyromitrin's product of hydrolysis, monomethylhydrazine (MMH), is a very toxic carcinogenic compound used in the manufacture of rocket fuel. Gyromitrin poisoning has puzzled scientists for many years because of the very narrow threshold between complete absence of discomfort and severe poisoning or even death. This is due to the volatile nature of gyromitrin, which is removed by the process of cooking or drying *providing it has a chance to escape.* Gyromitras cooked in a closed pan can cause severe poisoning, and inhalation of the vapors is dangerous. Raw Gyromitras, of course, pose the greatest threat.

The picture is complicated by significant differences in the toxicity of different geographical strains. For instance, *Gyromitra esculenta* in Europe has caused numerous fatalities (second only to the deadly Amanitas), while in California it appears to be much less toxic.

Symptoms and Treatment

The symptoms, which appear 2-24 hours after ingestion, include headaches, abdominal distress, cramps, severe diarrhea, and vomiting. In severe cases the liver, kidney, and red blood cells are damaged (much as in poisoning by Amanita toxins), which may result in death. Treatment is largely supportive; a physician should be consulted.

MUSCARINE

Mushrooms: *Inocybe* species, *Clitocybe dealbata, Clitocybe rivulosa, Omphalotus* species, and certain red-pored *Boletus* species.

Muscarine was originally isolated in *Amanita muscaria,* but occurs in that mushroom in extremely minute concentrations. However, many Inocybes contain large amounts of muscarine—enough so that they sometimes cause fatalities.

Symptoms and Treatment

The effects, which manifest themselves 15-30 minutes after ingestion, are primarily on the parasympathetic (involuntary) nervous system. They include excessive salivation, perspiration, tears, and lactation (in pregnant women), followed by severe vomiting and diarrhea. These may be accompanied by visual disturbances, irregular pulse rate, decreased blood pressure, and difficulty in breathing. The victim normally recovers within 24 hours, but in severe cases death may result from respiratory failure. Atropine is a specific antidote, but must be administered by a physician.

IBOTENIC ACID/MUSCIMOL

Mushrooms: *Amanita muscaria, Amanita pantherina*

There are many contradictions in the literature regarding the principal toxins of *Amanita muscaria* and *A. pantherina.* Muscarine was originally believed to be the toxin, and then bufotenine was put forth as a candidate. It turns out, however, that the active principal is ibotenic acid, which is converted by the human body into muscimol, a more powerful form that passes out through the urine.

Amanita muscaria is apparently one of the oldest intoxicants known. Its use by certain Siberian tribes has been extensively documented and R. Gordon Wasson, in his book *SOMA: The Divine Mushroom of Immortality,* makes a convincing case for it being the mystical Soma plant of the RgVedas (sacred Hindu texts). It may have been used throughout Eurasia in ancient times, but if so, its use has been successfully suppressed. Curiously, many Europeans fear *A. muscaria* more than its deadly cousin, *A. phalloides.* John Allegro's attempt to link it to the origins of Christianity *(The Sacred Mushroom and the Cross)* is far-fetched and abstruse.

Amanita muscaria is erroneously listed in older books as deadly poisonous. It can be fatal in large doses, but so can practically any poisonous mushroom. According to most sources, *A. pantherina* is somewhat more dangerous. Deliberate ingestion of these mushrooms has increased in this country now that it has been shown they are not as dangerous as once believed. However, their effects vary greatly from person to person. As each person's body chemistry is different and the concentrations of the toxins in each mushroom are different, there is no way of predicting what one's reaction will be. Some people experience extreme discomfort, others have vivid dreams, still others experience no effects whatsoever. Their use is definitely *not* recommended here. Not all of the toxins have been identified as yet. For instance, neither pure ibotenic acid nor muscimol produce the nausea and vomiting frequently experienced by *A. muscaria*-users.

Symptoms and Treatment

Symptoms normally appear 30 minutes to 2 hours after ingestion, and last for several hours. Nausea and vomiting are common, but the principal effects are on the central nervous system: confusion, mild euphoria, loss of muscular coordination, profuse sweating, chills, visual distortions, a feeling of greater strength, and sometimes hallucinations, delusions, or convulsions. (An inordinate number of "trippers" seem to think they are Jesus Christ.) Drowsiness is also a common phenomenon—in fact, the person frequently falls asleep ("swoons")—to awaken hours later with little or no memory of his or her experiences. There is no "hangover" effect as with alcohol, but most people who try it (including myself) do not wish to repeat the experience. Since muscimol passes out through the urine, Siberian users "recycled" their *A. muscaria* by drinking their own urine. I know of no one in California who has tested this approach.

Treatment is largely supportive—reassuring the victim that the effects are temporary. In the mistaken belief that muscarine was the principal toxin, older texts prescribe atropine as an antidote. Atropine, however, is likely to exacerbate the effects of ibotenic acid/muscimol.

PSILOCYBIN/PSILOCIN

Mushrooms: *Psilocybe baeocystis, P. cubensis, P. semilanceata,* and many others; also certain *Panaeolus* and *Conocybe* species.

These indole derivatives are well known for their psychedelic properties, and "psilocybin mushrooms" are often consumed for recreational purposes. Several hallucinogenic mushrooms played an important role in the religious and medicinal rites of Native Americans in Mexico and Central America. But the Spaniards suppressed their use to such an extent that their existence was seriously doubted by early 20th century botanists. They were "rediscovered" in Oaxaca in the 1930s, and 20 years later they were identified as belonging principally to the genus *Psilocybe.* Since then their properties have been so publicized that Oaxaca has been inundated by pleasure-seeking gringos. It has subsequently been discovered that many psilocybin-containing mushrooms grow in this country as well.

Psilocin (a dephosphorylated version of psilocybin) is about ten times as active as psilocybin. Most psilocybin-containing mushrooms contain only traces of psilocin, but the human body converts psilocybin into psilocin. A blueing reaction associated with the presence of psilocybin and psilocin is caused by an enzyme that oxidizes psilocin. However, not all mushrooms that stain blue contain psilocybin or psilocin, and not all "psilocybin mushrooms" stain blue.

Symptoms and Treatment

Symptoms are similar to those of LSD. Shortly after ingestion, and for a duration of several hours, the "victim" experiences heightened color perception, visual distortions, rapidly shifting shapes and images, a "kaleidoscope effect" with eyes closed, elation or hilarity, and hallucinations or delusions. Nausea and vomiting are rare. Some people report the sensation of leaving their bodies, or of traveling into the future or past, or other highly subjective experiences. Others experience profound anxiety.

In case of accidental ingestion or a "bad trip," the person should be repeatedly assured that the effects are temporary. A factor to bear in mind is that transferring the person to an unfamiliar environment can be frightening, and that sedatives may worsen the effects, especially if administered forcibly. LSD, incidentally, was derived from another fungus, the wheat ergot, *Claviceps purpurea.*

GASTROINTESTINAL IRRITANTS

Mushrooms: Many, including: *Agaricus "californicus," A. hondensis, A. meleagris, A. xanthodermus; Boletus satanas, B. erythropus, B. pulcherrimus; Entoloma rhodopolium, E. lividum,* and relatives; *Gomphus floccosus; Hebeloma* species; many acrid *Lactarius* species; *Laetiporus sulphureus* and *Lepiota naucina* (sometimes); *Naematoloma fasciculare; Omphalotus olivascens; Ramaria formosa* and relatives; many acrid *Russula* species; and several *Tricholoma* species (particularly *T. pardinum* and *T. pessundatum*).

As evidenced by the list, this is by far the most prevalent group of mushroom toxins. Very few of the principles have been identified chemically because they are rarely fatal. The most frequent culprits in gastrointestinal poisoning are the phenol-smelling *Agaricus* species, undoubtedly because of their resemblance to edible types. The most dangerous are *Entoloma* species (see *E. rhodopolium*), *Hebeloma* species (see *H. crustuliniforme*), *Tricholoma pardinum, Boletus satanas* (raw), and *Naematoloma fasciculare.* Allergic reactions to edible mushrooms normally take the form of gastrointestinal upset.

Symptoms and Treatment

Symptoms usually appear shortly after ingestion (20 minutes-4 hours). They include nausea, vomiting, cramps, and diarrhea, which pass after the irritant is expelled. Severe cases, however, may require hospitalization. Treatment is largely supportive—aiding the body in trying to eliminate that which it is not equipped to handle. Though not as serious as other types of mushroom poisoning, gastrointestinal upsets are not to be taken lightly—as evidenced by the fact that many people acquire a lingering distaste for mushrooms after an all-night bout with nausea and diarrhea.

MISCELLANEOUS TOXINS

Coprinus atramentarius contains a disulfram-like compound (coprine) that reacts with alcohol in the body to produce a peculiar but transitory set of symptoms: reddening of the ears and nose, a metallic taste in the mouth, lightheadedness, rapid heart beat, throbbing sensation, and sometimes nausea and vomiting. Recovery is normally spontaneous and complete. The alcohol needn't be consumed simultaneously with the mushrooms to produce a reaction—therefore anyone who indulges regularly in alcohol should not eat *Coprinus atramentarius.* Individual reactions vary greatly, suggesting that some people may be more sensitive or the mushrooms themselves may vary in coprine content. It has also been suggested that raw *Coprinus atramentarius* does not actually contain coprine, but that it is formed in the process of cooking.

Paxillus involutus is said to be toxic raw but is eaten by many people (especially Europeans) after being pickled or parboiled. However, the human body apparently develops a sensitivity to it—manufacturing antibodies that destroy red blood cells. Thus, someone who has eaten it for years may suddenly be poisoned.

Cortinarius orellanus and some close relatives have a mortality rate of about 15%. They contain toxins which, like the amanita-toxins, attack the liver and kidneys. Symptoms do not appear for up to three weeks after ingestion of the mushrooms—which makes diagnosis and treatment much more difficult. There are unconfirmed reports of this mushroom from the West Coast, so all dry-capped *Cortinarius* species are best avoided.

Naematoloma fasciculare, a common wood-loving species, can also cause liver and kidney damage. Fortunately, it is rarely eaten because of its bitter taste. An east coast strain of *Gymnopilus spectabilis* (perhaps a distinct species) is said to be hallucinogenic. The active principle, however, has not been identified.

Last but not least, there's the danger of contamination by pesticides and other environmental poisons. Always be aware of this possibility, especially when picking mushrooms in towns, along roads, and in forests or range land where herbicides like 2,4-D have been used.

A mature clump of *Gymnopilus spectabilis* growing from a buried pine stump.

SUGGESTED READINGS AND REFERENCES

Atkins, F.C. 1966. *Mushroom Growing Today.* New York: MacMillan. How to grow *Agaricus bisporus* on a large-scale basis.

Duffy, Thomas, and Paul Vergeer. 1977. *California Toxic Fungi.* San Francisco Mycological Society. A modest 30-page handbook on poisonous mushrooms.

Grigson, Jane. 1975. *The Mushroom Feast.* New York: Alfred Knopf. An excellent mushroom cookbook with a continental slant.

Harris, Bob. 1976. *Growing Wild Mushrooms.* Berkeley: Wingbow Press. Tells how to grow edible and hallucinogenic mushrooms.

Hesler, L.R., and Alexander H. Smith. 1963. *North American Species of Hygrophorus.* Knoxville: University of Tennessee Press. One of the few monographs that can be used by amateurs.

Lange, Morton, and F. B. Hora. 1963. *Collins Guide to Mushrooms and Toadstools.* London: Collins. Well-illustrated handbook.

Largent, David, and others. 1977. *How to Identify Mushrooms to Genus.* Eureka: Mad River Press. Designed primarily for serious mushroom students. Two volumes deal with macroscopic characteristics, two with microscopic features.

Lincoff, Gary, and D. H. Mitchell. 1977. *Toxic and Hallucinogenic Mushroom Poisoning.* New York: Van Nostrand Reinhold. A handbook for physicians and mushroom hunters.

McIlvaine, Charles, and Robert K. MacAdam. Reprinted 1973. *One Thousand American Fungi.* New York: Dover Books. Originally published in 1900, this tome isn't much help in identification, but anything by the mad mycophagist McIlvaine is of interest to toadstool-testers.

Miller, Orson K. 1972. *Mushrooms of North America.* New York: Chanticleer Press. Beautiful color pictures; a bargain in paperback.

Oss, O.T., and O.N. Oeric. 1976. *Psilocybin: Magic Mushroom Growers Guide.* Berkeley: And/Or Press. Outlines techniques for raising *Psilocybe (Stropharia) cubensis.*

Ott, Jonathan, and Jeremy Bigwood. 1978. *Teonanácatl: Hallucinogenic Mushrooms of North America.* Seattle: Madrona. 1978. Extracts from the Second International Conference on Hallucinogenic Mushrooms, October 27-30, 1977.

Overholts, Lee O. 1967. *The Polyporaceae of the United States, Alaska, and Canada.* Ann Arbor: University of Michigan Press. A useful monograph on polypores and bracket fungi.

Peterson, Ronald (editor). 1971. *Evolution in the Higher Basidiomycetes: An International Symposium.* Knoxville: University of Tennessee Press. A collection of papers by leading mycologists.

Puget Sound Mycological Society. 1973. *Oft Told Mushroom Recipes.* Seattle: Pacific Search. Recipes for wild mushrooms with an Oriental slant.

Ramsbottom, John. 1953. *Mushrooms and Toadstools.* London: Collins. A fascinating introduction to mushrooms, with a good deal of history and folklore thrown in.

Rice, Miriam. 1974. *Let's Try Mushrooms for Color.* Santa Rosa, CA: Thresh Publications. How to dye yarn with mushrooms—an interesting little book.

Rinaldi, Augusto, and Vassili Tyndalo. 1974. *The Complete Book of Mushrooms.* New York: Crown Publishers. Despite the pretentious title, this is a lavishly illustrated, comprehensive, and informative book.

Savonius, Moira. 1973. *All Color Book of Mushrooms and Fungi.* London: Octopus Books. One of several inexpensive color picture books printed in Europe. Useful in conjunction with a field guide.

Singer, Rolf. 1975. *The Agaricales in Modern Taxonomy,* 3rd edition. Weinheim, Germany: J. Cramer. A standard reference work.

Smith, Alexander H. Reprinted 1973. *Mushrooms in their Natural Habitats.* New York: Hafner Press. Original edition of this classic comes with a set of 33 stereo-viewer reels. Text includes excellent chapter on microscope technique.

Smith, Helen V., and Alexander Smith. 1973. *How to Know the Non-Gilled Fleshy Fungi.* Dubuque, Iowa: William Brown. Keys to common boletes, polypores, teeth fungi, puffballs, etc.

Stamets, Paul. 1978. *Psilocybe Mushrooms and Their Allies.* Seattle: Homestead Book Company. A detailed, well-illustrated handbook.

Stevens, Russell B. 1974. *Mycology Guidebook.* Seattle: University of Washington Press. Published by the Mycological Society of America—a must for aspiring mycologists.

Thiers, Harry D. 1975. *California Mushrooms: A Field Guide to the Boletes.* New York: Hafner. Despite misleading title, a scholarly and useful book on the boletes. Illustrated with microfiche.

Wasson, R. Gordon. 1968. *SOMA: The Divine Mushroom of Immortality.* New York: Harcourt Brace Jovanovich. All you ever wanted to know about *Amanita muscaria.*

Wasson, Valentina P., and Gordon Wasson. 1957. *Mushrooms, Russia, and History.* 2 vols. New York: Pantheon Books. A classic ethnobotanical text, but difficult to get a copy.

Webster, J. 1977. *Introduction to the Fungi.* Cambridge, England: University of Cambridge Press. A good beginning for those interested in learning about the biology and ecology of fungi.

GLOSSARY

acrid taste burning or peppery
acute pointed or sharp
adnate gills attached broadly to stalk (p. 19)
adnexed gills attached narrowly to stalk (p. 19)
agaric a mushroom with gills
amyloid staining blue, gray, or black in iodine solution (Melzer's reagent)
anastomosing gills connected by cross-veins
angular spores 4- to 6-sided, with sharp corners or angles
annulus ring formed by the veil
apex top
apical at or near the top
apical pore in certain puffballs, the mouth at the top of the spore sac through which spores are released; in spores, a germ pore
apiculate furnished with an apiculus
apiculus short projection on either end of a spore
apothecium the fruiting body of many Ascomycetes in which the asci are arranged in a hymenium
appendiculate cap margin hung or adorned with veil remnants
appressed flattened down or pressed against
areolate cap cracked into small plaques or blocks
ascocarp fruiting body of an Ascomycete
ascus (pl., **asci**) saclike cell in which spores of Ascomycetes are formed (p. 4)

basal at or near the base
basidiocarp fruiting body of a Basidiomycete
basidium (pl., **basidia**) a cell, usually club-shaped, on which spores of Basidiomycetes form (p. 4)
bolete a fleshy mushroom with tubes on underside of cap
boletivore one who eats boletes
brown rot carbonizing decay
buff general color term, usually a pale tan to pale yellow, toned with gray
bulbous stalk with an enlarged base (p. 19)
button a young fruiting body before it has opened up
butt rot a rot confined to the base or roots of a tree

cap the caplike part of the fruiting body which supports the spore-producing surface
capillitium modified, threadlike often branched hyphae enmeshed in the spore mass of most puffballs
carbonizing decay a cellulose-decomposing decay
cartilaginous stalk not fleshy; thin and hollow, tough or fragile
cellular cap cuticle composed of round or pear-shaped cells (p. 22)
cellulose a compound composed of glucose units—it is a major constituent of wood and of plants' cell walls
cespitose (caespitose) tufted or clustered
circumscissile volva that breaks around the circumference of the cap to form a collar or free rim at base of stalk (p. 226)
clamp connection a small bump, loop, or swollen area formed at the cross wall between hyphae in the process of cell division
clamps mycological jargon for clamp connections
class a grouping of related orders
clavate club-shaped
club-shaped stalk thickened noticeably toward base; basidia thickened toward spore-bearing end
columella sterile tissue or extension of the stalk projecting into the spore mass of certain Gasteromycetes (Hymenogastrales)

compound fruiting body with more than one cap arising from a common stalk or common base

conidia asexual spores

conifer a cone-bearing tree; one that has needles like a pine or redwood, or scales like a cypress

context the flesh of the cap or stalk

convergent gill hyphae projecting upward toward the cap as seen in cross-section; converging toward the center (p. 22)

convex cap rounded (p. 19)

convoluted wrinkled like a brain

coprophilous dung-loving; growing on dung

cuticle the skin or surface layer of the cap, more specifically one differentiated from the flesh

cystidium (pl., **cystidia**) specialized sterile cell projecting from the gills, tubes, cap, or stalk (p. 22)

daedeloid pores greatly elongated or meandering, like a labyrinth

decurrent gills running down the stalk (p. 19)

delignifying decay lignin-decomposing rot

deliquescing gills dissolving into a fluid; liquefying

depressed cap concave; center sunken below the level of the margin (p. 19)

dextrinoid staining red-brown or brown in iodine solution (Melzer's reagent)

dichotomous forking or dividing in pairs

differentiated different; not the same throughout

disc center of the cap

distant gills widely spaced

divergent gill hyphae projecting downward (away from cap) as seen in cross-section; diverging from the center (p. 22)

dry cap or stalk neither viscid nor hygrophanous

duplex flesh of two distinct textures

eccentric stalk off-center

echinulate spores spiny like a sea urchin

egg the button stage of a mushroom with a volva (e.g., *Amanita*); also, spore-containing capsule in a bird's nest fungus

ellipsoid spores elliptical in 3 dimensions; used here interchangeably with elliptical

elliptical spores rounded at both ends with sides curved slightly

endemic native to a region and generally restricted to it

endoperidium the inner layer of the spore sac in puffballs

entire gills with even edges; not serrate or toothed

epiphragm the thin membrane covering the mouth of many young bird's nest fungi

equal stalk of more or less uniform thickness throughout

evanescent transitory; disappearing

exoperidium the outer layer of the spore sac in puffballs

expanded cap fully developed; spread out

fairy ring a circle or arc of mushrooms (p. 7)

family a grouping of related genera

farinaceous odor or taste like fresh meal

fetid (foetid) nauseating or repulsive

fibril a fine fiber or hair

fibrillose covered with or composed of fibrils

fibrous composed of tough, stringy tissue

filamentous cap cuticle composed of threadlike cells or filaments (p. 22)

flaccid lacking firmness; flabby

flesh the tissue of the cap or stalk; the meaty portion

fleshy having substance (e.g., a fleshy fungal fructification) *or* soft as opposed to tough

floccose woolly or cottony; dry and loosely arranged
fluted stalk ribbed; with sharp longitudinal ridges
free gills not attached to stalk (p. 19)
friable easily crumbling
Friesian pertaining to Elias Fries (the "father" of mushroom taxonomy), and to his classification system based on macroscopic characteristics
fructification fruiting body
fruiting body the reproductive structure of a fungus; a mushroom
fulvous reddish-cinnamon-brown
fungus any member of a large group of organisms that lack chlorophyll, reproduce by means of spores, and have a filamentous vegetative phase
funiculus the cord attaching peridiole to the "nest" in certain bird's nest fungi
furfuraceous scurfy; roughened by minute particles
fuscous dark smoky-brown, sometimes with a violet tint
fusiform spores spindle-shaped; elongated and tapering from the middle to both ends
fusoid fusiform

gelatinous jelly-like in consistency or appearance
generic pertaining to genus
genus (pl., **genera**) grouping of closely related species
germ pore a soft spot in wall of certain spores, through which initial germination takes place
gills spore-producing blades on underside of an agaric
glabrous bald
glandular dots resinous spots on stalk in certain boletes (p. 402)
gleba the spore mass of a Gasteromycete (e.g., puffballs)
globose spherical
glutinous slimy or very sticky
granulose covered with granules
gregarious growing close together but not in clusters

habitat natural place of growth
hardwood used here loosely to denote any tree that is not a conifer
heart rot a rot of the heartwood
homogeneous the same throughout; not differentiated
humus decaying organic material in soil
hyaline spores colorless under microscope
hygrophanous cap changing color radically as it loses moisture; usually watery-looking when wet and opaque when dry
hymenium a layer or palisade of spore-producing cells
hypha (pl., **hyphae**) a threadlike fungal cell, the basic structural unit of any fungus or mushroom
hypogeous fruiting underground

incurved cap margin curved inward toward stalk
inferior ring located near base of stalk
innate a part of; not superficial or easily removed
inner veil a protective covering stretching from the stalk to the cap margin in many young mushrooms
inrolled cap margin curved in toward gills and rolled up; tucked under
interwoven gill hyphae entwined or tangled as seen in cross-section; not forming a regular pattern (p. 22)

KOH the chemical symbol for potassium hydroxide (potash)

lamellae the gills
lamellulae short gills that extend only part way to stalk
lateral stalk attached to side of cap
latex a juice or milk, as in *Lactarius*
leathery tough, pliant, not easily breaking
lignicolous wood-inhabiting

lignin a major constituent of wood

lubricous somewhat slippery or greasy to the touch but not viscid or slimy

macroscopic discernible without a microscope

margin the edge of cap or gills

marginate gills with edges differently colored than faces

mealy having a granular appearance *or* smelling like fresh meal

median ring at or near middle of stalk

Melzer's reagent an iodine test solution: 40 parts (by weight) water, 2 parts potassium iodide, 1 part iodine, and 40 parts chloral hydrate (poisonous!)

membranous membranelike; skinlike

metagrobolizing puzzling, bewildering, confounding, confusing, perplexing

micrometer see micron

micron (μm) microscopic unit of measure; 0.001 mm

microscopic discernible only with a microscope

mushroom the fruiting body of a fungus, especially one which has gills; also, any fungus that produces a fleshy fruiting body

mushrump a hump in the humus caused by a developing mushroom

mycelium a complex network of hyphae, the vegetative portion of a fungus

mycologist one who studies fungi

mycology the study of fungi

mycophagist one who eats mushrooms

mycophile one who loves mushrooms

mycophobe one who despises or fears mushrooms

mycorrhiza a mutually beneficial relationship between a fungus and the rootlets of a plant (especially trees), in which nutrients are exchanged

nodulose spores covered with small bumps or nodules

notched gills abruptly adnexed, as though a small wedge-shaped piece of tissue had been removed at the point of attachment to the stalk (p. 19)

oblong spores elongated, with approximately parallel sides

obtuse blunt; not pointed

ochraceous yellow or yellow-orange with a brownish tinge

order a grouping of related families

ornamentation any discontinuity (warts, ridges, etc.) on cap or stalk; not bald

outer veil a protective covering that envelops all or most of the fruiting body in certain mushrooms

ovate spores egg-shaped

ovoid egg-shaped, used here interchangeably with ovate

pallid pale or of an indefinite whitish color

parallel gill hyphae arranged more or less parallel to each other as seen in cross-section (p. 22)

paraphyses unspecialized sterile cells (p. 6)

parasitic growing on another living organism

partial veil inner veil

pedicel a slender stalk

pellicle a skinlike covering that peels easily and is often viscid

pendant ring skirtlike (p. 274); hanging down

peridiole small spore capsule in bird's nest fungi and *Pisolithus*

peridium the wall of the spore sac in Gasteromycetes such as puffballs; the "nest" in the bird's nest fungi

perithecium a flasklike "nest" of asci (in the Pyrenomycetes)

peronate ring sheathing the stalk; sheathlike (p. 274)

persistent persisting; not evanescent

pileus the cap
pip-shaped shaped like an apple seed
plane cap having a flat surface (p. 19)
pocket rot a rot producing hollow pockets in a tree
pores the mouths of the tubes in boletes and polypores
poroid having pores or resembling pores
pruinose powdery or appearing finely powdered
pseudocarp anything that resembles a mushroom but is not
pseudorhiza a rootlike extension of the stalk; "tap root"
pubescent minutely hairy; downy
punctate dotted with minute scales or points
putrescent readily decaying

resupinate lying flat on substrate; without a stalk or well-defined cap
reticulate stalk marked with lines crossed like the meshes of a net (p. 402)
rhizomorph a rootlike bundle of mycelial hyphae
ring a ring of tissue left on the stalk by a collapsed veil
rufous brownish-red
rugose wrinkled

saclike volva shaped like a sack, pouch, or cup (p. 226)
saprophytic living on dead or decaying matter
sap rot decay of the sapwood
scabrous stock decorated with rough tufted scales (p. 402)
scales pieces of differentiated tissue on the cap or stalk, usually of a different color than background (but exclusive of warts)
scaly furnished with scales; volva with rings of concentric scales at base of stalk (p. 226)
sclerotium an underground knot or body of hyphae in certain fungi; a resting stage that fruits periodically
seceding gills pulling away from stalk as the cap expands
septate partitioned; with one or more cross walls
serrate gill edges toothed like a saw
sessile lacking a stalk
setae pointed, elongated, thick-walled sterile cells (cystidia)
simple fruiting body unbranched; not compound
sinuate gills notched (p. 19)
sinuous crooked
sordid dingy or dirty in appearance
spawn the mycelium
species a particular kind of organism; the fundamental unit of taxonomy
sphaerocyst a round or swollen cell in *Russula, Lactarius,* and relatives
spore the reproductive unit of a fungus, usually a single cell
spore sac the large chamber that contains the spores in Gasteromycetes
squamose furnished with scales
squamulose furnished with small scales
stalk the stemlike structure that supports the cap in most mushrooms
stellate star-shaped
sterigma (pl., **sterigmata**) prong on the basidium on which a spore is formed
sterile not producing spores; infertile
sterile base the sterile chambered base beneath the spore mass in many puffballs
stipe the stalk
stipitate furnished with a stalk
striate finely furrowed with radiating lines or striations
stuffed stalk stuffed with a pith
subdistant gills fairly well spaced
subperonate somewhat or slightly peronate
substrate the material to which a fruiting body is attached

subtomentose finely or slightly tomentose
sulcate conspicuously furrowed; deeply striate
superficial scales, warts, etc. easily removable; not innate
superior ring located at or near top of stalk

tacky slightly sticky but not truly viscid
tawny the color of a lion
taxonomy the classification of organisms to reflect natural relationships
tenacious tough
terrestrial growing on the ground
toadstool a mushroom, especially one that is poisonous
tomentose covered with soft hairs
top rot a rot confined to the top of a tree
translucent-striate cap with the gills showing through to give a striate appearance
truncate appearing chopped off or flattened at one end
trunk rot decay found throughout the entire trunk of a tree
tuberculate spores with low bumps
tuberculate-striate striate with small bumps
tubes the tubelike structures on the underside of boletes and polypores, in which spores are produced
turbinate top-shaped

umber a deep dull brown
umbilicate cap with a navel-like central depression (p. 19)
umbo a knob or bump at center of cap
umbonate cap furnished with an umbo (p. 19)
universal veil outer veil

veil see inner veil and outer veil
ventricose swollen in the middle
vinaceous the color of red wine or somewhat paler
viscid slimy or sticky to the touch, at least when moist
volva remains of the outer veil at the base of the stalk in certain mushrooms, usually in the form of a sack, collar, or series of concentric rings (p. 226)
volval patch a patch of tissue from the volva deposited on the cap

warts small pieces of volval tissue deposited on the cap
white rot a delignifying decay

zonate cap concentrically zoned

GENERAL INDEX

Bold-face numbers indicate a full description of the subject, usually accompanied by a photograph.

* indicates a line drawing or photograph unaccompanied by a description.

A

B

C

D

E

F

G

H

N

O

P

INDEX TO GENERA AND SPECIES

* indicates an illustration unaccompanied by a description.

Bold-face numbers indicate a full description of the mushroom, usually accompanied by a photograph.

A

D

The author with some giant morels. (Joel Leivick)